MW00653452

Evidence-Based Technical Analysis

Founded in 1807, John Wiley & Sons is the oldest independent publishing company in the United States. With offices in North America, Europe, Australia and Asia, Wiley is globally committed to developing and marketing print and electronic products and services for our customers' professional and personal knowledge and understanding.

The Wiley Trading series features books by traders who have survived the market's ever changing temperament and have prospered—some by reinventing systems, others by getting back to basics. Whether a novice trader, professional or somewhere in-between, these books will provide the advice and strategies needed to prosper today and well into the future.

For a list of available titles, please visit our Web site at www.Wiley Finance.com.

Evidence-Based Technical Analysis

Applying the Scientific Method and Statistical Inference to Trading Signals

DAVID R. ARONSON

John Wiley & Sons, Inc.

Published by John Wiley & Sons, Inc., Hoboken, New Jersey.
Published simultaneously in Canada.

For general information on our other products and services or for technical
support, please contact our Customer Care Department within the United States
at (800) 762-2974, outside the United States at (317) 572-3993 or fax
(317) 572-4002.

Wiley also publishes its books in a variety of electronic formats. Some content
that appears in print may not be available in electronic books. For more
information about Wiley products, visit our web site at www.wiley.com.

Library of Congress Cataloging-in-Publication Data:

Aronson, David R., 1945–
    Evidence-based technical analysis : applying the scientific method and
statistical inference to trading signals / David R. Aronson.
      p.   cm.—(Wiley trading series)
    Includes bibliographical references and index.
    ISBN-13: 978-0-470-00874-4 (cloth)
    ISBN-10: 0-470-00874-1 (cloth)
    1. Investment analysis. I. Title. II. Series.
HG4529.A77   2007
332.63'2042—dc22

                                          2006014664

10 9 8 7 6 5 4 3 2 1

To Jack and Belma

Contents

Acknowledgments

Though a book is attributed to its author(s), it truly reflects the efforts of many more people. I wish to acknowledge those individuals without whom this book would have been impossible or a much lesser work.

I am most indebted to Dr. Timothy Masters, whom I have had the pleasure of knowing for over 10 years. His patient and intelligent guidance kept me on a solid statistical footing. Tim not only gave me important feedback on technical issues but was responsible for coding and running the ATR rule experiments and the statistical routines used to test the over 6,400 rules examined. Tim also innovated the Monte Carlo permutation method as an alterative to the patented method of White, called Reality-Check, for testing the statistical significance of rules discovered by data mining. Tim has graciously decided to put the method in the public domain and has allowed it to be published for the first time here.

Also crucial were the programming talents of Stuart Okorofsky and the database creation by Dr. John Wolberg. I am indebted Dr. Halbert White, inventor of Reality-Check and for the help of Professor David Jensen, director of the Knowledge Discovery Lab at the University of Massachusetts–Amherst.

I also wish to express my appreciation to the following people for reviewing and commenting on various chapters. Their feedback was essential: Charles Neumann, Lance Rembar, Dr. Samuel Aronson, Dennis Katz, Hayes Martin, George Butler, Dr. John Wolberg, Jay Bono, Dr. Andre Shlefier, Dr. John Nofsinger, Doyle Delaney, Ken Byerly, James Kunstler, and Kenny Rome.

Special thanks to the helpful folks at John Wiley & Sons: Kevin Commins, for seeing the value of a critical appraisal of technical analysis, and Emilie Herman, for her steady hand in editing the book. Thanks as well to Michael Lisk and Laura Walsh.

About the Author

David Aronson is an adjunct professor of finance at Baruch College's Zicklin School of Business in New York, where he teaches a graduate-level course in technical analysis to MBA and financial-engineering students, and vice-president of Hood River Research Inc., a firm that develops signal filters and predictive models. He was formerly a proprietary trader and technical analyst at Spear, Leeds and Kellogg and president of Raden Research Group Inc., a consulting firm that developed the data-mining software PRISM and filters and systems for various trading firms. Prior to that, he founded AdvoCom Corporation, which managed client funds in portfolios of futures trading advisors using portfolio optimization. He received a BA in philosophy from Lafayette College in 1967 and served in the Peace Corps in El Salvador.

Introduction

Technical analysis (TA) is the study of recurring patterns in financial market data with the intent of forecasting future price movements.[1] It is comprised of numerous analysis methods, patterns, signals, indicators, and trading strategies, each with its own cheerleaders claiming that their approach works.

Much of popular or traditional TA stands where medicine stood before it evolved from a faith-based folk art into a practice based on science. Its claims are supported by colorful narratives and carefully chosen (cherry picked) anecdotes rather than objective statistical evidence.

This book's central contention is that TA must evolve into a rigorous observational science if it is to deliver on its claims and remain relevant. The scientific method is the only rational way to extract useful knowledge from market data and the only rational approach for determining which TA methods have predictive power. I call this evidence-based technical analysis (EBTA). Grounded in objective observation and statistical inference (i.e., the scientific method), EBTA charts a course between the magical thinking and gullibility of a true believer and the relentless doubt of a random walker.

Approaching TA, or any discipline for that matter, in a scientific manner is not easy. Scientific conclusions frequently conflict with what seems intuitively obvious. To early humans it seemed obvious that the sun circled the earth. It took science to demonstrate that this intuition was wrong. An informal, intuitive approach to knowledge acquisition is especially likely to result in erroneous beliefs when phenomena are complex or highly random, two prominent features of financial market behavior. Although the scientific method is not guaranteed to extract gold from the mountains of market data, an unscientific approach is almost certain to produce fool's gold.

This book's second contention is that much of the wisdom comprising the popular version of TA does not qualify as legitimate knowledge.

KEY DEFINITIONS: PROPOSITIONS AND CLAIMS, BELIEF AND KNOWLEDGE

I have already used the terms *knowledge* and *belief* but have not rigorously defined them. These and several other key terms will be used repeatedly in this book, so some formal definitions are needed.

The fundamental building block of knowledge is a *declarative statement*, also known as a *claim* or a *proposition*. A declarative statement is one of four types of utterances that also include exclamations, questions, and commands. Declarative statements are distinguished from the others in that they have truth value. That is to say, they can be characterized as either true or false or probably true or probably false.

The statement "Oranges are on sale at the supermarket for five cents a dozen" is declarative. It makes a claim about a state of affairs existing at the local market. It may be true or false. In contrast, the exclamatory statement "Holy cow, what a deal," the command "Go buy me a dozen," or the question "What is an orange?" cannot be called true or false.

Our inquiry into TA will be concerned with declarative statements, such as, "Rule X has predictive power." Our goal is to determine which of these declarative statements warrant our belief.

What does it mean to say, "I believe X."? "With regard to states of affairs in general (i.e., 'matters of fact' or 'what will happen') believing X amounts to expecting to experience X if and when we are in a position to do so."[2] Therefore, if I believe the claim that oranges are on sale for five cents a dozen, it means that I expect to be able to buy oranges for five cents a dozen if I go to the store. However, the command to buy some oranges or the exclamation that I am happy about the opportunity, set up no such expectation.

What does all this all means for us? For any statement to even be considered as a candidate for belief, it must "assert some state of affairs that can be expected.[3] Such statements are said to have *cognitive content*— they convey something that can be *known*. "If the statement contains nothing to know then there is nothing there to be believe."[4]

Although all declarative statements presumably have cognitive content, not all actually do. This is not a problem if the lack of cognitive content is obvious, for example, the declaration "The square root of Tuesday is a prime number."[5] This utterance is, on its face, nonsense. There are other declarative statements, however, whose lack of cognitive content is not so obvious. This can be a problem, because such statements can fool us into thinking that a claim has been made that sets up an expectation, when, in fact, no claim has really been put forward. These pseudo-declarative-statements are essentially *meaningless claims* or *empty propositions*.

Although meaningless claims are not valid candidates for belief, this does not stop many people from believing in them. The vague predictions made in the daily astrology column or the nebulous promises made by promoters of bogus health cures are examples of meaningless claims. Those who believe these empty propositions simply do not realize that what they have been told has no cognitive content.

A way to tell if a statement has cognitive content and is, thus, a valid candidate for belief is the *discernible-difference* test[6] described by Hall. "Utterances with cognitive content make claims that are either true or false; and whether they are true or false makes a difference that can be discerned. That is why these utterances offer something to believe and why there is no point in trying to believe an utterance that makes no such offer"[7] In other words, a proposition that passes the discernible-difference test sets up an expectation such that the state of affairs, if the statement were true, is recognizably different from the state of affairs, if the statement were false.

The discernible-difference criterion can be applied to statements purporting to be predictions. A prediction is a claim to know something about the future. If a prediction has cognitive content, it will be clearly discernible in the outcome if the prediction was accurate or not. Many, if not most, of the forecasts issued by practitioners of popular TA are devoid of cognitive content on these grounds. In other words, the predictions are typically too vague to ever determine if they were wrong.

The truth or falsity of the claim *oranges are on sale for five cents a dozen* will make a discernible difference when I get to the market. It is this discernible difference that allows the claim to be tested. As will be described in Chapter 3, testing a claim on the basis of a discernible difference is central to the scientific method.

Hall, in his book *Practically Profound*, explains why he finds Freudian psychoanalysis to be meaningless when examined in light of the discernible-difference test.

"Certain Freudian claims about human sexual development are compatible with all possible states of affairs. There is no way to confirm or disconfirm either 'penis envy' or 'castration complex' because there is no distinguishable difference between evidence affirming and evidence denying these interpretations of behavior. Exactly opposite behaviors are equally predictable, depending on whether the alleged psychosexual stress is overt or repressed." The requirement of "cognitive content rules out all utterances that are so loose, poorly formed or obsessively held (e.g., conspiracy theories) that there is no recognizable difference between what would be the case if they were so, and what would be the case if they were not."[8] In a like vein, the Intelligent Design Theory carries no cognitive freight in the sense that no matter what life form is observed it is consistent with the notion that it manifests an underlying form specified by some intelligent designer.[9]

What then is *knowledge?* Knowledge can be defined as *justified true belief*. Hence, in order for a declarative statement to qualify as *knowledge*, not only must it be a candidate for belief, because it has cognitive content, but it must meet two other conditions as well. First, it must be true (or probably true). Second, the statement must be believed with justification. A belief is justified when it is based on sound inferences from solid evidence.

Prehistoric humans held the false belief that the sun moved across the sky because the sun orbited the earth. Clearly they were not in possession of knowledge, but suppose that there was a prehistoric person who believed correctly that the sun moved across the sky because of the earth's rotation. Although this belief was true, this individual could not be described as possessing knowledge. Even though they believed what astronomers ultimately proved to be true, there was no evidence yet to justify that belief. Without justification, a true belief does not attain the status of knowledge. These concepts are illustrated in Figure I.1.

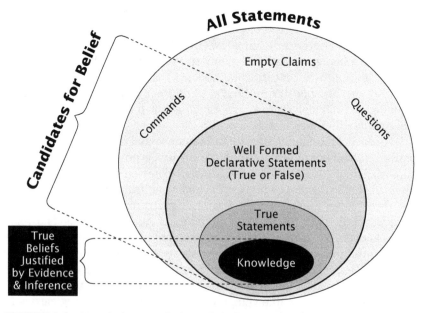

FIGURE I.1   Knowledge: justified true belief.

From this it follows that *erroneous beliefs* or *false knowledge* fail to meet one or more of the necessary conditions of knowledge. Thus, an erroneous belief can arise either because it concerns a meaningless claim or because it concerns a claim that, though meaningful, is not justified by valid inferences from solid evidence.

Still, even when we have done everything right, by drawing the best possible inference from sound evidence, we can still wind up adopting erroneous beliefs. In other words, we can be justified in believing a falsehood, and honestly claim to know something, if it appears to be true according to logically sound inferences from the preponderance of available evidence. "We are entitled to say 'I know' when the target of that claim is supported beyond reasonable doubt in the network of well-tested evidence. But that is not enough to guarantee that we do know."[10]

Falsehoods are an unavoidable fact of life when we attempt to know things about the world based on observed evidence. Thus, knowledge based on the scientific method is inherently uncertain, and provisional, though less uncertain than knowledge acquired by less formal methods. However, over time, scientific knowledge improves, as it comes to describe reality in a progressively more accurate manner. It is a continual work in progress. The goal of EBTA is a body of knowledge about market behavior that is as good as can be had, given the limits of evidence gathering and the powers of inference.

ERRONEOUS TA KNOWLEDGE: THE COST OF UNDISCIPLINED ANALYSIS

To understand why the knowledge produced by the popular version of TA is untrustworthy, we must consider two distinct forms of TA: subjective and objective. Both approaches can lead to erroneous beliefs, but they do so in distinct ways.

Objective TA methods are well defined repeatable procedures that issue unambiguous signals. This allows them to be implemented as computerized algorithms and back-tested on historical data. Results produced by a back test can be evaluated in a rigorous quantitative manner.

Subjective TA methods are not well-defined analysis procedures. Because of their vagueness, an analyst's private interpretations are required. This thwarts computerization, back testing, and objective performance evaluation. In other words, it is impossible to either confirm or deny a subjective method's efficacy. For this reason they are insulated from evidentiary challenge.

From the standpoint of EBTA, subjective methods are the most problematic. They are essentially meaningless claims that give the illusion of conveying cognitive content. Because the methods do not specify how they are to be applied, different analysts applying it to the same set of market data can reach different conclusions. This makes it impossible to determine if the method provides useful predictions. Classical chart pattern analysis,[11] hand-drawn trend lines, Elliott Wave Principle,[12] Gann patterns, Magic T's and numerous other subjective methods fall into this category.[13] Subjective TA is religion—it is based on faith. No amount of cherry-picked examples showing where the method succeeded can cure this deficiency.

Despite their lack of cognitive content and the impossibility of ever being supported by sound evidence, there is no shortage of fervent believers in various subjective methods. Chapter 2 explains how flaws in human thinking can produce strong beliefs in the absence of evidence or even in the face of contradictory evidence.

Objective TA can also spawn erroneous beliefs but they come about differently. They are traceable to faulty inferences from objective evidence. The mere fact that an objective method has been profitable in a back test is not sufficient grounds for concluding that it has merit. Past performance can fool us. Historical success is a necessary but not a sufficient condition for concluding that a method has predictive power and, therefore, is likely to be profitable in the future. Favorable past performance can occur by luck or because of an upward bias produced by one form of back testing called data mining. Determining when back-test profits are attributable to a good method rather than good luck is a question that can only be answered by rigorous statistical inference. This is discussed in Chapters 4 and 5. Chapter 6 considers the problem of data-mining bias. Although I will assert that data mining, when done correctly, is the modern technician's best method for knowledge discovery, specialized statistical tests must be applied to the results obtained with data mining.

HOW EBTA IS DIFFERENT

What sets EBTA apart from the popular form of TA? First, it is restricted to meaningful claims—objective methods that can be tested on historical data. Second, it utilizes advanced forms of statistical inference to determine if a profitable back test is indicative of an effective method. Thus, the prime focus of EBTA is determining which objective methods are worthy of actual use.

EBTA rejects all forms of subjective TA. Subjective TA is not even wrong. It is worse than wrong. Statements that can be qualified as wrong (untrue) at least convey cognitive content that can be tested. The propositions of subjective TA offer no such thing. Though, at first blush, they seem to convey knowledge, when they are examined critically, it becomes clear they are empty claims.

Promoters of New Age health cures excel at empty claims. They tell you that wearing their magic copper bracelet will make you will feel better and put more bounce in your step. They suggest your golf game will improve and maybe even your love life. However, the claim's lack of specificity makes it impossible to nail down exactly what is being promised or how it can be tested. Such claims can never be confirmed or contradicted with objective evidence. On these same grounds, it can be said that the propositions of subjective TA are empty and thus insulated from empirical challenge. They must be taken on faith.

In contrast, a meaningful claim is testable because it makes measurable promises. It states specifically how much your golf game will improve or how bouncy your steps will be. This specificity opens the claim to being contradicted with empirical evidence.

From the perspective of EBTA, proponents of subjective methods are faced with a choice: They can reformulate the method to be objective, as one practitioner of the Elliott Wave Principle has done,[14] thus exposing it to empirical refutation, or they must admit the method must be accepted on faith. Perhaps Gann lines actually provide useful information. In their present form, we are denied this knowledge.

With respect to objective TA, EBTA does not take profitable back tests at face value. Instead, they are subjected to rigorous statistical evaluation to determine if profits were due to luck or biased research. As will be pointed out in Chapter 6, in many instances, profitable back tests may be a data miner fool's gold. This may explain why many objective TA methods that perform well in a back testing perform worse when applied to new data. Evidence-based technical analysis uses computer-intensive statistical methods that minimize problems stemming from the data-mining bias.

The evolution of TA to EBTA also has ethical implications. It is the ethical and legal responsibility of all analysts, whatever form of analysis they practice, to make recommendations that have a reasonable basis and not to make unwarranted claims.[15] The only reasonable basis for asserting an analysis method has value is objective evidence. Subjective

TA methods cannot meet this standard. Objective TA, conducted in accordance with the standards of EBTA can.

EBTA RESULTS FROM ACADEMIA

Evidence-based technical analysis is not a new idea. Over the past two decades, numerous articles in respected academic journals[16] have approached TA in the rigorous manner advocated by this book.[17] The evidence is not uniform. Some studies show TA does not work, but some show that it does. Because each study is confined to a particular aspect of TA and a specific body of data, it is possible for studies to reach different conclusions. This is often the case in science.

The following are a few of the findings from academic TA. It shows that, when approached in a rigorous and intellectually honest manner, TA is a worthwhile area of study.

- Expert chartists are unable to distinguish actual price charts of stocks from charts produced by a random process.[18]
- There is empirical evidence of trends in commodities[19] and foreign exchange markets that can be exploited with the simple objective trend indicators. In addition, the profits earned by trend-following speculators may be justified by economic theory[20] because their activities provide commercial hedgers with a valuable economic service, the transference of price risk from hedger to speculator.
- Simple technical rules used individually and in combinations can yield statistically and economically significant profits when applied to stock market averages composed of relatively young companies (Russell 2000 and NASDAQ Composite).[21]
- Neural networks have been able to combine buy/sell signals of simple moving-average rules into nonlinear models that displayed good predictive performance on the Dow Jones Average over the period 1897 to 1988.[22]
- Trends in industry groups and sectors persist long enough after detection by simple momentum indicators to earn excess returns.[23]
- Stocks that have displayed prior relative strength and relative weakness continue to display above-average and below-average performance over horizons of 3 to 12 months.[24]
- United States stocks, selling near their 52-week highs, outperform other stocks. An indicator defined as the differential between a stock's current price and its 52-week high is a useful predictor of fu-

ture relative performance.[25] The indicator is an even more potent predictor for Australian stocks.[26]

- The head-and-shoulders chart pattern has limited forecasting power when tested in an objective fashion in currencies. Better results can be had with simple filter rules. The head-and-shoulders pattern, when tested objectively on stocks, does not provide useful information.[27] Traders who act on such signals would be equally served by following a random signal.
- Trading volume statistics for stocks contain useful predictive information[28] and improve the profitability of signals based on large price changes following a public announcement.[29]
- Computer-intensive data-modeling neural networks, genetic algorithms, and other statistical learning and artificial-intelligence methods have found profitable patterns in technical indicators.[30]

WHO AM I TO CRITICIZE TA?

My interest in TA began in 1960 at the age of 15. During my high-school and college years I followed a large stable of stocks using the Chartcraft point and figure method. I have used TA professionally since 1973, first as a stock broker, then as managing partner of a small software company, Raden Research Group Inc.—an early adopter of machine learning and data mining in financial market applications—and finally as a proprietary equities trader for Spear, Leeds & Kellogg.[31] In 1988, I earned the Chartered Market Technician designation from the Market Technicians Association. My personal TA library has over 300 books. I have published approximately a dozen articles and have spoken numerous times on the subject. Currently I teach a graduate-level course in TA at the Zicklin School of Business, Baruch College, City University of New York. I freely admit my previous writings and research do not meet EBTA standards, in particular with regard to statistical significance and the data-mining bias.

My long-standing faith in TA began to erode in response to a very mediocre performance over a five-year period trading capital for Spear, Leeds and Kellogg. How could what I believed in so fervently not work? Was it me or something to do with TA in general? My academic training in philosophy provided fertile grounds for my growing doubts. My concerns crystallized into full fledged skepticism as a result of reading two books: *How We Know What Isn't So* by Thomas Gilovich and *Why People Believe Weird Things*, by Michael Shermer. My conclusion: Technical analysts, including myself, know a lot of stuff that isn't so, and believe a lot of weird things.

TECHNICAL ANALYSIS: ART, SCIENCE, OR SUPERSTITION?

There is a debate in the TA community: Is it an art or a science? The question has been framed incorrectly. It is more properly stated as: Should TA be based on superstition or science? Framed this way the debate evaporates.

Some will say TA involves too much nuance and interpretation to render its knowledge in the form of scientifically testable claims. To this I retort: TA that is not testable may sound like knowledge, but it is not. It is superstition that belongs in the realm of astrology, numerology, and other nonscientific practices.

Creativity and inspiration play a crucial role in science. They will be important in EBTA as well. All scientific inquiries start with a hypothesis, a new idea or a new insight inspired by a mysterious mixture of prior knowledge, experience and a leap of intuition. Yet, good science balances creativity with analytical rigor. The freedom to propose new ideas must be married to an unyielding discipline that eliminates ideas that prove worthless in the crucible of objective testing. Without this anchor to reality, people fall in love with their ideas, and magical thinking replaces critical thought.

It is unlikely that TA will ever discover rules that predict with the precision of the laws of physics. The inherent complexity and randomness of financial markets and the impossibility of controlled experimentation preclude such findings. However, predictive accuracy is not the defining requirement of science. Rather, it is defined by an uncompromising openness to recognizing and eliminating wrong ideas.

I have four hopes for this book: First, that it will stimulate a dialogue amongst technical analysts that will ultimately put our field on a firmer intellectual foundation; second, that it will encourage further research along the lines advocated herein; third, that it will encourage consumers of TA to demand more "beef" from those who sell products and services based upon TA; and fourth, that it will encourage TA practitioners, professional and otherwise, to understand their crucial role in a human-machine partnership that has the potential to accelerate the growth of legitimate TA knowledge.

No doubt some fellow practitioners of TA will be irritated by these ideas. This can be a good thing. An oyster irritated by a grain of sand sometimes yields a pearl. I invite my colleagues to expend their energies adding to legitimate knowledge rather than defending the indefensible.

This book is organized in two sections. Part One establishes the methodological, philosophical, psychological, and statistical foundations of EBTA. Part Two demonstrates one approach to EBTA: testing of 6,402 binary buy/sell rules on the S&P 500 on 25 years of historical data. The rules are evaluated for statistical significance using tests designed to cope with the problem of data-mining bias.

PART I

Methodological, Psychological, Philosophical, and Statistical Foundations

CHAPTER 1

Objective Rules and Their Evaluation

T his chapter introduces the notion of objective binary signaling rules and a methodology for their rigorous evaluation. It defines an evaluation benchmark based on the profitability of a noninformative signal. It also establishes the need to detrend market data so that the performances of rules with different long/short position biases can be compared.

THE GREAT DIVIDE: OBJECTIVE VERSUS SUBJECTIVE TECHNICAL ANALYSIS

Technical analysis (TA) divides into two broad categories: objective and subjective. Subjective TA is comprised of analysis methods and patterns that are not precisely defined. As a consequence, a conclusion derived from a subjective method reflects the private interpretations of the analyst applying the method. This creates the possibility that two analysts applying the same method to the same set of market data may arrive at entirely different conclusions. Therefore, subjective methods are untestable, and claims that they are effective are exempt from empirical challenge. This is fertile ground for myths to flourish.

In contrast, objective methods are clearly defined. When an objective analysis method is applied to market data, its signals or predictions are unambiguous. This makes it possible to simulate the method on historical data and determine its precise level of performance. This is called back testing. The back testing of an objective method is, therefore, a repeatable experiment which allows claims of profitability to be tested and possibly refuted with statistical evidence. This makes it possible to find out which objective methods are effective and which are not.

The acid test for distinguishing an objective from a subjective method is the *programmability criterion: A method is objective if and only if it can be implemented as a computer program that produces unambiguous market positions (long,[1] short,[2] or neutral[3])*. All methods that cannot be reduced to such a program are, by default, subjective.

TA RULES

Objective TA methods are also referred to as mechanical trading rules or trading systems. In this book, all objective TA methods are referred to simply as *rules*.

A rule is a function that transforms one or more items of information, referred to as the rule's input, into the rule's output, which is a recommended market position (e.g., long, short, neutral). Input(s) consists of one or more financial market time series. The rule is defined by one or more mathematical and logical operators that convert the input time series into a new time series that consists of the sequence of recommended market position (long, short, out-of-the-market). The output is typically represented by a signed number (e.g., +1 or –1). This book adopts the convention of assigning positive values to indicate long positions and negative values to indicate shorts position. The process by which a rule transforms one or more input series into an output series is illustrated in Figure 1.1.

A rule is said to generate a *signal* when the value of the output series changes. A signal calls for a change in a previously recommended market position. For example a change in output from +1 to –1 would call for closing a previously held long position and the initiation of a new short position. Output values need not be confined to {+1, –1}. A complex rule, whose output spans the range {+10, –10}, is able to recommend positions that vary in size. For example, an output of +10 might indicate that 10 long positions are warranted, such as long 10 contracts of copper. A change in the output from +10 to +5 would call for a reduction in the long position from 10 contracts to 5 (i.e., sell 5).

Binary Rules and Thresholds

The simplest rule is one that has a *binary output*. In other words, its output can assume only two values, for example +1 and –1. A binary rule

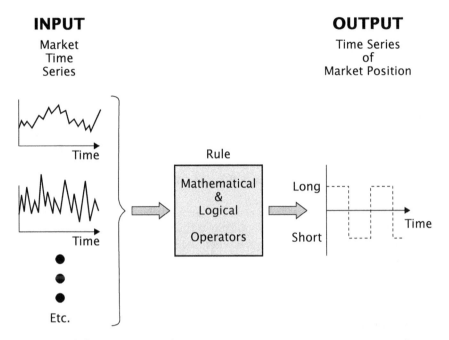

FIGURE 1.1 TA rule transforms input time series into a time series of market position.

could also be designed to recommend long/neutral positions or short/neutral positions. All the rules considered in this book are binary long/short {+1, −1}.

An investment strategy based on a binary long/short rule is always in either a long or short position in the market being traded. Rules of this type are referred to as *reversal rules* because signals call for a reversal from long to short or short to long. Over time a reversal rule produces a time series of +1's and −1's that represent an alternating sequence of long and short positions.

The specific mathematical and logical operators that are used to define rules can vary considerably. However, there are some common themes. One theme is the notion of a *threshold*, a critical level that distinguishes the informative changes in the input time series from its irrelevant fluctuations. The premise is that the input time series is a mixture of information and noise. Thus the threshold acts as a filter.

Rules that employ thresholds generate signals when the time series crosses the threshold, either by the rising above it or falling beneath it. These critical events can be detected with logical operators called *inequalities* such as *greater-than* (>) and *less-than* (<). For example, if the time series is greater than the threshold, then rule output = +1, otherwise rule output = –1.

A threshold may be set at a fixed value or its value may vary over time as a result of changes in the time series that is being analyzed. Variable thresholds are appropriate for time series that display trends, which are large long-lasting changes in the level of the series. Trends, which make fixed threshold rules impractical, are commonly seen in asset prices (e.g., S&P 500 Index) and asset yields (AAA bond yield). The moving average and the Alexander reversal filter, also known as the zigzag filter, are examples of time series operators that are commonly used to define variable thresholds. The operators used in the rules discussed in this book are detailed in Chapter 8.

The moving-average-cross rule is an example of how a variable threshold is used to generate signals on a time series that displays trends. This type of rule produces a signal when the time series crosses from one side of its moving average to the other. For example;

If the time series is above its moving average, **then** *the rule output value = +1, otherwise the rule output value = –1.*

This is illustrated in Figure 1.2.

Because it employs a single threshold, the signals generated by the moving-average-cross rule are, by definition, mutually exclusive. Given a single threshold, there are only two possible conditions—the times series is either above or below[4] the threshold. The conditions are also exhaustive (no other possibilities).[5] Thus, it is impossible for the rule's signals to be in conflict.

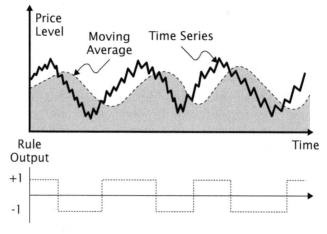

FIGURE 1.2 Moving-average-cross rule.

Rules with fixed value thresholds are appropriate for market time series that do not display trends. Such time series are said to be *stationary*. There is a strict mathematical definition of a stationary time series, but here I am using the term in a looser sense to mean that a series has a relatively stable average value over time and has fluctuations that are confined to a roughly horizontal range. Technical analysis practitioners often refer to these series as *oscillators*.

Time series that display trends can be *detrended*. In other words, they can be transformed into a stationary series. Detrending, which is described in greater detail in Chapter 8, frequently involves taking differences or ratios. For example the ratio of a time series to its moving average will produce a stationary version of the original time series. Once detrended, the series will be seen to fluctuate within a relatively well-defined horizontal range around a relatively stable mean value. Once the time series has been made stationary, fixed threshold rules can be employed. An example of a fixed threshold rule using a threshold of value of 75 is illustrated in Figure 1.3. The rule has an output a value of +1 when the series is greater than the threshold and a value of –1 at other times.

Binary Rules from Multiple Thresholds

As pointed out earlier, binary rules are derived, quite naturally, from a single threshold because the threshold defines two mutually exclusive and exhaustive conditions: the time series is either above or below threshold. However, binary rules can also be derived using multiple thresholds, but employing more than one threshold creates the possibility that the input

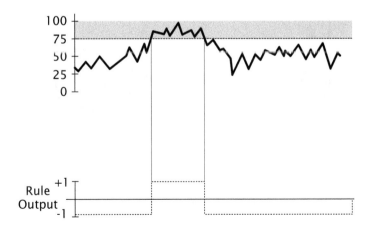

FIGURE 1.3 Rule with a single fixed threshold.

time series can assume more than two conditions. Consequently, multiple threshold rules require a more sophisticated logical operator than the simple inequality operator (greater-than or less-than), which suffices for single threshold rules.

When there are two or more thresholds, there are more than two possible conditions. For example, with two thresholds, an upper and lower, there are three possible conditions for the input time series. It can be above the upper, below the lower, or between the two thresholds. To create a binary rule in this situation, the rule is defined in terms of two mutually exclusive events. An event is defined by the time series crossing a particular threshold in a particular direction. Thus, one event triggers one of the rule's output values, which is maintained until a second event, which is mutually exclusive of the first, triggers the other output value. For example, an upward crossing of the upper threshold triggers a +1, and a downward crossing of the lower threshold triggers a −1.

A logical operator that implements this type of rule is referred to as a *flip-flop*. The name stems from the fact that the rule's output value *flips* one way, upon the occurrence of one event, and then *flops* the other way, upon the occurrence of the second event. Flip-flop logic can be used with either variable or fixed threshold rules. An example of a rule based on two variable thresholds is the moving average band rule. See Figure 1.4. Here, the moving average is surrounded by an upper and lower band. The bands may be a fixed percentage above and below the moving average, or the deviation of the bands may vary based on of the recent volatility of the times, as is the case with the Bollinger Band.[6] An output value of +1 is triggered by an upward piercing of the upper threshold. This value is retained

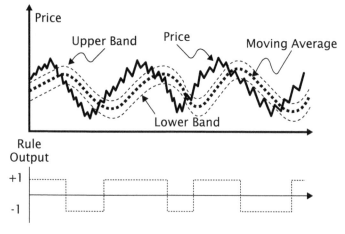

FIGURE 1.4 Moving average bands rule.

until the lower threshold is penetrated in the downward direction, causing the output value to change to –1.

Obviously, there are many other possibilities. The intent here has been to illustrate some of the ways that input time series can be transformed into a time series of recommended market positions.

Hayes[7] adds another dimension to threshold rules with *directional modes*. He applies multiple thresholds to a stationary time series such as a diffusion[8] indicator. At a given point in time, the indicator's mode is defined by the zone it occupies and its recent direction of change (e.g., up or down over the most recent five weeks). Each zone is defined by an upper and lower threshold (e.g., 40 and 60). Hayes applies this to a proprietary diffusion indicator called Big Mo. With two thresholds and two possible directional modes (up/down), six mutually exclusive conditions are defined. A binary rule could be derived from such an analysis by assigning one output value (e.g., +1) to one of the six conditions, and then assigning the other output value (i.e., –1) to the other five possibilities. Hayes asserts that one of the modes, when the diffusion indicator is above 60 and its direction is upward, is associated with stock market returns (Value Line Composite Index) of 50 percent per annum. This condition has occurred about 20 percent of the time between 1966 and 2000. However, when the diffusion indicator is > 60, and its recent change is negative, the market's annualized return is zero. This condition has occurred about 16 percent of the time.[9]

TRADITIONAL RULES AND INVERSE RULES

Part Two of this book is a case study that evaluates the profitability of approximately 6,400 binary long/short rules applied to the S&P 500 Index. Many of the rules generate market positions that are consistent with traditional principles of technical analysis. For example, under traditional TA principles, a moving-average-cross rule is interpreted to be bullish (output value +1) when the analyzed time series is above its moving average, and bearish (output value of –1) when it is below the moving average. I refer to these as *traditional* TA rules.

Given that the veracity of traditional TA maybe questionable, it is desirable to test rules that are contrary to the traditional interpretation. In other words, it is entirely possible that patterns that are traditionally assumed to predict rising prices may actually be predictive of falling prices. Alternatively, it is possible that neither configuration has any predictive value.

This can be accomplished by creating an additional set of rules whose

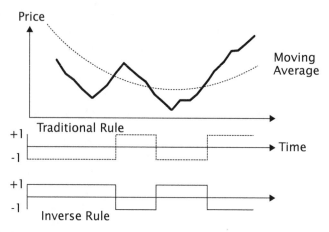

FIGURE 1.5 Traditional rules and inverse rules.

output is simply the opposite of a traditional TA rule. I refer to these as *inverse* rules. This is illustrated in Figure 1.5. The inverse of the moving-average-cross rule would output a value of −1 when the input time series is above its moving average, and +1 when the series is below its moving average.

There is yet another reason to consider inverse rules. Many of the rules tested in Part Two utilize input series other than the S&P 500, for example the yield differential between BAA and AAA corporate bonds. It is not obvious how this series should be interpreted to generate signals. Therefore, both up trends and down trends in the yield differential were considered as possible buy signals. The details of these rules are taken up in Chapter 8.

THE USE OF BENCHMARKS IN RULE EVALUATION

In many fields, performance is a relative matter. That is to say, it is performance relative to a benchmark that is informative rather than an absolute level of performance. In track and field, competitors in the shot-put are compared to a benchmark defined as best distance of that day or the best ever recorded in the state or world. To say that someone put the shot 43 feet does not reveal the quality of performance, however if the best prior effort had been 23 feet, 43 feet is a significant accomplishment!

This pertains to rule evaluation. Performance figures are only informative when they are compared to a relevant benchmark. The isolated fact that a rule earned a 10 percent rate of return in a back test is meaningless. If many other rules earned over 30 percent on the same data, 10 percent would indicate inferiority, whereas if all other rules were barely profitable, 10 percent might indicate superiority.

What then is an appropriate benchmark for TA rule performance? What standard must a rule beat to be considered good? There are a number of reasonable standards. This book defines that standard as the performance of a rule with no predictive power (i.e., a randomly generated signal). This is consistent with scientific practice in other fields. In medicine, a new drug must convincingly outperform a placebo (sugar pill) to be considered useful. Of course, rational investors might reasonably choose a higher standard of performance but not a lesser one. Some other benchmarks that could make sense would be the riskless rate of return, the return of a buy-and-hold strategy, or the rate of return of the rule currently being used.

In fact, to be considered good, it is not sufficient for a rule to simply beat the benchmark. It must beat it by a wide enough margin to exclude the possibility that its victory was merely due to chance (good luck). It is entirely possible for a rule with no predictive power to beat its benchmark in a given sample of data by sheer luck. The margin of victory that is sufficient to exclude luck as a likely explanation relates to the matter of *statistical significance*. This is taken up in Chapters 4, 5, and 6.

Having now established that the benchmark that we will use is the return that could be earned by a rule with no predictive power, we now face another question: How much might a rule with no predictive power earn? At first blush, it might seem that a return of zero is a reasonable expectation. However, this is only true under a specific and rather limited set of conditions.

In fact, the expected return of a rule with no predictive power can be dramatically different than zero. This is so because the performance of a rule can be profoundly affected by factors that have nothing to do with its predictive power.

The Conjoint Effect of Position Bias and Market Trend on Back-Test Performance

In reality, a rule's back-tested performance is comprised of two independent components. One component is attributable to the rule's predictive power, if it has any. This is the component of interest. The second, and unwanted, component of performance is the result of two factors that have nothing to do with the rule's predictive power: (1) the rule's long/short position bias, and (2) the market's net trend during the back-test period.

This undesirable component of performance can dramatically influence back-test results and make rule evaluation difficult. It can cause a rule with no predictive power to generate a positive average return or it can cause a rule with genuine predictive power to produce a negative average return. Unless this component of performance is removed, accurate rule evaluation is impossible. Let's consider the two factors that drive this component.

The first factor is a rule's *long/short* position bias. This refers to the amount of time the rule spent in a +1 output state relative to the amount of time spent in a −1 output state during the back test. If either output state dominated during the back test, the rule is said to have a position bias. For example, if more time was spent in long positions, the rule has a long position bias.

The second factor is the *market's net trend* or the average daily price change of the market during the period of the back test. If the market's net trend is other than zero, and the rule has a long or short position bias, the rule's performance will be impacted. In other words, the undesirable component of performance will distort back-test results either by adding to or subtracting from the component of performance that is due to the rule's actual predictive power. If, however, the market's net trend is zero or if the rule has no position bias, then the rule's past profitability will be strictly due to the rule's predictive power (plus or minus random variation). This is demonstrated mathematically later.

To clarify, imagine a TA rule that has a long position bias but that we know has no predictive power. The signals of such a rule could be simulated by a roulette wheel. To create the long position bias, a majority of the wheel's slots would be allocated to long positions (+1). Suppose that one hundred slots are allocated as follows; 75 are +1 and 25 are −1. Each day, over a period of historical data, the wheel is spun to determine if a long or short position is to be held for that day. If the market's average daily change during this period were greater than zero (i.e., net trend upward), the rule would have a positive expected rate of return even though the signals contain no predictive information. The rule's expected rate of return can be computed using the formula used to calculate the expected value of a random variable (discussed later).

Just as it is possible for a rule with no predictive power to produce a positive rate of return, it is just as possible for a rule with predictive power to produce a negative rate of return. This can occur if a rule has a position bias that is contrary to the market's trend. The combined effect of the market's trend and the rule's position bias may be sufficient to offset any positive return attributable to the rule's predictive power. From the preceding discussion it should be clear that the component of performance due to the interaction of position bias with market trend must be eliminated if one is to develop a valid performance benchmark.

At first blush, it might seem as if a rule that has a long position bias during a rising market trend is evidence of the rule's predictive power. However, this is not necessarily so. The rule's bullish bias could simply be due to the way its long and short conditions are defined. If the rule's long condition is more easily satisfied than its short condition, all other things being equal, the rule will tend to hold long positions a greater proportion of the time than short positions. Such a rule would receive a performance boost when back tested over historical data with a rising market trend. Conversely, a rule whose short condition is more easily satisfied than its long condition would be biased toward short positions and it would get a performance boost if simulated during a downward trending market.

The reader may be wondering how the definition of a rule can induce a bias toward either long or short positions. This warrants some explanation. Recall that binary reversal rules, the type tested in this book, are always in either a long or short position. Given this, if a rule's long (+1) condition is relatively easy to satisfy, then it follows that its short condition (–1) must be relatively difficult to satisfy. In other words, the condition required for the –1 output state is more restrictive, making it likely that, over time, the rule will spend more time long than short. It is just as possible to formulate rules where the long condition is more restrictive than the short condition. All other things being equal, such a rule would recommend short positions more frequently than long. It would be contrary to our purpose to allow the assessment of a rule's predictive power to be impacted by the relative strictness or laxity of the way in which its long and short conditions are defined.

To illustrate, consider the following rule, which has a highly restrictive short condition and, therefore, a relatively lax long condition. The rule, which generates positions in the S&P 500 index, is based on the Dow Jones Transportation Average.[10] Assume that a moving average with bands set at +3 percent and –3 percent is applied to the DJTA. The rule is to be short the S&P 500 while the DJTA is below the lower band, by definition a relatively rare condition, and long at all other times. See Figure 1.6. Clearly, such a rule would benefit if the S&P were in an uptrend over the back-test period.

Now let's consider the back test of two binary reversal rules which are referred to as rule 1 and rule 2. They are tested on S&P 500 data over the period January 1, 1976 through December 2004. During this period of approximately 7,000 days, the S&P 500 had an average daily return of +0.035 percent per day compounded, or +9.21897 percent annualized. Assume that rule 1 was in a long state 90 percent of the time and rule 2 was in a long state 60 percent of the time. Also, suppose that neither rule has predictive power—as if their output values were determined by a roulette wheel with 100 slots. The output for rule 1 is based on a roulette wheel

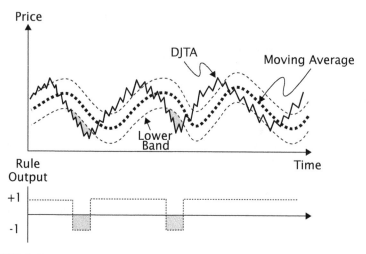

FIGURE 1.6 Rule with restrictive short condition and long position bias.

with 90 slots assigned a value of +1 and the remaining 10 assigned a value of −1. The output for rule 2 is based on a wheel with 60 slots assigned a +1 value and 40 a value of −1. By the Law of Large Numbers,[11] it is reasonable to expect that over the 7,000 days, rule 1 will be long very close to 90 percent of the time and rule 2 will be long approximately 60 percent of the time. Although the rules have different long/short biases, they have equal predictive power—none. However, their expected rates of return will be quite different over this segment of market history.

The expected return of a rule depends upon three quantities; (1) the proportion of time the rule spent in long positions, (2) the proportion of time spent in short positions (1 minus the proportion of time long) and (3) the market's average daily price change during the historical test period. The expected return (ER) is given by the following equation.

Expected Return

$$ER = [p(L) \times ADC] - [p(S) \times ADC]$$

Where
p(L) – probability of long position (proportion long)
p(S) – probability of short position (proportion short)
ADC: average daily change in market traded

Based on this calculation, the expected return for rule 1 is .028 percent per day or 7.31 percent annualized.[12] The expected return for rule 2 is

0.007 percent per day or 1.78 percent annualized.[13] This demonstrates that the rules' historical performance misleads us in two ways. First, both rules generate positive returns, yet we know that neither has any predictive power. Second, rule 1 appears to be superior to rule 2 even though we know they have equal predictive power—none.

When testing actual trading rules, one way to remove the deceptive effect due to the interaction of position bias and market trend would be to do the following: Subtract the expected return of a nonpredictive rule with the same position bias as the rule tested from the observed return of the tested rule. For example, assume that we did not know rules 1 and 2 had no predictive power. Simply by knowing their historical position bias, 90 percent long for rule 1 and 60 percent for rule 2, and knowing the market's average daily return over the back-test period, we would be able to compute the expected returns for rules with no predictive power having these position biases using the equation for the expected return already shown. The expected returns for each rule and would then be subtracted from each rule's observed performance. Therefore, from rule 1's back-tested return, which was 7.31 percent, we would subtract 7.31 percent, giving a result of zero. The result properly reflects rule 1's lack of predictive power. From rule 2's return of 1.78 percent, we would subtract a value of 1.78 percent, also giving a value of zero, also revealing its lack of predictive power.

The bottom line is this: by adjusting the back-tested (observed) performance by the expected return of a rule with no predictive power having an equivalent position bias, the deceptive component of performance can be removed. In other words, one can define the benchmark for any rule as the expected return of a nonpredictive rule with an equivalent position bias.

A Simpler Solution to Benchmarking: Detrending the Market Data

The procedure just described can be quite burdensome when many rules are being tested. It would require that a separate benchmark be computed for each rule based on its particular position bias. Fortunately there is an easier way.

The easier method merely requires that the historical data for the market being traded (e.g., S&P 500 Index) be detrended prior to rule testing. It is important to point out that the detrended data is used only for the purpose of calculating daily rule returns. It is not used for signal generation if the time series of the market being traded is also being used as a rule input series. Signals would be generated from actual market data (not detrended).

Detrending is a simple transformation, which results in a new market data series whose average daily price change is equal to zero. As pointed out earlier, if the market being traded has a net zero trend during the backtest period, a rule's position bias will have no distorting effect on performance. Thus, the expected return of a rule with no predictive power, the benchmark, will be zero if its returns are computed from detrended market data. Consequently, the expected return of a rule that does have predictive power will be greater than zero when its returns are computed from detrended data.

To perform the detrending transformation, one first determines the average daily price change of the market being traded over the historical test period. This average value is then subtracted from each day's price change.

The mathematical equivalence between the two methods discussed, (1) detrending the market data and (2) subtracting a benchmark with a equivalent position bias, may not be immediately obvious. A detailed mathematical proof is given in the Appendix, but if you think about it, you will see that if the market's average daily price change during the historical testing period is equal to zero, then rules devoid of predictive power must have an expected return of zero, regardless of their long/short position bias.

To illustrate this point, let's return to the formula for computing the expected value of a random variable. You will notice that if the average daily price change of the market being traded is zero, it does not matter what p(long) or p(short) are. The expected return (ER) will always be zero.

ER = [p (long) × avg. daily return] – [p (short) × avg. daily return]

For example, if the position biases were 60 percent long and 40 percent short, the expected return is zero.

0 = [(0.60) × 0] – [(0.40) × 0] Position Bias: 60 percent long, 40 percent short

If, on the other hand, a rule does have predictive power, its expected return on detrended data will be greater than zero. This positive return reflects the fact that the rule's long and short positions are intelligent rather than random.

Using Logs of Daily Price Ratio Instead of Percentages

Thus far, the returns for rules and the market being traded have been discussed in percentage terms. This was done for ease of explanation. However, there are problems with computing returns as percentages. These problems can be eliminated by computing daily returns as the logs of daily price ratios which is defined as:

$$\text{Log}\left(\frac{\text{current day's price}}{\text{prior day's price}}\right)$$

The log-based market returns are detrended in exactly the same way as the percentage changes. The log of the daily price ratio for the market being traded is computed for each day over the back-test period. The average is found, and then this average is deducted from each day. This eliminates any trend in the market data.

OTHER DETAILS: THE LOOK-AHEAD BIAS AND TRADING COSTS

It is said the devil lives in the details. When it comes to testing rules, this truth applies. There are two more items that must be considered to ensure accurate historical testing. They are (1) the look-ahead bias and the related issue, assumed execution prices, and (2) trading costs.

Look-Ahead Bias and Assumed Execution Prices

Look-ahead bias,[14] also known as "leakage of future information," occurs in the context of historical testing when information that was not truly available at a given point in time was assumed to be known. In other words, the information that would be required to generate a signal was not truly available at the time the signal was assumed to occur.

In many instances, this problem can be subtle. If unrecognized, it can seriously overstate the performance of rule tests. For example, suppose a rule uses the market's closing price or any input series that only becomes known at the time of the close. When this is the case, it would not be legitimate to assume that one could enter or exit a position at the market's closing price. Assuming this would infect the results with look-ahead bias. In fact, the earliest opportunity to enter or exit would be the following day's opening price (assuming daily frequency information). All of the rules tested in Part Two of this book are based on market data that is known as of the close of each trading day. Therefore, the rule tests assume execution at the opening price on the following day. This means that a rule's daily return for the current day (day_0) is equal to the rule's output value (+1 or –1) as of the close of day_0 multiplied by the market's change from the opening price of the next day (open day$_{+1}$) price to the opening price on day after that (open day$_{+2}$). That price change is given as the log of the ratio defined as opening price of day$_{+2}$ divided by the opening price on day$_{+1}$, as shown in the following equation:

$$\text{Pos}_0 \times \text{Log}\left[\frac{O_{+2}}{O_{+1}}\right]$$

Where:

POS_0 = Rule's market position as of the close of day$_0$

O_{+1} = Open S&P 500 on day$_{+1}$

O_{+2} = Open S&P 500 on day$_{+2}$

This equation does not show the detrended version of rule returns, as shown here:

$$\text{Pos}_0 \times \left[\text{Log}\left[\frac{O_{+2}}{O_{+1}}\right] - \text{ALR}\right]$$

Where:

POS_0 = Rule's market position as of the close of day$_0$

O_{+1} = Open S&P 500 on day$_{+1}$

O_{+2} = Open S&P 500 on day$_{+2}$

ALR = Average Log Return over Back Test

Look-ahead bias can also infect back-test results when a rule uses an input data series that is reported with a lag or that is subject to revision. For example, the back-test of a rule that uses mutual fund cash statistics,[15] which is released to the public with a two-week delay, must take this lag into account by lagging signals to reflect the true availability of the data. None of the rules tested in this book use information reported with a lag or that is subject to revision.

Trading Costs

Should trading costs be taken into account in rule back-tests? If the intent is to use the rule on a stand-alone basis for trading, the answer is clearly yes. For example, rules that signal reversals frequently will incur higher trading costs than rules that signal less frequently and this must be taken into account when comparing their performances. Trading costs include broker commissions and slippage. Slippage is due to the bid-asked spread and the amount that the investor's order pushes the market's price—up when buying or down when selling.

If, however, the purpose of rule testing is to discover signals that contain predictive information, then trading costs can obscure the value of a rule that reverses frequently. Since the intent of the rule studies conducted in this book are aimed at finding rules that have predictive power rather than finding rules that can be used as stand-alone trading strategies it was decided not to impose trading costs.

CHAPTER 2

The Illusory Validity of Subjective Technical Analysis

The difference between a crank and a charlatan is the charlatan knows he is dealing in snake oil, the crank does not.

—Martin Gardner

The chapter has two purposes. First, it is intended to encourage an attitude of skepticism toward subjective TA, a body of propositions that are untestable because they lack cognitive content. Second, it underscores the need for a rigorous and objective approach to knowledge acquisition, to combat the human tendency to form and maintain strong beliefs in the absence of solid evidence or even in the face of contradictory evidence.

Besides what we take on faith, most of us are under the impression that our beliefs are justified by sound reasoning from good evidence. It can be said that we know something when we have a belief that is true and we hold it because we have drawn a correct inference from the right evidence.[1] We know that ice cream is cold, gravity is real, and some dogs bite, on the basis of first-hand experience, but without the time or expertise to acquire all requisite knowledge directly, we willingly accept wisdom from secondhand sources we deem reliable. However we come by it, we do not adopt knowledge willy-nilly, or so we believe.

Unfortunately, this belief and many others that we hold are erroneous. Without realizing it, by a process that is as automatic as breathing, we adopt all sorts of beliefs without rational thought or reliable evidence. According to a growing body of research, this is due to a variety of cognitive errors, biases, and illusions. This is a serious liability, because once a

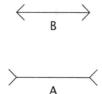

FIGURE 2.1 Senses can deceive us.

falsehood is adopted, it tends to persist even when new evidence shows it to be wrong. This longevity is also attributable to various cognitive errors that lead us to defend existing beliefs.

A visual illusion is an example of an erroneous belief that persists even after it has been pointed out. In Figure 2.1, line segment A appears longer than segment B, but if you apply a ruler, you will see they are of equal length. However, this knowledge does not undo the illusion. Seeing can be deceiving, and the deception lasts.

Figure 2.2[2] depicts another visual illusion. The table top on the right appears more elongated. If you compare them you will see they have the same dimensions.

Under normal circumstances, sensory impressions as interpreted by the brain produce accurate beliefs about the world. The selective pressures of evolution assured the development of such a vital capability. However, as well adapted as the eye/brain system is, it is not perfect. Under adverse conditions, conditions outside of those that shaped its evolution, the system can be fooled.

Just as there are illusory perceptions, there is illusory knowledge. It seems valid, but it is not, and similar to perceptual illusions, false knowledge tends to occur in situations beyond those that shaped the evolution

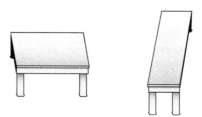

FIGURE 2.2 Both table tops have same size and shape.
"Turning the Tables" from MIND SIGHTS by Roger N. Shepard. Copyright © 1990 by Roger N. Shepard. Reprinted by permission of Henry Holt and Company, LLC.

of our cognitive abilities. Under such adverse conditions, our generally successful learning strategies fail, and we come to "know" what is not so.[3]

Over the last 30 years, cognitive psychologists have discovered that erroneous knowledge is often the result of systematic errors (biases) in the way we process information about complex and uncertain situations. Financial market behavior is complex and uncertain, so it should be no surprise that informal (subjective) analysis would produce illusory knowledge.

A systematic error, unlike a random error, occurs over and over again in similar situations. This is good news because it means the error is predictable and steps can be taken to avoid it. The first step is realizing that such errors are common.

SUBJECTIVE TA IS NOT LEGITIMATE KNOWLEDGE

As defined in Chapter 1, subjective TA is any method of analysis that, because of vagueness, cannot be defined as an algorithm that can be back tested by computer. Though the subjective domain of TA is comprised of many different methods, they share a faith that valid knowledge about financial markets can be discovered in an informal and nonscientific manner. I contend this faith is misplaced.

As discussed in the Introduction, subjective TA cannot be called wrong, because to call a method wrong implies it has been tested and contradicted by objective evidence. Subjective TA is immune to empirical challenge because it is untestable. Thus, it is worse than wrong; it is meaningless.

Beliefs that cannot be tested must be accepted on faith, anecdotal evidence, or authoritarian pronouncement . In this way, subjective TA is similar to practices such as New-Age medicine, astrology, numerology, and a host of other untestable claims, none of which can legitimately be classified as knowledge.

However, many TA practitioners and consumers believe strongly in the validity of subjective methods, and if asked, no doubt each would assert that their belief is justified and supported by evidence. I contend this is a consequence of the same cognitive flaws that underlie erroneous beliefs in general and the unscientific manner in which traditional TA is practiced.

TA is certainly not the only field to suffer the ill effects of nonscientific methods. Medicine and psychology, where the penalties for faulty wisdom are much greater, are also burdened with erroneous knowledge. This has spawned an emerging movement called evidence-based medicine that appeals to doctors to restrict themselves to practices with proven efficacy. There is a similar movement in psychotherapy. A journal called the *Scientific Review of Mental Health Practice*[4] describes its mission as ridding the field of unsubstantiated and untested treatments. Unfortunately, it is unlikely that traditional doctors and psychotherapists will abandon their ingrained ways. Old beliefs are hard to change. However, new practitioners may be persuaded, and it is their patients who will benefit from methods with proven efficacy.

Although this chapter is a critique of subjective TA, objective TA is also vulnerable to erroneous knowledge. However, it comes about in an entirely different manner. Whereas subjective TA suffers from a lack of quantitative evidence, objective TA suffers from faulty inferences drawn from quantitative evidence. This problem and possible solutions are explored in Chapter 6.

A PERSONAL ANECDOTE: FIRST A TRUE TA BELIEVER, THEN A SKEPTIC

A book on the necessity of quantitative objective evidence may be a strange place for personal anecdotes. Nevertheless, I offer a firsthand account of my initial conversion to a true believer in TA, my fall from faith, and my rebirth as a scientific skeptic who believes TA can offer value when researched in a disciplined manner.

I first learned of TA as a teenager and wanted to believe its claims were true. Making money from chart patterns seemed magical yet plausible. Until that time, my earnings were derived from summers spent tending lawns, digging clams on Long Island's North Shore, and working on a garbage truck at a local resort. Though I've never shied away from physical labor, the idea of making money without sweat had great appeal.

Like most TA true believers, my initial convictions came secondhand, reading the revealed wisdom of the field's self-proclaimed authorities. It never occurred to me that their claims might not be grounded in sound research. The very term *technical analysis* had a scientific ring to it. Later it became clear that in many instances the authorities were not basing their claims on firsthand research but merely regurgitating what they had read from even earlier self-proclaimed experts. Humorist and philosopher Artemus Ward has said, "It's not so much the things we don't know that get us into trouble as the things we know that just ain't so."

My first read was *How I Made Two Million Dollars in the Stock Market* by Nicholas Darvas, a professional dancer. He attributed his success to a charting method called the Box Theory. As my first exposure to TA, the idea that buy-and-sell signals could be derived from a stock's behavior was entirely novel and exciting. Darvas based his analysis on a staircase-like arrangement of price ranges that he called boxes. Soon I learned this was old wine in a new bottle—the good old-fashioned support and resistance zones of TA. My enthusiasm was undeterred. Next I studied Chartcraft's Point and Figure Method and began keeping charts on a large stable of stocks. For my sixteenth birthday my parents gave me the bible, *Technical Analysis of Stock Trends*, by Edwards and Magee, and my conversion was complete.

Before long, I was giving stock tips to my chemistry teacher, Mr. Corn. My initial success with a stock called Cubic made several other teachers fans of my mysterious charts. I picked several more winners. No one, not even I, considered the possibility that these early successes might have been nothing more than a run of good luck. There was no reason to. None of the TA books I studied ever discussed the roles of randomness in market behavior or luck in the performance of an investment method. My early scores were plausible because they were consistent with the anecdotes that filled the books, but it did not last. My track record began to blemish and my fans faded. However, my enthusiasm for TA continued to grow because it was always possible to explain away my failures. After the fact, I could always see where I had misread the chart. I'd get it right next time.

In high school I was a good science student, although I now realize I was scientifically illiterate. Later, college courses in the philosophy of science taught me that science is more than a set of facts. First and foremost, it is a method for distinguishing real from illusory knowledge. It would take me the better part of 40 years to see the connection between the philosophy of science and TA.

My skepticism grew out of my experience as a proprietary or "prop" trader for the firm of Spear, Leeds & Kellogg from the fall of 1996 through the spring of 2002. Prop traders have the ultimate fun job. They are given the freedom to speculate with a firm's capital. My trading strategy was based on what I had learned about TA over the prior 35 years. I made profits during the first three and one-half years, October 1996 through February 2000. Because my trading methods were subjective, it is not clear if these gains were the result of my abilities with TA or my ever-bullish bias coinciding with an upward-trending market. I suspect it was the latter because an analysis of my monthly returns relative to a market benchmark indicated I was not beating the market but merely matching it. In other words, I had not generated a significantly positive alpha.[5] Also suggestive was the fact that I gave back all my gains in the two years after the market trend turned down in March 2000. Over the full five-and-one-half-year period, my results, to put it generously, were lackluster.

Prior to joining Spear, Leeds & Kellogg, I had been a proponent of objective trading methods, so while at Spear, I made efforts to develop a systematic trading program in hopes that it would improve my performance. However, with limited time and development capital, these plans never came to fruition. Thus, I continued to rely on classical bar-chart analysis, supplemented with several indicators that I interpreted subjectively.

However, I was objective in several ways. Early in my trading career with Spear, I began keeping a detailed journal. Prior to each trade I would note its TA rationale. In addition, each trade was based on an objectively falsifiable prediction—a defined point of adversity where I would admit the trade was wrong. My managers insisted on this. I maintained the journal daily over the five-plus years of trading. After each transaction was completed, I did a postmortem analysis. This practice made it hard for me to rationalize my failures. There they were staring me in the face. This accelerated my fall from faith in subjective TA.

Because my results were for only one person, I considered the possibility I was not properly implementing the dictates of the TA texts I had been studying for the past 30+ years. Yet, I also began to wonder if what they said was correct or if what they said was even substantive.

When I discussed my growing skepticism with colleagues, their response was that TA was obviously valid. Trends and patterns in historical charts were simply too evident to be illusory. A widely used TA text[6] asserts that TA is valid on these grounds. This did not satisfy me. When I learned that the same patterns and trends,[7] to which TA attributes such significance, also appear with regularity in purely random data, my faith in chart analysis was shaken to the core. Moreover, it came to my attention that studies have shown that expert chart readers cannot reliably distinguish actual market charts from charts produced by a random process.[8] Such charts, which are generated by random draws from a sample of actual price changes, are, by design, devoid of authentic trends and patterns and, therefore, impossible to predict, but, to experienced chartists, they looked just like authentic price charts. On this basis, it would seem that predictions based on authentic charts could not be trusted. Clearly, "obvious validity" is an inadequate standard for judging the validity of market patterns.

With inspiration from two books, *How We Know What Isn't So* by Thomas Gilovich,[9] and *Why People Believe Weird Things* by Michael Shermer,[10] I came to the realization that TA must be approached with the skepticism and rigor of the scientific method.

THE MIND: A NATURAL PATTERN FINDER

We are predisposed to look for and find predictive patterns. Human nature is repulsed by the unpredictable and the unexplained, so our cognitive machinery tends to perceive order, pattern, and meaning in the sensory stimuli we receive from the world regardless of whether it truly is ordered, patterned, or meaningful. "In many instances, what we experience is nothing more than the vagaries of chance at work."[11] "The appearance of a face on the surface of the moon, the perception of Satanic messages when rock music is played backwards, or seeing the face of Jesus in the wood grain of a hospital door are examples of the mind imposing order on random visual sensory stimuli."[12]

The tendency to perceive order evolved because this ability was crucial for our survival.[13] The early humans who were best at it produced the most offspring, and we are descended from them. Unfortunately, evolution did not endow us with an equal ability to distinguish valid from invalid patterns. As a consequence, along with the valid knowledge came many falsehoods.

Acquiring knowledge, whether in prehistoric times or today, can fail in two ways: learning a falsehood or failing to learn a truth. Of these two mistakes, we seem to be more prone to adopting falsehoods than we are to overlooking vital truths. Evolutionary biologists speculate that the acquisition of false ideas was less detrimental to the survival of early humans than failing to learn something vital. The belief that a ritual dance prior to a hunt would promote success is a learned falsehood with minimal cost—a little wasted dancing—but the failure to learn the importance of standing downwind of an animal during a hunt was an error with a significant survival cost.

As a result, our brains evolved to have a voracious, although indiscriminate, appetite for predictive patterns and causal relations. The false beliefs that accumulated along the way were a price worth paying. Sometimes, a successful hunt did follow a ritual dance, so the superstitious practice was reinforced. Also, performing a ritual reduced anxiety by giving an illusory sense of control over outcomes that were largely a matter of chance.

Modern civilized life has changed this picture considerably. Not only are decisions more complex today, but the costs of learned falsehoods are greater. Consider the debate on global warming. Are rising temperatures indicative of a real long-term danger or are they a false alarm? If those convinced that it is a false alarm are later proven wrong, future generations will pay dearly. However, the cost of treating global warming as a serious threat would be more modest if that view turns out to be mistaken.

The evolution of human intelligence has been a slow process. Our intellectual capacities developed over a several-million-year period, most of which took place under conditions referred to as the ancestral environment of adaptation. In this environment, the mandates were few and clear: Survive and reproduce. Human intellectual capacities and thinking strategies were adapted for those conditions, not for the complexities of modern civilization, which date back a mere 10 to 15 thousand years. In other words, 99 percent of human evolution took place in an environment dramatically less complex than the one we face today. It is not surprising, then, that our intelligence would be maladapted to the complex judgment and decision-making tasks we face today. We seem to be as superstitious today as the cave dweller who believed in ritual dances.

THE EPIDEMIC OF WEIRD BELIEFS

A voracious but indiscriminate appetite for knowledge inevitably leads to weird beliefs. Our susceptibility to the adoption of false beliefs was evidenced dramatically in a 1990 Gallup survey of 1,236 adult Americans. The proportion of people believing in all manner of nonsense including the paranormal is frightening.[14] These are statistics presented by Shermer.[15]

Astrology 52 percent

Extrasensory perception 46 percent

Witches 19 percent

Aliens from space landing on earth 22 percent

A previously existing continent called Atlantis 33 percent

Humans and dinosaurs living at the same time 41 percent

Communicating with the spirits of the dead 42 percent

Ghosts 35 percent

Personal psychic experiences 67 percent

Astronomer Carl Sagan[16] lamented that more people believe in astrology than the theory of evolution. He attributed this widespread irrationality and superstition to a high rate of scientific illiteracy, which surveys estimate to be over 95 percent. "In such an atmosphere, pseudo science thrives. Strange beliefs, such as New-Age health practices, are supported in ways that purport to be scientific but really are not. The evidence offered is insufficient, and facts that point in other directions are given short shrift. However, the ideas they offer survive and thrive because they speak to powerful emotional needs that science often leaves unfulfilled."[17] As Sagan said, it's no fun to be skeptical. It is a burdensome attitude that leaves our need to believe in fun and comforting ideas, like the tooth fairy and Santa Claus, unsatisfied.

COGNITIVE PSYCHOLOGY: HEURISTICS, BIASES, AND ILLUSIONS

Cognitive psychology is concerned with how we process information, draw conclusions, and make decisions. It studies the mental processes by which sensory input is transformed, reduced, elaborated, stored, and re-covered.[18]

Over the last 30 years cognitive psychologies have been investigating the origins of unreliable knowledge. The good news is that common sense and intuitive interpretations of experience are mostly correct. The bad news is that human intelligence is maladapted to making accurate judgments in situations characterized by uncertainty. Under conditions of uncertainty, intuitive judgments and informally acquired knowledge are often wrong. Because financial market behavior is highly uncertain, erroneous knowledge in this domain is to be expected.

The pioneering research of Daniel Kahneman, Paul Slovic, and Amos Tversky showed that illusory knowledge[19] originates in two ways. First, people are plagued by various cognitive biases and illusions that distort what we experience and how we learn from that experience. Second, to compensate for the mind's limited abilities to process information, human intelligence has evolved various mental shortcuts called judgment heuristics. These rules of thought, which operate quite automatically beneath our conscious awareness, are the basis of our intuitive judgments and probability assessments. They are a mark of human intelligence crucial to everyday living. Though these quick and dirty rules of thinking are generally successful, in certain kinds of situation they cause us to make biased decisions and acquire erroneous knowledge.

Erroneous knowledge is especially problematic because of its resilience. Studies have shown that once a belief has been adopted, it can survive the assault of new evidence contradicting it or even a complete discrediting of the original evidence that led to the belief's formation.

The sections that follow will discuss a variety of cognitive errors responsible for erroneous knowledge. For purposes of presentation, each will be discussed separately. In actuality, however, they operate conjointly, feeding into and off one another, creating an illusion of validity for subjective TA. This is illustrated in Figure 2.3.

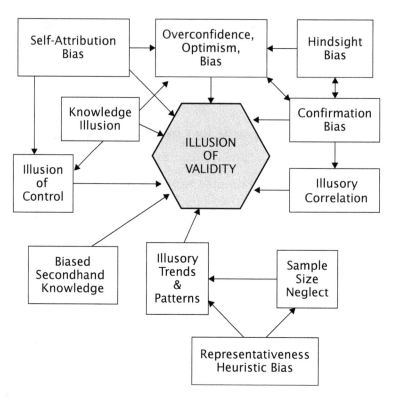

FIGURE 2.3 Illusion of validity.

HUMAN INFORMATION PROCESSING LIMITATIONS

Despite its awesome power, the information-processing capabilities of the human brain are limited. Nobel Laureate Herbert Simon called this the principle of bounded rationality. "The capacity of the human mind for formulating and solving complex problems is very small compared with size of the problems whose solution is required."[20] Consequently, we attend to only a small fraction of the torrent of information the world presents and process it in simplistic ways.

The number of separate chunks of information that can be held in conscious memory at a given time is estimated to be seven, plus or minus two.[21] Even more limited is the mind's ability to handle problems requiring configural thinking. A configural-thinking problem requires that a multitude of factors (variables) be considered simultaneously as an inseparable configuration. Research indicates that the mind is only able to handle a maximum of three factors when they must be evaluated in a configural fashion.[22] Medical diagnosis is typically a configural-thinking problem. A set of symptoms and lab results, if considered conjointly, can distinguish one disease from another, but taken in isolation they may be nothing more than a set of disconnected uninformative facts.

Configural thinking is a more demanding mode of thought than sequential or linear thinking. In a sequential/linear problem, the relevant variables can be analyzed independently, so even though there may be a multitude of variables, the message conveyed by each variable is unaffected by what others variables are saying. Therefore, once each variable has been interpreted on its own, the set of individual messages can be combined in a linear fashion (i.e., added algebraically[23]), to derive their collective meaning. Suppose, for example that a sequential problem involves seven variables, each of which can assume a value of either +1 or −1. Further, assume that five of the variables have the value +1 and two have the value −1. The linear or additive combination[24] would be equal to +3 or [(+5) + (−2)]. Research has shown that, when experts make multifactored decisions in a subjective fashion, they primarily rely on a linear combining rule,[25] though they do it less effectively than formal linear regression models.[26] These studies have shown that human experts are less effective than linear regression models because they fail to combine the information in the consistent manner of a formal mathematical model.

The combining of information in a linear fashion that satisfies the requirements of a sequential-thinking problem falls short when the problem demands a configural solution. In a configural problem, the relevant information is contained in the web of relationships (interactions) between the variables. This means that the variables cannot be evaluated in isolation as they can in a sequential/linear problem. To clarify what is meant by interactions, imagine a configural problem involving only three variables, A, B, and C. Further suppose that each variable can assume only two readings, high or low (i.e., the variables are binary). In a configural problem, a high reading on factor A may mean one thing when B is low and C is high, whereas a high reading on A can mean something entirely different when B is high and C is low. In a sequential/linear problem, a high reading on factor A carries the same message irrespective of the readings on B and C.

The difference between the two configurations—Configuration 1 (A-high, B-low, C-high) and Configuration 2 (A-high, B-high, C-low)—are illustrated in the Figures 2.4 and 2.5. The eight cells of the three-dimensional space show that there are eight distinctly different possible configurations of three binary variables. However, a linear combination of three binary variables can only assume four[27] distinct values.

The type of thinking problem faced by a subjective market analyst attempting to make a forecast by combining the readings on five indicators (variables), a relatively modest number, is likely to be configural rather

A—High, B—Low, C—High

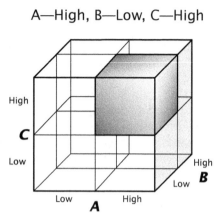

FIGURE 2.4 Configuration 1.

than sequential.[28] Simply determining which of the five indicators should be combined (some may be redundant or irrelevant) to produce an informative prediction is a huge configural problem in itself. With only five indicators, the predictive power of 26 possible combinations must be evaluated (10 pairs, 10 triplets, 5 quadruplets, and 1 quintuplet). Then, once a good combination has been identified, applying the multi-indicator rule would also entail configural thinking. As seen earlier, even if the indicators are binary, the simplest possible, 3 binary variables can have eight distinct configurations. Four binaries have 16 possible distinct configurations and 5 binary variables have 32. Subjective analysts who believe they

A—High, B—High, C—Low

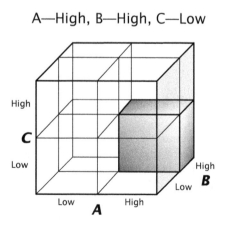

FIGURE 2.5 Configuration 2.

can perform such a feat are too confident—way too confident! This is not surprising. It is merely one example of the overconfidence bias.

TOO DANG CERTAIN: THE OVERCONFIDENCE BIAS

In general people are too confident. The overconfidence bias is the documented[29] tendency for people's self-assessments to err on the high side of the truth. They tend to view their personal attributes and abilities as better than objective evidence would indicate. People view themselves as above average in many ways, including how much they know and how accurately they know it. In other words people tend to be arrogant about their knowledge.

The tendency is so pervasive that psychologists think overconfidence is inborn, and they are quite confident about that. Biologists have speculated that high confidence is a feature of successful mating strategies, so we are most likely the offspring of swaggering parents. High confidence confers benefits on humanity as a whole, even if the daring individual trying something new and dangerous dies. After enough attempts, someone succeeds, and we all benefit. In addition, overconfidence is reinforced by yet other cognitive biases that distort what is learned from experience, including the self-attribution bias, the confirmation bias, and the hindsight bias, which are discussed later.

Columbia University psychologist Janet Metcalfe summed up research on human overconfidence with these humbling words:[30]

> *People think they will be able to solve problems when they won't; they are highly confident that they are on the verge of producing the correct answer when they are, in fact, about to produce a mistake; they think they have solved problems when they haven't; they think they know answers to information questions when they don't; they have the answer on the tip of their tongue when there is no answer; they think they produced the correct answer when they didn't, and furthermore, they say they knew it all along; they believe they have mastered learning material when they haven't; they think they have understood, even though demonstrably they are still in the dark."[31]*

Some specific findings about overconfidence:

- Overconfidence is most extreme for difficult or impossible tasks.[32] Studies have shown extreme overconfidence in tasks such as predicting the outcome of horse races,[33] distinguishing European from American handwriting, and predicting rising versus falling stock prices. In the domain of TA, the analogous task would be that of combining a multitude of indicator readings into a market forecast by subjective configural reasoning.

- Overconfidence is related to an inability to properly assess the difficulty of various tasks and is more pronounced the more difficult the task. TA analysts may not be aware of the configural reasoning demanded by subjective data analysis.
- Confidence increases as the number of pieces of information are increased, though prediction accuracy does not.[34] Increased confidence would only be justified if the individual bits of information were nonredundant, were useful, and could be successfully integrated.
- Confidence increases as the level of agreement among multiple inputs increases. When inputs are independent (uncorrelated) and have predictive information, increased confidence may be justified. When inputs are redundant, it is not. Many TA indicators that appear to be distinct because of naming conventions and specific calculations actually measure similar market attributes. This can encourage unwarranted confidence.
- Doctors who were 88 percent confident they had correctly diagnosed pneumonia were correct in only 20 percent of the cases.[35] Physicians were similarly overconfident in diagnosing skull fractures.[36]
- Many other professionals were overconfident about their specific areas of expertise. For example, when managers of a chemical company were 90 percent confident about company facts (i.e., they expected to be wrong only 10 percent of the time) they were right only 50 percent of the time.[37] Executives of a computer company were 95 percent confident about general business facts but were correct 80 percent of the time. With respect to specifics about their own company, they were 95 percent confident but correct only 58 percent of the time.[38]
- The overconfidence of Wall Street's analysts with respect to their ability to forecast quarterly earnings is attested to by the frequency of earnings surprises. According to one study, average forecast error was 44 percent. This statistic was based on over 500,000 individual earnings predictions.[39] People are surprised when outcomes fall outside of predicted ranges, and setting ranges too narrowly is a sign of overconfidence.
- Individual investors are overconfident in their ability to predict short-term market trends and pick stocks that will do better than the market, as evidenced by the level of their trading activity.[40]
- Wall Street strategists exhibit overconfidence in the forecasts for the general stock market and are frequently surprised by actual out-

comes. However, they maintain their confidence in spite of these mistakes.[41] If strategists were indeed learning to curb their confidence, they would make subsequent predictions with wider bands of uncertainty, and outcomes would be less likely to fall outside of those bands. They do not appear to do this.

Given the pervasiveness of overconfidence, it is likely that practitioners of subjective TA would be afflicted with it as well. It seems likely that their overconfidence would manifest with respect to three areas; (1) the predictive power of specific methods, (2) the efficacy of subjective data analysis and informal inference as a means of knowledge discovery, and (3) the ability to perform configural reasoning as in synthesizing a market forecast from a multitude of indicator reading and patterns. Both the complexity of the financial markets and the known limits of unaided human intelligence suggest that high confidence with respect to any of these areas is unwarranted.

According to one study, there are two forecasting professions that have managed to avoid overconfidence: meteorologists and horse-race handicappers. Their estimates of their predictive abilities are well calibrated because: "They face similar problems every day; they make explicit (falsifiable) probabilistic predictions; and they obtain swift and precise feedback on outcomes. When these conditions are not satisfied, overconfidence should be expected for both experts and non-experts."[42]

It is impossible for subjective TA practitioners to obtain accurate feedback in the context of historical research simply because their methods for generating forecasts and evaluating forecast accuracy are not well defined. Feedback is only possible with objective methods. However, in the context of real-time forecasting, subjective practitioners could obtain feedback if they were willing to make falsifiable forecasts. A falsifiable forecast is one that has cognitive content. That is to say, it sets up a clearly discernable difference between the outcomes that would indicate the forecast had been correct and outcomes that would indicate the forecast has been in error. Consider the following as an example of a falsifiable forecast:

The S&P 500 will be higher twelve months from today, and will not decline more than 20 percent from current levels within that time.

If the market is not higher 12 months hence or if it drops more than 20 percent from the current level within the next 12 months, it is clear that the forecast was in error. Unfortunately, falsifiable forecasts are rarely given by subjective practitioners, thereby preventing feedback for them and their customers. Overconfidence persists.

It's Going to Be Great: Optimism Bias

The optimism basis is overconfidence that extends to a generalized and unwarranted hopefulness about the future.[43] As a consequence, most people think their lives will be sprinkled with more favorable and fewer unfavorable events than the lives of their peers.

The optimism bias suggests that TA analysts' beliefs about their predictive prowess will persist even if their prior predictions have not worked out well. This is borne out by data provided by the *Hulbert Digest*,[44] a newsletter that tracks the performance of market forecasters by translating their recommendations into a portfolio whose value can be tracked. Some newsletter writers have attempted to explain away their poor performance ratings by claiming that Hulbert's evaluation methods are flawed. According to Hulbert, these claims are leveled primarily at the assumptions he is required to make to turn a newsletter's vague recommendations into specific recommendations whose performance can be measured. Many newsletters tracked by Hulbert give clear advice, making such assumptions unnecessary.

Despite their dismal long-term performance, newsletter writers continue to make confident predictions, and subscribers continue to believe they will be helpful. Both groups are optimistically biased. If subscribers were realistic, they would cancel their subscriptions and the writers could not continue in business. Obviously, something other than predictive success keeps faith alive. One possible explanation is that both subscribers and newsletter authors have bought into a story that explains why the underlying method should work, even if it does not work in practice. As is explained later, a compelling story can overcome statistical evidence because the mind has evolved a greater taste for stories than abstract facts. (See the secondhand information bias and the power of narratives.)

Self-Attribution Bias: Rationalizing Failure

The tendency toward overconfidence is amplified by other biases that distort what we learn from experience. The self-attribution bias refers to the tendency to interpret past successes and failure in a biased and self-serving manner. "Numerous studies across a wide range of situations have found that people attribute positive outcomes to their abilities while attributing failures to external circumstances."[45] As a result, we come away with a falsely optimistic assessment of our strategies and abilities. Whereas the feedback of past failures might motivate change and improved performance, self-serving interpretations short-circuit such learning. This may explain how newsletter writers can maintain confidence in the face of performance that, by any objective standard, would be regarded as negative.

In addition to making us feel good, self-serving explanations make intuitive sense. When we exert ourselves and succeed, the causal chain-linking effort to a good outcome is easy to understand and has the ring of truth. Attributing success to good luck or some other factor not under our control not only has less emotional appeal, it also seems less plausible. We all prefer the plausible. However, a failure despite our best efforts seems more likely to be attributable to bad luck. Common sense tends to overlook the role of luck (randomness) in favorable outcomes. That's the job of the statistician.

Studies of the self-attribution bias among gamblers are revealing.[46] By evaluating past losses in a biased manner, they are able to maintain a faith in their abilities in the face of growing losses. Surprisingly, past losses are not ignored. Actually the gamblers devote a great deal of cognitive energy to failures thereby recasting them in a more favorable light. Losses are treated as near wins or attributed to bad luck. Wins, on the other hand, are credited to genuine betting skill.[47] In the end, both wins and losses wind up feeding the gambler's sense of competence.

As a trader I frequently heard self-serving rationalizations. I was guilty of it myself until I started keeping a trading log early in my trading career with predefined exit points where I was forced to admit my earlier forecast was in error. Even though my forecasts were based on subjective TA, my evaluation criteria were objectively defined in advance. I did not start to question my abilities until a considerable amount of negative feedback jarred my faith.

Sure, I Know That!: The Knowledge Illusion

The knowledge illusion is a false confidence in what we know—both in terms of quantity and quality. It is based on the false premise that more information should translate into more knowledge.[48] When horse-race handicappers were given more items of information, they grew more confident in their forecasts, but their actual accuracy did not improve.[49] The additional facts created the illusion of more knowledge.

The knowledge illusion is relevant to TA because it is most likely to occur in situations characterized by large amounts of data. Not only do financial markets generate a torrent of individual time series, but each one can be transformed into a far greater number of derivative time series called technical indicators. This provides ample opportunity for TA practitioners to see themselves as more knowledgeable than they really are.

The knowledge illusion stems in part from an overconfidence in the mind's ability to perform configural reasoning, the simultaneous interpretation of a multitude of variables. In fact the unaided mind is able to deal with only two or three variables in a configural fashion (see Part Two). By failing to appreciate these limits, people easily assume that considering more variables (indicators) will lead to greater knowledge and a more informed opinion.

I Can Handle That: The Illusion of Control

The illusion of control is an unwarranted belief in our ability to control outcomes. People who feel in control are happier and more relaxed than people who do not.[50] This cognitive distortion is fed by the self-attribution bias and it, in turn, feeds the overoptimism bias.

According to Nofsinger, activities that are most likely to induce the illusion of control have the five following characteristics[51]:

1. A high level of personal involvement
2. A large range of choice
3. A great amount of information available to consider (Knowledge Illusion)
4. A high level of familiarity with the task
5. Early success in the activity

The first four clearly apply to subjective TA. A high level of personal involvement is engendered by the frequent analysis of market data, the creation of new indicators and new ways to interpret them, the drawing and redrawing of trend lines, the counting and then recounting of Elliott waves, and so forth. There is also a large degree of choice: which markets to follow, which indicators to use, where to place a trend line, and so on. The various methods used become familiar as they are studied and used regularly. The fifth factor, early success, is a matter of chance. Some will experience initial success and because of the self-attribution bias are likely to attribute it to their expertise and the efficacy of the TA methods rather than chance. All of these factors can induce and maintain an unjustified sense of control and an ability to earn market-beating returns.

The Hindsight Bias: I Knew Things Would Turn Out That Way

The hindsight bias creates the illusion that the prediction of an uncertain event is easier than it really is when the event is viewed in retrospect, after its outcome is known. Once we learn the upshot of an uncertain situation, such as which team won a football game or in which direction prices moved, subsequent to a TA pattern, we tend to forget how uncertain we really were prior to knowing the outcome. See Figure 2.6.

This cognitive distortion can be understood in terms of the way memories are stored in the brain. Past events are stored in categories of similar events (e.g., sports events) rather than as a sequential temporal record. For this reason similar types of events that occurred at different times become intermixed. As a result, after the outcome of a football game becomes known, the pregame state of knowledge (uncertainty) becomes intermixed with definitive postgame knowledge. Our state of knowledge prior to the game was uncertain because of the ambiguous nature of the pregame evidence. One could have made the case for either team winning. The intermixing of pregame knowledge with postgame knowledge happens immediately and unconsciously, leaving us unable to recall what we knew before the game or our state of doubt. Consequently, the pregame evidence, which was in fact quite uncertain, seems less uncertain after the winner became known. This creates a false sense of confidence in our ability to make predictions. It is because of this very pitfall that scientists are especially careful about defining procedures for making predictions and evaluating their accuracy.

Subjective TA is especially prone to the hindsight bias because it lacks clearly defined rules for pattern identification, forecast generation,

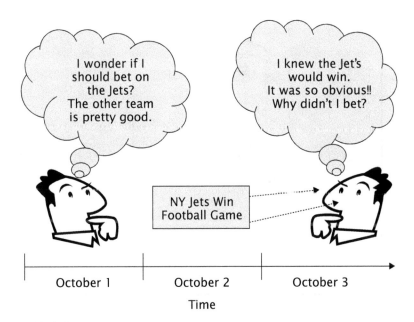

FIGURE 2.6 The hindsight bias.

and prediction evaluation. In real time, the practitioner of subjective TA faces a task of overwhelming ambiguity. A single chart contains a mind-boggling number of possible predictive cues that range from the extremely bearish to the extremely bullish. However, when the same chart is viewed in retrospect, the ambiguities that had faced the analyst trying to make a prediction fade away because outcomes are known. This creates a false credibility for subjective chart analysis.

Let's consider a hypothetical example illustrating how outcome knowledge might minimize the true ambiguities in a chart, thus overstating the predictive power of subjective chart analysis. Consider Figure 2.7 and what was knowable as of time A. The pattern could be interpreted as bullish: a prior uptrend with a bullish flag consolidation temporarily interrupting the uptrend.

Or the same chart could be interpreted as bearish: a head-and-shoulder pattern, with a neckline breach and then a return rally providing an ideal time for a short sale. This interpretation is illustrated in Figure 2.8. Note that both charts are identical up to point A, except for the price swings that have been highlighted and the forecast made based on the pattern.

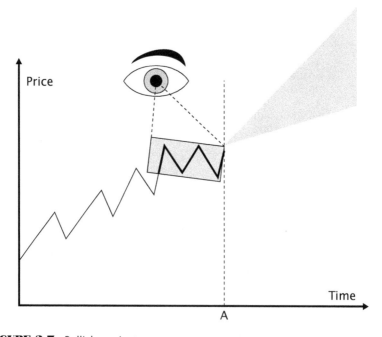

FIGURE 2.7 Bullish conjecture.

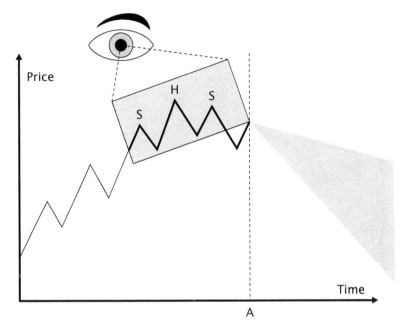

FIGURE 2.8 Bearish conjecture.

In reality, at point A the chart is an ambiguous mixture of technical features that could support either a bullish or bearish forecast. The true uncertainty, which is depicted in Figure 2.9, explains why chartists shown the same history will often express a variety of predictions

Now let's alter the situation by imagining how chartists might look at the same chart at a later time, point B. We will look at two different outcomes paths subsequent to point A. This is intended to illustrate how the hindsight bias can obscure the ambiguity that existed at time A, thereby creating an illusion of validity for subjective chart analysis, irrespective of which path prices actually took.

First consider an analyst's impression looking at the chart for the first time at time B in Figure 2.10. This is the same chart shown previously with an uptrend tacked on after point A. This observer knows an uptrend took place between A and B. It is my contention that the hindsight bias would encourage the subjective analysts to notice the bullish flag pattern rather than the bearish head-and-shoulder pattern. In other words, the possession of outcome knowledge tends to make patterns that gave incorrect predictions less noticeable while making patterns that predicted accurately more noticeable. What was in fact an ambiguous pattern to an observer only possessing knowledge up to point A appears as an obviously

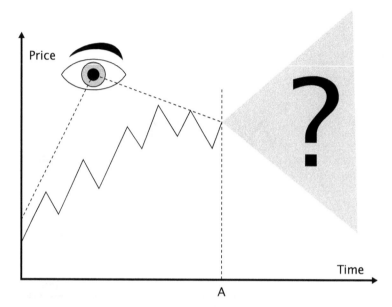

FIGURE 2.9   The true uncertainty of foresight.

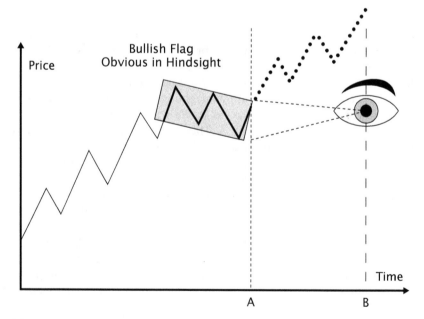

FIGURE 2.10   The false certainty of hindsight.

bullish bull flag to an observer looking back from point B. Similarly, the outcome knowledge possessed by the observer at point B renders the bearish head-and-shoulders pattern less noticeable. The observer at point B comes away with the impression that the evidence on the chart supports the validity of chart analysis.

Alternatively, if the price path from time A to time B had been a downtrend, as depicted in Figure 2.11, I contend that the hindsight bias would cause an observer at point B to notice a head-and-shoulders top pattern that predicted successfully, but the observer would not notice the bullish flag whose forecast proved erroneous.

These illustrations were contrived to make a point. Whatever the outcome, it is always possible to selectively notice chart features that seemingly predicted correctly, amongst what is truly an ambiguous mixture of bullish and bearish cues. The vague manner in which subjective chart patterns are defined, the lack of objective evaluation criteria, and the operation of the hindsight bias create an illusion of validity for subjective chart analysis.

Who among us, upon first learning of the head-and-shoulder pattern,

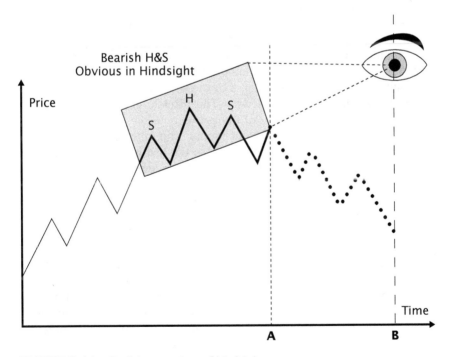

FIGURE 2.11 The false certainty of hindsight.

did not peruse historical charts to find examples of the head-and-shoulders pattern to see if it worked as claimed? And who among us did not come away with the impression, "This stuff actually works!" Were we merely victims of the hindsight bias?

There is persuasive experimental evidence[52] that people are afflicted with hindsight bias. In one typical study, students were asked to rate the probability of various outcomes in advance of President Nixon's trip to China in 1972. For example, they were asked to predict if a meeting would take place between President Nixon and chairman Mao Tse-tung and if the United States would establish a diplomatic mission in China but not grant the diplomatic recognition that China wanted. Both events were uncertain prior to the trip. Two weeks after the trip, when the events that did take place were known, the students were asked to recall what they had previously predicted. After a two-week interval, 67 percent of the students remembered their predictions as being more accurate than they actually were. In other words, they were unable to recall their prior uncertainty. After several months, the percentage of students afflicted with hindsight bias jumped from 67 percent to 84 percent.

The hindsight bias has been found to operate powerfully in trial testimony. Witnesses believe they are giving accurate accounts, but their recall of the order of events and of specific details are altered by knowing how matters actually turned out.[53]

The hindsight bias infects historical accounts. Historians, having the benefit of hindsight, will often point out that the rise of the Third Reich was quite predictable. They claim that the seeds of Nazism were obvious in various writings that preceded the Third Reich. In actuality, the rise of the Third Reich was only one of numerous possible interpretations that could have been read into these accounts. The outcome, the rise of the Third Reich, which seems so inevitable to the historians, when looked at in retrospect, was merely one among an infinite number of possible paths that history could have taken.

Other experimental evidence shows that strategies aimed specifically at reducing the hindsight bias are not effective.[54] Even when people are warned about hindsight bias and told to avoid it, it still occurs. It appears to be beyond rational control. Not even professional expertise is helpful. In one study, a group of doctors were asked to evaluate the diagnostic errors made by other doctors. The doctors doing the evaluations were armed with the knowledge of the disease that was ultimately confirmed by a pathology report. The evaluators were unable to understand how such errors could have been made by a trained physician. Again, outcome knowledge makes the past appear as if it should have been more predictable than it really was.

What cognitive processes are responsible for hindsight bias? Though the matter is not settled, it seems to go beyond a desire to see ourselves as smart and in control. One conjecture that has received some support suggests that it has to do with the way memory works, or, better said, fails to work.[55] In simplified terms, the recording of memories by the brain is not a passive process in which events are stored in proper temporal sequence ready for replay in that sequence. Rather, memory involves an active deconstruction of events for storage and then an active reconstruction of events when they are recalled. As events are experienced, they are sliced and diced and stored by associative categories, rather than by time of occurrence. An encounter with a dog last month at a friend's house in the country is dissected and stored in distinct categories and neural locations; memories of dogs, memories of friends, and memories of trips to the country, all of which may have occurred at various times in the past. When we attempt to recall the last month's visit to the country, the mind reconstructs the memory by splicing together bits of information stored in these separate associative locations. Psychologists have speculated that our brains evolved this way because it is generally effective and efficient. However, because time of occurrence is not an important feature of the storage system, it becomes difficult to recall the order of events. And it is the order of events, such as when we received a bit of knowledge, that is most critical when we are assessing our predictive abilities.

In the process of deconstructing events for storage, new experience gets mixed in with old experience. Just as a drop of ink in a glass of clear water becomes thoroughly and irreversibly intermixed, recently acquired knowledge, such as the outcome of an uncertain event, becomes inextricably intermixed with what was known prior to the outcome. Post-outcome knowledge becomes indistinguishable from pre-outcome knowledge and seems as if it were known all along. This explains why it is so difficult for people to reconstruct prior states of uncertainty.

Can subjective TA analysts overcome the hindsight bias? To answer this question we must consider the analyst in the context of two different tasks: (1) pattern research—the search for patterns with predictive power in historical data, and (2) real-time forecasting—applying the patterns in current time to make new predictions. The task of pattern research is exemplified by the early investigations of Charles H. Dow, originator of the Dow theory, or of Ralph N. Elliott, originator of the Elliott Wave Principle. In the process of formulating their ideas, they informally proposed and tested various hypotheses about which chart patterns had predictive power. The task of making real-time predictions by applying those patterns in current time would be exemplified by Dow theorist Richard Russell applying the Dow theory today or Robert Prechter, an Elliott-wave expert, making a forecast today.

In the context of historical pattern research, I contend that hindsight bias is unavoidable because it is impossible to shield oneself from outcome knowledge. Simply knowing the path that prices took biases the analyst's perception of the predictive power of whatever method is being evaluated. Only objective TA methods offer the opportunity of avoiding hindsight bias because only information known at a given point in time is used to generate signals, and signals are evaluated in an objective manner.

In the context of current-time forecasting, subjective analysts could protect themselves from hindsight bias if they were willing to make falsifiable forecasts. A forecast is falsifiable if, at the time a forecast is made, the analyst specifies (1) outcomes that would constitute a forecast error, or (2) the procedure that will be used to evaluate the forecast as well as when the procedure will be employed. For example:

> *The market will be higher six months from now, and within that time frame the market will not decline more than 20 percent from current levels, or*

> *The market will advance 20 percent from current levels before it declines 20 percent from current levels.*

> *A buy signal has been given. Hold long position until a sell signal is given.*

The first two forecasts specify outcomes that would clearly define a forecast error. For example, if the market were to drop 20 percent before it advanced 20 percent, the prediction would be wrong. End of story! The third forecast, a signal, implies a clear procedure for evaluation—compute the gain or loss from date of the buy until the date of the sell signal. Falsifiable forecasts would provide the analysts and their customers with valuable feedback. Unfortunately, few subjective forecasters do this.

SECOND-HAND INFORMATION BIAS: THE POWER OF A GOOD STORY

No one has the time, much less the expertise, to obtain all necessary knowledge via direct experience. Therefore, by necessity, most of what we know we learn secondhand from those who purportedly do know.

Among the myriad ways knowledge is communicated, the narrative account or story is by far the most popular. Biologist Stephen Jay Gould called humans "the story-telling primate." We have been sharing ideas this way for thousands, perhaps millions of years. Consequently much of what we know, even including how to do arithmetic, is stored in the mind in a narrative format.[56]

For this reason, good stories are more powerful persuaders than objective facts. Psychologists speculate that concrete, colorful, and emotionally interesting tales have a powerful impact on our beliefs because such stories call to mind pre-existing mental scripts.[57] Concepts and abstractions simply cannot light up the brain's story networks the way a lively tale can. Philosopher Bertrand Russell said that when we learn things informally (nonscientifically), we are impacted by the "emotional interest of the instances, not by their number"[58] It is for this very reason that scientists train themselves to react in exactly the opposite way, that is to discount dramatic stories and pay attention to objective facts, preferably those that can be reduced to numbers.

Not all stories are equally compelling. To command attention, a story must be interesting and understandable yet not bore us with what we already know. We are most captivated by vivid accounts about real people, preferably people we know. Stories that speak to our emotional needs while being entertaining and informative sell the best. A good tale not only enlivens us, but it gains a life of its own, as it is told and retold over and over again.

The Conflict between Truth and Tale

A conflict exists between our desire for knowledge and our desire that it be delivered in the form of a good story. Humorist H. L. Mencken put it eloquently; "What ails the truth is that it is mainly uncomfortable and often dull. The human mind seeks something more amusing and more caressing." Reality tends to be full of inconsistencies, so an audience must rely on the integrity of the storyteller to tell it like it is rather than how they would like to hear it.

Regrettably, even when the primary intent of a secondhand account is the delivery of knowledge, it is often biased to satisfy the audience's appetite for an engaging story. Storytellers know full well that information delivered with too many qualifiers is unappealing. Consequently, inconsistencies and ambiguities are minimized while cohesive aspects are amplified.[59] Although these editorial modifications make the account more digestible, they can rob it of its essential truth. In the end, the audience comes away with an exaggerated impression of the information's clarity and validity. This even occurs when the findings of scientific papers are summarized and communicated. Over numerous retellings, the truth gets left further and further behind. What started out as a result with possible significance may end up being reported as a discovery of high significance.

Especially persuasive are accounts that link events with the chain of cause and effect. The perception of causal relationships is a natural cognitive capacity[60] and causal chains satisfy our need to explain events in the world around us.[61] Studies of jury decisions show that the best causal narratives win in the courtroom.[62] The side offering the story that best ties the evidence into a coherent and credible sequence often carries the day.[63]

The problem is that cause-effect explanations that are, in fact, fallacious are hard to detect when they are plausible and appeal to a sense of the ironic. One story that has been making the rounds since the 1950s is as follows: "The Ten Commandments contain 297 words. The Declaration of Independence has 300 words, Lincoln's Gettysburg Address has 266 words, but a directive from the government's Office of Price Stabilization to regulate the price of cabbage contains 26,911 words." The truth is the Office of Price Stability never made such a directive. Nevertheless, the tale had such appeal, it remained alive despite the agency's efforts to convince the public it was false. Even the dissolution of the Office of Price Stability did not stop the story. It was merely modified so that the directive was described as a "federal directive."[64] The story would not die because of its irony and the plausibility of long-winded bureaucrats.

Elliott's Tale

The power of a good story may explain the enduring appeal of the Elliott Wave Principle (EWP), one of TA's more grandiose conjectures. The Elliott Wave Principle holds that price waves express a universal order and form that is found not only in the fluctuations of financial markets but throughout the natural world, including the shapes of sea shells, galaxies, pine cones, sunflowers, and numerous other natural phenomena.

According to EWP, market trends are fractal—a nested hierarchy of waves sharing the same form but ranging in magnitude and duration from microwaves that last only minutes to grand millennial macrowaves that can last for thousands of years.[65] This shared form, called the Elliott wave, is an eight-segment configuration of rising and falling price movements. In fact this universal pattern of growth and decay is alleged to describe not only the evolution of prices in financial markets; it is also manifested in the evolution of trends in mass psychology, the rise and fall of civilizations, cultural fashions, and other social trends. The theory claims to describe just about anything that goes through cycles of growth and change. Even the business career of Elliott wave's leading advocate Robert Prechter, according to Prechter himself, has followed a series of ups and downs that conform to the Elliott Wave Principle. This all ties in with a sequence of numbers called the Fibonacci series and the golden ratio phi, which does have many fascinating mathematical properties.[66]

However, that which purports to explain everything explains nothing. The Elliott Wave Principle, as popularly practiced, is not a legitimate theory but a story, and a compelling one that is eloquently told by Robert Prechter.[67] The account is especially persuasive because EWP has the seemingly remarkable ability to fit any segment of market history down to its most minute fluctuations. I contend this is made possible by the method's loosely defined rules and the ability to postulate a large number of nested waves of varying magnitude. This gives the Elliott analyst the same freedom and flexibility that allowed pre-Copernican astronomers to explain all observed planet movements even though their underlying theory of an Earth-centered universe was wrong. The analogy between the medieval astronomer fitting epicycle upon epicycle to their data and EWP analysts fitting wave within nested wave to market data is strong. Thus, even if the fundamental notion of EWP is wrong, the method of analysis will still be able to obtain a very good fit to past data.[68]

In fact, any sufficiently flexible model can fit a prior set of observations with perfection. For example, a polynomial function with a sufficient number of terms (equal in number to the number of data points) can also produce a perfect retrofit. However, a model or method with an unlimited ability to fit past observations but which cannot make testable (falsifiable[69]) predictions of future observations is neither meaningful nor useful.

Though the Elliott Wave Principle is said to hold even the heavens, where galaxies conform to the logarithmic spiral, its performance here on earth has been less than stellar.[70] What then, explains its enduring appeal? I contend that it is attributable to the fact that EWP is a comprehensive cause-effect story that promises to decipher the market's past and divine its future better than any other TA method. Some stories are too good to let die.

Stories Shaped by Self-Interest

Self-interest can motivate distortion in secondhand accounts. People with an ideological or theoretical position tend to selectively sharpen some aspects of a story and minimize others to bring it into better alignment with their point of view. Purveyors of specific TA methods or of TA in general have clear ideological and financial interests at stake.

This charge can be leveled at me[71] or any author arguing a position. However, when the storyteller is constrained by objective evidence and repeatable procedures, there is less leeway for the distorting effects of self-interest to operate.

CONFIRMATION BIAS: HOW EXISTING BELIEFS FILTER EXPERIENCE AND SURVIVE CONTRADICTING EVIDENCE

"Once a belief forms, we filter information in ways that sustain it."[72] The confirmation bias is the tendency to view as credible new evidence that confirms our prior beliefs but to view as incredible evidence that contradicts them.[73] This tendency inhibits learning from new experience and stifles the elimination of incorrect ideas. The confirmation bias explains why we get stuck with erroneous beliefs.

The Confirmation Bias Has a Rational Basis

In many instances it is rational to give weight and preference to evidence that supports an existing belief and to view with skepticism that which contradicts it. Beliefs would be highly unstable without such a rule.

The use of prior knowledge as an interpretive filter is a mark of human intelligence, so long as the prior knowledge is well supported. Scientists were justifiably skeptical of a claim that nuclear fusion had been achieved at room temperatures in an apparatus constructed from parts available at the local hardware store.[74] Their doubts were subsequently borne out by objective tests that were unable to reproduce the so-called cold-fusion effect. Few of us would accept at face value the supermarket-tabloid headline: "Elvis Returns on UFO & Will Build an Alien Theme Park." However, when prior beliefs are unjustified because they lack the support of sound inferences from solid evidence, it is not rational to grant them the status of intellectual gatekeeper. The problem is that people are often not aware of which of their held beliefs are unjustified. Consequently, the confirmation bias operates even when it should not.

Biased Perception

The confirmation bias is a consequence of the way perception works. Beliefs shape expectations, which in turn shape perceptions, which then shape conclusions. Thus we see what we expect to see and conclude what we expect to conclude. As Henry David Thoreau put it, "We hear and apprehend only what we already half know." The truism, *I'll believe it when I see it* might be better stated *I'll see it when I believe it.*

The potent effect of expectations on perception was demonstrated in the following experiment. When subjects were given a drink that they thought contained alcohol, but in fact did not, they experienced reduced social anxiety. However, other subjects who were told they were being given nonalcoholic beverages when they were, in fact, alcoholic did not experience reduced anxiety in social situations.[75]

Not only do we fail to perceive new information that is in conflict with prior beliefs, we are also reluctant to draw conclusions that are at odds with what we already believe to be so. As a result we tend to accept at face value information that is consistent with pre-existing thinking while we critically scrutinize and discount information that is inconsistent with prior beliefs. The confirmation bias explains why our beliefs fail to change in response to new information as much as they should.[76]

It gets worse. The confirmation bias, operating in conjunction with the laws of chance, predicts that erroneous beliefs will strengthen with time and familiarity.[77] A TA method with no predictive power (e.g., a signal based on a coin flip) will enjoy occasional success due to chance. Over time, these confirming instances will accumulate and, because of the confirmation bias, will be given greater weight than instances where the method fails. The result is a vicious cycle of growing self-deception. This suggests that the belief in a flawed method's efficacy will increase over time irrespective of its actual merit. It also implies that TA practitioners most experienced with a useless method will be the least able to recognize its flaws because of more lengthy exposure to the method's chance-based successes.

Motivational Factors

The confirmation bias is also driven by motivational factors. TA practitioners have a large emotional and financial investment in their favored method. This is especially true of practitioners whose professional lives are tied to a particular method.

There is also a strong motive to maintain consistency within our system beliefs and attitudes. The theory of cognitive dissonance formulated by Festinger[78] contends that people are motivated to reduce or avoid psychological inconsistencies.[79] The discomfort provoked by evidence that contradicts what we believe makes it hard to digest such evidence.

Biased Questions and Search

The confirmation bias also slants the way questions are framed, thereby biasing the search for new evidence. This search bias increases the chance of encountering new evidence that supports the prior belief while reducing the possibility of encountering nonconfirming or contradictory facts. This occurs in the context of subjective TA research. By definition, it is confined to the search for supportive anecdotal examples. Contradictory examples are difficult, if not impossible, to find because subjectively defined patterns do not specify the conditions of a prediction error.

People trained in the scientific method do two things to combat this tendency. First, at the inception of a test, they establish objective criteria for evaluating outcomes. Second, they actively pursue evidence that might contradict prior beliefs and assumptions. Scientists are guided by the notion that ideas that can survive a vigorous search for contradictory evidence have greater validity than ideas that are merely backed by confirmatory evidence discovered by a search directed at exactly that.

The confirmation bias can occur in the context of objective TA as well. Consider an analyst searching for profitable rules with back testing. If the first rule that is tested gives unsatisfactory performance, the search for a rule with good performance continues. This involves testing a sequence of rules with altered parameters, logic, indicators, and so forth until a good one is found. This is data mining. Because the decision about when to end this process is entirely up to the analyst, the scope of the search is unbounded. This guarantees that ultimately a rule with good past performance will be discovered. The researcher's initial belief that a good rule will be found is thus confirmed.

In fact, the past performance of a rule discovered by data mining overstates its likely performance in the future. This overstatement is called the data-mining bias and is discussed in Chapter 6. This problem is not data mining per se. In fact, when done properly, data mining is a productive research method. The error is the failure to take into account the upward bias caused by data mining. As will be explained in Chapter 6, by taking into account the extent of the search that led to the discovery of the good rule, it is possible to draw sound inferences about the rule's future profit potential.

How Vague Evaluation Criteria Contribute to the Confirmation Bias

Because subjective TA is vague about how its forecasts should be evaluated, evidence of its success and failure is ambiguous. This facilitates the analyst's ability to point to prior predictions that worked (confirmation bias) while at the same time preventing the identification of prediction errors. This effectively immunizes subjective practitioners from the negative feedback that might cause them to change their beliefs.[80]

Prediction errors of a subjective method can be obscured in a number of ways. One is what I refer to as pattern renaming. An upside breakout pattern that fails is relabeled a successful bull trap. According to TA doctrine, upside breakouts are alleged to predict upward trends. This is illustrated in Figure 2.12.

When an uptrend does not materialize it should be counted as a prediction error. If instead, the pattern is renamed a bull trap,[81] we wind up

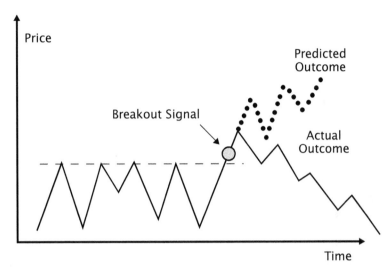

FIGURE 2.12 Breakout failure.

with a successful signal from a different pattern as shown in Figure 2.13. Objective pattern definitions and clearly predefined evaluation criteria would prevent such after-the-fact evidence fiddling.

Another way prediction errors are obscured is when forecasts lack a clear endpoint. The endpoint of prediction is a future time or event that calls for the prediction to be evaluated.. A forecast or signal that does

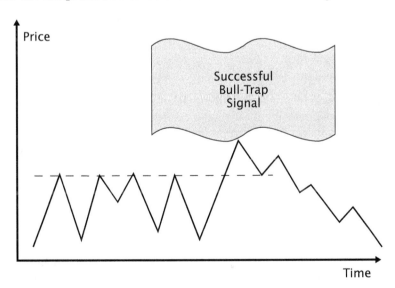

FIGURE 2.13 Prediction error obscured with pattern renaming.

specify or imply a clear endpoint is effectively meaningless. The talking heads of TA typically issue predictions without clear endpoints: "I'm bullish for the intermediate-term." This vague pronouncement provides the forecaster with enough postprediction wiggle room to avoid getting nailed with a bad call. Either a defined time period or a specific subsequent event, such as a certain percentage of adverse price movement, prevents the forecaster from engaging in an after-the-fact, free-for-all hunt for any evidence that portrays the forecast in a good light. However, the statement "I expect the market to advance at least 5 percent from current levels before it declines 5 percent" leaves no room for fudging. Objective signaling methods imply a clear endpoint—the subsequent signal to exit the position.

The freedom to alter the forecast evaluation criterion after the fact makes it likely that supportive evidence will be found. This is precisely why science has a dual personality. It is flexible and receptive to all testable ideas, yet rigidly orthodox about how testing and evaluation are to be carried out. In fact, much of what scientists do can be understood as the use of strict procedures for determining when an idea is worthless. If people were to use similar procedures in their everyday lives, they would be much less likely to adopt erroneous beliefs.[82] People are highly adept at concocting ideas, theories, and explanations for their experience that have a semblance of plausibility.[83] However, they are not nearly as good at testing those beliefs once they have taken root. One of the biggest reasons is the failure to precisely define which outcomes qualify as supportive evidence and which do not. Without objective evaluation criteria, the opportunity and motivation to find supportive evidence for what we already believe is left unchecked and runs rampant.

The Confirmation Bias and Vague Evidence

The precise way in which the confirmation bias functions to substantiate prior beliefs depends upon the clarity of the new evidence. When the new evidence is vague, the confirmation bias operates unfettered. Because vague evidence can be interpreted as either contradictory or supportive, it is simply taken as supportive.

Subjective TA methods are vague on two counts: with respect to how patterns and signals are defined, and with respect to how predictions based on said patterns and signals are to be evaluated. This invites the discovery of evidence that is weakly supportive. Weak evidence is not strong enough to compel the belief that the method works, but because weak evidence is open to interpretation, it can be interpreted as being consistent with a belief that the method works. The hallmark of weak evidence is that it can be interpreted as being consistent with several different points of view. For example, the appearance of a certain portion of a price chart could be consistent with a five-wave Elliott impulse pattern, or an entirely different subjective pattern, or purely random price movement.[84] Objectively defined patterns and evaluation criteria permit no such leeway. Either the data is an example of a particular pattern or it is not. Either the outcome is consistent with the pattern's prediction or it is not.

The Confirmation Bias and Clearly Contradictory Evidence

Let's now consider how the confirmation bias operates when there is evidence that clearly contradicts a prior belief. In many situations, the evidence is a mixture. Some evidence clearly confirms the belief and some clearly contradicts it. In these situations the confirmation bias still operates, but in a more complex manner.

It might be thought that the dissonant evidence would simply be ignored or twisted into being supportive. But, this tends not to happen because people value seeing themselves as rational and cognitively consistent. "They are reluctant to simply disregard pertinent evidence that is contradictory in order to see what they expect to see and believe what they expect to believe."[85] However, what they do is to alter the dissonant information in order to reduce its conflict with prior cherished beliefs. In other words, the confirmation bias encourages subtle cognitive manipulations to the clearly dissonant evidence to reduce its importance and reduce its clash with confirming evidence and cherished belief.

One way people discount discordant evidence is by applying a harsher standard of acceptance.[86] The standard applied to evidence that supports a favored position is the gentle requirement that it have a ring of plausibility or the possibility of being valid. In contrast, the standard applied to evidence that conflicts with cherished beliefs is that it must be *convincing beyond any possible doubt.* For believers in faith healing, a colorful corroborating account is accepted without question. However, a controlled scientific study denying the efficacy of faith healing would be faulted on any and every possible ground, reasonable or otherwise. By demanding that dissonant evidence be so strong that it be compelling beyond any doubt, while only requiring that harmonious evidence be weakly consistent, holders of erroneous beliefs are able to keep their faith alive.

One of the most surprising findings about the confirmation bias is that evidence that contradicts a prior belief can actually have the effect of strengthening that belief. One would think that a mixture of pro and con evidence should at least reduce the strength of the prior belief. Studies have shown otherwise. For example, in one experiment, subjects were presented with clear and convincing evidence that was both pro and con capital punishment.[87] The subjects were of two types: those with a prior belief that capital punishment was good and those with a prior belief that capital punishment was bad. Both groups were given summaries and critiques to two different studies on capital punishment. One study presented evidence showing that capital punishment was an effective deterrent against crime while the other provided evidence showing it was not effective.[88] The experiment showed that participants perceived the study that was consistent with their prior belief to be valid and important evidence, whereas the study that conflicted with their view was seen as flawed research and weak evidence. After being exposed to evidence on both sides of the issue, participants came away from the experiment with their prior beliefs strengthened. In other words a mixture of pro and con evidence caused the two groups to become more polarized.

It is also informative to consider what subjects in the study did not do. Hostile evidence was neither misconstrued to be favorable nor ignored. Rather, it was scrutinized for flaws, thus reducing its import. In other words, significant cognitive effort was expended to explain away or minimize contradictory evidence.[89]

An experiment that is closer to TA examined how the confirmation bias encouraged unsuccessful bettors to maintain their delusions of gambling greatness despite swelling losses. Losing money would seem to be unambiguous evidence of failure, yet bad gamblers remained optimistic. Thomas Gilovich showed they accomplished this by evaluating their wins and losses in a biased manner.[90] As was true for subjects in the study on capital punishment, the gamblers did not forget or ignore discordant evidence (losses). Rather, they applied significant cognitive effort to transform their losses into less derogatory evidence. This was displayed in journals kept by the gamblers. It was found that they devoted more commentary to losses than gains, and gains and loses were interpreted differently. Gains were easily attributed to the gambler's betting acumen (self-attribution bias) whereas losses were attributed to bad luck and, with a bit of fine tuning to the betting system, would have been wins.

These findings predict how subjective TA practitioners might react if presented with objective evidence contradicting the validity of a favored method.[91] For example, suppose a subjective method was to be transformed into an objective method, and tests indicated the method was not effective. It is likely that devotes of the method would find any number of grounds to criticize the study. There is no study in any field of science that cannot be criticized on some grounds. It is also likely that the subjective practitioner would trot out cherry-picked examples showing instances where their method was successful. In the end, it is probable that the practitioners would come away from the exercise more convinced than ever in the value of their method while muttering about ivory-tower academics having their heads stuck in the clouds or somewhere worse.

Beyond the Confirmation Bias: The True Believer

We have seen that erroneous beliefs thrive on vagueness and can even grow stronger in the face of evidence that would, at the very least, call for reduced belief. However, belief longevity goes beyond even this. Studies have shown that once a belief takes root, it can even survive a complete discrediting of the evidence that gave rise to the belief in the first place.

It has been demonstrated that, when subjects are tricked into forming an erroneous belief, their belief survives even after they are told that they had been tricked. One study is particularly relevant to TA because it involves pattern discrimination. Subjects were asked to distinguish authentic suicide notes from fictitious ones.[92] Initially, experimenters gave the subjects fake feedback, thus deceiving them into believing that they had learned to discriminate authentic suicide notes from fakes. In reality, the subjects had not learned how to perform this task. Later, the experimenters told the subjects of the deceit. Even with such clear discrediting evidence, the subjects continued to believe, to a considerable degree, that they were able to discriminate real from fake suicide notes. Other experiments conducted along similar lines have found the same effect: a belief can survive a total discrediting of its original basis.[93]

These findings predict how believers might react if Ralph Elliott, W.D. Gann, or Charles Dow were to return from the grave and announce that their methods had been intentional scams. It is likely that many current-day practitioners would continue to believe. Given that Elliott wave analysis, or at least one version of it, has now been reduced to an objective algorithm, it will be interesting to see the reactions of EWP believers if objective tests fail.[94]

Subjective Methods Most Likely to Suffer the Confirmation Bias

Some subjective TA methods are more likely to encourage the confirmation bias than others. These methods will possess three characteristics: (1) an elaborate causal explanation or compelling story about why the method works, (2) high retrofit power—the ability to fit or explain past market behavior accurately, and (3) no ability to generate falsifiable (testable) predictions.

TA methods fitting this profile include Elliott waves, Hurst cycle theory, astrology-based forecasting, and W.D. Gann analysis, among others. For example, the Elliott Wave Principle is based on an elaborate causal explanation invoking universal forces that shape, not only the physical world, but mass psychology, culture, and society as well. Moreover, it has high retrofit power. By employing a large number of nested waves that can vary in both duration and magnitude, it is possible to derive an Elliott wave count (i.e., fit) for any prior segment of historical data. However, except for one objective version[95] of Elliott waves, the method does not generate testable/falsifiable predictions.

Let's consider the first element, an elaborate causal explanation. TA methods that are based on intricate causal stories are able to withstand empirical challenges because they speak to the deeply felt human need to make sense of the world. Because we are compelled to explain our experience, we have highly developed abilities to generate plausible stories after the fact. "To live, it seems, is to explain, to justify, and to find coherence among diverse outcomes, characteristics and causes. With practice we have learned to perform these tasks quickly and effectively."[96] Studies in which people are encouraged to form erroneous beliefs and then requested to construct rationales for those beliefs are more resistant to belief change than subjects who were not asked to formulate explanations.[97] Subjects who developed reasons to explain their beliefs became so stuck in their opinions that, even after they were told that they had been manipulated into adopting a false belief, they continued to believe.[98] In fact, they continued to believe almost as strongly as other subjects who were manipulated to form false beliefs but were not told of the manipulation.

The second and third elements that make a TA method immune to evidentiary challenge is a high capacity to retrofit past market movements combined with an inability to make testable (falsifiable) predictions of future movements. The ability to bring all past market movement into conformity with the method has the effect of eliminating any contradictory evidence. When forecast errors do occur because outcomes are so completely out of whack with forecasts that even subjective evaluation is unable to hide the error, the standard explanation is that the error was caused by a misapplication of the method rather than a flaw in the method itself. This fallacious reasoning is then supported by reapplying the method so it fits the discordant outcome. The ability to always obtain a good retrospective fit combined with the inability to make testable predictions eliminates the possibility that any evidence will ever surface that contradicts the method.

In science, the rationale for eliminating an erroneous theory is the fact that its predictions of future observations are shown to conflict with those observations. This is the scientist's signal that the theory needs to be eliminated or reformulated. If the latter, the new version of the theory is then tested against a subsequent set of future observations. This essential mechanism for pruning away false theories is illustrated in Figure 2.14 and is discussed in depth in Chapter 3.

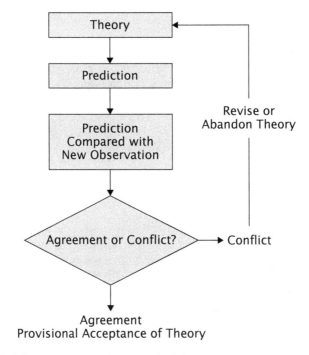

FIGURE 2.14 How science eliminates bad theories.

The entire motivation for revising or abandoning a TA method, or any theory for that matter, comes from seeing clear examples where its predictions are wrong. If it is easy to make after-the-fact adjustments that eliminate all errors, the rationale to abandon the method is lost.

Other research suggests that some people are more prone to the confirmation bias than others. Strangely, they are the most intelligent people. Harvard psychologist David Perkins conducted an interesting study showing that the higher a person's intelligence (measured in IQ points), the better they are able to construct articulate rationales for their beliefs and defend them.[99] However, Perkins also found that because of their strong ability to rationalize existing beliefs, highly intelligent people are less able to consider alternative explanations and points of view. Hence they are more apt to form beliefs that are resistant to change. Social scientist Jay Stuart Snelson calls this ideological immunity. He claims that intelligent and successful adults rarely change their most fundamental presuppositions.[100] This effect is most pronounced in people who have accumulated significant knowledge in a particular area. This suggests that the most intelligent and experienced subjective practitioners will be the least able to abandon a method in which they previously believed.

ILLUSORY CORRELATIONS

The studies discussed up to this point have dealt with people's erroneous beliefs about themselves and their abilities. We now consider studies that examined people's beliefs about the world at large, specifically whether a predictive relationship exists between a pair of variables.[101] These have shown that people have a tendency to perceive illusory correlation. An illusory correlation is the false perception of a relationship between a pair of variables. It is a significant problem for subjective TA practitioners.

Subjective TA Methods Represented as Binary Variables

A pair of variables is said to be correlated when one, referred to as the predictor, can be used to predict the other, referred to as the outcome or dependent variable. Although subjective TA methods are not usually described in these terms, all such methods can be viewed as asserting the existence of a correlation between a pair of variables. The predictor is a TA pattern or signal such as the head-and-shoulders top pattern. The outcome is the post-pattern price movement the pattern is purported to predict. A head-and-shoulders top pattern is supposed to predict a downtrend upon the pattern's completion. In fact, the entire enterprise of TA, both objective and subjective, can be viewed as the search for such correlations. These are then used individually, though more often in combination, to forecast market trends.

It can also be said of subjective patterns, that both the predictor and the outcome are binary variables. That is to say, they assume only two possible values. With respect to the predictor variable, the pattern or signal is either (1) currently present or (2) not present.[102] With respect to the outcome variable, the future price movement the pattern or signal is purported to predict, either (1) occurs or (2) does not occur.

For example, the head-and-shoulders top pattern is purported to be correlated with (predictive of) a postpattern downtrend. At a given point in time, a head-and-shoulder top pattern and neckline break signal is either present on the chart or it is not.[103] Following the signal the downtrend either occurs or it does not. All subjective patterns and signals can be interpreted within this framework.

The central contention of this chapter is that subjective TA knowledge possesses only illusory validity. This section examines a specific illusion of validity—illusory correlation. An illusory correlation is the perception of a correlation between two variables that are not truly related.

Why We Are Prone to Illusory Correlations

A substantial body of research indicates that people easily fall prey to the illusion of correlation.[104] These illusions seem to result from faulty information processing. The specific fault is paying too much attention to instances that confirm the existence of the correlation while paying too little attention to cases that either do not confirm the presumed correlations or that outrightly contradict its existence. In TA, confirmatory instances are those cases in which the pattern/signal occurs *and* the outcome that the pattern/signal is purported to predict also occurs. For example, the head-and-shoulders top pattern occurs and then a downtrend ensues. If you believe in the efficacy of a particular subjective pattern/signal, ask yourself if your belief is not entirely or primarily founded upon having seen instances in which the pattern has been successful (confirmatory examples). Now ask yourself if you are similarly aware of examples where it failed (false positive or false negative signals[105]).

However, confirmatory instances constitute only one type out of four possible types of outcomes that can occur between a pair of binary variables. The other three types are (2) the pattern/signal *does* occur but the market trend the pattern is supposed to predict *does not* occur, (3) the pattern/signal *does not* occur but the outcome the pattern is supposed to predict *occurs* anyway, and (4) the pattern/signal *does not* occur and the outcome the pattern/signal purports to predict *does not* occur either. Types one and four are correct predictions. Types two and three are prediction errors. Type two is called a false signal or false positive. Type three is called a failure to signal or false negative.

The Allure of the Upper Left Cell

The four possible outcomes between a pair of binary variables can be illustrated with a two-by-two (2×2) contingency table (Figure 2.15). This common data analysis tool is composed of four cells, one for each of the four possible outcome types. Into each cell goes a count of the number of instances of that type of outcome occurring within a sample of observations. Such a table would be useful to represent subjective TA patterns and their outcomes were it not for the fact that their subjectivity precludes obtaining the counts.

Studies show that people fall prey to illusory correlations because they pay excessive attention to the number of confirmatory instances, those falling into the upper-left cell of the table.[106] At the same time, they fail to take proper account of the number of cases falling into the other

	Predicted Outcome Occurs	Predicted Outcome Does NOT Occur
Pattern/Signal Occurs	**Correct Prediction** Confirmatory Instances	**Error** False Signal
Pattern/Signal Does NOT Occur	**Error** Failure to Signal	**Correct Prediction** No opportunity

FIGURE 2.15 2 × 2 contingency table.

three cells. We make this mistake for two reasons. The first has to do with the salience of the confirmatory instances, and the second has to do with a faulty intuitive notion of what constitutes sufficient evidence to conclude that a correlation exists.

The salience of evidence refers to how noticeable, vivid, or outstanding it is. Salient evidence is attention grabbing. Confirmatory examples are salient because they confirm a suspected hypothesis. In other words they are rewarding. When subjective technicians think they have discovered a useful pattern or signal, they typically will examine historical data to see if their initial supposition was correct. Thus, they are engaged in informal hypothesis testing. In this situation, confirmatory instances, examples in which the pattern occurred and it made a correct prediction, will be highly noticeable because they reward the analyst's initial conjecture. Consider what it might have been like for R. N. Elliott just after formulating his initial hunch that all market movements conform to the same fundamental pattern—a five-segment impulse wave followed by a three-segment corrective wave (5–3 pattern). At that point, his hypothesis had not yet attained the status of a strong belief. It was merely a suspicion. However, once that hypothesis was born in Elliott's mind, it motivated a search for additional confirming cases. In other words it was Elliott's initial conjecture itself that made confirmatory cases salient.

Necessary versus Sufficient Evidence

Once the confirmatory instances take front stage, a faulty intuition that is quite common enters the picture. This intuition, which is responsible for producing the illusion of a correlation, concerns the amount of evidence that is thought to be sufficient to establish a valid correlation. It is commonly thought that confirmatory evidence, by itself, is sufficient. This is incorrect!

It's not that this intuition is wrong so much as it is incomplete. Intuition correctly tells us that confirmatory instances (events in the upper left cell) are indeed *necessary* to establish the existence of a correlative relationship. If the head-and-shoulders pattern, or any pattern or signal for that matter, is a valid predictor, then there ought to be instances in which the pattern occurred and the expected outcome also occurred. However, it is a mistake to assume that a goodly number of confirmatory instances are sufficient to establish a correlative relationship. In other words, although confirmatory instances are necessary, they are not by themselves, *sufficient* to establish the existence of a correlative relationship. In reality, the number of instances falling into all four cells of the contingency table must be taken into account to determine if valid correlation exists.

It is because we fail to realize that a given belief is not supported by sufficient evidence that it takes on an illusion of validity. Thus we come to see it not as an opinion or an article of faith but as a reasonable inference from objective evidence.[107] Numerous studies[108] have shown that, when people rely on informal analysis to determine if there is a relationship between two variables, they tend to make two kinds of errors. They fail to detect correlations that are, in fact, valid, even when the correlation is relatively strong[109] (invisible correlations), and they falsely perceive correlations that are invalid (illusory correlations). Both errors are related to the observer's expectations stemming from pre-existing beliefs.

First, let's consider what happens when people are shown data for two variables[110] that are in fact related but which are not expected to be correlated. Experiments have shown that they are unable to detect the relationships unless the correlation exceeds approximately 0.70, on a scale of 0 to 1.0, where 1.0 represents a perfect correlation and zero represents no correlation. A correlation of 0.70 is far stronger than anything likely to be encountered within the domain of TA.[111] This finding suggests that subjective TA analysts relying on informal/intuitive data analysis methods will be prone to missing valid correlations that they do not expect to exist.

What is even more relevant to the problem of illusory TA knowledge is the tendency to perceive correlations that do not exist. When observers have a prior belief that a relationship exists between pattern and outcome, or there is a motivation to find one, the confirmation bias, discussed previously, makes it likely that a correlative relationship will be detected even if none exists. It is hard to imagine a TA analyst who is not impacted either by prior belief, motivation, or both.

Even if there is no prior belief or no motivation to believe, people still display a pronounced tendency to perceive illusory correlations. Smedslund performed one of the earliest experiments showing this tendency.[112] Nurses were shown 100 cards that were supposed to represent actual patients. Each card indicated if the patient manifested a particular symptom or not (the binary predictor) and whether that patient was ultimately diagnosed with a specific disease (the binary outcome). The nurses' task was to determine if the symptom was truly correlated with the disease. The data shown to the nurses is summarized in the contingency table in Figure 2.16.

Over 85 percent of the nurses said the symptom was correlated with the disease. They were persuaded by the 37 salient confirmatory instances falling in the upper left cell (symptom present and disease present). However, their conclusion was not supported by the data. A proper analysis of this data, which takes all cell counts into consideration, indicates that the symptom is not correlated with the disease.

	True Diagnosis	
	Disease Present	Disease NOT Present
Symptom Present	**Cell A** **37** instances	**Cell B** **17** instances
Symptom NOT Present	**Cell C** **33** instances	**Cell D** **13** instances

FIGURE 2.16 Data evaluated by nurses—Smedslund study (1963).

Giving All Cells Their Due

A formal statistical test that considers all cell counts would be the rigorous way to determine if the nurses' data was indicative of a valid correlation. However, one need not even resort to a formal test to see that there is no correlation between the symptom and the disease. All cells can be taken into consideration by computing some simple ratios of the cell counts. For example, the proportion of patients that manifested the symptom and who ultimately proved to have the disease was approximately 0.69 (cell A divided by [cell A + cell B], 37/54 = 0.685). However, the proportion of patients that did not have the symptom that ultimately were diagnosed with the disease was almost the same or 0.72 (cell C divided by [cell C + Cell D], 33/46 = 0.717). This quick-and-dirty calculation shows that likelihood of having the disease was about the same (.69 and .72) regardless of whether the symptom was present. Had the symptom really been correlated with the disease, the two proportions would have been quite different, such as 0.90 of those with the symptom had the disease whereas only 0.40 of those without the symptom had the disease. This would not necessarily suggest that the symptom was a cause of the disease but only that it was a valid predictor of it.

In light of the fact that even simple ratios showed no correlation between symptom and disease, it is surprising that 85 percent of the nurses concluded that the symptom was a reliable predictor of the disease. The nurses were presented with other data sets as well. Overall, the factor that best explained whether the nurses perceived a correlation was simply the number of confirmatory instances (cell A: symptom and disease both occur). Their judgments were unaffected by the relative proportions that went into the calculation done earlier. In other words, the nurses did not pay attention to the number of cases in the other three cells. As previously noted, many psychological studies have supported Smedslund's findings.[113]

The statistically correct way to detect a correlation between two binary variables is the Chi-square test.[114] The test determines whether the number of instances falling into each cell differs significantly from the number that would be expected in each cell if there were no correlation between the variables. In other words, the test determines if cell counts depart significantly from a random sprinkling of the instances among the four cells. When cell counts do depart significantly[115] from a random pattern, the Chi-square statistic takes on a large value. This is legitimate evidence of a correlation.

In Figure 2.17 the data from the nurses' study have been altered to illustrate how cell counts might appear for a symptom that is correlated with the disease. Each cell also contains the number of instances that

	Final Diagnosis		
	Disease Present	Disease NOT Present	
Symptom Present	**Cell A** **47** Expected = 37.8	**Cell B** **7** Expected = 16.2	**54**
Symptom NOT Present	**Cell C** **23** Expected = 32.2	**Cell D** **23** Expected = 13.8	**46**
	70	**30**	**100**

FIGURE 2.17 Evidence of valid correlation.

would be expected if there were no predictive relation between symptom and disease (the random pattern). For example, in cell B, there were only 7 occurrences of disease with the symptom present (a false signal). If the instances conformed to a random pattern, one would expect about 16 false signals. Thus, the relative proportion of disease, if symptom is present, is 0.87 versus 0.50 when the symptom is not present. The difference in the proportions shows that the symptom is correlated with the disease.

The Role of Asymmetric Binary Variables in Illusory Correlation

Illusory correlations are especially likely to emerge when the variables involved are binary variables of a particular type—asymmetric binary variables.[116] Binary variables can be either symmetric or asymmetric. A binary variable is said to be of the symmetric type if each of its possible values is associated with the presence of an attribute (red/blue or Republican/Democrat) or the occurrence of an event (rain/snow or flood/fire). However, in the case of an asymmetric binary variable, one of the variable's two values depicts the absence of an attribute or the nonoccurrence of an event. For example, (attribute present/attribute not present) or (event occurred/event did not occur). In other words, one of the variable's states represents something not happening or a feature *not being* present.

Research[117] shows that when both the predictor and outcome variables are of the binary asymmetric type, the confirmatory instances (pattern occurs and expected outcome occurs) are extraordinarily salient and especially likely to consume the attention of the informal data analyst. This attentional shift to the upper left cell strongly encourages the perception of illusory correlations. Recall that when the variables are asymmetric binaries, the other three cells of the contingency table contain instances in which one or both of the variables are registering the absence of the pattern, the nonoccurrence of the expected outcome or both pattern absence and outcome nonoccurrence.

The nonoccurrence of an event, or the absence of an attribute, is easily overlooked, because people have difficulty conceptualizing and evaluating this kind of evidence. The research just alluded to has shown it takes more cognitive effort to evaluate instances where something does not occur than instances where something does. To illustrate the extra cognitive effort required to process a statement involving the nonoccurrence of an event or the absence of an attribute, consider the following two statements. Although they both convey the same information, the meaning of the first, which is given in an affirmative form, is intuitively obvious. However, the meaning of the second, which is given in the negative form, requires some thought.

Statement 1: *All humans are mortal.*

Statement 2: *All nonmortals are nonhumans.*

Many of the propositions of subjective TA assert the existence of a correlation between a pair of asymmetric binary variables: a signal/pattern that is either present on the chart or not and an outcome that the signal/pattern is supposed to predict, which either occurs or does not. Thus the psychological research described earlier suggests that subjective TA practitioners will be especially likely to fall prey to illusory correlations. They will tend to be overly impressed with confirmatory instances, in which the pattern/signal did occur and the expected outcome also occurred, and give too little attention and weight to the three other types of instances. Some examples of subjective patterns along with their expected outcomes are illustrated Table 2.1.

TABLE 2.1 Subjective Patterns and Their Expected Outcomes

Pattern/Signal	Expected Outcome
Head-and-shoulders top	Downtrend
Completed 5th Elliott wave	Corrective wave
Strong uptrend, then flag	Continuation of uptrend
Extremely bullish sentiment readings	Bear market

Hidden or Missing Data Compounds the Problem of Illusory Correlations

The discussion so far shows how people come to believe in bogus correlations because of an insufficient consideration of all relevant information in a contingency table. However, the subjective technician's plight does not end here. Further compounding the propensity to detect illusory correlations is the problem of missing data. The cell counts needed to fill in the contingency table are not even readily available. The missing data problem is yet another consequence of subjective analysis.

Without objectively defined signals/patterns and without objectively defined standards for evaluating their outcomes, it is impossible obtain the requisite counts that are needed to fill the cells of the contingency table. Without these counts, the true efficacy of the signal/pattern cannot be evaluated. This applies even to the confirmatory instances found in the upper left cell of the table, although subjective practitioners seem never to run short of confirmatory examples.[118] Objective definitions are the only solution to the missing data problem. Until TA adopts objectivity, it will continue to operate on the basis of magical thinking and myth.

Once an illusory correlation is accepted as fact, two previously mentioned cognitive errors assure the misconception's longevity. The mere belief in the specious relationship increases the likelihood that additional supportive evidence will be noticed (confirmation bias). Moreover, the alleged correlation is easily assimilated into one's system of beliefs. As Gilovich points out, once a phenomenon is suspected to exist, people are easily able to come up with an explanation about why it exists and what it means. In other words humans are very good at inventing stories after the fact.[119] Studies show that when people are falsely informed that they are either above average or below average at some task, they can readily invent a reason that explains why.[120] Part of the appeal of subjective TA is the fascinating story offered about why it works. The story itself helps sustain belief.

A Behaviorist's Explanation of Illusory Correlations

Thus far, the discussion has explained the birth and longevity of erroneous beliefs in terms of cognitive psychology. A separate subdiscipline of psychology, behaviorism, offers a somewhat different account of why erroneous beliefs as to the efficacy of subjective TA should be so durable.

Behavioral psychology is concerned with roles of reward (positive reinforcement) and punishment (negative reinforcement) in the learning of habitual behaviors. If a pigeon is put in a cage and rewarded with a food pellet each time it pecks at a button, it will eventually learn the habit of pecking the button. Once this behavior has been acquired, the bird will continue pecking the button so long as the food pellets keep coming. However, if the reward is stopped, the bird eventually learns that the behavior no longer pays, and the learned behavior is extinguished.

One area of interest within behavioral psychology is the relationship between the strength of a habit, indicated by the degree to which it resists extinction, and the specific type of reinforcement schedule that originally led to the habit's formation. The question is which type of reinforcement schedule produces the strongest habits. The simplest type of reinforcement is rewarding every action—each peck earns a pellet. Another is partial reinforcement, in which rewards come only at fixed time intervals, such as every 60 seconds, or fixed behavior intervals, such as every tenth peck. It has been discovered that partial reinforcement schedules produce slower learning (habit takes longer to form) but stronger habits.

Most relevant to the domain of TA is the fact that of all the partial reinforcement schedules investigated, random reinforcement[121] produces habits that are most resistant to extinction. Under random reinforcement, the organism's behavior is not truly associated with the receipt of a reward. Behavior is rewarded by chance. In one experiment, a pigeon pecked at a colored button and received random reinforcement for a mere 60 seconds. However, the pecking behavior continued for 3.5 hours after the reward was stopped. In other words, the pathetic bird engaged in a fruitless activity for a period that was 210 times longer than the random reinforcement period that produced the habit.[122]

Random reinforcement is precisely the type of reward received by someone who believes in an illusory TA correlation. Every so often, by chance, the signal/pattern is followed by the expected outcome, thus reinforcing the belief. Behaviorist studies would predict that such a belief would be extremely resistant to extinction. Superstitions and compulsive gambling, two habits that rest on illusory correlations, are known to be extremely difficult to cure.[123]

When I worked on the floor of the American Stock Exchange, I met several traders who displayed superstitious behavior. One fellow insisted on wearing the same tie every day, which contained an accurate historical record of his tastes in soup. Another was adamant about entering the trading floor through one particular door of the several available. Another refused to use a red pen. Each of these odd habits was probably initiated by an accidental pairing of the behavior with a desired or undesirable outcome and then perpetuated by random reinforcement.

MISPLACED FAITH IN CHART ANALYSIS

Subjective technicians, irrespective of the specific method they practice, believe in the efficacy of visual chart analysis. Price charts are presumed to be a valid method for detecting exploitable order in financial market data. The pioneers of TA used charts to discover the discipline's foundational principles, and today they remain the primary analysis tool. This section explains why confidence in chart analysis is misplaced.

This is not to say that charts have no role in TA. They can serve as a source of inspiration that leads to the formation of testable hypotheses about market behavior. However, unless and until these conjectures are vigorously and objectively tested, they remain mere suppositions rather than trustworthy knowledge.

An Informal Search for Order Is Sure to Find It

Humans have both the need and the capacity to find order and meaning in their experience. "It may have been bred into us through evolution because of its general adaptiveness: We can capitalize on ordered phenomena in ways that we cannot on those that are random. The predisposition to detect patterns and make connections is what leads to discovery and advance. The problem is that the tendency is so strong and so automatic that we sometimes detect coherence even when it does not exist."[124]

A trait of intuitive, nonscientific thinking is the tendency to accept without question surface impressions and obvious explanations. Unfortunately, what is obvious at first blush is not necessarily valid. To the ancients it seemed obvious the sun orbited the earth. To the pioneers of TA it seemed obvious that financial market prices formed patterns and trends. Just as early observers of the heavens perceived mythical figures like Leo the Lion and Orion the Hunter in the random arrangements of stars, the first technicians saw heads-and-shoulders, double and triple tops, and other patterns in the meandering movements of stock and commodity prices. These patterns form the lexicon of subjective chart analysis.

Our nervous system seems to be wired to see shapes regardless of whether they are real. Dr. John Elder,[125] a noted authority on predictive modeling and data mining, calls this the "bunnies in the clouds" effect. There is, however, good reason to question the validity of chart analysis, and by extension, to question the validity of knowledge based on it. I contend that trends and patterns on charts that appear real to the eye may often be illusions born of the mind's voracious, though indiscriminate, appetite to perceive order.

This is not meant to imply that financial markets are devoid of authentic trends and patterns. In fact, there is sound empirical evidence that patterns exist which have predictive power.[126] It does mean, however, that visual inspection of charts is an inadequate means for discovering or verifying the authenticity of patterns. Studies[127] have shown that even expert chartists cannot reliably distinguish between authentic stock charts and simulated charts produced by a random process. A method of analysis that cannot discriminate real charts from fakes cannot provide reliable analysis of the real. A jeweler who can't tell the difference between authentic diamonds and dime-store costume jewelry is in no position to appraise a diamond necklace.

Illusory Trends and Patterns in Financial Data

Statistician Harry Roberts said that technical analysts fall victim to the illusion of patterns and trends for two possible reasons. First, "the usual method of graphing stock prices gives a picture of successive (price) levels rather than of price changes and levels can give an artificial appearance of *pattern* or *trend*. Second, chance behavior itself produces *patterns* that invite spurious interpretations."[128]

Roberts showed that the same chart patterns to which TA attaches importance[129] appear with great regularity in random walks. A random walk is, by definition, devoid of authentic trends, patterns, or exploitable order of any kind. However, Roberts' random-walk charts displayed head-and-shoulder tops and bottoms, triangle tops and bottoms, triple tops and bottoms, trend channels, and so forth.

You can create a random-walk chart from a sequence of coin flips by starting with an arbitrary price, say $100, and adding one dollar for each head and subtracting one dollar for each tail. In other words, the face of the coin represents a price change and the chart shows a sequence of simulated price levels. Each simulated price in the sequence is equal to the cumulative algebraic sum of all prior random changes added to the starting value. If you carry out this process for three hundred or so flips, you may be amazed at the patterns that appear. Many will be similar to the patterns found on actual charts of financial assets. Clearly the patterns or trends that appear on a coin-flip chart cannot predict its future evolution.

This raises an important question: if chartist-like patterns can appear with such regularity in random walks, and it is known that these patterns cannot be predictive, how can the same patterns be considered predictive simply because they happen to appear on a real chart?

Perhaps we should not trust the eye of Roberts. He was a statistician, not an expert in TA. If an expert chartist were able to spot the patterns occurring in random-walk charts as fakes the way a competent jeweler can spot a counterfeit diamond, then Roberts's random-walk experiment would not prove anything other than his lack of chart expertise. Certainly, expert chartists should claim that they can tell the difference between patterns occurring in random walks and those occurring on real charts. After all, if the patterns on actual markets charts form as a result of changes in supply and demand and/or oscillations in market mood, as TA claims, they should look different from the accidental meanderings on a random-walk chart![130]

Unfortunately expert chartists have been unable to tell the difference between real and fake charts. Arditti[131] put them to the test. When presented with an assortment of real charts mixed with random-walk charts, the chartists examined by Arditti were no more accurate at telling the real from the fake than a guess. This result was subsequently confirmed in an informal study[132] by Professor Jeremy Siegel of the Wharton Business School.[133] Siegel presented the graphs shown in Figure 2.18 (four real and four random) to a group of top Wall Street stockbrokers who considered themselves competent chart readers. Again, the experts were unable to reliably distinguish the real from the random. I conducted a similar experiment using graduate business students who had just completed a course in technical analysis. Their accuracy was consistent with guessing. The real charts are indicated by the X.

What can we conclude from these results? First, they do not imply that financial markets are random, and hence devoid of valid trends and patterns. But they do call into question the efficacy of subjective/visual chart analysis as a means of knowledge acquisition and forecasting. If chart reading were a valid skill, it should at least be possible to distinguish an actual chart from a random fake.

Evidence of Illusory Trends in Sports

Financial markets are not the only arena in which observers are plagued by the illusion of order. Many sports fans and athletes believe in performance trends, periods of hot and cold performance. What baseball fan or

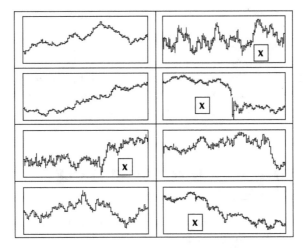

FIGURE 2.18   Real and randomly generated stock charts.
Siegel, Jeremy J., *Stocks for the Long Run*, 3rd Edition, Copyright 2002, 1998, 1994, McGraw-Hill; the material is reproduced with the permission of The McGraw-Hill Companies.

player does not think batting slumps or hitting streaks are real? Basketball fans, players, coaches, and sports commentators speak of the so-called hot hand, a trend of above-average shooting accuracy.

These beliefs are widely held because trends in athletic performance seem so obvious. However, rigorous statistical analysis of player performance[134] indicates that the hot hand phenomenon is an illusion. The fans have been duped by their intuition. This erroneous belief stems from a faulty notion about how random phenomena ought to behave.[135] Common sense would have us believe that streaks (a sequence of strike-outs, or a sequence of successful shots, and so forth) should not occur in a random process. Rather, intuition incorrectly tells us that random processes should display something resembling an alternating pattern of positive and negative outcomes.

The truth is that sports trends are, by and large a cognitive illusion. What appears to be a batting slump or a hitting streak is often nothing more than a run of similar outcomes, a phenomenon that is quite common in random processes. A valid trend is a streak of longer duration than those that are ordinary in random data. That is to say, a real trend is a streak of sufficient length that it would be rare in a random process.

Gilovich points out that "although a player's performance does not display longer streaks than those allowed by chance, it does not mean that the player's performance is chance determined. It is not. Whether a given shot is hit or missed is determined by a host of non-chance factors, foremost among them being the skill of the offensive and defensive players involved. However, one factor that does not influence or predict the outcome is the player's recent hit rate."[136]

To understand why sports fans, athletes, and chart analysts fall prey to the illusion of trends and patterns in data that may in fact be random we must delve a bit deeper into the nature of intuitive judgment.

THE INTUITIVE JUDGMENT AND THE ROLE OF HEURISTICS

"To simplify, there are basically two types of thought processes: automatic and controlled."[137] "Intuition is automatic. It is our capacity for direct knowledge, for immediate insight without observation or reason."[138] It is perception-like, rapid, and effortless, notes Princeton University psychologist Daniel Kahneman. In contrast, "deliberate or controlled thinking is reasoning-like, critical, and analytic."[139] The prototype of controlled thought is scientific reasoning. The prototype of intuition is the brilliant medical diagnostician who always seems to sniff the underlying disease. Subjective technicians rely primarily on intuition, and they do so to their detriment.

Human intelligence has limits. We can only pay attention to an extremely small fraction of the information that comes to us through our sensory organs. Moreover, the mind is not well suited to complex tasks such as estimating probabilities and making decisions in a logically and probabilistically correct manner in situations characterized by uncertainty.

To cope, we must simplify. We reduce the complexities of estimating and decision making by resorting to a variety of quick and dirty rules of reasoning known as judgment heuristics. They focus our attention on a limited portion of the total information picture and utilize relatively simple forms of information processing and reasoning to arrive at conclusions quickly. All of this is done without awareness or exertion. We make intuitive judgments as automatically and effortlessly as we recognize someone's face, a task for which the mind is very well suited.

We acquire judgment heuristics from life experience. The term *heuristic* refers to the notion of discovery by trial and error, and this is how these rules of thought are acquired. Moreover, they slip into usage so subtly that we are unaware of how or when we learned them. And we adopt them because, in general, they work. However, they work imperfectly and when they fail our judgment suffers.

The good news is that heuristic judgment tends to err in a consistent manner. In other words, the judgments are biased—they tend to be wrong in the same way over and over again.[140] This consistency makes it possible to predict the conditions under which heuristic judgments will fail and how they will fail—whether the deviation from true value will be a positive or a negative one.

In general, heuristic judgments tend to err in situations characterized by uncertainty.[141] Financial markets are highly uncertain, so intuitive judgments in this arena are likely to be biased. The specific bias that afflicts subjective technicians is the propensity to see trends and patterns in data where such structures are not truly present. In other words, there is a systematic tendency to perceive order where only random behavior exists. This may explain why chartists are unable to distinguish real charts from pseudocharts produced from random data.

In the words of Professor Burton Malkiel, "Randomness is a difficult notion for people to accept. When events come in clusters and streaks, people look for explanations and patterns. They refuse to believe that such patterns—which frequently occur in random data—could equally be derived from tossing a coin. So it is in the stock market as well."[142] Malkeil takes the extreme position that the market is random. I do not share this conviction but agree that people misperceive order in data that is random. For this reason visual inspection of price charts cannot be trusted.

The illusion of trends and patterns in data that is truly random may be attributable to the failure of a specific judgment heuristic called *reasoning by representativeness*. That is to say, a faulty application of the generally useful representativeness rule biases us toward the perception of order where it does not exist.

Heuristic Bias and the Availability Heuristic

To recap, heuristics help us make complex decisions rapidly in spite of the limitations of human intelligence, but they can cause those decisions to be biased. The notion of heuristic bias is easily explained by considering the *availability heuristic*.

We rely on the *availability heuristic* to estimate the likelihood of future events. It is based on the reasonable notion that the more easily we can bring to mind a particular class of events, the more likely it is that such events will occur in the future. Events that are easily brought to mind are said to be *cognitively available*. For example, plane crashes are a class of events with high cognitive availability.

The availability heuristic makes a certain amount of sense. The ability to recall a class of events is indeed related to how frequently they have occurred in the past, and it is also true that events that have happened frequently in the past are generally more likely to occur in the future. This is in keeping with one theory of probability that asserts that the future likelihood of an event is related to its historical frequency.[143] Taken as a class, thunderstorms have been more frequent in the past than asteroid impacts, and they do indeed have a higher future likelihood.

The problem with the availability heuristic is that there are factors that can enhance an event's cognitive availability that have nothing to do with its historical frequency and are, therefore, irrelevant to estimating its future likelihood. Consequently, our judgments of likelihood are sometimes falsely inflated by the intrusion of these irrelevant factors. Two factors that have no relevance to an event's likelihood but that do increase its cognitive availability are recency and vividness. That is to say, how recently[144] an event of the type in question took place and how vivid the event was both impact how easily we can bring such events to mind. Consider plane crashes as a class of events. A plane crash that just occurred is both vivid and recent. As a result, in the period right after a well-publicized plane crash many people tend to overestimate the likelihood of future plane crashes and are inordinately fearful of flying. Note the bias in the judgment is one of overestimating a probability. The availability heuristic never causes us to underestimate an event's likelihood. The error is always one of overestimating the probability.

The Representativeness Heuristic: Reasoning by Similarity

The *representativeness* heuristic, which was first identified by Tversky and Kahneman[145] is of particular relevance to subjective TA. We use this rule to make intuitive classification judgments. In other words, it is used to estimate the probability that a particular object, for example the dog before me, belongs to a particular class of objects, for example the class of poodles. The underlying premise of the representativeness heuristic is that each member of a class should display the key common attributes that define the class. It is quite reasonable to expect that objects from the same class should possess a similar set of characteristics. In arriving at a judgment by representativeness about whether a given object belongs to a particular class, we unconsciously consider the degree of similarity or match between the attributes of the object and the set of attributes presumed to be representative of that class. This is why this heuristic is referred as a reasoning by *representativeness*.

In this section and the next, I will argue that visual chart analysis is inherently flawed because of a bias toward the perception of order and pattern even in data that is truly random. I will contend that this bias is due to a misapplication of the representativeness heuristic. In other words, a bias stemming from a faulty application of the representativeness heuristic can explain why subjective technicians fall prey to an illusion of order in charts that were, in fact, produced by a random process.

To explain how chartists make this mistake, which is rather subtle, we will take a brief detour by considering a more easily understood case of heuristic bias caused by representativeness reasoning.

As mentioned earlier, reasoning by representativeness is premised on the notion that a class of objects or events can be represented by a class stereotype—a typical example that possesses the class's key distinguishing characteristics. Often this line of reasoning works well. However, it fails when an object's most noticeable features are not reliable indicators of the object's class. In other words, when the characteristics that most draw our attention are not relevant in judging the object's class[146] reasoning by representativeness tends to fail. Unfortunately, intuitive judgment tends to be based on the most obvious features of an object or event regardless of whether these features are truly useful indicators of its class.

Reasoning by representativeness estimates the probability than an object belongs to a given class by considering the degree of match between the object's most salient attributes and the most salient attributes of the class stereotype. The greater the number of matching attributes, the higher the adjudged probability that the object is indeed a member of the class in question. "Modern psychologists hypothesize that our concepts of categories (classes) like bank tellers, feminists, microcomputers, skunks, and all kinds of things are represented cognitively as lists of attributes that we believe are defining characteristics of those entities."[147] This is illustrated in Figure 2.19. In many instances this fast and frugal classification rule gives accurate results. People would not use such a rule it if it did not.

Let's consider an example where the application of the representativeness rule leads to an erroneous judgment about an object's class. Imagine that you have just taken your seat on a commercial airline flight and you become concerned that a person (the object) seated next to you may be a terrorist (the class). Your apprehension is aroused because the person has the following obvious characteristics: man of apparently Middle Eastern origin, mustache, 25–30 years of age, wearing a turban, reading the Koran, and appearing nervous. Your conclusion that the man may very well belong to the class of terrorists occurred quite spontaneously because his obvious characteristics are similar to a set of characteristics that was also possessed by (i.e., is representative of) the terrorists who conducted the attacks of September 11, 2001. Your inference was based on the representativeness heuristic. Now consider how you would have reacted if the passenger were a young Middle Eastern man but was wearing blue jeans and a tee-shirt with an obscene logo, had on a New York

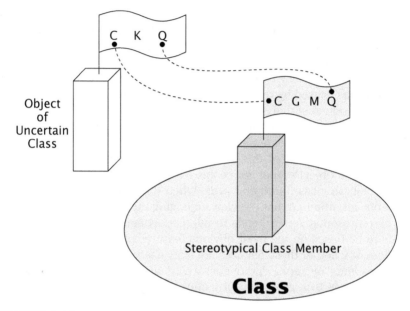

FIGURE 2.19   Classification by number of matching attributes.

Yankee baseball cap instead of a turban, was reading a copy of *Playboy* instead of the Koran, and was listening to rock music on an iPod while blowing chewing-gum bubbles. You would not have been worried. Intuitive judgments of class rest on the assumption that the most obvious characteristics of an individual are reliable indicators of that individual's class.

Judgments based on representativeness can err because they fail to take into account statistical and/or logical elements of a situation that are truly relevant to an accurate judgment about its class. The probabilistically correct way of estimating the class of an event or object is called Bayes' theorem,[148] which is derived from the axioms of probability theory. If it were applied to the airline passenger suspected of being a terrorist, it would take into account such things as the proportion of terrorists in the world (i.e., the base rate of the class of terrorists), the proportion of people in the world that possess the set of observed characteristics (i.e., the base rate of the pattern), and the proportion of terrorists that have this pattern of characteristics (i.e., the conditional probability that these characteristics are present given that the individual is in fact a terrorist). When these values are plugged into the equation that expresses Bayes' theorem we obtain the conditional probability that the person is a terrorist, given that they possess the pattern of characteristics.

Because intuition operates on the basis of representativeness, rather than Bayes' law, we tend to commit an error called the *base rate fallacy*. This is the failure to consider the base rate statistics characterizing a situation. Terrorists, fortunately, are very rare (i.e., have a very low base rate). Thus, among the entire set of people who possess the same salient characteristics as the terrorists of 9/11/01, the fraction that are actually terrorists is extremely small. Perhaps only one person in a million with these traits is actually a terrorist. This fact is highly relevant to judging the likelihood that the person seated next to us is dangerous. However, we tend to neglect base-rate statistics because intuitive judgment is focused on the attention-grabbing features of a situation or object rather than relevant facts such as a base-rate.

An example of fallacious reasoning by representativeness was displayed by market analysts who predicted that a deflationary depression would follow the stock market crash of October 1987. They were captivated by the very noticeable similarity between the behavior of the stock market in 1929, which did lead to a deflationary depression, and its behavior in 1987. Both witnessed market crashes. This glaring similarity took analysts' attention away from significant dissimilarities between 1987 and 1929. In other words, 1987 and 1929 were different with respect to factors that do have some predictive information with respect to deflationary collapses. An examination of market crashes over the last 100 years shows that a price crash is not a reliable predictor of a deflationary depression.

Another error associated with representative reasoning is called the *conjunction fallacy*, a failure to take into account a basic law of logic telling us that a proper subset must contain a smaller number of objects than the larger set to which it belongs. The set *horses* is a proper subset of the larger set, *animals*. It follows that horses must be fewer in number than animals in general, which includes horses, bluebirds, aardvarks, and so forth. However, when people rely on the representativeness rule, they seem to ignore this law of logic and commit the conjunction[149] fallacy. In one experiment conducted by Tversky and Kahneman,[150] subjects were presented with the following description:

> *Linda is 31 years old, single, outspoken, and very bright. She majored in philosophy. As a student, she was deeply concerned with issues of discrimination and social justice, and also participated in antinuclear demonstrations. Which possibility is most likely? (1) Linda is a bank teller, or (2) Linda is a bank teller AND is active in the feminist movement.*

Astoundingly, 85 percent of the subjects responded that it was more likely that Linda was a bank teller AND active in the feminist movement than that Linda was simply a bank teller. This conclusion ignores the logical relationship between a set and a proper subset. Subjects became so fixated on the fact that Linda possessed a set of salient characteristics that matched an intuitive stereotype of a feminist, that they committed the conjunction fallacy. Clearly, the set of women who are both bank tellers *and* active in the feminist movement is a subset of a larger category which contains all female bank tellers including those who are feminists and those who are not. Other studies confirmed these findings and led Tversky and Kahneman to conclude that people's probability judgments are biased by the addition of salient detail. Even though each additional detail describing an object reduces the probability that such an object exists,[151] when people reason by representativeness, additional detail increases the number of characteristics that match a class stereotype, thus increasing an intuitive estimate of probability. The conjunction fallacy is illustrated in Figure 2.20.

The conjunction fallacy can have disastrous consequences when it seeps into jury verdicts. For example, consider which of two possibilities would seem more likely[152]:

1. The defendant left the scene of the crime.
2. The defendant left the scene of the crime for fear of being accused of murder.

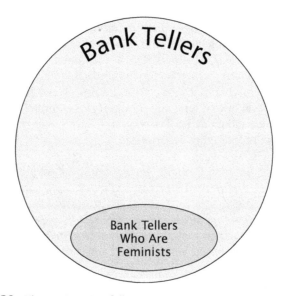

FIGURE 2.20 The conjunction fallacy.

The second hypothesis involves a conjunction of "left the scene" *and* "fear of accusation." Because the second alternative is a subset of the first, it is by definition less probable. Clearly, there are reasons for someone's leaving a crime scene other than fear of being accused, like going to pick up the dry cleaning. However, the additional detail of the second hypothesis lends a ring of plausibility because it increases a sense of match to actions that would be representative of a guilty party.

THE REPRESENTATIVENESS HEURISTIC AND THE ILLUSION TRENDS AND PATTERNS IN CHARTS: REAL AND FAKE

So far the representativeness heuristic has been discussed with respect to its use in classifying objects. In fact, the heuristic is also involved in a more abstract type of classification judgment that is central to the practice of subjective TA: judging that a sample of data evidences trends and patterns and is, therefore, worthy of further analysis *or* alternatively that the data is a random hodge-podge not worthy of further analysis.

Bear in mind the judgment about whether a data set appears random or nonrandom is not made with conscious awareness or intention. It occurs as automatically and unconsciously as the judgment involved in recognizing the face of a friend. All heuristic judgments, including reasoning by representativeness, occur automatically and without conscious awareness. As a result, when a chartist concludes that a sample of price history contains authentic patterns and trends (i.e., that the data is nonrandom) and is, therefore, worthy of analysis, it is not a matter of controlled thinking. That is to say, the chartist does not consciously pose the question: "Does this data appear as if it contains exploitable order and structure."

Although heuristic judgments slip into our thinking unnoticed, they can have a profound influence on our beliefs. The problem is that heuristic thinking fails to take into account important features of the data that are relevant to determining if it does contain authentic patterns and trends that might be exploited with further analysis.

In a previous section, I asked you to create an artificial price history (random-walk chart) by flipping a coin 300 times. If you did not do so then, I urge you to do so now. Not only will it make this section more meaningful, it may permanently change the way you look at charts. To quote Martha Stewart, "that's a good thing."

If this was your first exposure to data generated by a random process, you may be surprised by how nonrandom it looks. You may not have expected to see formations that look like chart patterns (head-and-shoulders, double top, etc.). The question we must consider is this: Why does this sequence, which we know to be random in origin, give the appearance of having authentic patterns and trends. Or, said differently, why does data generated by a purely random process appear as if it were generated by a process governed by rules, which, if discovered, would make prediction possible?

Your chart may have looked something like Figure 2.21.

The bottom line is this: That which appears to be nonrandom is not necessarily nonrandom. My contention is that the perception of trends and patterns in randomly generated data occurs because of a faulty application of the representativeness heuristic. Specifically, the heuristic creates a faulty intuitive notion of how random data is supposed to look. That is to say, it produces a false stereotype of randomness. Thus, when we view data that does not appear to match this false stereotype, we automatically and erroneously conclude that the data is nonrandom. From this flawed conclusion, it is a short leap to the equally false perception of patterns and the equally false notion that the patterns contain predictive information.

One consequence of representativeness-based reasoning is the expectation that an effect should resemble its cause. This is often reasonable. The Earth (big cause) is responsible for gravity (big effect), while a mere pebble in our shoe causes only a minor annoyance. However, the rule that an effect should resemble its cause does not always hold. The 1918 flu pandemic, a big effect, was caused by a creature of submicroscopic proportions.

How does this relate to charts of asset prices? A set of data on a chart can be seen as an effect of a process, the activity of a financial market. The process is the cause whereas the data is the effect. A chart of our

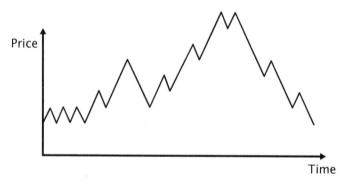

FIGURE 2.21 Data from a random process that appears ordered.

body's hourly temperature over a 24-hour period is an effect caused by a process that happens to be our body's metabolism.

Because representativeness-based thinking operates involuntarily beneath conscious awareness, when we view the chart of an asset's price history, we tend to draw an automatic conclusion about the nature of the process that generated the chart. Perhaps, if stock charts looked something like the trace in Figure 2.22, the pioneers of TA would have been less likely to see exploitable structure, and the practice of TA would never have been born. This data is supposed to approximate an intuitive stereotype of randomness: haphazard, disorderly, and without any hint of trend.

On the basis of the representativeness heuristic, we presume that if a process (the cause) is random, its effect (the data) should also appear random. As a consequence of this assumption, any sample of data that deviates from the presumed stereotype of randomness, because it manifests some sense of pattern or trend, is concluded to be the product of a nonrandom process. Stock charts give the appearance of having been generated by a nonrandom process. In other words they match an intuitive notion of order and predictability. Bear in mind that financial markets may indeed be nonrandom to some degree and hence be amenable to prediction. However, that is not the issue here. Rather the issue is can nonrandom structure that is amenable to prediction be detected by visual inspection and intuitive appraisal?

As mentioned previously, the deficiencies of reasoning by representativeness are due to an excessive focus on obvious appearances and the simultaneous disregard of important statistical and logical features. As will be explained in Chapter 4, one of the most important features of a sample of data, from the standpoint of data analysis, is the number of observations comprising the sample. Valid conclusions about a sample of data must take the number of observations into account. Moreover, the statistical

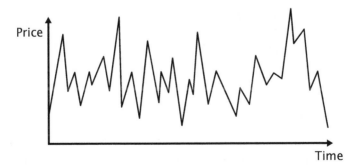

FIGURE 2.22 Intuitive stereotype of random data: haphazard, disordered, nontrending.

characteristics of a large number of observations are required to accurately represent the true nature of the process that generated the data (e.g., random or nonrandom). Conversely, small samples of data often convey the illusion of patterns and trends because the statistical characteristics of a small sample of data can be wildly unrepresentative of the data generating process.

I contend that the belief that visual chart analysis is a valid method for detecting trends and patterns is based on a flawed chain of thinking that goes something like this:

1. On the basis of the representativeness heuristic, it is erroneously thought that data generated by a random process should look random—a formless haphazard flip-flop without any hint of patterns, organized shapes or trends.

2. This stereotype is erroneously assumed to manifest in all samples of random data, irrespective of the number of observations comprising the sample.

3. A small sample of data is examined and it appears not to match the intuitive stereotype of randomness.

4. The data is thus deemed to be the product of a nonrandom process.

5. Nonrandom processes are amenable to prediction, hence it would be reasonable to look for patterns and trends in the data to make predictions.

This is illustrated in Figure 2.23.

The principal flaw in this chain of reasoning is the failure to consider the matter of sample size (step 2 of the preceding list). The presumption that a sample of data can accurately reflect the nature of the data generating process, irrespective of the number of observations comprising the sample, violates an important principle of formal data analysis, the Law of Large Numbers. Reasoning by representativeness fails to respect the Law of Large Numbers. In other words, it commits the crime of small numbers or sample size neglect. The penalty is automatic membership in The Fools of Randomness[153] club.

The Law of Large Numbers and the Crime of Sample Size Neglect

The Law of Large Numbers tells us that sample size is of paramount importance because it determines the confidence we can have in inferences based on a sample of data. Also known as the Law of Averages, the Law of Large Numbers tells us that only samples comprised of large numbers of

Does The Data Contain Predictable Order?
Yes: Data sample does not match intuitive stereotype of randomness

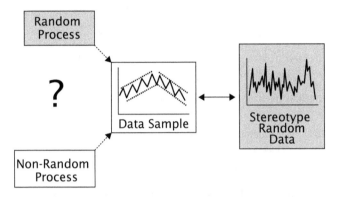

FIGURE 2.23   Data is presumed to be amenable to prediction because it does not match an intuitive stereotype of randomness.

observations reliably and accurately reflect the characteristics of the process that generated the sample. Or, said differently, only large samples can inform us about the characteristics of the population from which the sample came. Thus, the larger the number of coin tosses, the more closely the proportion of heads in the sample will reflect an essential truth about fair coins: the probability of heads is 0.50. The bottom line is we can have greater confidence in what we learn from large samples than from small ones. The Law of Large Numbers will be discussed in greater depth in connection with statistics in Chapter 4. For the present discussion, what is important is the connection between the Law of Large Numbers and the appearance of illusory patterns and trends in small samples of data.

Small samples can be misleading because they can manifest characteristics that are very different from the true characteristics of the process that generated the sample. This explains why a small segment of a pseudo-stock chart—one that was actually generated by a random process—gives the appearance of authentic patterns and trends. Of course, by design, such a chart cannot have real trends and patterns. Thus, a reliable conclusion about whether a sample of data was the result of a random or non-random process cannot be obtained from a small sample. This is depicted by Figures 2.24 and 2.25. When the parts (small samples) of the chart look nonrandom, an illusion of nonrandomness is created in the entire chart, when they are put together.

Coin-toss experiments illustrate how small samples can produce misleading impressions. The obvious statistical characteristic of this random

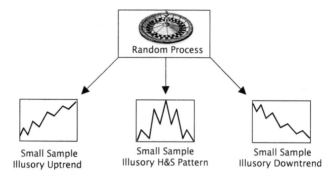

FIGURE 2.24 The illusion of trends and patterns in small samples—data generated by a random process.

process is that there are two equally likely outcomes. This is the basis for an expectation that the proportion of heads is 0.50. This intuition is indeed correct when the number of tosses is large. In a sample of 100,000 tosses, the proportion of heads will be extremely close to 0.50. If one were to repeat this experiment many times, the proportion of heads would always be very close to 0.50. In fact, it would be unlikely to fall outside the range of 0.497–0.503.[154]

The problem is intuition pays no attention to sample size or the Law of Large Numbers. So we also expect 0.50 heads to appear in all samples. Although it is true that the expected proportion of heads in any sample is always 0.50, even for just two tosses, the proportion of heads that will ac-

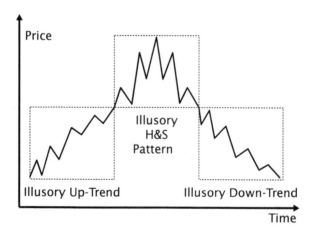

FIGURE 2.25 If small parts of a chart look orderly, the whole chart assumes a nonrandom look.

tually appear in a given small sample can depart significantly from 0.50. In ten tosses, for example, three heads (0.30) or seven heads (0.70) can easily happen. In a sample of 100,000 tosses, 0.30 heads (30,000) or 0.70 (70,000) would be virtually impossible with a fair coin.

Another faulty intuition about random processes is that outcomes should alternate (up/down, head/tail) more than they really do. When people are asked to imagine what a sequence of coin tosses would be like, they tend to imagine sequences that show far more head /tail alternation than would really occur in a random sequence.[155] In reality, random process displays less alternation and longer streaks of similar outcomes (up, up, up) than is widely believed. Therefore, when a set of data does not match the false expectation of an alternating sequence, it gives rise to the illusion of a trend. For example, it seems intuitively correct that a coin toss would be more likely to produce the sequence H,T,H,T,H,T than the sequence H,H,H,H,H. However, both sequences are, in fact, equally probable,[156] so we come away with the erroneous impression that the former sequence suggests a random process whereas the latter suggests a process that displays a trend.

Because random sequences actually alternate less and streak more than our intuitive conception, sequences that actually are random appear as if they are nonrandom. For example, the average basketball player makes about 50 percent of their shots, similar to the probability of getting heads. Thus, there is a reasonably good chance of making four, five, or even six shots in a row if 20 shots are taken in a game. In other words, chance favors the appearance of what sports fans call a hot-hand,[157] which is, in fact, nothing more than a streak typical of a random sequence.

The erroneous notion that random processes should alternate more and streak less is responsible for two false perceptions: (1) the *clustering illusion,* and (2) the *gambler's fallacy.* In this context, the term *cluster* refers to a clump, either in time or space, of similar events. A cluster of similar outcomes in a random time series gives the illusion of a trend that has momentum and this creates the false expectation that the trend should persist. The gambler's fallacy is the equally false expectation that a cluster of similar outcomes should not occur, and when one does, it gives rise to the false expectation that a reversal is due. The gambler's fallacy is exemplified by a person who thinks a tail is more likely after a string of heads.

It is an observer's prior beliefs about a process that determines whether he will fall prey to the clustering illusion or the gambler's fallacy. Suppose a person is observing a process that is, in fact, random but does not realize that it is. That person will tend to fall prey to the clustering illusion if they hold a prior belief that the process is nonrandom and that it should manifest trends. Sooner or later a streak occurs, and the prior belief is confirmed. The observer has fallen prey to the clustering illusion.

In contrast, if the observer has a prior belief that the process is random, it is more likely that they will fall prey to the gambler's fallacy. Sooner or later a streak occurs, for example four heads in a row, which is then followed by a tail. Although this would be quite normal in a random process, the appearance of the tail reinforces the false belief that a tail was due. Therefore, when a process is truly random both the observer who thinks the process is nonrandom and believes that trends (clusters) should occur and the observer who thinks the process is random and that the trends should reverse will have their beliefs rewarded. In truth, when a process is random both observers' expectations are false. Random walks have no memory, and prior outcomes have no effect on subsequent events.

The clustering illusion can also occur in a spatial context. The perception of illusory shapes in random data is simply another manifestation of a false expectation about randomness. The false expectation is that random data should not display any hint of organization or form. Any departure from this expectation is interpreted, falsely, as a sign of a nonrandom process at work. A case in which illusory spatial patterns in random data encouraged the formation of erroneous perceptions occurred during the World War II bombing of London by German V-1 and V-2 missiles.[158] The newspapers ran maps of missile impact sites, and readers had the immediate perception that the strikes were clustered. This gave rise to an equally false, after-the-fact interpretation that impact patterns were evidence of an effort by the Germans to avoid hitting certain parts of London, which in turn spawned fallacious causal reasoning. Londoners came to believe that these areas were spared V-2 attacks because they housed German spies. However, a formal analysis of the missile impact sites showed that they were entirely consistent with a random pattern.

A more recent example of illusory spatial clustering that fostered erroneous causal reasoning was the so-called cancer-cluster hysteria in California. People became alarmed if the number of diagnosed cases of cancer of a particular type (e.g., lung cancer caused by asbestos) was far above average in their community. It turns out that clusters can occur by chance. What is not apparent to the statistically unsophisticated is this: Given 5,000 census tracts in California and 80 possible environmental cancers, there will be some tracts in which the number of cancer cases will be far above average simply due to chance. In some cases, such clusters really are attributable to environmental toxins, but not always and not nearly as often as intuition would suggest.

This brings us back to TA and the appearance of orderly patterns like double tops, head-and-shoulders bottoms, and so forth. The occurrence of such shapes is not consistent with an intuitive notion of data produced by a random process. Such data is erroneously presumed to be completely haphazard and shapeless, so, we jump to the conclusion the patterns must be the by-product of a nonrandom process that is not only amenable to visual analysis but that the patterns themselves are useful for making predictions. As Roberts showed, random walks can easily trace the patterns that subjective technicians hold so dear.

In summary, people have a hard time telling when a set of data is random or not. Because the mind is predisposed to the perception of order and adept at inventing stories that explain why that order exists, it is not at all mysterious that the pioneers of TA would find patterns and trends in price charts and then invent theories about why such patterns should occur. Methods more rigorous than visual analysis and intuition are needed to find the exploitable order that may exist in financial market fluctuations.

THE ANTIDOTE TO ILLUSORY KNOWLEDGE: THE SCIENTIFIC METHOD

This chapter examined many ways we can be fooled into adopting erroneous knowledge. The best antidote ever invented for this problem is the scientific method, the subject of the next chapter.

CHAPTER 3

The Scientific Method and Technical Analysis

T A's central problem is erroneous knowledge. As it is traditionally practiced, much of TA is a body of dogma and myth, founded on faith and anecdote. This is a consequence of the informal, intuitive methods used by its practitioners to discover patterns with predictive power. As a discipline, TA suffers because it is practiced without discipline.

Adopting a rigorous scientific approach would solve this problem. The scientific method is not a cookbook procedure that automates knowledge discovery. Rather it is "a set of methods designed to describe and interpret observed or inferred phenomena, past or present aimed at building a testable body of knowledge open to rejection or confirmation. In other words, (it) is a specific way of analyzing information with the goal of testing claims."[1] This chapter summarizes its logical and philosophical foundations and discusses the implications of its adoption by TA practitioners.

THE MOST IMPORTANT KNOWLEDGE OF ALL: A METHOD TO GET MORE

"Of all the kinds of knowledge that the West has given to the world, the most valuable is the scientific method, a set of procedures for acquiring new knowledge. It was invented by a series of European thinkers from about 1550 to 1700."[2] Compared to informal approaches it is unsurpassed in its ability to separate fact from falsehood. The dramatic increase in our understanding of and control over the natural world over the last 400 years attests to the power of the scientific method.

The method's rigor protects us from the frailties of mind, which often impair what we learn from experience using less formal methods. Although informal knowledge acquisition works well for many of the obvious truths of daily living, sometimes what seems obvious is not true. It was obvious to the ancients that the sun revolved around the earth. It took science to show this was false. Informal observation and intuitive inference are especially prone to failure when phenomena are complex or highly random. Financial market behavior displays both.

Historically, TA has not been practiced in a scientific manner, but this is now changing. In academia and the business world, a new breed of practitioners, known as quants, have been adopting a scientific approach. Indeed, some of the most successful hedge funds are using strategies that could be called scientific TA.

Unsurprisingly, many traditional TA practitioners have resisted this change. Vested interests and habitual ways of thinking are hard to abandon. No doubt there was opposition when folk medicine evolved into modern medicine, when alchemy progressed into chemistry, and when astrology advanced into the science of astronomy. Rancor between traditional and scientific practitioners is to be expected. However, if history is any guide, traditional TA will, in the end, be marginalized. Astrologers, alchemists, and witch doctors still practice, but they are no longer taken seriously.

THE LEGACY OF GREEK SCIENCE: A MIXED BLESSING

The Greeks were the first to make an effort at being scientific, though their legacy proved to be a mixed blessing. On the positive side of the ledger was the invention of logic by Aristotle. The formal reasoning procedures he developed remain a pillar of today's scientific method.

On the negative side were his faulty theories of matter and motion. Instead of being generalized from prior observations and tested against freshly observed facts, as is the practice in modern science, his theories were deduced from metaphysical principles. When observations conflicted with theory, Aristotle and his disciples were prone to bending the facts rather than altering or abandoning the theory. Modern science does the opposite.

Aristotle ultimately realized that deductive logic was insufficient for learning about the world. He saw the need for an empirical approach based on inductive logic—observation followed by generalization. Its invention was his most significant contribution to science. However, he failed in the application of his own invention. At his institution of higher learning, the famed Lyceum in Athens, Aristotle and his students made meticulous observations on a wide range of natural phenomena. Unfortunately, the inferences they drew from these facts were biased by Aristotelian dogma and often based on inadequate evidence.[3] There was too much theorizing from too little evidence. When facts contradicted favored first principles, Aristotle would contort the facts to conserve the principle.

Ultimately the Aristotelian legacy would prove to be an obstruction to scientific progress. Because his authority was so great, his flawed theories were transmitted as unquestioned dogma through the next 2,000 years. This hindered the growth of scientific knowledge, or at least the sort of knowledge that we now characterize as scientific.[4] In a like manner, the teachings of TA's pioneers like Dow, Schabacker, Elliott, and Gann have been passed along unquestioned and untested. Just as there is no room for dogma in science, neither should there be in TA.

THE BIRTH OF THE SCIENTIFIC REVOLUTION

"Science was the major discovery, or invention, of the seventeenth century. Men of that time learned—and it was a very revolutionary discovery—how to measure, explain, and manipulate natural phenomena in a way that we call scientific. Since the seventeenth century, science has progressed a great deal and has discovered many truths, and it has conferred many benefits that the seventeenth century did not know, but it has not found a new way to discover natural truths. For this reason, the seventeenth century is possibly the most important century in human history."[5]

The revolution began in Western Europe around 1500 in an atmosphere of intellectual stagnation. At that time, all knowledge was based on authoritarian pronouncements rather than observed facts. The doctrines of the Roman Church and the dogma of Greek science were taken as literal truths. On Earth, objects were assumed to be governed by Aristotelian physics. In the heavens, the laws invented by the Greek astronomer Ptolemy and later endorsed by the Church were thought to rule. The Ptolemaic system held that the earth was the center of the universe and that the sun, stars, and planets orbited about it. To the casual observer, the facts seemed to agree with the Church's orthodox theory.

Everyone was happy until people began to notice facts that conflicted with these accepted truths. Artillerymen observed that projectiles hurled by catapults and shot from cannons did not fly in conformity with

Aristotle's theory of motion (Figure 3.1). The objects were repeatedly observed to follow arced paths—a distinct departure from the trajectory predicted by Greek theory, which would have had them fall directly to earth as soon as they left the apparatus. Either the theory was wrong or the solders were deceived by their senses. The notion of testing the validity of a theory by comparing its predictions with subsequent observations is fundamental to the modern scientific method. This was an early step in that direction.

Also, at that time, observations of the heavens began to collide with the Church's theory of an Earth-centered universe. Increasingly accurate astronomical measurements revealed that planets did not move as the theory said they should. For a time, bewildered astronomers were able to patch up the Church's theory to make it agree with observed planetary paths. As discordant observations occurred, new assumptions were added to the theory, in the form of smaller orbits revolving about a planet's principal orbit. These ad hoc fixes, called epicycles, permitted the theory to account for the troublesome observations. For example, epicycles were able to explain why planets were sometimes seen to move backwards (retrograde motion) rather than follow a continuous path across the sky. Over time, a succession of epicycle fixes transformed the fundamentally incorrect theory of an Earth-centered universe into an unwieldy monstrosity of complexity with epicycles upon smaller epicycles upon even smaller epicycles.

A landmark in scientific history took place when the telescope of Galileo Galilei (1564–1642) showed that four moons circled the planet Jupiter. This observation contradicted Church orthodoxy that all celestial objects must revolve around the Earth. Galileo's findings would have called for the rejection of deeply held beliefs and the destruction of the Church's view of reality. Religious authorities were not about to face these facts. Though Galileo had originally been given permission by the Church to publish his findings, it subsequently withdrew the permission and

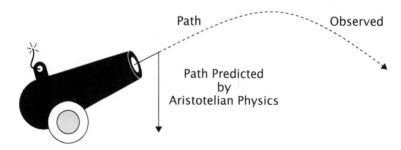

FIGURE 3.1 Prediction versus observation.

found him guilty ex post facto. As punishment, he was forced to give up astronomy and live out his days under house arrest.[6]

Eventually, the Church's theory of the heavens was replaced by the far simpler and more correct Copernican model. It placed the sun at the center of the universe and managed to explain astronomical observations with far fewer assumptions. Today we know that the sun is not the center of the universe, but at the time the Copernican model represented a true increase in man's knowledge of the heavens.

FAITH IN OBJECTIVE REALITY AND OBJECTIVE OBSERVATIONS

Science makes a fundamental assumption about the nature of reality; there is an objective reality that exists outside and independent of those who observe it, and this reality is the source of the observer's sensory impressions. This faith is the basis of science's emphasis on observation. It is properly characterized as a faith because there is no experiment or logic that can prove the existence of an objective reality. For example, I cannot prove that my perception of a red traffic signal is caused by a light that exists outside of myself rather than by something that arose entirely within my own mind.

One might ask why we should make a big deal about a fact that seems so obvious to common sense. Everyone can see there is a world out there. However, in the eyes of science this issue is a mountain and not a molehill, and it points to an important difference between knowing scientifically and knowing intuitively. Science does not accept something as true simply because it seems to be so. The history of science has shown repeatedly that the obvious is not necessarily true. Science assumes the truth of an independent objective reality, not because it is self-evident, but because it is consistent with a principle that shapes much of the scientific enterprise—*the principle of simplicity.*

The principle says simpler is better. Thus, when judging which of several theories is most likely to be true, when all theories are equally good at fitting a set of observed facts, the principle of simplicity urges us to accept the simplest theory. This is the theory that invokes the fewest and least complicated assumptions. The principle of simplicity, also known as Okaum's Razor, tells us to cut away a theory's excess complexity. The Copernican model of the universe was preferable to the Church's model because it replaced a complex arrangement of epicycles with one orbit for each planet. In a like manner, if a segment of market history can be explained either as a random walk, which assumes very little, or as an Elliott wave pattern that assumes waves embedded within waves, golden ratios, Fibonacci sequences, and a host of other complexities, the random walk is the preferred explanation. That is, unless the Elliott Wave Principle is able to make more accurate predictions than the random-walk theory.

Assuming the existence of an external reality simplifies matters greatly. To do otherwise would require a far more complex set of assumptions to explain why two people, observing the same phenomenon, will come away with generally the same impression. Explaining why I see other cars stopping when I see the traffic signal turning red is simple if I assume that there really is a traffic light out there. However, without that assumption, many more complicated assumptions would be required to explain why other motorists stop when I do.

As a consequence of its faith in an objective reality, science holds that objective and subjective perceptions are essentially different. My objective observation of a red traffic signal and my subjective experience of being annoyed because it will make me late for work are not the same. Objective observations can be shared with and confirmed by other observers. For this reason, objective observations lend themselves to the establishment of knowledge that can be shared with and confirmed by others. Subjective thoughts, interpretations, and feelings cannot, and this flaw alone is sufficient to disqualify subjective TA as legitimate knowledge.

THE NATURE OF SCIENTIFIC KNOWLEDGE

Albert Einstein once said; "One thing I have learned in a long life: that all our science, measured against reality is primitive and childlike—and yet it is the most precious thing we have."[7] Scientific knowledge is different than wisdom gained by other modes of inquiry such as common sense, faith, authority, and intuition. These differences, which account for science's higher reliability, are considered in this section.

Scientific Knowledge Is Objective

Science strives for maximum objectivity by confining itself exclusively to facts about the world out there, although it is understood that perfectly objective knowledge is never attainable. This eliminates from consideration subjective assessments that are inherently private and accessible by only one person. Inner thoughts and emotive states cannot be shared accurately with others, even when that is the intent of an artist, poet, writer, or composer. In *Naked Lunch,* William Burroughs attempts to convey his personal experience of heroin. However, I will never know his experience and may take away from those passages something quite different than Burroughs's experience or that of someone else reading it. Scientific knowledge is, therefore, public in the sense that it can be shared with and verified by as many people as possible. This promotes maximum possible agreement among independent observers.

Scientific knowledge is empirical or observation based. In this way it differs from mathematical and logical propositions that are derived from and consistent with a set of axioms but need not refer to the external world or be confirmed by observation. For example, the Pythagorean Theorem tells us that the squared length of the hypotenuse of a right triangle, c, is equal to the sum of the squares of the other two sides a and b or

$$c^2 = a^2 + b^2$$

However, this truth was not derived by studying thousands of examples of right triangles and generalizing from those many observations. Rather, it is derived from a set of accepted mathematical postulates.

Scientific Knowledge Is Quantitative

The notion that the world is best understood when described in quantitative terms originated with the Greek mathematician Pythagoras [569 B.C.–approx. 475 B.C.]. It was his contention that both the world and the mind are essentially mathematical. The importance science places on quantification cannot be overemphasized. "Wherever mankind has been able to measure things, which means transform or reduce them to numbers, it has indeed made great progress in understanding them and controlling them. Where human beings have failed to find a way to measure, they have been much less successful, which partly explains the failure of psychology, economics, and literary criticism to acquire the status of science."[8]

Observations must be reduced to numbers if they are to be analyzed in a rational and rigorous fashion. Quantification makes it possible to apply the powerful tool of statistical analysis. "Most scientists would say that if you cannot describe what you are doing in mathematical terms, you are not doing science."[9] Quantification is the best way to ensure the objectivity of knowledge and to maximize its ability to be shared with and tested by all qualified practitioners.

The Purpose of Science: Explanation and Prediction

The goal of science is the discovery of rules that predict new observations and theories that explain previous observations. Predictive rules, often referred to as scientific laws, are statements about recurring process, such as 'event A tends to predict event B,' but laws don't try to explain why this happens.

Explanatory theories go further than predictive rules by telling us why it is that B tends to follow A, rather than simply telling us that it does. Chapter 7 will describe some theories advanced by the field of behavioral finance that attempt to explain why the behavior of financial markets is, at times, nonrandom. These theories give hope to TA and may explain why certain methods of TA can work.

Scientific laws and theories differ with respect to their generality. The most prized are the most general—that is, they predict and/or explain the widest range of phenomena. A TA rule that is effective on all markets and all time scales would have higher scientific stature than one that works only on copper futures on hourly data.

Laws also differ with respect to their predictive power. Those that depict the most consistent relationships are the most valuable. All other things being equal, a TA rule that is successful 52 percent of the time is less valuable than one that works 70 percent of the time.

The most important type of scientific law is the functional relationship. It summarizes a set of observations in the form of an equation. The equation describes how a variable that we wish to predict (dependent variable) typically denoted by the letter Y, is a function of (i.e., dependent on) one or more other variables called predictors, usually designated by the letter X. This is illustrated as

$$Y = f(X_i)$$

Typically the values of the predictors are known, but the value of the dependent variable is not. In many applications, this is because the dependent variable Y refers to a future outcome, whereas the X variables refer to values that are currently known. Once a functional relationship has been derived, it is possible to predict values for the dependent variable by plugging in known values of the predictor variables.

Functional relationships can be derived in two ways. They can be deduced from explanatory theories or they can be estimated (induced) from historical data by function fitting (e.g., regression analysis). Currently, TA is primarily constrained to the latter because theories of TA are just now being formulated (see Chapter 7).

THE ROLE OF LOGIC IN SCIENCE

Scientific knowledge commands respect, in part because its conclusions are based on logic. By relying on logic and empirical evidence to justify its conclusions, science avoids two of the common fallacies that contaminate informal reasoning: *appeals to authority* and *appeals to tradition*. An appeal to authority offers as proof the statement of a purportedly knowledgeable person. An appeal to tradition offers a long-standing way of doing things as proof.

To its detriment, much of popular TA is justified on grounds of tradition or authority rather than formal logic and objective evidence. In many instances, current authorities merely quote prior authorities who, in turn, quote yet earlier experts and so on back to an original source whose knowledge was primarily intuitive. Thus the fallacies of authority and tradition are mutually reinforcing.

The First Rule of Logic: Consistency

Aristotle (384–322 B.C.) is credited with the invention of formal logic, which evolved from geometry. The Egyptians had been making accurate measurements of lines and angles and calculating areas for over two thousand years, but it was the "Greeks who extended these basic notions and transformed them into a compelling system of irrefutable conclusions derived from mathematical definitions (axioms)."[10]

Formal logic is the branch of mathematics concerned with the laws of correct reasoning that are used to formulate and evaluate the validity of arguments. In contrast to informal inference, if the rules of formal logic are followed, a true conclusion is guaranteed.

The most fundamental principle of formal logic is the rule of consistency. It is expressed in two laws: the *Law of the Excluded Middle* and the *Law of Noncontradiction*. "The law of the excluded middle requires that a thing must either possess or lack a given attribute. There is no middle alternative. Or said differently, the middle ground is excluded."[11] A statement is either true or false. It cannot be both. However, the law is only properly applied to situations that are binary and is easily misapplied to situations that are not truly two-state.

"Closely related to the law of the excluded middle is the law of noncontradiction. It tells us that a thing cannot both be and not be at the same time."[12] A statement cannot be true and not true at the same time. An argument that allows for its conclusion to be true and not true at the same time is said to be a self-contradictory.

As will be shown in subsequent sections, these laws of logic are used to great effect in science. Although observed evidence, such as the profitable back test of a TA rule, cannot logically prove that the rule has predictive power, that same evidence can be used to logically disprove (contradict) the assertion that the rule is devoid of predictive power. By the Law of Noncontradiction, this indirectly proves that the rule does possess predictive power. This method of proving empirical laws, called the method of indirect proof or proof by contradiction, is the logical basis of the scientific method.

Propositions and Arguments

Logical inference takes two distinct forms: deduction and induction. We will consider each separately and then see how they are used together in the logical framework of modern science, the hypothetico-deductive method. However, before considering these forms of inference some definitions are in order.

- *Proposition:* a declarative statement that is either true or false sometimes referred to as a claim. For example, the statement *The head-and-shoulder pattern has more predictive power than a random signal* is a proposition. A proposition differs from other kinds of statements that do not possess the attribute of truth of falsity such as exclamations, commands, and questions. Therefore, only propositions may be affirmed or denied.
- *Argument:* a group of propositions, one of which is referred to as the *conclusion*, which is claimed to follow logically from the other propositions, called *premises*. Thus, an argument asserts that its premises provide the evidence to establish the truth of its conclusion.

Deductive Logic

As mentioned earlier, the there are two forms of logic, deductive and inductive. This section considers deductive logic; the next considers inductive.

Categorical Syllogisms. A deductive argument is one whose premises are claimed to provide conclusive, irrefutable evidence for the truth of its conclusion. A common form of deductive argument is the categorical syllogism. It is comprised of two premises and a conclusion. It is so named because it deals with logical relations between categories. It begins with a premise that states a general truth about a category, for example *All humans are mortal*, and ends with a conclusion that states a truth about a specific instance, for example *Socrates is mortal*.

Premise 1: *All humans are mortal.*

Premise 2: *Socrates is a human.*

Therefore: *Socrates is mortal.*

Notice that the argument's first premise establishes a relationship between two categories, humans and mortals: *All humans are mortal*. The second premise makes a statement about a particular individual member of the first category: *Socrates is a human*. This forces the conclusions that this individual must also be a member of the second category: *Socrates is mortal*.

The general form of a categorical syllogism is as follows:

Premise 1: *All members of category A are members of category B.*

Premise 2: *X is a member of category A.*

Therefore: *X is a member of category B.*

Deductive logic has one especially attractive attribute—certainty. A conclusion arrived at by deduction is true with complete certainty, but this is so if and only if two conditions are met: the premises of the argument are *true* and the argument has *valid* form. If either condition is lacking, the conclusion is false with complete certainty. Therefore, a valid argument is defined as one whose conclusion must be true if its premises are true. Or, said differently, it is impossible for a valid argument to have true premises and a false conclusion.

In summary, conclusions arrived at by deduction are either true or false. If either valid form or true premises are lacking, then the conclusion is false. If both are present, the conclusion is true. There is no middle ground.

It is important to note that *truth* and *validity* are two distinct properties. Truth, and its opposite, falsity, are properties that pertain to an individual proposition. A proposition is true if it conforms to fact. Because premises and conclusions are both propositions, they are aptly characterized as either true or false. The premise *All pigs can fly* is false. The premise *Socrates is a man* is true as is the conclusion *Socrates is mortal*.

Validity is a property that pertains to the form of an argument. In other words validity refers to the logical relationships between the propositions comprising the argument. Validity or lack thereof describes the correctness of the logical inference linking the premises to the conclusion, but validity makes no reference to the factual truth of the argument's premises or conclusion. An argument is said to be valid if, when its premises are true, its conclusion must also be true.

However, an argument can be valid even if is composed of false propositions so long as the logical connections between the propositions

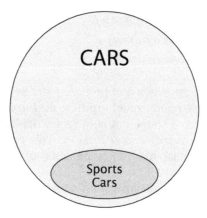

FIGURE 3.2 Euler circles.

are sound. The categorical syllogism that follows has valid form because its conclusion is logically compelled by its premises, yet its premises and conclusion are clearly untrue.

> *All humans are immortal.*
> *Socrates is a human.*
> *Therefore, Socrates is immortal.*

Because validity has nothing to do with matters of fact, validity can best be demonstrated with arguments or diagrams of arguments, called Euler circles, which make no factual references whatsoever. In a Euler diagram, the set of elements comprising a category is represented by a circle. To show that one category, such as sports cars, is a subset of the more general category—cars in general—the circle representing sports cars resides within the larger circle representing cars. See Figure 3.2.

Figure 3.3 makes clear why argument 1 is valid but argument 2 is not. Argument 1 is valid because its conclusion, *X is a B*, follows necessarily from (i.e., is compelled by) its premises. However, Argument 2 is not valid because it conclusion, *X is an A*, is not logically compelled by its premises. X may belong to category A but not necessarily. The Euler diagrams portray validity more forcefully than the argument itself because the argument alone requires some thinking.

Argument 1
All A's are B's.
X is an A.
Therefore, X is a B.

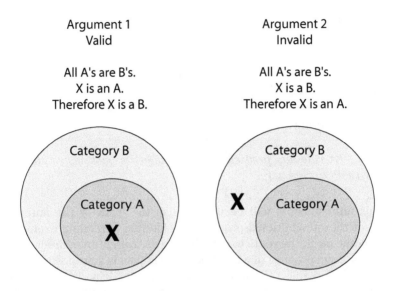

FIGURE 3.3 Valid and invalid categorical syllogisms.

Argument 2

All A's are B's.

X is a B.

Therefore, X is an A.

Conditional Syllogisms: The Logic of Scientific Arguments.
Another form of deductive argument, and the one that is central to scientific reasoning, is the *conditional* syllogism. It is the logical basis for establishing the discovery of new knowledge.

Like the categorical syllogism, the conditional syllogism is also composed of three propositions: two premises and a conclusion. It is so named because its first premise is a conditional proposition.

A conditional proposition is a compound statement that combines two simple propositions using the words *If–then*. The proposition following *if* is referred to as the *antecedent* clause and the proposition following *then* is referred to as the *consequent* clause. The general form of a conditional proposition is

If (antecedent clause), then (consequent clause)

For example:

If it is a dog, then it has four legs.

In the example, *it is a dog* is the antecedent clause and *it has four legs* is the consequent clause. A second example that is closer to the purpose at hand would be

If the TA rule has predictive power, then its back tested rate of return will exceed zero.

Our ultimate goal will be to establish the truth of the antecedent clause of these conditional propositions like the preceding example. As will become clear, the route to establishing its truth is an indirect one! The second premise of a conditional syllogism is a proposition that either affirms or denies the truth of either the antecedent clause or the consequent clause of the first premise. Referring to the prior example, the second premise could be one of the following four statements:

It is a dog: Affirms the truth of the antecedent.

It is not a dog: Denies the truth of the antecedent.

It has four legs: Affirms the truth of the consequent.

It does not have four legs: Denies the truth of the consequent.

The conclusion of the conditional syllogism affirms or denies the truth of the remaining clause of the first premise. In other words, the conclusion references the clause that is not mentioned in the second premise. For example, if the second premise refers to the antecedent clause of the first premise, *It's a dog*, then the conclusion would refer to the consequent clause, *It has four legs*.

An example of a conditional syllogism is as follows:

If it is a dog, *then it has four legs.*

It is a dog (affirms the truth of the antecedent).

Therefore, it has four legs (affirms the truth of the consequent).

When a conditional syllogism possesses valid form, its conclusion is logically compelled by the two premises. Moreover, if it has valid form and its premises are factually true, then the conclusion of the conditional syllogisms must also be true.

Valid Forms of the Conditional Syllogism.   There are two valid forms of the conditional syllogism; *affirming the antecedent* and *denying the consequent.* In an argument that *affirms the antecedent,* the second premise affirms the truth of the antecedent clause of the first premise. In an argument that *denies the consequent,* the second premise asserts that the consequent clause of the first premise is not true. These two valid forms of argument are shown here. They assume all dogs possess four legs.

Affirming the antecedent:

Premise 1: *If it is a dog, then it has four legs.*

Premise 2: *It is a dog.*

Valid Conclusion: *Therefore, it has four legs.*

In this valid form, the second premise *affirms the antecedent* clause by stating *It is a dog.* These two premises deductively compel the conclusion *It has four legs.* The general form of a conditional syllogism in which the antecedent is affirmed is

Premise 1: *If A is true, then B is true.*

Premise 2: *A is true.*

Valid Conclusion: *Therefore, B is true.*

The other valid form of the conditional syllogism is *denial of the consequent.* In this form, the second premise asserts that the consequent clause of premise 1 is a falsehood. From this, one may conclude that the antecedent clause of premise 1 is also false. This is illustrated by the following example:

Premise 1: *If it is a dog, then it has four legs.*

Premise 2: *It does NOT have four legs.*

Valid Conclusion: *Therefore, it is not a dog.*

Denial of the consequent follows the general form:

Premise 1: *If A is true, then B is true.*

Premise 2: *B is not true.*

Valid Conclusion: *Therefore, A is not true.*

This is sometimes shortened to

If A, then B.
Not B.
Therefore, not A.

Notice that this form of argument uses evidence (creature does not have four legs) to prove that antecedent (*It is a dog*) is false. It is this form of reasoning that is used in science to prove that a hypothesis is false. The hypothesis plays the role of the antecedent. We hypothesize that the creature is a dog. The consequent clause predicts what will be observed if the hypothesis is true. That is, if the creature is truly a dog, then, when it is observed, it will be seen to possess four legs. In other words, the conditional proposition, *If A, then B*, predicts that B would be observed in an experiment if the hypothesis (A) were in fact true. The second premise states that when the observation was made, the observation contradicted the prediction, that is, B was not observed. Given this, we can validly deduce that the hypothesis A is false.

As will be shown in due course, if we can prove that hypothesis A is false, we can indirectly prove that some other hypothesis is true. That other hypothesis is the new knowledge that we wish to establish as true, for example that a new vaccine is more effective than a placebo or that some TA rule predicts more effectively than a randomly generated signal.

Invalid Form of the Conditional Syllogism. An important reason for using formal logic is the difficulty people often have when reasoning informally about conditional syllogisms. Consistent with the numerous biases and illusions discussed in Chapter 2, psychological studies[13] have shown that people tend to commit two fallacies when reasoning about conditional propositions: the fallacy of *affirming the consequent*, and the fallacy of *denying the antecedent*. An example of the fallacy of affirming the consequent is

Premise 1: *If it is a dog, then it has four legs.*
Premise 2: *It has four legs.*
Invalid Conclusion: *Therefore, it is a dog.*

The fact that a creature has four legs certainly does not compel the conclusion that the creature is a dog. It may be a dog. The evidence is consistent with the fact that it is a dog. However, the evidence is also consistent with other conclusions. It could just as easily be a cow, a horse, or any other four-legged creature. The fallacy of affirming the consequent has the general form:

Premise 1: *If A is true, then B is true.*

Premise 2: *B is true.*

Invalid Conclusion: *Therefore, A is true.*

This fallacy is a very common error in poor scientific reasoning and one committed in many articles on TA. Consider the following syllogism, which commits the fallacy of affirming the consequent.

Premise 1: *If TA rule X has predictive power, then it should produce profits in a back test.*

Premise 2: *The back test was profitable.*

Invalid Conclusions: *Therefore, the TA rule has predictive power.*

Both of these premises may be true, but the conclusion is not necessarily true. With respect to the first premise, it is true that if the TA rule X does possess predictive power it should back test profitably. In other words, a profitable back test would be consistent with the supposition that the rule has predictive power. However, a profitable back test could also be consistent with the supposition that the rule was merely lucky. Similarly, just as evidence of four legs is consistent with a dog, it is also consistent with all other four-legged creatures.[14] The fallacy of affirming the consequent is the reason that empirical evidence cannot be used to prove that a hypothesis is true. As we shall see, one philosopher of science, Karl Popper, contended that the scientific method must, therefore, rest on denial (falsification) of the consequent, which, as pointed out earlier, is a valid form of inference.

The other fallacy associated with conditional syllogisms is the fallacy of denying the antecedent. It is illustrated here:

Premise 1: *If it is a dog, then it has four legs.*

Premise 2: *It is not a dog.*

Invalid Conclusion: *Therefore, it does not have four legs.*

The fact that a creature is not a dog does not preclude its having four legs. The general form of this fallacy is

Premise 1: *If A is true, then B is true.*

Premise 2: *A is not true.*

Invalid Conclusion: *Therefore, B is not true.*

In logical shorthand

If A, then B.
Not A.
Therefore, not B.

Invalid arguments can be hard to notice when they concern complex subjects. The best way to reveal them is to plug in commonplace items for A and B and see if the conclusion follows from the premises.

Figures 3.4 and 3.5 summarize the preceding discussion of the conditional syllogism.

As mentioned, the great strength of deductive reasoning is its ability to deliver conclusions that are true with certainty. However, deductive logic has a great weakness; it is unable to reveal new knowledge about the world. All that a deductive argument can do is to reveal truths that were already implicit in its premises. In other words, deductive reasoning can only tease out truths that were already present in the premises though they may not have been evident.

This is not meant to minimize or trivialize deduction but to clarify its role. It may well be that a conclusion implied by the premises is far from obvious. Great mathematical discoveries are exactly that—the revealing of truths that had been implicit in the axioms of a mathematical system but that had not been understood prior to being proven. Such was the case with the much-publicized proof of Fermat's last theorem. It was first

Valid	Invalid
Affirming the Antecedent	**Denying the Antecedent**
If A, then B. A. Therefore, B.	If A, then B. Not A. Therefore, Not B.
Denying the Consequent	**Affirming the Consequent**
If A, then B. Not B. Therefore, Not A.	If A, then B. B. Therefore, A.

FIGURE 3.4 Conditional syllogisms: general form.

Valid	Invalid
Affirming The Antecedent If a dog, then has 4 legs. It is a dog. Therefore, has 4 legs.	**Fallacy: Denying Antecedent** If a dog, then has 4 legs. It is not a dog. Therefore, not 4 legs.
Denying The Consequent If a dog, then has 4 legs. Legs not equal to 4. Therefore not a dog.	**Fallacy: Affirming Consequent** If a dog, then has 4 legs. Has 4 legs. Therefore dog.

FIGURE 3.5 Conditional syllogisms: example.

hinted at in the margin of a book in 1665 but not proven until 1994, by Andrew Wiles and Richard Taylor.

Inductive Logic

Induction is the logic of discovery. It aims to reveal new knowledge about the world by reaching beyond the knowledge contained in the premises of an inductive argument. However, this new knowledge comes with a price—uncertainty. Conclusions reached by induction are inherently uncertain. That is, they can only be true with some degree of probability. Thus, the notion of probability is intimately connected with induction.

Induction proceeds in a manner opposite to deduction. We saw that deduction progresses from a premise expressing a general truth that is held to apply to an unlimited number of instances, *All men are mortal* to a conclusion about a specific instance *Socrates is mortal*. In contrast, inductive reasoning moves or, better said, leaps from a premise based on a limited number of observed instances to a general conclusion about an unlimited number of similar but not-yet-observed instances. Thus, this form of inference is often referred to as inductive generalization. It is in leaping beyond what has been directly experienced by observation that induction incurs uncertainty—the possibility that its conclusion may be wrong.

Inductive generalization is illustrated by the following:

Premise: *Each of one thousand healthy dogs had four legs.*

General conclusions: *All healthy dogs will have four legs.*

The conclusion, in this example, is called a universal generalization, because it asserts that *all* members of the class dog have the attribute four legs. Universal generalizations have the form

All X's are Y's.

or

100 percent of X's have the attribute Y.

Generalizations need not be universal. Nonuniversal generalizations have the form

P percent of X's are Y's.

or

P percent of X's have attribute Y.

or

X's have attribute Y with probability P.

Again, we see that probability is inextricably tied to the concept of generalization. In fact, nonuniversal generalizations are also known as probabilistic generalizations. An example would be: *A higher percentage of bulldogs are prone to violence than poodles.* This statistically sound nonuniversal generalization[15] does not claim all bulldogs are prone to violent behavior, nor does it claim that even a majority are so inclined. However, it does say that, as a group, statistics show that bulldogs have a higher probability of being dangerous than poodles.

Aristotle's defeat as scientist was in part attributable to his failure to appreciate that nonuniversal generalizations convey useful knowledge. His fascination with the certainty of deductive proofs led him to restrict his search to universal generalizations. He was unable to see that many important regularities of the natural world are inherently probabilistic.

Induction by Enumeration

The most common form of inductive argument is based on enumeration. It proceeds from a premise that enumerates the evidence contained in a set of observations, and then draws a general conclusion that pertains to all similar observations outside the enumerated set.

Premise: *Over the past 20 years there have been 1,000 instances in which TA rule X gave a buy signal and in 700 of those instances the market moved higher over the next 10 days.*

Conclusion: In the future, when rule X gives a buy signal, there is a 0.7 probability that the market will be higher at the end of 10 days.

This conclusion or any conclusion reached by induction is inherently uncertain because it extends to observations that have not yet been made. However, some inductive arguments are stronger than others, and hence, arrive at conclusions that are more certain. The strength of an inductive argument and the certainty of its conclusion depend upon the quantity and quality of the evidence enumerated in its premise. The more numerous the instances cited and the higher their quality, the more likely the conclusion will generalize accurately to future observations.

Suppose that the conclusion about TA rule X had been based on only 10 instances with a 70 percent success rate instead of 1,000. In such a case, the conclusion would have been at least 10 times more uncertain.[16] This means we should be less surprised if the signal's future accuracy differs greatly from its historic success rate. In science, the evidence offered in support of a conclusion is typically evaluated with statistical methods. This allows one to make quantitative statements about the conclusion's uncertainty. This topic is discussed in Chapters 5 and 6.

The strength of an inductive argument also depends upon the quality of the evidence. Evidence quality is an entire subject unto itself, but suffice it to say that some observational methods produce higher quality evidence than others. The gold standard in science is the controlled experiment, where all factors but the one under study are held constant. TA does not permit controlled experiments, but there are better and worse ways to make observations. One issue that is relevant to TA is the matter of systematic error or bias. As will be discussed in Chapter 6, objective TA research is prone to a particular type of systematic error called *data mining bias* if careful steps are not taken.

Also relevant to the strength of an inductive argument is the degree to which the evidence cited is representative of the kinds of observations that are likely to be encountered in the future. An inference about a rule that generates long/neutral (+1,0) signals that was back-tested only during rising markets is unlikely to be accurate about the rule's performance in a declining market environment. Even if the rule had no predictive power, its restriction to long or neutral positions makes it likely that it would have generated a profit because it was tested during a rising market period.

The most common fallacy of induction is the hasty generalization—an induction based on too little evidence or evidence of poor quality. Rule studies that cite a small number of successful signals as a basis for concluding that the rule has predictive power are likely to be hasty generalizations.

THE PHILOSOPHY OF SCIENCE

The philosophy of science seeks to understand how and why science works. It explains such things as: the nature of scientific propositions and how they differ from nonscientific and pseudoscientific propositions; the way scientific knowledge is produced; how science explains, predicts, and, through technology, harnesses nature; the means for determining the validity of scientific knowledge; the formulation and use of the scientific method; and the types of reasoning used to arrive at conclusions.[17]

That the scientific method is one of man's greatest inventions and is by far the most effective method for acquiring objective knowledge about the natural world is beyond question. "The part of the world known as the Industrial West could, in its entirety, be seen as a monument to the Scientific Revolution. . . ."[18] Humankind's ability to predict and control the natural world has improved more in the last 400 years, since the scientific revolution began, than it had in the prior 150,000 years that modern humans, *homo sapiens*, walked the face of the Earth.

Strange as it may seem, the invention of the scientific method and its first fruits came before it was understood why the method worked as well as it did. That insight came gradually, over the course of several centuries, as practicing scientists and their erstwhile critics, the philosophers of science, wrestled with perfecting the method and, in parallel, developed an understanding of how and why it worked.

The mere fact that the scientific method did work was not enough. It was seen as necessary to understand why. What philosophers found so vexing was the following apparent contradiction. On the one hand were the great victories of science, such as Newton's laws of motion and gravity and humanity's expanding technological control over nature. On the other was the fact that scientific knowledge was inherently uncertain, because conclusions arrived at by logical induction were inherently uncertain. How could so much useful knowledge result from such a flawed method of inference?

This section discusses the keys steps in the method's development and the milestones in our deepening understanding of how and why it works. The reader may wish to skip this historical development and go directly to the summary of the key aspects of the scientific method.

Bacon's Enthusiasm

Without invitation, philosophers poke their noses into all sorts of matters. It's their nature. They tell us how to act (ethics), how governments should rule (political philosophy), what is beautiful (aesthetics), and of greatest concern to us, what constitutes valid knowledge (epistemology) and how we should go about getting it (philosophy of science).

The scientific revolution was, in part, a revolt against Aristotelian science. The Greeks regarded the physical world as an unreliable source of truth. According to Plato, mentor of Aristotle, the world was merely a flawed copy of the truth and perfection that existed in the world of *Forms*, a metaphysical nonmaterial realm, where archetypes of the perfect dog, the perfect tree, and every other imaginable thing could be found.

When the revolt against this view of reality finally arrived, it was harsh and unremitting.[19] The new school of thought, empiricism, resoundingly rejected the Greek paradigm. It contended that, not only was the natural world worthy of study, but that careful observation could lay bare its truths. A pioneer of empiricism and perhaps the first philosopher of science was Francis Bacon (1561–1626). "Nature, for Bacon was an open book that could not possibly be misread by an unprejudiced mind."[20] In his famous work the *Novem Organum* (the new tool) Bacon extolled the power of observation and induction. He held science to be a completely objective rational practice that could conclusively confirm or falsify knowledge simply by observing without bias or prejudice and then generalizing from those observations. In many situations, this approach seemed to work.

However, empiricism was not the perfect tool Bacon and his disciples claimed, and philosophers made it their business to say why. First, they pointed out that empiricism, an observation-based enterprise, rested on a crucial assumption that could not be confirmed by observation, the assumption that nature was uniform over all time and space. That assumption was critical in justifying the empiricists' position that if a scientific law was observed to hold true here and now it would also hold true everywhere and forever. Because the uniformity of nature assumption could not be confirmed by observation, it had to be taken on faith. Second, science often deals with phenomena and concepts that defy direct observation: atomic structure, the force of gravity, and electric fields. Though their effects are observable, these constructs could not be arrived at exclusively by observation and induction. They are better understood as human inventions that explain and predict rather than observable physical realities.

Nevertheless, Bacon's contributions to the development of the scientific method were important. He promoted the idea of experiment and made room for doubt by taking special note of discordant observations. Both ideas eluded the Greeks.

Descartes's Doubt

If philosophers are good for anything it's raising doubt, and no one was better than Rene Descartes (1596–1650). Regarded as the father of modern philosophy and a key figure in the birth of science, Descartes shared Bacon's skepticism for the authoritarian knowledge of the Greeks and the dogma of the Roman Church. However, Descartes was just as skeptical of the claims made by the empiricists about the power of observation and inductive generalization. His famous expression, "I think, therefore I am," expressed the position that science must start by doubting everything except the existence of the person who experiences doubt. From that point of solidity, knowledge must be built purely by deductive reasoning without being contaminated by error-prone observations made with the imperfect five senses.

As a consequence of Descartes' anti-empirical stance and penchant for theorizing in a factual vacuum, his scientific findings were almost meaningless.[21] However, his contributions to science were lasting. Skepticism is central to the scientific attitude. In addition, Descartes' invention of analytic geometry paved the way for Newton's invention of the calculus which, in turn, allowed him to specify his famous equations of motion and gravity.

Hume's Critique of Induction

Another dose of doubt was administered by Scottish empiricist and philosopher David Hume (1711–1776). His seminal work, the *Treatise on Human Nature*, published in 1739, grappled with a central problem of epistemology: how to distinguish knowledge from lesser forms of knowing, such as opinions that happen to be true. Prior to Hume's publication, philosophers generally agreed that the distinction was related to the quality of the method used to acquire the knowledge. What justified calling one bit of wisdom knowledge but not another was the pedigree of the method of inquiry.[22]

Philosophers could not, however, agree on the best method of knowledge acquisition. Empiricists argued that objective observation followed by inductive generalization was the route to wisdom. Rationalists, on the other hand, contended that pure deductive reasoning from self-evident truths was the correct method.

Hume took issue with both schools of thought and ultimately even with himself. As an empiricist, Hume disparaged the rationalists' purely deductive approach because it was disconnected from observed facts. Also, in the spirit of empiricism, Hume said that it was wise to adjust the strength of one's beliefs in proportion to the evidence and that theories should be evaluated by the degree to which they matched observation. But then Hume went on to contradict himself by attacking the logical basis of empiricism. He denied the validity of inductive generalization and disparaged the ability of science to establish causal laws. His searing critique of induction has come to be known as Hume's problem.

Hume's attack on induction was on both psychological and logical grounds. First, he said the belief that induction could establish correlative or causal connections between events was a nothing more than a by-product of human psychology. Hume asserted that the perception of cause and effect was merely an artifact of the mind. The belief that A causes B or is even correlated to B, simply because A has always been followed by B was nothing more than a habit of mind, and a bad habit at that.

From a logical perspective, Hume claimed that induction was flawed because no amount of observed evidence, no matter how objectively collected, can compel a conclusion with the force of a valid deduction. Moreover, he said that there was no rule of induction that tells us when we have evidence of sufficient quantity or quality to justify the leap from a finite set of observations to a conclusion about an infinite number of similar but not yet observed instances. A rule of induction would, itself, have had to be the result of a prior valid induction made on the basis of an even earlier rule of induction, and so forth and so on, ad infinitum. In other words, an attempt to justify induction inevitably rests on an infinite regress—a logically impossible absurdity.

In light of Hume's attack, supporters of induction retreated to a narrower claim saying inductive generalizations were merely correct in a probabilistic sense. So as evidence accumulates in favor of a relationship between A and B, the probability that the relationship is authentic also increases. However, philosophers were quick to point out that a probabilistic justification of induction was also flawed. As will be pointed out in Chapter 4, the probability that A predicts B is equal to the number of times that A was followed by B divided by the total number of instances of A regardless of whether it was followed by B.[23] Because the future holds an infinite number of instances, the probability will always be zero, no matter how numerous the past observations (any number divided by an infinitely large number is still zero).

Thus, Hume and his allies created a paradox. On one hand were their seemingly valid concerns about the flaws of induction. On the other hand was the accumulation of stunning scientific discoveries. If science was based on such a flawed logic, how could it have managed to be so successful?

William Whewell: The Role of Hypothesis

It took philosophers and scientists two hundred years of watching the scientific method succeed to understand how it worked and why it had been so triumphant. By the middle of the nineteenth century, it was becoming clear that science employs a synergistic combination of inductive and deductive logic. In 1840, William Whewell (1794–1866) published *The History and Philosophy of Inductive Sciences*.

Whewell was the first to understand the crucial role of induction in the formulation of a hypothesis. Whewell called it a happy guess, He said that scientific discovery starts with a bold inductive leap to a new hypothesis, but it is followed by deduction. That is to say, after a hypothesis has been induced, a prediction is deduced from said hypothesis. This prediction takes the form of a conditional statement:

> *If the hypothesis is true, then specific future observations are predicted to occur.*

When the observations are made, they will either be consistent with the prediction, thus confirming the hypothesis, or conflict with the prediction, thus contradicting the hypothesis.

What is a scientific hypothesis? It is a conjecture of a suspected pattern, for example:

> *X predicts Y.*

> or

> *X brings about Y.*

This conjecture is spawned by a scientist's prior experience—noticing repeated pairings of X and Y. Once the XY hypothesis has been put forward, a testable prediction is deduced from it. This takes the form of a conditional proposition, which is composed of two clauses: an antecedent and a consequent. The hypothesis serves as the antecedent clause, and the prediction serves as the consequent clause. In situations where it is merely asserted that X is correlated (predicts) with Y the following conditional proposition would apply:

> *IF X predicts Y, then future instances of X will be followed by instances of Y.*

In cases where the hypothesis asserts that X causes Y, the following conditional proposition would apply:

IF X causes Y, then if X is removed, Y should not occur.

The predictions embodied in the consequent clause of the conditional proposition are then compared with new observations. These must be observations whose outcome is not yet known. This is crucial! This does not necessarily mean that the observations concern some future event. It simply means that when the prediction is made, the outcome of the observations is not yet known. In historical sciences like geology, archeology, and so forth, the observations are about events that have already taken place. However, the outcomes have not yet been observed.

If it turns out that future observations of X are not followed by Y or if removal of X does prevent the occurrence of Y, then the hypothesis (antecedent) is proven to be false by the valid deductive form falsification of the consequent.

If X, then Y.
Not Y.
Valid Deduction: *Therefore, not X.*

If, however, future instances of X are indeed followed by Y, or if the removal of X does cause the disappearance of Y, the hypothesis is not proven! Recall that affirming the consequent is not a valid deductive form.

If X, then Y.
Y.
Invalid: *Therefore, X.*

That the prediction has been confirmed merely offers tentative confirmation of the hypothesis. The hypothesis survives for the moment, but more stringent tests of it are sure to follow.

Whewell agreed with Hume that inductive conjecture was a habit of human thought, but the habit that Hume so disparaged Whewell regarded as fruitful though mysterious. He was unable to explain the mental processes that gave rise to such creative thoughts though he believed inductive generalization was part of it. He called the ability to conjure a hypothesis an unteachable inventive talent but a crucial one, because, without a hypothesis, a set of observations remain nothing more than a disconnected collection of facts that could neither predict nor explain. However, with one came the breakthroughs of science.

Whewell's description of this crucial creative aspect of science reminds me of a conversation I had many years ago with Charles Strauss, a prolific composer of some of Broadway's most successful musicals. In my early twenties at the time, short on tact and long on audacity, I asked him to explain how he managed to be so productive. With more forbearance than I deserved, Charles described a daily discipline of religiously sitting at the piano from 8 until 11 each morning and from 2 until 5 each afternoon, whether he felt inspired or not. He told me he treated composing music like a job. During this time he would test tentative melodies—musical hypotheses. He modestly attributed his high productivity to 99 percent discipline and 1 percent creative talent. However, as I thought about this conversation years later, it seemed otherwise. With an almost infinite number of note combinations, his success at creating infectious tunes had to be a creative talent—some special ability to see which of those musical conjectures had the potential to be melodies and which did not. This was what Whewell called the happy guess—that unteachable talent of seeing a theme that meaningfully relates a disparate set of observations or notes that eludes the average person. A few folks have it. The vast majority do not.

Whewell's realization that proposing a hypothesis was an act of invention no less than the creation of the steam engine or the light bulb represented a profoundly important advance in thinking about science.[24] Induction could not produce truths on its own, but it was a necessary first step. This was a profound departure from the prior notion of science as a systematic objective investigation followed by inductive generalization. Whewell saw the scientist as a creator as much as an investigator.

Karl Popper: Falsification and Bringing Deduction Back into Science

In two landmark works, *The Logic of Scientific Discovery*[25] and *Conjectures and Refutations*,[26] Karl Popper (1902–1994) extended the insight of Whewell and redefined the logic of scientific discovery by clarifying the role of deduction. Popper's central contention was that a scientific inquiry was unable to prove hypotheses to be true. Rather, science was limited to identifying which hypotheses were false. This was accomplished by using observed evidence in combination with the valid deductive form of falsification of the consequent.

If hypothesis H is true, **then** evidence E is predicted to occur under specified conditions (e.g., back test of a TA rule).

Evidence E did not occur under the specified conditions.

Therefore, hypothesis H is false.

In taking this stance, Popper challenged the prevailing view advocated by a school of philosophy called logical positivism. Just as Francis Bacon had revolted against the strictures of the Greek tradition, Popper was in revolt against the Vienna Circle, the home of logical positivism. Logical positivists believed that observations could be used to prove hypotheses to be true. Popper demurred, saying that observed evidence could only be used to prove a hypothesis false. Science was a baloney detector, not a truth detector.

Popper justified his method, called falsificationism, as follows. A given set of observations can be explained by or is consistent with numerous hypotheses. Therefore, the observed data, by itself, cannot help us decide which of these hypotheses is most likely correct.[27] Suppose the data is that one of my shoes is missing. One hypothesis that might explain this observation is that I'm a disorganized housekeeper who is always misplacing things. Another hypothesis, which is equally consistent with the observation of a missing shoe, would be that my house was burglarized by a one-legged thief who only had use for one shoe. In fact, an infinite number of hypotheses could be proposed that are consistent with (explain) the missing shoe.

We have already seen that data cannot be used logically to deduce the truth of a hypothesis. Attempts to do so commit the fallacy of affirming the consequent.[28] However, and this is the key to Popper's method of falsificationism, data can be used to validly deduce the falsehood of a hypothesis by denial of the consequent. In other words, disconfirming evidence can be used to reveal a false explanation. For example, finding the other shoe would be evidence that would falsify the one-legged thief hypothesis. The logical argument is as follows:

> Premise 1: *If a one-legged thief is responsible for my missing shoe, then I will not find the shoe in my home.*
>
> Premise 2: *Missing shoe is found (consequent denied).*
>
> Conclusion: *Therefore, the one-legged thief hypothesis is false.*

Popper's method of falsification runs against the grain of common sense, which is biased in favor of confirmatory evidence. As pointed out in Chapter 2, intuition often tells us to test the truth of a hypothesis by seeing if confirmatory evidence can be found. We do so under the mistaken impression that confirmatory evidence is sufficient to establish truth. However, using evidence in this way commits the fallacy of affirming the consequent. We are not wrong to suspect that confirmatory evidence should be found if the hypothesis is true, but we are wrong to think that confirmatory evidence is sufficient to establish its truth. Said differently, confirmatory evidence is a necessary condition of a proposition's truth but not a sufficient condition.[29] Popper's point was that the absence of necessary evidence is sufficient to establish the falsity of a hypothesis, but the presence of necessary evidence is not enough to establish its truth. Having four legs is a necessary condition of a creature being a dog, but the presence of four legs is not sufficient to establish that a creature is a dog. However, the observation that the creature does not have four legs is sufficient to falsify the contention it is a dog. Popper's logic of falsification can be seen as a protection against the confirmation bias that infects informal inference (see Chapter 2).

One final example may help clarify the power of falsifying evidence and the weakness of confirmatory evidence. It is the famous problem of the black swan posed by philosopher John Stuart Mill (1806–1873). Suppose we wish to ascertain the truth of the proposition: 'All swans are white.' Mill said, and Popper concurred, that no matter how many white swans have been observed—that is, no matter how voluminous the confirmatory evidence—the proposition's truth is never proven. A black swan may lurk just around the next corner. This is the limitation of induction that so upset Hume. However, by merely observing a single non-white swan, one may declare with certitude that the proposition is false. The conditional syllogism below shows that the falsity of the proposition *All swans are white* is based on the valid deductive form falsification of the consequent.

> Premise 1: *If it is true that all swans are white, then all future observations of swans will be white.*
>
> Premise 2: *A nonwhite swan is observed.*
>
> Valid Conclusion: *The proposition that all swans are white is false.*

The general form of argument used to test a hypothesis under Popper's method of falsification is:

> Premise 1: *If the hypothesis is true, then future observations are predicted to have property X.*
>
> Premise 2: *An observation occurs that lacks property X.*
>
> Valid Conclusion: *Therefore, hypothesis is false.*

As will be seen in Chapters 4 and 5, this is the logic used to test statistical hypotheses.

The Provisional and Cumulative Nature of Scientific Knowledge.
One implication of Popper's method of falsification is that all existing sci-

entific knowledge is provisional. Whatever theory is currently accepted as correct is always a target for empirical challenge and the possibility of its being replaced by a more correct theory always exits. Today Einstein's Theory of Relativity is taken as correct. Though its predictions have withstood countless tests, tomorrow a new test may show it to be false or incomplete. Thus, science is a never-ending cycle of conjecture, prediction, testing, falsification, and new conjecture. It is in this way that the body of scientific knowledge continually evolves toward an ever more accurate representation of objective reality.

In most instances when older theories are replaced, it is not because they are proven false so much as they are shown to be incomplete. When Newton's laws of motion were replaced by Einstein's theories, Newtonian physics was still mostly correct. Within the limited domain of everyday experience, where bodies travel at normal speeds (approximately less than 90 percent of the speed of light), Newton's laws still held true. However, Einstein's theory was correct in a wider domain, which not only included the motions of everyday objects, but also objects traveling up to and including the speed of light. In other words, Einstein's theory, which built upon Newton's, was more general and thus subsumed it.

The net result of building upon prior successful ideas (those whose predictions have been confirmed) and pruning away wrong ideas (those whose predictions have been falsified) is a body of knowledge that continually improves. This cannot be said of any other intellectual discipline, where new styles are introduced but where newer is not necessarily better. The fact that a scientist in any field of science knows more today than even the best one living just a generation ago is beyond debate. However, whether gangsta rap is better or worse than Mozart could be argued endlessly.

The Restriction of Science to Testable Statements. Another implication of Popper's method is that science must restrict itself to testable hypotheses—propositions that generate predictions about observations not yet made. To say that a hypothesis has been tested and has survived or has been tested and falsified means that predictions deduced from it have either been confirmed or contradicted by new observations. The comparison of predictions with new observations is the crucial mechanism that fosters the continual improvement of scientific knowledge. For this reason, propositions that do not generate testable predictions must be excluded from the domain of scientific discourse.

The term *prediction*, in the context of hypothesis testing, warrants some clarification, because TA is essentially an enterprise dedicated to prediction. When we speak of prediction as it pertains to testing a hypothesis, it does not necessarily mean foretelling the future though the predicted observations may indeed lie in the future. Rather, the term *prediction* refers to the fact that the observations' outcomes are not yet known.

Predictions made in historical sciences, such as geology, refer to events that have already taken place perhaps eons ago. For example, geology's dominant theory, plate tectonics, may predict that specific geologic formations that were created millions of years ago would be observed if an investigation of some specific location were to be carried out tomorrow. In finance, the efficient market's hypothesis predicts that if a TA rule were to be back tested, its profits, after adjustment for risk, would not exceed the risk adjusted return of the market index.

Once the prediction has been deduced from the hypothesis, the operations necessary to produce the new observations are carried out. They may involve a visit to the location of the predicted geologic formation or the back test of the TA rule. Then it becomes a matter of comparing prediction with observation. Measuring the degree of agreement between observation and prediction and making the decision about whether the hypothesis is left intact or falsified is what statistical analysis is all about.

What is important from the standpoint of science is that the hypothesis is able to make predictions about observations whose outcomes are not yet known. This is what allows a hypothesis to be tested. Observations whose outcomes are known cannot serve this purpose because it is always possible to fashion an explanation, after-the-fact that is consistent with said observations. Therefore, activities that are unable or unwilling to make testable predictions, thus opening them to the possibility of falsification, do not qualify as scientific.

The Demarcation Problem: Distinguishing Science from Pseudoscience. An important consequence of Popper's method was that it solved a key problem in the philosophy of science—defining the boundary between science and nonscience. The domain of science is confined to propositions (conjectures, hypotheses, claims, theories, and so forth) that make predictions that are open to refutation with empirical evidence. Popper referred to such propositions as falsifiable and meaningful. Propositions that cannot be challenged in this manner are unfalsifiable or meaningless. In other words they do not say anything of substance, something that sets up a testable expectation.

Unfalsifiable propositions may appear to assert something, but, in fact, they do not. They cannot be challenged because they do not say, with any degree of specificity, what can be expected to happen. In effect, they are not informative. Hence, the falsifiability of a proposition is related to its information content. Falsifiable propositions are informative because they make specific predictions. They may prove to be wrong, but at least they say something of substance. A proposition that cannot generate falsifiable predictions essentially says any outcome can happen. For example, a weather forecast that says, *It will be cloudy or sunny, wet or dry, windy or calm, and cold or hot,* allows for all possible outcomes. It cannot be falsified. The only thing good that can be said about it is that its lack of information is completely obvious.

The problem is that pseudoscientists and pseudoforecasters are clever about the way they word their predictions so as to obscure their lack of information and nonfalsifiability. Consider the astrologer's forecast "You will meet a tall dark stranger, and your life will be changed." This statement is impossible to refute no matter what the outcome. Should you ever go back for a refund, you will be given one of two answers: (1) be patient—you will meet the stranger soon, or (2) you already did meet a dark stranger and you life is indeed different, but you are oblivious to the change. These answers cannot be challenged because the prediction was vague. It neither stated when your life would change or in what measurable (verifiable) manner. This is a far cry from the prediction, "Before 7:00 P.M. next Wednesday you will see a man wearing one red shoe, walking east on 42nd Street whistling 'Satin Doll.'" By 7 P.M. next Wednesday, the evidence will be in and you will have had the opportunity to evaluate the prediction as true or false. Even if the prediction turns out to be false, it was at least falsifiable allowing you to decide if future visits to the astrologer are worthwhile.

The infomercial pitchmen that inhabit late-night television are masters of the meaningless claim. "Wearing our copper bracelet will improve your golf game." What does *improve* mean? How is it to be measured and when? As with the astrologer's forecast, the claim's vagueness makes it impossible to deduce a testable (falsifiable) prediction. However, it is quite easy to imagine after-the-fact anecdotal evidence that is seemingly confirmatory. "Holy cow, I feel so much more relaxed wearing my copper bracelet. I used get all tensed up before teeing off. Now my drives seem straighter. Last week I almost had a hole in one, and I don't curse nearly as much as I used to. My wife even says I look more handsome in my golf outfit, and I think my hair has stopped falling out." Although meaningless claims invite confirmatory anecdotes, they are protected from objective falsifying evidence. The claimant never gets nailed and the claim gains support from seemingly confirmational anecdotal reports.

In contrast, the statement, "Wearing a copper bracelet will increase the length of your drives by 25 yards," is informative and meaningful because it generates a testable prediction. You hit 100 golf balls not wearing the copper bracelet and determine their average distance. The next day, do the same thing while wearing a copper bracelet and get their average distance. Repeat this alternating series of experiments for 10 days. If the

drives on copper-bracelet days are less than 25 yards better, evidence refuting the claim would be in hand.

Limitations of Popper's Method. As important as Popper's method
of falsification is to modern science, it has been criticized on a number of
grounds. Critics assert that Popper's contention that hypotheses can be
definitively falsified overstates matters. Although the observation of a
black swan can neatly and logically falsify the universal generalization
that *all* swans are white, the hypotheses of real science are far more complex[30] and probabilistic (nonuniversal). They are complex in the sense
that a newly proposed hypothesis rests on numerous auxiliary hypotheses
that are assumed to be true. Thus, if a prediction deduced from the new
hypothesis is later falsified, it is not clear whether the new hypothesis was
in error or one of the many auxiliary hypotheses was incorrect. This proved
to be the case when the solar system's eighth planet, Neptune, was discovered. The aberrant path of Uranus was not due to flaws in Newton's laws
but in the auxiliary hypothesis that the solar system contained only seven
planets. However, when the theory did fail early in the twentieth century,
it was indeed because of imperfections in Newton's laws. Doing real science is tricky business. TA is a long way from facing these problems because we are still at the at the point of scratching the data for reliable
predictive rules.

Moreover, because many of the hypotheses of science are probabilistic, as would be the case in TA, an observation that contradicts the hypothesis can never be taken as certain evidence of falsity. The aberrant
observation may be a chance occurrence. It is here that statistical analysis
enters the picture. As will be pointed out in Chapters 4 and 5, the decision
to reject a hypothesis on the basis of observed evidence runs a certain
probability of being wrong. Statistics helps us quantify this probability.

Despite these and other limitations that go beyond our concerns here,
Popper's contributions to the development of the scientific method have
been enormous.

The Information Content of Scientific Hypotheses

To recap, a hypothesis is informative if it can make testable predictions.
This opens it to the possibility of being found false. Thus, the falsifiability
of a hypothesis and its information content are related.

Within the domain of scientifically meaningful hypotheses, there are
degrees of information content and falsifiability. Some hypotheses are
more information rich and hence more falsifiable than others.

When Popper referred to a *bold conjecture* he was speaking of a
highly informative hypothesis from which many falsifiable predictions

could be deduced. The scientist's job, therefore, is to continually attempt to refute an existing hypothesis and to replace it with an even more informative one. This spurs the improvement of scientific knowledge.

An information-rich hypothesis makes many precise (narrow ranged) predictions about a broad range of phenomena. Each prediction presents an opportunity to show the hypothesis is false. In other words, the more informative a hypothesis the more opportunities it presents for falsification. In contrast, low information, timid hypotheses make fewer or less-precise predictions. Consequently they are more difficult to falsify. For example, a TA rule that claims high profitability on any instrument in any time frame makes a bold and information-rich claim that that could be falsified by showing that it is unprofitable on one market in one time frame. In contrast, a method that only claims to be marginally profitable on S&P futures on the one-week bar time scale is timid, has low information content, and is hard to falsify. The only opportunity to refute it would be limited to back test of the S&P 500 on a weekly showing that was not at all profitable.

Some TA methods that are seemingly informative are not. Elliott Wave Principle is a case in point. On the surface, it bravely proclaims that all price movement in all markets over all time scales can be described by a single unifying principle. This proposition is seemingly confirmed by the ability of EWP practitioners to produce a wave count for any prior segment of price data. In fact, EWP is timid to the point of being meaningless because it makes no falsifiable predictions of future price motion.[31]

A second case in point, one more pleasing to the TA community, is the Efficient Markets Hypothesis (EMH). In this context, the term *efficiency* refers to the speed with which prices reflect all known and knowable information that is relevant to the future returns of an asset. In an efficient market, relevant information is presumed to be reflected in price almost instantaneously. EMH comes in three flavors. In descending order of boldness, information content, and falsifiability they are: EMH strong, EMH semistrong, and EMH weak.

EMH strong asserts that financial markets are efficient with respect to all information, even private inside information. This version predicts that all investment strategies, be they based on an inside tip from the president about an impending takeover, or based on public information of a fundamental or technical nature, will be useless in earning market-beating (excess) returns. This most audacious version of EMH is also seemingly the most informative and falsifiable because any evidence of abnormal profits from any investment strategy whatsoever, irrespective of the type of information or form of analysis used, would be sufficient to refute EMH strong. However, because information that is known privately can never be confirmed, this version is not testable in a practical sense.

The semistrong version of EMH makes a less informative and narrower claim, saying that the market is only efficient with respect to public information. This version of EMH can be falsified with any evidence of market-beating returns produced by an investing strategy based on either public fundamental data (P/E ratios, book values, and so forth) or technical data (relative strength rank, volume turnover ratios, and so forth). In effect, EMH semistrong denies the utility of fundamental and technical analysis.

Finally we have EMH weak, which makes the least bold and least informative claim. It asserts that the market is only efficient with respect to past price, volume, and other technical data. Because EMH weak only denies the utility of technical analysis, it presents the smallest and hardest-to-hit target by would-be falsifiers. Their only hope would be to present evidence that shows excess returns generated by an investment strategy based on TA.

Because EMH weak is the hardest version to falsify and is thus the least likely to be proven false, its falsification would also generate the most surprise. In other words, of all versions of EMH, falsification of EMH weak would generate the biggest increase in knowledge. This points out a general principle of science: the largest gains in knowledge occur when the most timid and hardest to falsify hypotheses are falsified. A test showing that inside information, like the tip from a corporate president, was able to generate excess returns (i.e., falsification of EMH strong) would not be surprising nor would we learn very much from it. Big deal, so inside information generates profits. What else is new? In contrast, the falsification of EMH weak would be a highly informative event for both TA practitioners and EMH supporters. Not only would it mean the final destruction of the EMH, an important principle of finance for over 40 years, but it would be an important confirmation of TA's validity. Both would represent large changes in the current state of knowledge.

Thus, it can be said that the gain in knowledge that occurs upon falsification of a hypothesis is inversely related to its information content. Likewise, it can be said that the knowledge gained by confirmation of a hypothesis (observations consistent with its predictions) is directly related to the information content of the hypothesis. The most informative hypotheses make the most audacious claims of new knowledge. They attempt to bring within the realm of understanding the broadest range of phenomena with the greatest degree of precision while at the same time involving the fewest assumptions. When such a hypothesis is falsified, we are not very surprised nor do we learn very much. Few would have expected the hypothesis to be confirmed, except perhaps for the bold scientist proposing it. For example, suppose a bold new theory of physics is put forward, one of whose predictions is that it is possible to build an antigravity device. If true, such a theory would represent a major increase in knowledge. However, if the device fails to work, no one would be surprised by the prediction's failure. However, it is exactly the opposite when a timid hypothesis is falsified. For example a timid hypothesis would be one that merely asserts that the currently accepted theories of physics are true and predicts that the antigravity device should fail. The falsification of this weak hypothesis via observations of the antigravity device working would result in a very significant gain in knowledge—the verification of new physics.

The most timid hypothesis that can be put forward is one that asserts that there have been no new discoveries. In other words, it says that all that is currently known is all that there is to know. This hypothesis denies the truth of any other hypothesis that asserts that something new has been discovered. The timid hypothesis that asserts that nothing new had been discovered has a special name in science. It is called the *null hypothesis* and it is the starting assumption in the investigation of any claim that a new discovery has been made. Whether that claim asserts that a new vaccine will cure a dreaded disease, that a new principle of physics tells us how to nullify gravity, or that a TA rule has predictive power, we always start by assuming that the null hypothesis is true. Then, if evidence can be produced that falsifies the null hypothesis, a most timid claim, it generates a big gain in knowledge.

Thus, science proceeds as follows. Every time a bold new hypothesis is put forward, it spawns an opposing claim, the null hypothesis. The null is as timid as the new hypothesis is bold. Jonas Salk's bold hypothesis that his vaccine would prevent polio better than a placebo spawned a competing claim, the null hypothesis. It made the timid prediction that the vaccine's ability to prevent infection would be no better than a placebo. This was a timid prediction because every prior attempt to develop a vaccine against polio had failed. These two competing claims left no middle ground. If one hypothesis could be falsified, by logic's Law of the Excluded Middle, we know that the other must be true. Salk's experimental evidence made it clear that the rate of infection among those receiving the real vaccine was significantly less than those receiving the placebo. In other words it was sufficient to falsify the null's prediction. This was a surprising result that represented a huge increase in medical knowledge!

How Scientists Should Respond to Falsification

How should a scientist respond when a hypothesis or theory that has survived many prior tests is ultimately falsified because recent observations conflict with predictions? The proper response is whatever leads to the biggest increase in knowledge. Because scientists are human beings, they sometimes fail to do what is scientifically correct.

There are two possible responses that increase knowledge. The first is to preserve the existing hypothesis by using it to predict new, previously unknown facts. If these new facts are confirmed and can explain why the observations that had been in conflict with the hypothesis are no longer in conflict, then the hypothesis deserves to be retained. The new facts represent an increase in what we know about the world. A second proper response is to throw out the old hypothesis and propose a new one that not only accounts for all observations that had been explained by the prior hypothesis but also explains the new discordant observations. This also represents an increase in knowledge in the form of a new hypothesis with greater explanatory or predictive power. However, in either case the correct response is to do whatever advances the frontier of knowledge the most.

Unfortunately the interests of science sometimes take a back seat to personal agendas. Human nature gets in the way of good science. Emotional, economic and professional ties to a prior hypothesis can motivate attempts to explain away the discordant evidence in a way that reduces the information content and falsifiability of their cherished hypothesis. This moves the frontier of knowledge backward. Fortunately science is a collective self-correcting enterprise. The community of scientists happily takes their fallen brothers to task when they stray from the path of righteousness in this way.

Some examples will clarify these abstract concepts. First, I present an example of a proper response to predictions being contradicted by new observations. In this case, new facts were predicted to rescue an established theory from falsification. This high road was taken by two astronomers during the nineteenth century, and it led to new knowledge in the form of a new planet being discovered. At that time, Newton's laws of motion and gravity were the accepted physics of planetary motion. They had been confirmed and reconfirmed by countless observations, but then, to the surprise of astronomers of that day, new and more powerful telescopes showed the planet Uranus was deviating from the orbit predicted by Newton's laws. A rigid and improper application of falsificationism would have called for an immediate rejection of Newtonian mechanics. However, all theories rest on a bed of auxiliary assumptions. A key assumption in this case was that the solar system contained only seven planets with Uranus being the seventh and furthest from the sun. This led astronomers Adams and Leverrier to boldly predict the existence of a yet undiscovered eighth planet (the new fact), lying beyond Uranus. If this were true, that new planet's gravitational effects could explain the aberrant motion of Uranus, which seemed to be in conflict with Newton's laws.

In addition, if an eighth planet did exist, one of Newton's laws would predict the exact spot in the sky where the new planet would be observable. This was a bold, informative, and highly falsifiable prediction that put Newton's laws to a most stringent test. The astounding prediction made by Adams and Leverrier about where the new planet would appear in the sky was indeed confirmed in 1846 with the discovery of Neptune. They saved Newton's laws from falsification by demonstrating that the theory was not only able to explain the deviant behavior of Uranus but was also able to make a highly accurate prediction. This is the kosher way to retain a theory when it is confronted with dissonant observations.

In the end, however, Newton's laws proved to be provisionally true, as is ultimately the case for all laws and theories. Although Newton's laws had worked perfectly for more than 200 years, early in the twentieth century more precise astronomical observations were found to be truly inconsistent with the theory's predictions. The old theory had finally been falsified and it was time for a new one. In 1921, Albert Einstein responded properly by putting forward his new and more informative Theory of General Relativity. Today, almost one hundred years later, Einstein's theory has survived all attempts to falsify it.

Newton's theory qualified as scientific because it was open to empirical refutation. In fact, Newton's theory was not wrong so much as it was incomplete. Einstein's General Theory of Relativity not only accounted for all of the phenomena covered by the Newtonian model, but it accommodated the new observations that conflicted with Newton's more limited theory. This is how science progresses. Longevity and seniority mean nothing. Predictive accuracy and explanatory power are everything.

The case of Adams and Leverier make clear why claims must be open to empirical refutation. Falsifiability alone gives scientific knowledge a large advantage over conventional wisdom. The ability to jettison false or incomplete ideas and replace them with ever more informative ones produces a body of knowledge that is self-correcting and in a continual state of improvement. This in turn provides a stable base upon which new ideas can be erected that reach ever higher levels of understanding. Intellectual activities that have no procedure for eliminating erroneous knowledge inevitably get bogged down in nonsense. This is precisely the problem with the popular version of TA.

Now we will consider an example of an improper response to falsification. It occurs in the field of finance. The injection of science into finance is relatively recent. Perhaps this explains the defensive, unscientific response of those who support the efficient markets hypothesis. When observations collided with their favorite theory, they tried to save it from falsification by reducing its information content. As mentioned earlier, its least informative version, EMH weak, predicts that investment strategies based on TA[32] will not be able to earn risk adjusted returns that beat the market index. When EMH supporters were faced with studies showing that TA-based strategies were able to earn excess returns,[33] they responded by trying to immunize their theory from falsification. They did so by inventing new risk factors and claimed that the excess returns earned by TA were merely compensation for risks inherent in pursuing such a strategy. In other words, EMH defenders claimed that investors who followed the TA strategy were exposing themselves to a risk that was specific to that strategy. This allowed the EMH supporter to characterize the TA strategy's returns as non-market-beating. Recall EMH does not claim that earning returns higher than the market is impossible. It only says that higher returns entail the assumption of additional risk. If the returns earned by the TA strategy were indeed compensation for bearing higher risk, then EMH would remain intact despite the studies that show TA strategy earning a return higher than the market index.

There was one problem with the way EMH supporters did this. They cooked up the risk factor after the TA studies had been performed.[34] This is not kosher science. It would have been scientifically correct if EMH had defined the risk factor in advance of the study and predicted that a test of the TA method would generate what appeared to be market-beating returns. Had they done this, the status of EMH would have been enhanced with a successful prediction. Instead, EMH supporters took the low road to save their favored hypothesis by giving themselves the license to invent a new risk factor any time they needed to explain away findings that conflicted with their favored theory. In so doing, EMH supporters rendered their hypothesis unfalsifiable, thereby draining it of any information content.

The precedent for this knowledge-regressive method of immunizing the EMH hypothesis against falsification had already been established by earlier flawed defenses of EMH. These earlier, and similarly misguided, efforts to save EMH were in response to studies that had shown that public fundamental information, such as the price-to-book ratio and PE ratio, could be used to generate excess returns.[35] In response to this inconvenient evidence, EMH defenders claimed that low price-to-book ratios and low PE ratios were merely signals of stocks with abnormally high risk. In other words, the fact that a stock's price is low relative to its book value is an indication that the company is facing difficulties. Of course, this reasoning is circular. What is key here is the fact that EMH advocates had not defined low price-to-book or low PE as risk factors in advance of the studies showing that stocks with these traits were able to earn excess returns. Had EMH theorists done so, it they would have bolstered the information content of EMH with an additional dimension of risk. Instead, EMH theorists invented these risk factors after the fact, for the specific purpose of explaining away discordant observations that had already been made. Such explanations are termed ad-hoc hypotheses—explanations invented after the fact for the specific purpose of saving a theory or hypothesis from being falsified. Popper referred to this knowledge regressive, save-the-theory-at-any-cost behavior as falsification immunization.

Had Popper known of it, he would have chastised the die-hard supporters of EMH, but he would have probably applauded the efforts of those advocating behavioral finance. This relatively new field has proposed testable hypotheses that explain the profitability of strategies based on public technical and fundamental data as arising from the cognitive biases and illusions of investors. It is ironic that erroneous beliefs in the validity of subjective TA and the valid profitability of some forms of objective TA may both be the result of cognitive foibles.

The Scientific Attitude: Open yet Skeptical

Falsificationism makes a clear distinction between two phases of scientific discovery: proposal and refutation. These phases demand different mindsets—openness and skepticism. The coexistence of these opposite mindsets defines the scientific attitude.

An attitude of openness to new ideas is vital when hypotheses are being formulated. The willingness[36] to see things in a new way, to advance new explanations and take bold inductive leaps characterizes the proposal phase. Most practitioners of TA function well in this mode. New indicators, new systems, and new patterns get proposed all the time.

However, once a bold conjecture has been made, receptivity must morph into skepticism. Doubt about the new idea motivates a relentless search for its flaws. Thus, there is an ongoing tension in the scientist's mind between speculative curiosity and hard-nosed disbelief. However, the doubt is not an unremitting skepticism but one that yields to persuasive new evidence. This is the quasi-schizoid state that defines the scientific attitude.

Beyond the distrust of the new hypothesis, another form of skepticism thrives in the mind of a scientist: doubt about the mind itself. This springs from a profound awareness of the all-too-human tendency to generalize hastily and leap to unfounded conclusions (see Chapter 2). The procedures of science can be seen as safeguards against these tendencies.

THE END RESULT:
THE HYPOTHETICO-DEDUCTIVE METHOD

Some would say there is no such thing as the scientific method.[37] "The scientific method, as far as it is a method is nothing more than doing one's damnedest with one's mind no holds barred."[38] At its essence it is intelligent problem solving.

The problem-solving method used in science today has come to be known as the hypothetico-deductive method. It is commonly described as having five stages: observation, hypothesis, prediction, verification, and conclusion. "In actual scientific work these stages are so intertwined that it would be hard to fit the history of any scientific investigation into this rigid scheme. Sometimes the different stages are merged or blurred, and frequently they do not occur in the sequence listed."[39] Rather, it is a useful way to think about the process.

The hypothetico-deductive method was initiated by Newton in the seventeenth century, but was not formally named until after Popper's contributions were introduced. It is the outgrowth of several hundred years of tussling between scientists and philosophers. The method integrates both inductive and deductive logic, paying heed to their individual limits while leveraging their respective powers.

The Five Stages

1. **Observation:** A possible pattern or relationship is noticed in a set of prior observations.

2. **Hypothesis:** Based on a mysterious mixture of insight, prior knowledge, and inductive generalization, it is hypothesized that the pattern is not an artifact of the particular set of observations but one that should be found in any similar set of observations. The hypothesis may merely assert that the pattern is real (scientific law) or it may go further and offer an explanation about why the pattern exists (scientific theory).

3. **Prediction:** A prediction is deduced from the hypothesis and embodied in a conditional proposition. The proposition's antecedent clause is the hypothesis and its consequent clause is the prediction. The prediction tells us what should be observed in a new set of observations if the hypothesis is indeed true. For example: **If** the hypothesis is true, **then** X should be observed if operation O is performed. The set of outcomes defined by X makes clear which future observations would confirm the prediction and, more importantly, which future observations would be in conflict with it.

4. **Verification:** New observations are made in accordance with the operations specified and compared to the predictions. In some sciences the operation is a controlled experiment. In other sciences it is an observational study.

5. **Conclusion:** An inference about the truth or falsity of the hypothesis is made based on the degree to which the observations conform to the prediction. This stage involves statistical inference methods such as confidence intervals and hypothesis tests, which are described in Chapters 4 and 5.

An Example from TA

The following is an example of the hypothetico-deductive method as it would be applied to testing a new idea about technical analysis.

1. **Observation:** It is noticed that when a stock market index, such as the Dow Jones average or the S&P 500, rises above its 200-day moving average, it generally continues to appreciate over the next several months (probabilistic generalization).

2. **Hypothesis:** On the basis of this observation, inductive generalization, and prior findings of technical analysis, we propose the following hypothesis: Upward penetrations of the 200-day moving average by the DJIA will, on average, produce profitable long positions over the next three months. I'll refer to this hypothesis as 200-H.

3. **Prediction:** On the basis of the hypothesis, we predict that an observational investigation, or back test, will be profitable. The hypothesis and the prediction are turned into the following conditional statement: **If** 200-H is true, **then** the back test *will be profitable.* However this prediction creates a logical problem. Even if the back test is profitable it will not be helpful in proving the truth of 200-H because, as previously pointed out, while a profitable back test would be consistent with the truth of 200-H, it cannot prove that 200-H is true. An attempt to do so would commit the fallacy of affirming the consequent (see argument 1 below). If, on the other hand, the back test turns out to be unprofitable, it would be valid to conclude 200-H is false by the valid logical form falsification of the consequent. See Argument 2 below.

Argument 1

Premise 1: *If 200-H is true, then a back test will be profitable.*

Premise 2: *The back test was profitable.*

Invalid Conclusion: Therefore, 200-H is true. (fallacy of affirming the consequent)

Argument 2

Premise 1: *If 200-H is true, then a back test will be profitable.*

Premise 2: *The back test was NOT profitable.*

Valid Conclusion: *Therefore, 200-H is false.*

However, our objective is to prove the truth of 200-H. To get around this logical problem, suppose we had formulated a null hypothesis at stage 2, specifically, *Upward penetrations of a 200-day moving average do not generate profits over the following three months.* Let's refer to this as Null-200. From this we can formulate the following conditional proposition: **If Null-200 is true, then a back-test will NOT be profitable.** If the back test does turn out to be profitable, we can validly argue that the null hypothesis has been falsified (falsifying the consequent). By the Law of the Excluded Middle, either 200-H is true or Null-200 is true. There is no middle ground; there is no other hypothesis possible. Thus by disproving the null we will have indirectly proven that 200-H is true. Thus we have the following conditional syllogism:

Premise 1: *If Null-200 is true, then the back test will be unprofitable.*

Premise 2: *The back test was NOT unprofitable (i.e., it was profitable).*

Valid Conclusion: Null-200 is false, therefore 200-H is true.

4. **Verification:** The proposed rule is back tested and its profitability is observed.

5. **Conclusion:** Determining the meaning of the results is a matter of statistical inference, the topic treated over the next three chapters.

RIGOROUS AND CRITICAL ANALYSIS OF OBSERVED RESULTS

The fifth phase of the hypothetico-deductive method points to another important difference between science and nonscience. In science, observed evidence is not taken at face value. In other words, the obvious implication of the evidence may not be its true implication. The evidence must be subjected to rigorous analysis before a conclusion can be drawn from it. The evidence of choice in science is quantitative data, and the tool of choice for drawing conclusions is statistical inference.

An important scientific principle is the preference for simpler explanations (Okam's Razor). As such, astounding hypotheses are given serious consideration only after more commonplace hypotheses have been rejected. Sightings of a UFO are not immediately interpreted as evidence of an alien visit. More mundane accounts such as ball lightning, weather balloons, or a new aircraft must first be discredited before an invasion from outer space is taken seriously.

Thus a scientific attitude toward an extraordinarily profitable rule back test would first consider and reject other explanations before entertaining the possibility that a significant TA rule has been discovered. The possible explanations of good performance unrelated to a rule's predictive power are good luck due to sampling error (see Chapters 4 and 5) and systematic error due to data-mining bias (see Chapter 6).

SUMMARY OF KEY ASPECTS OF THE SCIENTIFIC METHOD

The following is a summary of the key points of the scientific method:

- No matter how voluminous the evidence, the scientific method can never conclusively prove a hypothesis to be true.
- Observed evidence used in combination with the deductive form falsification of the consequent can be used to disprove a hypothesis with a specified degree of probability.
- Science is restricted to testable hypotheses. Propositions that are not testable are not within the domain of scientific discourse and are considered to be meaningless.
- A hypothesis is testable if and only if predictions about yet-to-be-made observations can be deduced from the hypothesis.
- A hypothesis that can only explain past observations but that cannot make predictions about new observations is not scientific.
- A hypothesis is tested by comparing its predictions with new observations. If predictions and observations agree, the hypothesis is not proven, but merely receives tentative confirmation. If they don't agree, the hypothesis is taken to be false or incomplete.
- All currently accepted scientific knowledge is only provisionally true. Its truth is temporary until a test shows it to be false, at which point it is replaced or subsumed by a more complete theory.
- Scientific knowledge is cumulative and progressive. As older hypotheses are shown to be false, they are replaced by newer ones that more accurately portray objective reality. Science is the only method of inquiry or intellectual discipline which can claim that newer is better.

Though knowledge, styles, and methods in other disciplines, such as music, art, philosophy, or literary criticism, may change over time, it cannot be claimed that new is necessarily better.

• Any set of past observations (data) can be explained by an infinite number of hypotheses. For example, Elliott Wave Theory, Gann Lines, classical chart patterns, and a roster of other interpretive methods can all explain past market behavior according to their own paradigm of analysis. Therefore, all these explanations are said to be empirically equal. The only way to decide which ones are better is by seeing how well they can predict observations whose outcomes are not yet known. Those methods that cannot generate testable (falsifiable) predictions about new observations can be eliminated immediately on the grounds that they are scientifically meaningless. Those methods that can generate predictions that are found to conflict with future observations can be eliminated on grounds that they have been falsified. Thus, only methods that can make testable predictions that display genuine predictive power deserve to be retained in the body of TA knowledge.

IF TA WERE TO ADOPT THE SCIENTIFIC METHOD

This section examines consequences of TA adopting the scientific method.

The Elimination of Subjective TA

The most important consequence of TA adopting the scientific method would be the elimination of subjective approaches. Because they are not testable, subjective methods are shielded from empirical challenge. This makes them worse than wrong. They are meaningless propositions devoid of information. Their elimination would make TA an entirely objective practice.

Subjective TA would be eliminated in one of two ways: by transformation into objective methods or abandonment. Perhaps Gann Lines, subjective divergences, trend channels, and a host of subjective patterns and concepts embody valid aspects of market behavior. In their present subjective form, however, we are denied this knowledge.

Transforming a subjective method into an objective version is not trivial. To illustrate a case where this has been done, I discuss an algorithm for the automated diction of head and shoulder patterns and test results in the section "Objectification of Subjective TA: An Example."

Elimination of Meaningless Forecasts

It is not practical to assume that all subjective practitioners will follow my call to objectify or close up shop. For those who continue to use subjective approaches, there is an important step that can be taken to make their output, if not their methodology, objective. Henceforth, they would issue only falsifiable forecasts. This would at least make the information they provide meaningful and informative. In this context, informative does not necessarily mean correct but rather that the forecasts have cognitive content that passes the discernable difference test discussed in the Introduction. In other words, the forecast would convey something of substance, the truth of which can be clearly determined by subsequent market action. In other words, the forecast will make explicit or clearly imply which outcomes would show it to be wrong. As stated previously, a forecast that does not make clear what future events constitute prediction errors in essence says that any outcome can happen.

At the present time, most subjective forecasts, often referred to as market calls, are meaningless. In all likelihood, this is not obvious to either consumers or the analysts issuing the forecasts. First, consider a forecast that is clearly meaningless: "My indicators are now predicting the market will either go up an infinite percentage, down 100 percent, or something in between." On its face, the statement is unfalsifiable because there is no outcome that could possibly conflict with the prediction. The only good thing about the forecast is that its lack of meaning and lack of falsifiability are transparent. A more typical market call goes something like this: "On the basis of my indicators [fill in one or more TA methods], I am bullish." This unfalsifiable statement is just as meaningless, but its lack of substance is not obvious. Though there is a prediction of a rise, the prediction leaves unclear when it might occur or under what circumstances the prediction would be wrong.

This bullish stance could have been made meaningful by clearly excluding certain outcomes. For example, *I expect the market to rise more than 10 percent from current levels before it declines by more than 5 percent from current levels.* Any instance of a decline of greater than 5 percent before a rise of 10 percent would be sufficient to classify the forecast as an error.

If you ever suspect that you are being fed a meaningless prediction, here are some good antidotes. Ask the following question: "How much adverse movement (opposite to the direction predicted) would have to occur for you to admit this forecast is mistaken?" Or "What outcomes are precluded by your prediction?" Or "When, and under what conditions, can the forecast be evaluated, such as the passage of time, change in price (adverse or favorable), or a specific indicator development?" Reader, I warn you not to do this if you are squeamish about watching people squirm.

Making subjective forecasts meaningful with an up-front statement of when and how the forecast will be evaluated would eliminate the market guru's after-the-fact wiggle room. Some ways of adding meaning to a subjective forecast include (1) defining a future point in time when the forecast will be evaluated, (2) defining the maximum degree of adverse movement that would be allowed without declaring the prediction wrong, and (3) predicting a specified magnitude of favorable movement prior to a specified magnitude of unfavorable movement (X percent favorable before Y percent unfavorable). Steps like these would allow a subjective practitioner to develop a track record of meaningful market calls. Meaningful track records can also result from specific transaction recommendations made in real time.

One limitation of this recommendation is that it would still leave unclear what the profitable track record represents. This is because subjective forecasts are derived in an undefined way, so even if a profitable track record of meaningful predictions is built up over time, it cannot be known that they were the result of a consistent analysis procedure that can be repeated in the future. In fact, it is likely that the method of analysis is not stable over time. Studies of expert subjective judgment indicate that experts do not combine information in a consistent manner from one judgment to the next. "Intuitive judgments suffer from serious random inconsistencies due to fatigue, boredom, and all the factors that make us human."[40] In other words, given the exact same pattern of market data at different times, it is quite possible that a subjective analyst would not give the same forecast.[41]

Paradigm Shift

Refashioning TA into an objective practice would be what Thomas Kuhn calls a paradigm shift. In his highly influential book, *The Structure of Scientific Revolutions*, Kuhn rejected Popper's notion that science evolves strictly by falsification and conjecture. Instead, Kuhn saw the evolution of a science as a sequence of paradigms, or world views. While a given paradigm is in place, practitioners indoctrinated in that point of view confine their activities to posing questions and hypotheses that are consistent with and answerable within that view.

A large number of TA analysts have been indoctrinated with the nonscientific, intuitive analysis paradigm developed by TA pioneers like Dow, Gann, Shabacker, Elliott, Edwards and Magee, and so forth. They established the subjective research tradition and postulated the background wisdom that is accepted as true and taught to aspiring practitioners. The certification exam given by the Market Technicians Association to aspiring Chartered Market Technicians (CMT) exemplifies this tradition.

The shift to an evidence-based objective approach would challenge much of this material as either meaningless or not sufficiently supported by statistical evidence. Many of the teachings will go the way of early Greek physics and astronomy. Some methods will survive objectification and statistical testing and will warrant a position in a legitimate body of TA knowledge.

Lest the reader think my position too harsh, I am not advocating that the falsifiability criterion be used to cut off all research in budding TA methods just as they are being formulated. Many of the brilliant theories of science began as half-backed prescientific ideas on the wrong side of the falsifiability criterion. These ideas needed time to develop, and one day some turned into meaningful science. One example in TA is the new field of socionomics, an outgrowth of Elliott Wave Theory. At the current time, I regard this newly developing discipline as prescientific, though it may have the potential to become a science. According to a conversation I had with Professor John Nofsinger, who is working within the field of socionomics, at this time the discipline is not yet able to make testable predictions. This will require the quantification of social mood, the key determinant of market movement according to socionomics.

Nascent areas of research such as this and others should not be short-circuited simply because they are not at this time able to generate testable predictions. One day they may be able to do so.

OBJECTIFICATION OF SUBJECTIVE TA: AN EXAMPLE

One of the challenging aspects of moving TA to a science will be transforming subjective chart patterns into objectively defined testable patterns. This section presents an example of how two academic technicians, Keving Chang and Carol Osler (C&O) objectified the head-and-shoulders pattern).[42] Not all elements of their pattern are included here. Rather, I have included enough of their rules and the problems they faced and solved to illustrate the challenges of transforming a subjective method into an objective one. For further details please refer to their original articles.

Descriptions of the head-and-shoulders pattern can be found in many TA texts[43] and are typically accompanied by a diagram similar to the one in Figure 3.8. It represents the pattern as a sequence of noise-free price swings. When the pattern manifests in perfect textbook form, even a beginning student of TA can spot it.

The problem occurs when an actual chart pattern departs from this ideal. Even seasoned chartists can debate whether a given pattern qualifies as a legitimate head and shoulders, an unavoidable consequence of the lack of an objective pattern definition. Subjective pattern definitions generally describe how the head-and-shoulders pattern should look, but they do not provide clear rules for discriminating patterns that do qualify as head and shoulders from patterns that possess some head-and-shoulders-like features but do not qualify. In other words, the definitions lack clear rules for which patterns to exclude. This problem is conceptualized in Figure 3.6.

Without objective rules for deciding what does and what does not qualify as a legitimate head-and-shoulders pattern it is impossible to evaluate the pattern's profitability or predictive power. The solution to the problem is to define objective rules that discriminate valid head-and-shoulders patterns from those that are not.[44] This notion is illustrated in Figure 3.7. The challenge of turning a subjective pattern into an objective one can be thought of as the problem of defining the pattern as a clear subset in the super-set of all possible TA price patterns.

C&O defined the head-and-shoulders top pattern as composed of five pivot or price reversal points that, in turn, define the pattern's three peaks and two troughs. These pivots are denoted by letters A through E on Figure 3.8. All eight texts consulted by C&O were clear that the head, denoted by letter C, must be higher than the two surrounding peaks (shoulders) denoted by letters A and E. There has been some debate among chartists about several auxiliary features including the Adam's apple, the double chin, and the cowlick. However, the TA manuals consulted by C&O were inconsistent on these aspects and they were not included.

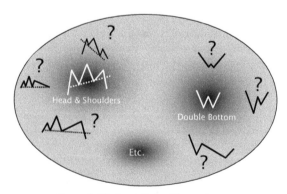

Set of All Possible Chart Patterns

FIGURE 3.6 Subjective patterns—no definitive exclusion rules.

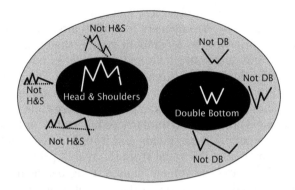

FIGURE 3.7 Objective patterns—definitive exclusion rules.

One challenge that faces the real-world chartist is the fact that actual price oscillations do not trace out clearly identifiable peaks and troughs. Rather, peaks and troughs occur at numerous oscillation scales from tiny waves lasting minutes to very large ones lasting years or decades. This property, called fractal scaling, imposes a burden on the subjective analyst trying to identify a head-and-shoulders pattern. The analyst must visually filter the price behavior to isolate peaks and troughs at one particular scale of interest. This is relatively easy in retrospect, but it is quite difficult as the pattern is actually unfolding in real time.

C&O addressed this problem by using a percentage filter, also known as an Alexander filter[45] or a zigzag indicator, which is discussed by Merrill

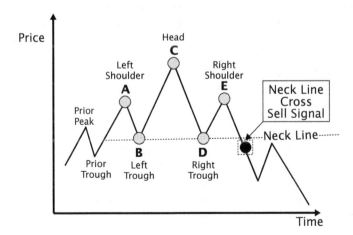

FIGURE 3.8 Head and shoulders.

in *Filtered Waves.*[46] It is an objective method for identifying peaks and troughs as prices evolve. Troughs are identified after prices have moved up from a recent price low by an amount greater than a specified threshold percentage and peaks are identified after prices have moved down from a recent price high by the threshold percentage. The problem is that the identification occurs with a time lag, the time it takes for prices to move the threshold amount. For example, if the threshold is set at 5 percent, then a peak is not detected until prices have fallen at least 5 percent from the most recent price maximum, and troughs are not detected until prices have risen at least 5 percent from the recent price minimum. The minimum required price movement causes a lag between the time the peak or trough actually occurred and the time at which it is detected by the zigzag filter.

Next, C&O addressed how to determine the correct threshold percentage to define the zigzag filter. Different filter thresholds would reveal head-and-shoulders patterns of different size (scale). For example, a 3 percent filter might reveal a head-and-shoulders pattern that a 10 percent filter would completely ignore. This makes it possible for multiple head-and-shoulders patterns of differing scale to exist simultaneously. C&O addressed this problem by subjecting each financial instrument (stock or currency) to 10 different zigzag filters employing a range of threshold values. This allowed them to identify head-and-shoulders patterns on a variety of scales.

This raised yet another problem. What should the 10 filter thresholds be? Clearly, a set of thresholds that would be good for one instrument may not be good for another because they are characterized by different levels of volatility. Realizing this, C&O take each instrument's recent volatility into account to arrive at the set of 10 filter thresholds used for that instrument. This insight allowed their head-and-shoulders algorithm to generalize across markets with different volatilities. C&O defined a market's volatility, V, as the standard deviation of daily percentage price changes over the most recent 100 trading days. The 10 thresholds were arrived at by multiplying V by 10 different coefficients; 1.5, 2.0, 2.5, 3.0, 3.5, 4.0, 4.5, 5.0, 5.5, 6.0. This resulted in 10 zigzag filters with varying sensitivity. The validity of the set of coefficients chosen by C&O were confirmed by visual inspection of price charts by TA practitioners who agreed that the 10 zigzag filters did a reasonable job of identifying head-and-shoulders patterns.

Next C&O addressed the problem of defining rules that qualify a candidate pattern as a valid head-and-shoulders. These rules were applied to the instrument once its price had been zigzag filtered and the peaks and troughs at a given scale had been identified.

First, the head and shoulders identified by C&O's algorithm had to satisfy the following basic rules:

1. The head of the pattern must be higher than both the left and right shoulders.

2. The instrument must be in an uptrend prior to the formation of the head-and-shoulders pattern. Thus, the pattern's left shoulder has to be above the prior peak (PP) and the pattern's left trough has to be above the prior trough (PT).

Next C&O grappled with more subtle and complex issues to qualify a candidate pattern as a valid head-and-shoulders. They accomplished this with a set of innovative measurements that qualified the pattern in terms of its vertical and horizontal symmetry and the time it took for the pattern to complete. These rules allowed them to definitively label a candidate pattern as either head-and-shoulders or a non–head-and-shoulders.

Vertical Symmetry Rules

The vertical symmetry rules exclude patterns with necklines that are too steeply sloped. The pattern in Figure 3.9 has acceptable vertical symmetry.

The rules compare the price levels of the right and left shoulders (A and E) and the price levels of the right and left troughs (B and D) with a price level defined by the midpoint of segment AB, designated as point X, and the midpoint of segment DE designated as point Y. To qualify as a

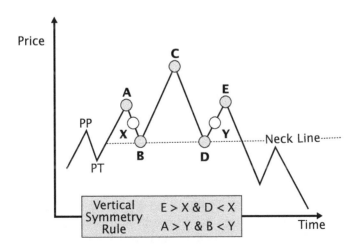

FIGURE 3.9 Good vertical symmetry.

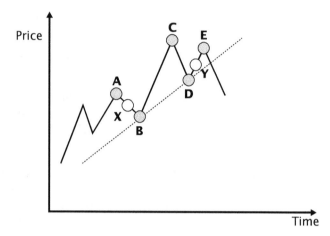

FIGURE 3.10 Poor vertical symmetry—neckline slope too steep.

vertically symmetrical head-and-shoulders, the pattern must satisfy the following rules.

1. The price level of the left shoulder peak, point A, must exceed the price level of point Y.
2. The price level of the right shoulder peak, point E, must exceed the price level of point X.
3. The price level of the left trough, point B, must be less than the price level of point Y.
4. The price level of the right trough, point D, must be less than the price level of point X.

Figures 3.10 and 3.11 show two head-and-shoulders patterns that would be excluded because the vertical symmetry criteria have not been satisfied.

Horizontal Symmetry Rule

Another feature used by C&O to distinguish head-and-shoulders patterns from non-head-and-shoulders patterns was horizontal symmetry. A pattern with good horizontal symmetry is one for which the head, at point C, is roughly equidistant from the peaks representing the pattern's two shoulders (points A and E). C&O's rule was that the distance from the head to

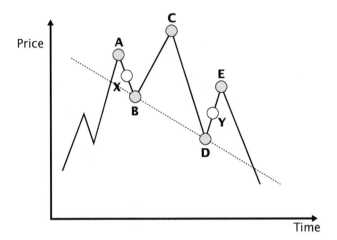

FIGURE 3.11   Poor vertical symmetry—neckline slope too steep.

one shoulder should not be greater than 2.5 times the distance of the head to the other shoulder. There is nothing magical about the value 2.5 other than it seemed reasonable. See Figure 3.12.

Figure 3.13 is an example of a pattern that fails the test for horizontal symmetry. Note the right shoulder is stretched too far to the right. A pattern with excessive leftward stretch would also be disqualified.

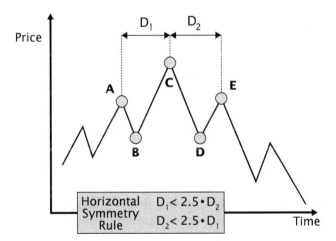

FIGURE 3.12   Good horizontal symmetry.

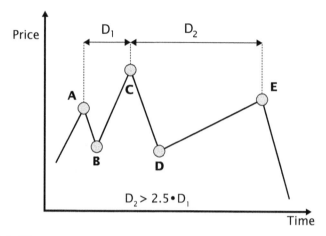

FIGURE 3.13   Poor horizontal symmetry.

Pattern Completion Rule: Maximum Time to Neckline Penetration

C&O also specified a rule that excludes patterns that take too long to penetrate the neckline once the right shoulder, point E, has been formed. As with other features, this criterion is defined in terms of the pattern's internal proportions rather than some fixed number of time units. This allows the rule to be applied to all patterns irrespective of their time frame or scale.

The maximum time allowed for the movement from the right shoulder, point E, until the penetration of the neckline is the temporal distance separating the two shoulders, points A and E. The pattern in Figure 3.14 meets the time to completion criterion because the temporal distance from the right shoulder until neckline penetration (D4) is less than the temporal separation of the shoulders (D3). The pattern in Figure 3.15 does not qualify because D4 exceeds D3.

Future Information Leakage: Look-Ahead Bias

In their simulation of head-and-shoulders patterns, C&O took precautions against the future information leakage or look-ahead bias problem. This problem afflicts back tests that assume the possession of knowledge that was not truly available when a trading decision was made. In the context of back testing, this can make results appear more profitable than would be possible in actual trading. An extreme example would be assuming access to the *Wall Street Journal* the day before its publication.

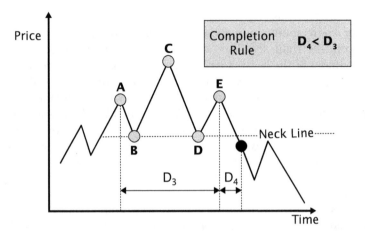

FIGURE 3.14 Pattern completion rule satisfied.

In the context of back testing the head-and-shoulders pattern, future information leakage can occur if the zigzag threshold percentage is larger than the percentage distance between the right shoulder peak and the neckline. It would not be legitimate to assume a short-sale signal due to a neckline penetration until the right shoulder (point E) has been detected. However, it is possible for prices to cross the neckline before the right shoulder is identified by the zigzag filter. To clarify, suppose the right shoulder, point E, lies only 4 percent above the neckline, but the threshold

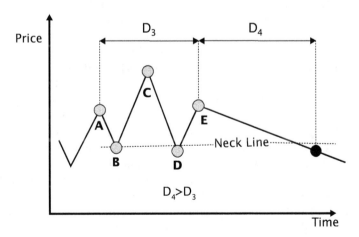

FIGURE 3.15 Pattern completion rule not satisfied.

for the zigzag filter is 10 percent. It would not be legitimate to assume that a trader knew about the neckline penetration because a 10 percent decline from the right shoulder would have been required to identify the right shoulder of the head-and-shoulders pattern. In this example, assuming an entry price only 4 percent below the right shoulder would be more favorable than waiting for a price 10 percent below the right shoulder, the price movement required to have a fully formed head-and-shoulders pattern. To avoid this problem, C&O assumed an entry after the right shoulder had been objectively identified by the zigzag filter. Though this was a less favorable entry price in some instances, the back test was unencumbered by look-ahead bias. I mention this because it shows C&O's attention to detail.

C&O's pattern definition also deals with numerous other issues regarding entry and exit of positions, stop-loss levels, and so forth, but the point has been made that it is possible to transform subjective chart patterns into objective testable patterns. Readers may take exception to arbitrary aspects of C&O's pattern. All well and good if the reader has a better objective definition to offer.

As a final sanity check, C&O showed patterns that had been identified by their automated head-and-shoulders algorithm to a number of chartists. C&O claim that the chartists agreed that the patterns identified by the objective head-and-shoulders algorithm did indeed conform to subjective head-and-shoulders criteria.

Head-and-Shoulders Back Test Results

Does the head-and-shoulders pattern carry predictive information with respect to stocks or currencies? In a word, the pattern hailed as a cornerstone of charting is a bust. Tests by C&O show that it is worthless on stocks and only modestly profitable on currencies. The pattern was profitable in two out of six currencies tested, but the relatively complicated head-and-shoulders algorithm was far outperformed by a much simpler objective signal based on zigzag filters. Moreover, when C&O tested the occurrence of a head-and-shoulders in conjunction with the zigzag rule either as a confirming or disconfirming signal, the head-and-shoulders pattern added no value. In other words, zigzag signals did no better when the head-and-shoulders signal was in the same direction as the zigzag signal and the zigzag did no worse when the head-and-shoulders signal was in the opposite direction. The bottom line for currency traders: the value of head-and-shoulders is doubtful.[47]

The head-and-shoulders performed worse on stocks. C&O evaluated the head-and-shoulders on 100 randomly selected equities[48] over the period from July 1962 until December 1993. On average, each stock gave one head-and-shoulders signal per year, counting both long and short signals, giving a sample of over 3,100 signals. To test the pattern's profitability on actual stock prices, C&O established a benchmark based on the pattern's performance on pseudo-price histories. These simulated price histories were generated from actual historical price changes strung together in a random fashion. By using actual price changes, the pseudo-price histories had the same statistical characteristics as real stocks, but any predictability due to authentic temporal structure—the structure TA patterns are intended to exploit—was eliminated Despite the fact that the pseudo-price histories were randomly generated, head-and-shoulders patterns that fit C&O's definition still emerged. This confirms the results of Harry Roberts referred to earlier.

If the head-and-shoulders patterns appearing in real stock data are useful, they should generate profits superior to those achieved by trading the patterns appearing in the fake stock price histories. C&O found that head-and-shoulders patterns in actual stock prices lost slightly more money than the signals on pseudo-price histories. According to the study "the results uniformly suggest that head-and-shoulders trading are not profitable." The signals lose on average about 0.25 percent over a 10-day holding period. This compares with an average loss of 0.03 percent for head-and-shoulders patterns in the pseudo-stock data. C&O referred to traders using the pattern as "noise traders," speculators who mistake a random signal for an informative one.

Confirming C&O's findings is the work of Lo et al.[49] Lo used an alternative method of objectifying the H&S pattern based on kernel regression, a sophisticated local[50] smoothing technique. Their study was unable to unseat the null hypothesis that the head-and-shoulders pattern is useless.[51]

Bulkowski[52] found the head-and-shoulders was profitable, but his research falls short. He does not provide an objective pattern definition that back-testable pattern or entry and exit rules. In other words, his study is subjective TA. In addition, his results fail to adjust for the trend of the general stock market over the time period in which he tested the patterns.

SUBSETS OF TA

Given the preceding discussion, TA can be seen as comprised of four subsets: (1) subjective TA, (2) objective TA with unknown statistical significance, (3) objective TA that is not statistically significant, and (4) objective TA that is statistically significant.

The first subset, subjective TA, has already been defined as methods that cannot be reduced to a back-testable algorithm. Subsets two, three, and four refer to objective methods.

The second subset is comprised of objective methods of unknown value. Though these methods are objective and may have been back tested, their results have not been evaluated for statistical significance. Here, it is simply a matter of applying the methods discussed in Chapters 4, 5, and 6. This is not meant to suggest that applying statistical methods to back test results is simple, but rather that the decision to do so is.

The third subset, which I refer to as useless TA, consists of objective TA rules for which results have been comprehensively back tested and evaluated with statistical methods, but have been reveled to add no value either on a stand-alone basis or when used in combination with other methods. In all likelihood, the majority of objective TA methods will fall into this subset. This is to be expected because financial markets are extremely difficult to predict due to their inherent complexity and randomness. In fact, in all fields of science, most proposed ideas do not work. Important discoveries are rare. This is not obvious because the numerous failures are typically not reported in the lay press or even in scientific journals. What is most important is having a procedure in place for getting rid of methods that do not work.

The fourth subset, useful TA, consists of objective methods that produce statistically significant or, better yet, economically significant results. Though some rules will be useful on a stand-alone basis, the complexity and randomness of financial markets make it likely that most

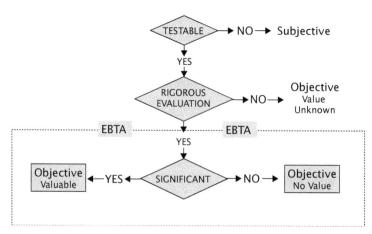

FIGURE 3.16 Subsets of Technical Analysis.

rules will add value when used in combination with other rules to form complex rules.

Evidence-based technical analysis (EBTA) refers to subsets (3) and (4)—objective TA that has been back tested and subjected to statistical analysis. Given the preceding discussion, the categorization of TA is illustrated in Figure 3.16.

The next three chapters discuss the application of statistical analysis to back-test results.

CHAPTER 4

Statistical
Analysis

S tatistics is the science of data.[1] In the late nineteenth century, renowned British scientist and author H.G. Wells (1866–1946) said that an intelligent citizen in a twentieth-century free society would need to understand statistical methods. It can be said that an intelligent twenty-first-century practitioner or consumer of TA has the same need. This chapter and the next two address aspects of statistics that are particularly relevant to TA.

Statistical methods are not needed when a body of data conveys a message loudly and clearly. If all people drinking from a certain well die of cholera but all those drinking from a different well remain healthy, there is no uncertainty about which well is infected and no need for statistical analysis. However, when the implications of data are uncertain, statistical analysis is the best, perhaps the only, way to draw reasonable conclusions.

Identifying which TA methods have genuine predictive power is highly uncertain. Even the most potent rules display highly variable performance from one data set to the next. Therefore, statistical analysis is the only practical way to distinguish methods that are useful from those that are not.

Whether or not its practitioners acknowledge it, the essence of TA is statistical inference. It attempts to discover generalizations from historical data in the form of patterns, rules, and so forth and then extrapolate them to the future. Extrapolation is inherently uncertain. Uncertainty is uncomfortable.

The discomfort can be dealt with in two ways. One way is to pretend it does not exist. The other is the way of statistics, which meets uncertainty head on by acknowledging it, quantifying it, and then making the best decision possible in the face of it. Bertrand Russell, the renowned British mathematician and philosopher said, "Uncertainty, in the presence of vivid hopes and fears, is painful, but must be endured if we wish to live without the support of comforting fairy tales."[2]

Many people are distrustful or disdainful of statistical analysis and statisticians are often portrayed as nerdy number-crunching geeks divorced from reality. This shows up in jokes. We deride what we do not understand. There is the story about the six-foot-tall man who drowns in a pond with an average depth of only two feet. There's the tale about three statisticians who go duck hunting. They spot a bird flying overhead. The first shoots a foot too far to the left. The second shoots a foot too far to the right. The third jumps up and exclaims, "We got it!!" Even though the average error was zero, there was no duck for dinner.

Powerful tools can be put to bad purpose. Critics often charge that statistics are used to distort and deceive. Of course, similar ends can be achieved with words, although language is not held liable. A more rational stance is needed. Rather than viewing all claims based on statistics with suspicion or taking them all at face value, "a more mature response would be to learn enough about statistics to distinguish honest, useful conclusions from skullduggery or foolishness."[3] "He who accepts statistics indiscriminately will often be duped unnecessarily. But, he who distrusts statistics indiscriminately will often be ignorant unnecessarily. The middle ground we seek between blind distrust and blind gullibility is an open-minded skepticism. That takes an ability to interpret data skillfully."[4]

A PREVIEW OF STATISTICAL REASONING

Statistical reasoning is new terrain for many practitioners and consumers of TA. Trips to strange places are easier when you know what to expect. The following is a preview of the next three chapters

For reasons discussed in Chapter 3, it is wise to start with the assumption that all TA rules are without predictive power and that a profitable back test was due to luck. This assumption is called the null hypothesis. *Luck*, in this case, means a favorable but accidental correspondence between the rule's signals and subsequent market trends in the historical data sample in which the rule was tested. Although this hypothesis is a reasonable starting point, it is open to refutation with empirical evidence. In other words, if observations contradict predictions made by the null hypothesis, it is abandoned and the alternative hypothesis, that the rule has predictive power, would be adopted. In the context of rule testing, evidence that would refute the null hypothesis is a back-tested rate of return that is too high to be reasonably attributed to mere luck.

If a TA rule has no predictive power, its expected rate of return will be zero on detrended[5] data. However, over any small sample of data, the profitability of a rule with no predictive power can deviate considerably from zero. These deviations are manifestations of chance—good or bad luck. This phenomenon can be seen in a coin-toss experiment. Over a small number of tosses, the proportion of heads can deviate considerably from 0.50, which is the expected proportion of heads in a very large number of tosses.

Generally, the chance deviations of a useless rule from a zero return are small. Sometimes, however, a useless rule will generate significant profits by sheer luck. These rare instances can fool us into believing a useless rule has predictive power.

The best protection against being fooled is to understand the degree to which profits can result from luck. This is best accomplished with a mathematical function that specifies the deviations from zero profits that can occur by chance. That is what statistics can do for us.

This function, called a probability density function, gives the probability of every possible positive or negative deviation from zero. In other words, it shows the degree to which chance can cause a useless rule to generate profits. Figure 4.1 shows a probability density function.[6] The fact that the density curve is centered at a value of zero reflects the null hypothesis assertion that the rule has an expected return of zero.

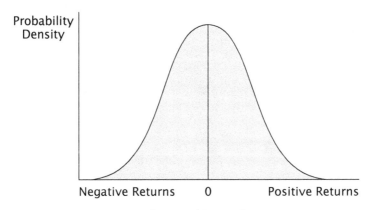

Back-Tested Rate of Return

FIGURE 4.1 Probability density of chance performance—range of possible performance for a useless TA rule.

In Figure 4.2, the arrow indicates the positive rate of return earned by a rule when it was back tested. This raises the question: Is the observed rate of return sufficiently positive to warrant a rejection of the null hypothesis that the rule's true rate of return is zero? If the observed performance falls well within the range of the deviations that are probably attributable to chance, the evidence is considered to be insufficient to reject the null hypothesis. In such a case, the null hypothesis has withstood the empirical challenge of the back-test evidence, and a conservative interpretation of the evidence would suggest that the rule has no predictive power.

The strength of the back-test evidence is quantified by the fractional area[7] of the probability density function that lies at values equal to or greater than the rule's observed performance. This portion of the density function is depicted by the darkened area to the right of the vertical arrow in Figure 4.2. The size of this area can be interpreted as the probability that a rate of return this high or higher could have occurred by chance under the condition that the rule has no predictive power (expected return = 0, or the null hypothesis is true). When this area occupies a relatively large fraction of the density curve, it means that there is an equivalently large probability that the positive performance was due to chance. When this is the case, there is no justification for concluding that the null hypothesis is false. In other words, there is no justification for concluding that the rule does have predictive power.

However, if the observed performance is far above zero, the portion of the probability density function lying at even more extreme values is

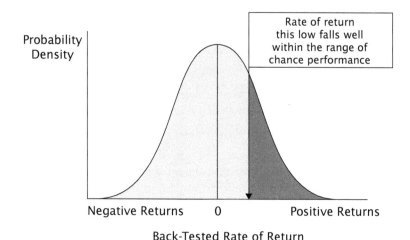

FIGURE 4.2 Probability of chance performance for a useless rule.

small. Performance this positive would be inconsistent with the assertion that the rule has no predictive power. In other words, the evidence would be sufficient to refute the null hypothesis. Another way to think of this is as follows: If the null hypothesis were true, a level of performance this positive would have a low probability of occurrence. This probability is quantified by the proportion of the density function that lies at values equal to or greater than the observed performance. This is illustrated in Figure 4.3. Note that the observed performance lies in the extreme right tail of the density curve that would pertain if the rule were devoid of predictive power.

It is important to understand what this evidence does not tell us. It tells us nothing about the probability that either the null hypothesis or the alternative hypothesis is true. It only speaks to the probability that the evidence could have occurred under the assumption that the null hypothesis is, in fact, true. Thus, the probability speaks to the likelihood of the evidence, not the likelihood of the truth of the hypothesis. Observed evidence that would be highly improbable, under the condition that the null hypothesis is true, permits an inference that the null hypothesis is false.

Recall that, in Chapter 3, it was shown that evidence that a creature has four legs cannot conclusively establish the truth of the hypothesis: *The creature is a dog.* Although evidence of four legs would be consistent with the hypothesis that the creature is a dog, it is not sufficient to prove, deductively, that the creature is a dog. Similarly, while the observation of positive performance would be consistent with the hypothesis that a rule has predictive power, it is not sufficient to prove that it does. An argument that attempts to prove the truth of a hypothesis with observed evidence

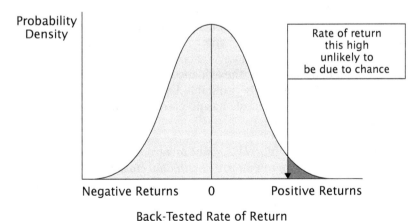

FIGURE 4.3 Probability of chance performance for a good rule.

that is consistent with the hypothesis commits the logical fallacy of affirming the consequent.

> *If the creature is a dog, **then** it has four legs.*
> *The creature has four legs.*
> Invalid Conclusion: *Therefore, the creature is a dog.*

> *If a rule has predictive power, **then** it will have a profitable back test.*
> *Back test was profitable.*
> Invalid Conclusion: *Therefore, rule has predictive power.*

However, the absence of four legs is sufficient to prove that the hypothesis, *the creature is a dog*, is false.[8] In other words, observed evidence can be used to conclusively prove that a hypothesis is false. Such an argument uses the valid deductive form, *denial of the consequent*. The general form of an argument, in which the consequent is denied, is as shown:

> *If P is true, **then** Q is true.*
> *Q is not true.*
> Valid Conclusion: *Therefore, P is not true (i.e., P is false).*

> *If the creature is a dog, **then** it has four legs.*
> *Creature does not have four legs.*
> Valid Conclusion: *Therefore, it is false that the creature is a dog.*

The argument just given uses the evidence, the absence of four legs, to conclusively falsify the notion that the creature is a dog. However, this level of certitude is not possible in matters of science and statistics. One can never conclusively falsify a hypothesis. Nevertheless, a similar logic can be used to show that certain evidence is highly unlikely if the hypothesis were true. In other words, the evidence gives us grounds to challenge the hypothesis. Thus, a highly profitable back test can be used to challenge the hypothesis that the rule has no predictive power (i.e., that it has an expected return of zero).

> *If a rule's expected return is equal to zero or less, **then** a back test should generate profits that are reasonably close to zero.*
> *The back-tested performance was not reasonably close to zero; in fact, it was significantly above zero.*
> Valid Conclusion: *Therefore, the contention that the rule's expected return is equal to zero or less is likely to be false.*

How unlikely or rare must the positive performance be to reject the notion that the rule is devoid of predictive power? There is no hard and fast rule. By convention most scientists would not be willing to reject a hypothesis so unless the observed performance has a 0.05 probability or less of occurrence under the assumption the null is true. This value is called the statistical significance of the observation.

The discussion so far pertains to the case where only one rule is back tested. In practice, however, TA rule research is typically not restricted to testing a single rule. Economical computing power, versatile back-testing software, and plentiful historical data make it easy, almost inviting, to test many rules with the aim if selecting the one with the best performance. This practice is known as data mining.

Although data mining is an effective research method, testing many rules increases the chance of a lucky performance. Therefore, the threshold of performance needed to reject the null hypothesis must be set higher, perhaps much higher. This higher threshold compensates for the greater likelihood of stumbling upon a useless rule that got lucky in a back test. This topic, the data mining bias, is discussed in Chapter 6.

Figure 4.4 compares two probability density functions. The top one would be appropriate for evaluating the significance for a single rule back test. The lower density curve would be appropriate for evaluating the sig-

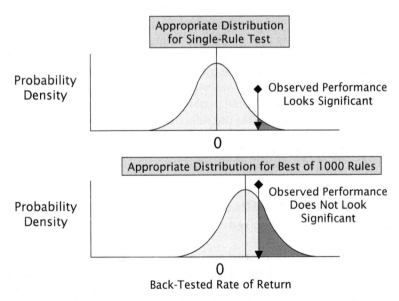

FIGURE 4.4 Great performance in a single rule back test is only mediocre when 1,000 rules are tested.

nificance of the best-performing rule out of 1,000 back-tested rules. This density curve takes into account the increased likelihood of luck that results from data mining. Notice that if this best rule's observed performance were to be evaluated with the density curve appropriate for a single rule, it would appear significant because the performance is far out in the right tail of the distribution. However, when the best rule's performance is evaluated with the appropriate probability density function it does not appear statistically significant. That is to say, the rule's rather high performance would not warrant the conclusion that it has predictive power or an expected return that is greater than zero.

THE NEED FOR RIGOROUS STATISTICAL ANALYSIS

The tools and methods of a discipline limit what it can discover. Improvements in them pave the way to greater knowledge. Astronomy took a great leap forward with the invention of the telescope. Though crude by today's standards, the earliest instruments had 10 times the resolving power of the unaided eye. Technical analysis has a similar opportunity, but it must replace informal data analysis with rigorous statistical methods.

Informal data analysis is simply not up to the task of extracting valid knowledge from financial markets. The data blossoms with illusory patterns whereas valid patterns are veiled by noise and complexity. Rigorous statistical analysis is far better suited to this difficult task.

Statistical analysis is a set of well-defined procedures for the collection, analysis, and interpretation of data. This chapter and the next two will introduce the way statistical tools and reasoning can be used to identify TA rules that work. This overview is necessarily condensed, and in many instances I have sacrificed mathematical rigor for the sake of clarity. However, these departures do not dilute the essential message: If TA is to deliver on its claims, it must be grounded in a scientific approach that uses formal statistical analysis.

AN EXAMPLE OF SAMPLING AND STATISTICAL INFERENCE

Statistical reasoning is abstract and often runs against the grain of common sense. This is good and bad. Logic that runs counter to informal inference is good because it can help us where ordinary thinking lets us down. However, this is exactly what makes it difficult to understand. So we should start with a concrete example.

The central concept of statistical inference is extrapolating from samples. A sample of observations is studied, a pattern is discerned, and this pattern is expected to hold for (extrapolated to) cases outside the observed sample. For example, a rule observed to be profitable in a sample of history is projected to be profitable in the future.

Let's begin to think about the concept in the context of a problem that has nothing to do with technical analysis. It comes from an excellent book: *Statistics, A New Approach* by Wallis and Roberts.[9] The problem concerns a box filled with a mixture of white and grey beads. The total number of beads and the numbers of grey and white beads are unknown. The task is to determine the fraction of beads that are grey in the entire box. For purposes of brevity, this value will be designated as *F-G* (fraction-grey in box).

To make this situation similar to statistical problems faced in the real world, there is a wrinkle. We are not allowed to view the entire contents of the box at one time, thus preventing a direct observation of F-G. This constraint makes the problem realistic because, in actual problems, observing all the items of interest, such as all beads in the box, is either impossible or impractical. In fact, it is this constraint that creates the need for statistical inference.

Although we are not allowed to examine the box's contents in its entirety, we are permitted to take samples of 20 beads at a time from the box and observe them. So our strategy for acquiring knowledge about F-G will be to observe the fraction of grey beads in a multitude of samples. In this example 50 samples will be taken. The lowercase f-g stands for the fraction of grey beads in a sample.

A sample is obtained as follows: The bottom of the box contains a sliding panel with 20 small depressions, sized so that a single bead is captured in each depression. The panel can be slid out of the box by pushing it with a similar panel that takes its place. This keeps the remaining beads from dropping out of the bottom. Consequently, each time the panel is removed, we obtain a sample of 20 beads and have the opportunity to observe the fraction grey (f-g) in that sample. This is illustrated in Figure 4.5.

After the fraction of grey beads (f-g) in a given sample has been determined, the sample beads are placed back into the box and it is given a thorough shaking before taking another sample of 20. This gives each bead an equal chance of winding up in the next sample of 20. In the parlance of statistics, we are making sure that each sample is random. The entire process of taking a sample, noting the value f-g, putting the sample back in the box, and shaking the box is repeated 50 times. At the end of the whole procedure we end up with 50 different values for f-g, one value for each sample examined.

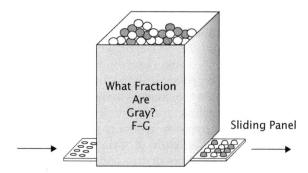

FIGURE 4.5 Determining f-g for each sample.

By placing each sample back in the box before taking another sample, we are maintaining a stable concentration for the fraction of grey beads in the box. That is to say, the value for F-G is kept constant over the course of the 50 samplings. Problems in which the statistical characteristics remain stable over time are said to be stationary. If the beads were not replaced after each sample the value F-G would change over the course of the 50 samplings, as groups of beads were permanently removed from the box. A problem in which the statistical characteristics change over time is said to be nonstationary. Financial markets may indeed be nonstationary, but for pedagogical purposes, the box-of-beads problem is designed to be stationary.

It is important to keep in mind the distinction between F-G and f-g. F-G refers to the fraction of grey beads in the entire box. In the language of statistics, all the observations in which we are interested are called a *population*. In this example, the term population refers to the color of all the beads in the box. The term *sample* refers to a subset of the population. Thus, F-G refers to the population while f-g refers to the sample. Our assigned task is to gain as much knowledge as possible about the value of F-G by observing the value f-g over 50 separate samples.

It is also important to keep clear the distinction between two numbers: the number of observations comprising a sample—in this case 20 beads—and the number of samples taken—in this case 50.

PROBABILITY EXPERIMENTS AND RANDOM VARIABLES

Probability is the mathematics of chance.[10] A *probability experiment* is an observation on or a manipulation of our environment that has an uncertain outcome.[11] This would include actions such as noting the precise time of arrival after a long trip, observing the number of inches of snow that falls in a storm or the face of a coin that appears after the tossing of a coin.

The quantity or quality observed in a probability experiment is called a *random variable* such as the face of a coin after a flip, the number of inches of snow that fell, or a value that summarizes a sample of observations (e.g., a sample average). This quantity or quality is said to be random because it is affected by chance. Whereas, an individual observation of a random variable is unpredictable, by definition, a large number of observations made on a random variable may have highly predictable features. For example, on a given coin toss, it is impossible to predict head or tails. However, given one thousand tosses, that the number of heads will lie within a specified range of 500 is highly predictable.

Depending on how it is defined, a random variable assumes at least two different values, though it can assume more—perhaps even an infinite number. The random variable in a coin toss, the face visible after the toss, can assume two possible values (heads or tails). The random variable, defined as the temperature at noon taken at the base of the Statue of Liberty, can assume a very large number of values, with the number limited only by the precision of the thermometer.

Sampling: The Most Important Probability Experiment

The most important probability experiment in statistical analysis is sampling. It involves the extraction of a subset of observations from a population. Here the random variable at issue is called a sample statistic. It is any computable characteristic of the sample. The value f-g is an example of a sample statistic.

Sampling can be done in a number of different ways, but it is crucial that the observations that are selected for the sample be chosen in a random manner and that they be selected independently of each other. This means that all observations that could possibly end up in the sample have an equal chance of doing so. Because no particular observation has a better chance of appearing in the sample than any other, the observations that wind up in the sample do so by chance. Samples must be constructed in this manner because the principles of probability, upon which statistical reasoning rests, assume that the observations that wind up in the sample got there randomly.

Consider the test of a new medicine on a sample of volunteers. The sample must be constructed so that anyone who might eventually take the medicine has an equal chance of being selected for the test group. If the subjects in the experiment are not selected this way, the results of the test will not lead to a sound conclusion. A medical experiment that selects test subjects who are expected to respond favorably to the medication will produce a biased conclusions. In other words, the estimates of the medication's efficacy in the general population will be too optimistic.

Imagine taking a single bead at random from the box with your eyes closed and then observing its color. This is a sampling experiment with a sample size of one. The bead's color, grey or white, is the random variable. Now imagine randomly selecting 20 beads from the box. Here the sample size is 20 and the fraction grey in that sample (f-g) is a sample statistic that is also a random variable.

As discussed earlier, we will call this random variable f-g. It is a random variable because its value is affected by chance. It can assume 21 different values {0, 0.05, 0.10, 0.15, . . . , 1.0}. Now let's get back to the goal: increasing our knowledge about the value of F-G.

The Knowledge Gleaned from One Sample

Suppose the first sample contains 13 grey beads out of 20. The value of the sample statistic f-g is 0.65 (13/20). What does this tell us about F-G? With only this information, some might be tempted to conclude that we have solved the problem, and that 0.65 is the fraction grey for the entire box (i.e., F-G = 0.65). This view tacitly and naively assumes that a single sample can provide perfect knowledge. At the opposite extreme are those who just as wrongly conclude that the sample is too small to supply any information.

Both conclusions are wrong. First, there is no basis for thinking that we could acquire perfect knowledge from one sample. Though it is possible that a single sample of 20 beads might be a perfect replica of the entire contents of the box, it is not likely. For example, if the true value of F-G were 0.568, a 20-bead sample could never produce such a value. An f-g value of 0.55 (11 grey of 20) is as close as one could get. Ten grey beads in the sample would give an f-g of 0.50, 11 would give 0.55, and 12 would give 0.60.

Those who assert that nothing has been learned are also mistaken. On the basis of this sample alone, two possibilities can be eliminated. We can reject with absolute certainty that F-G = 1.0 (i.e., all beads grey) because there were 7 white beads in the sample. With equal certainty, we can reject the proposition that F-G is 0, because there were 13 grey beads in the sample.

However, more precise estimates of F-G on the basis of the single observed value of f-g are subject to uncertainty. Even if we were to take numerous samples and have numerous values of f-g, the value of F-G would remain uncertain. This is because a sample is, by definition, a partial representation of the full contents of the box. Only by observing every bead in the population could all uncertainty about F-G be eliminated. And this is prohibited.

However, with what has been learned from the single sample, some intelligent guesses can be made that go beyond the certain knowledge that F-G is neither 0 nor 1.0. For example, although a claim that F-G is as low as 0.10 cannot be conclusively ruled out; no one would take it seriously. The observed f-g value of 0.65 obtained from the first sample is too far above 0.10 for it to be a credible estimate of F-G. If F-G really were as low 0.10, the probability of getting a sample with an f-g of 0.65 would seem unlikely just based on common sense. We could apply the same kind of logic to dispense with a claim that F-G = 0.95. An f-g reading of 0.65 would seem too low if the entire box were composed of 95 percent grey beads. The bottom line: It is fair to say that a single sample does provide some knowledge about F-G.

What Can Be Learned from 50 Samples?

Greater knowledge about F-G can be obtained by analyzing more samples. Assume another 49 samples are taken and the value f-g for each sample is measured. The first thing we would notice is that f-g varies in an unpredictable fashion from sample to sample. This particular form of random behavior is one of the most important phenomena in all of statistics. It is called *sampling variability* or *sampling variation*.

Sampling variation is important because it is responsible for the uncertainty in statistical conclusions. Greater sampling variability translates to greater uncertainty. The greater the fluctuations in f-g from one sample to the next , the greater will be the uncertainty about the value of F-G.

Regrettably, this important phenomenon, sampling variability, is unfamiliar to many people who analyze data. This is understandable because real world problems do not offer the luxury of looking at more than one independent sample. The box-of-beads provides this opportunity.

As will be seen, by conducting 50 sampling experiments, the random variation in f-g becomes obvious. This is quite different from the situation faced by rule researchers. They typically have a single historical sample of the market, and if all that data is used to test a rule, only one observed value of the performance statistic is obtained. This provides no opportunity to see how the rule's performance would vary if it were tested in numerous independent samples. The bottom line is this: Sampling variation is an important fact that may not be obvious to data analysts unfamiliar with statistical analysis. This is a huge blind spot!

Sampling variation can be seen in a table of the 50 f-g values. See Table 4.1.

TABLE 4.1 Fraction of Grey Beads in 50 Different Samples

Sample Number	f-g	Sample Number	f-g	Sample Number	f-g
1	0.65	18	0.60	35	0.60
2	0.60	19	0.40	36	0.55
3	0.45	20	0.60	37	0.50
4	0.60	21	0.45	38	0.50
5	0.45	22	0.55	39	0.45
6	0.45	23	0.45	40	0.50
7	0.55	24	0.50	41	0.55
8	0.40	25	0.70	42	0.45
9	0.55	26	0.55	43	0.55
10	0.40	27	0.60	44	0.60
11	0.55	28	0.70	45	0.60
12	0.50	29	0.50	46	0.60
13	0.35	30	0.70	47	0.65
14	0.40	31	0.50	48	0.50
15	0.65	32	0.90	49	0.50
16	0.65	33	0.40	50	0.65
17	0.60	34	0.75		

Not surprisingly, the value of f-g, a random variable, fluctuates from sample to sample. This is an example of chance in operation. However, f-g's value is not entirely determined by chance. Its value is also strongly influenced by the value of F-G, the proportion of grey beads in the entire box.

Thus, it can be said that each observed value of f-g is the result of two influences; the underlying phenomenon, F-G, and randomness caused by sampling. F-G acts like a center of gravity, always keeping f-g within a certain range. In some samples, randomness nudged the value f-g above F-G. In other samples, randomness nudged f-g below F-G. From sample to sample the value of f-g oscillates randomly around this center of gravity. This is sampling variability.

Another important aspect of this situation is that the number of observations impacts our level of uncertainty about the value of F-G. The greater the number of observations comprising the sample, the more precisely the value f-g will reflect the value F-G. Suppose that, instead of taking a 20-bead sample, we took a 200-bead sample. The random variation in f-g around F-G would be smaller. In fact, it would be about one third of what it is for a 20-bead sample. This is a very important point: the larger the sample size, the smaller the impact of randomness. Two hundred beads dampen the ability of any single bead to push f-g away from F-G. In a one-bead sample, the single selected bead will produce an f-g of either 0 or 1.0. In a two-bead sample, f-g can be 0, 0.50 or 1.0. In a three-bead sample, f-g can be 0, 0.33, 0.66, or 1.0. Thus, the larger the sample size, the smaller will be the magnitude of random variation in f-g. Large samples give F-G, the truth that we wish to know, the ability to reveal itself. This is an effect of the *Law of Large Numbers*: Large samples reduce the role of chance. In other words, it can be stated that the larger the size of a sample, the more tightly the values of f-g will cluster about the value F-G. This is one of the most important principles in statistics.

We have learned an important concept of statistics that can be stated as follows: even though the value of F-G does not change over the course of the 50 sampling experiments, the value f-g can vary considerably from sample to sample. The phenomenon is called *sampling variability*. It is present whenever a random sample of observations is used to form a conclusion about a larger universe (i.e., population). Sampling variability is the source of the uncertainty that is addressed by statistical inference.[12]

Frequency Distribution of the Sample Statistic f-g

In the box-of-beads experiment, the random variable f-g can assume 21 possible values ranging from zero, when there are no grey beads in a sample, to 1.0, when the sample is composed entirely of grey beads. The 50 observed values of f-g are shown in Table 4.1. A casual examination shows that some values of f-g occurred with greater frequency than others. Values in the range of 0.40 to 0.65 occurred quite often, whereas values less than 0.40 and greater than 0.65 almost never occurred. In the 50 samples taken, f-g assumed the value 0.50 nine times, 0.55 eight times, and 0.60 ten times. Note that the value 0.65, which characterized the first sample, appeared only five times. Therefore, that value was not among the most common values, but it was not particularly unusual either.

A plot called a frequency distribution or frequency histogram communicates this information more forcefully than words or a table. It displays how frequently each of f-g's possible values occurred over the 50 sampling experiments. The term *distribution* is apt, because it depicts how a set of observations on a random variable are distributed or sprinkled across the variable's range of possible values.

Arrayed along the horizontal axis of the frequency distribution is a sequence of intervals, or bins, one for each possible value of f-g. The height of the vertical bar over each interval represents the number of times that a specific value of f-g occurred. Figure 4.6 shows the frequency distribution of the 50 f-g values.

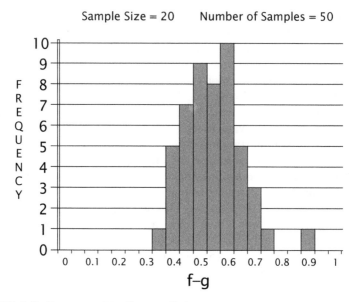

FIGURE 4.6   Frequency Distribution: (f-g).

The Equivalence of Frequency and Area

Frequency distributions depict an important relationship between the frequency of a particular value or set of values and the area covered by the bars representing that value or set of values. This concept can be understood if we first consider the entire distribution. In Figure 4.6, all the grey bars comprising the frequency distribution represent all 50 of the observed values of f-g. Thus, the area covered by all the vertical bars corresponds to 50 observations. You can verify this by summing the counts associated with all of the vertical bars. They will add up to 50.

The same principle applies to any fraction of the distribution's area. If you were to determine the fraction of the frequency distribution's total area covered by the area of a single bar, you would find that the bar's fractional area is equal to the fraction of the total observations represented by that bar. For example, the vertical bar associated with the f-g value 0.60 shows a count (frequency) of 10. Thus, the bar represents 20 percent (10/50) of the observed values. If you were to then measure the area covered by this vertical bar, you would find that its area represents 0.20 of the total area covered by the entire distribution. This idea is illustrated in Figure 4.7.

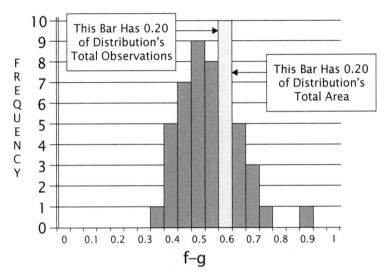

FIGURE 4.7 Proportion of observations equals proportion of distribution's total area.

Although this idea may seem obvious, even trivial, it is an essential aspect of statistical reasoning. Ultimately, we will use the fractional area of a distribution to measure the probability that the back-test profits of a rule could have occurred by chance under the assumption that the rule has no predictive power. When that probability is small, we are led to the conclusion that the rule does have predictive power.

Relative Frequency Distribution of f-g

The *relative* frequency distribution is similar to the ordinary frequency distribution discussed earlier. The height of a bar in an ordinary frequency distribution represents an absolute number or count of the number of times a particular value of a random variable was observed to occur. In the relative frequency distribution, the height of a bar represents the number of observed occurrences relative to (divided by) the total number of observations comprising the distribution. For example, f-g assumed the value 0.60 on 10 out of 50 observations. Thus the value 0.60 had a relative frequency of 10/50 or 0.20. The distribution's bar for the value 0.60 would be drawn to a height of 0.20 along the vertical scale. This is illustrated in Figure 4.8.

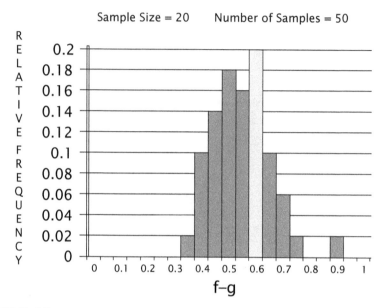

FIGURE 4.8 Relative frequency distribution: (f-g).

The equivalence between frequency and area that applies to ordinary frequency distributions also applies to relative frequency distributions. The relative frequency of all bars is equal (adds up) to 1.0. This simply says that a random variable always (1.0 of the time) assumes a value somewhere in the range encompassed by all bars. If you were to add up the relative frequencies associated with all of the individual bars comprising the distribution, they would sum to 1.0 (100 percent of the observations). This has to be so because each bar represents the fraction of observations falling into that interval, and, by definition, all the bars together represent all (1.0) the observations.

The relative frequency of any single bar or group of contiguous bars is equal to their proportion of the distribution's total area. Thus the relative frequency of an f-g value of 0.65 and larger is equal to 0.10 + 0.06 + 0.02 + 0.02 = 0.20. This is equivalent to saying that the combined area of the contiguous bars associated with f-g values of 0.65 and larger is 20 percent of the distribution's total area. We will be making statements similar to this when testing claims about TA rules. Based on this, it can be said that the relative frequency of f-g values equal to or greater than 0.65 is 0.20. This is illustrated in Figure 4.9.

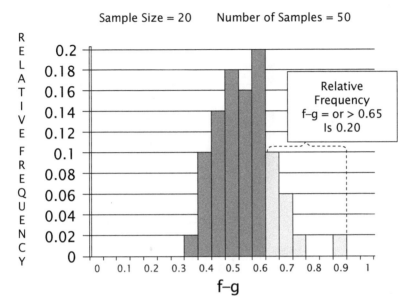

FIGURE 4.9 Relative frequency distribution: (f-g).

What Knowledge Has Been Gained about F-G from Sampling?

So far, sampling has increased our level of knowledge about F-G. In the first 20-bead sample, f-g had a value of 0.65. Based on this observation, two possibilities were conclusively ruled out: that F-G is equal to 0, and that F-G is equal to 1.0.

Not being content with these meager morsels of wisdom, another 49 samples were taken, and the value f-g was observed in each. These 50 values showed that f-g varies randomly from sample to sample. However, despite the unpredictability of any single f-g value, an organized pattern emerged from the randomness that was informative. The f-g values coalesced about a central value forming a well-organized hump. We suspect that this central tendency is related to the value F-G, yet F-G's precise value remains uncertain because of the random variation in f-g. However, in light of the hump's relatively narrow width, it seems reasonable to conjecture that F-G lies somewhere in the range 0.40 to 0.65.

Given that we started with no knowledge of F-G and given that we were precluded from examining the contents of the box in its entirety, a lot was learned from these 50 samples.

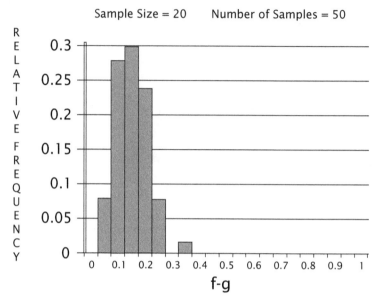

FIGURE 4.10 Relative frequency distribution box 2: (f-g).

A Second Box of Beads

Now we will use sampling to learn the color proportions of a second box of beads. It too is a mixture of grey and white. The objective is the same—to learn the relative proportion of grey beads to the total number of beads in a second box. We call this quantity F-G 2.

As before, we are not allowed to examine the full contents of box 2, but we are permitted to take 50 samples, each composed of 20 beads. The value f-g 2, which refers to the proportion of grey beads in a sample from box 2, is measured in each sample. Again, note the distinction between the terms F-G 2 and f-g 2. F-G 2 refers to the proportion of grey beads in the entire box 2 whereas f-g 2 refers to the proportion of grey beads in an individual sample. F-G 2 is not observable while f-g 2 is.

Figure 4.10 is the relative frequency distribution for 50 values of f-g 2. There are several things to notice:

1. The general shape of the distribution for box 2 is similar to that of box 1, a hump clustering about a central value.

2. The central value of the distribution for box 2 is different than that of box 1. The distribution for box 1 was centered near a value of 0.55. The central value for box 2's distribution is near 0.15. This is clearly

seen in Figure 4.11, which shows both distributions on the same horizontal scale. An arrow has been placed above each distribution at their approximate central values. Thus the arrows represent average values for f-g and f-g 2. From this we can conclude that box 1 has a higher concentration of grey beads than box 2.

3. Even though the samples from box 1 and box 2 were both affected by random variation, the degree of random variation differs. Box 2's results are less variable than those of box 1. This is evidenced by box 2's narrower clustering about its central value. Given the lower degree of sampling variation in box 2, it would be fair to say that we know the value of F-G 2 with greater certainty than we know F-G.

What the Box Experiments Taught Us about Statistics

Yogi Berra, former manager of the New York Yankees, said you can observe a lot just by looking. If he were a statistician, he might have said that you can learn a lot just by sampling. Even though a sample is only a portion of a larger universe (population), it can teach us a lot about that pop-

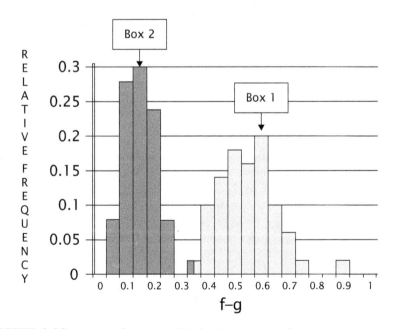

FIGURE 4.11 Relative frequency distributions compared.

ulation. However, there are limits to what a sample can tell us, limits imposed by randomness.

A fundamental task of statistics is to quantify the uncertainty due to sampling variability. This makes it possible to quantify the reliability of statements of knowledge based on samples. Without such quantification, such statements are of limited value. Statistics cannot eliminate uncertainty, but it can inform us about it, and in so doing, it tempers assessments of how much we know or how accurately we know it. Thus, statistical analysis is a powerful antidote to the tendency to be overconfident.

STATISTICAL THEORY

The box-of-beads experiments touched on many of the key ideas of statistical inference. We will now mix in some theory to extend those ideas to the evaluation of TA rules.

The Six Elements of a Statistical Inference Problem

Evaluating a claim that a TA rule has predictive power, that a new vaccine can prevent illness, or any other claim of knowledge are examples of a statistical inference problem. Generally, such problems can be reduced to six key elements: (1) a population, (2) a sample consisting of a set of observations randomly selected from the population, (3) a population parameter, (4) a sample statistic, (5) an inference, and (6) a statement about the reliability of the inference. Each of these elements will be discussed as they relate to the box-of-beads experiments and then to the evaluation of TA rules.

The Population.   A population consists of all possible observations of a random variable. It is a large—perhaps infinitely large—but a well-defined universe of observations. In the typical statistical inference problem, we want to learn some fact about the population, but it is either impractical or impossible to observe the population in its entirety. In the box-of-beads experiments, the population consisted of the set of beads filling a box. The color was the random variable. With respect to testing a TA rule, the population consists of all conceivable daily returns[13] that would be earned by the rule's signal over the *immediate practical future*.

To what does the term *immediate practical future* refer? It would be unreasonable to assume that the dynamics of financial markets are stationary, and so it would be unreasonable to expect that the profitability of a rule will endure in perpetuity. For this reason, the population with respect to TA rules cannot refer to returns occurring over an infinite future.

A more reasonable notion is what I refer to as the *immediate practical future*. The immediate practical future refers to a finite future time period, over which it would be reasonable to expect a useful rule's profitability to persist, even though markets are nonstationary. Any endeavor to find predictive patterns must make some assumption about the continuity of predictive power. In other words, unless one is willing to assume some persistence in predictive power, all forms of TA are pointless. The assumption being made here is that a rule will continue to work long enough to compensate the researcher for the effort of discovering it. This is consistent with the position taken by Grossman and Stiglitz in "On the impossibility of informationally efficient markets."[14] It is also consistent with the idea that profitable rules signal opportunities to earn a risk premium,[15] a topic discussed in Chapter 7.

Therefore, the immediate practical future refers to all possible random realizations of market behavior over a finite future. It is as if there were an infinite number of parallel universes, where all universes are an exact duplicate except for the random component of the market's behavior. In each realization, or universe, the pattern that accounts for the rule's profitability is the same, but the random component of the market is different. This idea is illustrated in Figure 4.12.

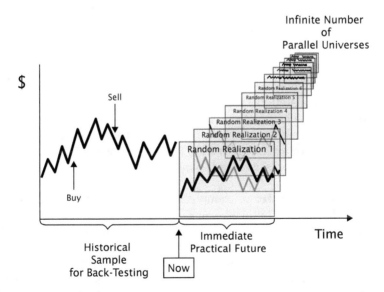

FIGURE 4.12 Different realizations of randomness in an infinitude of parallel universes.

The Sample.   The sample is a subset of the population that is available for observation. In the box-of-beads case, we were able to observe 50 independent samples. In the case of a TA rule, we typically observe a single sample of the rule's performance by back testing it over a segment of market history. This sample is composed of a sequence of daily returns generated by the rule's signals. The sequence of returns is reduced to a single number, a sample performance statistic.

The Population Parameter.   The population parameter is a fact or characteristic about the population that we would like to know. It is typically numerical, but it need not be.

Unfortunately, the population parameter is unknown because the entire population cannot be observed. The essence of statistical inference is the attempt to increase our knowledge about a population parameter, despite the impossibility of observing the population in its entirety. In the box-of-beads case, the population parameter of interest was the fraction of grey beads in the box (i.e., F-G, and F-G 2). In the case of a TA rule, the population parameter is the rule's expected performance over the immediate practical future. Performance can be defined in many ways. Some common measures include average rate of return, Sharpe ratio, profit factor, and so forth. In this book, our measure of performance is the annualized average daily return on detrended market (zero-centered) data.

In many statistical problems, it is safe to assume the population parameter never changes (i.e., it is a constant). In the box-of-beads experiment, the proportion of grey beads remained constant. Statistical problems in which the population parameter remains fixed are said to be stationary.[16] Now imagine a wrinkle on that situation. Suppose, unbeknownst to the experimenter, an invisible demon secretly removes or adds grey beads between samplings. Now the population parameter, F-G, is unstable, or nonstationary."[17]

Earlier in this chapter, I said that it is best to start with an assumption that any rule we test has no predictive power. That is, we assume that it has an expected return equal to zero. Or, to put it in statistical terms, the population parameter is assumed equal to be zero.

The Sample Statistic.   A sample statistic is a measurable attribute of a sample.[18] Its value is known because it has been observed. In this book, the term *sample statistic* is restricted to numerical facts, for example a proportion, a percentage, a standard deviation, an average rate of return, a trimmed average,[19] a Sharpe ratio, and so forth. In a statistical inference problem, the *sample statistic* typically refers to the same measurable attribute as the population parameter. In the case of the box-of-beads, the sample statistic, f-g, referred to the fraction of grey beads in an individual sample. The population parameter, F-G, referred to the fraction of grey beads in the whole box.

The bottom line is this: A sample statistic is important because it sheds light on the population parameter. Beyond this, it is a fact of no particular importance. Some market historians seem to be unmindful of this essential truth.

If a back test should result in a positive rate of return, it raises the following question: Is the positive performance a random deviation above zero due to sampling variability or is it attributable to the rule's predictive power (i.e., the rule has an expected return greater than zero)? Answering this question requires the tools of statistical inference. This is illustrated in Figure 4.13.

An Inference. Statistical inference is the inductive leap from the observed value of a sample statistic, which is known with certainty but which is true only for a specific sample of data, to the value of a population parameter, which is uncertain but which is deemed to hold true for a wide, perhaps infinite, number of unobserved cases.

When a rule's positive past performance can reasonably be attributed to sampling variability, the reasonable inference is that its expected return over the immediate practical future is zero or less. However, if the positive performance is too high to be reasonably attributed to sampling variability (luck), the reasonable inference would be that the rule possesses genuine predictive power and has a positive expected return over the immediate practical future.

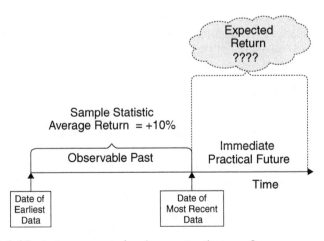

FIGURE 4.13 Is the parameter's value greater than zero?

A Statement about the Reliability of the Inference. Because a sample can not represent the population perfectly, inferences based on a sample statistic are subject to uncertainty. In other words, it is possible that the inference is wrong. We have already seen how sample statistics vary randomly around the true value of the population parameter value. The science of statistics goes beyond simply admitting that its inferences are uncertain. It quantifies their reliability. This makes statistical conclusions considerably more useful than those reached by informal methods that do not provide such information.

The inference can be wrong in two ways. One error is concluding the rule has predictive power when it does not. This is a case of good luck shining on a worthless rule. This type of mistake translates into taking market risks that will not be compensated. The other error is concluding the rule has no predictive ability when it really does. This mistake results in missed trading opportunities.

DESCRIPTIVE STATISTICS

The field of statistics subdivides into two main areas: descriptive and inferential. The most important for TA is statistical inference, which was discussed in the preceding sections. However, before making an inference, we must describe the sample data in a succinct and informative way. The tools of descriptive statistics serve this purpose.

The goal of descriptive statistics is data reduction, that is, reducing a large set of observed values to a smaller, more intelligible set of numbers and plots. Descriptive statistics tell the story of the forest rather than the individual trees. Three descriptive tools will be important for the work that lies ahead: (1) frequency distributions, (2) measures of central tendency, and (3) measures of variation.

Frequency Distributions

Frequency distributions have already been discussed in connection with the box-of-beads experiments. They were used to reduce a set of 50 observations on random variable f-g into an informative plot.

With only 50 observations, one might be able to form an overall impression of the data simply by looking at a table of numbers. Then again, if the number of observations were 500 or 5,000, a table would not be as informative as a frequency distribution.

Plotting a frequency distribution is usually the first step in analyzing a set of data. It provides a quick visual impression of two key features of a sample of observations: the central tendency (e.g., average value) and the degree of dispersion or variation about the central value. For example, Figure 4.11 showed that the two boxes of beads had different central values and different degrees of dispersion.

A visual impression of a sample is useful, but quantification improves matters. For our purposes, we will need to quantify two features of the frequency distribution: its central tendency and its variability or dispersion about its central tendency.

Statistics That Measure Central Tendency

There are many measures of central tendency. Three of the most common are the average, the median, and the mode. The average, also known as the arithmetic mean, is used in many TA applications and is the summary statistic used in this book. It is the sum of the observed values divided by the number of observations.

It is important to distinguish the population mean from the sample mean. The sample mean is a statistic, a known quantity that is computed from observed values and varies randomly from one sample to the next. The population mean, in contrast, is unknown and does not vary in stationary problems. The formula for the mean of a sample is given in Figure 4.14 in two forms.

Sample Mean for Variable X

$$\overline{X} = \frac{X_1 + X_2 + X_3 + \ldots X_n}{n}$$

$$\overline{X} = \frac{\sum_{i=1}^{n} x_i}{n}$$

Where x_i is an individual observation on variable X

FIGURE 4.14 Sample mean for variable X.

Statistical Measures of Variability (Dispersion)

Measures of variability describe the degree to which the observations in a sample are dispersed about their central tendency. In other words, measures of variability quantify the width of a frequency distribution.

Among the widely used measures of dispersion are the variance, the mean absolute deviation, and the standard deviation. They are important in the traditional approach to statistics (i.e., classical statistics). The standard deviation is the square root of the average squared deviation of each observation from the mean of the data. The formula for the standard deviation of a sample is shown in Figure 4.15.

An intuitive notion of dispersion is best conveyed with pictures. Figure 4.16 shows a number of idealized frequency distributions with differing degrees of variation and different central tendencies. They are idealized in the sense that the stair-step look that characterizes real frequency distributions has been smoothed away. The key point of Figure 4.16 is that central tendency and variation (dispersion) are independent characteristics of a frequency distribution. In row 1 of Figure 4.16, the four distributions have the same degree of variation but different central values. In row 2 the distributions have the same central value but different degrees of variation. In row 3 all distributions have different central values and different degrees of variation.

Standard Deviation of a Sample of Observations

$$ S = \sqrt{\frac{\sum (X_i - \bar{X})^2}{n}} $$

Where:

X_i Is an individual observation on variable X

$\bar{X}$ Is the sample mean on variable X

n Is number of observations in the sample

FIGURE 4.15 Standard deviation of a sample of observations.

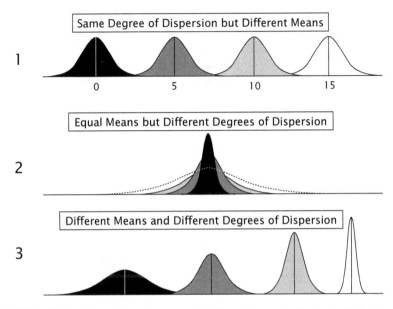

FIGURE 4.16 Central tendency and dispersion are distinct attributes of a distribution.

PROBABILITY

The notion of probability is important in statistics because it is used to quantify uncertainty. A conclusion reached via statistical inference is uncertain; that is, there is a chance of error. Thus, an inference about the value of a population parameter has some chance of being wrong. This chance is given in terms of a probability.

We routinely use informal notions of probability to form expectations and make choices. Is the person I find so wonderful now, likely to remain so after marriage? What is the chance I will find gold if I dig in a certain spot? Is it probable I will feel fulfilled pursing a career in law? Should I buy that stock, and if I do, how much profit am I likely to make?

The informal usage of probability is connected to a cluster of interchangeable terms illustrated in Figure 4.17.

For our purposes, something more definitive is required. The definition of probability that makes the most sense for the work that lies ahead is based on the notion of relative frequency. The relative frequency of an event is the number of times the event actually occurred divided by the total number of opportunities on which the event could have occurred. Relative frequency is given as a fraction between 0 and 1. It could rain every

FIGURE 4.17 Common notions of probability.

day, but in the month of April the relative frequency of rain has actually been 0.366 (11 out of 30 days). If rain never occurred, then its relative frequency would be 0. If rain occurred every day, its relative frequency is 1.0. Thus, the relative frequency of an outcome is equal to:

$$\frac{\text{Number of occurrences of an event}}{\text{Number of possible opportunities for the event to occur}}$$

In the box-of-beads experiment the value of f-g was measured 50 times. This was the maximum number of opportunities for any specific f-g value to occur. In fact, the value f-g = 0.65 occurred on 5 out of 50. Therefore, it had a relative frequency of 5/50 or 0.10.

Probability is the relative frequency of an event over the long run—the very long run. That is to say, the probability of an event is its relative frequency of occurrence given an infinite number of opportunities for its occurrence. Probability is stated as a number that lies in the range of 0 to 1 inclusive. A probability value of 0 means the event never occurs, whereas a value of 1.0 means it always occurs.

Probability is a theoretical notion because it is never possible to observe an infinite number of anything. For practical purposes, however, when the number of observations becomes very large, relative frequency approaches theoretical probability.

The Law of Large Numbers

The tendency of relative frequencies to converge to theoretical probabilities, as the number of observations becomes large, is called the Law of Large Numbers.[20] The operation of the Law of Large Numbers can be illustrated with coin tossing. The possible outcomes (events) are heads or tails and the probability of heads is known to be 0.50. The Law tells us that the relative frequency of heads will *converge* to its theoretical value, 0.5, as the number of coin tosses becomes large. However, even for a large number of tosses, a departure from 0.50 can still occur, though the likely size of the departures decreases as the number of tosses increases. For small samples, however, The Law of Large Numbers warns us that the relative frequency of heads can differ substantially from 0.50. When the number of tosses is only three, a value of 1.0 can easily occur—three heads in three tosses.

Figure 4.18 shows the fraction of heads in a coin-toss experiment as the number of tosses grows from one to one thousand. When the number of tosses (observations) is less than 10, the fraction of heads experienced two large deviations from 0.50. At 3 tosses the fraction of heads reached 0.66 (2 out of 3). At 8, the fraction was 0.375 (3 out of 8). However, as the number of tosses increased the random variable, fraction heads, experienced progressively smaller deviations from the expected value of 0.50. This is exactly what the Law of Large Numbers predicts.

Now imagine a naive coin flipper. Upon observing five heads in five tosses, he loudly proclaims, "I've found the holy grail of coins. It always comes up heads." The Law of Large Numbers says that the poor fellow's optimism is unwarranted. This is also likely to be true for the TA researcher who finds a rule with five historical signals, all of which were correct. Optimism is most likely unwarranted. Chapter 6 will show that if this rule was selected because it was the best performing rule out of a large universe of back-tested rules, that is to say, it was discovered by data mining, there would be even less reason to be optimistic about its future performance.

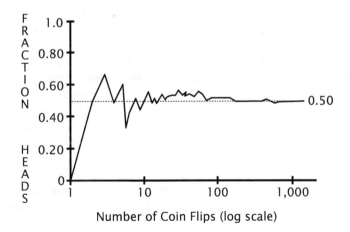

FIGURE 4.18 Law of Large Numbers.

Theoretical versus Empirical Probability

There are two kinds of probabilities: theoretical and empirical. "Theoretical probabilities can be determined with a good degree of confidence purely on logical grounds. They are derived independent of prior experience, most often based on arguments of symmetry."[21] In other words, they can be deduced without any reference to the world of experience. The probability of a head in a coin toss is a theoretical probability. There is no need to toss it ten thousand times to predict that over the long run the probability of heads is 0.50. Simply the fact that the coin is fair, that it has two faces, and that it is unlikely to land on its edge is sufficient grounds for suspecting heads and tails are equally likely. The probabilities for being dealt a royal flush in poker, the occurrence of a six in a dice roll, and the chance of winning Lotto are also theoretical because each can be determined by a logical analysis of the situation.

Empirical probabilities are based on observed frequencies. Technical analysis is concerned with this type of probability. The chance of new snowfall on Mount Hood during the month of July or the likelihood of a rise in the stock market following a 2 percent drop in interest rates are examples of empirical probabilities. They can only be determined by observing numerous past instances of the specified conditions (Mount Hood in July), and determining the relative frequency of the event (new snow).

When determining empirical probabilities, it is vitally important that each instance be characterized by the same set of conditions. In TA this is a practical impossibility. Each past instance of a 2 percent drop in interest rates is similar with respect to that specific condition, but there are numerous other conditions that may not be the same. For example, the level of interest rates prior to the 2 percent drop may differ from observation to observation. In one instance, interest rates were at 5 percent prior to the drop whereas in another they were 10 percent. Of course, the level of interest rates could be added to the set of conditions that define each instance, but that has the downside of reducing the number of comparable instances. Moreover, there will always be other conditions that are not part of the specified condition set. The inability to control all potentially relevant variables is an unfortunate fact of life in nonexperimental/observational sciences. In contrast, the experimental scientist enjoys the supreme advantage of being able to hold constant all or nearly all relevant variables except the one being investigated. Imagine being able to do that in TA! I am told this is how it is in the afterlife.

PROBABILITY DISTRIBUTIONS OF RANDOM VARIABLES

A probability distribution shows how often we can expect the different possible values of a random variable to occur (i.e., their relative frequencies). The probability distribution of a random variable is a relative frequency distribution built from an infinite number of observations.

The concept of a probability distribution can be understood by thinking of a sequence of relative frequency distributions, each built from increasing numbers of observations and progressively narrower bins or intervals. Gradually, the relative frequency distribution becomes a probability distribution. With increasing numbers of observations, more discrete intervals of decreasing width can be created.[22] As the number of observations approaches infinity, the number of intervals approaches infinity and their widths shrink to zero. Thus, the relative frequency distribution morphs into what is called a probability distribution, more technically referred to as a probability density function.[23]

Figures 4.19 though 4.23 show how a relative frequency distribution evolves into a probability density function as the number of intervals is increased and their interval widths are decreased. The height of each bar represents the relative frequency of events falling within the bar's interval. The figures presume that the random variable is a measure of price change.

This succession of diagrams shows that a probability density function is, in effect, a relative frequency distribution composed of an infinite number of observations whose intervals are infinitely narrow. Here is where things get a bit strange. If the intervals of a probability distribution have

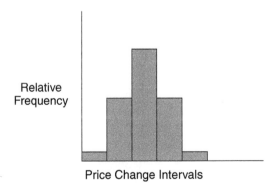

Price Change Intervals

FIGURE 4.19 Relative frequency distribution based on five intervals.

FIGURE 4.20 Relative frequency distribution based on seven intervals.

FIGURE 4.21 Relative frequency distribution based on fifteen intervals.

FIGURE 4.22 Relative frequency distribution based on twenty nine intervals.

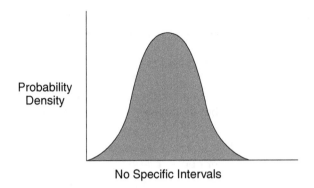

FIGURE 4.23 Probability density function.

zero width, then there are zero observations per interval. This seems to make no sense! However, it is quite common for mathematical concepts to be at odds with common sense. In geometry, a point has location but occupies no space (i.e., length, width, and breadth equal zero), a line has length but zero width, and so forth.

The fact that an interval has zero observations has a strange implication—the probability that any single value of a continuous random variable will ever occur is equal to zero. For this reason, it only makes sense to speak of the probability that a random variable will assume a value within a specified range of values. In other words, it makes sense to speak of the probability that a random variable will assume a value between specified minimum and maximum values. It also makes sense to speak of the probability that a random variable will assume a value that is equal to or greater than some specified value or less than or equal to a specified value. For example, we can speak of the probability that a value of 3.0 or greater will occur. However, it would make no sense to speak of the probability of a value of exactly 3.0.[24]

This somewhat counterintuitive idea fits nicely with rule testing. When testing the statistical significance of a rule's past rate of return, we will be concerned with the probability that a rate of return of +10 percent or higher could have occurred by chance under the condition that the rule has no predictive power. Probability density functions can provide such information.

RELATIONSHIP BETWEEN PROBABILITY AND FRACTIONAL AREA OF THE PROBABILITY DISTRIBUTION

Let's recap what has been established up to this point:

1. The probability of an event is its relative frequency of occurrence given an infinite number of instances in which the event could have occurred.

2. A probability density function is a relative frequency distribution built from an infinite number of observations and intervals of zero width.

3. The relative frequency of a random variable taking on a value within a given interval is equal to the fractional area of the frequency distribution sitting on top of that interval. See Figure 4.24.

We are now ready to take the final step in this sequence of thinking. It is analogous to point 3 in the preceding list, except that the term *relative frequency* distribution is replaced with *probability density function*. The probability that a continuous random variable will assume a value within a specified range is equal to the fraction of the probability density func-

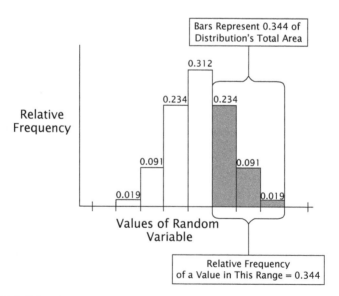

FIGURE 4.24 The correspondence of relative frequency and fractional area of a distribution.

tion encompassed by (sitting above) that range. This concept is illustrated in Figure 4.25. It shows the probability that X, a continuous random variable, will assume a value within the range A-B is equal to 0.70.

In many instances, the interval in question refers to the extreme or tail of the distribution. For example, Figure 4.26 shows the probability that random variable X will assume a value of B or greater. The probability is 0.15.

The probability distribution of a random variable is a very useful concept. Even though an individual future observation on random variable X is not predictable, a large number of observations form a highly predictable pattern. This pattern is the random variable's probability density function.

Now, here is where these ideas start to come together for us. Chapter 5 will show that when a hypothesis is represented by the probability distribution of a random variable we will be able to use an observed value of the random variable to test the veracity of the hypothesis. This will enable us to conclude if a rule's back-tested profitability was due to luck or genuine predictive power.

The probability distribution used for this purpose is a specific type. It is called a sampling distribution—perhaps the most important one in all of statistics and certainly the most important for TA analysts.

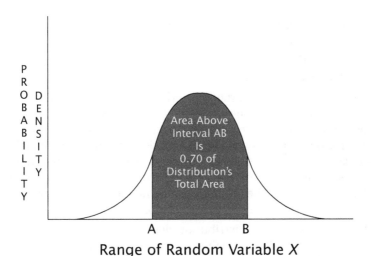

FIGURE 4.25 The probability random variable X will assume a value between A and B equals the fraction of the distribution's total area above the interval A,B.

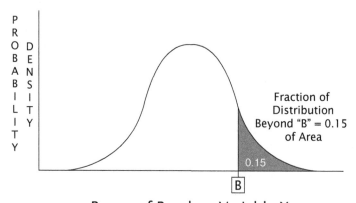

Range of Random Variable X

FIGURE 4.26 The probability random variable X will assume a value equal to or greater than B equals the fraction of the distribution's total area equal to or greater than B.

THE SAMPLING DISTRIBUTION: THE MOST IMPORTANT CONCEPT IN STATISTICAL INFERENCE

To recap:

1. A random variable is the outcome of a probability experiment.

2. Taking a sample of a given number of observations from a population and computing the value of a statistic such as *the sample's* mean is a probability experiment.[25]

3. A sample statistic[26] is a random variable in the sense that it fluctuates unpredictably from one sample of observations to the next. The sample statistic fluctuates randomly because chance determines which specific observations wind up in a particular sample, and it is that particular set of observations that determines the value of the statistic for that sample. In the box-of-beads experiment, the value f-g varied randomly from one 20-bead sample to the next because the particular set of beads that wound up in a given sample was determined by chance.

4. A relative frequency distribution describes how often the possible values of a random variable occur over a very large number of observations.

We are now ready to meet the sampling distribution, the most important concept in statistical inference.

The Sampling Distribution Defined

The sampling distribution is the probability distribution of a random variable, and that random variable happens to be a sample statistic. In other words, the sampling distribution shows the various possible values the sample statistic can assume, and their associated probabilities.[27] For example, "the sampling distribution of the sample mean refers to the probability distribution of all possible means for all possible random samples of a given size from some population."[28] Here, the sample statistic is the *mean*.

The sample statistic in the box-of-beads experiments was f-g. Its random variation across 50 samples, each comprised of 20 beads, was shown by the relative frequency distribution in Figure 4.8. If, instead of 50 values we were to take all possible 20-bead samples—a very large number—this theoretical distribution would be f-g's sampling distribution.

In rule back testing, the sample statistic is a measure of performance observed in a back test. In this book that sample statistic will be the rule's average rate of return. A back test typically produces a single observed value for the performance statistic because we have a single sample of market history. Now imagine what it would be like if we were able to test a rule in an infinite number of independent samples of market history. This would provide an infinite number of values for the performance statistic. If this set of data were then converted into a relative frequency distribution, it would be the statistic's exact sampling distribution. This is obviously not possible because we do not have an infinite number of independent samples of historical data. However, statisticians have developed several methods to get something that approximates the exact sampling distribution closely enough to be useful, despite the fact that we have only one sample of historical data and one value of the sample statistic. Two of these methods will be discussed later in this chapter.

The Sampling Distribution Quantifies Uncertainty

The sampling distribution of a statistic is the foundation of statistical inference because it quantifies the uncertainty caused by the randomness of sampling (sampling variability).

As stated above, the sampling distribution displays the relative frequencies of a statistic if it were to be measured in an infinite number of random samples of the same size, drawn from the same parent population. The box-of-beads experiments showed that the value of a statistic, f-g fluctuated randomly from sample to sample. Figure 4.8 showed that these values tend to fall into a well-behaved pattern, not a random chaotic mess. The fact that the pattern of random variation is well behaved is what makes statistical inference possible.

It may seem ironic that a sample statistic would show such a regular pattern given that it is, in fact, a random variable. Thankfully for statisticians, it does. Figure 4.8 revealed a central value (i.e., the mean of the sampling distribution) of approximately 0.55. It also showed a well-defined pattern of dispersion about this central value. This pattern allowed us to conclude, with a fair degree of assurance, that the value of the population parameter F-G was contained within the range 0.40 to 0.65. It also allowed us to conclude, although with somewhat diminished confidence, that F-G was more accurately pinned in the range between 0.50 and 0.60. It was the degree of dispersion in f-g's sampling distribution that permitted these statements to be made about the value of the population parameter F-G.

The dispersion of the sampling distribution quantifies the uncertainty of our knowledge about the population parameter F-G. The distribution's central tendency conveys information about the most likely value of F-G, approximately 0.55. Knowing this is nice, but it is not enough. It is also important to know about the reliability of the value 0.55. In other words, how accurately does the sampling distribution's central tendency of 0.55 portray the true value of F-G?

The reliability (degree of certainty) is conveyed by the dispersion of the sampling distribution. The greater the distribution's dispersion around its central value, 0.55, the less certain we can be that 0.55 accurately informs us about the true value F-G, the proportion of grey beads in the entire box.

To illustrate this point consider the two following sampling distributions. Both have central values of 0.55 but their dispersions are quite different. The first shown in Figure 4.27 is a narrow dispersion thereby delivering a strong impression that F-G is in the vicinity of 0.55. The distribution in Figure 4.28 is wider thus conveying a less certain message about F-G value. It is saying that the true value F-G may be considerably different from the central value of the sampling distribution.

In summary, certainty is directly related to the dispersion of the sampling distribution. And the certainty of a conclusion about a population parameter depends upon the width of the statistic's sampling distribution—greater width means greater uncertainty.

Suppose it is hypothesized that a rule's expected return is equal to zero. Also suppose the rule's back-tested return turns out to be greater than zero. Is the positive return sufficient evidence to conclude that the hypothesized value of zero is false? The answer will depend on how far above zero the back-tested return is relative to the width of the sampling distribution. If the relative deviation is large the hypothesis can be rejected. Quantifying the relative deviation and the reasoning behind a

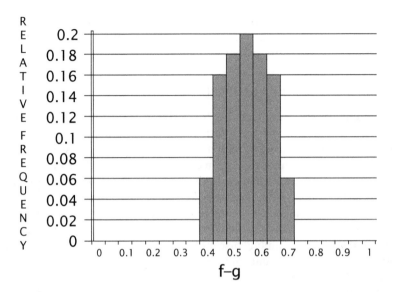

FIGURE 4.27 Relative frequency distribution: f-g. (sample size = 20, number of samples=50).

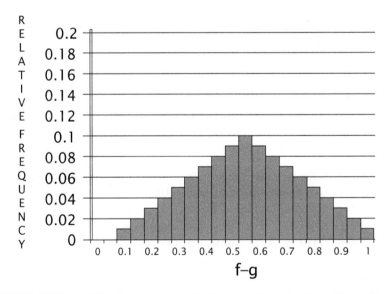

FIGURE 4.28 Relative frequency distribution: f-g. (sample size = 20, number of samples=50).

decision to reject or not to reject the hypothesis will be treated in Chapter 5. The important point for now is that the width of the sampling distribution is critically important in answering this question.

Sampling Distribution of Trading Performance

A sampling distribution can be formed for any statistic: the average (mean), the median, the standard deviation, and many other statistics used in statistical inference.[29] Each has its own sampling distribution.

This discussion here is confined to the sampling distribution of the mean because the performance statistic used to evaluate TA rules in this book is a rule's mean rate of return. However, there are many other performance measures that might be used: the Sharpe ratio,[30] the profit factor,[31] the mean return divided by the Ulcer Index,[32] and so forth. It should be pointed out that the sampling distributions of these alternative performance statistics would be different from the sampling distribution of the mean.

It should also be pointed out that the methods used in this book to generate the sampling distribution of the mean may be of limited value in generating sampling distributions for performance statistics with elongated right tails. This can occur with performance statistics that involve ratios such as the Sharpe ratio, the mean-return-to-Ulcer-Index ratio, and the profit factor. However, this problem can be mitigated by taking the log of the ratio to shorten the right tail.

The Three Distributions of Statistical Inference

Statistical inference actually involves three different distributions, one of which is the sampling distribution. They are easy to confuse. This section is intended to clarify their differences. In the context of rule testing the three distributions are:

1. *Data distribution of the population*: an infinite sized distribution comprised of all possible daily rule returns, which we assume extends into the immediate practical future.

2. *Data distribution of the sample*: a distribution comprised of a finite number (N) of daily rule returns from the past.

3. *Sampling distribution*: an infinite-sized distribution of the sample statistic—in this case it is the rule's mean return. It represents the mean returns of the rule, if it were to be tested in an infinite number of random samples of size N extracted from the population.

There are two points to emphasize. First, the observations comprising the data distribution of the population and the data distribution of the sample (1 and 2 in the preceding list) are comprised of single-day rule returns. In contrast, the observations comprising the sampling distribution are sample statistics in which each observation represents the mean return of the rule computed over a sample of days. Second, both the population distribution and the sampling distribution are theoretical in the sense that they refer to an infinite number of possible observations. In contrast, the data distribution of the sample is composed of a finite number of observations from a historical back test.

The relationship between these three distributions can be visualized by imagining an experiment similar to the box-of-beads experiment. In this case, however, you are to imagine a population distribution of daily rule returns that is infinite in size. Imagine taking 50 independent samples from the population, where each sample is comprised of a substantial number of daily rule returns. Next, determine the mean return for each sample and then plot the sampling distribution of the 50 means. This is illustrated in Figure 4.29.[33]

The Real World: The Problem of One Sample

The preceding discussion was theoretical in the sense that we imagined what it would be like if we could observe 50 independent samples from a

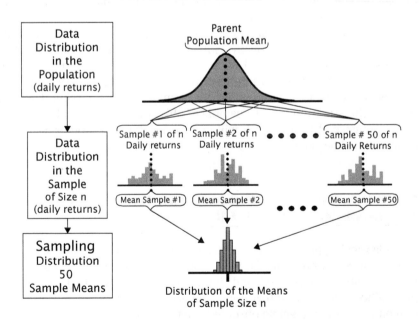

FIGURE 4.29 The three distributions of statistical inference.

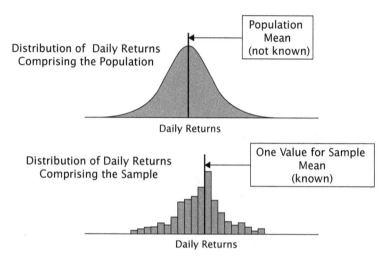

FIGURE 4.30 The real world: one sample and one value of the test statistic.

parent population. In most real-world statistical problems, there is only one sample of observations and thus one value for the sample mean. The problem is that with only one sample mean available we have no notion of the sample statistic's variability. The problem of one sample and one mean is illustrated in Figure 4.30.

Fortunately, we can learn a lot about a sample statistic's variability and its sampling distribution by looking at the single available sample. The discovery of how to do this, early in the twentieth century, is what made the field of statistical inference possible. In fact, statisticians have developed two distinct approaches for estimating the sampling distribution of a statistic from a single sample of observations: classical and computer intensive. Although both will be discussed, the computer-intensive approach will be used for the rule tests performed in Part Two.

DERIVING THE SAMPLING DISTRIBUTION: THE CLASSICAL APPROACH

This classical approach is the one most often taught in basic statistics courses. It is attributed to the two fathers of mathematical statistics, Sir Ronald Fisher (1890–1962) and Jerzy Neyman (1894–1981). It utilizes probability theory and integral calculus to derive the sampling distribution on the basis of a single observed sample. It provides estimates of the sampling distribution's dispersion, its mean, and its basic shape (normal).

In other words, it provides everything needed to quantify the reliability of an inference based on a single sample of observations.

The Sampling Distribution of the Sample Mean

Every statistic has its own sampling distribution. This discussion will focus on the sampling distribution of the mean (average), because it is the statistic used in Part Two to evaluate TA rules.

Classical statistical theory tells us several things about the sampling distribution of the mean.

1. The mean of a large sample is a good estimate of the mean of the population distribution from which the sample was obtained. The larger the sample, the more closely the sample mean conforms to the population mean.

2. The dispersion of the sampling distribution depends on the size of the sample. For a given population, the larger the sample, the narrower the sampling distribution.

3. The dispersion of the sampling distribution also depends on the amount of variation within the parent population data. The bigger the variation in the parent population, the wider the sampling distribution.

4. Under the conditions that apply to the evaluation of TA rules, the shape of the sampling distribution of the mean will tend towards the so-called normal or bell shape, with the conformity to the normal shape increasing as the sample size increases. Other sample statistics, such as ratios, can be profoundly nonnormal.

Each of these concepts is now explained.

The Mean of a Large Sample Is a Good Estimate of the Population Mean. This is a manifestation of The Law of Large Numbers, which we met previously in the context of a coin-flipping experiment. To recap, The Law of Large Numbers tells us that the larger the number of observations comprising the sample, the more closely the sample mean will approximate the population mean. There are some qualifying conditions[34] attached to this promise, but they need not concern us here.

The graph of the coin-flipping experiment illustrated the action of the Law of Large Numbers (Figure 4.18). As the number of coin tosses increased, the proportion of heads gradually converged to its theoretically correct value of 0.50. In the early stages of the experiment, when the sample size was small, there were large departures from 0.50. These departures illustrate the large role that chance plays in small samples. In four tosses, though values of 0.75 or 0.25 are not the most probable, they are quite common. However, when the number of coin tosses reaches 60, the probability of 0.75 or 0.25 is less than 1 in 1,000. The important lesson: Increased sample size diminishes the role of chance.

The Dispersion of the Sampling Distribution Depends on the Size of the Sample: the Larger the Sample the Less the Dispersion. Imagine a very large population of observations on some variable whose standard deviation is 100. Usually, we do not know the population standard deviation, but in this case we will assume that we do.

In Figure 4.31, I show the parent population distribution at the bottom. Above it are two sampling distributions for the variable's mean for sample sizes of 10 and 100. Notice that the width of the sampling distribution is cut by approximately one-third each time the sample size is increased by a factor of 10. One of the lessons from classical statistics is that the standard deviation of the sampling distribution of the mean is inversely proportional to the square root of the sample size.[35] Thus, if the sample size is increased by a factor of 10, the width of the sampling distribution is reduced a factor of 3.16, the square root of 10. The parent distrib-

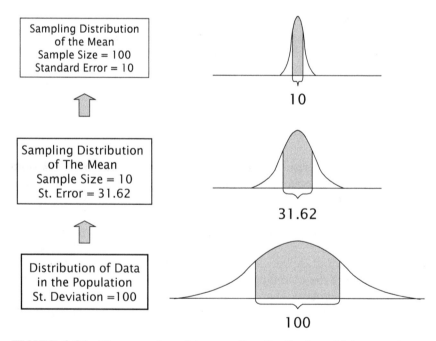

FIGURE 4.31 The narrowing of the sampling distribution with increased sample size.

ution can be thought of as a sampling distribution with a sample size of one (one mean—the population mean). The sampling distribution for a sample size of 100 is one-tenth the width of the parent population. The essential message is the larger the sample size, the less the uncertainty about the value of a sample statistic. Incidentally, the standard deviation of the sampling distribution of the mean is given a special name in statistics, the *standard error of the mean* (see later explanation).

With some qualifications,[36] the Law of Large Numbers tells us that the larger the sample size, the more accurate our knowledge of the population's average. With some caveats,[37] therefore, we would like to work with samples that are as large as possible so as to minimize the width of the sampling distribution as much as possible.

The Dispersion of the Sampling Distribution of the Mean Also Depends On the Amount of Variation within the Data Comprising the Parent Population. There is another factor that impacts the width of the sampling distribution—the amount of variation within the parent population from which the sample was taken. The greater the variation within the population data, the greater will be the variation (dispersion) of the sampling distribution.

You can visualize this by thinking about a population that has no variation at all. For example, if all people in the population weighed 150 lbs, every sample is going to have an average weight of 150 lbs. Therefore, zero variation among the members of the population would lead to zero variation in the sample average, and consequently a sampling distribution that has no dispersion whatsoever. Conversely, if there is great variation among the individuals comprising the population, there is going to be greater variation in the sample averages, which translates to a fat sampling distribution.

Shape of the Sampling Distribution Tends Toward Normal. The Central Limit Theorem, a foundational principle of classical statistics, states that as the size of a sample gets larger, the sampling distribution of the mean, with some qualifications,[38] converges toward a specific shape irrespective of the shape of the population distribution. In other words, no matter how weirdly shaped the distribution of the data in the parent population, the shape of the sampling distribution approaches a specific shape that statisticians refer to as the *normal distribution*, also known as the Gaussian distribution.

The *normal distribution* is the shape of the most common probability distribution. Often referred to as the bell curve because it has the silhouette of the Liberty Bell, the normal distribution characterizes continuous variables that describe many real-world phenomena.

There are a few points about the normal distribution that should be understood:

- It is completely described by its mean and its standard deviation. If these two facts are known, you know every thing that there is to know about the distribution.
- About 68 percent of the observations lie within one standard deviation of the mean, and about 95 percent lie within two standard deviations of the mean.
- The tails of the distribution become quite thin beyond two standard deviations. Thus values beyond three standard deviations are rare and beyond four are extremely rare.

The normal distribution, which is illustrated in Figure 4.32, is so common that it has been called a fundamental feature of the natural world. Its shape is caused by the additive effects of many independent factors acting on the same situation. For example, systolic blood pressure is affected by genetic factors, diet, weight, lifestyle, aerobic conditioning, and a multitude of other factors. When they interact, the probability distribution of blood pressures in a large group of randomly selected people will have the bell-shaped distribution.

Figure 4.33[39] shows several very nonnormal population distributions along with the shape of the sampling distribution of the mean. Note how the sampling distribution converges to a normal shape as a sample size is increased irrespective of the shape of the distribution of the data in the

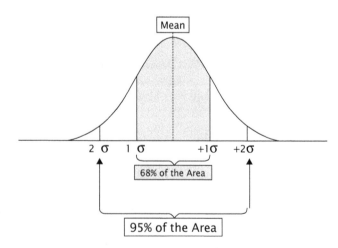

FIGURE 4.32 The normal distribution.

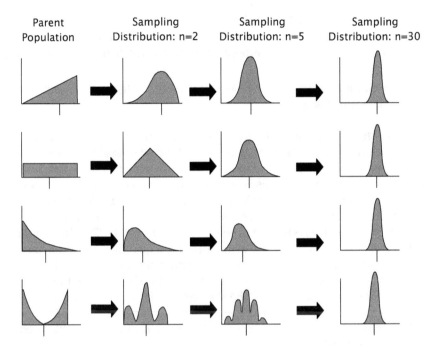

FIGURE 4.33 Given sufficient sample size the sampling distribution of the mean approaches normal shape irrespective of the variable's distributional shape.

parent population. There is nothing magical about the number 30. The rate at which the sampling distribution converges to a normal shape as a function of sample size depends on the shape of the parent distribution. Note that for three of the cases in the figure, a sample size of five produces a nearly normally shaped sampling distribution of the mean. However, for the bottom case in the figure, the sampling distribution of the mean does not become normal-like until a sample size of 30.

The Standard Error of the Mean

We are now in a position to take the final step toward defining the sampling distribution of the mean as it is done in classical statistics. So far, it has been established that:

1. The sampling distribution of the mean converges to the shape of a normal distribution as the sample size is increased.
2. A normal distribution is fully described by its mean and its standard deviation.

3. The standard deviation of the sampling distribution of the mean, also known as the standard error of the mean, is directly related to the standard deviation of the population from which the samples were taken.

4. The standard error of the mean is inversely related to the square root of the sample size.

The standard error of the mean is equal to the standard deviation of the population divided by the square root of the sample size. This is a true statement but not of practical use because the standard deviation of the population is not known. This is simply a consequence of the fact that the full population is not observable. However, the standard deviation of the population can be estimated from the sample. This estimate, which is designated by sigma-hat, is shown in equation in Figure 4.34. The little roof or hat over the sigma is statistical symbolism for a quantity that has been estimated. You will note that the divisor within the radical sign is $n - 1$, rather than n. This modification compensates for the fact that the sample standard deviation understates the standard deviation of the population.

This expression is used to estimate the standard deviation of the parent population, which is then used in the equation in Figure 4.35 to estimate the standard error of the mean.

With the standard error of the mean in hand, and the assumption that the sampling distribution is normal, it is now possible to form a good esti-

Estimate of Population Standard Deviation Based on a Sample of Observations

$$\hat{\sigma} = \sqrt{\frac{\sum (x_i - \bar{x})^2}{n - 1}}$$

Where:

X_i Is an individual observation on variable X in the population

$\bar{X}$ Is the sample mean on variable X

n Is number of observations in the sample

FIGURE 4.34   Estimate of population standard deviation based on a sample of observations.

$$\text{Standard Error of the Mean} = \frac{\hat{\sigma}}{\sqrt{n}}$$

FIGURE 4.35 The standard error of the mean.

mate of the sampling distribution of the mean. And recall all this was on the basis of a single sample.

There is one problem with the traditional approach. It assumes that the sampling distribution is normally shaped (bell curve). If this proves not to be so, the conclusions reached will be inaccurate. For this reason, I have chosen to use an alternative method for estimating the sampling distribution of the mean, based on computer simulation.

DERIVING THE SAMPLING DISTRIBUTION WITH THE COMPUTER-INTENSIVE APPROACH

Until about 30 years ago there was no alternative to the classical approach for deriving the sampling distribution from a single sample. Now there is— the computer-intensive approach. By systematically resampling the single available sample many times, it is possible to approximate the shape of the sampling distribution. This procedure is described in this section.

The next chapter will present two computer-based methods: bootstrap resampling and Monte Carlo permutation. Although each method has its limitations, as is true for any statistical method, they are useful alternatives to the classic approach.

The bootstrap is so named because it seemingly lifts itself up, as if by its own bootstraps, to approximate the shape of the sampling distribution. In this book, it will be used to approximate the shape of the sampling distribution of the *average return* for rules that have no predictive power. The Monte Carlo permutation method is named after the famed European gambling casino because it uses the computer as if it were a roulette wheel.

By whatever means it is generated, the sampling distribution serves the same purpose. It tells us how much the back-tested return of a nonpredictive rule can vary above or below zero due to the random effects of sampling. Thus, it serves as the benchmark for evaluating rule performance. If the rule's mean return is too high to be due to sampling variability, the rule is judged to have predictive power.

PREVIEW OF NEXT CHAPTER

We have already made a number of references to using statistical inference to test claims. The official title for this activity is hypothesis testing. The next chapter discusses the rationale and mechanics of hypothesis testing.

It will also consider another use of statistical inference, estimating confidence intervals. A confidence interval is a range that contains the true value of the population parameter with a specified level of confidence. For example, if the observed mean return of a rule is 15 percent the 95 percent confidence interval might indicate that the rule's true return lies between 5 percent return and 25 percent return. The width of the confidence interval, in this case 20 percentage points, is derived from the same sampling distribution that is used for hypothesis testing.

CHAPTER 5

Hypothesis Tests and Confidence Intervals

TWO TYPES OF STATISTICAL INFERENCE

Statistical inference encompasses two procedures: hypothesis testing and parameter estimation. Both are concerned with the unknown value of a population parameter. A hypothesis test determines if a sample of data is consistent with or contradicts a hypothesis about the value of a population parameter, for example, the hypothesis that its value is less than or equal to zero. The other inference procedure, parameter estimation, uses the information in a sample to determine the approximate value of a population parameter.[1] Thus, a hypothesis test tells us if an effect is present or not, whereas an estimate tells us about the size of an effect.

In some ways both forms of inference are similar. Both attempt to draw a conclusion about an entire population based only on what has been observed in a sample drawn from the population. In going beyond what is known, both hypothesis testing and parameter estimation take the inductive leap from the certain value of a sample statistic to the uncertain value of a population parameter. As such, both are subject to error.

However, important differences distinguish parameter estimation from hypothesis testing. Their goals are different. The hypothesis test evaluates the veracity of a conjecture about a population parameter leading to an acceptance or rejection of that conjecture. In contrast, estimation is aimed at providing a plausible value or range of values for the population parameter. In this sense, estimation is a bolder endeavor and offers potentially more useful information. Rather than merely telling us whether we should accept or reject a specific claim such as a

217

rule's average return is less than or equal to zero, estimation approximates the average return and provides a range of values within which the rule's true rate of return should lie at a specified level of probability. For example, it may tell us that the rule's estimated return is 10 percent and there is a 95 percent probability that it falls within the range of 5 percent to 15 percent. This statement contains two kinds of estimates; a *point estimate*, that the rule's return is 10 percent, and an *interval estimate*, that the return lies in the range 5 percent to 15 percent. The rule studies discussed in Part Two use estimation as an adjunct to the hypothesis tests.

HYPOTHESIS TESTS VERSUS INFORMAL INFERENCE

If a rule has been profitable in a sample of historical data, this sample statistic is an indisputable fact. However, from this fact, what can be inferred about the rule's future performance? Is it likely to be profitable because it possesses genuine predictive power or are profits unlikely because its past profits were due to chance? The hypothesis test is a formal and rigorous inference procedure for deciding which of these alternatives is more likely to be correct, and so can help us decide if it would be rational to use the rule for actual trading in the future.

Confirmatory Evidence: It's Nice, It's Necessary, but It Ain't Sufficient

Chapter 2 pointed out that informal inference is biased in favor of confirmatory evidence. That is to say, when we use common sense to test the validity of an idea, we tend to look for confirmatory evidence—facts consistent with the idea's truth. At the same time, we tend to ignore or give too little weight to contradictory evidence. Common sense tells us, and rightly so, that if the idea is true, instances where the idea worked (confirmatory evidence) should exist. However, informal inference makes the mistake of assuming that confirmatory evidence is sufficient to establish its truth. This is a logical error. Confirmatory evidence does not compel the conclusion that the idea is true. Because it is consistent with the idea's truth, it merely allows for the possibility that the idea is true.

The crucial distinction between necessary evidence and sufficient evidence was illustrated in Chapter 4 with in the following example. Suppose we wish to test the truth of the assertion: *The creature I observe is a dog.* We observe that the creature has four legs (the evidence). This evidence is consistent with (i.e., confirmatory of) the creature being a dog. In other words, if the creature is a dog, then it will necessarily have four legs. However, four legs are not *sufficient* evidence to establish that the creature is a dog. It may very well be another four-legged creature (cat, rhino, and so forth).

Popular articles on TA will often try to argue that a pattern has predictive power by presenting instances where the pattern made successful predictions. It is true that, if the pattern has predictive power, then there will be historical cases where the pattern gave successful predictions. However, such confirmatory evidence, while necessary, is not sufficient to logically establish that the pattern has predictive power. It is no more able to compel the conclusion that the pattern has predictive power than the presence of four legs is able to compel the conclusion that the creature is a dog.

To argue that confirmatory instances are sufficient commits the fallacy of affirming the consequent.

If p is true, then q is true.

q is true.

Invalid Conclusion: *Therefore, p is true.*

If the pattern has predictive power, then past examples of success should exist.

Past examples of success exist, and here they are.

Therefore, the pattern has predictive power.

Chapter 3 showed that although confirmatory evidence is not sufficient to prove the truth of an assertion, contradictory evidence—evidence that is incompatible with an assertion's truth—is sufficient to establish that the assertion is false. The fact that a creature lacks four legs is sufficient to falsify the assertion that the creature is a dog. This is the valid form of argument called denial of the consequent.

If p is true, then q is true.

q is not true.

Therefore, p is not true (i.e., p is false).

If the creature is a dog, then the creature has four legs.

Creature does not have for legs.

Therefore, creature is not a dog.

The logical basis of the hypothesis test is falsification of the consequent. As such, it is a potent antidote to the confirmation bias of informal inference and an effective preventative of erroneous belief.

What Is a Statistical Hypothesis?

A statistical hypothesis is a conjecture about the value of a population parameter. Often this is a numerical characteristic, such as the average return of a rule. The population parameter's value is unknown because it is unobservable. For reasons previously discussed, it is assumed to have value equal to or less than zero.

What an observer does know is the value of a sample statistic for a sample that has been drawn from the population. Thus, the observer is faced with a question: Is the observed value of the sample statistic consistent with the hypothesized value of the population parameter? If the observed value is *close* to the hypothesized value, the reasonable inference would be that the hypothesis is correct. If, on the other hand, the value of the sample value is *far away* from the hypothesized value, the truth of the hypothesis is called into question.

Close and *far* are ambiguous terms. The hypothesis test quantifies these terms making it possible to a draw a conclusion about the veracity of the hypothesis. The test's conclusion is typically given as a number between 0 and 1.0. This number indicates the probability that the observed value of the sample statistic could have occurred by chance under the condition that (given that or assuming that) the hypothesized value is true. For example, suppose it is hypothesized that a rule's expected return is equal to zero, but the back test produced a return of +20 percent. The conclusion of the hypothesis test may say something like the following: *If the rule's expected rate of return were truly equal to zero, there is a 0.03 probability that the back-tested return could be equal to or greater than +20 percent due to chance.* Because there is only a 3 percent probability that a 20 percent return could have occurred by chance if the rule were truly devoid of predictive power, then we can be quite confident that the rule was not simply lucky in the back test.

Falsifying a Hypothesis with Improbable Evidence

A hypothesis test begins by assuming that the hypothesis being tested is true. Based on this assumption, predictions are deduced from the hypothesis about the likelihood of various new observations. In other words, if the hypothesis is true, then certain outcomes would be probable to occur whereas other outcomes would be improbable. Armed with this set of expectations an observer is in a position to compare the predictions with subsequent observations. If predictions and observations agree, there is no reason to question the hypothesis. However, if low probability outcomes are observed—outcomes that would be inconsistent with the truth of the hypothesis—the hypothesis is deemed falsified. Thus, it is the occurrence of unexpected evidence that is the basis for refuting a hypothesis. Though this line of reasoning is counterintuitive, it is logically correct (denial of the consequent) and extremely powerful. It is the logical basis of scientific discovery.

To give a concrete example, suppose I view myself as an excellent social tennis player. My *hypothesis* is *David Aronson is an excellent social tennis player.* I join a tennis club with members whose age and years of play are similar to mine. On the basis of my hypothesis, I confidently predict to other club members that I will win at least three-quarters of my games (predicted win rate = 0.75). This prediction is merely a deductive consequence of my hypothesis. I test the hypothesis by keeping track of my first 20 games. After 20 games I am shocked and disappointed. Not only have I not scored a single victory (observed win rate = 0), but most losses have been by wide margins. This outcome is clearly inconsistent with the prediction deduced from my hypothesis. Said differently, my hypothesis implied that this evidence had a very low probability of occurrence. Such surprising evidence forcefully calls for a revision (falsification) of my hypothesis. Unless I prefer feel-good delusions to observed evidence, it is time to abandon my delusions of tennis grandeur.[2]

In the preceding situation, the evidence was overwhelmingly clear. I lost every one of 20 games. However, what if the evidence had been ambiguous? Suppose I had won two-thirds of my games. An observed win rate of 0.66 is below the predicted win rate of 0.75 but not dramatically so. Was this merely a random negative deviation from the predicted win rate or was the deviation of sufficient magnitude to indicate the hypothesis about my tennis ability was faulty? This is where statistical analysis becomes necessary. It attempts to answer the question: Was the difference between the observed win rate (0.66) and the win rate predicted by my hypothesis (0.75) large enough to raise doubts about the veracity of the hypothesis? Or, alternatively: Was the difference between 0.66 and 0.75 merely random variation in that particular sample of tennis matches? The hypothesis test attempts to distinguish prediction errors that are small enough to be the result of random sampling from errors so large that they indicate a faulty hypothesis.

Dueling Hypotheses: The Null Hypothesis versus the Alternative Hypothesis

A hypothesis test relies on the method of indirect proof. That is, it establishes the truth of something by showing that something else is false. Therefore, to prove the hypothesis that we would like to demonstrate as correct, we show that an opposing hypothesis is incorrect. To establish that hypothesis *A* is true, we show that the opposing hypothesis *Not-A* is false.

A hypothesis test, therefore, involves two hypotheses. One is called the *null hypothesis* and the other the *alternative hypothesis*. The names are strange, but they are so well entrenched that they will be used here. The alternative hypothesis, the one the scientist would like to prove, asserts the discovery of important new knowledge. The opposing or null hypothesis simply asserts that nothing new has been discovered. For example, Jonas Salk, inventor of the polio vaccine, put forward the alternative hypothesis that his new vaccine would prevent polio more effectively than a placebo. The null hypothesis asserted that the Salk vaccine would not prevent polio more effectively than a placebo. For the TA rules tested in this book, the alternative hypothesis asserts the rule has an expected return greater than zero. The null hypothesis asserts that the rule does *not* have an expected return greater than zero.

For purposes of brevity, I will adopt the conventional notation: H_A for the alternative hypothesis, and H_0 for the null hypothesis. A way to remember this is the null hypothesis asserts that zero new knowledge has been discovered, thus the symbol H_0.

It is crucial to the logic of a hypothesis test that H_A and H_0 be defined as mutually exclusive and exhaustive propositions. What does this mean? Two propositions are said to be *exhaustive* if, when taken together, they cover all possibilities. H_A and H_0 cover all possibilities. Either the polio vaccine has a preventive effect or it does not. There is no other possibility. Either a TA rule generates returns greater than zero or it does not.

The two hypotheses must also be defined as mutually exclusive. Mutually exclusive propositions cannot both be true at the same time, so if H_0 is shown to be false, then H_A must be true and vice versa. By defining the hypotheses as exhaustive and mutually exclusive statements, if it can be shown that one hypothesis is false, then we are left with the inescapable

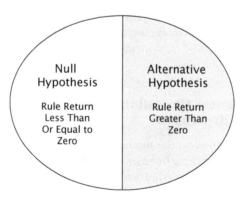

FIGURE 5.1 Mutually exclusive and exhaustive hypotheses.

conclusion that the other hypothesis must be true. Proving truth in this fashion is called the method of indirect proof. These concepts are illustrated in the Figure 5.1.

RATIONALE OF THE HYPOTHESIS TEST

Two aspects of the hypothesis test warrant explanation. First, why the test is focused on the null hypothesis. Second, why the null hypothesis is assumed to be true rather than the alternative hypothesis. This section explains the reasoning behind both aspects.

Why Is the Null Hypothesis the Target of the Test?

As discussed in Chapter 3, evidence can be used to logically deduce that a hypothesis is false, but it cannot be used to deduce that it is true.[3] Therefore, hypothesis testing must be about trying to falsify something. The question is: Which of the hypotheses, H_0 or H_A, should be the target of this effort?

Of the two competing claims, H_0 presents a better target for falsification because it can be reduced to a single claim about the value of the parameter. This means that only one test must be performed. If that single value can be successfully challenged with evidence, H_0 will have been falsified. In contrast, the alternative hypothesis represents an infinite number of claims about the parameter's value. With no unique value to shoot at, an infinite number of tests would have to be performed to falsify the alternative hypothesis.

In fact, both H_0 and H_A represent an infinite number of claims about the rule's expected return, but H_0 can be reduced to a single claim. First, let's consider why H_A represents an infinite number of claims. In asserting that the rule's return is greater than zero, H_A effectively says that the rule's expected return, over the immediate practical future, might be any one of an infinite set of values greater than zero: + 0.1 percent, or +2 percent or +6 percent or any other positive value. This is illustrated in Figure 5.2. Given that H_A makes an infinite number of claims, an infinite number of tests would have to be conducted to conclusively refute it. Clearly this is impractical.

H_0 also makes an infinite number of claims about the value of the population parameter. It asserts that the rule's average return is equal to zero or some value less than zero. However, only one of these claims really matters—that the rule's average return is equal to zero.

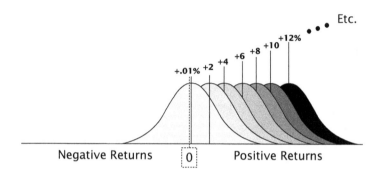

H₁ Asserts:
Rule's Expected Return > 0%.

FIGURE 5.2 The alternative hypothesis makes an infinite number of claims about the rule's expected rate of return.

The attempt to falsify a single claim is a practical goal. If the most positive of these claims (return = 0) can be called into question by the rule's back-test profitability, then all lesser claims (e.g., the rule's return = –1.3 percent) are contradicted but to an even greater degree. This is how H_0 reduces to the single claim that the rule's return is zero. This is illustrated in Figure 5.3.

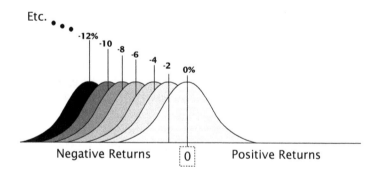

H_0 Asserts:
Rule's Return < or = 0%.

FIGURE 5.3 The null hypothesis makes an infinite number of claims about the population mean, but only one matters.

Why Is the Null Hypothesis Assumed to Be True?

The hypothesis test assumes H_0 is true on two grounds: scientific skepticism and the principle of simplicity (parsimony).

Skepticism. The assumption that H_0 is true is consistent with science's skeptical attitude toward all new claims of knowledge. As explained in Chapter 3, this conservative stance is justified because making claims is easy but making genuine discoveries is hard. The burden of proof should be on the claimant.

Science has a legitimate concern with protecting the storehouse of knowledge from contamination with falsehoods and weird beliefs. A useful analogy can be made to the criminal justice system. Free societies have a legitimate concern with protecting the lone citizen from the vast prosecutorial power of the state. For this reason the defendant in a criminal prosecution starts off with a presumption of innocence. This places the burden of proving guilt—falsifying the assumption of innocence—on the state, and it is indeed a substantial burden. To gain a conviction, the state must provide evidence of guilt beyond a reasonable doubt, a very high threshold. The initial assumption of innocence and the high threshold of proof can be seen as the legal system's way of preventing the jails and gallows from being contaminated with innocent citizens.

Following the scientific tradition, the hypothesis test places the burden of proof on those asserting new knowledge. In fact, whenever the back-tested performance of a rule is greater than zero, the sample evidence actually favors H_A—that the rule's expected return is greater than zero. However, the hypothesis test demands more than merely reasonable evidence. It demands compelling evidence before abandoning the assumed truth of H_0. Those asserting that a TA rule has predictive power (H_A) must meet a large burden of proof before they can reasonably expect their claim to be accepted by scientific practitioners of TA.

Simplicity. An additional reason to grant priority to H_0 is the principle of simplicity. This fundamental precept of science says that simpler theories are more likely to capture the true patterns of nature than more elaborate ones. This principle, known as *Occam's Razor*, says that if a phenomenon can be explained by more than one hypothesis, then the simplest hypothesis is more likely to be correct. H_0, which explains a rule's past success as luck, is simpler than H_A, which asserts that profits stem from a recurring market pattern with predictive power.

Simpler explanations (theories, rules, hypotheses, models, and so forth) are more likely to be correct because they are less likely to fit data by chance. The more complex an explanation—that is, the more numerous its assumptions, its conditions, and constraints—the more likely it is to fit a set of observations by chance. This is illustrated when fitting a mathematical function to a set of data. A function can be thought of as a mathematical hypothesis that explains a given set of observations. In Figure 5.4, two mathematical functions have been fitted to the same set of data. One function is linear. It is relatively simple in that it is defined by only two coefficients or degrees of freedom: its slope and where it cuts the vertical axis (Y-intercept). In other words, the line's fit to the data can be improved by manipulating only these two factors.

The other function is a complex polynomial with 10 coefficients. Each coefficient allows the curve to make an additional bend. With this degree of flexibility, the curve can weave and bend so that it touches every data point. In fact, when a function is fit to data using a method called least-squares regression, a perfect fit is guaranteed if the function is allowed to contain as many degrees of freedom (coefficients) as there are data points. Although the linear function does not manage to touch every observed point, it does describe the general tendency of the data; increasing values of X are associated with increasing values of Y. In other words, the simple function captures the essential feature of the data, making it more likely that it represents the real relationship between X and Y. In contrast, the complex function is most likely a detailed description of the data's random fluctuations in addition to the positive correlation between X and Y.

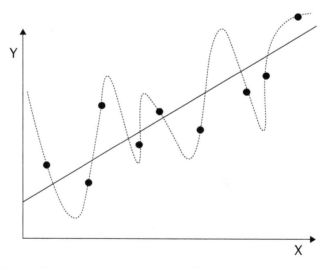

FIGURE 5.4 The superiority of simplicity—all else being equal.

This is not to suggest that complex curves are never justified. If there is enough data and it was generated by a complex process, an elaborate model may very well be justified. However, all else being equal, the simpler explanation is more likely to be correct.

Strong and Weak Decisions

A hypothesis test leads to one of two decisions; reject H_0 or retain H_0. The decisions are qualitatively different: the first is a strong decision while the second is a weak one.[4] Rejection is a strong decision because it is compelled by improbable, informative evidence that forcefully contradicts H_0. In contrast, the decision to retain H_0 is a relatively weaker choice because the evidence is nothing more than consistent with what we had already expected and assumed to be so, that H_0 is true. In others words, the observed value of the test statistic is unsurprising and hence uninformative.

Had tests of Salk's polio vaccine shown that recipients of the real vaccine had the same risk of getting the disease as recipients of the placebo, H_0 would be left intact, and no one would have been surprised by the vaccine's failure. Nothing had worked up to that point, so it would have been just another frustrating day at the lab. Of course this is not what actually happened, and the course of medical history was changed. Salk's decision to reject H_0 was compelled by a rate of infection in the treated group that was surprisingly less than the placebo group.

It is in this way that a decision to reject H_0 is fundamentally a stronger decision than one to retain H_0. It is a decision forced by evidence that is strong enough to rebut an initial and entirely reasonable doubt that new knowledge has been discovered. In contrast, the decision to retain H_0 is due to an absence of compelling evidence. The absence of compelling evidence does not mean the null is necessarily true or even probably true.[5] It simply means that it could be true. Because science takes a conservative stance toward new knowledge, in the absence of compelling evidence, the more reasonable conclusion is that nothing new has been discovered.

HYPOTHESIS TESTING: THE MECHANICS

"Three ingredients are usually necessary for a hypothesis test: (1) a hypothesis, (2) a *test statistic*, and (3) some means of generating the probability distribution (sampling distribution) of the test statistic under the assumption that the hypothesis is true."[6] The term *test statistic* refers to the sample statistic that is being used to test a hypothesis. Thus, the terms are interchangeable.

To recap these items as they pertain to rule testing: (1) the hypothesis H_0 is that the rule has an expected return of zero or less, (2) the test statistic is the rule's mean return obtained by back testing it in a historical sample of data, and (3) the sampling distribution represents the random variation in the rule's mean return if it were to be tested in many independent samples. The sampling distribution is centered at a mean return of zero, reflecting the assumption asserted by H_0.

As discussed in Chapter 4, the sampling distribution can be derived in two ways: the analytical approach of classical statistics and via computer simulation. There are two computer-based approaches: Monte-Carlo permutation and the bootstrap. Both will be used in the case study presented in Part Two.

The Question: Is the Test Statistic Improbable?

The basic idea of a hypothesis test is simple: an outcome (observation) that would rarely happen under the condition that the hypothesis were true is good evidence that the hypothesis is not true."[7] If my hypothesis that *I am a good tennis player* were true, then it would be rare (improbable) for me to lose 20 games in a row. To my surprise and embarrassment I did lose 20 games in a row. That evidence implies my hypothesis is false.

Suppose a TA rule called MA50 is back tested. The MA50 rule is defined as follows: If S&P 500 close is greater than a 50-day moving average, hold a long position in the S&P 500, otherwise hold a short position. The alternative hypothesis (H_A) asserts that the rule has predictive power and is, therefore, expected to earn a rate of return greater than zero on detrended data.[8] Zero is the rate of return expected for a rule with no predictive power. The null hypothesis (H_0) asserts that the MA50's expected return is equal to zero or less. H_0's assertion is depicted in Figure 5.5.

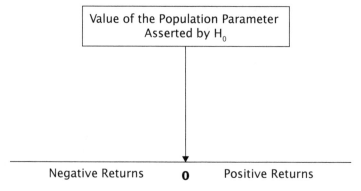

FIGURE 5.5 Value of population parameter asserted by H_0.

The horizontal axis represents expected return over the immediate practical future.

MA50's mean return is obtained by back testing the rule in a sample of historical data. When this value is plotted on the same axis as the hypothesized value for population parameter, we get Figure 5.6.

Note that in Figure 5.6 there is a positive deviation between the value predicted by H_0 and the performance of the rule obtained in the back test. This raises the question: Is the positive deviation so surprising that H_0 should be rejected as an implausible hypothesis?

There are two possible explanations for the positive deviation. It could simply be due to sampling error—the rule got lucky in the particular sample of data used for back-testing—or, it could be because the hypothesized value of zero is wrong—the rule does have predictive power and its expected return is indeed greater than zero. The objective of the hypothesis test is to determine if the evidence, specifically the size of positive deviation, is sufficiently rare, surprising, or improbable that it would warrant a rejection of H_0.

To assess the improbability of the evidence, the observed average return, in particular its deviation from the hypothesized value, is evaluated in light of the sampling distribution. Recall, the sampling gives the probability for various sized deviations between the observed value of the sample statistic and its expected value due to sampling error. If the observed value's deviation is greater than what could reasonably be attributed to sampling error, then H_0 is rejected and the alternative hypothesis, H_A, is adopted. In other words, we conclude that the rule has predictive power.

Figure 5.7 gives us an intuitive sense of the values of the sample statistic

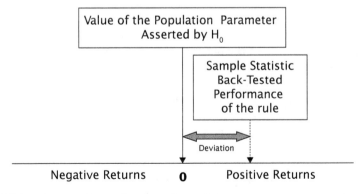

FIGURE 5.6 Hypothesized value of population parameter compared to back-tested performance.

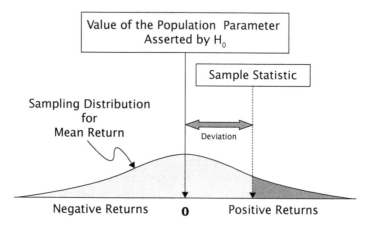

FIGURE 5.7 Unsurprising evidence lies well within the range of sampling variation; H_0 not rejected.

that could occur due to sampling variability. Note that the sampling distribution is positioned so that the most likely value of the return is zero. This merely reflects the value of the population parameter asserted by H_0. Also note that the observed (back tested) value of the rule's average return falls well within the range of random variation allowed by the sampling distribution. This is an unsurprising result. In other words, the deviation between the observed value of the test statistic and the hypothesized (predicted) value could easily be due to sampling error. Hence the evidence is not strong enough to warrant a rejection of H_0.

Figure 5.7 makes it clear that the width of the sampling distribution is critical in deciding if the deviation between the observed return and the hypothesized return is large enough to warrant a rejection of H_0. We saw in Chapter 4 that the width of a statistic's sampling distribution is determined by two factors: (1) the amount of variation within the parent population which gave rise to the sample, and (2) the number of observations comprising the sample. With respect to the first factor, the greater the variability of the data comprising the population, in this case daily rule returns, the larger the width of the sampling distribution. With respect to the second factor, the larger the number of observations comprising the sample, the smaller the width of the sampling distribution.

In Figure 5.8 the sampling distribution is relatively narrow. The observed value of the sample statistic lies in the outer right tail of the sampling distribution. This would be considered an improbable or surprising observation and one that would be incompatible with the hypothesized value. Such evidence would warrant a rejection of H_0.

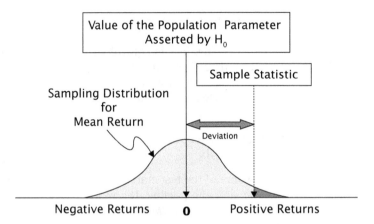

FIGURE 5.8 Surprising (improbable) evidence at the outer edge of the range of sampling variation; H_0 rejected.

These diagrams convey an intuitive sense of how the size of the deviation between an observed value and a hypothesized value (the value predicted by the hypothesis) is used to falsify a hypothesis. To be rigorous, this intuition must be quantified. This is done by translating the observed value's deviation into a probability— specifically the probability of observing a deviation that large under the condition that the hypothesized value is true. A probability that is contingent on the existence of a specified condition, in this case that the hypothesized value is true, is called a *conditional probability*. Said differently, a conditional probability is a probability that is conditional upon some other fact being true.

In a hypothesis test, this conditional probability is given the special name *p-value*. Specifically, it is the probability that the observed value of the test statistic could have occurred conditioned upon (given that) the hypothesis being tested (H_0) is true. The smaller the p-value, the greater is our justification for calling into question the truth of H_0. If the p-value is less than a threshold, which must be defined before the test is carried out, H_0 is rejected and H_A accepted. The p-value can also be interpreted as the probability H_0 will be erroneously rejected when H_0 is in fact true. P-value also has a graphical interpretation. It is equal to the fraction of the sampling distribution's total area that lies at values equal to and greater than the observed value of the test statistic.

Let's consider how all of this pertains to the test of a rule. For example, if a rule's return in a back test was +3.5 percent, we mark the value +3.5 percent on the horizontal axis upon which the sampling distribution sits. We then determine the fraction of the sampling distribution's area occupying values equal to or greater than +3.5 percent. Suppose that this area equals 0.10 of the sampling distribution's total area. The value 0.10 is the sample statistic's p-value. This fact is equivalent to saying that if the rule's true return were zero, there is a 0.10 probability that its return in a back test would attain a value as high as +3.5 percent or higher due to sampling variability (chance). This is illustrated in Figure 5.9.

p-value, Statistical Significance, and Rejecting the Null Hypothesis

A second name for the p-value of the test statistic is the *statistical significance of the test*. The smaller the p-value, the more statistically significant the test result. A *statistically significant* result is one for which the p-value is low enough to warrant a rejection of H_0.

The smaller the p-value of a test statistic, the more confident we can be that a rejection of the null hypothesis is a correct decision. The p-value can be looked upon as the degree to which the observed value of the test statistic conforms to the null hypothesis (H_0). Larger p-values mean greater conformity, and smaller values mean less conformity. This is simply another way of saying that the more surprising (improbable) an observation is in relation to a given view of the world (the hypothesis), the more likely it is that world view is false.

How small does the p-value need to be to justify a rejection of the H_0? This is problem specific and relates to the cost that would be incurred by an erroneous rejection. We will deal with the matter of errors and their costs in a moment. However, there are some standards that

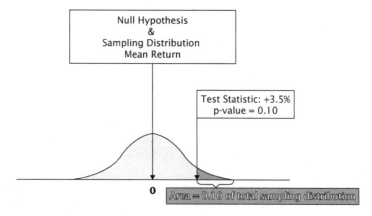

FIGURE 5.9 P-Value: fractional area of sampling distribution greater than +3.5%, conditional probability of +3.5% or more given that H_0 is true.

are commonly used. A p-value of 0.10 is often called possibly significant. A p-value of 0.05 or less is typically termed statistically significant and is usually considered to be the largest p-value that would give a scientist license to reject H_0. When the p-value is 0.01 or less it is called called very significant and values of 0.001 or less are termed highly significant.

Test Conclusions and Errors

A hypothesis test leads to one of two possible conclusions: (1) reject H_0, or (2) accept H_0. What is actually true also has two possibilities: (1) H_0 is true, that is, the expected return of the rule is zero or less); or (2) H_0 is in fact false, that is, the rule's expected return is greater than zero because it possesses some degree of predictive power. Given that the test has two possible conclusions, and the truth has two possible states, there are four possible outcomes. They can be illustrated by a table with four cells shown in Figure 5.10.

The hypothesis test can err in two ways. A *type I error* is said to occur when a low p-value leads us to reject H_0, but in reality H_0 is true. This would be the case when a rule is truly devoid of predictive power, but by luck it generates a sufficiently profitable back test that its p-value is low enough to justify rejecting H_0. This is a case of the rule researcher being fooled by randomness. The second type of error, called a *type II error*, occurs when a high p-value leads us to retain H_0, when it is in fact false. In other words, the back test fooled us into concluding the rule has no predictive power, but it actually does and its expected return is greater than zero.

		Truth (The Reality Only Known to God)	
		H_0 True Rule Return < = 0	H_0 False Rule Return > 0
Test Result & Conclusion	High P-value H_0 Not Rejected	**Correct Decision** TA Rule Useless We Discard It	**Type II Error** TA Rule Good We Don't Use It Opportunity Loss
	Low P-value H_0 Rejected	**Type I Error** TA Rule Useless We Use it Earn Zero Return & Take Risk	**Correct Decision** TA Rule Good We Use Rule & Make Profits

FIGURE 5.10 Possible outcomes of a hypothesis test.

At the time the hypothesis test is conducted, only God knows for certain if an error has occurred and of which type. Mere mortals relying on statistical inference must accept the reality that the test's conclusion may be in error.

From the standpoint of an objective technician, the two types of errors have different consequences. A type I error, where H_0 is mistakenly rejected, leads to the use of a worthless rule. This exposes trading capital to risk without the prospect of compensation. A type II error causes a useful rule to be ignored, resulting in lost trading opportunities. Of the two kinds of error, type I is more serious. Lost trading capital is worse than lost opportunities. When capital is exhausted one is out of the game, whereas there will always be other trading opportunities.

The hypothesis test can also be right in two ways: a correct rejection of H_0, when the rule does have merit, and a correct acceptance of the H_0, when the TA rule is useless.

COMPUTER-INTENSIVE METHODS FOR GENERATING THE SAMPLING DISTRIBUTION

As previously mentioned, hypothesis testing requires a method for estimating the shape of the sampling distribution of the test statistic. There are two ways to do this: the traditional approach of mathematical statistics, and the more recently developed computer-intensive randomization methods. This section discusses two computer-based methods: bootstrapping and the Monte Carlo permutation.

Both the traditional and computer-intensive approaches solve the problem of estimating the degree of random variation in a test statistic when there is only a single sample of data and, therefore, only a single value of the test statistic. As previously stated, a single value of a statistic cannot convey a sense of its variability.

Computer-intensive methods estimate the sampling distribution's shape by randomly resampling (reusing) the original sample of observation so as to produce new computer- generated samples. A test statistic is then computed for each resample. This procedure can be repeated as many times as desired, perhaps thousands of times, thus producing a large set of values for the sample statistic. The sampling distribution is developed from this large set of computer-generated values. It might seem strange that reusing the original sample of observations over and over again would allow one to approximate the variability of a sample statistic, yet it does! Not only does this work quite well in practice, the approach is grounded in sound mathematical theory.

The two computer-intensive methods, the bootstrap and Monte Carlo permutation, are similar in that they both rely on randomization. That is, they randomly resample the original sample. However, the two methods are different in several important respects. First, they test slightly different versions of H_0. Although, in both, H_0 asserts that the rule being tested has no predictive power, they do so in slightly different ways. The H_0 tested by the bootstrap asserts that the population distribution of rule returns has an expected value of zero or less. In contrast, the H_0 tested by the Monte Carlo permutation method asserts that the rule's output values (+1 and –1) are randomly paired[9] with future market price changes. In other words, it asserts that the rule's output is uninformative noise that could have just as easily been generated by a roulette wheel.

Because the bootstrap and the Monte Carlo methods test somewhat different versions of the null hypothesis, they require different data. The bootstrap utilizes a daily history of rule returns. The Monte Carlo uses a daily history of the rule's output values (i.e., a sequence of +1 and –1's) and a daily history of price changes for the market being traded.

The two methods also use different random sampling methods. The bootstrap uses a randomization method called resampling with replacement, whereas the Monte Carlo randomly pairs rule output values with market returns without replacement. This distinction will be clarified in the description of each method's algorithm.

Because of these differences, the methods generate somewhat different sampling distributions. Therefore, it is possible that the conclusion to reject or not to reject H_0 may not always be the same. However, extensive simulations conducted by Dr. Timothy Masters, developer of the Monte Carlo permutation method, show that both methods generally do agree when they are applied to detrended market data. For this reason, the hypothesis tests conducted in this book use detrended market data for both the bootstrap and Monte Carlo methods.

The final distinction of the Monte Carlo permutation method is that it is in the public domain, whereas the bootstrap method that is suitable for rule testing is a patented product that is available only from its developer, Quantmetrics.[10]

The Bootstrap

The bootstrap method was first described by Efron[11] in 1979 and then refined in several later publications cited in Eric Noreen's *Computer Intensive Methods for Testing Hypotheses*.[12] The bootstrap derives a sampling distribution of the test statistic by resampling with replacement from an original sample.

The bootstrap is based on a truly amazing mathematical fact, the bootstrap theorem. A mathematical theorem deduces a previously unrecognized truth from the established theorems and foundational assumptions (axioms) of a mathematical system. Assuming that certain reasonable conditions are satisfied, the bootstrap theorem assures us that it will converge to a correct sampling distribution as the sample size goes to infinity. From a practical standpoint, this means that given a single sample of observations bootstrapping can produce the sampling distribution needed to test the significance of a TA rule.

In its basic form, the bootstrap is not suitable for evaluating the statistical significance of rules discovered by data mining. However, a modification invented and patented by Dr. Halbert White, professor of economics at the University of California, San Diego, extended the application of the bootstrap to rules discovered by data mining. This modification to the bootstrap, which is incorporated in software called "Forecaster's Reality Check," is discussed in Chapter 6 and utilized in Chapter 9 to evaluate the statistical significance of over 6,000 rules for trading the S&P 500.

Bootstrap Procedure: White's Reality Check. The description that follows pertains to the use of bootstrapping in the context of testing the statistical significance test of a single TA rule. Thus, the following description does not address the issue of data mining. Figure 5.11 illustrates

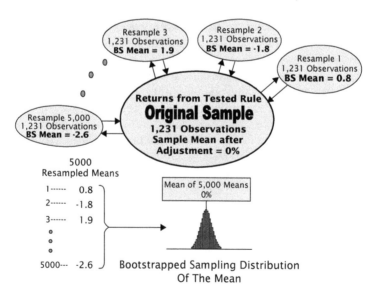

FIGURE 5.11 How bootstrapping produces the sampling distribution for the sample mean return.

the bootstrap procedure. The double arrows between each resample and the original sample indicate that the sampling is being done with replacement (explained below).

There are several things worthy of note in Figure 5.11. First, the original sample, represented by the large oval, is comprised of the daily returns earned by the rule on detrended data. As discussed in Chapter 1, the detrended market data has an average daily change of zero.

Second, before the resampling operation begins, the daily returns of the rule are adjusted by a procedure called zero-centering, not to be confused with the detrending. The zero-centering adjustment makes the mean daily return of the rule equal to zero. In other words, if the rule was able to earn a nonzero return on detrended data, its returns must be zero centered. This serves the purpose of bringing the daily returns into conformity with the H_0, which asserts that their average value is equal to zero. This step is accomplished by first computing the mean daily return of the rule and then subtracting that mean value from each daily rule return. Once the rule's daily returns have been zero centered in this fashion we are in a position to generate a sampling distribution that conforms to H_0's assumption.

Third, the number of daily observations comprising each resample must be exactly equal to the number of observations in the original sample. The bootstrap theorem only holds true if the number of observations in each resample is equal to the number of observations in the original sample. In the figure, the original sample is composed of 1,231 observations. Thus, each bootstrapped resample is also comprised of 1,231 observations.

Fourth, each resample is produced by sampling with replacement. This means that after a daily rule return has been selected at random from the original sample and its value has been noted, it is then replaced back into the original sample before another daily return is selected at random. This makes it possible for an individual daily return to be selected more than once or for it never to be selected at all for a given resample. It is this element of randomness that enables the bootstrap procedure to model the variability in the sample statistic.

Fifth, the diagram shows 5,000 resamples being taken. A mean is computed for each resample. These 5,000 means are used to construct the sampling distribution of the mean.

The sequence of steps involved in bootstrapping the sampling distribution of the mean is:

1. Calculate the mean daily return for the rule over the observations in the original sample (1,231 in Figure 5.11).
2. Zero centering: Subtract the mean daily return from each day's return in the original sample.

3. Place the zero-centered data in a bucket.

4. Select a daily return at random from the bucket and note its value.

5. Place that return back in the bucket, and then thoroughly stir the bucket (some statisticians prefer their samples shaken rather than stirred).

6. Perform steps 4 and 5 exactly N – 1 more times (e.g., 1,230) creating a total of N (1,231) randomly selected observations. This completes the first bootstrapped sample.

7. Compute the mean return for the N (1,231) observations in the first resample. This is one value of the bootstrapped mean.

8. Perform steps 6 through 9 a large number of times (5,000) yielding a large number of bootstrapped means.

9. Form the sampling distribution of the means.

10. Compare the observed mean return of the rule to the sampling distribution and determine the fraction of the 5,000 means comprising the sampling distribution that exceed the observed mean return of the rule to determine the p-value. See Figure 5.12.

Monte Carlo Permutation Method [MCP]

Monte Carlo simulation, invented by Stanislaw Ulam (1909–1984), is a general method for solving mathematical problems by random sampling. The Monte Carlo permutation method for rule testing was developed by Dr. Timothy Masters. He is the first to propose this approach as a way to

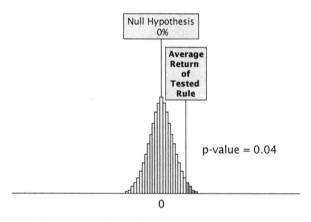

FIGURE 5.12 Comparing the rule's mean return to the bootstrapped sampling distribution of the mean.

produce the sampling distribution to test the statistical significance of a rule's back-tested performance. It is presented as an alternative to White's reality check.

Although the Monte Carlo method has been in existence for a long time, it had not been previously applied to rule testing. This was made possible by Dr. Masters' insight that the Monte Carlo method could generate the sampling distribution of a rule with no predictive power. This is accomplished by randomly pairing or permuting the detrended daily returns of the market (e.g., S&P 500) with the ordered[13] times series representing the sequence of daily rule output values. Recall that the H_0 tested by the Monte Carlo permutation method asserts that the returns of the rule being evaluated are a sample from a population of returns that were generated by a rule with no predictive power. The daily returns of such a rule can be simulated by randomly pairing the rule's output values (+1 and −1) with the market's price changes. The random pairing of the rule output values with market changes destroys any predictive power that the rule may have had. I refer to this random pairing as a *noise rule*.

The process of randomly pairing market-price changes with rule output values is illustrated in Figure 5.13. The daily time series of rule output values are simply those that were produced by the rule that is being evaluated in their original order. After the sequence of output values has been randomly paired with what is effectively a scrambled version of the market's history, the mean daily return of the noise rule can be computed. This value appears in the grey box at the end of each row. To produce the sampling distribution we need many such values.

Time Series of Rule Output Values	+1	+1	+1	+1	-1	-1	-1	-1	-1	-1	
Randomized SP500 Return₁	-0.8	+0.3	-0.9	-2.6	+3.1	+1.7	-0.8	-2.6	+1.2	-0.4	Mean Return₁
Randomized Rule Return₁	-0.8	+0.3	-0.9	-2.6	- 3.1	-1.7	+0.8	+2.6	-1.2	+0.4	**-0.62**
Randomized SP500 Return₂	-0.4	+1.2	-2.6	-0.8	+1.7	+3.1	-2.6	-0.9	+0.3	-0.8	Mean Return₂
Randomized Rule Return₂	-0.4	+1.2	-2.6	-0.8	-1.7	- 3.1	+2.6	+0.9	-0.3	+0.8	**-0.34**
Randomized SP500 Return₃	-2.6	+1.7	-0.4	-0.9	-0.8	-0.8	+0.3	+1.2	-2.6	+3.1	Mean Return₃
Randomized Rule Return₃	-2.6	+1.7	-0.4	-0.9	+0.8	+0.8	-0.3	-1.2	+2.6	-3.1	**-0.26**

FIGURE 5.13 Monte Carlo permutation method.

To produce additional values of noise rule mean returns, the same time series of actual rule output values is paired with (permuted with) numerous scrambled (randomized) versions of market-price changes. The illustration shows only three Monte Carlo permutations but in practice it would be done a large number of times, perhaps 5,000. The 5,000 values for average return are then used to form the sampling distribution of the mean return earned by a noise rule—a rule with no predictive power.

Procedure. The sequence of steps to generate the sampling distribution by the Monte Carlo permutation method is as follows:

1. Obtain a sample of one-day market-price changes for the period of time over which the TA rule was tested, detrended as described in Chapter 1.

2. Obtain the time series of daily rule output values over the back-test period. Assume for this illustration that there were 1,231 such values, one rule output value for each day on which the rule was tested.

3. Place the market's detrended one-day-forward price changes on a piece of paper. Place them in a bin and stir.

4. Randomly select a market-price change from the bin and pair it with the first (earliest) rule output value. Do not put the price change back in the bin. In other words this sampling is being done without replacement.

5. Repeat step 4 until all the returns in the bin have been paired with a rule output value. In this example there will be a total of 1,231 such pairings.

6. Compute the return for each of the 1,231 random pairings. This is done by multiplying the rule's output value (+1 for long, −1 for short) by the market's one-day-forward price change.

7. Compute the average return for the 1,231 returns obtained in step 6.

8. Repeat steps 4 through 7 a large number of times (e.g., 5,000).

9. Form the sampling distribution of the 5,000 values obtained in step 8.

10. Place the tested rule's rate of return on the sampling distribution and compute the p-value (the fraction of random rule returns equal to or greater than the tested rule's return).

Application of Computer Intensive Methods to Back-Test of a Single Rule

This section demonstrates the application of the two computer-intensive hypothesis testing methods to a single rule: 91 day channel breakout[14] using the Dow Jones Transportation Index (input series 4) as the rule's input series. This rule, which is designated as TT-4-91, and all others tested in Part Two of this book are described in detail in Chapter 8. The main point for current purposes is to demonstrate the hypothesis test. The rule was used to generate long and short signals on the S&P 500 index from November 1980 through June 2005. Over this period of time, the rule earned an annualized return of 4.84 percent using detrended S&P 500 data to compute the rule's daily returns. The expected annual return of a rule with no predictive power is zero on detrended data.

Both the bootstrap and the Monte Carlo permutation methods were used to test the null hypothesis that the rule has no predictive power. The question is this: Is TT-4-91's +4.84 percent return sufficient to reject the null hypothesis?

Testing Rule Performance Using Bootstrap: White's Reality Check. To generate the sampling distribution of the average return, the specific steps taken starting with the detrended S&P 500 data are:

1. Zero Centering the Daily Rule Returns: Because the rule generates a positive return (+4.84 percent) on the detrended market data, the average daily return of the rule (approximately 0.0192 percent per day) is subtracted from the return earned by the rule each day. This transformation creates a set of daily returns whose average value is zero, thereby making the data conform to H_0. Note—this is not to be confused with the detrending of the S&P 500 data.

2. Resampling the Daily Returns: The zero-centered daily returns as computed in the preceding step are sampled with replacement. This must be done exactly 6,800 times (the number of observations in the original sample) for the Bootstrap Theorem to hold true.

3. Compute the Mean Return: The mean daily return is computed for the 6,800 resampled returns. This is the first bootstrapped mean.

4. Repeat steps 2 and 3 5,000 times. This obtains 5,000 values for the resampled mean.

5. Create the bootstrapped distribution of resampled means.

6. Compare rule's +4.84 percent return to the sampling distribution to determine the fraction of the sampling distribution's area that lies at values equal to or greater than +4.84 percent per annum. This is done by counting the fraction of the 5,000 bootstrapped means that have values equal to or greater than this return.

Results: H_0 Rejected—Rule Possibly Has Predictive Power. Figure 5.14 shows the bootstrapped sampling distribution with the actual

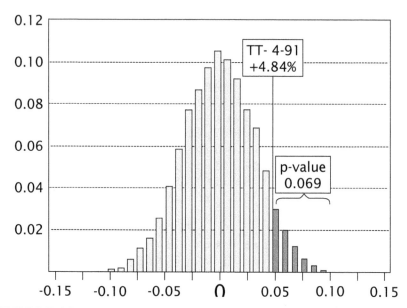

FIGURE 5.14 Bootstrapped sampling distribution for rule TT-4-91 and its p-value.

performance of rule TT-4-91 superimposed. The p-value of 0.0692 indicates that .069 of the 5,000 bootstrapped means were equal to or greater than +4.84 percent. This means that if the rule's expected return were truly equal to zero, about 7 times out of 100, the rule would earn a return of +4.84 percent or greater simply due to chance (sampling variability). Statisticians would regard such a result as possibly significant. As will be seen in Chapter 6, the amount of searching that led to the discovery of the rule, specifically whether the rule was found amongst a large group of back-tested rules, can impact the p-value and the rule's significance. Consequently, the results quoted here assume that this was the only rule proposed for back testing.

Testing Rule Performance with Monte Carlo Permutation Method. The following steps describe the process of applying the Monte Carlo Permutation Method to a rule's back-tested performance:

1. The time series of daily rule output values is laid out in its proper sequence over the time period of the rule back test. As stated earlier there will be 6,800 of these daily +1 and –1 values.

2. Each of the 6,800 detrended one day forward price changes is inscribed on a ball. These 6,800 balls are placed in a bin.

3. The bin is shaken, and then, one at a time, the balls are drawn at random and paired with an individual rule output value. Thus, each of the rule's daily output values is matched with a single one day forward S&P 500 return. This is done without replacement until all balls have been paired with a rule output value. Because there are exactly 6,800 daily market returns and 6,800 rule output values, the bin will be empty when this step is complete.

4. Multiply each rule value (+1 or –1) by the associated S&P 500 return. This gives the return that would be earned by the noise rule over the next day. This step will produce 6,800 daily rule returns.

5. Average the 6,800 values obtained in step 4. This is the first Monte Carlo permuted mean return for a noise rule.

6. Steps 3 through 5 must be repeated 5,000 times.

7. Produce the sampling distribution from the 5,000 Monte Carlo means.

8. Compare the return of the TT-4-91 rule with the sampling distribution and determine the fraction of Monte Carlo means that equal or exceed the return earned by the rule. This is the p-value.

Monte Carlo Results: Rule Possibly Has Predictive Power. Confirming the bootstrapped result, the Monte Carlo method gives a p-value that is almost identical.

ESTIMATION

Estimation is the other form of statistical inference. In contrast to hypothesis testing, which is oriented to the acceptance or rejection of a claim made about the value of a population parameter, estimation's purpose is to approximate the value of the population parameter. In our case, it will be used to estimate the expected return of a rule.

Point Estimates

There are two kinds of estimates: point and interval. A point estimate is a single value that approximates the population parameter, for example *the rule has an expected return of 10 percent*. An interval estimate is a range of values within which the population parameter lies with a given level of probability. The following statement would exemplify this: *The rule's expected return lies within the range 5 percent to 15 percent with a probability of 0.95.*

Actually, we already have been making point estimates, but they have not been described as such. Every time we compute a sample mean and use it to approximate the population mean, we are making a point estimate. This fact is easily overlooked. Some commonly used point estimators are: the mean, median, standard deviation, and the variance. The estimate is computed from a sample of observations taken from the population. In other words, a point estimate is a sample statistic. The formula to compute a sample mean is shown in Figure 5.15.

The use of means (averages) is so ubiquitous in TA that it is taken for granted, yet the sample mean turns out to be an elegant and powerful estimator. It provides a single value that is, in an important sense, the best (most informative) estimate of the population's mean. This is an important fact.

Just how informative the sample mean is becomes clear when we consider the criteria used to judge the quality of an estimator. Good estimators should be: *unbiased, consistent, efficient, and sufficient.* In terms of these four criteria, it can be shown that the sample mean is the best estimator of the population mean.[15]

An estimator is unbiased if its expected value is equal to the population value. Said differently, if an estimator is unbiased its deviations from the true population value have an average value of zero. The sample mean's deviations from the population mean are unbiased. This allows us to say that a rule's mean return in a historical sample is an unbiased estimate of its mean return in the immediate practical future.

Another criterion of a point estimator's goodness is its *consistency.* An estimator is said to be consistent if its value converges to the value of

Sample Mean of Variable X

$$\overline{X} = \frac{X_1 + X_2 + X_3 + \ldots X_n}{n}$$

$$\overline{X} = \frac{\sum_{i=1}^{n} X_i}{n}$$

Where X_i is an individual observation on variable X

FIGURE 5.15 Sample mean of variable X.

the population parameter as sample size is increased. The Law of Large Numbers tells us that this is so for the sample mean.

Estimators should also be *efficient*. This criterion relates to the width of its sampling distribution. As mentioned earlier, an estimator is a sample statistic, and thus has a sampling distribution. The most efficient estimator is the one that produces the narrowest sampling distribution. In other words, the most efficient estimator has the smallest standard error.[16] Both the sample mean and the sample median are unbiased and consistent estimators of the population mean for populations that are distributed symmetrically. However, the sample mean is more efficient than the sample median. For large samples, the standard error of the mean is about 80 percent smaller than the sample median's standard error.[17]

The final trait of a good point estimator is called its *sufficiency*. "An estimator is sufficient if it makes such use of all the available sample data that no other estimator would add any information about the parameter being estimated."[18] The sample mean is sufficient in this sense.

Interval Estimates—The Confidence Interval

More informative than the point estimate is the interval estimate, also known as a confidence interval. It is described in this section.

What Do Confidence Intervals Tell Us?   A point estimate has limited value because it conveys no sense of the uncertainty in the estimate due to sampling error. The confidence interval solves this problem by combining the information of the point estimate with the information about the estimator's sampling distribution.

A confidence interval is a range of values that surround the point estimate. The interval is defined by upper and lower values called bounds. In addition, the interval is accompanied by a probability number that tells us how likely it is that the true value of the population parameter falls within the bounds of the confidence interval. By convention the probability is stated as a percentage rather than a fraction. Thus, a 90 percent confidence interval for the mean has a 0.90 probability of enclosing within its bounds the population's true mean value.

When thinking about what a confidence interval tells us, it is best to think of what would happen if one were to construct a large number of 90 percent confidence intervals, each based on an independent sample of data taken from the population. If this were to be done, about 90 percent of the intervals would actually encompass the value of the population's parameter. By extension, about 10 percent of the confidence intervals would fail to include the population parameter. This is illustrated in Figure 5.16 for 10 confidence intervals. Ten is a small number, which I used to

True Population Mean

μ

Means
&
90% Confidence
Intervals
For
10 Independent
Samples

Error
90% CI
Fails To
Enclose
Population
Mean

FIGURE 5.16   90 percent confidence intervals (.90 probability correct).

keep the figure simple. The true, but unknown, population mean is indicated by the Greek letter μ (mu). The sample mean is identified by the dot
within each confidence interval. Note that one of the confidence intervals
fails to enclose the population mean.

The researcher can choose whatever confidence level is desired. For
example a 99 percent confidence level contains the true population mean
with a probability of 0.99. Of course, there is a price to be paid for the
higher level of confidence—the interval is wider. In other words, the price
for higher confidence is reduced precision. Note in Figure 5.17, by increasing the confidence level to 99 percent, the error made by the 90 percent

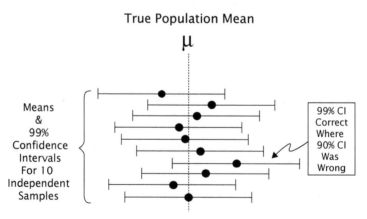

FIGURE 5.17   99 percent confidence intervals (.99 probability correct).

confidence interval in Figure 5.16 has been eliminated. The reduced error rate was accomplished by using a wider (less precise) confidence interval.

If a rule were to be back tested on one hundred independent samples of data and a 90 percent confidence interval were constructed about the mean return observed in each sample, approximately 90 percent of these confidence intervals would contain the rule's true or expected return in the population. Figure 5.18 shows a 90 percent confidence interval for a rule that earned a 7 percent return in a back test. We can be certain, with a probability of 0.90, that the rule has an expected return between 2 percent and 12 percent.

The Confidence Interval and Its Connection to the Sampling Distribution. Confidence intervals are derived from the same sampling distribution that is used to compute the p-values for a hypothesis test. Given what we have already learned about sampling error (sampling variability), it can be said that the value of a sample mean is equal to the unknown value of the population mean, plus or minus its sampling error. This relationship is shown by the upper formula in Figure 5.19. By rearranging the terms of this formula we get the lower formula in Figure 5.19. It says that the value of the population mean is equal to the known value of the sample mean plus or minus sampling error.

The bottom formula tells us that, although we do not know the precise value of the population mean, we can take the value of the sample mean, which we do know, and the sampling distribution of the mean, which we also know, and obtain a range of values that contains the population mean with a specified level of probability. In operational terms, this tells us that if we were to repeat the following procedure 1,000 times—*compute a sample mean and a 90 percent confidence interval*—

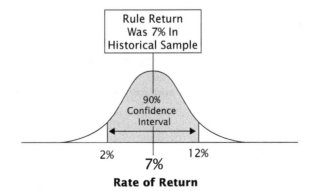

FIGURE 5.18 90 percent confidence interval for rule back test.

The known sample mean is
the unknown population mean with error

$$\overline{X} = \mu \ +/- \ \text{Sampling Error}$$

The unknown population mean is
the known sample mean with error

$$\mu = \overline{X} \ +/- \ \text{Sampling Error}$$

FIGURE 5.19 The known sample mean is the unknown population mean with error.

the population mean would lie within approximately 900 of the 1,000 confidence intervals. This concept is illustrated when the procedure is repeated only 10 times in Figure 5.20. Note that one of the 10 confidence intervals fails to include the population mean. The point of this section is that the confidence interval's width is derived from the width of the sampling distribution.

As was said earlier, the confidence interval is based on the same sampling distribution that is used in the hypothesis test. However, in the case of the confidence interval, the sampling distribution is simply shifted from the position it occupies in a hypothesis test. In the hypothesis test, the sampling distribution is centered at the hypothesized value of the population mean, for example, zero. In the case of a confidence interval, the sampling distribution is centered over the sample mean, for example, 7 percent. This concept is illustrated in Figure 5.21.

Generating Confidence Intervals with the Bootstrap. Bootstrapping can be used to derive confidence intervals. The procedure is almost identical to the one used to generate the sampling distribution for a hypothesis test.

There are numerous methods for computing bootstrap confidence intervals. The one presented here, the *bootstrap percentile method*, is popular, easy to use, and generally gives good results. More sophisticated methods are beyond the scope of this text.

It should be pointed out that the Monte Carlo permutation method cannot be used to generate confidence intervals. This is because the

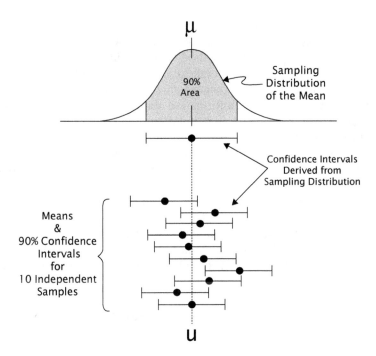

FIGURE 5.20 The connection between the confidence interval and the sampling distribution.

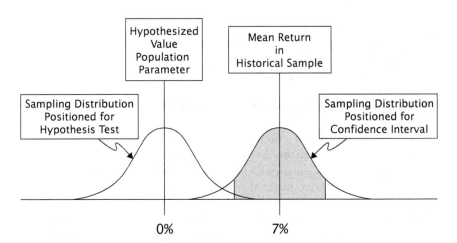

FIGURE 5.21 The sampling distribution positioned for a hypothesis test and positioned for a confidence interval.

method has nothing to do with estimating the value of a population parameter or testing a claim made about its value. As previously mentioned, the Monte Carlo permutation method tests a claim about the information content of the rule's signals. Specifically, the H_0 asserted under the Monte Carlo permutation method is that the long and short positions dictated by the rule are devoid of useful information about future market changes. Because there is no reference to a population parameter (e.g., mean rule return) there is nothing to create a confidence interval for!

The bootstrap percentile procedure for constructing the confidence intervals works as follows: Suppose the rule's returns have been resampled 5,000 times and a mean is computed for each resample. This would result in 5,000 different values for the resampled mean return. We know that because of sampling variability, these means will differ. Next suppose that the set of 5,000 values is arranged in rank order from highest mean to lowest. Then, depending on the confidence interval desired, the highest x percent and lowest $>x$ percent of values are removed from the ordered list, where

$$X = \frac{100 - \text{Confidence Interval Desired}}{2}$$

So if a 90 percent confidence interval is desired, one would remove the highest 5 percent and the lowest 5 percent of the values in the 5,000 resampled means. This would require removing the highest 250 and the 250 lowest values of the resampled mean. After these extreme values are removed, the highest remaining resampled mean would be the upper bound of the 90 percent confidence interval and the lowest remaining resampled mean is the lower bound. The 99 percent confidence interval would result by removing only the highest 25 (top .5 percent) and the lowest 25 (bottom .5 percent) from the set of 5,000 resampled means comprising the sampling distribution.

Hypothesis Tests versus Confidence Intervals: Potential Conflict. Some astute readers may have envisioned a problem. It is possible for a hypothesis test and a confidence interval to lead to different conclusions about a rule's expected return. This prospect stems from the fact that a hypothesis test focuses on the right tail of the sampling distribution whereas the confidence interval focuses on the left tail of the sampling distribution. This means it is possible for the lower bound of a 90 percent confidence interval to imply that there is a 5 percent probability that a rule's expected return is less than zero, while a hypothesis test conducted at the .05 significance level rejects H_0. In other words, it is possible for the confidence interval to tell us that the rule does not have predictive power while the hypothesis tells us that it does. In theory, the hypothesis test and the confidence interval should come to the same conclusion on this issue. That is to say, if the lower bound of a 90 percent confidence interval tells us that the rule's expected return is less than 0 percent, then a hypothesis test at the .05 significance level would presumably not reject the null hypothesis.

Conflicting conclusions can arise when the sampling distribution is not symmetrical (i.e., is skewed to the right or left). This is illustrated in Figure 5.22. The sampling distribution, which is clearly skewed to the left, is shown in two positions. In the lower portion of Figure 5.22, the sampling distribution is positioned as it would be for conducting a test of H_0. Because less than 5 percent of the sampling distribution's right tail lies above the mean return of the back-tested rule, the test indicates the rule is significant at the .05 level. In other words, H_0 can be rejected in favor of the alternative hypothesis, H_A, that claims the rule has an expected return that is greater than zero.

The upper portion of Figure 5.22 shows the sampling distribution as it would be positioned to construct a 90 percent confidence interval using the bootstrap percentile method. Note that the lower bound of the confidence interval is below a zero rate of return. This tells us there is greater than a .05 probability that the rule's true rate of return is less than zero. In other words, the 90 percent confidence interval leads to a conclusion that is opposite to the conclusion of the hypothesis test. The

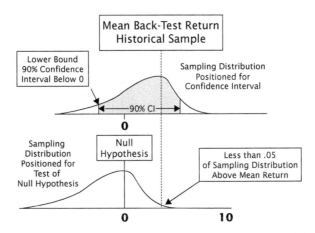

FIGURE 5.22 Potentially conflicting conclusions: hypothesis test versus confidence interval.

figure shows that the ambiguity is due to the asymmetrical shape of the sampling distribution.

Fortunately this problem does not afflict the research conducted in this book, which uses the sample mean as a performance statistic. The all-important Central Limit Theorem assures us that the sampling distribution of the mean will not be seriously skewed (asymmetrical) as long as the sample size is large. To recap, the Central Limit Theorem tells us that, as sample size increases, the sampling distribution of the mean tends toward a symmetrical bell shape. Other performance statistics may not behave this way. In situations where the sampling distribution is not symmetrical, there are bootstrap techniques, which involve pivoting the sampling distribution to alleviate this problem. Unfortunately, these other methods can have problems of their own. In any case, this all makes the mean return an attractive performance statistic to use in rule testing.

Confidence Intervals for the TT-4-91 Rule.   This section gives an example of the confidence interval for the rule TT-4-91. Figure 5.23 shows the 80 percent confidence interval superimposed on the bootstrapped

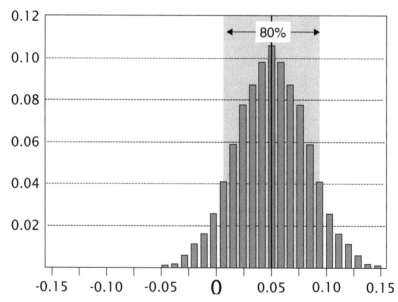

FIGURE 5.23 Sampling distribution and 80 percent confidence interval for rule TT-4-91.

sampling distribution positioned at the rule's observed back-tested return of +4.84 percent. The lower bound of the 80 percent confidence interval is +0.62 percent. The upper bound is +9.06 percent. This tells us that if rule TT-4-91 were to be back tested on 100 independent samples of data and an 80 percent confidence interval were to be placed around the mean return in each sample, in approximately 80 of the samples, the true expected return of the rule would be enclosed by the confidence interval.

CHAPTER 6

Data-Mining Bias: The Fool's Gold of Objective TA

In rule data mining, many rules are back tested and the rule with the best observed performance is selected. That is to say, data mining involves a performance competition that leads to a winning rule being picked. The problem is that the winning rule's observed performance that allowed it to be picked over all other rules systematically overstates how well the rule is likely to perform in the future. This systematic error is the data-mining bias.

Despite this problem, data mining is a useful research approach. It can be proven mathematically that, out of all the rules tested, the rule with the highest observed performance is the rule most likely to do the best in the future, provided a sufficient number of observations are used to compute performance statistics.[1] In other words, it pays to data mine even though the best rule's observed performance is positively biased. This chapter explains why the bias occurs, why it must be taken into account when making inferences about the future performance of the best rule, and how such inferences can be made.

I begin by introducing this somewhat abstract topic with several anecdotes, only one of which is related to rule data mining. They are appetizers intended to make later material more digestible. Readers who want to start on the main course immediately may choose to skip to the section titled "Data Mining."

The following definitions will be used throughout this chapter and are placed here for the convenience of the reader.

- **Expected performance:** the expected return of a rule in the immediate practical future. This can also be called the true performance of the rule, which is attributable to its legitimate predictive power.

- **Observed performance:** the rate of return earned by a rule in a back test.
- **Data-mining bias:** the expected difference between the observed performance of the best rule and its expected performance. *Expected difference* refers to a long-run average difference that would be obtained by numerous experiments that measure the difference between the observed return of the best rule and the expected return of the best rule.
- **Data mining:** the process of looking for patterns, models, predictive rules, and so forth in large statistical databases.
- **Best rule:** the rule with the best observed performance when many rules are back tested and their performances are compared.
- **In-sample data:** the data used for data mining (i.e., rule back testing).
- **Out-of-sample data:** data not used in the data mining or back-testing process.
- **Rule universe:** the full set of rules back tested in a data mining venture.
- **Universe size:** the number of rules comprising the rule universe.

FALLING INTO THE PIT: TALES OF THE DATA-MINING BIAS

This following account is apocryphal. Some years ago, before I took up the study of statistics, I was approached by an impresario seeking backers for a show business venture that he claimed would be enormously profitable. The show was to feature a monkey that could write Shakespearian prose by dancing on the keyboard of a word processor.

At each show, the literate monkey, whom the promoter had named the Bard, would be placed at a keyboard and a large screen would display to an audience what the monkey wrote, as it was being written. Surely, people would rush to see the Bard, and my share of ticket sales would yield a handsome return on the required investment of $50,000. At least, that was the promoter's claim. "It can't miss!" was his refrain.

I was intrigued, but wanted some proof that the monkey could actually produce Shakespearian prose. Any investor would. I was given proof ... of a sort. It was what accountants call a cold-comfort letter. The letter said, "We have examined the Bard's previous works and he has in fact written the words 'To be or not to be, that is the question.' We are, however, unfamiliar with the circumstances under which these words were written."

What I really wanted was a live demonstration. Regrettably, my request could not be accommodated. The impatient promoter explained the monkey was temperamental and besides, there were many other anxious investors clamoring to buy the limited number of shares being offered. So I seized the opportunity and plunked down $50,000. I was confident it was just a matter of time before the profits would start flowing in.

The night of the first show arrived. Carnegie Hall was packed to capacity with a crowd that anxiously awaited the first words. With everyone's eyes glued to the big screen, the Bard's first line of text appeared.

lkas1dlk5jf wo44iuldjs sk0ek 123pwkdzsdidip'adipjasdopiksd

Things went downhill quickly from there. The audience began screaming for refunds, I threw up, and the Bard defecated on the keyboard before scampering off the stage. My investment went up in a cloud of smoke.

What happened? Thinking it unimportant, the promoter failed to disclose a key fact. The Bard had been chosen from 1,125,385 other monkeys, all of whom had been given the opportunity to dance on a keyboard every day for the past 11 years, 4 months, and 5 days. A computer monitored all their gibberish to flag any sequence of letters that matched anything ever written by Shakespeare. The Bard was the first monkey to ever do so.

Even in my state of statistical illiteracy, I doubt I would have invested had I known this. Mere common sense would have told me that chance alone favored the occurrence of some Shakespearian quote in such a large mass of nonsense. The freedom to data mine the trillions of letters generated by an army of monkeys raised the probability of a lucky sequence of letters to a virtual certainty. The Bard was not literate, he was just lucky.

The fault, Dear Brutus, lay with the sincere but statistically naïve promoter. He was deluded by the data-mining bias and attributed too much significance to a result obtained by data mining. Despite my loss, I've tried not to judge the promoter too harshly. He sincerely believed that he had found a truly remarkable monkey. He was simply misled by intuition, a faculty inadequate for evaluating matters statistical and probabilistic.

By the way, the promoter has kept the Bard as a pet and still allows him to dance on that once-magical keyboard in hopes of new evidence of literacy. In the meanwhile, to keep body and soul together, he is now selling technical trading systems developed along similar lines. He has a throng of dancing monkeys developing rules, some of which seem to work quite well, in the historical data.

Proving the Existence of God with Baseball Stats

Collectors of sports statistics have also been seduced by the data-mining bias. For example, there is Norman Bloom, who concluded that interesting and unusual patterns found in baseball statistics prove the existence of God. After thousands of searches through his database, the dedicated data miner found patterns he believed to be so amazing they could only be explained by a universe made orderly by God.

One of Bloom's patterns was as follows: George Brett, the *third* baseman for Kansas City, hit his *third* home run in the *third* game of the play-offs, to tie the score *3-3*. Bloom reasoned that, for the number three to be connected in so many ways, compelled the conclusion it was the handiwork of God. Another interesting pattern discovered by Bloom had to do with the stock market: The Dow Jones Industrial Average crossed the 1,000 level 13 times in 1976, miraculously similar to the fact that there were 13 original colonies that united in 1776 to form the United States.

As pointed out by Ronald Kahn,[2] Bloom committed several errors on the way to his unjustified conclusions. First, he did not understand the role of randomness and that seemingly rare coincidences are in fact quite probable if one searches enough. Bloom found his mystical patterns by evaluating thousands of possible attribute combinations. Second, Bloom did not specify what constituted an important pattern before he began his searches. Instead, he took the liberty of using an arbitrary criterion of importance defined after the fact. Whatever struck his fancy as interesting and unusual was deemed to be important. Kahn points out that one is guaranteed to discover "interesting" patterns when they are searched for in such an undisciplined manner.

Discovering Hidden Predictions in the Old Testament

Even Bible scholars have fallen into the data mining pit. In this instance, the well intentioned but statistically unsophisticated researchers found predictions of major world events encoded in the text of the Old Testament. Knowledge of the future would certainly imply that the words had been inspired by an omniscient Creator. However, there was one small problem with these predictions, known as Bible Codes. They were always discovered after the predicted event had taken place. In other words, the codes predict with 20/20 hindsight.[3]

The Bible Codes are clusters of words imbedded in the text that are discovered by linking together letters separated by a specific number of intervening spaces or other letters. These constructed words are referred to as equal letter sequences or ELS. Code researchers grant themselves the freedom to try any spacing interval they wish and allow the words comprising the cluster to be arranged in virtually any configuration so long as the cluster occurs in what the researcher deems[4] to be a compact region of the original text. What constitutes a compact region and what words constitute a prediction are always defined after a code has been discovered. Note the use of an *evaluation* criterion defined *after the fact.* This is not scientifically kosher.

The Bible Code scholars contend that the occurrence of a code is so statistically unlikely that it can only be explained by its having been put there by God. Their fundamental error—the error made by all naive data miners—is the failure to understand that given enough searching (data mining), the occurrence of such patterns is actually highly probable. Thus, it is likely that researchers will find codes that correspond to names, places, and events of historical importance. For example, the word *1990* in the same region of text as *Saddam Hussein* and *war* are not rare events requiring a metaphysical explanation. However, when found in 1992, after the first Iraq war had taken place, the word pattern seemingly predicted the 1990 Iraq war. Bear in mind that the words *Bush, Iraq, invasion*, and *desert storm* would serve just as nicely as a code that also appears to predict the 1990 Iraq war. Indeed, there are a huge number of word combinations that would correspond to the 1990 war, after the particulars of that historical event are known.

In his 1997 book, *The Bible Code*, author Michael Drosnin, a journalist with no formal training in statistics, describes the research of Dr. Eliyahu Rips. Dr. Rips is an expert in the mathematics of group theory, a branch of mathematics that is not particularly relevant to the problem of data-mining bias. Though Drosnin claims that the Bible Codes have been endorsed by a roster of famous mathematicians, 45 statisticians who reviewed Rips's work found it to be totally unconvincing.[5] Data-mining bias is, at its heart, a problem of faulty statistical inference.

Statisticians take a dim view of the unconstrained searching practiced by Bible Code researchers. It commits a mathematical sin called the excessive burning of degrees of freedom. To the statistical sophisticate, the stench produced by this incineration is most foul. As pointed out by Dr. Barry Simon, "A Skeptical Look at the Torah Codes,"[6] in Chumash, just one of the 14 books comprising the Torah, approximately 3 billion possible words can be produced from the existing text when the ELS spacing interval is allowed to vary from 1 to 5,000. Searching this set of manufactured words for interesting configurations is no different than searching through tons of gibberish written by an army of monkeys dancing on keyboards.

The foolishness of the Bible Code scholars' search algorithms becomes apparent when they are applied to non-Biblical texts of similar length, such as the Sears catalogue, *Moby Dick*, Tolstoy's *War and Peace*, or the Chicago telephone directory. When these texts are searched, coded after the fact predictions of historical events are also found. This suggests the codes are a by-product of the search method and not of the text being searched.

In a more recent book by Drosnin, *The Bible Code II: The Countdown*, he shows how the codes "predicted" the terrible events of 9/11/01. Why, you ask, didn't he warn us before the events happened? He did not because he could not. He discovered the predictions after the tragedy occurred. Drosnin is another example of a well-intentioned but naïve researcher fooled by the data-mining bias.

Data-Mining Newspaper Reporters

Newspaper reporters have also been duped by the data-mining bias. In the mid 1980s, they reported the story of Evelyn Adams, who had won the New Jersey state lottery twice in four months.[7] Newspaper accounts put the probability of such an occurrence at 1 in 17 trillion. In fact, the probability of finding a double winner was far higher and the story far less newsworthy than the reporters had thought.

The before-the-fact (a priori) probability that Ms. Adams or any other individual *will win* the lottery winner twice is indeed 17 trillion to one. However, the after-the-fact probability of finding someone who *has already won* twice by searching the entire universe of all lottery players is far higher. Harvard statisticians Percy Diaconis and Frederick Mosteller estimated the probability to be about 1 in 30.

The qualifier *after-the-fact* is the key. It refers to a perusal of data after outcomes are known. Just as the probability that any individual monkey will in the future produce a Shakespearian quote is extremely small, the probability that there exists some monkey, among millions of monkeys, that has already produced some literate prose, is substantially higher. Given enough opportunity, randomness produces some extraordinary outcomes. The seemingly rare is actually quite likely.

Mining the UN Database for Gold
and Finding Butter

David J. Leinweber, on the faculty of California Institute of Technology and formerly a managing partner at First Quandrant, a quantitative pension management company, has warned financial market researchers about the data-mining bias. To illustrate the pitfalls of excessive searching, he tested several hundred economic time series in a UN database to find the one with the highest predictive correlation to the S&P 500. It turned out to be the level of butter production in Bangladesh, with a correlation of about 0.70, an unusually high correlation in the domain of economic forecasting.

Intuition alone would tell us a high correlation between Bangladesh butter and the S&P 500 is specious, but now imagine if the time series with the highest correlation had a plausible connection to the S&P 500. Intuition would not warn us. As Leinweber points out, when the total number of time series examined is taken into account, the correlation between Bangladesh butter and the S&P 500 Index is not statistically significant.

The bottom line: whether one searches sport statistics, the Bible, the random writings of monkeys, the universe of lottery players, or financial market history, data mining can lead to false conclusions if the data mining bias is not taken into account.

THE PROBLEM OF ERRONEOUS KNOWLEDGE IN OBJECTIVE TECHNICAL ANALYSIS

TA is comprised of two mutually exclusive domains—subjective and objective. To recap, objective TA is confined to methods that are sufficiently well defined that they can be reduced to a computerized algorithm and back tested. Everything else is, by default, subjective TA.

Both domains are contaminated with erroneous knowledge, but the falsehoods are of very different types. The loosely defined propositions of subjective TA carry no cognitive freight, generate no testable predictions,[8] and are, therefore, shielded from empirical challenge. Without this crucial procedure for excising worthless ideas, falsehoods accumulate. As a result, subjective TA is not a legitimate body of knowledge but a collection of folklore resting on a flimsy foundation of anecdote and intuition.

Objective TA methods have the potential to be valid knowledge but only if back-test results are considered in light of randomness (sampling variability) and data-mining bias. Because many objective practitioners are unaware of these effects, falsehoods accumulate in this domain as well.

Erroneous objective TA manifests as out-of-sample[9] performance deterioration—a rule that performs well in the sample used for back testing but then performs worse in out-of-sample data. This problem is illustrated in Figure 6.1.

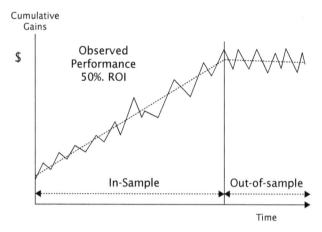

FIGURE 6.1 Out-of-sample performance deterioration.

Explanations for Out-of-Sample Deterioration: Old and New

Out-of-sample performance deterioration is a well-known problem.[10] Objective technicians have proposed a number of explanations. I propose a relatively new one, based on data-mining bias.

The least plausible explanation attributes the problem to random variation. Although it is true that a rule's performance will vary from one sample of history to another due to sampling variability, this explanation does not even fit the evidence. If random variation were responsible, then out-of-sample performance would be higher than in-sample performance about as frequently as it is lower. Anyone experienced with back testing knows that out-of-sample performance is inferior far more often.

A second rationale is that the market's dynamics changed when the out-of-sample period began. It is reasonable to assume that financial markets are nonstationary systems.[11] However, it is not reasonable to assume that each time a rule fails out of sample it is because market dynamics have changed. It would be odd, almost fiendish, for the market to always change its ways just when a rule moves from the technician's laboratory to the real world of trading. It is simply implausible to suggest that a market's dynamics change as frequently as rules fail out of sample.

An even more elaborate explanation, also based on changing market dynamics, invokes the additional assumption that the change occurred because the rule has been adopted by too many traders. This story asserts that the buying and selling of the traders using the rule has destroyed the market pattern that accounted for the rule's back-test profitability. This rationale also lacks plausibility. Given that there are an almost infinite number of rules that could be formulated, it would be unlikely that a large enough number of participants would adopt any particular rule. Even when numerous traders adopt similar rules, as is the case with futures trading funds that employ objective trend-following methods, reduced rule performance seems to be due to changes in market volatility that are not related to the usage of technical systems.[12]

A more plausible explanation[13] of out-of-sample performance breakdown is based on randomness. It asserts that market dynamics are a combination of systematic or patterned behavior and randomness or noise. Valid rules exploit the market's systematic features. Because the systematic component should continue to manifest in out-of-sample data, it is a dependable source of rule profits. In contrast, the random component is a nonrecurring phenomenon that will manifest differently in each sample of data. It is reasoned that a portion of a rule's in-sample performance was luck—a coincidental correspondence between the rule's signals and the market's nonrecurring noise. These lucky profits will not manifest out of sample, and so future performance will fall below past performance. This explanation is closer to the mark, but it is incomplete. Randomness is only one villain.

A more complete account of out-of-sample performance deterioration is based on the data-mining bias. It names two villains: (1) randomness, which is a relatively large component of observed performance and (2) the logic of data mining, in which a best-performing rule is selected after the back-tested performances of all tested rules are available for the data miner's examination. When these two effects combine, they cause the observed performance of the best rule to overstate its future (expected) performance. Thus, it is likely that the best rule's future performance will be worse than the level of performance that caused it to be selected from the universe of rules tested.

The data-mining bias explanation for out-of-sample performance deterioration is superior to the one based on changed market dynamics. Both explanations fit the data in the sense that they are both consistent with the fact that out-of-sample performance tends to be worse. However, the latter explanation invokes the assumption that market dynamics have changed. The data-mining bias explanation does not. It simply says that the process of data mining favors the selection of rules that benefited from good luck during the back test. When choosing among a set of explanations that are equally adept at accounting for a phenomenon, it is wisest to choose the one making the fewest assumptions. This is the principle of simplicity known as Occam's Razor, which was discussed in Chapter 3.

As will be shown, the observed performance of a rule can be decomposed into two independent components: randomness and the rule's inherent predictive power. Of these two, randomness is by far the more dominant component. Thus, the rule with the best-observed performance was most likely the beneficiary of good luck. That is to say, randomness boosted the rule's performance above the level attributable to its true predictive power, if it possessed any. The opposite is the case for the rule with the worst observed performance. It was most likely negatively impacted by luck. By selecting the rule with the highest observed performance, the data miner winds up picking a rule that experienced a large component of good luck. Because luck cannot be counted on to repeat, this rule's out-of-sample performance is likely to settle back toward a level that is representative of its inherent predictive power. This makes it probable that out-of-sample performance will be lower than the level of performance that allowed the rule to win the performance competition. The bottom line: out-of-sample performance deterioration of the best rule is most probably a fall from an unrealistically high expectation rather than an actual decline in the rule's predictive power.

DATA MINING

Data mining is the extraction of knowledge, in the form of patterns, rules, models, functions, and such, from large databases. The limitations and biases of human intelligence make this task nearly impossible for the unaided mind when the knowledge involves multiple variables, nonlinear relationships, or high levels of noise. Thus, data mining relies on computerized algorithms for knowledge extraction. An excellent discussion of the principal methods used in data mining can be found in *Elements of Statistical Learning*,[14] *Predictive Data Mining: A Practical Guide*,[15] and *Data Mining: Practical Machine Learning Tools and Techniques*.[16]

Data Mining as a Multiple Comparison Procedure

Data mining is based on a problem solving approach called a multiple comparison procedure[17] (MCP). The basic idea behind an MCP is to test many different solutions to the problem and pick the one that performs the best according to some criterion. Three elements are required to apply an MCP: (1) a well-defined problem, (2) a set of candidate solutions, and (3) a figure of merit or scoring function that quantifies the goodness of each candidate's performance. After all scores are in, they are compared and the candidate with the highest score (best-observed performance) is selected as the best solution for the problem.

Consider how this problem-solving paradigm applies in the context of rule data mining:

1. **The problem:** timing long and short positions in a financial market to generate profits.

2. **A set of candidate solutions** (solution universe or solution space): a set of rules proposed by the objective technician.

3. **Figure of merit:** a measure of financial performance such as the average rate of return over a historical test period, Sharpe ratio, return to Ulcer Index.[18]

The performances of all rules are determined by back testing, and the rule achieving the highest performance is selected.

Rule Data Mining as a Specification Search

Data mining can be understood as a specification search. That is to say, it is a hunt for the specifications of the rule that produces the highest performance. The specifications are a set of mathematical and/or logical operations applied to one or more market data series thus transforming them into a time series of market positions dictated by the rule.

Suppose the rule defined below turned out to be the best performing rule:

> *Hold a long position in the S&P 500 if the ratio of Dow Jones Transportation Average close divided by the S&P 500 close is greater than its 50-day moving average, else hold a short position.*

The rule is specified by two mathematical operators: *ratio* and *moving average*; two logical operators: the inequality operator *greater-than*, the conditional *if, then, else*; a single numerical constant: *50*; and two data series: *Dow Jones Transports* and *S&P 500*. Data mining discovered that this set of specifications produced better performance than any alternative set of specifications that was tested.

Types of Searches

Data mining searches range from the simple to the sophisticated. One of the ways in which they differ is how broadly the search universe is defined. This section considers three definitions of the search universe, starting with the narrowest search and progressing to the broadest. All approaches to data mining, whether they search simply and narrowly or broadly using the most advanced methods are subject to data-mining bias.

Parameter Optimization.   The narrowest form of data mining is parameter *optimization*. Here, the search universe is confined to rules with the same form differing only in terms of their parameter values. Thus, the search is restricted to finding the parameter value(s) of the highest-performing rule of a particular form.

An example of a rule form would be the dual-moving-average crossover rule. It is specified by two parameters; look-back periods for the short-term and long-term moving average. Signals are given when the short-term moving average crosses above (buy) and below (sell) a longer-term moving average. Parameter optimization searches for the pair of parameter values that yields the highest performance.

The maximum number of dual-moving-average crossover rules that can be searched is equal to the product of the number of values tested for the short-term parameter and number of values tested for the long-term parameter. A search that considers all these combinations is referred to as an exhaustive or brute-force search.

There are more intelligent search methods that restrict the search to combinations that are more likely to yield good results. This is accomplished by using the performances of parameter combinations tested early in the search to guide the combinations that will be tested at later stages. One such intelligent search method is the genetic algorithm, a technique based loosely on the principles of biological evolution. Its demonstrated ability to find parameter combinations that are close to optimal relatively quickly makes it especially useful when the number of possible parameter combinations is high. Genetic algorithms have also proven to be effective when performance is impacted strongly by randomness, which renders more conventional guided search methods based on calculus impractical. Excellent discussions of optimization methods can be found in Pardo,[19] and a review of various advanced methods can be found in Katz and McCormick[20] and Kaufman.[21]

Rule Searching.   A broader version of data mining is *rule searching*. Here, the universe of rules differ in their conceptual form as well as their parameter values. The dual-moving-average crossover rule is one formalism for trend-following. Thus, it is simply one form in the broader category of trend-following rules that also include channel breakouts, moving-average bands, and so forth. The general category of trend-following rules is merely one technical analysis category among others that include counter-trend (mean-reversion) rules,[22] extreme value rules, divergence rules,[23] diffusion rules, and so forth. Each category can be realized with numerous specific rule forms.

Part Two of this book presents a data-mining case study that is based on rule searching. The study will focus on three rule categories or themes: trends, extreme-values and transitions, and divergence. Each theme is realized with a specific rule form, which is defined in Chapter 8.

Though rule searching considers a multitude of rule forms, each rule's complexity remains fixed throughout the course of the search. Complexity refers to the number of parameters required to specify the rule. In other words rule searching, as defined herein, does not involve combining simple rules to produce more complex rules

Rule Induction with Variable Complexity. The broadest and most ambitious form of data mining is rule induction. Here the search considers rules of undefined complexity. As the search proceeds, rules of ever-greater complexity are considered. A complex rule might be thought of as a composition of a simpler rule conjoined by logical operators or combined with a mathematical function as in a multivariate model. Thus rule-induction data mining is concerned with finding the rule of optimal complexity.

In contrast to less ambitious forms of data mining in which a rule's complexity is defined at the outset of the search, rule induction uses machine learning (autonomous induction) to find the degree of complexity that produces the best performance. One scheme for rule induction starts by testing individual rules. Next, pairs of rules are considered to see if their performance is better than the best individual rule. Gradually, progressively more complex rules are tested and evaluated. In effect, rule-induction methods learn how to combine rules to optimize performance.

Genetic algorithms, neural networks, recursive partitioning, kernel regression, support-vector machines, and boosted trees are some of the methods used for these most ambitious of data-mining ventures. An excellent discussion of various methods and supporting statistical theory can be found in *The Elements of Statistical Learning* by Hastie, Tibshirani, and Friedman.[24]

OBJECTIVE TA RESEARCH

The goal of the objective technician is the discovery of a rule(s) that will be profitable in the future. The research method is back testing, which produces an observable measure of performance. On the basis of this statistic, an inference is made about a population parameter, the rule's future or expected performance. It can be said, therefore, that the essence of objective TA is statistical inference.

Why Objective Technicians Must Data Mine

The problem of out-of-sample performance failure has encouraged some practitioners of objective TA to reject data mining. This is neither a wise nor viable position. Today, an objective technician who refuses to data mine is like the taxi driver who refuses to abandon the horse-drawn carriage—a charming relic but no longer suitable for getting to one's destination efficiently.

Several factors compel the adoption of data mining as the preferred method of knowledge acquisition. First, it works. Experiments presented later in this chapter will show that under fairly general conditions, the greater the number of rules back tested the greater the likelihood of finding a good rule.

Second, technological trends favor data mining. The cost effectiveness of personal computers, the availability of powerful back-testing and data-mining software, and the availability of historical databases now make data mining practical for individuals. As recently as a decade ago, the costs limited data mining to institutional investors.

Third, at its current stage of evolution, TA lacks the theoretical foundation that would permit a more traditional scientific approach to knowledge acquisition. In developed sciences, such as physics, a single hypothesis can be deduced from established theory and its predictions can be tested against new observations. In the absence of theory, a data-mining approach is called for, in which a multitude of hypotheses (rules) are proposed and tested. The risk of this shotgun approach is fool's gold—rules that fit the data by accident. Steps that can minimize this risk are discussed later in this chapter.

Single-Rule Back-Testing versus Data Mining

Not all back testing is data mining. When just a single rule is proposed and back tested, there is no data mining. This mode of research is illustrated in Figure 6.2. If the rule's back test proves to be unsatisfactory, the research stops and other more practical means of earning a living are considered.

Data mining involves the back testing of many rules and picking one based on its superior performance. This process is illustrated in Figure 6.3. Note that as depicted here an initial unsatisfactory performance by

FIGURE 6.2 Single rule back testing.

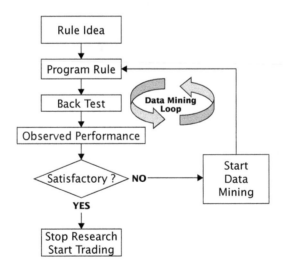

FIGURE 6.3 Rule Data mining.

the first rule tested does not stop the research. The rule is refined or a new rule is defined, and it is tested and its performance is evaluated. The cycle continues until a rule with good performance is produced. This process may involve testing tens, hundreds, thousands, or even greater numbers of rules.

Legitimate Uses of Observed Performance

For this discussion, the assumed performance statistic is the mean rate of return over the back-test period. The observed performance statistic can play a legitimate role both in single-rule back testing and in data mining. However, the roles are different. In single-rule back testing, observed performance serves as an estimator of future performance. In data mining, observed performance serves as a selection criterion. Problems arise for the data miner when observed performance is asked to play both roles.

In single-rule back testing, the tested rule's mean return can legitimately be used as an unbiased estimate of the rule's expected return. In other words, the tested rule's most likely future return is its back tested return. This is merely a restatement of a something covered in Chapter 4. There, we learned that a sample mean provides an unbiased estimate of the mean of the parent population that gave birth to the sample. The sample mean may err due to the random variation of sampling. It may be greater than the population mean or less than it, but neither error is more likely. This principle pertains to the case of a single-rule back test. The rule's mean return in a back test is an unbiased estimate of its expected return in the future. And although its historic mean return is indeed its most likely return in the future, its performance may prove to be higher or lower, with neither being more likely. This is illustrated in Figure 6.4.

In data mining, the back-test performance statistic plays a very different role than it does in single-rule back testing. In data mining, back-

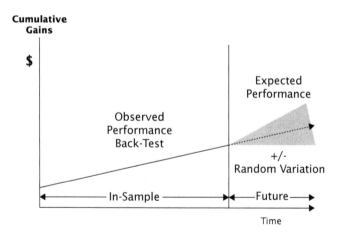

FIGURE 6.4 Expected performance for single rule back test.

tested performance serves as a selection criterion. That is to say, it is used to identify the best rule. The mean returns of all back-tested rules are compared and the one with the highest return is selected. This, too, is a perfectly legitimate use of the back test (observed) performance statistic.

It is legitimate in the sense that the rule with the highest back-tested mean return is in fact the rule that is most likely to perform the best in the future. This is certainly not guaranteed, but it is the most reasonable inference that can be made. A formal mathematical proof of this statement is offered by White.[25]

The Data Miner's Mistake: Misuse of Observed Performance

Let's recap two key points. In a single-rule back test, past performance can be used as an unbiased estimate of future performance. In multiple-rule back testing (i.e., data mining), past performance can be used as a selection criterion.

The data miner's mistake is using the best rule's back-tested performance to estimate its expected performance. This is not a legitimate use of back-tested performance because the back-tested performance of the best-performing rule is positively biased. That is, the level of performance that allowed the rule to win the performance competition overstates its true predictive power and its expected performance. This is the data-mining bias. This concept is illustrated in Figure 6.5.

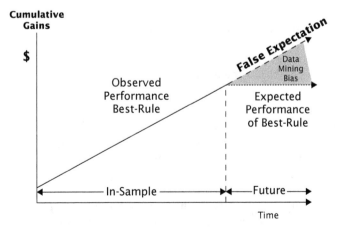

FIGURE 6.5 Expected performance of best data-mined rule.

The best rule's performance does not truly deteriorate out of sample. It only appears that way as the out-of-sample performance assumes a level that reflects the rule's true predictive power without the good luck that allowed it to beat the other rules. Its in-sample performance was a combination of some level of predictive power, possibly zero, and a big component of good luck. The good luck that shined on the rule during the back test is now shining elsewhere. In a like manner, the monkey did not suffer a loss of literary skill on the night of the big show. His performance merely reflected his true literary ability minus the good luck that allowed him to produce letters that happened to match a segment of Shakespearian prose.

DATA MINING AND STATISTICAL INFERENCE

This section discusses the connection between data-mining bias and statistical inference. This section will cover the following points: (1) the distinction between biased and unbiased estimators, (2) the distinction between random error and systematic error (i.e., bias), (3) the fact that unbiased estimators are afflicted with random error but biased estimators are afflicted with both random error and systematic error, (4) statistical statements hold true for a large number of observations, such as a large number of estimates, and (5) the data-mining bias is an effect that shows up generally over many instances of data mining; thus we cannot say that any particular data-mined result is biased.

Unbiased Error and Systematic Error

All scientific observations are subject to error. Error is defined as the difference between an observed value and the true value:

$$\text{Error} = \text{observed} - \text{true}$$

A positive error is said to occur when the observed value is greater than true value. Negative error is the reverse. If a scale indicates a person weighs 140 lbs but they actually weight 150, the error is negative 10 lbs.

There are two distinct types of error: unbiased and biased (systematic). All observations are infected with some degree of unbiased error. No measuring instrument or technique is perfect. This type of error has an expected value of zero. This means that if a large number of observations are made on some phenomenon, such as the return of a rule, and those observations are afflicted only with unbiased error, the observed values will be haphazardly distributed about the true value. If an average were to be computed for all these errors the average would be approximately zero. See Figure 6.6.

In contrast, observations afflicted with systematic error tend to lie on one side of the truth. Such observations are said to be biased. When the errors of many biased observations are averaged, the average error will be distinctly nonzero. See Figure 6.7. In the illustration the observations are positively biased and their average error (observed – true) is positive.

Suppose a chemist observes the weight of a residue left by a chemical reaction on one hundred separate instances. Unbiased error might be attributable to random variations in laboratory humidity over the course of the one hundred weighings. The amount of moisture in the residue affects its weight. Systematic error, if present, could be due to an imperfection in the scale, always causing the observed weight to be lower than the true weight.

Unbiased and Biased Statistics

Interpreting a large sample of observations is difficult. As was discussed in Chapter 4, a sensible first step is data reduction. This reduces the large

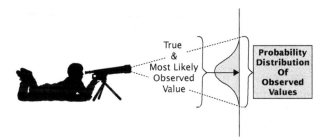

FIGURE 6.6 Unbiased observations.

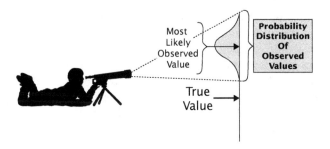

FIGURE 6.7 Observations with systematic error.

set of measurements to a smaller set of summary statistics: sample mean, sample variance, and other computed measures that describe the entire set of observations.

Chapter 4 also pointed out that a sample statistic, such as the mean, is subject to a particular type of random error called sampling error. This error is unbiased. Here, the term *error* refers to the deviation between a sample mean and the mean of population from which the sample was taken. Because the sample does not represent the population perfectly, the mean of the sample will deviate to some degree from the mean of the population.

Relating this back to objective TA, a rule back test produces a large sample of observations—the rule's daily, weekly, or monthly returns. This sample is made more intelligible by reducing it to a performance statistic (e.g., annualized average return, Sharpe ratio, and such). As is true of any sample statistic, the performance statistic is subject to random error. However, the statistic may also be subject to systematic error or bias.

To state the obvious, a historical performance statistic cannot be put in the bank or be used to buy a Ferrari. Its sole economic utility is the inference it allows us to make about future performance of the rule that produced it. Objective technicians use back-tested performance to make an inference about a rule's expected performance in the form of a confidence interval or a hypothesis test. In either case, the accuracy of the inference will depend on the type of error: unbiased or systematic, and its magnitude.

Biased statistics are afflicted with systematic error. As stated previously in a single-rule back test, the mean return is an unbiased statistic. Therefore, inferences about the rule's expected return based on back-test performance will be subject only to a form of unbiased error called sampling variability.

This, however, is not the case for the best rule found via data mining. The observed average return of the best-performing rule is a positively biased statistic. As a result, inferences based on it will be systematically in error. This means that when conducting a hypothesis test, one would be prone to reject the null hypothesis more frequently than the significance level would suggest. For example, at a significance level of 0.05 one expects to reject the null hypothesis in error only 5 times in 100. However, if the observed performance is positively biased, then H_0 will be rejected more frequently than it should, perhaps far more frequently. This will result in trading using rules that appear to have predictive power but in fact do not. The question is: What causes the back-tested return of the best rule, the rule picked by the data miner, to overstate its true predictive power?

The Mean versus the Maximum

Single-rule back testers and data miners are looking at two entirely different statistics. The single-rule back tester is observing the mean of a single sample. The data miner is observing the maximum mean among a multitude of sample means. It is easy to overlook the fact that these are two entirely different statistics.

To be clear, in the case of a single-rule back test there is one set of results—the rule's daily returns generated over the back-test period. They are summarized by a performance statistic (e.g., mean daily return). In data mining, many rules are back tested, and so there are many sets of results and many performance statistics. If 50 rules have been back tested the data miner has the opportunity to observe 50 mean returns prior to selecting the rule that produced the maximum mean return.

The set of 50 means returns can be considered as a set of observations, which, in turn, could be summarized with a statistic. For example one could compute the *mean of the means*. That is the mean return of all 50 rules. Another statistic that could be computed for this set of observations would be the *minimum mean*—the mean return of the rule that did the worst. Yet another statistic would be the *maximum mean*—the mean return of the rule that did the best.

The statistic observed by the data miner is the *maximum mean* from among the 50 rules. This is illustrated in Figure 6.8, where all rules are assumed to be useless and have an expected return equal to zero. Each dot represents the observed mean return of a different rule. Note that the mean return of the rule that had the maximum return (37 percent) is not at all representative of that rule's expected return (0 percent). It simply got lucky in the back test. When many rules are back tested, the one with

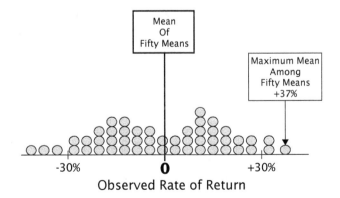

FIGURE 6.8 Observed performance of 50 rule back tests.

the highest average return will almost always have been the beneficiary of good luck. This is why its back-tested performance is likely to overestimate its expected performance. In a different sample, with less luck, the rule is likely to do worse.

This is the key lesson to take away from this: The observed performance of the best-performing rule, amongst a large set of rules, is a positively biased estimate of that best rule's expected performance because it incorporates a substantial degree of good luck. Data miners who don't understand this are likely to be disappointed with this rule's out-of-sample performance.

Sound Inference Requires the Correct Sampling Distribution

Sound statistical inference depends on using the correct sampling distribution. Each test statistic has a sampling distribution that is appropriate for testing its statistical significance. The sampling distribution that would be correct for testing the significance of a single sample mean or constructing its confidence interval would not be correct if the test statistic being observed were, in fact, a maximum mean among a multitude of sample means.

Therefore, to make sound inferences, the data miner requires the sampling distribution of the maximum mean among a multitude of means because that is the statistic being considered when evaluating the best rule found by data mining. The central tendency of the sampling distribution of the maximum mean reflects the role that good luck can play in data mining. The central tendency of a sampling distribution of a single sample mean does not.

Now let's consider how all this impacts a test of significance. As discussed in Chapter 5, in a traditional test of significance, the null hypothesis asserts that the trading rule has an expected return equal to zero or less. The test statistic is the rule's observed mean return. In this case let's assume the return was +10 percent annualized. The sampling distribution of the test statistic is centered at the hypothesized value of zero. The p-value is the area of the sampling distribution that is equal to or greater than a 10 percent return. This area represents the probability that, if the rule's expected return were truly equal to zero, the rule could have produced a return of +10 percent or higher by chance. If the p-value is smaller than a preset value, such as 0.05, the null hypothesis would be rejected and the alternative hypothesis, that the rule's expected return is greater than zero, would be accepted. So long as the performance of only one rule was being evaluated this is all well and good.

Now consider significance testing in the data mining case. Continuing with the data mining example from the prior section, assume that 50 rules have been back tested. The rule with best performance earned annualized return of +37 percent. A traditional test of significance, with a significance level of 0.05, would look like the one in Figure 6.9. The sampling distribution shown is centered at zero, reflecting the null's assumption that the expected return of a rule with no predictive power would generate a return of zero. This sampling distribution does not account for the data-mining bias. Experimental results presented later in this chapter will show that this assumption is wrong. They will demonstrate that even when all rules tested during data mining have expected returns equal to zero, the best performing rule is likely to display a much higher performance than zero.

Note in Figure 6.9 that the observed performance of +37 percent falls far out in the right tail of the sampling distribution giving a p-value of less than 0.05. On the basis of this evidence, the null hypothesis would be rejected and the inference would be that the rule has an expected return greater than zero (i.e., has predictive power). This conclusion is wrong!

If, however, the observed performance of this best rule of 50 were to be subjected to a more advanced test of statistical significance that does take into account the data-mining bias, the picture would look considerably different. This is shown Figure 6.10, where the observed mean return for best-rule-of-50 is compared to the correct sampling distribution. This is the sampling distribution of the statistic *maximum-mean among 50 means*. This sampling distribution properly reflects the biasing effects of data mining. Note that the sampling distribution is no longer centered at zero. Rather, it is centered at +33 percent. Against

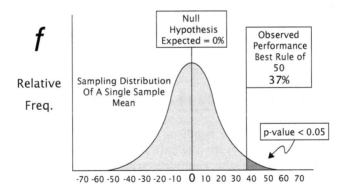

FIGURE 6.9 Traditional sampling distribution (does not account for data-mining bias).

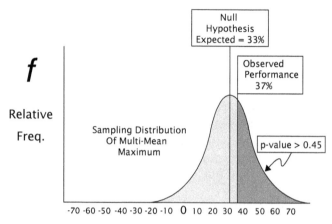

FIGURE 6.10 Correct sampling distribution (accounts for data-mining bias).

this backdrop, the best rule's performance no longer appears significant. The fraction of the sampling distribution that is equal to or greater than the observed return of 37 percent is nearly half (0.45) of the distribution total area. In other words, if the expected return of each of the 50 rules were zero, then there is a 0.45 probability that the mean return of the best rule would be greater than or equal to 37 percent due to luck. From this, it is clear that 37 percent is not a statistically significant result. The particular sample of data in which the rule excelled just happened to favor the rule.

Figure 6.10 shows that randomness (good luck) can inflate the performance of a rule with no predictive power. It turns out that randomness is only one of two factors that jointly cause the data-mining bias. The other cause is the selection principle that underlies all multiple comparison procedures: picking the candidate with the best-observed performance.

DATA-MINING BIAS: AN EFFECT WITH TWO CAUSES

The data-mining bias is the result of a conjoint effect: (1) randomness and (2) the selection imperative of data mining or any multiple comparison procedure—picking the candidate with the best-observed performance. This section will examine how these two factors combine to cause the observed performance of the best rule to overstate its expected performance.

Two Components of Observed Performance

The observed performance of a rule can be factored into two components. One component of observed performance is attributable to the rule's true predictive power, if it has any. This is the component of performance due to a recurring feature of market behavior that is exploited by the rule and that should continue to manifest in the immediate practical future. This is the rule's expected performance.

The second component of observed performance is attributable to randomness. Randomness can manifest as either good luck or bad luck. Good luck boosts observed performance above expected performance whereas bad luck pushes observed performance below expected. The component of observed performance attributable to randomness cannot be expected to repeat in the immediate practical future.

This discussion is summed up by the equation in Figure 6.11.

The Spectrum of Randomness

It is useful to think of a spectrum of randomness. This concept is depicted in Figure 6.12.[26] At one end of the spectrum, observed performance is

$$\begin{array}{c}\text{Observed} \\ \text{Performance}\end{array} = \left(\begin{array}{c}\text{Expected} \\ \text{Performance}\end{array}\right) +/- \left(\text{Randomness}\right)$$

FIGURE 6.11 The two components of observed performance.

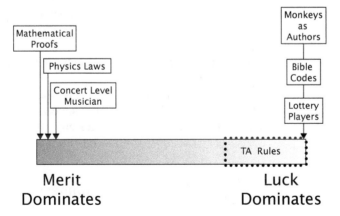

FIGURE 6.12 Spectrum of randomness—relative contributions of merit versus luck in observed outcomes.

dominated by randomness. At this extreme, all performances are purely a matter of luck. Here we find literary works of monkeys dancing on word processors and outcomes of lottery players. At the other end of the spectrum, observed performance is dominated by merit or systematic behavior. At this extreme, it is only merit that matters. Producing a valid proof of a mathematical theorem resides here. Very nearby are the observed performances of concert-level musicians. Also, in this neighborhood we find the the laws of physics whose highly accurate predictions are made possible by the orderly behavior of certain aspects of nature.

Toward the middle of the randomness spectrum lie the most interesting data mining problems. The farther to the random end of the spectrum one goes, the greater the risk of data-mining bias. Toward the right end of the continuum, we find a region that contains the TA rules. The complexity and randomness of financial markets assure us that even the most potent rules will be weakly predictive. In this zone, the magnitude of the data-mining bias will be large.

Now we come to an important principle. The larger the contribution of randomness (luck) relative to merit in observed performance, the larger will be the magnitude of the data-mining bias. The reason is this: The greater the role of luck relative to merit, the greater the chance that one of the many candidate rules will experience an extraordinarily lucky performance. This is the candidate that will be selected by the data miner. However, in situations where observed performance is strictly or primarily due to a candidate's true merit, the data-mining bias will be nonexistent or very small. In these cases, a candidate's past performance will be a reliable predictor of future performance and the data miner will rarely fill the hopper with fool's gold.

Because financial markets are extremely difficult to predict, most of a rule's observed performance will be due to randomness rather than its predictive power. Thus the equation previously given in Figure 6.11 might be better illustrated as it is in Figure 6.13. The large role of randomness relative to merit (i.e., predictive power) makes it likely that TA rule data mining will be infected with a large bias.

The range of problems to which multiple comparison procedures might be applied can be visualized as lying along the spectrum of randomness. Toward the random end of the spectrum is a range associated with

$$\frac{\text{Observed}}{\text{Performance}} = \left(\begin{smallmatrix}\text{Predictive}\\\text{Power}\end{smallmatrix}\right) +/- \left[\text{Randomness}\right]$$

FIGURE 6.13 Relative contributions of randomness and predictive power in observed performance.

TA rule data mining. I used a range to represent rule data mining rather than a single location to indicate that the level of randomness will vary from one mining venture to the next. As will be demonstrated later in this chapter, the level of randomness in any given data mining venture is determined by five independent factors.[27] When these factors are taken into consideration, it becomes possible to develop statistical significance procedures that are better able to deal with the data-mining bias. In other words, it becomes possible to compute the statistical significance of or confidence interval for a rule that was discovered by data mining. These procedures alleviate the key problem facing objective TA practitioners using data mining for knowledge discovery.

The Effectiveness of Multiple Comparison Procedures under Differing Conditions of Randomness

Multiple comparison procedures are applied to problems where a best solution is sought. A universe of candidate solutions is proposed. A figure of merit quantifies the observed performance of each candidate and the one with the best-observed performance is selected.

Many people presume that MCP delivers on two promises: (1) The candidate with the highest observed performance is most likely to perform the best in the future, and (2) the observed performance of the best-performing candidate is a reliable estimate of its future performance. It does deliver on the first promise. However, in the domain of TA rule back testing, it does not deliver on the second.

With regard to the first promise, that the candidate with the highest observed performance is also the one most likely to do best in the future, this was proved to be true by White[28] as the number of observations approaches infinity. White showed that, as the sample size approaches infinity, the probability that the candidate rule with the highest expected return (i.e., the truly best rule) will make itself known by having the best observed performance approaches 1.0. This tells us that the basic logic of data mining is sound! The rule with the highest observed performance is the rule that should be selected. The validity of this assumption will also be demonstrated by mathematical experiments presented later in this chapter: Experimental Investigation of the Data-Mining Bias. These results show that when a sufficient number of observations are used to compute a rule's performance statistic (e.g., its mean return), the rule with the highest observed performance does have a higher expected return than a rule picked at random from the universe of rules tested. Data mining must, at the very least, pass this minimal test of efficacy for it to be considered a worthwhile research method, and it does!

With regard to the second promise, that the observed performance of the selected candidate is a reliable estimate of its future performance, the news is not good. Jensen and Cohen[29] point out that, when MCP is applied in situations where randomness plays a significant role in observed performance, the observed performance of the best-performing candidate overestimates its expected (future) performance. In other words, when observed performance is significantly determined by luck, it is gives a positively biased estimate. This is the case in TA rule data mining.

Observed performance is a reliable estimate of the best candidate's future performance in situations where randomness is nonexistent or so low that it can never influence the choice of the wining candidate. Such is the case in a music competition or a competition at doing mathematical proofs, where it is merit, not luck, that carries the day.

The bottom line: the MCP selected candidate is the candidate most likely to do best in the future so long as a large number of observations are used to compute the performance statistic. Nevertheless, in problems where randomness has a significant impact, observed performance is positively biased, and the selected candidate's future performance will, in all probability, be worse than the performance that allowed it to win the competition.

MCP Efficacy in Low Randomness Situations

First, consider the application of MCP to problems with low randomness. At this end of the spectrum, a candidate's observed performance is dominated by merit, and MCP is effective in identifying superior merit.

This problem is exemplified by the task of hiring a new first violinist for a symphony orchestra.[30] The universe of candidates consists of the set of musicians applying for the job. Each is asked to perform a challenging composition, without prior rehearsal, for a panel of judges. The judges' evaluation is the figure of merit. This acid test of instrumental competence, known as sightreading, is effective because great performances do not occur by luck. If luck is a factor, it is a minor one. For example, a great musician may have an off day because of a marital spat or a flat tire on the way to the audition, but even these random influences will have only a small effect on a truly meritorious musician.

In this situation, observed performance is an accurate indicator of true merit and an excellent predictor of future performance. This is depicted in Figure 6.14. Each candidate's merit, which is equivalent to his expected performance, is indicated by the arrow. Both musicians are excellent, although one is slightly better. The distribution of possible performance surrounding each candidate's merit is narrow, indicating the minor impact of randomness on observed performance. Note

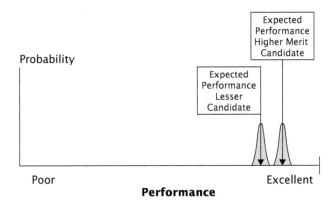

FIGURE 6.14 Low randomness—small merit differential. True merit shines through thin fog of randomness.

that there is no overlap in the distributions so that even if the better candidate has an unlucky performance (i.e., at the extreme low end of the distribution) and the lesser candidate has an extremely lucky one, the better candidate will still be selected. This is another way of saying that randomness is unlikely to inflate the inferior competitor's performance sufficiently such that it would be selected over the higher merit candidate.

MCP Efficacy in High Randomness

Now consider a situation at the opposite end of the randomness spectrum, TA rule data mining. Here, randomness has a major impact on observed performance, for even the most potent TA rules or models possess relatively little predictive power. This is a consequence of the complex and highly random nature of financial markets. The probability distribution of observed performance of a rule with an expected return of zero is illustrated in Figure 6.15. Although zero is the most likely return, far higher or lower returns are possible due to good or bad luck. If the rule is unlucky in the back test, observed performance will be negative. Even more problematic for the objective technician is when good luck shines on the worthless rule and it earns a positive rate of return. This may fool the objective technician into believing that TA gold has been found. In fact, the rule's signals coincided favorably with the market's fluctuations purely by accident.

Although an extremely positive or negative average return is unlikely for an individual rule, it becomes increasingly likely as more rules are back tested. Just as the greater the number of people playing the lottery

FIGURE 6.15 Probability distribution of observed performance.

increases the chance that there will be someone lucky enough to win twice, the greater the number of rules back tested increases the chance that a rule will have an extraordinarily lucky observed performance. This is the rule that would be picked by the data miner. The bottom line: when observed performance is primarily due to randomness, it is likely that the best observed performance, among a large set of observed performances, will be largely an effect of randomness.

To see how luck might impact a data miner, imagine that you are observing a data miner at work. Furthermore, imagine that you are in the fortunate position of knowing what no data miner ever knows, the true expected return of each rule that is back tested. Suppose the data miner back tests twelve different rules, and you know that each of the rules has an expected return of 0 percent. All the data miner knows are the observed returns produced by each rule's back test. In Figure 6.16, each rule's observed performance is depicted by an arrow on the probability distribution. Each distribution is centered at zero, reflecting the fact that each rule has an expected rate of return of zero. Notice that one rule got lucky, producing an observed return of +60 percent. This is the rule that would be selected by the data miner. In this case, the data-mining bias was a positive 60 percent.

If the data miner were to test an even greater number of rules, the chance of an even more positive observed performance would be increased. As will be discussed, the number of rules tested during data mining is one of five factors that impact the size of the data-mining bias. In Figure 6.17, 30 rules are tested, and one managed to produce an observed performance of 100 percent. This is the rule that would be selected by the data miner. You know it is highly probable that its future performance will be disappointing.

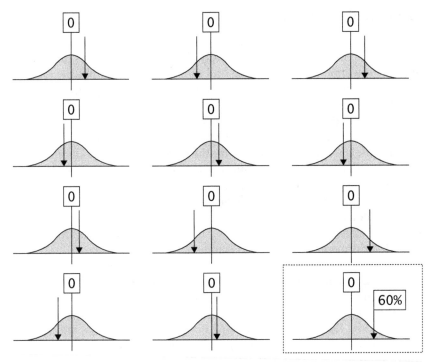

FIGURE 6.16 Twelve different rules (each has an expected return of 0 percent).

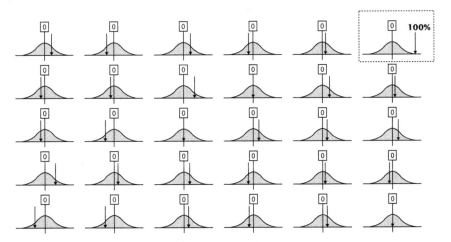

FIGURE 6.17 Data mining more rules increases probability of more extreme luck.

The Risk of Picking an Inferior Rule

The prior examples assumed that all rules were of equal merit (all had expected returns equal to zero). Naturally, the data miner hopes that there is at least one superior rule amongst all those tested, and that the superior rule's observed performance will identify it as such. Unfortunately, this is not always the case.

This is another negative consequence of high randomness. The superior rule, the one with highest expected return, may not get picked, because an inferior rule's lucky performance wins the data mining competition. An intuitive sense of the likelihood of this unfortunate result is portrayed in Figure 6.18. It shows the distribution of observed performance for two rules with nearly identical expected performances, but one is indeed superior. However, the considerable overlap of the distributions gives a sense there is a substantial chance the rule of lesser merit will produce the highest observed performance, causing it to get picked.

However, when the difference in expected returns (merit) between the truly best rule and the next best rule is large enough, the data miner can be more confident that best-observed performance will reliably point to the superior rule. This is illustrated in the Figure 6.19. In other words, when the difference in merit between the best rule and its nearest competitor is large, merit will be more likely to shine through the fog of randomness. This is the illumination that guides the data miner to the gold.

Practically speaking, the data miner is never aware of the risk of picking an inferior rule. That would require knowledge of true merit (expected return), which is a population parameter and hence never known. The

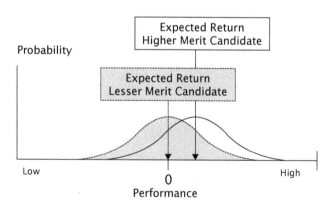

FIGURE 6.18 High randomness and small merit difference.

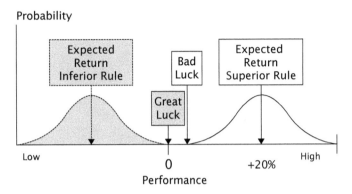

FIGURE 6.19 High randomness and large merit difference (superiority overcomes randomness).

data miner never gets to see the full consequences of the data-mining bias until, as the song says, the future is past.

Five Factors Determine the Magnitude of the Data-Mining Bias

Let us recap briefly what has been established thus far:

- The data-mining bias is defined as the expected difference between the observed performance of a rule that wins the data mining competition and its true expected performance.
- Observed performance refers to the level of performance achieved by a rule in back testing. Expected performance refers to the rule's theoretical performance in the future.
- The observed performance of the highest-performing rule found by data mining is positively biased. Therefore, its expected performance out of sample will be less than the in-sample observed performance that allowed it to beat other rules tested.
- Observed performance is a combination of randomness and predictive power. The greater the relative contribution of randomness, the larger will be the magnitude the data-mining bias.

The relationship between the data-mining bias and the relative contribution of randomness is illustrated in Figure 6.20. As explained in the next section, the degree of randomness encountered in a given data mining venture depends on five factors that characterize the venture.

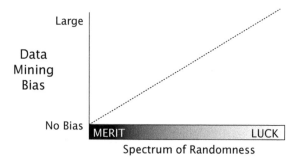

FIGURE 6.20 Relationship of data-mining bias to degree of randomness.

The Five Factors Defined. Five factors determine the degree of data-mining bias. They are:

1. **Number of rules back-tested:** This refers to the total number of rules back tested during the data-mining process en route to discovering the highest-performing rule. The larger the number of rules tested, the larger the data-mining bias.
2. **The number of observations used to compute the performance statistic:** The larger the number of observations, the smaller the data-mining bias.
3. **Correlation among rule returns:** This refers to the degree to which the performance histories of the rules tested are correlated with each other. The less correlated they are, the larger the data-mining bias.
4. **Presence of positive outlier returns:** This refers to presence of very large returns in a rule's performance history, for example a very large positive return on a particular day. When these are present, the data-mining bias tends to be larger, although this effect is reduced when the number of positive outliers is small relative to the total number of observations that are used to compute the performance statistic. In other words, more observations dilute the biasing effect of positive outliers.
5. **Variation in expected returns among the rules:** This refers to the variation in true merit (expected return) among the rules back tested. The lower the variation, the greater the data-mining bias. In other words, when the set of rules tested have similar degrees of predictive power, the data-mining bias will be larger.

How Each Factor Impacts the Data-Mining Bias. Figures 6.21 through 6.25 depict the relationships between each of the five factors and

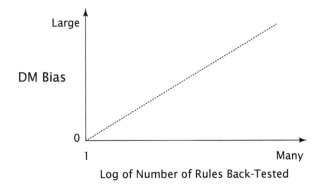

FIGURE 6.21 Number of rules back tested (1).

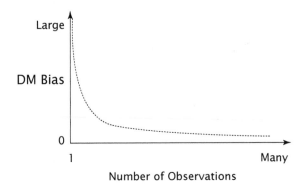

FIGURE 6.22 Number of observations used to compute performance statistic (2).

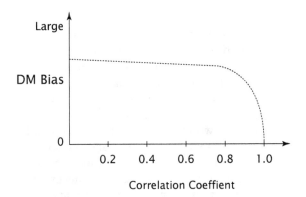

FIGURE 6.23 Correlation among rule returns (3).

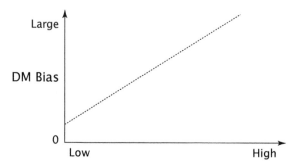

Number & Magnitude of Outliers Relative to Number of Observations Used to Compute Performance Statistic

FIGURE 6.24 Presence of positive outlier returns (4).

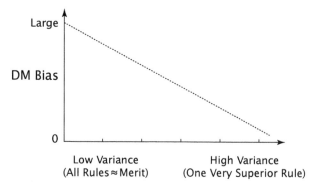

FIGURE 6.25 Variance in expected ROI—degree of difference in merit in rule universe(5).

the magnitude of the data-mining bias. These relationships pertain specifically to data mining ventures where the performance statistic being used is the rule's mean rate of return. Because the sampling distribution of other performance statistics, such as the Sharpe ratio, will differ from the distribution of the mean return, the relationships between the five factors and the data mining bias may also be different.

The astute reader will wonder how such curves could have been developed, given that a rule's expected performance is never known (it is a population parameter) but must be known to measure the data-mining bias. The reader is correct; the data-mining bias is never known for actual rules. However, it can be known for *artificial rules* and can therefore be investigated. An artificial rule is a computer-simulated trading signal whose accuracy (fraction of correct signals) can be set experimentally. This makes it possible to know the expected return of the artificial rule. The preceding curves were based on a set of tests done on artificial rules. The results of these tests, which are described in the next section, show how the five factors impact the data-mining bias.

EXPERIMENTAL INVESTIGATION OF THE DATA-MINING BIAS

Scientists make observations and draw inferences from them. Sound inferences depend on accurate observations. Thus, a key task is determining the accuracy of the procedure used to make observations. The process of measuring the random and systematic error that may be present in an observational procedure is called calibration. One way to calibrate the accuracy of a procedure is to test it on a problem whose correct answer is known. This makes it possible to measure its random and/or systematic errors.

Objective technicians are the scientists of the TA world. Their primary procedure is rule back testing. The observable produced is a performance statistic. On the basis of this statistic, an inference is made about a rule's predictive power or expected performance. Therefore, objective technicians are properly concerned with the random and or systematic error that that may be present in performance statistics obtained by back testing. Chapter 4 showed that performance statistics are subject to random error due to sampling variability. This chapter is concerned with a form of systematic error that stems from data mining—the data-mining bias.

This section describes the results of experiments that investigate the data-mining bias by examining how each of the five factors impacts the size of the bias. This is done by data mining a universe of artificial trading rules (ATRs). Unlike real TA rules, ATRs are ideal for this purpose because their expected return can be known because it is under experimental control. This allows us to measure the data-mining bias associated with the rule that had the best-observed performance. This, in turn, tells us how accurately its observed performance, a statistic which is known to the data miner, portrays its expected performance, the population parameter the data miner wishes to know.

Artificial Trading Rules and Simulated Performance Histories

The ATR performance histories produced in these experiments are composed of monthly returns. The expected return of an ATR is controlled by manipulating the probability of a profitable monthly return. This probability can be expected to manifest over a very large number of months, a manifestation of the Law of Large Numbers. However, over any small sample of months, the actual fraction of profitable months will vary randomly about the specified probability level. This variation introduces the crucial element of randomness into the experiments. An ATR performance history can be generated for any specified number of months (e.g., 24).

When the probability of a profitable month is known, as it is with an ATR, its expected return can be determined precisely. This, in turn, allows the data-mining bias associated with the rule to be measured. The expected return of an ATR is given by the formula used to compute the expected value of a random variable:

$$EV = p(\text{profitable month}) \times \text{average gain} - p(\text{losing month}) \times \text{average loss}$$

The average gain and average loss are also known because the ATRs were applied to the absolute monthly percentage changes for the S&P 500 over the period August 1928 through April 2003. The term *absolute* means the sign of the S&P's actual monthly change was ignored. In the ATR tests the algebraic sign (+ or −) of the ATR's monthly return was determined by a random process that is described below. Over this time period, comprising nearly 900 monthly observations, the average absolute monthly return for the S&P 500 was equal to 3.97 percent. Thus, the formula for calculating an ATR's expected return is:

$$ER = ppm \times 3.97 - (1 - ppm) \times 3.97$$

Where *ppm* is defined as the probability of a profitable month.

ATR performance histories were generated by Monte Carlo simulation. Specifically, the absolute monthly changes in the S&P 500 were sampled with replacement from the 900-month history. A monthly return, without its sign, was chosen at random, and a roulette wheel, simulated by a computer, determined if that particular month was a gain or loss. This represented one month of the ATR's performance history. The probability of a profitable month was set by the experimenter. A probability of 0.70 would be as if the roulette wheel had 100 slots with 70 designated as profit and 30 designated as loss. This procedure for generating monthly ATR returns was repeated for a specified number of months, another variable under experimental control. The performance history is then summarized with a statistic—mean monthly return, annualized. This procedure is illustrated in Figure 6.26.

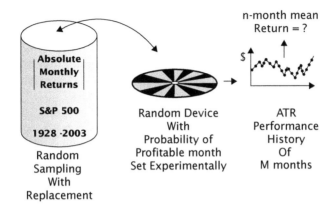

FIGURE 6.26 Monte Carlo generation of ATR performance histories.

Let's consider what the expected return for an ATR would be under four different settings for probability of a monthly gain: 1.0, 0.63, 0.50, and 0.0. An ATR with p(gain) set at 1.0 (all months profitable) would have an expected monthly return equal to the S&P 500's average absolute monthly return of +3.97 percent per month or a 47.6 percent annualized noncompounded return. This value can be obtained by plugging into the formula for the expected value of a random variable. The same formula tells us that an ATR with probability of a gain month set to 0.63 would have an expected return of +12.4 percent. An ATR with probability of gain set to 0.50 would have an expected return of zero whereas a probability of gain equal to zero would earn a return of –3.97 percent per month or –47.6 percent per year.

Bear in mind that these are expected values that would be earned over a very large number of months. Over any small number of months, the ATR's observed mean return can vary from this value. The smaller the number of months comprising the ATR's performance history, the larger will be the random variation from the expected mean return.

To simulate the effect of data mining, for example picking the best-performing ATR of 10, 10 ATR performance histories were generated. The one with highest mean return was selected, and its observed return was noted. This process was repeated a total of 10,000 times. The 10,000 observations were used to form the sampling distribution for the statistic— mean return of the highest performing ATR selected from 10.

Experiment Set 1: Data Mining ATRs of Equal Merit

In the first set of experiments, all ATRs were specified to have equal predictive power. This was accomplished by setting p(gain) to 0.50 for all ATRs, thus giving them all an expected return of zero.

Factor 1: Number of Rules Tested. All else being equal, the more rules back tested to find the best rule, the larger the data-mining bias. More monkeys dancing on keyboards increases the probability that one will get lucky enough to type something that appears literate. Similarly, back testing a larger number of rules increases the chance that one will enjoy extraordinary luck.

In the tests that follow, each ATR was simulated over a 24-month period. First let's look at the no-data-mining case—only one rule is back tested. There is no data mining and no data-mining bias. Although an ATR with p(gain) set at 0.50 has an expected return equal to zero, sampling variability makes it possible for any given 24-month history to produce a mean return that varies above and below zero.

To demonstrate this, 1,000 ATR performance histories, each of 24 months' duration, were produced by computer simulation. The sampling distribution for the statistic *mean annualized return* is shown in Figure 6.27. As expected, the distribution is centered at zero, which is indeed the expected return of an ATR with p(gain) set 0.50. Also as expected, the mean return displays a wide range of variation around zero because 24 observations is a relatively small sample size. A few ATRs, those out in the right tail of the sampling distribution, had very good luck (more than 50 months wound up profitable). In the left tail of the distribution, we find the performance histories with bad luck. However, it is the center of the sampling distribution that tells the story. On average, under the condition of no data mining, an ATR with no predictive power can be expected to

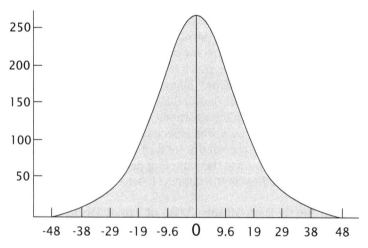

FIGURE 6.27 Mean annualized percent return (single ATR, 24 month history, 1,000 replications).

earn a mean return of zero. As the next tests will show, when a best-performing ATR is picked from two or more ATRs, the best is likely to show a return greater than zero, even though it has an expected return of zero.

Now we will be data mining by picking a best ATR from two or more. To examine the relationship between the size of the data mining bias and the number of rules from which the best is selected we will vary the size of the ATR universe—the number from which the best is picked. Specifically, the bias is measured for the best ATR of 2, 10, 50, and 400. For example, if the number of ATRs was set at 10, the best-performing one of 10 was picked, and its observed mean return was noted. This procedure was repeated 10,000 times and the sampling distribution for the statistic (*observed return of the best ATR*) was plotted. All performance histories are 24 months, all rules are set to p(gain) = 0.50 (expected return = 0), and all rules are set to have independent returns (no correlation). Because all ATRs had expected returns equal to zero, the data-mining bias is simply equal to the observed return of the best performer averaged over 10,000 replications.

Figure 6.28 shows the sampling distribution of observed performance for the best ATR out of two. The sampling distribution is centered at +8.5 percent. In other words, when only two ATRs are tested and the best is selected, the bias is a positive 8.5 percent. The data miner would be expecting +8.5 percent in the future, but we know the true expected return is 0 percent.

If the number of ATRs is increased to 10, and the best is selected, the data-mining bias increases to +22 percent. However, we know that the selected ATR has a p(gain) of 0.50 and an expected return of 0 percent.

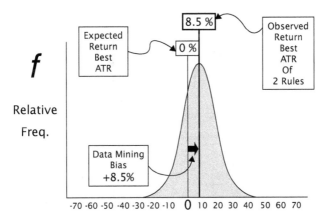

FIGURE 6.28 Sampling distribution —mean return best of two ATRs.

Figure 6.29 is similar to 6.28, except it shows the sampling distribution for the mean observed return for the best-of-10 ATRs. The observed performance of the best-of-10 ATRs is biased by +22 percent.

When the size of the data-mined universe is expanded to 50 ATRs the bias increases to +33 percent. Figure 6.30 shows the sampling distribution for the mean return of the best-of-50 ATRs.

A similar plot, in Figure 6.31, shows that the data-mining bias increases to a +48 percent for the best-of-400 ATRs.

The relationship between number of ATRs tested and the data-mining bias can be seen in Figure 6.32. It summarizes the results obtained for

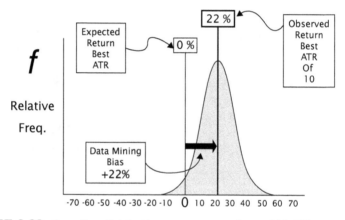

FIGURE 6.29 Sampling distribution—mean return best of 10 ATRs.

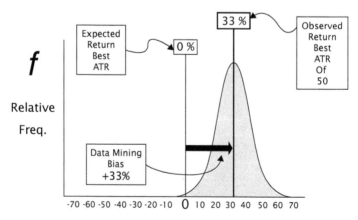

FIGURE 6.30 Sampling distribution—mean return best of 50 ATRs.

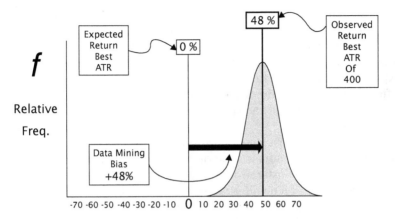

FIGURE 6.31 Sampling distribution—mean return best of 400 ATRs.

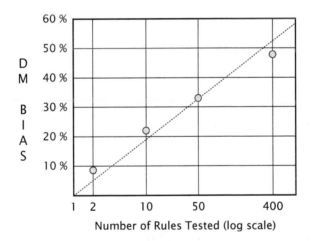

FIGURE 6.32 Data-mining bias versus number of rules tested (annualized percent return): 24-month performance history.

best-of 2, 10, 50, and 400 ATRs. The vertical axis represents the magnitude of the data-mining bias—the differential between the observed returns for the best performing ATR and its expected return. The horizontal axis represents the number of ATRs back tested to find the best. The relationship is summarized by fitting a curve through the four data points. It is nearly linear when number of rules tested is plotted in log terms—log (base10). The main point to take away from these experiments is this: The larger the number of rules tested to find a best rule, the greater the data-mining bias.

It should be pointed out that the particular magnitudes of data-mining bias shown in the preceding tests are valid only for the particulars of this test: a particular set of S&P 500 monthly returns, a 24-month performance history, all rules have independent returns, and all rules having an expected return equal to zero. In a different data-mining venture, with different particulars, the same principle would apply (more rules produce a bigger bias) but the specific levels of the data-mining bias would be different.

For example, had a longer performance history been used to compute mean return—48 months instead of 24—the distribution of mean ATR returns would have clustered more tightly around the expected return of zero. This is merely a manifestation of the Law of Large Numbers. Consequently, the bias associated with the highest performing ATR would have been less. This tells us that the number of observations used to compute the performance statistic is an important factor in determining the magnitude of the data-mining bias.

Let's consider what was said in the previous sentence. The greater the number of monthly observations used to compute the performance statistic, the smaller the dispersion of the statistic's sampling distribution. In other words, the larger the sample size used to compute the performance statistic, the less the degree of randomness in observed performance and the less the opportunity for an extraordinarily lucky performance. Whatever reduces the degree of randomness in observed performance reduces the data-mining bias.

The importance of sample size on data-mining bias can be seen in Figure 6.33. It is similar to the preceding Figure 6.32. It is a plot of data-mining bias, represented on the vertical axis, as a function of number of ATR's compared to find the best one, on the horizontal axis. However, in this plot there are four curves instead of one. Each curve is based on using a different number of monthly observations to compute each rule's mean return; 10, 24, 100, and 1,000 months. The dotted line for 24 months is the same curve seen in Figure 6.32. Two points are worthy of note. First, all curves rise as the number of rules back tested is increased. This is consistent with the finding discussed in the preceding section—the data-mining bias increases as the number of ATR's tested is increased. Second, and perhaps most important, is the fact that the magnitude of the bias is reduced by increasing the number of months used to compute the mean return. For example, when only 10 months of data are used, the bias for the best-of-1,024 ATRs is approximately 84 percent. When 1,000 months of data are used, the bias for the best of 1,024 rules shrinks to less than 12 percent. In the next section, we will see why the number of observations is so important in determining the size of the data-mining bias.

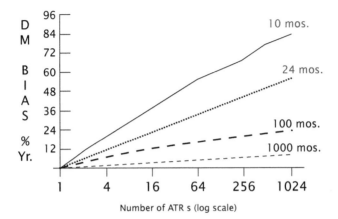

FIGURE 6.33 Data-mining bias versus number of ATRs tested for different sample sizes.

Factor 2: Number of Observations Used to Compute the Performance Statistic. Figure 6.33 tells us that increasing the number of observations used to compute the performance statistic reduces the magnitude of the data-mining bias. In fact, of all the factors impacting the size of the bias, sample size may be the most important. The more observations used, the less opportunity there is for a few lucky observations (profitable months) to result in a high mean return. We saw this in Chapter 4, where it was demonstrated that the sampling distribution is reduced in width when a larger number of observations are used to compute the sample statistic. With only a few observations, a sample mean can stray considerably above or below the true population mean. The message conveyed by a wide sampling distribution is that there is a greater opportunity for a rule to generate a very profitable return in a back test by luck rather than by predictive power. This is illustrated in Figure 6.34, which shows two sampling distributions for the same rule, for which expected return is zero. Note the sampling distribution based on fewer observations is wider. A mean return computed from a short performance history is more likely to produce a very lucky result than a mean computed from a larger number of observations (i.e., a longer performance history).

The next set of experiments examine the effect of the number of monthly observations used to compute mean ATR return on the size of the data-mining bias. The number of months was varied from one month to 1,000 months, in 50-month increments, with data-mining bias computed at each increment. This was done for two cases: the best-of-10 and

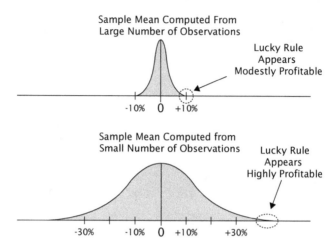

FIGURE 6.34 Narrow versus wide sampling distributions.

the best-of-100 ATRs. As in prior experiments all ATRs were set to have expected returns equal to zero.

Figure 6.35 shows the relationship between the data-mining bias on the vertical axis versus the number of observations used to compute ATR mean returns on the horizontal axis. Because the expected return for all ATRs is equal to zero, the data-mining bias is equal to the average observed performance of the best. Thus, the vertical axis, which is labeled *data-mining bias*, could as easily have been labeled *average performance of the best rule*. Note the steep decline in the magnitude of

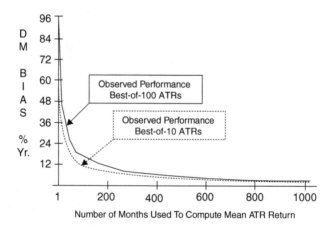

FIGURE 6.35 Data-mining bias versus number observations.

the bias as the number of observations used to compute the mean return is increased. This is the Law of Large Numbers working in favor of the data miner.

The lesson here is this: Be very skeptical of performance statistics computed from a small number of signals or time intervals. Another important message from Figure 6.35 is that when the number of observations (months) becomes quite large, 600 or so, the difference in the bias between best-of-10 and the best-of-100 ATRs becomes tiny. This finding has very important implications for the data miner—when the number of observations is sufficient, one can data mine a much larger number of rules without significantly increasing the data-mining bias. The Law of Large Numbers rules!

Factor 3: Degree of Rule Correlation. The third factor affecting the size of the data-mining bias is the degree of similarity among the rules tested. Rules are said to be similar when they generate performance histories that are strongly correlated. That is to say, their monthly or daily returns are correlated. The stronger the correlation between the rules tested, the smaller will be the magnitude of the bias. Conversely, the lower the correlation (i.e., the greater the degree of statistical independence) between rules returns, the larger will be the data-mining bias.

This makes sense because increased correlation among the rules has the consequence of shrinking the effective number of rules being back tested. Imagine a large set of rules that are completely identical. Naturally, they will generate perfectly correlated performance histories. In effect, this large set of rules is really just one rule, and we already know that the data-mining bias shrinks to zero when only one rule is back tested. Backing off from this extreme case, when rules are highly similar, and thus have highly correlated returns, the chance of an extraordinarily lucky performance is reduced. The more dissimilar the rules, the greater will be the opportunity for one to have a great coincidental fit to the historical data and achieve high performance. So high correlation amongst the rules shrinks the effective number of rules back tested and hence shrinks the data-mining bias.

In practical terms, rule correlation is most likely to be high when data mining involves optimizing the parameters of a specific rule form. Suppose a dual moving average crossover rule is being optimized. This means that every rule tested is the same except for the parameter values—the number of days used to compute the short-term and long-term moving averages. The rule using values of 26 days and 55 days will produce returns that are highly correlated with a rule using values of 27 and 55.

Figure 6.36 shows the relationship between the magnitude of the data-mining bias for the best rule (vertical axis) and the degree of correlation

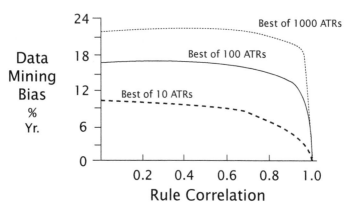

FIGURE 6.36 Data-mining bias versus rule correlation (annualized percent return number of monthly observations = 100).

(horizontal axis) among the rules. Rule correlation was simulated as follows: An initial ATR performance history was generated. In the generation of a second ATR history, a biased random device was consulted to determine the monthly returns of ATR history 2. The bias was set to the desired level of correlation. For example, if a .7 correlation was desired, a coin flip was simulated with the probability of heads = 0.70. If the coin landed on heads, then the monthly return for the second ATR would be the same as the monthly return of the initial ATR. This was continued for subsequent ATR histories.

Each ATR was simulated over a 100-month history. Three different tests were run, each based on a different number of ATRs: 10, 100, 1,000. In other words, one test measures the data-mining bias associated with the best ATR rule out of 100. As in prior tests, all rules had expected returns equal to zero. The vertical axis of the plot represents the data-mining bias. The factor being examined here, rule correlation, was varied from 0 to 1.0. Note that the bias remains high until rule correlations approach a level of 1.0. Thus, rule correlation does not have a major impact in reducing the data-mining bias until there is a high level of correlation in their returns. Also note that the data-mining bias is higher for the best of 1,000 rules than it is for best of 10. This is simply a manifestation of factor 1, the greater the number of rules from which the best is selected, the greater the data-mining bias.

Factor 4: Presence of Positive Outliers in Rule Returns. A sample of rule returns (daily, weekly, or monthly) that contains a few extremely large positive observations has the potential to create a large data mining bias. The size of the bias will depend on how extreme the values are and the number of observations used to compute the mean. If a small number of observations are used, one extremely positive value can boost the sample mean dramatically. A large number of observations will lessen the impact of an occasional extreme value.

Distributions that contain extreme values are said to have heavy tails. The tails of a distribution are the outer right and left zones where the extreme but rare observations lie. Heavy-tailed distributions extend farther away from the distribution's center than light-tailed distributions. The normal distribution has light tails. Figure 6.37 illustrates this distinction. The distribution in the upper portion of Figure 6.37 has the normal bell shape. Note how quickly the tails disappear as one moves away from the distribution's center. This tells us that extreme observations are rare to the point of being virtually nonexistent. People's heights are normally distributed. It is rare to see someone over seven feet tall. No one has ever seen a person over 10 feet. The distribution in the lower portion of the figure is heavy tailed. Although extreme observations are also rare, they occur more frequently than in light-tailed distributions. Were people's heights distributed this way, you might meet someone 20 feet tall!

As mentioned earlier, when the distribution of daily (weekly, monthly) returns contains extreme observations, a sample mean, computed from these observations, can also take on an extreme value. This occurs when one or more of the extreme values wind up in the sample and the sample size is small. From this it follows that heavy tails in the return distribution tend to cause tail heaviness of the sampling distribution of the mean.

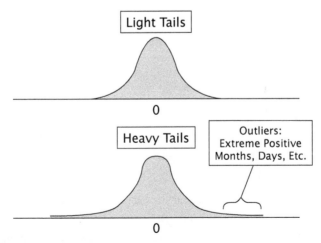

FIGURE 6.37 Light- versus heavy-tailed return distributions.

Nevertheless, the value of a sample mean is never as extreme as the most extreme value found in a sample. This is simply the effect of averaging. Therefore, the sampling distribution of the mean return will always have lighter tails than the distribution of interval returns. This is illustrated in Figure 6.38. Two return distributions are depicted. On the left is a return distribution with heavy tails. The sampling distribution of the mean based on this distribution also has heavy tails, although they are lighter than the return distribution itself. On the right is a thin-tailed return distribution. A sampling distribution of the mean based on it necessarily has light tails.

Note that both of the sampling distributions in the Figure 6.38 are based on the same sample size. Sample size is a separate factor influencing tail heaviness of the sampling distribution. I wanted to hold sample size constant so as not to confuse the issue.

Now let's consider the effect of sample size on the sampling distribution's tail heaviness. When more observations are used to compute the sample mean, the effect of tail heaviness in the return distribution is minimized. The greater the number of observations used to compute the sample mean, the lighter will be the tails of the sampling distribution. This is illustrated in Figure 6.39. The return distribution clearly has heavy tails. On the left is the sampling distribution of the mean based on a small sample size. Its tails, though not as heavy as the return distribution itself, are still heavy. On the right is a sampling distribution of the mean derived from the same return distribution, except that a larger sample size is used

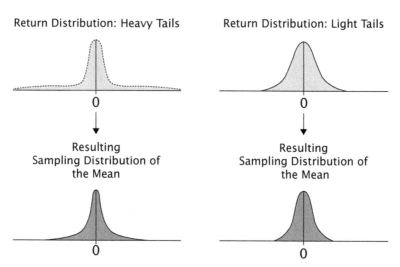

FIGURE 6.38 Impact of extremes in return distribution on sampling distribution: equal sample size.

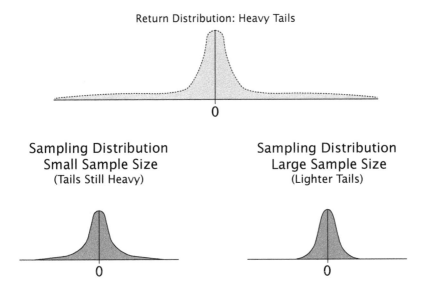

FIGURE 6.39 Impact of sample size on tail heaviness of the sampling distribution.

to compute the sample mean. The tails of this sampling distribution are lightened as a result.

What is the relevance of all this to the data-mining bias? A heavy-tailed sampling distribution is saying that randomness is playing a large role in the mean return. Randomness is always bad news for the data miner.[31] Imagine two rules. Both have expected returns of zero. One has a heavy-tailed sampling distribution. The other has a sampling distribution with light tails. The heavy tails tell us that there is a greater probability that the rule will produce a mean return, in a back test, that is much higher than its expected return. If this rule is picked by the data miner, its data-mining bias will be large and its out-of-sample performance is likely to be disappointing. This is illustrated in Figure 6.40. The heavy-tailed sampling distribution shows that it is within the realm of probability for the rule to earn mean return of greater than 30 percent in a back test. In the case of the sampling distribution with light tails, a return that high would have a probability of almost zero.

It is widely recognized that the distribution of stock market returns and the returns of other financial asset have relatively heavy tails compared to a normal distribution.[32] A rule that was short, by coincidence, when the market crashed may win the data-mining-performance competition, but it will have won for the wrong reason.

The issue of tail heaviness and its resultant impact on the data-mining

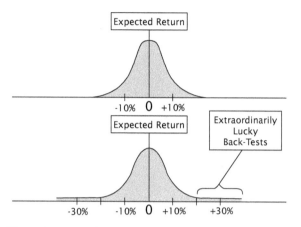

FIGURE 6.40 Light- versus heavy-tailed sampling distributions.

bias was examined experimentally. The data-mining bias was compared for two sets of ATRs. One set used the S&P 500 monthly returns, a distribution with tails that are heavier than those of the normal distribution, to generate performance histories. The other set of ATRs used a return distribution with intentionally light tails. As in the other experiments, the ATR with the best-observed performance was selected and its data-mining bias was measured. The results of these experiments were clear. The data-mining bias was much less pronounced for the ATRs that were based on the light-tailed return distribution. This finding is of practical value only when data-mining rules exit at fixed targets. This has the effect of eliminating extreme outcomes. This in turn has the effect of reducing tail heaviness in the sampling distribution of the performance statistic. In most instances, however, rule researchers are stuck with the return distributions produced by financial market behavior. Because markets are subject to extreme events, mean rule returns will tend to be extreme as well.

Factor 5: Variation in Expected Returns among the ATRs. This factor refers to the degree of variation in the expected returns among the set of rules considered during data mining. The ATR experiments discussed thus far have considered ATRs with uniform predictive power. All have had expected returns set at zero. When all rules are of equal merit, be that merit none, low, or high, any differences in their observed performances are due entirely to luck. In such a case, the winner of the data-mining performance competition will simply be the luckiest rule. Thus, the difference between its observed mean return and its expected return will be large. Therefore, when all rules possess equal expected returns, the data-mining bias will be large.

However, if the universe of rules explored during data mining differs with respect to their expected returns, the data-mining bias will tend to be smaller. Under certain conditions, it will be very small. The following experiments investigate how variation in expected returns with the rule universe impacts the data-mining bias. This is accomplished by creating a universe of ATRs that have differing levels of expected return. Recall, that an ATR's expected return is entirely determined by its designated probability of a profitable month.

Let's first consider what the following experiments should show. Suppose a universe of ATRs contains one that is truly superior to all the others. It has an expected return of +20 percent, whereas the others all have expected returns of zero. We would expect its true superiority to reveal itself by producing the highest-observed performance most of the time (on any given test it is not guaranteed to do so). Consequently, most of the time the superior ATR will get picked and the data-mining bias associated with it will tend to be small. The bias will tend to be small because its observed performance was earned the old-fashioned way, by dint of predictive power rather than luck.

Experiment 2: Data Mining ATRs with Differing Expected Returns

The following tests investigate the data-mining bias within a universe populated by ATRs whose expected returns differ. In these tests, the majority of ATRs have expected returns equal to zero or close to zero. However, a few ATRs with returns significantly greater than zero are sprinkled in. This is intended to replicate the world a rule data miner can reasonably hope to encounter—there really is some TA gold in the mountains of data although it is rare.

In addition to investigating the magnitude of the data-mining bias, this set of tests also addresses another question: Does data mining rest on a sound premise? That is, does picking the rule with the best-observed performance do a better job of identifying authentic predictive power than randomly selecting a rule from the universe of rules. Data mining must, at the very least, pass this *minimal* test of efficacy to establish that it is a reasonable research approach. Figure 6.41 shows the expected return for an ATR given its specified probability of a profitable month. Bear in mind that this graph is specific to the monthly SP returns used in these simulation experiments.

Recall that an ATR's expected return is determined entirely by its probability-of-profitable-month (PPM). The following tests assume that rules with high expected returns are rare. To simulate this assumption, the PPM assigned to each ATR was drawn at random from a distribution of

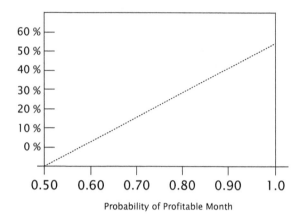

FIGURE 6.41 Expected return (f) probability of profitable month.

PPMs. The distribution used for this purpose has a shape similar to the distribution of wealth in a society. It has a long tail out to the right, indicating that wealthy individuals, like Bill Gates, are extremely rate while a great many are poor. The distribution of expected returns used for these experiments was defined such that an ATR with an expected return of 19 percent per year or greater had a frequency of occurrence of about 1 in 10,000. The expected return for the average ATR in the universe was +1.4 percent per year. The approximate shape of the distribution used is illustrated in Figure 6.42.

Although the specific assumptions underlying this distribution may not be accurate, they are probably correct to within one order of magnitude. This is based on the performance of the best hedge funds using

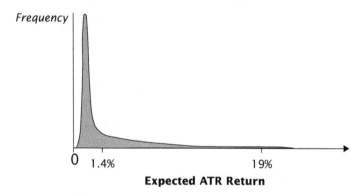

FIGURE 6.42 Distribution of ATR expected returns.

technical analysis. However, for purposes of these experiments, the specifics are not crucial. The real purpose here is to measure the data-mining bias in a universe of rules whose expected returns differ and to investigate how the bias can thwart the objective of data mining, finding merit in a universe where it is rare.

Is Data Mining Based on a Sound Premise?— A Qualified Yes!

This section addresses the important fundamental question: Is data mining based on a sound premise? This is really two questions. First, is observed mean return a useful indicator of rule merit in the sense that the rule with the highest observed mean return has a higher expected return than a rule picked at random? If a randomly selected rule is as likely to perform well in the future as a rule that performed well in a back test, then data mining is a pointless activity. Second, is more data mining better? That is, does testing a larger number of rules lead to the discovery of a rule with higher expected returns? If so, then back testing 250 rules would be a better idea than back testing only ten.

Fortunately for the field of data mining, the answer to both questions is a qualified yes. The qualification relates to the number of observations that are used to compute the rule's mean return or other performance statistics. If a sufficient number of observations is used, then the answer to both questions is yes. This is very good news for the data miner. However, when the number of observations is small, data mining does not work. One would do just as well picking a rule by guess, and data mining a larger number of rules will not produce better rules.

Because the number of observations used is crucial, no doubt the reader would like to know how many are sufficient. Unfortunately, there is no simple answer. The requisite number depends on the performance statistic and the nature of the raw data. The best I can do is to provide representative charts that give a general sense of requisite sample sizes.

In prior plots, the vertical axis represented the data-mining bias in annualized percent return per year. Take note, however, that in Figure 6.43, the vertical axis represents the true merit or expected return of the rule with the highest-observed performance—the rule that would be selected by the data miner. Clearly, such a plot could not be produced for actual TA rules because their expected returns are never known. The horizontal axis represents the number of ATRs tested to find the one with the best-observed performance. The set of numbers considered was: 1 (no data mining), 2, 4, 8, 16, 32, 64, 128, and 256. There are three curves on the plot. Each curve is based on a different number of monthly observations used

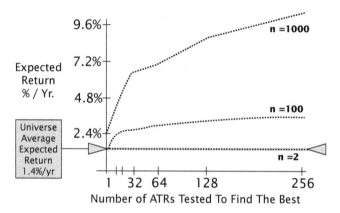

FIGURE 6.43 Expected return of best performing ATR versus number of ATRs back tested.

to compute the ATR's mean annual return. The number of monthly observations used for these three cases were: 2, 100, and 1,000.

The second question posed was the following: Does testing more rules lead to the discovery of a rule with a higher expected return? If so, the curve of expected return should rise as the number of ATRs examined to find the best one goes up. In other words, the expected return of the ATR with the best-observed performance should be positively correlated with the number tested to find the best. On the other hand, if the curve does not rise, it would be telling us that more searching does not lead to rules of higher merit. This would mean that data mining is a fruitless activity.

In Figure 6.43, two of the three curves rise—the one based on 100 monthly observations and the one based on 1,000. This tells us that back testing more rules leads to the discovery of higher merit rules. The curve based on 1,000 rises more steeply than the one based on 100. This is telling us that when performance statistics are computed from a larger number of observations, data mining more reliably leads to better rules. This is good news for data miners who pay attention to the issue of sample size.

The curve in Figure 6.43 that does not rise also tells a story: When too few observations are used to compute the performance statistic, data mining does not work. That is to say, testing more rules does not lead to the discovery of better rules. The flat curve shows that when only two months were used to compute the mean return of each ATR, the expected return of the best performing ATR out of 256 ATRs was no higher than the best performing ATR when only one was tested (i.e., no data mining). The importance of sample size cannot be over emphasized!

Now let's go back and address the first question: Does data mining select rules with higher expected returns than simply picking one at random from the universe? Figure 6.43 speaks to this question as well. Note the curve based on two observations remains stuck at +1.4 percent as the number of ATRs tested is increased. A return of +1.4 percent is the expected return of the average ATR in the ATR universe. In other words, if one were to grab an ATR at random from the universe and note its expected return and repeat this many times, on average the expected return of the randomly selected rule would be +1.4 percent. Figure 6.41 tells us that when only two months of observations are used, picking the ATR with the best-observed performance is no better than picking an ATR at random. The fact that the curve is flat says that it does not matter how many ATRs are tested. However, the curves based on 100 and 1,000 observations rise well above the universe average. For example, when a best is picked from 256 ATRs using 1,000 months of history to compute the observed mean return, its expected return is +10 percent a year, far above the universe average of +1.4 percent. The bottom line: *When there are a sufficient number of observations a rule's observed rate of return is a useful, though positively biased, indicator of its expected rate of return. However, when there are too few observations, the observed rate of return is virtually useless.*

Data-Mining Bias as a Function of Universe Size: In a Universe of Variable Merit

The previous section established that the payoff from data mining increases as the number of rules tested is increased, given sufficient sample size. This shows that observed performance of the best rule is a useful, though positively biased, gauge of its expected return. The question is: How large is this bias associated with the best rule (highest observed return) when the universe is composed of rules that differ in terms of their expected returns?

The figures that follow (Figures 6.44, 6.45, 6.46, 6.47) are plots of the data-mining bias (vertical axis) versus the number of rules back tested in a rule universe where merit is distributed according to the distribution displayed in Figure 6.42. Each plot is based on a different number of monthly observations for computing mean return: 2, 100, and 1,000 months, respectively. First, each curve is shown individually (Figures 6.44, 6.45, and 6.46). Figure 6.47 shows the three curves placed on top of one another. It gives a sense of the relative magnitude of the data-mining bias at different sample sizes.

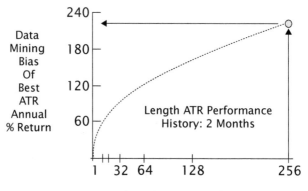

FIGURE 6.44 Data-mining bias versus number of ATRs tested in variable merit rule universe using a two-month performance history.

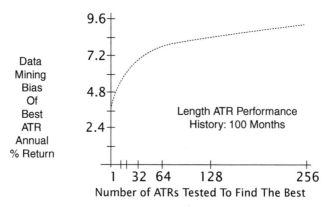

FIGURE 6.45 Data-mining bias versus number of ATRs tested in variable merit rule universe using a 100 month performance history.

Figure 6.44 is based on using only two months of observations to compute each ATR's observed return. The figure clearly shows the problem created by using a small sample size. For example, the observed performance of the best performing ATR out of 256 ATRs overstates its expected return by over 200 percent per year. For short performance histories, the data-mining bias is extreme. However, for the 100-observation case, shown in Figure 6.43, and for the 1,000 observation case shown in Figure 6.44, the bias is dramatically smaller. For example, the bias associated with the best ATR of 256 is approximately 18 percent when 100 months are used and less than 3 percent when 1,000 months are used.

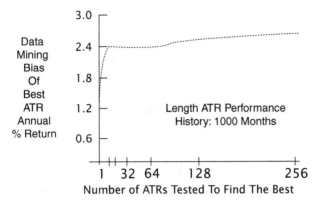

FIGURE 6.46 Data-mining bias versus number of ATRs tested in variable merit rule universe using a 1,000-month performance history.

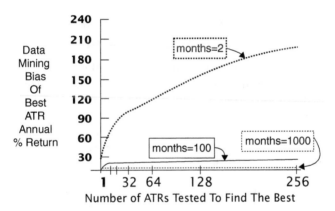

FIGURE 6.47 Data-mining bias versus number of ATRs tested in variable merit rule universe.

There are two messages expressed by Figures 6.44, 6.45, and 6.46. First, the number of observations has a major impact on data-mining bias. Second, when the number of observations used to compute rule performance is large, the bias levels out quickly. This is seen Figure 6.46 based on 1,000-month performance histories. The data-mining bias of the best of 16 ATRs is not much worse than the best of 256. Figure 6.47 superimposes the prior three figures. It shows that searching a larger number of ATRs to find a best (i.e., more data mining) does not increase the magnitude of the bias once the number of ATRs tested exceeds a modest number. In other words, the penalty for testing more rules does not increase, once a rather low threshold number of rules has been exceeded, provided, of course, that a sufficient number of observations has been used to compute the performance statistic.

How quickly the data-mining bias stabilizes once this threshold is passed can be seen more clearly in Figure 6.48, which is a portion of the curve for the 100-month observation case magnified. It shows the region along the horizontal axis where the number of ATRs tested is between 1 and 40. After approximately 30 ATRs have been examined, increasing the number tested has a minimal effect on the size of the data-mining bias. This is good news for the data miner who utilizes an adequate number of observations. The bottom line: testing a larger number of rules is a good thing, and the penalty for doing so drops off quickly if a sufficient number of observations are used to compute the performance statistic that is used for rule selection.

Data-Mining Bias as a Function of Number of Observations: In a Universe of Variable Merit

This section presents a series of plots showing the relationship between the magnitude of the data-mining bias (vertical axis) and the number of monthly observations used to compute the observed performance statistic (horizontal axis). This effect was visible on prior plots by showing separate curves of the bias versus number of ATRs for distinct values of 2, 100, and 1,000 months. However, the plots presented in this section show the relationship between the bias and number of observations along a continuum of the number of months.

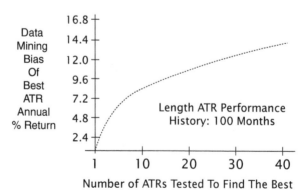

FIGURE 6.48 Data-mining bias stabilizes quickly when sample size is sufficient.

Each plot shows the data-mining bias as a function of number of observations, with that number ranging from 1 month to 1,024 months. What we would expect to see, on the basis of previous findings, is for the bias to be large when the number of observations is small. This is indeed what occurs. The message to the data miner is clear: Heed the Law of Large Numbers. Figures 6.49, 6.50, and 6.51 show the data-mining bias versus the number of observations used to compute mean ATR return for three different cases: best ATR of 2, best of 10, and best of 100, respectively. Figure 6.52 shows the three curves superimposed.

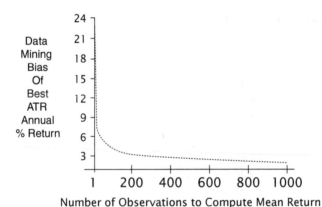

FIGURE 6.49 Data-mining bias versus number of observations for best ATR of 2.

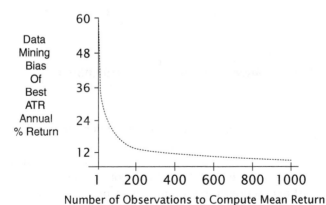

FIGURE 6.50 Data-mining bias versus number of observations for best ATR of 10.

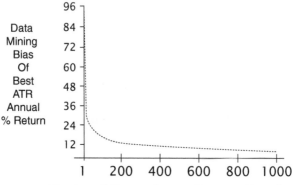

FIGURE 6.51 Data-mining bias versus number of observations for best ATR of 100.

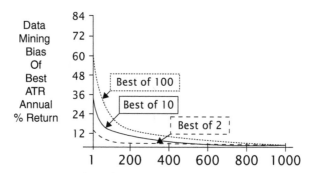

FIGURE 6.52 Data-mining bias versus number of observations for best ATR of 2, 10, and 100.

Observed Performance and Expected Performance versus Number of Observations in a Universe of Variable Merit

Figures 6.53 and 6.54 display two curves. The upper curve is the observed performance of the best-performing ATR amongst, say, 10 ATRs. The lower curve shows the expected return for that best-performing ATR. The vertical axis represents annualized return, both observed and expected. The horizontal axis represents the number of monthly observations. So, for example, in Figure 6.53, point A on the upper curve represents the observed performance of the best ATR out of 10 when 400 observations were

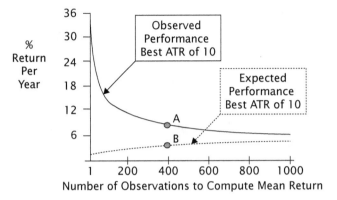

FIGURE 6.53 Observed and expected performance best ATR versus number of observations based on 10 ATRs.

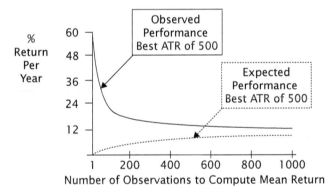

FIGURE 6.54 Observed and expected performance best ATR versus number of observations.

used to compute the ATR's observed mean return. Point B represents that ATR's expected return. The vertical distance between them is the data-mining bias, given these specific conditions: best of 10 ATRs and 400 monthly observations.

Here is what we should anticipate, given the results of prior experiments. When the number of observations is small, randomness will dominate merit, and observed performance will be much greater than expected performance—a large data-mining bias. This will show up on the plot as the two curves being far apart. The large vertical gap between the curves occurs when the performance statistic is based on few observations because this permits one ATR to get very lucky. However, as more observations are used to compute mean return, the curves should converge as observed performance more truly represents expected performance. However, the curve of observed performance will always lie above the curve of expected performance because a best-of-selection criterion will always induce some positive bias when luck plays a role in observed performance.

These tests were run for two cases. Figure 6.53 shows the curves for the best ATR of 10. Figure 6.54 shows them for the best ATR of 500. As expected, the bias shrinks as the number of observations is increased (the curves converge). Also, as expected, the bias is greater for the 500 ATR case than for the 10 ATR case due to the greater opportunity for luck when more ATRs are examined to find a best.

Data-Mining Bias as a Function of Rule Correlation: In a Universe of Variable Merit Based on 500 ATRs

We have previously seen that when the returns of the candidate rules are correlated, it reduces the data-mining bias. Correlation shrinks the bias because correlation reduces the effective number of rules being examined. In the extreme case, where all rules have perfectly correlated returns, there is really only one rule being tested. In this situation, no data mining takes place, and so the data-mining bias shrivels to zero. These results were for a universe of rules of equal merit; all had expected returns of zero. Now results for a variable-merit universe are presented.

Figure 6.55 plots the expected return (vertical axis) of the universe's best-performing ATR as the number of ATRs examined (horizontal axis) is varied from 1 to 256. There are four curves, each

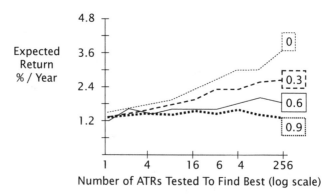

FIGURE 6.55 Expected return of best ATR versus number of ATRs. Tested at four levels of correlation: 0, 0.3, 0.6, 0.9. Number of observations= 100.

representing a different level of correlation in returns amongst the ATRs from which the best is selected. The correlation levels are: 0.0, 0.3, 0.6, and 0.9. The number of monthly observations used to compute ATR mean return is set at 100 months.

The first thing to note about Figure 6.55 is that the higher the level of correlation, the less the expected return of the best-performing one. This is consistent with the previous finding that when fewer ATRs are back tested, there is less opportunity to discover better ones (see Figure 6.43). Higher correlation means we are effectively searching through a smaller universe than the actual number of ATRs tested would suggest. As pointed out earlier, in the extreme case in which correlation is 1.0, there is no data mining at all. When the correlation among the ATR returns is nearly perfect, 0.9, the expected return of the best of 256 ATRs is only +1.4 percent. This is the same as an ATR picked at random. In other words, at a correlation of 0.9 the effective number of ATRs being tested is quite small (little data mining). Less data mining means less opportunity to find good rules. Conversely, when correlation among rule returns is zero, the effective size of the universe is maximized—we really are searching among 256 different ATRs. Consequently, the expected return of the best ATR out of 256 is nearly 4 percent, considerably above the universe average of +1.4 percent (data mining works!).

Summary of Findings Regarding the Data-Mining Bias

This section has presented the results of numerous experiments. It is worthwhile, at this point, to summarize our findings. They make clear the nature of the problem that must be solved by the methods presented in the next section.

1. The observed performance of a rule discovered by data mining—that is, the best performer in a set of back-tested rules—is positively biased. Its expected future return is less than its observed historical performance. Its likely performance in any sample of data from the future will be lower than the back-tested performance that allowed it to win the performance competition.

2. The magnitude of the data-mining bias is profoundly affected by the number of observations used to compute the performance statistic used to select the best rule. The number of observations affects both the width and tail thickness of the performance statistic's sampling distribution.

   a. The larger the number of observations, the narrower the sampling distribution and the smaller the data-mining bias.

    b. The larger the number of observations, the lighter the tails of the sampling distribution and the smaller the data-mining bias.

3. The larger the number of rules searched, the larger the data-mining bias.

4. The smaller the variability in true quality (expected return) among the rules tested, the larger will be the data-mining bias. In other words, the more equivalent the predictive power of the rules back tested, the greater will be the bias. This point was not explored experimentally.

5. Data mining works when the sample size is large. The more rules tested, the higher the expected performance of the rule ultimately selected. Data mining does not work when the sample size is too small.

SOLUTIONS: DEALING WITH THE DATA-MINING BIAS

Data mining works but its results are positively biased. Hence, if the set of candidate rules examined by the data miner contains any rules with superior expected returns, data mining can be an effective way to find them. However, their future performance will, in all probability, be less than their back-tested performance. This out-of-sample performance deterioration is simply a fact of life in the data-mining business.

A worse problem occurs when all candidate rules are worthless—all have expected returns of zero or less. In this instance, the data miner runs the risk of being fooled by the data-mining bias and choosing a rule whose expected return is zero. This is the fool's gold of the objective technician. This section discusses some ways to reduce this risk.

Three approaches have been proposed: out-of-sample testing, a data-mining correction factor proposed by Markowitz and Xu, and randomization methods. Out-of-sample testing involves excluding one or more subsets of the historical data from the data mining (out-of-sample). This data is then used to evaluate the best rule discovered in the mined data (in-sample). The selected rule's performance on the data that was insulated from mining operations provides an unbiased estimate of its expected return in future data. A number of schemes for partitioning the historical data into in-sample and out-of-sample segments have been proposed. I summarize several of them later.

A second approach, one that has not been widely discussed outside the academic literature, is based on randomization methods like bootstrapping and Monte Carlo. This approach offers a number of advantages. First, it allows the data miner to test as many rules as desired. Testing a greater number of rules increases the chance of finding superior rules.

Second, it does not require holding data aside, as is done in out-of-sample testing, thereby allowing all available historical data to be used for data mining. Third, it permits significance testing, and, sometimes, approximate confidence intervals can be produced.

A third approach, the data-mining correction factor developed by Markowitz and Xu, deflates the observed performance of the rule that did the best. The reader is directed to source material for this approach. As a point of interest, limited experiments conducted with this method suggest it can work surprisingly well, but it can also fail miserably, depending on the conditions.

Out-of-Sample Testing

Out-of-sample testing is based on the valid notion that the performance of a data-mined rule,[33] in out-of-sample data, provides an unbiased estimate of the rule's future performance. Of course, due to sampling variation, the rule may perform differently in the future than it does in its out-of-sample test, but there is no reason to presume it will do worse. Because out-of-sample performance is unbiased, it makes sense to reserve data for out-of-sample testing.

This raises the issue of how to best segment the historical data into in-sample and out-of-sample subsets. Various schemes have been proposed. The simplest is to create two subsets; the early portion of the historical data is used for data mining while the later portion is reserved for out-of-sample testing. See diagram A in Figure 6.56.[34] A more sophisticated segmentation scheme breaks the historical data up in a checkerboard pattern such that both in-sample and out-of-sample data come from all parts of the history. See diagrams B and C in Figure 6.56.

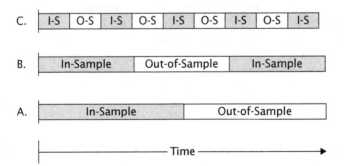

FIGURE 6.56 In-sample and out-of-sample segmentation of historical data.

Walk-Forward Testing. Another data segmentation approach specific to financial market trading applications is walk-forward testing. It is described in Pardo,[35] De La Maza,[36] Katz and McCormick,[37] and Kaufman.[38] It employs a moving data window, which itself is divided into an in-sample and out-of-sample segment. The terminology used for the in-sample and out-of-sample segments is somewhat different, however. Because walk-forward testing has a dynamic aspect, in which the rule is being modified over time as the market evolves, the terminology alludes to a rule that is learning from its experience. Thus the in-sample segment is referred to as the *training* data set because the best parameter values for the rule are learned in this portion of the data. The out-of-sample segment is referred to as the *testing* data set, because the parameter values that were learned in the training test are tested for performance in this data segment.

The notion of a moving data window is well known in time series analysis and technical analysis. Moving averages, moving max-min price channels, and rate-of-change indicators, to name a few, employ a data window that slides along the time axis. Mathematical operations, such as determining the maximum value or the average value, are confined to the data in the window.

In the context of rule testing, the data window (training set + testing set) that is walked forward is sometimes referred to as a *fold* (see Figure 6.57). An out-of-sample performance estimate is computed for each fold. Because there are typically numerous folds and hence numerous out-of-sample estimates, it becomes possible to determine the variance of the performance statistic. This allows a confidence interval to be computed. Moreover, the moving data window adds a dynamic adaptive aspect to rule testing. A new rule can be formulated in each new realization of the data window. This makes walk-forward testing especially attractive for nonstationary phenomena such as financial markets. Hsu and Kuan found adaptive trading rules (they referred to them as learning strategies) effective in their test of over 36,000 objective rules.[39]

In a walk-forward scheme, the training segment is used for data mining, and then the best rule found there is tested on the testing segment. This yields an unbiased estimate of its out-of-sample performance. Then, the entire window is moved forward and the process is repeated.

The walk-forward process is illustrated in Figure 6.57. Note, the window is moved forward by a sufficient amount so that testing data segments in separate folds do not to overlap. In this way, the of out-of-sample performance estimates are independent of each other.

Limitations of Data Out-of-Sample Testing Methods. As an antidote to the data-mining bias, out-of-sample testing suffers from several deficiencies. First and foremost, the virginal status of the data reserved

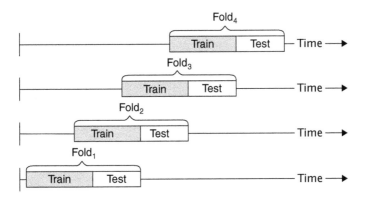

FIGURE 6.57 Walk-forward data testing two data segments.

for out-of-sample testing has a short life span. It is lost as soon as it is used one time. From that point forward, it is no longer able to provide unbiased estimates of rule performance.

A second deficiency is that it eliminates certain portions of the data from mining operations. Thus it reduces the amount of data available to find patterns. When noise is high and information is low, more observations are extremely valuable.

Third, the decision about how to apportion the data between the in-sample and out-of-sample subsets is arbitrary. There is no theory that suggests what fraction of the data should be assigned to training and testing. Results can be very sensitive to these choices. Often it's a seat-of-the-pants call.

Markowitz/Xu Data Mining Correction Factor

A formula for estimating the data-mining bias has been proposed by Markowitz and Xu[40] (MX) and described for practical implementation in an Excel spreadsheet by De La Maza.[41] Markowitz is well known for his pioneering work in modern portfolio theory, for which he shared the 1990 Nobel prize in economics.

The MX method does not require data segmentation. What is required, though, is the complete set of interval returns (e.g., daily, weekly, monthly, and such) for all rules examined by the data miner en route to selecting a best-performing rule. The method corrects for the data-mining bias by shrinking the observed performance of the best rule back toward the average performance of all rules tested. The degree of shrinkage is determined by several factors including: (1) the degree of variation in each rule's daily returns around the grand mean daily return for all rules tested, (2) the degree of variation in each rule's mean return around the mean return for all rules tested, (3) the number of rules examined, and (4) the number of time intervals (e.g., days) of returns.

The article by De La Maza, which was referred to earlier, lays out the details for constructing a spreadsheet that computes the value of a shrinkage factor, **B**, which is a number between zero and one. This value is then plugged into the formula

$$H' = R + \boldsymbol{B}(H - R)$$

Where

H' is the expected return for the best-performing rule after adjustment for the data-mining bias.

R is the average return of all the tested rules.

H is the observed performance of the best rule.

$\boldsymbol{B}$ is the shrinkage factor.

The corrected or shrunken performance estimate for the best rule, H', will lie somewhere between its observed performance and the average for all rules tested. When $\boldsymbol{B}$ equals zero, then the expected return for the best rule is simply equal to the average return of all rules (R). As $\boldsymbol{B}$ approaches a value of 1, the expected return of the best rule approaches its back-tested return. This occurs in a case where no data-mining bias was detected and thus no need to shrink the observed return of the best rule.

The result given by MX is very approximate. Under some conditions, the shrunken performance estimate can be quite good. However, under other conditions easily encountered in practice, its results can be seriously in error. MX is best used as a rough guideline.

Randomization Methods

Chapter 5 introduced two randomization methods that can be used to test the statistical significance of a rule's observed performance in a back test. They were bootstrapping and Monte Carlo permutation. As pointed out in Chapter 5, these significance tests were only valid for a single rule back test, that is, where there was no data mining used to discover the rule. However, with modifications described in this section, these procedures can also be used to test the statistical significance of a rule discovered with data mining.

Both randomization methods allow the data miner to use all historical data for rule discovery. This circumvents the arbitrary decisions required with out-of-sample testing: how to partition the data into in-sample and out-of-sample, how much to use for training versus testing, and so on. However, the randomization methods require that certain information about each rule tested during data mining be retained. Because the specific information that must be retained depends on whether Monte Carlo or bootstrapping is used, the information requirements of each method will be discussed separately.

A brief review is in order to explain how randomization methods can be used for significance testing. The sampling distribution of a test-statistic is the foundation of statistical inference. It describes the degree of random variation in a statistic. This distribution is vital in judging the statistical significance of a rule's observed performance. Chapter 5 pointed out that the sampling distribution can be derived by bootstrapping or the Monte Carlo permutation.

Bootstrapping the Sampling Distribution: White's Reality Check. White's Reality Check (WRC) was invented and patented by economist Halbert White, a professor at the University of California at San Diego. It uses the bootstrap[42] method to derive a sampling distribution that is appropriate to test the statistical significance of the best rule found by data mining. The software can be acquired from Quantmetrics,[43] a firm owned by Dr. White.

Prior to WRC, bootstrapping could be used to generate the sampling distribution to test the significance of a single rule. White's innovation, for which he was granted a patent, allows the bootstrap to be applied to the best rule found by data mining. Specifically, WRC permits the data miner to develop the sampling distribution for the best of N-rules, where N is the number of rules tested, under the assumption that all of the rules have expected returns of zero. In other words, WRC generates the sampling distribution to test the null hypothesis that all the rules examined during data mining have expected returns of zero.

Let's take a highly simplified example to explain the procedure WRC uses. Suppose the data miner has back tested only two rules ($N = 2$) over 10 days. I will refer to the rules as R_1 and R_2. Over the 10-day period R_1 earned a mean daily return of 1 percent, whereas R_2 earned a mean daily return of 2 percent. The data miner picks rule 2 as the best performer, but then wonders, as one should, if the 2 percent was the result of data-mining bias and if its true expected return is actually zero. To generate the sampling distribution that would be appropriate for this data-mining venture, the following steps are taken:

1. The rules are tested over 10 trading days. Thus 10 slips of paper are used to represent each date of trading. They are numbered from 1 through 10 and placed in a bucket for sampling.

2. The slips of paper are then sampled with replacement 10 times. Each time a date is withdrawn from the bucket, the date number is noted. The number of samplings is 10 because that was the length of each rule's performance history. This is a requirement of the Bootstrap Theorem. Suppose the following dates were selected: 5, 3, 5, 5, 7, 2, 5, 8, 1, 2.

3. Using the dates obtained in step 2, a pseudo-track record based on the actual daily returns associated with these dates is created for R_1. This procedure is also carried out for R_2. We now have a randomly generated performance history of length 10 for each rule.

4. Recall that our goal is to generate the sampling distribution for the best-performing rule in a universe of rules which have expected returns equal to zero. Because it is possible, in fact it is our hope, that at least one of the rules tested has an expected return greater than zero, the raw historical returns of R_1 and R_2 must be adjusted to have mean returns of zero. To accomplish this, WRC determines the mean daily return for each rule tested and subtracts this amount from each individual daily return.[44] In this example, R_1's mean daily return is 1 percent and R_2's is 2 percent. Thus 1 percent is deducted from each of R_1's daily returns whereas 2 percent is deducted from each of R_2's daily returns. This has the effect of shifting the distribution of daily returns for each rule so that it is centered over zero. These adjusted daily returns are now used.

5. The adjusted returns of R_1 for days 5, 3, 5, 5, 7, 2, 5, 8, 1, 2 are averaged. The adjusted returns for R_2 are also averaged.

6. The larger of these two mean values is held aside as the first value used to form the sampling distribution of the maximum mean return of N rules. In this case $N = 2$.

7. Steps 2 through 6 are repeated many times (e.g., 500 or more times).

8. The sampling distribution of the statistic, *maximum mean return in a universe of N (2) rules whose expected returns are zero* is formed from these 500 values.

9. With the sampling distribution now in hand, the p-value can be computed.

10. The p-value would simply be the fraction of the 500 values obtained at step 7 that exceed the average return of the tested rule. (See Chapter 5 for the procedure.)

The example described above was intentionally highly simplified. In a more realistic case the data miner would examine a much larger number of rules over a much longer time period. But the procedure for generating the sampling distribution would be the same. All this is done automatically by the WRC software, once it has been provided with the interval returns, (e.g., daily) of all rules tested. This set of data contains all the information WRC needs to derive the sampling distribution that is appropriate for a particular data-mining venture. When many rules are tested this can be a considerable amount of data. Currently, few data miners or data-mining systems save this valuable information.

In Part Two of this book I will perform a case study of 6,402 rules for trading the S&P 500 index. A version of WRC that incorporates some recent enhancements, which are described later, will serve as one method to test the statistical significance of the rules' observed performances.

The Monte Carlo Permutation Method. The Monte Carlo permutation method (MC) can also be used to generate the sampling distribution required to evaluate the statistical significance of rules found by data mining. As noted in Chapter 5, it uses different data than the bootstrap and it tests a different formulation of the null hypothesis, or H_0.

In terms of the data, MC uses the historical times series of a rule's output values (i.e., +1, –1) as well as the market's raw returns. In contrast, the bootstrap uses the rule's interval (e.g., daily) returns. In terms of the H_0, both WRC and MC test the notion that all rules examined during data mining have no predictive power. However, MC formulates H_0 somewhat differently. To simulate the performance of a rule devoid of predictive power, MC randomly pairs rule output values with daily market price changes. In contrast to WRC, MC's random coupling of output values and market changes is done without replacement. Presumably, if rule output values are randomly assigned to market changes, the performance would be consistent with the null hypothesis that the rule is worthless. The return earned by the random pairings becomes the benchmark against which the actual rule returns are compared. If a rule has genuine predictive power, then its informed pairing of output values and market changes should generate significantly better performance.

The performance of the random pairing is simply the rule's value (+1 or –1) multiplied by the market change randomly assigned to that day. Thus, if a rule output of +1 gets paired with a day when the market rose, the rule earns the market's price change. Likewise, if a –1 rule output gets randomly paired with a day on which the market fell, it earns that positive amount that day. Losses occur on days when the sign of the rule's output value is opposite to that of the market's price change.

After the full history of a rule's output values have been paired with a market price change, the mean return is computed. This is done for each rule in the universe of N rules giving N mean returns. The maximum mean return is selected, and this becomes the first value used to construct the

MC sampling distribution. This entire process is repeated many times (>500) with different random pairings each time. The sampling distribution is generated from this large number of values.

Note that there is no need to reposition each rule's return distribution to be centered over zero as is done with WRC because it assumes that all rules have an expected return of zero. In contrast, the MC sampling distribution's mean is the expected return of a useless rule in a data-mining venture. If, after randomly assigning rule values to market returns, the sampling distribution is situated at a value greater than zero, so be it. p-values can be computed directly from the MC generated sampling distribution, just as they would be with a sampling distribution generated by alternative methods. The p-value is the area in the right tail of the distribution that lies at or beyond the back-tested rule's mean return.

A limitation of the MC method compared to WRC is that it cannot be used to generate confidence intervals because it does not test a hypothesis about the rule's mean return. MC's null hypothesis is simply that all rules tested have output values that are randomly correlated with future market behavior.

To recap, the steps by which the MC permutation method generates the sampling distribution for a data miner are:

1. Obtain the daily rule output states for all N rules examined during the data-mining venture.
2. Each rule's output values are randomly paired with a scrambled version of the actual future market price changes. Note that it is important the same pairings be used for all rules. Thus, if a rule's output value for day 7 is paired with the market return for day 15, this same pairing must be done for all competing rules. This is done to preserve correlation structure that may be present in the rules, which is one of the five factors impacting the data-mining bias.
3. Determine the mean rate of return for each rule.
4. Out of these N rules, select the highest mean return. This value becomes the first value for the sampling distribution of the mean for the best mean among N useless rules.
5. Repeat steps 2, 3, and 4, M times (where $M = 500$ or some large number).
6. Form the sampling distribution from the M values obtained in steps 2 through 5.
7. The p-value for a back-tested rules can be determined by determining the fraction of the values obtained by step 6 that are equal to or greater than its mean return.

Potential Flaws in Initial WRC and MCP Methods. Both WRC and MC test the null hypothesis that all rules in the data-mined universe are useless. The rule miner hopes to reject this hypothesis in favor of the alternative hypothesis: that not all the rules examined are useless. As pointed out earlier, the meaning of the term *useless* depends on the randomization method used. In the context of WRC, a useless rule has an expected return equal to zero. In the context of the MC, useless refers to a rule whose output values are randomly paired with the market's future change.

As was discussed in Chapter 5, a hypothesis test can err in two ways. A type-I error occurs when the null hypothesis is true (all rules tested really are useless) is rejected in error. This occurs when a rule that is in fact useless managed to earning a high mean return and a low p-value by luck. This is the data miner's fool's gold.

A type-II error occurs when the null hypothesis is in fact false and should be rejected, but the rule's performance is too low to do so. That is to say, the rule really does have predictive power, but its virtue remains undetected because it experienced bad luck during the back test. The data miner winds up leaving real TA gold in the ground.

The ability of a hypothesis test to avoid making a type-II error is referred to as the test's *power*, not to be confused with a rule's predictive power. Here, we are speaking of the power of a statistical test to detect a false H_0. So a hypothesis test is characterized by two measures of goodness: its *significance* (probability of making a type-I error) and its *power* (probability of avoiding a type-II error). It is with respect to the issue of power that initial versions of WRC and MCP are open to criticism.

As pointed out by economist Peter Hansen,[45] WRC and, by extension, the MCP would both suffer a loss of power (increased likelihood of making a type-II error) when the data-mined universe contains rules that are worse than the benchmark. This refers to a situation in which one or more rules are actually worse than useless—they have expected returns that are less than zero. This could occur, for example, if one were to reverse the output value of a rule that has an expected return that is truly greater than zero. Because approximately half of the rules tested in Part Two of this book are obtained in this fashion (i.e., inverse rules), the research presented in Part Two of this book is vulnerable to the problem discussed by Hansen.

To evaluate Hansen's criticism, the power of both WRC and MCP was evaluated by Dr. Timothy Masters, on an ATR universe that contained rules that were both better than and worse than the benchmark. In other words, the evaluation simulated exactly the case that troubles Hansen. These tests showed that his concerns are justified for a situation in which a rule with negative expected returns has an extremely large variance in returns. This can drastically reduce the power of both WRC and MCP. However, in cases that one is more likely to encounter in TA rule data mining, both methods are reasonably resistant to this problem. Therefore, when there is one or more superior rules in the universe of examined rules, both WRC and the MCP method have a reasonable chance of detecting them.

Recent Enhancement to WRC and MCP. Despite the reasonable power of the initial versions of WRC and MCP methods, a recent paper by Romano and Wolf[46] recommends a modification that enhances the power of WRC and that also appears to enhance the power of MCP. Thus the Romano and Wolf enhancement reduces the probability of a Type-II error. This modification was introduced to the versions of WRC and MC used in Part Two's case study. However, at this time, there is no commercial version of WRC with this enhancement. The MCP version with the enhancement is being placed in the public domain and codes for it will be made available on a web site, www.evidencebasedta.com.

CHAPTER 7

Theories of Nonrandom Price Motion

At the risk of stating the obvious, if market fluctuations were completely random, TA would be pointless. TA is a justifiable endeavor if and only if price movements are nonrandom to some degree some portion of the time. This chapter offers several theories explaining why episodes of nonrandom price movements ought to occur in financial market prices.

Although the occurrence of nonrandom price motion is necessary to justify TA, this alone is not sufficient to justify any specific TA method. Each method must demonstrate, by objective evidence, its ability to capture some part of the nonrandom price motion. Part Two will evaluate a large number of TA rules with respect to their ability to do just that.

THE IMPORTANCE OF THEORY

Several new theories from the field of behavioral finance explain why price movements are nonrandom to some degree and therefore potentially predictable . Thus, these novel theories take a position that is contrary to the efficient markets hypothesis (EMH), a cornerstone of finance theory for over 40 years. EMH contends that price changes in financial markets are random and, therefore, unpredictable. Therefore, these new theories hold out hope for TA.

The reader may wonder why theoretical support for nonrandomness is even necessary. If a TA method has a profitable back test, isn't that all that should be needed? It could be asserted that a significantly profitable back test not only establishes that markets are nonrandom, it also establishes that the method is able to exploit some portion of the market's nonrandomness.

This view misses the importance of theoretical support. Even when all statistical precautions have been taken, a profitable back test that is not supported by sound theory is an isolated result and possibly still a lucky one. A successful back test always provokes the question: Will the rule continue to work in the future? Theory can be helpful here because a back test that is consistent with sound theory is less likely to be a statistical fluke. When a back test has theoretical foundation, it is no longer an isolated fact, but part of a larger cohesive picture in which theory explains fact and fact confirms theory.

For example, the profitability of technical trend-following systems in commodity futures can be explained as compensation (i.e., a risk premium) for providing a valuable service to commercial hedgers, that of risk transference. In other words, economic theory predicts that futures markets should manifest enough profitable trends to motivate trend followers to accept the price risks hedgers wish to shed.[1] This is discussed later in this chapter.

SCIENTIFIC THEORIES

In everyday speech, a theory is a speculative conjecture about why something is the way it is. As explained in Chapter 3, a scientific theory is something different. First, it offers a succinct explanation for a broad range of prior observations. Second, and most importantly, it makes specific predictions that are later confirmed by new observations.

Kepler's laws of planetary motion[2] concisely explained a large number of prior astronomical observations and made specific predictions that were subsequently confirmed by additional observations. However, as good as Kepler's laws were, Newton's theory of gravitation was better because it was broader in scope. It not only explained why Kepler's laws worked but explained a far wider variety of phenomena. Theories of nonrandom price motion need not predict with the accuracy of physical theories. However, to be useful, they must not only succinctly describe a wide variety of previously observed market behavior, but must also make testable predictions confirmed by subsequent observations.

WHAT IS WRONG WITH POPULAR TA THEORY?

Many TA texts offer no explanation about why their proposed methods work. The statement of John Magee, author of one of TA's seminal works[3] is typical. He said, "We can never hope to know why the market behaves as it does, we can only aspire to understand how. History obviously has repetitive tendencies and that's good enough."

Some TA texts do offer explanations, but these are typically ad-hoc rationales that generate no testable predictions. According to author John Murphy, the cornerstone premise of TA is "anything that can possibly affect the price—fundamentally, politically, psychologically, or otherwise—is actually reflected in the price of that market."[4] One would be hard pressed to extract testable predictions from such a vague statement.

Actually, this statement, which purports to explain why TA works, contains a logical contradiction. For, if it were true that price did reflect (i.e., discount) all possible information, it would imply that price was devoid of any predictive information. To understand why, assume a hypothetical price pattern has just occurred in stock XYZ, which is currently at $50, and based on the pattern a move to $60 is implied. Then, by definition, when the pattern occurs its predictive implication has yet to be reflected in prices. However, if the premise that price reflects all information were true, the price would already be at the level predicted by the pattern, thus negating the pattern's forecasting ability.

This logical contradiction is even more apparent when it is pointed out that EMH, a school of thought that rejects the efficacy of TA, rests on the very same premise; "prices fully reflect all available information."[5] Technical analysis cannot be based on the same premise as its mortal enemy. This contradiction is an example of cloudy uncritical thinking that is all too common in the popular version of TA.

Fortunately for TA, its cornerstone premise that price reflects all information appears to be contradicted by fact. One example is the so-called underreaction effect, which has been postulated by behavioral finance. It says that, because prices sometimes fail to respond to new information as rapidly as EMH theorists contend, a systematic price movement, or trend, toward a price level that does reflect the new information occurs. The failure of prices to respond rapidly is caused by a several cognitive errors that afflict investors, such as the conservatism bias and the anchoring effect. These are discussed later in this chapter.

Another popular justification of TA is based on pop psychology. By pop psychology, I mean principles of human behavior that seem plausible but lack scientific support. According to noted economist and authority in the field of behavioral finance, Robert Shiller, "In considering lessons from psychology, it must be noted that the many popular accounts of the psychology of investing are simply not credible. Investors are said to be euphoric or frenzied during booms or panic-stricken during market crashes. In both booms and crashes, investors are descried as blindly following the herd like so many sheep, with no minds of their own."[6] The fact is, people are more rational than these pop-psychology theories suggest. "During the most significant financial events, most people are preoccupied with other personal matters, not with the financial markets at all. So it is hard to imagine that the market as a whole reflects the emotions described by these psychological theories."[7] We will need to look beyond the platitudes of popular texts for TA's justification. Fortunately, theories developed in the field of behavioral finance and elsewhere are beginning to offer the theoretical support TA needs.

THE ENEMY'S POSITION: EFFICIENT MARKETS AND RANDOM WALKS

Before discussing theories that explain why nonrandom price movements should exist, we need to consider the enemy's position, the EMH. Recently, some have argued that EMH does not necessarily imply that prices follow unpredictable random walks,[8] and that efficient markets and price predictability can coexist. However, the pioneers of EMH asserted that random walks were a necessary consequence of efficient markets. This section states their case and examines its weaknesses.

What Is an Efficient Market?

An efficient market is a market that cannot be beaten. In such a market, no fundamental or technical analysis strategy, formula, or system can earn a risk-adjusted rate of return that beats the market defined by a benchmark index. If the market is indeed efficient, the risk-adjusted return earned by buying and holding the market index is the best one can hope for. This is so because prices in an efficient market properly reflect all known and knowable information. Therefore, the current price provides the best estimate of each security's value.

According to EMH, markets achieve a state of efficient pricing because of the vigorous efforts of numerous rational investors attempting to maximize their wealth. In their pursuit of true value, these investors are constantly updating their beliefs with the latest information in a probabilistically correct manner[9] so as to project each security's future cash flows. Although no single investor is all knowing, collectively they know as much as can possibly be known. This knowledge motivates investors to buy and sell in such a way that prices settle at the *equilibrium* or rational price level.

In such a world, prices change only when new information arrives. When it does, prices change almost instantly to a new rational price that properly reflects the news. Thus, prices do not gradually trend from one rational price level to the next, giving the trend analyst a chance to get on board. Not at all. In the world posited by EMH, prices trace a step function as they move almost instantly from one rational level to the next. If the news is favorable, prices rise, and if it's unfavorable, prices fall. Because it is not predictable whether the news will be favorable or unfavorable (it wouldn't be news if it was), price changes will be unpredictable as well. This is illustrated in Figure 7.1.

The Consequences of Market Efficiency: Good and Bad

Market efficiency has good and bad implications. They are good for the economy as a whole but bad—very bad—for TA. They are good for the economy because rational prices send vital signals of asset values that, in turn, encourage the efficient allocation of scarce resources, such as capital and labor. This fosters economic growth.[10]

However, prices in an efficient market are unpredictable rendering all forms of TA useless. According to Paul Samuelson, financial market prices

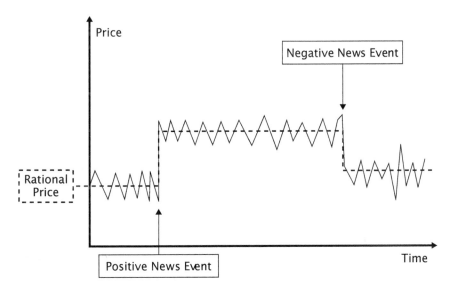

FIGURE 7.1 Efficient market's response to positive and negative news.

follow a random walk because of the actions of many intelligent/rational investors. In seeking to maximize wealth, they buy undervalued assets pushing their prices higher and sell overvalued assets pushing prices lower.[11] "Taken to its logical extreme, it means that a blindfolded monkey selecting stocks by throwing darts at a newspaper's financial pages could do just as well as one carefully selected by the experts."[12]

"EMH rules out the possibility of trading systems, based on available information, that have expected profits or returns in excess of equilibrium expected profit or return."[13] "In plain English, an average investor— whether an individual, pension fund, or a mutual fund—cannot hope to consistently beat the market, and the vast resources that such investors dedicate to analyzing, picking and trading securities are wasted."[14] Although, under EMH, it is still possible to generate positive returns from an investment strategy, when those returns are adjusted for risk, they will not be superior to the return of buying and holding the market index portfolio.

The efficient markets hypothesis also declares that when there is no news entering the market, prices tend to oscillate in a random and unbiased fashion above and below the rational price level. See Figure 7.2. Because this level is itself subject to uncertainty, no technical or fundamental indicator can reliably indicate when prices are above or below it. This means, for example, that in an efficient market stocks with a low price to book ratio, a well known fundamental indicator, are no more likely to appreciate than stocks with a high price to book ratio. This is a cold world for anyone looking for an edge.

FIGURE 7.2 Efficient market hypothesis (random and unbiased pricing errors).

False Notions of Market Efficiency

There are a number of commonly held but false notions about market efficiency. First is the idea that efficiency requires the market price to be equal to rational value at all times. In fact, market efficiency simply requires that price deviates from rational value in an unbiased fashion. Therefore, positive deviations from rational value are just as likely as negative deviations, and at any point in time there is a roughly equal chance that the asset's price will be above its rational value as below it. Moreover, these deviations are random. Thus the time series of pricing errors in an efficient market is a random variable whose probability distribution is centered at the rational price and is approximately symmetrical about it.

A second false notion about market efficiency is that it implies that no one can beat the market. Actually, in any given time period, about 50 percent of all investors will outperform the benchmark index, while the remaining 50 percent underperform. The notion that no single investor or money manager can beat the market over the long term is equally false. Given enough players, a small number are likely to have lengthy streaks of market beating returns even if their strategies are totally without merit. Nassim Taleb[15] shows that even if we assume money managers are no better than a blind monkey throwing darts[16] (probability of beating the market = 0.5) and the universe of managers is large enough, say 10,000, after five years there is likely to be about 312 firms who have beaten the market five years in a row. These lucky folks are the ones who will send salesmen calling. The other 9,682 are less likely to knock on your door.

The Evidence in Favor of EMH

As previously discussed, a scientific hypothesis plays a dual role: explanation and prediction. Its veracity is tested by comparing its predictions with new observations. As discussed in Chapter 3, predictions are meaningful only if they are specific enough to offer the possibility of empirical falsification. If new observations do contradict a hypothesis's predictions, the hypothesis is either reformulated and tested anew or thrown out. However, what should be inferred when observations and predictions agree?

On this issue there is debate. Philosophers in the camp of David Hume contend that no amount of confirmatory evidence is ever sufficient to prove a theory, but in the practical world of science, confirmation does add strength to a hypothesis. If test after test yields observations that are consistent with its predictions, that means something to most scientists.

So EMH advocates have put forward a roster of supporting evidence. Their evidence comes in two flavors because EMH comes in two testable flavors: semistrong and weak.[17] The semistrong form asserts it is impossible to beat the market with public information. Because this includes all fundamental and technical data, the semistrong form predicts that neither fundamental nor technical analysis can beat the market. This informal prediction is not sufficiently specific to be testable, but it is in agreement with the observation that people have great difficulty profiting consistently from market fluctuations—and a lot try.

The semistrong form also makes several specific predictions that are testable. One is that a security's price will react quickly and accurately to any news that bears on its value. The proper response of an efficient market to news is illustrated in Figure 7.3.

This prediction implies prices should neither overreact nor underreact to news. This is testable in the following way. Imagine for a moment that prices did not behave efficiently and did systematically over- or underreact to new information. If this were the case, it would imply that price movements would be predictable. To see why, consider what would happen if a stock overreacted to news either by going up too much in response to good news or down too much in response to bad. Because EMH says prices must stay close to rational values, overshooting rational value would necessarily lead to a corrective movement back toward rational value. This correction would not be random meandering but rather a pur-

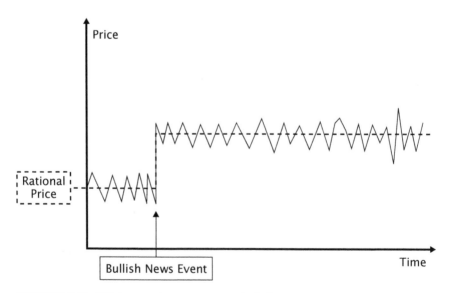

FIGURE 7.3 Efficient market response to bullish news.

poseful movement, as if the price were being magnetically drawn to the rational level. Such a movement would be, to some degree, predictable. Because EMH denies predictability, it must also deny the possibility of overreactions to news. A hypothetical overreaction to bullish news and a subsequent systematic movement back to rational levels is illustrated in Figure 7.4.

By the same logic, EMH must also deny the possibility of underreaction to news, where prices move less than the news justifies. In this case, a systematic price movement would also develop as prices continued to trend (drift) toward the new rational level implied by the news. Underreaction to bullish and bearish news events and the resultant nonrandom movement toward rational value are illustrated in Figure 7.5.

Evidence supporting EMH's prediction that overreactions and underreactions do not occur is presented in the event studies of Eugene Fama.[18] He examined all types of corporate news events such as earnings and dividend announcements, takeovers, mergers, and so forth and found that after an initial, almost instantaneous, nonexploitable price movement triggered by the news, there was no additional movement. These observations are consistent with EMH's prediction that the markets quickly and accurately discount news events.[19]

A second prediction of EMH is that prices should change only when news arrives. It follows then, that prices should not change dramatically in the absence of news or in response to noninformative events.[20] These

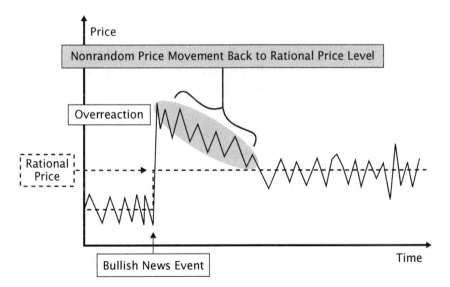

FIGURE 7.4 Overreaction to bullish news (implies nonrandom price movements).

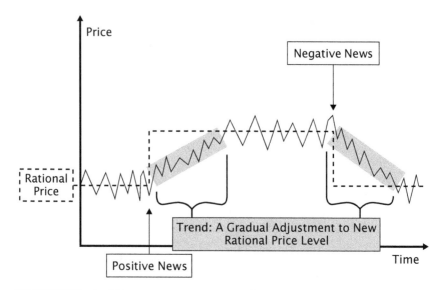

FIGURE 7.5 Underreaction to news can explain nonrandom trends.

two predictions suggest yet a third that is most crucial to TA. EMH implies that stale information, information already in the public domain, should have no predictive power and be of no value in making investment profits. Clearly, all information used by TA qualifies as stale. Thus, EMH predicts that all TA methods should fail. If this were to be confirmed, it's lights out for TA.

The prediction that all stale information strategies should have no predictive power seems cut and dried until one tries to test it. Recall, EMH says an investment strategy based on stale information should not be able to generate excess profits after risk adjustment. So the mere fact that a strategy based on stale information makes gains is not sufficient to rebut EMH. To contradict EMH, it must be demonstrated that the gains are excessive after adjusting for the strategy's risk.

The notion of judging investment strategies on the basis of risk-adjusted returns is entirely reasonable. For example, if a strategy makes 20 percent per year and the benchmark makes 10 percent, but the strategy exposes the investor to three times the risk, the strategy has not beaten the index after risk adjustment. The question is: How does one define and quantify risk?

Quantifying risk requires a risk model. The most well known is the capital asset pricing model[21] (CAPM), which explains systematic differences in the returns of securities in terms of a single risk factor, the security's relative volatility. This is to say, the risk of a stock is quantified by its volatility relative to the volatility of the market as a whole. Thus, if a stock is twice as volatile as the market index, its returns should be twice that of the market. Such a stock is said to earn excess returns when it earns more than twice the market return. This approach works well when measuring the risk of a single stock or a portfolio of long stock positions. However, CAPM cannot quantify the risk exposures of more complex strategies. In response to this limitation, capital market theorists have proposed other risk models. One of the best known is APT (arbitrage pricing theory), which attributes risk to several independent risk factors.[22]

However, EMH advocates have tacitly given themselves the liberty of cooking up new risk factors whenever they wish. This makes it nearly impossible to refute their claim that stale information strategies cannot beat the market. For, it is always possible to propose a new risk model that explains away a strategy's excess returns as compensation for risk. As explained in Chapter 3, this is not a scientific sin if the risk factor(s) were identified before the stale information strategy earning excess returns was discovered. However, proposing a new risk factor(s) after a market-beating strategy has been discovered is nothing more than an ad hoc hypothesis. This is an explanation cooked up after the fact for the specific purpose of immunizing a theory, in this case EMH, from falsification. This practice is frowned upon in science for good reason. Also, as discussed in Chapter 3, the information content of a scientific theory is roughly equivalent to the opportunities it presents for falsification. The unbridled ability to explain away any and all dissonant evidence effectively drains the theory of its information content. Thus, the freedom to concoct new risk factors to explain each and every investment strategy that beats the market with stale information effectively reduces EMH to a meaningless theory.

The evidence confirming the weak form of EMH, which states that stale prices and indicators derived from them—such as price momentum—are without value, is based on auto-correlation studies. They measure the degree to which price changes are linearly correlated with prior changes, at various lag intervals.[23] These studies have confirmed that price changes (i.e., returns) are indeed linearly independent. This means that a linear function of current and past returns cannot be used to predict future returns.[24] Based on these findings, it was concluded by EMH advocates, that security returns are an unpredictable random walk.

However, autocorrelation studies are relatively weak tests in the sense that they can only detect linear dependencies. Searching for linear structure is merely one way to determine if a time series is behaving in a nonrandom fashion. Edgar Peters[25] and Andrew Lo and A. Craig MacKinlay[26] have shown that alternative data analysis methods indicate that financial market time series do not behave like random walks. For example, the test statistic used by Lo and McKinlay, called the variance ratio, can detect more complex (nonlinear) nonrandom behaviors that would be invisible autocorrelation studies.

CHALLENGING EMH

A good theory is consistent in two ways. Its logic is internally consistent and it is consistent with observed evidence. Thus a theory can be challenged either by showing that it contradicts itself or that it is contradicted by evidence.

A theory is self-contradicting if it implies or predicts something that would contradict the theory. An example was given earlier in this chapter: I showed that a cornerstone premise of popular TA, which asserts that price perfectly reflects all information, contradicts another of its central premises, that price contains predictive information.

The Smart versus Dumb Paradox

One implication of market efficiency is that knowledgeable investors should not be able to earn higher returns than investors who are less knowledgeable. This follows from the premise that market efficiency means that whatever information is known or knowable has already been reflected in security prices. In an efficient market, there is no competitive advantage to being smart or disadvantage to being dumb.

However, this implication conflicts with another of EMH's assumptions—that the arbitrage activities of rational investors are able to drive prices toward rational levels. (See the heading titled "The Assumptions of EMH" later in this chapter.) Arbitrage can only act as an enforcer of rational prices if arbitrageurs have more trading capital and, thus, greater price-moving power than irrational, dumb investors. Having more trading capital implies that smart arbitrageurs must have earned higher returns in the past than less well informed (dumb) investors. Either market prices are set by the smartest, richest participants or they are not. EMH implies both. Paradoxical, isn't it!

The Cost of Information Paradox

Another logical inconsistency of EMH has to do with the cost of information. It is reasonable to assume that it costs time, money, and intelligence to gather information and process it into useful investing strategies. At the same time EMH contends that such information cannot earn incremental returns for investors who incur these costs. Remember, EMH contends that information is instantly reflected in prices. This implies that no matter how wide or deep the research effort, whatever is discovered will be of no value.

However, if EMH is correct that there is no payoff for information gathering and processing, then investors would lack the motivation to incur the costs of doing so. With no one to dig out the information and act on it, it would not get reflected in price. In other words, if it is costly to make markets informationally efficient, investors would be motivated to do it only if they were compensated with excess risk-adjusted returns. Thus the contradiction—EMH requires that information seekers be compensated for their efforts and simultaneously denies that they will be.

This paradox is argued persuasively by Grossman and Stiglitz in their article "On the Impossibility of Informationally Efficient Markets."[27] They contend that inefficiencies are necessary to motivate rational investors to engage in information gathering and processing. The returns they earn from the market's pricing errors are compensation for their efforts, which, in turn, have the effect of moving prices toward rational levels. The gains of these rational investors are financed by the losses of noise traders and liquidity traders. Noise traders are investors who buy and sell based on signals that they think are informative but that are not. Rational investors also earn profits from the losses of investors who trade to increase their cash reserves (liquidity traders). One way for the rational investor to gain would be if there were a delay between the time information is discovered and the time it is reflected in prices, but EMH denies the possibility of gradual price adjustments. This is yet another logical inconsistency of EMH.

A similar logic applies to the costs of acting on information (e.g., commissions, slippage, bid-asked spreads). Unless investors were compensated for incurring trading costs there would be no point to their trading activities, which are required by EMH to move the price to its rational level. The bottom line is that any factor that limits trading—costs to trade, costs to generate information, the rule that impairs short-selling, and so forth—limits the ability of the market to attain efficiency. It simply does not hold logically that there would be no compensation to those engaged in trading.

The Assumptions of EMH

To appreciate the arguments made by EMH's critics, it is necessary to understand that EMH rests on three progressively weaker assumptions: (1) investors are rational, (2) investors' pricing errors are random, and

(3) there are always rational arbitrage investors to catch any pricing errors. Let's examine each of these in a bit more detail.

First is EMH's contention that investors are, by and large, rational. To recap, rational investors, in aggregate, are purported to value securities correctly. This means prices will reflect, as accurately as possible, the present discounted value of a security's future cash flows and risk characteristics. As rational investors learn new information, they respond quickly, bidding up prices when news is good and letting the price fall when news is bad. As a consequence, security prices adjust, almost instantly, to new information.[28]

Even if this assumption were incorrect, EMH advocates still insist that prices adjust quickly to rational levels anyway because of their second assumption: The valuation mistakes of individual investors are uncorrelated. This means that if one investor erroneously values a security too high, that error will be offset by another investor's error of valuing it too low. Taken in aggregate, these valuation errors are self-canceling and have an average value of zero. That is to say pricing errors are unbiased. This is presumed to be true because the error-prone investors are likely to be using different, though useless, investment strategies. Therefore, their actions should be uncorrelated. To put it bluntly, as one foolish investor gets an uninformative signal to buy, another investment fool is equally likely to get an uninformative signal to sell. In effect they wind up trading with each other, leaving prices very close to rational levels.

Moreover, even if this second assumption fails to keep prices at rational levels, EMH invokes yet a third assumption. That is, if the valuation mistakes of irrational investors turn out to be biased (i.e., have an average value that is greater than or less than zero), arbitrage investors will come to the rescue. They will notice that prices have systematically diverged from rational values. The arbitrageurs will buy when prices are too low or sell when they are too high, thus forcing prices back to where they should be.

In the EMH world, arbitrage is as close as it gets to a free lunch. An arbitrage transaction incurs no risk, requires no capital, and earns a guaranteed return. As envisioned by efficient market advocates, an arbitrage trade goes something like this: Consider two financial assets, stocks X and Y, which sell at equal prices and which are equally risky. However, they have different expected future returns. Obviously, one of the two assets is improperly priced. If asset X has a higher future return, then to take advantage of the mispricing, arbitrageurs would buy asset X while short-selling Y. With the activities of like-minded arbitrageurs, the price of each stock will converge to its proper fundamental value.[29] Market efficiency attained in this manner assumes there are always arbitrageurs ready, willing, and able to jump on these opportunities. The better ones become very wealthy, thereby enhancing their ability to drive prices to proper levels, while the irrational investors eventually go broke losing their ability to push prices away from equilibrium levels. The uninformed, irrational investors are driven out of the market the way a weak species is driven from an ecosystem, while the rational, well-informed arbitrageurs thrive.

Flaws in EMH Assumptions

This section considers each of the assumptions of EMH and how they miss the mark.

Investors Are Rational. Investors do not appear to be as rational as EMH assumes. Many investors react to irrelevant information, what noted economist Fischer Black calls "noise signals."[30] Though they think they are acting intelligently, these investors can expect to earn the same return as an investor who buys and sells based on a coin flip. Investors who follow the advice of financial gurus who base their advice on noise signals are noise traders by proxy.

In fact, investors are guilty of numerous departures from rationality. For example, they fail to diversify, they trade too actively, they increase their tax liabilities by selling appreciated stocks but hold onto losing positions, and they trade mutual funds with high fees. Moreover, their failures are recurring. "Investors' deviations from the maxims of economic rationality turn out to be highly pervasive and systematic."[31] These departures from rationality can be classified into three areas: inaccurate risk assessments, poor probability judgments, and irrational decision framing. I discuss each of these in turn.

Investors typically do not assess risks in conformity with the normative ideal put forward by Neumann and Morgenstern, known as "expected utility theory." In a perfectly rational world, an individual faced with choosing among several options selects the one with the highest expected value. The expected value of a particular choice is equal to a sum of products, where each product is the probability of each possible outcome multiplied by the value or utility of that outcome to the decision maker. The problem is people do not actually behave this way. Research has shown that investors make numerous systematic errors when assessing risks and making choices.

These mistakes have been incorporated into a framework called Prospect Theory, which was proposed by Kahneman and Tversky (1979).[32] It explains how people actually make decisions under conditions of uncertainty. For example, it explains that investors hold onto losing stocks but sell profitable positions to avoid the psychic pain of realizing a loss. It also explains why investors overvalue low-probability long-shot speculations.

The second way investors depart from the rational ideal of EMH is in their judgments of probability. EMH assumes that, as investors receive new information, they update their probability assessments in accordance with Bayes' theorem, a formula for combining probabilities in a theoretically correct way. However, to their detriment, investors do not behave this way. One common error, discussed in Chapter 2, is the crime of small numbers—drawing grand conclusions from small samples of data. This explains why investors will rashly conclude that a corporation with a short string of successful quarterly earnings reports is likely to continue to grow rapidly. Their overreaction to this small sample of positive earnings changes causes the stock to become overpriced.

Lastly, investors' decisions can be strongly impacted by how choices are described (framed). By incorrectly framing a decision situation, investors tend to misperceive the true expected value of a choice. For example, when choices are framed in terms of potential gains, investors tend to choose the option most likely to earn a gain, even if it is insignificant in size. However, when the same choices are framed in terms of potential losses, investors will assume the risk of a very significant loss just to avoid the certainty of a small loss. This error, called the "disposition effect," is thought to explain why investors sell winners quickly, so as to be sure to earn a gain, even if it's small, but hold on to losers even if it means there is a chance the loss will turn into a much larger one.

Investor Errors Are Uncorrelated. The assumption that investors' errors are uncorrelated is contradicted by psychological research which shows people do not deviate from rationality randomly in situations characterized by uncertainty. In reality, most people tend to make similar mistakes in such situations and hence their deviations from rationality are correlated. Many investors will be tempted to buy the same stock because the stock appeals to a common heuristic rule of judgment that makes it look like a candidate for further appreciation. For example, a company that has three positive earning quarters can be perceived by many investors to be a growth stock that warrants a high price-to-earnings ratio or P/E. This problem is made worse by social interactions, or herding, between investors. "They follow each other's mistakes listening to rumors and imitating the actions of their fellow traders."[33]

Money managers, who should know better, make these mistakes as well. They are guilty of creating portfolios that are excessively close to the benchmarks against which they are measured, all in an effort to reduce the chance they will underperform. Professional money managers also engage in imitative behavior and move herd-like into the same stocks, for fear of falling behind the pack. They dress up their portfolios by adding stocks that have done well and eliminate those that have not, so year-end portfolio reports show the fund invested in the highest performing stocks.

Arbitrage Forces Prices to Rational Levels. This assumption fails because the power of arbitrage activities to push prices toward rational levels is limited. First, no one rings a bell when securities become mispriced. The rational price is the discounted value of a stream of future cash flows, which is, by definition, uncertain. Investors try to estimate future earnings, but their forecasts are prone to significant error.

Second, arbitrageurs do not have unlimited tolerance for adverse price movement—for example, when an underpriced stock that has been purchased continues to go lower, or an overpriced security that has been sold short continues to soar. The actions of noise traders can easily push prices further away from rational levels before they return to them. Therefore, even if an arbitrageur spots a truly mispriced security, the pricing error may grow larger before it is finally eradicated. Should this adverse price movement become too large, the arbitrageur may have to close the position with a loss. If this happens often enough, the noise traders can drive rational investors out of business. This is referred to as noise trader risk[34] and it limits the motivation and commitments of arbitrage traders. Behavioral finance expert Andre Shleifer says even an arbitrage trade that looks nearly perfect from the outside is in reality quite risky so the number of investors who go after it will be limited. The bottom line is arbitrage activities cannot always enforce rational pricing.

Noise trader risk was a factor in the blow-up of the Long Term Capital Management (LTCM) hedge fund in the fall of 1998. The fund's crash nearly took the entire financial market with it. Ultimately, the mispricings that LTCM had identified were corrected, but because they had overleveraged their positions, the fund lacked the staying power to hold its positions through a short-term period of even greater mispricing.

Improper use of leverage is yet another factor that can impair the role arbitrage plays in driving markets to efficiency. Thus, even if arbitrageurs can accurately identify over- and under-priced securities, if they use too much leverage they can get wiped out. There is an optimal leverage for favorable bets (i.e., speculations with a positive expectancy).[35] If this level is exceeded, the probability of ruin rises despite the positive expectation.

I show this to my students during a class I call Casino Night. We play a game in which everyone starts off with an imaginary $100. I have a friend come in to act as coin flipper. Before each flip, the students determine what fraction of their capital to bet on the next coin toss. If a head results, the payoff is twice the amount of the bet. If a tail results, only the amount of the bet is lost. We play the game for 75 flips. This game has a very favorable expectation.[36] However, even in a game with such a favorable expectancy, many students wind up losing money because they bet too aggressively (i.e., the fraction of capital wagered on a bet is too large). A formula worked out by Kelly, an electrical engineer at Bell Labs in the 1950s, now known as the Kelly Criterion, specifies the optimal fraction to bet on each coin flip so as to maximize the growth rate of the bettor's capital. The optimal fraction depends on the probability of a win and the ratio of the average win to average loss. In this particular game, the optimal fraction to wager on each bet is 0.25. If this level is exceeded, the bettor faces greater risk without the benefit of a faster growth of capital. If one were to employ a bet fraction of 0.58 it is likely all funds would be lost, despite the favorable expectation. This is what happens to an arbitrageur with good information who uses too much leverage.

Another constraint on an arbitrage's ability to enforce efficient pricing is the lack of perfect substitute securities. An ideal (riskless) arbitrage transaction involves the simultaneous purchase and sale of a pair of securities with identical future cash flows and identical risk characteristics. An arbitrage transaction based on securities that do not conform to this ideal necessarily involves risk. And it is risk that limits the degree to which arbitrage activity can force prices to efficient levels. When a broad class of assets, such as all stocks, become overpriced, as they did in the spring of 2000, there is no substitute security to use as the long-side hedge to a short sale of the entire stock market. Even in the case where the securities in an arbitrage transaction are close substitutes, there can be substantial risks. Each stock has its own specific or idiosyncratic risks, and this makes arbitrageurs wary. For example, if GM were undervalued and it were purchased against an offsetting short sale in Ford, there would be the risk that some bullish event unique to Ford or a bearish event unique to GM would create a loss for the arbitrage trader.

There are still other constraints that prevent arbitrage from playing the price-policing role envisioned by EMH. Arbitrageurs do not have unlimited funds to correct pricing errors nor do they have total freedom to pursue any and all opportunities. Most arbitrage investors manage money for other investors in the form of hedge funds. The management contracts under which the fund managers operate typically constrain their actions to some degree. Without a completely free hand and unlimited funds, some mispricings will remain unarbitraged.

As a result of these limits, the EMH assumption that all arbitrage opportunities will be eradicated appears to be an oversimplification.

Empirical Challenges to EMH

The EMH is not only riddled with logical inconsistencies, its predictions are contradicted by a growing body of empirical evidence. This section summarizes these findings.

Excessive Price Volatility. If security prices were as tightly connected to fundamental values as EMH asserts, then the magnitude of price changes should be similar to the magnitude of changes in the underlying fundamentals. However, studies show prices are far more volatile than fundamentals. For example, when fundamental value is defined as the net present value of future dividends,[37] changes in fundamental value are unable to explain the high volatility of prices. The technology stock bubble that ruptured in the spring of 2000 and the bubble in Japanese stock prices in the late 1980s are examples of price movements that cannot be explained by changes in fundamental value.

EMH also predicts that large price changes should occur only when significant new information enters the market. The evidence does not agree. For example, the stock market crash of October 1987 was not accompanied by news that would have justified a price drop that exceeded 20 percent. A 1991 study by Cutler cited by Shleifer[38] examined the 50 largest one-day price movements since the end of World War II. Many of these price events were not associated with significant news announcements. In a similar study, Roll[39] showed that fluctuations in the price of frozen orange juice futures often occurred without any developments in the weather, the major fundamental influence on that market. Roll also showed that individual stock movements are often not associated with corporate news events.

Evidence of Price Predictability with Stale Information. The evidence most damning to EMH are studies showing that price movements can be predicted to a meaningful degree with publicly known (stale) information. In other words, strategies based on stale information can generate risk-adjusted returns that beat the market. If it were true that prices quickly incorporate all known information, as EMH asserts, this should not be possible.

How Cross-Sectional Predictability Studies Are Performed. The April 2001 issue of *Journal of Finance* notes that many predictability studies show that publicly available information is not fully reflected in stock prices and that numerous strategies based on this information are profitable.[40] These studies measure the degree to which indicators based on public information are able to forecast the relative performance of stocks.[41] Indicators tested included a stock's price-to-earnings ratio, its price-to-book-value ratio, its recent relative price performance, and so forth.

Predictability studies employ a cross-sectional design. That is to say, they examine a large cross section of stocks at a given point in time, for example, all stocks in the S&P 500 Index as of December 31, 1999. For that date, the stocks are ranked on the basis of an indicator[42] that is being examined for its predictive power, such as a stock's rate of return over the past six months (price momentum). With this done, the stocks are arranged into a number of portfolios on the basis of rank, with each portfolio containing an equal number of stocks. Ten portfolios is a common number. Thus portfolio 1 would contain the top 10 percent of all stocks ranked by their prior six-month rate of return. That is to say, the portfolio is composed of those stocks whose prior six-month rate of return was in greater than the ninetieth percentile. A second portfolio is formed containing stocks ranked from the eightieth percentile to the eighty-ninth percentile, and so on until a final portfolio is formed from the 10 percent of stocks with the worst prior six-month performance.

To determine if six-month momentum has predictive power, the future performance of the top decile portfolio (1) is compared to the future performance of the bottom decile portfolio (10). The forward prediction horizon is typically one time period. Therefore, using monthly data, it would be one month.[43] Typically these studies quantify the indicator's predictive power as the return earned by a long portfolio versus a short portfolio. In other words, a long position is assumed to be taken in all portfolio 1 stocks and a short position in all portfolio 10 stocks. For example, if in a given time period, the long portfolio earned 7 percent while the short portfolio lost 4 percent (e.g., the stocks sold short went up 4 percent), the long-versus-short strategy would have earned 3 percent. Although in this example the indicator used to rank stocks was the six-month price momentum, any item of information that was known at the time the portfolios are constructed could be used. I illustrate this concept in Figure 7.6, where the indicator used is each stock's P/E ratio.

I just described how a cross-sectional study is carried out for a single month (December 1999). However, cross-sectional studies are carried out over many months (cross-sectional time series). Thus, the predictive power of an indicator is measured as the average return on portfolio 1 minus the average return on portfolio 10 over an extended period of time. Such studies often examine a number of candidate predictor variables. This idea is illustrated in Figure 7.7.

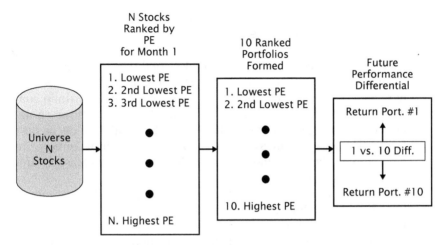

FIGURE 7.6 Cross-sectional study to determine the predictive power of P/E ratio.

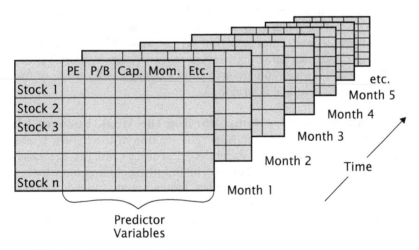

FIGURE 7.7 Cross-sectional time series study.

Predictability Studies Contradicting Semistrong EMH. The semistrong form of EMH is the boldest testable version of EMH.[44] It asserts that no information in the public domain, fundamental or technical, can be used to generate risk-adjusted returns in excess of the market index. The bottom line of numerous well-conducted cross-sectional time series studies is this: Price movements are predictable to some degree with stale public information, and excess risk-adjusted returns are possible. Here, I summarize some of these key findings:

- **Small capitalization effect:** A stock's total market capitalization, defined as the number of shares outstanding multiplied by its price per share, is predictive of future returns.[45] Stocks in a portfolio composed of the lowest decile portfolio of market capitalization earned about 9 percent per year more than stocks in the highest decile portfolio.[46] This effect is most pronounced in the month of January. Recent studies show this indicator's predictive power has disappeared since the mid to late 1980s.
- **Price-to-earnings ratio effect:** Stocks with low P/E ratios outperform stocks with high P/E ratios.[47]
- **Price-to-book-value effect:** Stocks with low price to book value ratios outperform stocks with high price to book value ratios.[48] The cheapest stocks, in terms of price to book, outperformed the most expensive stocks by almost 20 percent per year.
- **Earnings surprise with technical confirmation:** Stocks reporting unexpected earnings or giving earnings guidance that is confirmed by strong price and volume action on the day after the news is announced earn an annualized return spread (longs – shorts) over the next month of over 30 percent.[49] This strategy is a marriage of fundamental and technical information.

Predictability Studies Contradicting the Weak Form of EMH. The weak form of EMH is the least bold version of the theory. It claims that only a subset of public information, past prices, and price returns[50] is unhelpful in earning excess returns. The following studies show that stale prices and other data used in technical indicators are indeed useful. This is very good news for TA and very bad news for EMH. The narrowest, most timid, and most difficult to falsify version of EMH has been contradicted with evidence.

- **Momentum persistence:** Jegadeesh and Titman (1993)[51] showed that price momentum measured over the past six to twelve months persists. In other words, the stocks that have been strongest over the past 6 months, 7 months, 8 months, and so on, up to 12 months, tend to outperform over the following 6 to 12 months. Their study simulated a strategy of holding long positions in stocks with the highest returns over the prior 6 months (top decile) and holding short positions in stocks with the worst performance (lowest decile). The portfolio of long and short positions was then held for 6 months. This strategy earned an annualized return of 10 percent. In light of this evidence, even one of the high priests of EMH, Eugene Fama, had to admit that past stock returns can predict future stock returns.[52] Score a big one for TA!

- **Momentum reversal:** Although stocks with strong trends over the past 6 to 12 months tend to maintain those trends over the following 6 to 12 months, something different is observed when momentum is measured over longer time spans. Strong trends measured over the prior three to five years display a tendency to reverse. De Bondt and Thaler tested a strategy of buying stocks with the most negative five-year trends (losers) and selling short stocks with the most positive five-year trends (winners). The long-versus-short portfolio averaged an 8 percent annualized return over the next three years,[53] and most importantly, this return difference was not attributable to risk. The prior losers (future winners) were not more risky than the prior winners (future losers).[54] This contradicts a central proposition of EMH that higher returns can only be earned by assuming higher risks. Additionally, it bolsters the notion that a very simplistic form of TA is useful.

- **Nonreversing momentum:** When a stock's momentum is measured by its proximity to its 52-week high, rather than its prior rate of return, profits are greater and momentum does not reverse.[55] The author of this study speculates that investors become mentally anchored to prior 52-week price highs. Anchoring is known to prevent people from making appropriate adjustments to new information. The author of this study, Michael Cooper, conjectured that this prevents stocks near their 52-week highs from responding to new fundamental developments as rapidly as they should. Retarded news response engenders systemic price trends (momentum) that correct the mispricing.

- **Momentum confirmed by trading volume:** Further support for the validity of TA comes from studies showing that, when trading volume is used conjointly with price momentum, even higher returns can be earned. That is to say, a synergism can be attained by combining price and volume indicators. The return of the combination is 2 to 7 percent higher than the return can be earned using price momentum alone.[56] Stocks with high volume and positive price momentum do better going forward than stocks with positive price momentum alone. Moreover, stocks with high volume and negative price momentum do worse going forward than stocks that merely have negative price momentum. Said differently, the discrimination power of price momentum is greater for high-volume stocks.

EMH Digs for a Defense

When an established theory is contradicted with empirical evidence, its supporters do not simply roll over and say never mind. The cognitive mechanisms of belief persistence (see Chapter 2) don't work that way for trained scientists any more than they do for common folk. Cynical observers of science say adherents to a theory that has been falsified never really change their minds. They have far too much invested in its survival to do that. With time, they just fade away.

With EMH having served, and served well, for 40+ years, as the foundation of finance, its backers were just not about to go away with heads hanging low. Two of its standard bearers (read pall bearers), Eugene Fama and Kenneth French, said gains earned by stale-information strategies such as price-to-book value and market capitalization were nothing more than fair compensation for risk. Recall that EMH does not deny the possibility that stale public information can earn profits. It merely says that when those gains are adjusted for risk, they will not be better than investing in an index fund.

So long as the term *risk* is left undefined, EMH defenders are free to conjure up new forms of risk after the fact. As Elliott wavers have proven, after-the-fact fiddling allows any prior observations to be explained or explained away. And that, it seems to me, is what Fama and French did.[57] They invented a new, ad hoc risk model using three risk factors to replace the old standby, the capital asset pricing model,[58] which uses only one risk factor, a stock's volatility relative to the market index. Quite conveniently, the two new risk factors that Fama and French decided to add were the price-to-book ratio and market capitalization. By citing these as proxies for risk, Fama and French neatly explained away their predictive power. "According to the new risk model, stocks of smaller firms (low-market cap) or firms with low market-to-book ratios are fundamentally riskier companies and thus must offer higher average returns to compensate the investors willing to own them. Conversely, large capitalization stocks because they are safer, and high price-to-book ratio stocks, which are in effect growth stocks with more certain future prospects, earn lower average returns because they expose their owners to lower risk."[59]

This was nothing more than an ad hoc after-the-fact explanation conjured up to save a dying theory. Had Fama and French predicted that price-to-book and market capitalization were valid risk factors before these variables were discovered to earn excess returns, that would have been a much different story. It would have shown that EMH was a powerful theory whose deductive consequences were confirmed by subsequent observations. However, Fama and French did not do this. They invented the new risk factors after price-to-book and market cap had been shown to produce excess returns.

As pointed out earlier, Fama and French justified their new risk model by suggesting that low market-cap and low price relative to book are signals of corporations at higher risk of failure. If this were true, it would imply (predict) that value strategies (buying low price-to-book stocks) and small cap strategies would earn subpar returns in bad economic times, when distressed companies are most likely to suffer.

Empirical evidence contradicts this prediction. A 1994 study found no evidence that value strategies do worse when the economy suffers.[60] Also, the disappearance of the excess return to small-cap stocks in the last 15 years presents a problem. If cap size were indeed a legitimate risk factor, the returns to strategies based on it should continue to earn a risk premium. Finally, neither the Fama-French risk model, nor any other EMH model, is able to explain the predictive power of price momentum indicators or the conjoint effect of price momentum and trading volume.

BEHAVIORAL FINANCE: A THEORY OF NONRANDOM PRICE MOTION

New theory is needed when existing theory confronts dissonant evidence. EMH has now been bombarded with a lot of evidence that contradicts its predictions. It is time for a new theory.

The relatively new field of behavioral finance has come forward with several variations of a new theory of financial market behavior that explains phenomena that EMH cannot. These theories are scientifically meaningful in that they do not simply explain (fit) what has occurred, but they make testable predictions that have been confirmed by subsequent observational studies.

Behavioral finance incorporates elements of cognitive psychology, economics, and sociology to explain why investors depart from full rationality and therefore why markets depart from full efficiency. By considering the impact of emotions, cognitive errors, irrational preferences, and the dynamics of group behavior, behavioral finance offers succinct explanations of excess market volatility as well as the excess returns earned by stale information strategies.

Behavioral finance does not assume that all investors are irrational. Rather, it views the market as a mixture of decision makers who vary in their degree of rationality. When irrational investors (noise traders) trade with rational investors (arbitrageurs), markets can depart from efficient pricing. In fact, market efficiency is a rather special condition that is less probable than other more plausible market conditions, where prices are likely to diverge from rational levels and thus likely to experience systematic predictable movements toward those levels.[61] This explains why systematic strategies based on stale information can profit.

This is all quite ironic with respect to TA. As discussed in Chapter 2, cognitive errors can explain how people form erroneous beliefs in the validity of subjective TA in the absences of sound supportive evidence or even in the face of contradictory evidence. At the same time, however, cognitive errors may also explain the existence of market inefficiencies that spawn the systematic price movements that allow objective TA methods to work. That which explains the foolishness of subjective TA practitioners also explains the reasonableness of some objective TA methods.

Foundations of Behavioral Finance

Behavioral finance rests on two foundational pillars: The limited ability of arbitrage to correct pricing errors, and the limits of human rationality.[62] When both notions are combined, behavioral finance is able to predict specific departures from market efficiency that produce systematic price movements. For example, under certain circumstances, trends are predicted to persist, whereas, under other circumstances, trends are predicted to reverse. We will consider each of these pillars.

Limits of Arbitrage. To recap briefly, arbitrage is not the perfect enforcer of efficient pricing that EMH assumes. The lack of perfect security substitutes turns arbitrage from a risk-free, no-investment-required transaction into one that requires capital and incurs risk. Even where there are very good substitute securities, there is a risk that prices will diverge further from rational values before returning to them. Moreover, the investors who supply trading capital to arbitrageurs don't have unlimited patience, or unlimited capital. Consequently, they do not grant unlimited latitude to arbitrageurs in terms of the types of opportunities that can be considered for exploitation.

These constraints explain why security prices do not always react properly to new information. Sometimes, prices underreact, and sometimes, they overreact. Add to this the impact of noise traders, who act on uninformative signals,[63] and it becomes clear how security prices can systematically depart from rational levels for extended periods of time.

Limits of Human Rationality. The constraints on arbitrage predict that inefficiencies will occur, but they alone do not predict under what conditions the inefficiencies will manifest. For example, arbitrage constraints do not tell us under which circumstances markets are more likely to underreact to new information than overreact. That is where the second pillar of behavioral finance, the limits of human rationality, comes in.

As we learned in Chapter 2, cognitive psychology has revealed that, under conditions of uncertainty, human judgment tends to err in predictable (systematic) ways. By taking into account the systematic errors of human judgment, behavioral finance can predict the type of departure from market efficiencies that are most likely to occur in a given set of circumstances.

Of the two pillars of behavioral finance, more is understood about the limits of arbitrage than about investor irrationality. This is because arbitrageurs are expected to be rational, and economic theory has a firmer grasp on the behavior of rational actors than irrational ones. For example, it is not yet clear which specific cognitive biases and systematic judgment errors are most important in finance, but a picture is gradually emerging. This section describes the current state of behavioral finance's understanding of irrational investor behavior and the systematic price movements that arise as a result of them.

In contrast to traditional finance theory, behavioral finance asserts investors make biased judgments and choices. In effect, market prices systematically deviate from rational values because investors systematically deviate from full rationality. However, these mistakes are not a sign of ignorance, but rather a consequence of the generally effective ways human intelligence has developed to cope with complexity and uncertainty.

Behavioral finance and EMH are similar in that they both contend that the market eventually does get it right—that is, prices ultimately converge toward rational valuations. They merely differ about the character of these departures and their duration. EMH says prices depart from rational levels randomly and briefly. Behavioral finance says some departures are systematic and last long enough to be exploited by certain investment strategies.

Psychological Factors

In Chapter 2 we saw the way cognitive errors impact subjective technicians and result in erroneous beliefs. In the context of behavioral finance, we will consider how cognitive errors impact investors and result in systematic price movements. The cognitive errors discussed in the sections that follow are not completely distinct, nor do they operate independently. However, they are presented separately for the purpose of clarity.

Conservatism Bias, Confirmation Bias, and Belief Inertia.

The conservatism bias[64] is the tendency to give too little weight to new information. Consequently, people fail to modify their prior beliefs as much as the new information would warrant. Prior beliefs tend to be conserved. Because of this, investors tend to underreact to new information that is relevant to security values and so security prices fail to respond adequately. Over time, however, prices do systematically catch up with value. This gradual, purposeful adjustment appears on a chart as a price trend. This is illustrated in Figure 7.5.

This conservatism bias is encouraged by the confirmation bias, which causes people to accept evidence that is consistent with a prior belief and reject or give too little credence to evidence that contradicts it. Thus, when investors hold an existing view about a security and new information arrives that confirms that belief, they will tend to give it more weight than it deserves and overreact to it. Conversely, when new information arrives that contradicts the prior belief, they tend to treat it skeptically and underreact.

The confirmation bias also causes investors' beliefs, whatever they may be, to become more extreme over time. The reason is as follows: Over time, news items arrive as a random mixture of confirmatory and contradictory information. However, the confirmation bias causes them to be treated differently. Confirmatory information is given credence, thus strengthening the prior belief, while contradictory information will tend not to be believed and thus have a negligible impact on the investors' prior belief. Consequently, over time it is likely that prior beliefs strengthen.

However, prior beliefs can be subject to a radical and irrational weakening if several bits of contradictory information arrive in a streak. Even though streaks are common in a random sequence, investors may commit the crime of small numbers and attribute too much significance when several pieces of information that contradict the prior beliefs arrive sequentially. In other words, the random streak may be erroneously interpreted as an authentic trend. These ideas are illustrated in Figure 7.8.

Too Much Anchoring and Too Little Adjustment. In Chapter 2 we saw that, in uncertain situations, people rely on heuristics to simplify and speed complex cognitive tasks like estimating probabilities. One heuristic, not discussed thus far, is called anchoring. It is relied upon to estimate quantities. The rule is applied as follows: An initial estimate of the quantity is made, based on preliminary information called the anchor. Then upward or downward adjustments are made to the initial estimate based on additional information. The anchoring rule seems to make sense.

However, in practice, people commonly make two mistakes when applying this heuristic. First, initial estimates can be strongly influenced by a

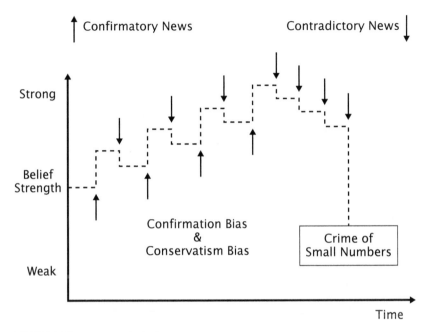

FIGURE 7.8 Revising beliefs.

completely irrelevant anchor. This occurs even when the anchor's irrelevance is completely obvious. Second, even in cases where the initial estimate is based on relevant anchoring information, there is a tendency for subsequent adjustments up or down to be too small (the conservatism bias). In other words, the additional information is given too little weight relative to the initial estimate.

The tendency to seize on an irrelevant anchor was demonstrated in a study in which people were asked to estimate the length of the Mississippi River (actual length = 2,348 miles). Subjects were first asked if the length was greater than or less than some arbitrary length. This number assumed the role of anchor in the subject's minds. When the question posed was: Is the length greater or less than 800 miles? Most people correctly said the Mississippi was longer than 800 miles. Subjects were then asked to give an estimate of its actual length. Other subjects were given the number 5,000 miles in the greater than or less than part of the question. Again, most people correctly said the river's length was less than 5,000 miles, but their estimates of the river's actual length were, on average, greater than the estimates given by subjects who were asked to make a comparison with 800 miles. This revealed that the subjects seized on the number of miles given in the question as an anchor, and then made inadequate adjustments from there. If the figure 800 or 5,000 were not truly influencing the estimate, the estimates of length would have been about the same, irrespective of whether the question involved a comparison with 800 miles or 5,000 miles.[65] The anchor had a strong influence.

Another experiment showed that people will anchor on a number even when it is obviously irrelevant.[66] Subjects were asked about facts that are typically not part of common knowledge—for example, "What is the percentage of African nations in the United Nations?" The answers to each question involved a percentage (0 to 100). Before each question, a wheel of fortune with 100 numbered slots was spun in front of the subjects. The study showed that the subjects' answers were strongly affected by the wheel's obviously random result. For example, if the wheel landed on the number 10, the median estimate was 25 percent, but when the wheel stopped on 65 the median estimate was 45 percent.

The anchoring heuristic is thought to be related to investor underreaction. Underreactions to bullish news cause asset prices to remain too cheap, whereas underreactions to bearish news leave prices too dear. Over time, the market's temporary state of inefficiency is resolved as prices drift (trend) to the rational level. Thus, anchoring can help explain the occurrence of price trends.

Anchoring may explain the profitability of a momentum strategy alluded to earlier.[67] It is based on a simple technical indicator, a stock's proximity to its 52-week high. Because this information is available in newspapers and on various web sites, investors may fixate (anchor) on it. In other words, investors may fixate or anchor on the 52-week high price if a stock is currently trading near that level. In effect, the stock gets stuck near its 52-week high. Thus the price fails to respond properly to new bullish information, and it becomes temporarily underpriced. Ultimately the pricing error is corrected as the stock responds with a systematic movement higher.

Anchoring to Stories. Investors not only become anchored to numbers; they can get stuck on intuitively compelling[68] stories, too. The effect is the same; prices do not respond efficiently to new information and thus depart from rational valuations.

Stories are compelling because "much of human thinking that results in action is not quantitative, but instead takes the form of storytelling and justification."[69] As pointed out in Chapter 2, investors rely more on causal narratives than on weighing and combining evidence to estimate probabilities and make decisions. People seem to need simple rationales to justify their actions.[70] The most compelling rationales are plausible, easily understood, easily retold, cause and effect chains filled with concrete and colorful details. These are the tales that captivate investors and incite buying and selling. These are the stories that get stuck in investors' minds.

Optimism and Overconfidence. To recap, people are generally too confident about the quality and precision of their knowledge. Thus, investors tend to be overconfident about their private interpretations of public information and overly optimistic about the profits they will achieve. The combined effect of overconfidence and overoptimism leads investors to overreact to their private information, and in turn pushes security prices too far. Overextended price movements lead to price reversals and systematic movements back toward rational levels.

The Crime of Small Numbers (Sample Size Neglect). The crime of small numbers is the failure to consider the number of observations comprising a sample being used to form a conclusion. Thus, it is fallacious to judge whether a datum was produced by a random or nonrandom process or to estimate a population parameter on the basis of a small sample. For example, if a sequence of 10 coin flips produces 7 heads, it would be invalid to conclude the coin has a 0.7 probability of producing heads. The true head rate for a coin can be reliably inferred from only a large number of flips.

Investors who neglect sample size are easily deceived when trying to decide if a time series is random or not. For example, by generalizing too hastily from too little evidence, investors may incorrectly conclude that a few quarters of positive earnings growth indicate that the company has established a valid growth trend. We have already seen that a small cluster of positive quarters can easily occur in a random-earnings stream. Thus, the crime of small numbers helps explain why investors may overreact to a short sequence of good earnings reports.

The crime of small numbers can cause two different judgment errors: the gambler's fallacy and the clustering illusion. Which of these two errors results depends on the observer's prior belief about the process being watched. Suppose an investor is watching a sequence of price changes that are truly independent of each other (a random walk).

If the investor holds a prior belief that the process is random, the error will most likely be the gambler's fallacy. Recall that on the basis of common sense we expect random processes to display more flip-flops and fewer streaks (trends) than actually do occur. As a result, a streak of positive price changes will lead naive observers to falsely conclude that a trend reversal (a negative price change) is due. Thus, after five heads, the observer erroneously concludes a tail is more likely than 50/50, its true likelihood. In reality, a random-walk sequence has no memory. Thus, the occurrence of a positive streak does not alter the probability of the next outcome in any way. The false expectation of a reversal is called the "gambler's fallacy" because the statistically naive tend to make this mistake when watching a roulette wheel; a sequence of black outcomes is thought to increase the chance of a red. Wrong!

The other fallacy stemming from sample-size neglect is the clustering illusion. It occurs when an observer has no prior belief about whether the process generating the data is random or nonrandom The clustering illusion is the misperception of order (nonrandomness) in data that is actually a random walk. Again, imagine someone observing the outcomes of a process that is truly a random walk trying to determine if the process is random or nonrandom (orderly, systematic).[71] Recall that small samples of random walks often appear more trended (clustered) than common sense would lead us to expect (the hot hand in basketball). As a result of the clustering illusion, a sequence of positive price or earnings changes is wrongly interpreted as a legitimate trend, when it is nothing more than an ordinary streak in a random walk.

Social Factors: Imitative Behavior, Herding, and Information Cascades[72]

We have just seen how investor behavior viewed at the level of the individual investor can explain several types of systematic price movement. This section examines investor behavior at the group level to explain systematic price movements. In contrast to conventional TA theories of investor psychology, we will see that some group behaviors are quite rational.

When faced with uncertain choices, people often to look to the behavior of others for cues and imitate their actions. This is what is meant by herd behavior. I should clarify that herd behavior is not defined by similarity of action. Similar actions by many individuals can also occur when individuals have made similar choices but those choices have been arrived at independently. Herd behavior refers specifically to similarity of action arising from imitation. As I will point out, the choice to imitate can be entirely rational.

There is a major difference between similar behaviors arising from herding and similar behaviors arising from many individual decision makers making the same choice independently. Herd behavior stops the diffusion of information throughout a group, but independent decision making does not. When information diffusion is impeded, it becomes more likely that investors will make the same mistakes and prices will systematically diverge from rational levels.

To see why herd behavior impedes the spread of information, consider the opposite case, where individuals evaluate information independently and make autonomous choices. Suppose a large number of investors are independently evaluating a stock. Some may mistakenly value it too high, while others mistakenly value it too low. Because the mistakes are made independently, they will tend to be offsetting, making the average valuation error close to zero. Here, each investor has made an individual appraisal and in effect acted on a unique signal. This makes it far more likely that all the available information about the stock will have been considered and built into the price of the stock. Even if no single investor was in full possession of all the facts, the group, taken as a whole, is likely to be nearly fully informed.

In contrast, when investors elect to imitate the behavior of others rather than deciding independently, all the relevant information about the stock is less likely to be fully diffused throughout the entire group, making it more likely that the stock's price will not reflect all relevant information. However, an individual investor electing to imitate may be making a perfectly rational choice. Not everyone has the time or expertise to evaluate a stock, so it can make sense to copy an investor with a good track record, such as Warren Buffett. Once Buffett does his analysis and makes his buy or sell decision known, investors may cease their own efforts to gather information and evaluate the stock. This makes it more likely that, if some factor has escaped Buffett's notice, it will remain unnoticed by the community of investors. So here is a case where individuals take actions that are fully rational on an individual basis but harmful to them as a group.

Why Do We Imitate?   At one time it was thought that imitative behavior was a consequence of social pressure to conform. Early experimental evidence seemed to confirm this.[73] In one study, an authentic subject was asked to estimate the length of line segments in the presence of fake subjects who also gave estimates. The fakes, who were actually part of the experiment, intentionally gave wrong answers. Even though the correct answer was obvious, the authentic subjects often went along with the group rather than give the obviously correct answer. However, a later experiment,[74] in which the authentic subject was isolated from the group of confederates, showed the subject still imitated the group's obviously wrong answer. This finding implied that social pressure does not explain imitative behavior. A better explanation emerged. The subjects seemed to be relying on a social heuristic: When one's own judgment is contradicted by the majority, follow the majority. In other words, people operate with an implicit rule: The majority is unlikely to be wrong.

"This behavior is a matter of rational calculation: in everyday living we have learned that when a large group of people is unanimous in its judgment on a question of simple fact, the members of the group are almost certainly right."[75] Similarly, most of us operate with the principle that, when an expert tells us something that contradicts our common sense, we tend to heed the expert. So it is entirely rational under conditions of uncertainty to look to the advice of experts or the actions of the majority.

Information Cascades and Herd Behavior. The uncertainties of investing make it likely that investors would rely on an imitation heuristic rather than independent decision making. This has important implications for the emergence of systematic price behavior because imitation gives rise to "information cascades."[76] An information cascade is a chain of imitative behavior that was initiated by the action of one or just a few individuals. In some instances that initiating action may have been a random choice.

The emergence of an information cascade can be illustrated with a hypothetical example. Suppose two new restaurants open for business on the same day, right next door to each other. The first hungry customer to arrive must choose one, and has little information on which to base a decision. That customer's choice is, therefore, a random decision. However, when the second customer arrives, there is an additional piece of information: one of the restaurants has a patron. This may trigger the second customer to go into the same place. Because the first customer's selection was a guess, we know that the second customer's choice was based on an uninformative signal. When the third customer arrives and sees one restaurant empty and the other with two customers, the chance is increased that the third customer will also make an imitative choice. In the end, a cascade of dependent choices, triggered by the first customer's random choice, may ultimately cause one establishment to thrive and the other to fail, and it is entirely possible that the failing establishment offered better food.

Thus, an initial random event sets the course of history down one particular path (restaurant 1 succeeds) rather than another path (restaurant 2 succeeds). As time goes on, the likelihood that one restaurant will thrive increases while the likelihood that the second establishment will fail increases. In the same way, an initial random price movement can trigger successive rounds of imitative investor behavior, resulting in a long-duration large amplitude price swing.

Now consider what would have happened if many customers had made independent restaurant choices, allowing both establishments to be sampled by many customers. By combining their findings, they would have discovered which was the better of the two restaurants. However, in an information cascade, imitative behavior prevents the accumulation and sharing of many independent appraisals. Thus, information cascades block the diffusion of information and rational choice.

The information cascade model reveals the flaw in the common sense notion that financial market prices are determined by a process like voting, in which many individuals make their own assessment.[77] In an information cascade, investors make the rational choice of copying the actions of others, rather than expending the considerable effort required to arrive at an independent choice. Voters do one thing, and investors sometimes do something entirely different.

The Diffusion of Information Among Investors. We have seen that information cascades can explain why the rational behavior of individual investors can impede the diffusion of information. This is important for TA because the rate at which information spreads among investors can explain the occurrence of systematic price movements. EMH assumes almost instantaneous information diffusion and, consequently, almost instantaneous price adjustments. Such price adjustments are too quick to be exploited by TA methods. However, information that diffuses slowly allows for gradual, systematic price movements that can be exploited by TA methods.

Despite the prevalence of advanced communications technology, the preferred method of exchanging investment information is still a good story told person to person. This predilection, a result of several million years of evolution, has been confirmed by the studies of behavioral-economist Robert Shiller. He has shown that the word-of-mouth effect is strong even among people who read a lot. A story about a hot new issue has greater impact in conversation than a statistic about the high failure rate of new companies.

The way stories spread among investors has been studied with mathematical models similar to those used by epidemiologists to study the spread of disease within a population. Unfortunately, these models have not been as accurate in the investor domain as they have been in the realm of biology. This is explained by the fact that the mutation rate of circulating ideas is far higher than the mutation rate of organisms. However, the models have been enlightening in another way; they explain how stories spread so rapidly.

One reason a "new" story can spread so rapidly is that it is not really new. Investors' minds are already infested with many familiar story scripts, and it does not matter that the panoply of stories residing in investors' minds contradict each other. For example, investors can be comfortable with the notion that the stock market cannot be predicted and at the same time hold the opposing notion that it can. No doubt, most investors have been exposed to experts who have espoused both points of view. Our minds are able to accommodate a wide variety of contradictory ideas because the scripts lie there inert with no demand that we choose one side or the other.

Nevertheless, this state of affairs can change rapidly. Even a slight random perturbation in the news or the market's behavior can cause an idea that had been hibernating in investors' minds to spring to life and consume their attention.

Shifts in Investor Attention.   Where investors are focusing their attention at any given moment can shift dramatically due to minor changes in the news. "The human brain is structured to have essentially a single focus of attention at a time and to move rapidly from one focus to another."[78] The brain had to evolve a capacity to selectively attend to only a tiny trickle of the torrent of information that pours in from the world. This filtering process is both a mark of human intelligence and a source of judgment error. Numerous instances of expert error are attributable to missing important details. However, before outcomes are known, we never know which details deserve our attention.

Among the automatic unconscious rules used by the brain to filter relevant from irrelevant information is the rule to look to other people for cues. In other words, we presume that what grabs the attention of others must be worthy of our attention as well. According to economist Robert Shiller, "the phenomenon of social attention is one of the great creations of behavioral evolution and is critical for the functioning of human society."[79] Although communal attention has great social value, because it promotes collaborative action, it has a downside. It can lead an entire group to hold an incorrect view and take similar mistaken actions.

In the opposite situation, where individuals form their own views independently, errors of attention would be random and self-canceling. Although this mode of thought makes it harder to organize joint efforts around common views and goals, it is less likely to overlook important details. Dramatic market movements can easily grab the attention of the community of investors and encourage them to act in ways that amplify the movement, even if there is no fundamental reason for it.

Robert Shiller has studied the way dramatic price movements capture investor attention and trigger herd behavior. Even institutional investors, who would be expected to select stocks in systematic ways based on statistically valid characteristics, are prone to buying a stock simply because it has experienced a rapid price increase.[80] This mechanism can explain how a market boom can be triggered just by a vivid initial price movement that calls attention to the stock market. Moreover, Shiller's studies show that investors are often not even aware that it was a dramatic price movement that motivated them to act.

The Role of Feedback in Systematic Price Movements.   Social interaction among investors creates feedback. Feedback refers to the channeling of a system's output back into the system as input. See

Figure 7.9, where two systems are compared—one with no feedback and one with feedback.

There are two types of feedback, positive and negative. One way to think of the difference is as follows. In the case of negative feedback, the system output is multiplied by a negative number and the result is feedback in. In the case of positive feedback the multiplier is a positive number. This is illustrated in Figure 7.10.

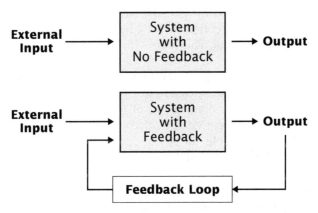

FIGURE 7.9 Feedback: output becomes input.

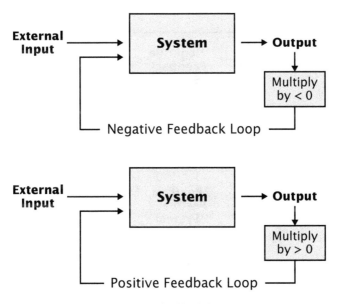

FIGURE 7.10 Positive and negative feedback loops.

Negative feedback has the effect of dampening system behavior, driving the output back toward a level of equilibrium. Positive feedback has the opposite effect, amplifying a system's behavior, thus driving its output further from equilibrium. This is illustrated in Figure 7.11.

An example of a negative feedback system is a household heating & air conditioning system. When the temperature falls below a desired or equilibrium level, the thermostat turns on the furnace, returning the system's output, the household temperature, back to the desired level. Temperature above the desired level turns on the A/C, bringing the temperature back down. This is all accomplished by feeding the system's output back into the system as an input. This allows the system to self-regulate its way toward equilibrium.

Positive feedback is illustrated by the growing screech in a public-address system when the speakers are placed too close to the microphone. The normal hum coming out of the speakers (output) gets fed back into the audio system via the microphone, where it is amplified by the system. With each cycle, the sound comes out louder, developing into a loud screech. Positive feedback is also known as the snowball effect or vicious cycle.

Financial markets, like other self-organizing self-regulated systems, rely on a healthy balance between negative and positive feedback.[81] Arbitrage provides negative feedback. Prices that are too high or too low

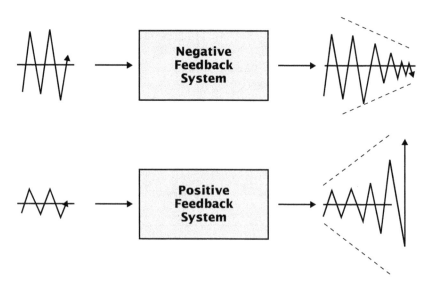

FIGURE 7.11 Positive and negative feedback loops: dampening versus amplifying.

trigger arbitrage trading that pushes prices back toward rational levels. Positive feedback occurs when investor decisions are dominated by imitative behavior rather than independent choice. In this regime, investors will hop aboard an initial price movement, buying after first signs of strength or selling after first signs of weakness, thus amplifying an initial small price movement into a large-scale trend. A TA approach, known as trend following, depends on large-scale price moves for its profitability and thus is most effective during times when positive feedback dominates.

Positive feedback can cause a vicious cycle of price increases or decreases, which take prices far beyond rational levels even if the initial price move that triggered the whole affair was justified. In other words, price trends can go far above or below rational levels simply due to the amplifying effect of positive feedback.

Positive feedback can also result from they way people adapt their expectations to recent changes. Although it generally makes sense to alter expectations when conditions change, people do it imperfectly. At times, they adjust insufficiently (the conservatism bias), whereas at other times they are overly sensitive to change and alter their expectations more than is justified. Investors are especially likely to overreact to new information that is prominent. Either a single large price change or a sequence of similar changes can induce investors to alter their expectations too much. These price changes can feed on themselves, thus generating price momentum that may lead to a bubble or crash.

A judgment error that sometimes contributes to positive feedback is mental accounting. This is the irrational tendency to think about money as if it belonged in separate accounts, which should be treated differently. Gains from prior speculative ventures may be assigned to the hot-action account, whereas money accumulating in the home-equity account is treated with greater conservatism. Rationally, all of an investor's money, regardless of how it was made or in which asset it is invested, should be treated in the same way. A dollar is a dollar. However, speculative gains from a recent market rise are often, irrationally, earmarked for further speculation, thus adding fuel to a rising market.

At some point, the increasing expectations that fuel a bubble run out. Common sense would suggest, and some analysts insist, that a price bubble necessarily ends in market crashes (i.e., a negative bubble). At times they do, but other bubble termination patterns are possible. Computer simulations of systems that incorporate feedback loops show that bubbles not only develop in a jagged fashion with many intervening pauses, but they can also deflate in a similar manner. If the late 1990s was a price bubble, it seems to be ending with many intervening pauses.

Self-Organizing Ponzi Schemes

The feedback theory of price bubbles is appealing because of its plausibility and the numerous historical examples that seem to confirm its validity. However, it is hard to prove that a simple feedback mechanism involving heightened investor focus, imitative behavior, and exaggerated investor confidence is truly operational in financial markets.

Nevertheless, Yale economist Robert Shiller believes actual cases of pyramid frauds known as Ponzi schemes offer evidence that confirms the feedback theory. The scheme, named after the infamous Charles Ponzi, who invented the idea in the 1920s, involves promising investors a high rate of return from some sort of business venture or investment. However, the investors' money is never put to work in the way promised. Instead, the commitments of new investors are used to pay off earlier investors. This serves two purposes: it makes the venture look legitimate and it encourages the first investors to spread the story of their success. As the tale gains popularity, new investors are motivated to make investments. Their funds are, in turn, used to pay off a prior round of investors, who now go out and tell their story. This cycle of using Peter's investment to pay off Paul to prove the success of the enterprise continues and grows. The number of people influenced by the scam follows a curve similar to the diffusion of an infection throughout a population. Ultimately, a saturation level is reached. The supply of noninfected speculators gets exhausted, and so there are no new investments with which to pay off the last round of investors. At this point, the scheme crashes.

Recently a housewife from a small town in Alaska collected an estimated \$10 to \$15 million over a six-year period by promising a 50 percent return. Her business was purportedly based on unused frequent flyer miles accumulated by large companies. In fact, this was very similar to Ponzi's original scheme, which was based on international postage coupons.

Ponzi scams evolve in a typical pattern. Initially, investors are skeptical and invest only small amounts, but once early investors reap profits and tell their success story, later-stage investors gain confidence and the flow of capital into the scheme gains momentum. Frequently there are rational skeptics issuing warnings, but the greedy pay no heed. Well-founded cynical arguments cannot compete with vivid accounts of fat profits. The moths dive into the flame.

Shiller contends that speculative bubbles are naturally occurring Ponzi schemes that emerge spontaneously in financial markets, without requiring the machinations of a fraudulent promoter.[82] Such self-organizing phenomena are common in complex systems. There is no need for false stories because there is always some buzz about the stock market anyway. A trend of rising prices acts as a call to action much like the gains of early investors in a Ponzi scheme. The message is then amplified by Wall Street's salesmen, and they need not tell lies. They simply pitch the upside potential while downplaying the risk side of the story. The parallels between Ponzi schemes and speculative bubbles are so clear in Shiller's opinion that the burden of proof is on those who deny the similarity.

Competing Hypotheses of Behavioral Finance

A mathematical model quantifies a scientific hypothesis about some aspect of the world, This allows quantitative predictions to be made that can be tested against future observations. Of course, those proposing the model hope its predictions will coincide with said observations. Nevertheless, if they should clash, a true scientist stands ready to formulate a new model that both explains the discordant observations and makes additional predictions that can be tested against further observations. This cycle of refinement never ceases because knowledge is never complete.

Pseudoscientific stories resemble legitimate scientific hypotheses, but only superficially. A scientific hypothesis is compact, yet it accounts for a wide range of observations. Pseudoscientific stories tend to be complicated. Scientific hypotheses make precise predictions that can be checked against future observation. Pseudoscientific accounts make vague predictions that are consistent with prior observations but never make predictions specific enough to permit clear refutation. Thus, pseudoscientific accounts survive in the minds of the gullible, no matter how far off the mark they may be.

On this basis, behavioral finance qualifies as science, albeit a young one. Although as yet, there is no agreement on a single theory, there has been substantial progress. Within the last decade behavioral-finance practitioners have proposed several hypotheses to explain investor behavior and key features of market dynamics. These are important to TA because they provide a rationale for the occurrence of systematic price movements, the "without-which-not" of TA.

The behavioral-finance hypotheses have been formulated as mathematical models, thus allowing them to generate testable predictions of how markets would behave if the hypothesis were correct. This opens the hypotheses to refutation if markets do not manifest the predicted behaviors. For example, if a model predicts the occurrence of trend reversals similar to those actually observed in market data, the hypothesis gains some confirmation. However, if the model's predicted scenarios are contradicted by actual market behavior, then the hypothesis would be refuted. This makes the hypotheses of behavioral finance scientifically meaningful.

Recall that the random-walk model of EMH predicts that systematic price motion should not be observed in market behavior. In contrast, the behavioral-finance hypotheses described later predict the occurrence of systematic price motion and offer an explanation about why they should occur. Even though none of the hypotheses provides a comprehensive theory of market behavior, they have a common a message of importance to TA: There is good reason to believe financial markets are not entirely random walks.

Biased Interpretation of Public Information: The Barberis, Shleifer, and Vishny (BSV) Hypothesis. Empirical studies show that investors display two distinct errors in response to news releases. Sometimes they underreact, and consequently prices change less than the new fundamentals say they should. At other times, investors overreact, causing prices to change more than is justified by the news. Ultimately, however, these pricing errors are rectified by systematic price movements toward price levels that accurately reflect the new information.

The puzzle is: Why do investors sometimes overreact while at other times they underreact? A hypothesis proposed by Barberis, Shleifer, and Vishny[83] (BSV) offers an explanation. First, BSV asserts that two distinct cognitive errors are involved: conservatism bias and sample-size neglect. Second, they assert that the particular error that is operative at a given point in time depends on circumstances.

To briefly recap: The conservatism bias describes the tendency to alter a prior belief less than new information would warrant. Existing opinions are sticky. Sample-size neglect, also known as the crime of small numbers, is the tendency to draw too grand a conclusion from a small sample of observations. Thus, the conservatism bias is the opposite of the crime of small numbers. In the former, new evidence is given too little weight; in the latter, it is given too much.

The conservatism bias is at work when investors underreact to news, leaving prices too low after good news or too high after bad news. However, as investors gradually realize the new information's true significance, prices make a gradual systematic march to a level that properly reflects the news. Thus, some price trends can be explained by investor underreaction.

The crime of small numbers explains investor overreaction. For example, if investors observe a small number of positive earnings changes, they may conclude, too hastily, that a valid growth pattern has been established. This stimulates overly aggressive buying that pushes prices higher than warranted. Investors can overreact in the same way to a few negative observations and push the price too low.

The mathematical model put forward by BSV makes the following simplifying assumptions: (1) the market has a single stock, (2) its earnings stream follows a random walk, but (3) investors do not realize this,[84] so (4) investors labor under the false impression that the stock's earnings stream shifts back and forth between two distinct regimes, a growth trend phase and a mean-reverting (oscillating) phase, but they do not consider the possibility that the earning may follow a random walk, (6) therefore, investors believe their job is to figure out which of these two regimes is operative at any given point in time.

Let's see how BSV's mythical investor might react to the releases of new earnings information. At any given time, the investors hold a belief that the earnings are in either one of two nonrandom regimes: a growth trend or mean reverting process. The possibility of a random walk is not considered. Recall that a random walk displays less mean reversion than a true mean-reverting process and also displays streaks that are shorter in duration than those found in a truly trending process. As we pick up the story, an investor holds some prior belief about the earnings regime and hears news about earnings. Suppose the news announcement contradicts the investor's belief. For example, if the investor had believed the stock's earnings had been in a growth trend, and a negative earnings report came out, the investor would be surprised. Similarly, if the investor had been under the belief that earnings were in a mean-reverting regime, a streak of similar changes would also be surprising. According to the BSV hypothesis, both kinds of surprises would trigger an underreaction by the investor due to the conservatism bias. In other words, regardless of whether the investor's prior belief was in a mean-reverting regime or in a growth regime, news contradicting the belief would be given too little weight causing prices to underreact to the new information. However, if news that is at odds with a prior belief continues to occur, the investor will become convinced that the regime has switched, either from mean reverting to growth or from growth to mean reverting. In this case, the BSV hypothesis predicts that investors will switch from the mistake of being too stuck with their prior beliefs and underreacting (the conservatism bias) to the mistake of committing the crime of small numbers and overreacting. Thus, the BSV model accounts for both kinds of investor error as well as the systematic price movement that corrects both forms of errors.

I illustrate the type of behavior predicted by BSV in Figure 7.12. Here I posit the case where investors initially believe that earnings are in a mean-reverting regime. Thus, they expect positive earnings reports to be followed by a negative report. For this reason, they underreact to the first two positive earnings reports. However, after the third positive

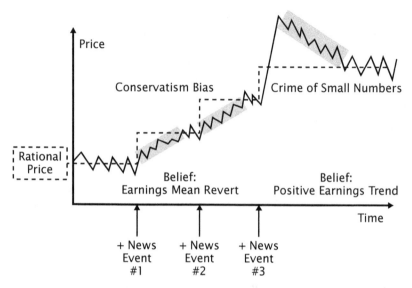

FIGURE 7.12 BSV: underreaction followed by overreaction.

report, not at all unusual in a random process (three heads in a row), they abandon their earlier belief and adopt the idea that earnings have entered a growth regime and have established an uptrend. Consequently they now expect that future reports will also be positive. This causes investors to overreact, pushing the stock above a rational level. The systematic price movements resulting from both types of investor error are highlighted in grey.

Thus BSV's model also shows how a feedback loop emerges from the crime of small numbers. When investors see earnings move in the same direction several times in succession, they switch from doubting the trend to assuming it is real.[85] However, the conservatism bias initially impedes the adoption of the new belief. The interaction between the crime of small numbers and the conservatism bias determines the speed at which speculative feedback develops.[86] Simulations of the BSV model show several kinds of actual market behavior such as price trends following surprising earnings, price momentum, long-term reversals, and the forecasting power of fundamental ratios such as price-to-book. Thus, the BSV model explains how investors' biased interpretations of public information can predict the occurrence of phenomena that are observed in actual market data. This suggests that the model does capture some of the dynamics of real financial markets.

Biased Interpretation of Private Information: The Daniel, Hirshleifer, and Subrahmanyam (DHS) Hypothesis. An alternative hypothesis proposed by Daniel, Hirshleifer, and Subrahmanyam (1998, 2001)[87] (DHS) suggests a different explanation for systematic price movements such as trend reversals and trend persistence (momentum). In contrast to BSV, the DHS hypothesis is founded upon investors' biased interpretations of private research. In addition, DHS emphasizes somewhat different cognitive errors: the endowment bias, the confirmation bias (see Chapter 2), and the self-attribution bias (see Chapter 2.).

Private research refers to an investor's independently derived interpretations of public information (i.e., proprietary research). The hypothesis put forward by DHS predicts that investors will be overly confident about the quality of their private research and hence will have a tendency to overreact to it. This prediction is based on the endowment bias—the predisposition to place too high a value on what we own or create. This overreaction pushes prices beyond rational levels, which ultimately leads to a price reversal back toward rational prices. So in DHS's view of the world, price reversals are an effect of overconfidence in privately derived signals.

DHS also explains price momentum (nonrandom price trends) as the result of two other cognitive biases: confirmation bias and self-attribution bias. They assert price momentum develops because news releases and price movements impact investors in a biased manner. Because of the confirmation bias, news or price movements that confirm an investor's prior beliefs, (i.e., those founded on their private signals and research), will be given excessive weight. News events and/or price movements that are confirmatory have the effect of increasing the investors' confidence that their private research was indeed accurate. This induces them to take additional action (buying or selling), which amplifies the momentum of the current price trend. The self-attribution bias also causes investors to view confirmatory news or price movement as a sign that their private research is good. Recall that self-attribution causes people to take credit for outcomes, even if they occur because of good luck, but to deny responsibility for bad outcomes by attributing them to bad luck. Thus, both the confirmation bias and self-attribution bias induce investors to overreact to confirmatory evidence, thereby amplifying the market's positive feedback.

Conversely, if public information or price behavior contradicts the investor's private research, it will be given too little weight (confirmation bias) and investors will attribute it to bad luck rather than to poor private research (self-attribution bias). Therefore, regardless of whether the news or the price movement confirms or contradicts the investor's private information, the DHS model predicts that investors' confidence in their private research will increase. "This unequal treatment of new information means initial overconfidence is on average followed by even greater overconfidence, thus generating price momentum."[88] However, after a sequence of contradictory public news signals, the investors' confidence in their private information will be shattered (crime of small numbers), and price trends will reverse.

Both DHS and BSV predict that investors are sometimes excessively optimistic and sometimes excessively pessimistic. In addition, these beliefs are predicted to be subject to reversal when a streak of disconfirming information arrives. If DHS and BSV are valid, then the profits earned by strategies that exploit trend reversals should be concentrated at the times of information releases. This predicted consequence, which opens both hypotheses to refutation, has been confirmed.[89] Indeed, a large fraction of the excess returns earned by buying value stocks (low price to book, low P/E, and so forth) and buying the weakest stocks of the past three to five years do occur near the times of earnings information releases.

News Traders and Momentum Traders: The HS Hypothesis. As just described, certain instances of price momentum can be explained by prices catching up with fundamentals due to an initial underreaction to news. Other trends can be explained by positive feedback, in which a price increase stimulates additional buying and price weakness stimulates additional selling.[90] Thus, some investors look for signals in recent price changes rather than news.

From the perspective of TA, trends spawned by positive feedback can be viewed as a cascade of progressively less sensitive trend-following signals being triggered. An initial price movement (news inspired or random) triggers the most sensitive trend signals (e.g., a very short-term moving average crossover signal). Transactions triggered by that signal push prices enough to trigger a somewhat less sensitive trend signal (e.g., medium-term moving average), which in turn triggers even less sensitive signals and so on. Whatever the mechanism, investor actions become correlated, forming a herd effect.

The hypothesis proposed by Hong and Stein[91] (HS) explains three market phenomena: momentum, underreaction, and overreaction. To do so, they postulate two classes of investors, news watchers (fundamentalists) and momentum traders (technicians). The HS hypothesis asserts that an interaction between these two classes of investors creates positive feedback and, therefore, price momentum. The HS assumption that there is more than one class of investors is grounded in the notion that investors, by dint of their intellectual limits, must confine their attention to a restricted portion of the available information. News watchers confine their attention to fundamental developments. On the basis of this information, they derive private estimates of future returns. In contrast, momentum traders confine their attention to past price changes and derive their private forecast of future trends.

Hong and Stein posit that news watchers pay little or no attention to price changes. As a result, their private assessments of the news fail to spread quickly throughout the community of news watchers. To understand how an exclusive focus on the fundamental news impedes the diffusion of information, consider what would happen if the news watchers also paid attention to price action. Watching price movements would allow them to infer, to some degree, the private information of other news watchers. For example, rising prices might imply that other news watchers were interpreting the news as favorable, whereas falling prices might imply the opposite. As we have seen, any investor behavior that slows the process by which prices incorporate new information can cause price trends. That is, instead of prices instantaneously adjusting to new information, they move gradually to a higher or lower level justified by new information. For momentum (trend-following) strategies to work, prices must change in a gradual enough fashion to allow signals based on an initial price change to predict additional price change. Thus, the failure of news traders to extract information from price action slows the rate at which prices adjust to new information, thus resulting in price trends.

Now consider the effect on market dynamics caused by momentum traders (trend-followers). The HS hypothesis claims that momentum traders only pay attention to signals from price behavior. Trend following assumes that newly emerging price trends are an indication that important new fundamental information is starting to diffuse throughout the market. Momentum traders make the bet that the diffusion is incomplete and that the price trend will continue after the initial momentum signal. Actions taken by subsequent waves of trend followers keep prices moving, thus generating positive price feedback. Ultimately, as more trend followers join the party, prices may carry further than fundamentals justify. The overshooting occurs because momentum traders are unable to judge the extent to which the news has been diffused and understood by all investors. When the news is fully diffused and all investors have acted on it, no further price movement is fundamentally justified. Thus, HS assert that the overshooting of rational price levels, resulting from the positive feedback of momentum traders, sets up the conditions for a trend reversal back toward rational levels based on fundamentals.

The Bottom Line. Behavioral finance has offered a number of testable hypotheses that attempt to explain systematic price motion. It is not yet clear which, if any, of these are correct. No doubt new hypotheses will be offered. So long as they generate testable (falsifiable) predictions, they should be entertained. What is of importance to TA is that these theories suggest that systematic price movements should occur in financial market prices.

NONRANDOM PRICE MOTION IN THE CONTEXT OF EFFICIENT MARKETS

The preceding section explained how systematic price movement can arise in markets that are not fully efficient. However, even if markets are fully efficient, the case for TA is not lost. A case cam be made for the existence of systematic price motion in markets that are fully efficient. This section presents this case.

How Systematic Price Motion and Market Efficiency Can Coexist

Some economists contend that systematic price movements are possible even if markets are fully efficient.[92] In other words, the existence of non-random price behavior and the possibility of price prediction does not necessarily imply that financial markets are inefficient.[93]

Other economists state the case more strongly, asserting that some degree of predictability is not only possible but necessary for markets to function properly. In their book *A Non-Random Walk Down Wall Street*, Andrew Lo and Craig MacKinlay say, "predictability is the oil that lubricates the gears of capitalism."[94] A similar position is taken by Grossman and Stiglitz.[95] They contend that efficient markets must offer profit opportunities to motivate investors to engage in the costly activities of information processing and trading. For it is these very activities that drive prices toward rational valuations.

In fact, there is only one special condition under which market efficiency necessarily implies that price movement must be random and, therefore, unpredictable. This occurs when all investors have the same attitude toward risk, a condition that is simply not plausible. Is there any type of risk about which all people have the same attitude? To see how far-fetched this assumption is, imagine for a moment a world in which all people have the same attitude toward risk. There would be either too many test pilots and high steel workers or not enough of them.

Either everyone would be into skydiving and alligator wrestling, or no one would.

It is far more realistic to assume a world of investors with highly diverse attitudes toward risk. In such a world, some investors would be more adverse to risk than others, and they would be willing to pay other investors to accept the burden of additional risk. Also, there would likely be risk-tolerant investors looking to profit from the opportunity to assume additional risk. All that would be needed in such a world is a mechanism by which risk can be transferred from the risk adverse to the risk tolerant and for compensation to be paid to those willing to accept said risk.

Let's step away from markets for a moment to consider one mechanism by which the risk adverse can compensate the risk inclined—the insurance premium. Homeowners dread the possibility of a fire, so they enter into a transaction with a fire insurance company. The homeowner transfers the financial risk of a fire to the insurance company and, in exchange, the insurance company earns a premium. This is a profitable business if the insurance company can predict the likelihood of a house burning down (over a large number of homes—Law of Large Numbers) and charge a premium that compensates it for that risk plus a bit more for profit. The bottom line: The insurance company provides a risk acceptance service and is compensated for doing so.

Participants in financial markets have exposures to various risks and vary in their tolerance for them. These ingredients motivate transactions that transfer risk from one party to another. In this situation, the investors willing to bear greater risks can reasonably demand compensation in the form of a higher return than that offered by riskless investments, just as test pilots and high steel workers can demand a premium salary for the additional risks they bear. In financial market terms, compensation for accepting increased risk is called a risk premium or economic rent.

Financial markets offer several kinds of risk premiums:

- **The equity market risk premium:** Investors provide working capital for new business formation and are compensated by receiving a return that is above the risk-free rate for incurring the risk of business failure, economic downturns, and such.
- **Commodity and currency hedge risk transfer premium:** Speculators assume long and short positions in futures to give commercial hedgers (users and producers of the commodity) the ability to shed the risk of price change. Compensation is in the form of profitable trends that can be captured with relatively simple trend-following strategies.
- **Liquidity premium:** Investors assume positions in less liquid securities and in securities being aggressively sold by investors with acute

short-term needs for cash. Compensation is in the form of higher returns for holding illiquid securities or in the form of short-term gains
for buying stocks that have recently been very weak (i.e., engaging in
countertrend strategies).

- **Information or price discovery premium for promoting market
efficiency:** This premium compensates investors for making buy-and-
sell decisions that move prices toward rational levels. Because these decisions are often based on complex models developed by sophisticated
research, this premium might also be called a complexity premium.[96]
For example, a strategy that sells overvalued stocks and buys undervalued stocks helps move prices back to rational values (price discovery).

The good news about returns that come in the form of a risk premium
is that they are more likely to endure into the future. Of course, it is every
analyst's dream to discover true market inefficiencies because the returns
earned from them do not entail additional risk.[97] However, inefficiencies
are ephemeral. Sooner or later they tend to be discovered and wiped out
by other diligent researchers. However, returns that are justified as a risk
premium are more likely to endure as they represent payment for service.

How do risk premiums explain the existence of systematic price
movements? Such price movements can provide a mechanism for risk-
accepting investors to be compensated. The investor who is willing to provide liquidity to a stockholder with a strong desire to sell winds up buying
stocks that have a systematic tendency to rise over the near term. These
stocks can be identified with countertrend strategies.[98]

Therefore, in the context of efficient markets, the profits-earned by
TA strategies may be understood as risk premiums; compensation for the
beneficial effect the strategy confers on other investors or the market as a
whole. In other words, TA signals may generate profits because they identify opportunities to assume risks that other investors wish to shed.

I should point out that the mere fact that an investor is willing to bear
a risk does not guarantee that a return will be earned. The risk taker must
be clever about it. Just as a careless high steel worker or test pilot may not
live long enough to collect a wage that includes the hazardous-duty premium, a careless seeker of risk premiums may not stay in the game long
enough to collect, either.

Hedge Risk Premium and the Gains to
Trend-Following Commodity Futures

This section describes how the profits to trend followers in the commodities markets may be explained as a risk transfer premium. The
commodities futures markets perform an economic function that is fun-

damentally different from the stock and bond markets. The stock and bond markets provide companies with a mechanism to obtain equity and debt financing[99] and provide investors with a way to invest their capital. Because stocks and corporate bond investments expose investors to risks that exceed the risk-free rate (government treasury bills), investors are compensated with a risk premium—the equity risk premium and the corporate-bond risk premium.

The economic function of the futures markets has nothing to do with raising capital and everything to do with price risk. Price changes, especially large ones, are a source of risk and uncertainty to businesses that produce or use commodities. The futures markets provide a means by which these businesses, called commercial hedgers, can transfer price risk to investors (speculators).

At first blush, it may seem puzzling that commercial hedgers would even need investors to assume their price risk. Because some hedgers need to sell, like the farmer who grows wheat, and some need to buy, like the bread company that uses wheat, why don't hedgers simply contract with each other? They do, but often there is an imbalance in their hedging needs. Sometimes wheat farmers have more wheat to sell than bakery companies and other commercial users of wheat need to buy. At other times, the situation is the opposite. Thus there is often a gap between the farmers' supply and the bakers' demand. This creates the need for a third group of market participants who are willing to buy or sell. That is, they are willing to fill the supply-demand gap that develops between commercial producers and commercial users.

The existence of a supply-demand gap is a predicable consequence of the law of supply and demand; as the price of wheat rises, supply goes up while demand goes down. As the price falls, supply goes down while demand goes up. Data from the Commodity Futures Trading Commission (CFTC), which tracks the buying and selling of commercial hedgers, confirms this is exactly what occurs in the futures markets. During rising price trends, commercial hedge selling exceeds hedge buying (i.e., hedgers are net sellers). During falling trends, commercial hedge buying exceeds commercial hedge selling (hedgers are net buyers).

In the futures markets, the amount sold and the amount bought must be equal just as in real estate transactions the number of homes sold must equal the number of homes bought. It cannot be otherwise. Given that a rising trend motivates more commercial hedge selling than hedge buying, there is a need for additional buyers during rising markets to accommodate the excess hedge selling. During falling trends, excessive commercial hedge buying creates the need for additional sellers.

Enter the price trend speculator who is willing to buy during uptrends to meet the unfilled needs of commercial hedge sellers and willing to sell short during falling price trends, to meet the unmet needs of the commercial hedge buyers. In other words the futures markets need speculators to be trend followers. And it is the invisible hand of the marketplace that creates the trends to compensate them for filling this need.

However, trend followers are exposed to significant risks. For example, most trend-following systems generate unprofitable signals 50 to 65 percent of the time. These occur when markets are trendless, which is the case a majority of the time. During these times, the trend followers experience the dreaded equity drawdown. During drawdowns it is not unusual for successful trend followers to lose up to 30 percent of their trading capital. Thus they need a strong motive to tolerate drawdown risk. That motive is the opportunity, though not the guarantee, to profit from price trends when they do occur. In other words, large-scale trends provide a profit opportunity to trend followers who are adequately capitalized and who manage leverage correctly.

The Mt. Lucas Management Index of Trend Following Returns

The risk premium earned by commodity trend followers has been quantified with the creation of a benchmark index called the Mt. Lucas Management Index (MLM). It is a historical record of the returns that can be earned by an extremely simplistic trend-following formula. In other words, it assumes no specialized knowledge of a complex forecasting model. If it did it could not legitimately be called a benchmark index, whose function is to estimate the returns that can be earned by investing in an asset class with no special skill.

The risk-adjusted returns earned by the MLM index suggest that commodity futures markets contain systematic price movements that can be exploited with relatively simple TA methods. The MLM index monthly returns, which have been computed back to the 1960s, are derived by applying a 12-month moving-average crossover strategy to 25 commodities markets.[100] At the end of each month, the price of the nearby futures contract for each of the markets is compared to its 12-month moving average. If the price is greater than the moving average, a long position is held in that market for the next month. If the price is below the average, a short position is held.

The annualized return[101] and risk, as measured by the standard deviation in annual returns, of the MLM index is compared with returns and risks of several other asset-class benchmarks in Figure 7.13.

The risk-adjusted excess return or Sharpe ratio for the MLM index, and the other asset classes are shown Figure 7.14. The trend follower earns a risk premium that is somewhat better than the other asset-class

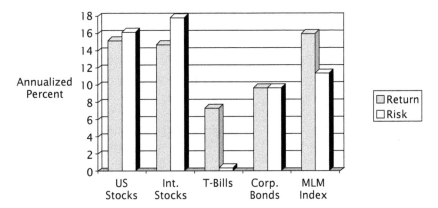

FIGURE 7.13 Returns and standard deviations for five benchmarks.

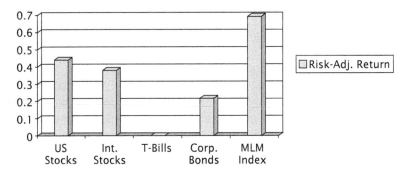

FIGURE 7.14 Risk-adjusted excess returns.

benchmarks.[102] The MLM index provides some evidence that the futures markets offer compensation in the form of systematic price movements.

If a risk-transfer premium is a valid explanation of trend-follower returns, then trend following in stocks should not be as rewarding as it is in the commodity futures markets. A trend follower in stocks is not providing a risk-transfer service. There are data suggesting that trend following in stocks is indeed a less rewarding enterprise.[103] Lars Kestner compared the performance of trend-following systems for a portfolio of futures and a portfolio of stocks. The futures considered were 29 commodities in 8 different sectors.[104] The stocks were represented by 31 large-cap stocks in 9 different industry sectors,[105] and 3 stock indices. Risk-adjusted performance (Sharpe ratio) was computed for 5 different trend-following systems,[106] over the period January 1, 1990 through December 31, 2001. The Sharpe ratio averaged over the five trend-following systems in futures was

.604 versus .046 in stocks. These results support the notion that futures trend followers are earning a risk premium that is not available to trend followers in stocks. See Figure 7.15.

Liquidity Premium and the Gains to Counter Trend Trading in Stocks

The stock market offers risk-taking stock traders a different form of compensation. They can earn a premium for providing liquidity to highly motivated sellers. In other words, there are systematic price movements in stocks that can be exploited with countertrend strategies that buy stocks that have been very weak over the recent past.

Owners of stock with an urgent need to liquidate their holdings need buyers. This suggests that the market should offer compensation to traders who are willing to meet unmet needs for liquidity. Evidence presented by Michael Cooper shows that buyers of oversold stocks can earn above-average short-term returns.[107] His study shows that stocks that have displayed negative price momentum on declining trading volume earn excess returns. In other words, the pattern identifies stocks with distressed sellers in search of buyers. The excess returns appear to be a liquidity premium. Cooper's study showed that stocks that have declined sharply over the prior two weeks on declining volume display a systematic tendency to rise over the following week. The declining volume aspect of this pattern is plausible because it can be interpreted to mean that there are insufficient buyers to meet the acute needs of the sellers. To guard against the possibility of data mining, Cooper used a walk-forward out-of-sample simulation to form portfolios of long and short positions over the period 1978 to 1993. The long/short portfolios, created from 300 large capitalization stocks, earned an annualized return of 44.95 percent versus a benchmark buy-and-hold return of 17.91

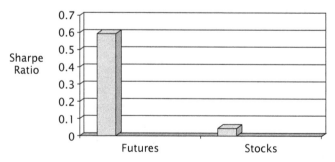

FIGURE 7.15 Risk-adjusted returns to trend-following futures versus stocks.

percent. Again, we see evidence of systematic price movements that can be explained as a risk premium, in this case a liquidity premium, which can be exploited with TA.

In the context of efficient equity and futures markets, signals given by TA methods can be viewed as identifying opportunities to fill a market need. In effect, they are want ads, "risk adopter for hire by hedgers," or "desperately seeking liquidity provider—will pay." TA traders profiting from these signals are not getting a free lunch. They are simply reading the market's Help Wanted advertisements.

CONCLUSION

In this chapter, I have made a case for the existence of nonrandom price movements in financial markets. Without them, there can be no justification for technical analysis. With them, TA has an opportunity to capture some portion of that nonrandom behavior. Ultimately, it is up to each method of TA to prove that it can.

Case Study: Signal Rules for the S&P 500 Index

CHAPTER 8

Case Study of Rule Data Mining for the S&P 500

T his chapter describes a case study in rule data mining, the results of which are reported in Chapter 9. The study evaluates the statistical significance of 6,402 individual TA rules back tested on the S&P 500 Index over the period from November 1, 1980 through July 1, 2005.

DATA MINING BIAS AND RULE EVALUATION

The primary purpose of the case study is to illustrate the application of statistical methods that take into account the effects of data-mining bias. To recap, data mining is a process in which the profitability of many rules is compared so that one or more superior rules can be selected. As pointed out in Chapter 6, this selection process causes an upward bias in the performance of the selected rule(s). In other words, the observed performance of the best rule(s) in the back test overstates its (their) expected performance in the future. This bias complicates the evaluation of statistical significance and may lead a data miner to select a rule with no predictive power (i.e., its past performance was pure luck). This is the fool's gold of the objective technician.

This problem can be minimized by using specialized statistical-inference tests. The case study illustrates the application of two such methods: an enhanced version of White's reality check and Masters's Monte-Carlo permutation method. Both take advantage of a recent improvement,[1] which reduces the probability that a good rule will be overlooked (Type II error). That is to say, the improvement increases the power of the tests.

A secondary purpose of the case study was the possible discovery of one or more rules that generate statistically significant profits. However, when the case study's rules were proposed, it was unknown if any would be found to be statistically significant.

AVOIDANCE OF DATA SNOOPING BIAS

In addition to data mining bias, rule studies can also suffer from an even more serious problem, the *data-snooping bias*. *Data snooping* refers to using the results of prior rule studies reported by other researchers. Because these studies typically do not disclose the amount of data mining that led to the discovery of whatever it was that was discovered, there is no way to take its effects into account and hence no way to properly evaluate the statistical significance of the results. As pointed out in Chapter 6, depending on which method is being used—White's Reality Check or the Monte Carlo permutation method—information about each rule tested must be available to construct the appropriate sampling distribution.

For example, suppose the case study in this book had included a rule developed by Dr. Martin Zweig known as the *double 9:1 upside/downside volume* rule. This rule signals long positions when the daily ratio of upside to downside volume on the NYSE exceeds a threshold value of 9 on two instances within a three-month time window. Note, this rule has three free parameters: the threshold value on the ratio (9), the number of instances on which the ratio exceeds the threshold (2), and the maximum time separation between the threshold violations (3 months). According to tests of this rule conducted by students in my technical analysis class, the signal does have predictive power over the following 3, 6, 9, and 12 months. In other words, the rule is statistically significant, but only under the assumption that Zweig did not engage in data mining to discover the parameter values he recommends: 9, 2, and 3. Zweig has not reported if he tested other versions of the rule using different parameter combinations or, if he did, how many combinations were tried to find the specific set that defines his rule. If Zweig's rule were to be included in the case study and it was selected as the best rule, it would be impossible to take into account the true amount of data mining that led to its discovery.

In an effort to avoid data-snooping bias, the case study did not explicitly include any rules discussed by other researchers. Even though it is possible, perhaps even likely, that some of the study's rules were similar to those tested in prior rule studies, these similarities were by accident, not by design. This precaution mitigated the data-snooping bias but could not eliminate it entirely because, in proposing the 6,402 rules tested, I could not help but be affected by rule studies I have previously read.

ANALYZED DATA SERIES

Although all rules were tested for their profitability on the S&P 500 Index, the vast majority of rules utilized data series other than the S&P 500 to generate buy-and-sell signals. These other data series included: other market indices (e.g., transportation stocks), market breadth (e.g., upside and downside volume), indicators that combine price and volume (e.g., on-balance volume), prices of debt instruments (e.g., BAA bonds), and interest-rate spreads (duration spread between 10-year treasury notes and 90-day treasury bills). This approach is in the spirit of intermarket analysis as discussed by Murphy.[2] All series and rules are detailed below.

TECHNICAL ANALYSIS THEMES

The 6,402 rules tested were derived from three broad themes of TA: (1) trends, (2) extremes and transitions, and (3) divergences. Trend rules generate long and short market positions based on the current trend of the data series analyzed by the rule. Extreme and transition rules generate long and short positions when the analyzed series reaches an extreme high or low value or as it makes a transition between extreme values. Divergence rules generate signals when the S&P 500 Index trends in one direction while a companion data series trends in the other. The specific data transformations and signal logic for each rule are described later in this chapter.

The rules employ several common analysis methods including moving averages, channel breakouts, and stochastics, which I refer to as channel normalization.

PERFORMANCE STATISTIC: AVERAGE RETURN

The performance statistic used to evaluate each rule was its average return over the period (1980 to 2005) when back tested on detrended S&P 500 data. As pointed out in Chapter 1, detrending involves subtracting the S&P 500's average daily price change over the back-test period from each day's actual price change. This results in a new data series for which the average daily change is equal to zero.

As discussed in Chapter 1, detrending eliminates any benefit or detriment that would accrue to a rule's performance as a result of either a long or short position bias. A binary rule can be position biased if one of its conditions (long or short) is restrictive relative to the other condition (long or short). For example, if the long-position condition is more difficult to satisfy than the short-position condition, the rule will have a short-position bias and tend to spend a majority of its time in short positions. If such a rule were to be applied to market data with a positive trend (average daily price change > 0), its average return would be penalized. This reduction in the rule's performance would have nothing to do with its predictive power and thus cloud its evaluation.

NO COMPLEX RULES WERE EVALUATED

To keep the scope of the case study manageable, it was restricted to tests of individual rules. Complex rules, which are derived by combining two or more individual rules with mathematical and/or logical operators, were not considered. The combining method can be as simple an unweighted average or as complex as an arbitrarily nonlinear function derived with sophisticated data-modeling software.

Limiting the case study to individual rules was detrimental for two reasons. First, few practitioners rely on a single rule to make decisions. Second, complex rules exploit informational synergies between individual rules. It is not surprising, therefore, that complex rules have demonstrated higher levels of performance. At least one study[3] has shown that complex rules can produce good performance, even when the simple rules combined to form the complex rule are individually unprofitable. Combining rules intuitively is extremely difficult, but there are now effective automated methods[4] for synthesizing complex rules.

THE CASE STUDY DEFINED IN STATISTICAL TERMS

The following section defines the case study in terms of the key elements of a statistical study: the population at issue, the parameter of interest, sample data used, the statistic of interest, the null and alternative hypotheses considered, and the designated significance level.

The Population

The population at issue is the set of daily returns that would be earned by a rule if its signals were to be applied to the S&P 500 over all possible realizations of the *immediate practical future*.[5] This is an abstract population, in the sense that its observations have not yet occurred and it is infinite in size.

Population Parameter

The population parameter is the rule's expected average annualized return in the immediate practical future.

The Sample

The sample consists of the daily returns earned by a rule applied to detrended S&P 500 Index prices over the back-test period from November 1, 1980 until July 1, 2005.

Sample Statistic (Test Statistic)

The sample statistic is the average annualized return earned by a rule when applied to the detrended S&P 500 price data from November 1, 1980 until July 1, 2005.

The Null Hypothesis (H_0)

The null hypothesis states that all 6,402 rules tested are without predictive power. This implies that any observed profits in a back test were due to chance (sampling variability).

In reality, there are two version of the null hypothesis in the case study. This stems from the fact that two different methods were used to assess statistical significance: White's reality check and Masters's Monte Carlo permutation method. Although both methods assert that all rules considered were devoid of predictive power, they implement this assumption differently. The null hypothesis tested by White's reality check is that all rules tested have expected returns equal to zero (or less). The null tested by Masters's Monte Carlo permutation is that all rules generated their long and short positions in a random fashion. In other words, long and short were randomly permuted with the market's one-day-forward price change.

The Alternative Hypothesis

This study's alternative hypothesis asserts that a rule's back-tested profitability stems from genuine predictive power. Again, the two methods assert this in slightly different ways. In the case of White's reality check, the alternative hypothesis says that there is at least one rule within the tested universe that has an expected return greater than zero. It should be noted that White's reality check does not assert that the rule with the highest observed performance is necessarily that best rule (i.e., the rule with the highest expected return). However, under fairly reasonable conditions, they are one and the same.[6] The alternative hypothesis declared by Masters's method is that a rule's back-tested profitability is the result of an informative pairing of its long and short positions with the market's one-day-forward price change. In other words, the rule has predictive power.

The Statistical Significance Level

A 5 percent level of significance was chosen as a threshold for rejection of the null hypothesis. This means there was a 0.05 probability of rejecting the H_0 hypothesis when the H_0 was, in fact, true.

Practical Significance

The practical significance of a result is different from its statistical significance. The latter is the probability that a rule that has no predictive power (i.e., H_0 is true) would earn a return as high as or higher than the return produced by the rule in a back test by luck. In contrast, practical significance relates to the economic value of the observed rule return. When sample sizes are large, as they are in the case study (i.e., over 6,000 days), the H_0 can be rejected even if a rule's return is positive by a very minor amount. In other words, a rule can be statistically significant even though its practical value is negligible. Practical significance depends upon a trader's objectives. One trader may be satisfied with a rule for which expected return is 5 percent whereas another may reject any rule for which expected return is less than 20 percent.

RULES: TRANSFORMING DATA SERIES INTO MARKET POSITIONS

A rule is an input/output process. That is to say, it transforms input(s), consisting of one or more time series, into an output, a new time series consisting of +1's and −1's that indicate long and short positions in the market being traded (i.e., S&P 500). This transformation is defined by the one or more mathematical,[7] logical,[8] or time series[9] operators that are applied to the input time series. In other words, a rule is defined by a set of operations. See Figure 8.1.

Some rules utilize inputs that are raw time series. That is to say, the one or more time series used as inputs to the rule are not transformed in any way prior to the rule's position logic being applied, for example the S&P 500 closing price. This is illustrated in Figure 8.2.

Other rules utilize input series that have been derived from one or more raw market series by applying various transformations to the market data. These preprocessed inputs are referred to as constructed data series or *indicators*. An example of an indicator is the *negative volume index*. It is derived from transformations of two raw data series; S&P 500 closing price and total NYSE daily volume. This is illustrated in Figure 8.3. The transformations used in the creation of the negative volume index and other indicators used in the case study are described in the following section.

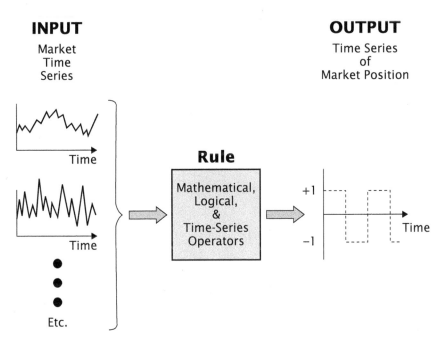

FIGURE 8.1 TA rule transforms input into output.

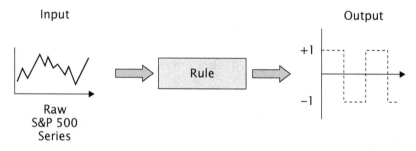

FIGURE 8.2   Raw market time series as rule input.

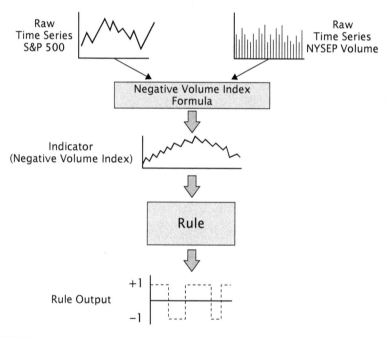

FIGURE 8.3   Transformed market time series as rule input.

TIME-SERIES OPERATORS

This section describes the time-series operators used in the case study to transform raw data series into indicators. Time-series operators are mathematical functions that transform a time series into a new time series. The case study utilized several common time-series operators: channel breakout, moving average, and channel normalization. The channel breakout operator is used to identify trends in a time series for rules that are based on trends. The moving-average operator, which can also identify trends, is used in the case study for smoothing. The channel-normalization operator, or stochastics, is used to eliminate the trend of a time series (i.e., detrending).

Channel Breakout Operator (CBO)

"The purpose of all trend identification methods is to see past the underlying noise in a time series, those erratic moves that seem to be meaningless, and find the current direction of the series."[10] One such method is the n-period channel-breakout operator.[11] Here, n refers to the number of time periods (days, weeks, and such) into the past that are examined to define the upper and lower channel boundaries that enclose the time series. The lower boundary is defined by the minimum value of the time series over the past n-periods, not including the current period. The upper boundary is defined by the time series' maximum value over the past n-periods, not including the current period. Despite its extreme simplicity, the channel-breakout operator has proven to be as effective as more complex trend-following methods.[12]

As conventionally interpreted, the channel breakout operator signals long positions if the analyzed series exceeds its maximum value established over the past n-periods. Conversely, short positions are signaled when the time series falls below its n-period minimum. This is illustrated in Figure 8.4. In practice, the channel is redrawn as each new data point

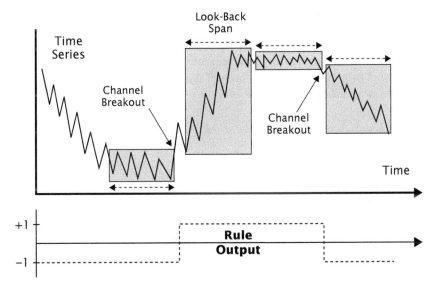

FIGURE 8.4 Channel-breakout operator.

becomes available, but in Figure 8.4 only several channels are shown to illustrate its function. Although the channel has a constant look-back span with respect to the time axis, its vertical width with respect to the axis that represents the value of the time series adjusts dynamically to the range of the series over the past n-periods. This feature may explain the effectiveness of the method. This is to say, the channel breakout's dynamic range may reduce the likelihood of false signals caused by an increase in the series' volatility rather than an actual change in its trend.

The n-period breakout operator has a single free parameter, its look-back span, the number of time periods into the past used to establish the channel's boundaries. In general, the larger the look-back span, the wider the channel, and hence, the less sensitive the indicator. Thus, larger values of n are used to identify larger trends. The case study tested 11 different look-back spans for which lengths were separated by a factor of approximately 1.5. The specific spans used were: 3, 5, 8, 12, 18, 27, 41, 61, 91, 137, and 205 days.

Moving-Average Operator (MA)

The moving average is one of the most widely used times-series operators in TA. It clarifies trends by filtering out high frequency (short-period) fluctuations while passing through low frequency (long-period) components. Thus, the moving-average operator is said to function as a low-pass filter. This is illustrated in Figure 8.5, where the moving average has been centered[13] (lagged by 0.5 × period −1). Note that the output of the moving-average operator is essentially the trend of the original time series with the high frequency oscillations about the trend removed.

The smoothing effect is accomplished by averaging the values of the time series within a moving data window called the *look-back span*. This eliminates or reduces the magnitude of fluctuations with durations that are equal to or less than the duration of the look-back span. Thus, a 10-day mov-

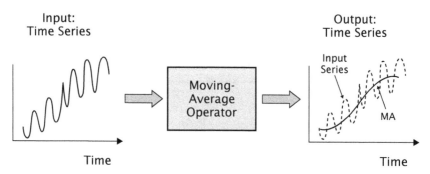

FIGURE 8.5 Moving-average operator: low-pass filter.

ing average will reduce the amplitude of fluctuations for which peak-to-peak or trough-to-trough duration is less than 10 days, and it will completely eliminate a fluctuation with a duration that is exactly equal to 10 days.

The benefit of smoothing comes at a cost—lag. In other words, fluctuations in the raw price that manifest in the smoothed version experience some delay. Thus, a trough in the raw price does not produce a trough in the moving average until some later date. The amount of lag depends upon the length of the look-back span. A longer look-back span produces more smoothing while producing more lag.

The lag induced by a *simple moving average*, which gives equal weight to all elements in the window, is equal to one-half of the look-back span minus one. Thus, the output of an 11-day simple moving average has a lag of $(11 - 1)/2$ or 5 days. This means that trend reversals in the input time series, which are of sufficient duration to manifest in the moving average, will not show up until 5 days later.

There are many types of moving averages, from the simple moving average that gives equal weight to each element in the data window, to sophisticated smoothing methods that use complex data-weighting functions. The benefit conferred by a complex weighting is improved filter performance—less lag for a given degree of smoothing. The field of digital signal processing is concerned with, among other things, the design of weighting functions that maximize filter performance. Digital filters that are relevant to TA are discussed in two books by Ehlers.[14]

The calculation for a simple moving average is given by the following formula.[15]

Moving Average Operator

$$MA_t = \frac{P_t + P_{t-1} + P_{t-2} \ldots + P_{t-n+1}}{n}$$

$$= \frac{\sum_{i=1}^{n} P_{t-i+1}}{n}$$

Where:
P_t = Price at time t
MA_t = Moving average at time t
n = Number of days used to compute moving average

The lag of a simple moving average can be reduced while maintaining the same degree of smoothing by using a linearly weighted moving average. As pointed out by Ehlers[16] the lag of a linearly weighted moving average with a look-back span of n days is $(n - 1)/3$ compared with $(n - 1)/2$ for a simple moving average. Thus, a linearly weighted moving average with a span of 10 days will have a lag of 3 days whereas a simple moving average with the same span will have a lag of 4.5 days. The linear-weighting scheme applies a weight of n to the most recent data point, where n is the number of days in the moving average look-back span, and then the weight is decreased by one for each prior day. The sum of the weights becomes the divisor. This is illustrated in the following equation:

Linear Weighted Moving Average

Weights

$$WMA_t = \frac{(n) \times P_t + (n-1) \times P_{t-1} + \ldots + (n-(t-n+1)) \times P_{t-n+1}}{n + n-1 + \ldots + n-(t-n-1)}$$

Sum of Weights

Where:
P_t = Price at time t
WMA_t = Weighted moving average at time t
n = Number of days used to compute moving average

The case study used a four-day linearly weighted moving average to smooth indicators used in rules that signal when the indicator crosses above or below a critical threshold. Smoothing mitigates the problem of excessive signals that an unsmoothed version of the indicator wiggling back and forth across the threshold would produce. The calculation of a four-day linearly weighted moving average is illustrated in the following equation:

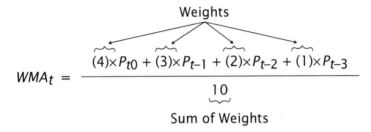

Four Day Linear Weighted Moving Average

Weights

$$WMA_t = \frac{(4) \times P_{t0} + (3) \times P_{t-1} + (2) \times P_{t-2} + (1) \times P_{t-3}}{10}$$

Sum of Weights

Where:
P_t = Price at time t
WMA_t = Weighted moving average at time t
n = Number of days used to compute moving average

Channel-Normalization Operator (Stochastics): CN

The channel-normalization operator (CN) removes the trend in a time series, thus clarifying short-term fluctuations around the trend. Channel normalization detrends the time series by measuring its current position within a moving channel. The channel is defined by the maximum and minimum values of the time series over a specified look-back span. In this way it is similar to the channel breakout operator discussed earlier.

The channel normalized version of a time series is scaled to the range 0 to 100. When the raw time series is at its maximum value within the look-back span, CN assumes the value of 100. When the series is at the minimum value within the look-back span the CN is equal to zero. A value of 50 indicates the series is currently midway between its maximum and minimum values.

The calculation of CN is illustrated in the following equation:

Channel Normalization Operator

$$CN_t = \left(\frac{S_t - S_{min-n}}{S_{max-n} - S_{min-n}} \right) 100$$

Where:
CN_t = n day channel normalized value on day t
S_t = Value of time series at time t
S_{min-n} = Minimum value of time series, last n days
S_{max-n} = Maximum value of time series, last n days
n = Channel look-back span in days

An example of the calculation is illustrated in Figure 8.6.
In terms of its filtering properties, the CN operator functions as a high-pass filter. In contrast to the moving average, a low-pass filter, CN expresses the short-period (high-frequency) oscillations in its output while filtering out the long-period fluctuations or trend. This is illustrated in Figure 8.7. Note that the input series has a distinct upward trend, but the output series has no trend.

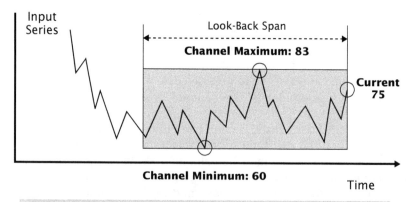

Channel Normalized Value = (75 – 60)/(83–60) = 0.65

FIGURE 8.6 Channel normalization.

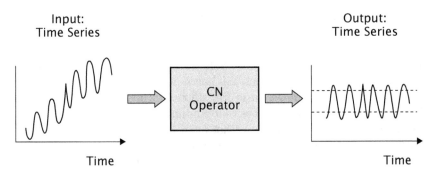

FIGURE 8.7 Channel normalization operator: a high-pass filter.

The CN operator has been known in TA at least as far back as 1965 when Heiby[17] used it to formulate divergence rules. He measured divergences by comparing the channel normalized value of the S&P 500 with the channel normalized value of a market breadth indicator. According to Heiby, a divergence occurred when one series was in the upper quartile of its 50-day range (CN > 74) while the other series was in the lower quartile of its range (CN <26). Sometime in the early 1970s, a virtually identical operator was described by George Lane,[18] who dubbed it *stochastic*. Unfortunately, the name is a misnomer. In reality, *stochastic* is a mathematical term that refers to the evolution of a random variable through time. There is nothing random about the CN operator, which is a completely deterministic data transformation. This text uses the term channel normalization (CN) rather than Lane's term, because it accurately describes what the operator does. Most TA writings continue use the term *stochastics*. The case study utilizes the CN operator for two types of rules: (1) extremes and transitions and (2) divergences. They are discussed in following sections.

Indicator Scripting

As discussed earlier, the time series that are used as inputs to the rules may either be in raw form, just as they comes from the market, or in the form of indicators—times series that have been created by applying one or more mathematical, logical, or time-series operators to one or more raw time series. The specification of an indicator may require the application of several operators. For example, the raw time series might first be smoothed with a moving average and then channel normalization is applied to the smoothed version. When the creation of an indicator involves multiple steps, it is convenient to express it in terms of an *indicator scripting language* (ISL). An ISL expression succinctly depicts the set of transformations used to create the indicator from raw time series.

My first exposure to an ISL was *Gener*, which was developed in 1983 for Raden Research Group by friend and colleague Professor John Wolberg. Today, ISLs are common. All rule back-testing platforms,[19] such as TradeStation, Wealth-Lab, Neuro-Shell, Financial Data Calculator, and so forth have an ISL. Though each ISL has features unique to it, they share similar syntaxes. The most basic ISL statement is a time-series operator followed by a set of parentheses that contain the arguments of the operator. The arguments are the items that must be defined for the operator to do its thing. Operators differ in terms of the number of arguments required. For example, the moving-average operator requires two arguments: a data series to which the operator will be applied and the number of periods in the look-back span. Thus a moving-average indicator would be specified by a statement such as this:

Moving Average Indicator = MA (input series, *N*)

Where:
MA is the moving average operator
N is the number of days in the moving average.

The general form of an indicator expression in scripting language is:

Indicator = Operator (Argument$_1$, Argument$_2$, . . . , Argument$_i$)

Where:
i is the number of arguments required by the operator.

Figure 8.8 shows the ISL syntax for the operators defined thus far: channel breakout, moving average, and channel normalization.

A key benefit of ISL is the ability to define complex indicators by nesting operators. In nesting, the output of one operator becomes an argument for a second operator and so on. For example, if one wanted to define an indicator that is the 60-day channel normalization of another time series that is a 10-day moving average of the Dow Jones Transportation Index, the expression for the indicator in ISL would look something like this:

Indicator = CN [MA(DJTA, 10), 60]

Channel-Breakout Operator (CBO)

Number of Arguments = 2:

Indicator = CBO (Time Series, n)

Moving-Average Operator (MA) or Linear Weighted MA (LMA)

Number of Arguments = 2:

Indicator = MA or LMA (Time Series, n)

Channel-Normalization Operator (CN)

Number of Arguments = 2:

Indicator = CN (Time Series, n)

FIGURE 8.8 Indicator scripting language for three TA operators.

INPUT SERIES TO RULES: RAW TIME SERIES AND INDICATORS

This section describes the 24 raw time series used in the case study as well as the 39 time series that were ultimately used as rule inputs. Ten of the 39 inputs were in the form of raw unprocessed time series: S&P 500 closing price, Dow Jones Transportations Index closing price, NASDAQ Composite Index closing price, and so forth. The additional rule 29 inputs were indicators derived from one or more raw time series.

Raw Time Series

The 24 raw time series used in the case study came from two sources: Ultra Financial Systems[20] and Market Timing Reports.[21] They are shown in Table 8.1.

Indicators

Twenty-nine of the 39 rule inputs were indicators derived by transforming one or more raw time series with various mathematical, logical, and

TABLE 8.1   Raw Time Series

Number	Raw Data Series	Abbreviation	Source
1	S&P 500 Daily Close	SPX	Ultra 8
2	S&P 500 Open	SPO	Ultra 8
3	DJIA High	DJH	Ultra 8
4	DJIA Low	DJL	Ultra 8
5	DJIA Close	DJC	Ultra 8
6	S&P Industrials	SPIA	Market Timing Reports
7	Dow Jones Transports	DJTA	Market Timing Reports
8	Dow Jones Utilities	DJUA	Market Timing Reports
9	NYSE Financial Index	NYFA	Market Timing Reports
10	Dow Jones 20 Bonds	DJB	Ultra 8
11	NASDAQ Composite Close	OTC	Ultra 8
12	Value Line Geometric Close	VL	Ultra 8
13	NYSE Advancing Issues	ADV	Ultra 8
14	NYSE Declining Issues	DEC	Ultra 8
15	NYSE Unchanged Issues	UNC	Ultra 8
16	NYSE New 52-Week Highs	NH	Ultra 8
17	NYSE New 52-Week Lows	NL	Ultra 8
18	NYSE Total Volume	TVOL	Ultra 8
19	NYSE Upside Volume	UVOL	Ultra 8
20	NYSE Downside Volume	DVOL	Ultra 8
21	3-Month T-Bill Yields	T3M	Market Timing Reports
22	10-Year T-Bond Yields	T10Y	Market Timing Reports
23	AAA Bond Yields	AAA	Market Timing Reports
24	BAA Bond Yields	BAA	Market Timing Reports

time-series operators. This section describes the transformations used to produce these indicators.

The indicators are presented in four categories: (1) price and volume functions, (2) market-breadth indicators, (3) prices-of-debt instruments, and (4) interest-rate-spread indicators.

Price & Volume Functions.   Fifteen (15) indicators were functions that combine price and volume information. A number of studies have shown that trading volume contains useful information both on its own and when used in conjunction with price.[22] Technical analysis practitioners have suggested a number of price and volume functions: on-balance volume, accumulation distribution volume, money flow, negative volume, and positive volume. Each of these functions is described below.

The price-volume functions were used to create two types of indicators: (1) cumulative sums and (2) moving averages. An indicator defined as a cumulative sum is the algebraic sum of all prior daily values of the price-volume function. The daily value of a price-volume function can either be a positive or negative quantity. Thus, an indicator defined as the cumulative sum of the on-balance volume, at a given point in time, is equal to the sum of all prior values of the daily on-balance-volume quantity. An indicator defined as a cumulative sum will display long-term trends similar to those observed in the levels of asset prices and interest rates. In other words, these indicators are nonstationary time series.

In contrast, a moving average of a price-volume function will be a stationary time series. In other words, it will not display trends. This is explained by the fact that a moving average only considers the observations within the look-back span. Since price and volume functions can assume both positive or negative values, a moving average will tend to remain within a relatively confined range near zero. See Figure 8.9.

FIGURE 8.9 Cumulative sum versus moving average of price-volume functions.

Cumulative On-Balance Volume.   Perhaps the first invented price & volume function was the cumulative on-balance-volume indicator, which is attributed to Joseph Granville and Woods and Vignolia.[23] It is a cumulative sum of signed (+ or –) total market volume. The algebraic sign of the volume for any given day is determined by the sign of the change in a market index for the current day, week, or whatever time interval is being used. The case study used daily market changes in the S&P 500 to determine the appropriate sign for the volume. If the price of the index rose on a given day, that day's entire NYSE volume was assigned a positive value and the number of shares traded was added to the prior cumulative sum. On days when the price declined, the NYSE volume was assigned a negative value and added to the prior cumulative sum (i.e., subtracted).

The computation for the cumulative on-balance volume is shown in the following equation:[24]

Cumulative On-Balance Volume (COBV)

$$COBV_t = COBV_{t-1} + (f_t V_t)$$

$$f_t = 1.0 \qquad \text{if } Pc_t > Pc_{t-1}$$
$$f_t = -1.0 \qquad \text{if } Pc_t < Pc_{t-1}$$
$$f_t = 0 \qquad \text{if } Pc_t = Pc_{t-1}$$

Where:
$OBV_t = (f_t V_t)$ = On-Balance Volume for day t
$COBV_t$ = Cumulative On-Balance Volume for day t
V_t = NYSE volume for day t
Pc_t = Closing price S&P 500 for day t

Moving Averages of On-Balance Volume.   In addition to the cumulative on-balance volume, two moving averages of daily on-balance volume were considered: for 10 and 30 days (OBV10, OBV30). In ISL they would be:

$$OBV10=MA(OBV,10)$$
$$OBV30=MA(OBV,30)$$

where OBV represents the on-balance volume for a given day.

Cumulative Accumulation-Distribution Volume (CADV). Another price-volume function, *accumulation distribution volume*, is attributed to Marc Chaiken.[25] However, there are several similar functions including: *Intra-day Intensity* developed by David Bostian and *Variable Accumulation Distribution* developed by Larry Williams. These transformations attempt to overcome a perceived limitation in on-balance volume, which treats the entire day's volume as positive (negative) even if the market index had a miniscule positive (negative) price change. It was felt that minor price changes should not be treated the same as large price changes. The proposed modifications to on-balance volume sought to ameliorate on-balance volume's all-or-none approach.

Chaiken proposed that a day's price activity could be more accurately characterized by quantifying the position of the closing price within the high-low range. Specifically, his calculation takes the difference between the closing price and the midpoint of the daily range and divides the difference by the size of the range. The assumption is that, when the market closes above the midpoint of its daily range, bullish or accumulation activity dominated the day's trading activity (accumulation) and should predict higher prices. Conversely when the market closes below the midpoint of its daily range, the day is said to be dominated by bearish or distribution activity and should predict lower prices. Only if the index closed at the low of the day or the high of the day is the entire day's volume assigned a negative (distribution) or positive (accumulation) value. More typically, the close is somewhere within the day's range resulting in some fraction of the volume being assigned to accumulation (positive volume) or to distribution (negative volume). The range factor, which is defined below, quantifies the position of the closing price within the day's range. The range factor is multiplied by the daily volume, and this figure is accumulated to produce the cumulative sum. The calculation is shown in the following equation.[26]

Cumulative Accumulation/Distribution Volume

$$CADV_t = CADV_{t-1} + (V_t \times Rf_t)$$

$$\text{Range Factor } (Rf_t) = \frac{(Pc_t - Pl_t) - (Ph_t - Pc_t)}{(Ph_t - Pl_t)}$$

Where:
$ADV_t = V_t \times Rf_t$ = Accumulation/Distribution Volume for day t
$CADV_t$ = Cumulative Accumulation/Distribution Volume for day t
V_t = NYSE volume for day t
Rf_t = Range factor for day t
Pc_t = Closing price Dow Jones Industrials for day t
Pl_t = Low price Dow Jones Industrials for day t
Ph_t = High price Dow Jones Industrials for day t

The case study used data for Dow Jones Industrials for the calculation of the accumulation-distribution function rather than the S&P 500 because daily high and low prices were not available for it. I assumed that the closing position of the Dow Industrials within its range would be similar to the closing position of the S&P 500 within its range.

Moving Averages of Accumulation Distribution Volume. Moving averages of daily accumulation/distribution values were constructed for 10- and 30-day periods. In ISL they are:

ADV10=MA(ADV,10)
ADV30=MA(ADV,30)

Cumulative Money Flow (CMF). Cumulative money flow (CMF) is similar to CADV with the exception that the product of volume and range factor is further multiplied by the price level in dollars of the S&P 500 Index. This is intended to measure the monetary value of the volume. The price level used is an average of the daily high, low, and closing prices. The computation is shown in the following equation:[27]

Cumulative Money Flow

$$CMF_t = CMF_{t-1} + (V_t \times Ap_t \times Rf_t)$$

$$\text{Range Factor } (Rf_t) = \frac{(Pc_t - Pl_t) - (Ph_t - Pc_t)}{(Ph_t - Pl_t)}$$

Where:

$MF_t = (V_t \times Ap_t \times Rf_t)$ = Money Flow for day t
CMF_t = Cumulative Money Flow for day t
Ap_t = Average price S&P 500 for day t: (Hi + Lo + Close)/3
V_t = NYSE volume for day t
Rf_t = Range Factor for day t
Pc_t = Closing price Dow Jones Industrials for day t
Pl_t = Low price Dow Jones Industrials for day t
Ph_t = High price Dow Jones Industrials for day t

Moving Averages of Money Flow. Moving averages of money flow were constructed for 10- and 30-day periods. In ISL they are:

MF10=MA(MF,10)
MF30=MA(MF,30)

Cumulative Negative Volume Index (CNV). Cumulative negative volume is an accumulation of price changes on days of lower trading volume. In other words, it is a continuous algebraic sum of daily percentage changes in a stock market index on days when volume is less than the prior day. When volume is equal to or greater than a prior day, the CNV remains unchanged.

The inventor of CNV is unclear. Several sources attribute it to Norman Fosback[28] but several sources, including Fosback, attribute the idea to Paul Dysart.[29] However, it seems clear that it was Fosback who developed objective signal rules for CNV and evaluated their predictive power.[30]

The notion of negative volume is based on the conjecture that "trading by unsophisticated investors occurs predominately on days of exuberantly rising volume, whereas informed buying and selling (i.e., smart-money activity) usually occurs during quieter periods of declining volume. Therefore, the direction that the market assumes on days of negative volume purportedly reflects accumulation (buying) or distribution (selling) of stock by those who are in the know."[31]

The computation of the index is as shown in the following equation:

Cumulative Negative Volume Index (CNV)

$$CNV_t = CNV_{t-1} + f_t$$

$$f_t = [(Pc_t/Pc_{t-1})-1] \times 100 \quad \text{if } V_t < V_{t-1}$$

$$f_t = 0 \quad\quad\quad\quad\quad\quad\quad\quad \text{if } V_t > \text{ or } = V_{t-1}$$

Where:

$NV_t = f_t$ = Negative Volume Index for day t

CNV_t = Cumulative Negative Volume Index for day t

V_t = NYSE volume for day t

Pc_t = Closing price S&P 500 for day t

Moving Averages of Negative Volume Index.   Moving averages of the daily value of negative volume index (i.e., index's percentage change on lower volume days) were constructed for 10- and 30-day periods. In ISL:

NV10=MA(NV,10)
NV30=MA(NV,30)

Cumulative Positive Volume Index (CPV).   Cumulative positive volume (CPV) is the opposite of CNV. It is an algebraic accumulation of market index changes for days when volume is greater than the prior day. Positive volume index is variously attributed to Fosback[32] and to Dysart. The calculation is presented in the equation that follows. It seems as if Dysart proposed the positive volume index and suggested ways of interpreting it in a subjective manner, whereas Fosback defined objective rules and formally tested them:

Cumulative Positive Volume Index (CPV)

$$CPV_t = CPV_{t-1} + f_t$$

$$f_t = [(Pc_t/Pc_{t-1})-1] \times 100 \quad \text{if } V_t > V_{t-1}$$

$$f_t = 0 \qquad\qquad\qquad \text{if } V_t < \text{ or } = V_{t-1}$$

Where:
$PV_t = f_t$ = Positive Volume Index for day t
CPV_t = Cumulative Positive Volume Index for day t
V_t = NYSE volume for day t
Pc_t = Closing price S&P 500 for day t

Moving Averages of Positive Volume. Moving averages of daily values of the positive volume index were constructed for 10- and 30-day periods (PV10 and PV30). In ISL:

$$PV10 = MA(PV, 10)$$
$$PV30 = MA(PV, 30)$$

Market Breadth Indicators. *Market breadth* refers to the spread or difference between the number of stocks advancing and the number declining on a given day, week, or other defined time interval. Breadth has been measured in a variety of ways, and they are reviewed in a scholarly study by Harlow.[33] For purposes of the case study, breadth is defined as the daily advance-decline ratio; that is, it is the difference between a day's advancing and declining issues divided by the total number of issues traded. The data is based on all issues traded on the NYSE rather than an alternative version that is restricted to NYSE common stocks. The series restricted to common stocks, which some have claimed is superior because it excludes closed-end stock and bond funds and preferred stocks, was not available in computer-readable form for the time period required.

The case study's breadth indicators are of two forms: cumulative sums of daily figures and moving averages of daily figures. For reasons previously explained, the breadth indicators that are cumulative sums display long-term trends, whereas moving-average breadth indicators tend to have reasonably stable mean values and fluctuation ranges.

Cumulative Advance-Decline Ratio (CADR). The cumulative advance decline ratio or CADR is a cumulative sum of the daily advance-decline ratio:

$$CADR_t = CADR_{t-1} + ADR_t$$

$$ADR_t = \frac{adv_t - dec_t}{adv_t + dec_t + unch_t}$$

Where:
$CADR_t$ = Cumulative Advance/Decline Ratio for day t
ADR_t = Advance/Decline Ratio for day t
adv_t = NYSE advancing issues for day t
dec_t = NYSE declining issues for day t
$unch_t$ = NYSE unchanged issues for day t

Moving Averages of Advance-Decline Ratio. Moving averages of daily advance-decline ratio (ADR) were constructed for 10- and 30-day periods (ADR10 and ADR30). In ISL they are:

$$ADR10=MA(ADR,10)$$
$$ADR30=MA(ADR,30)$$

Cumulative Net Volume Ratio (CNVR). Another measure of market breadth is the net volume ratio. It is based on the difference between daily upside and downside volume. Upside (downside) volume is the total number of shares traded in stocks that closed up (down) for the day. The innovation of calculating and analyzing upside and downside volume separately is attributed to Lyman M. Lowry in 1938.[34] The daily net volume ratio, a quantity that can assume either positive or negative values, is the difference between upside and downside volume divided by total trading volume. The case study used statistics released daily by the New York

Stock Exchange. The cumulative net volume ratio (CNVR) is the cumulative sum of daily ratios:

Cumulative Net Volume Ratio (CNVR)

$$CNVR_t = CNVR_{t-1} + NVR_t$$

$$NVR_t = \frac{upvol_t - dnvol_t}{upvol_t + dnvol_t + unchvol_t}$$

Where:
$CNVR_t$ = Cumulative Net Volume Ratio for day t
NVR_t = Net Volume Ratio for day t
$upvol_t$ = NYSE advancing volume for day t
$dnvol_t$ = NYSE declining volume for day t
$unchvol_t$ = NYSE unchanged volume for day t

Moving Averages of Net Volume Ratio.   Moving averages of the daily net volume ratio were constructed for 10- and 30-day periods (NVR10 and NVR30). In ISL:

$$NVR10=MA(NVR,10)$$
$$NVR30=MA(NVR,30)$$

Cumulative New Highs-Lows Ratio (CHLR).   A third measure of breadth, the cumulative new highs and new lows ratio (CHLR), takes a longer-term view. In contrast to CADR and CNVR, which are based on daily price changes and daily volumes, CHLR is based on a stock's current price relative to its maximum and minimum price over the preceding year. Specifically, CHLR is the cumulative sum of the daily new highs-new lows ratio (HLR), a quantity that can assume positive or negative values. The high-low ratio is defined as the difference between the number of stocks making new 52-week highs on the day and the number of stocks making new 52-week lows on the same day divided by the total number of issues traded that day. This figure is accumulated algebraically to obtain CHLR.

There is nothing particularly significant about using a look-back interval of 52 weeks. It is simply the mostly widely available statistic for new high and new low data. Prior to 1978, the number of issues making highs and lows was not based on a consistent 52-week look-back span. From the middle of March in any given year, the data were based only on the current calendar year. Prior to the middle of March, the figures were based on the current and prior years. Thus, over the course of a given year, the look-back span used to determine if a stock was making a new low or a new high varied from 2.5 months in mid-March to as long as 14.5 months just before mid-March. Most of the data used in this study was post-1978.

Despite the distortions created by the variable look-back span, rule tests based on pre-1978 high-low data suggested that the indicator's information content was robust to this distortion. For example, Fosback developed and tested an indicator called the high-low logic index over the period 1944 to 1980. His results showed that indicator demonstrated predictive power over the entire period even though the bulk of the data was infected with the variable look-back span distortion.[35] The formula for constructing the CHLR series is shown here:[36]

Cumulative New Highs New Lows (CHLR)

$$CHLR_t = CHLR_{t-1} + HLR_t$$

$$HLR_t = \frac{nuhi_t - nulo_t}{adv_t + dec_t + unch_t}$$

Where:
$CNHL_t$ = Cumulative New Highs New Lows on day t
HLR_t = New Highs New Lows on day t
$nuhi_t$ = NYSE new 52-week highs day t
$nulo_t$ = NYSE new 52-week lows day t
adv_t = NYSE advancing issues for day t
dec_t = NYSE declining issues for day t
$unch_t$ = NYSE unchanged issues for day t

Moving Averages of New Highs/New Lows Ratio (HLR1 and HLR30).   Moving averages of the daily high/low ratio were constructed for 10- and 30-day periods (HLR10 and HLR30). In ISL they are:

HLR10=MA(HLR,10)
HLR30=MA(HLR,30)

Prices-of-Debt Instruments from Interest Rates.   Typically, interest rates and stock price levels move inversely. However, by taking the reciprocal (1/interest rate) interest rates can be transformed into price-like time series that are, in general, positively correlated with stock prices. This reciprocal series can be multiplied by a scaling factor such as 100. Thus, a rate of 6.05 percent would be equivalent to a price of 15.38 (1/6.05 × 100).

This transformation was used in the case study and was performed on four interest rate series: three-month treasury bills, 10-year treasury bonds, Moody's AAA corporate bonds, and Moody's BAA corporate bonds.

Interest Rate Spreads. An interest-rate spread is the difference between two comparable interest rates. Two types of interest-rate spreads were constructed for the case study; the *duration* spread and the *quality* spread. The duration spread, also known as the *slope of the yield curve*, is the difference between yields on debt instruments having the same credit quality but having different durations (i.e., time to maturity). The duration spread used in the case study was defined as the yield on the 10-year treasury note minus the yield on the three-month treasury bills (10-year yield minus 3-month yield). The spread was defined in this way rather than 3-month minus 10-year so that an upward trend in the spread would presumably have bullish implications for the stock market (S&P 500).[37]

A quality spread measures the difference in yield between instruments with similar durations but with different credit qualities (default risk). The quality spread for the case study was based on two of Moody's[38] long-term corporate bond series: AAA,[39] which are the highest rated corporate debt, and BAA,[40] a lower rated grade of corporate debt. The quality spread is defined here as AAA yield –BAA yield. When rates on lower quality debt (higher default risk such as BAA rated bonds) are falling faster than rates on higher quality debt such as AAA rated bonds, it is interpreted as indication that investors are more willing to assume additional risk to earn the higher yields on lower quality debt. In other words, a rising trend in the quality spread is a signal that investors are willing to take higher risks to earn higher returns. By this reasoning, the quality spread should trend in the same direction as stocks.

TABLE OF 40 INPUT SERIES USED IN CASE STUDY

Table 8.2 lists all of the data series used as rule inputs in the case study.

TABLE 8.2   Input Series Used in the Case Study

Number	Description	Abbreviation	Form
1	S&P 500 Close	SPX	Raw
2	S&P 500 Open	SPO	Raw
3	S&P Industrials Close	SPIA	Raw
4	Dow Jones Transportation Index	DJTA	Raw
5	Dow Jones Utility Index	DJUA	Raw
6	NYSE Financial Index	NYFA	Raw
7	NASDAQ Composite	OTC	Raw
8	Value Line Geometric Close	VL	Raw
9	Cumulative On-Balance Volume	COBV	Indicator
10	On-Balance Volume 10-Day MA	OBV10	Indicator
11	On-Balance Volume 30-Day MA	OBV30	Indicator
12	Cumulative Accum. Distr. Volume	CADV	Indicator
13	Accum. Distr. Volume 10-Day MA	ADV10	Indicator
14	Accum. Distr. Volume 30-Day MA	ADV30	Indicator
15	Cumulative Money Flow	CMF	Indicator
16	Money Flow 10-Day MA	MF10	Indicator
17	Money Flow 30-Day MA	MF30	Indicator
18	Cumulative Negative Volume Index	CNV	Indicator
19	Negative Volume Index 10-Day MA	NV10	Indicator
20	Negative Volume Index 30-Day MA	NV30	Indicator
21	Cumulative Positive Volume Index	CPV	Indicator
22	Positive Volume Index 10-Day MA	PV10	Indicator
23	Positive Volume Index 30-Day MA	PV30	Indicator
24	Cum. Advance Decline Ratio	CADR	Indicator
25	Advance Decline Ratio 10-Day MA	ADR10	Indicator
26	Advance Decline Ratio 30-Day MA	ADR30	Indicator
27	Cum. Up Down Volume Ratio	CUDR	Indicator
28	Up Down Volume Ratio 10-Day MA	UDR10	Indicator
29	Up Down Volume Ratio 30-Day MA	UDR30	Indicator
30	Cum. New Highs/New Lows Ratio	CHLR	Indicator
31	New Highs/New Lows Ratio 10-Day MA	HLR10	Indicator
32	New Highs/New Lows Ratio 30-Day MA	HLR30	Indicator
33	NYSE Volume	TVOL	Raw
34	Dow Jones 20 Bond Index	DJB	Raw
35	Price 3-Month T-Bill	PT3M	Indicator
36	Price 10-Year Treasury Bond	PT10Y	Indicator
37	Price AAA Corporate Bonds	PAAA	Indicator
38	Price BAA Corporate Bonds	PBAA	Indicator
39	Duration Spread (10 Year –3 Month)	DURSPD	Indicator
40	Quality Spread (BAA–AAA)	QUALSPD	Indicator

THE RULES

The rules tested in the case study can be grouped into three categories, each representing a different theme of technical analysis: (1) trends, (2) extremes and transitions, and (3) divergence. The following sections describe the rules in each category.

Trend Rules

The first category of rules is based on trends. A foundational principle of TA is that prices and yields move in trends that can be identified in a sufficiently timely manner to generate profits. Practitioners have developed a variety of objective indicators to define the direction of the current trend and signal trend reversals. Among the most widely used are moving averages, moving-average bands, channel breakout, and Alexander filters also known as zigzag filters. These are described in Kaufman[41] and there is no need to cover them all here.

The trend rules in the case study used the channel breakout operator or CBO to define trends in the input time series. Thus, the CBO operator transformed the input time series into a binary valued time series consisting of +1 and –1. When the trend of the input series was in an uptrend, as determined by the CBO, the rule's output was +1. Conversely, when the analyzed series was determined to be in a downtrend, the output was –1.

The identification of trend reversals in the input series by CBO is subject to lag. All trend indicators necessarily incur lag—a delay between the time the input series experiences a trend reversal and the time the operator is able to detect it. Lag can be reduced by making the indicator more sensitive. For example, in the case of CBO, lag can be reduced by decreasing the number of periods in the look-back span. However, this fix creates a different problem—an increased number of false signals. In other words, there is a tradeoff between a trend-following indicator's lag and its accuracy. Therefore, all trend indicators attempt to strike a reasonable balance between signal accuracy and signal timeliness. Finding the optimum is a challenge in the design of any signaling system, be it a household smoke detector or a TA trend rule. In the end, optimal is whatever maximizes the indicator's performance, such as average return, risk-adjusted rate of return, and so forth. Since the behavior of financial market time series changes over time, the optimal look-back span for the CBO operator would change as well. Adaptive versions of CBO were not used in the case study.

Of the 40 input series depicted in Table 8.2, 39 were used as inputs for the trend rules. The open price of the S&P 500, input series 2 in Table 8.2, was excluded on grounds of being redundant of the S&P 500 close.

Each trend rule was defined by two parameters or arguments: the CBO look-back span and a time series chosen from the set of 39 candidates shown in Table 8.2. A set of 11 values were tested as look-back spans. They were 3, 5, 8, 12, 18, 27, 41, 61, 91, 137, and 205 days. The values were chosen to be separated by a multiplier of approximately 1.5. For example, the look-back span of 205 days is approximately 1.5 times 137 days. This resulted in a total of 858 trend rules, 429 (39 × 11) based on a traditional TA interpretation, and an additional 429 inverse-trend rules.

A traditional version of a trend rule produced an output value of +1 (long position in the S&P 500) when the input time series was determined to be in an upward trend by CBO operator, and an output value of −1 (short position in the S&P 500) when the time series was in downtrend according to CBO operator. Inverse trend rules simply produced the opposite signals (e.g., short S&P 500 when the analyzed series was determined to be in an uptrend).

In Chapter 9, where test results are reported, the following shorthand naming convention will be used for the traditional and inverse trend rules. A naming convention was necessitated by the large number of rules. The syntax of the naming convention is as follows (note this syntax is different from the syntax used for indicator scripting):

Rule (TT or TI) – Input Series Number – Look-back Span

Where TT stands for a traditional trend rule

and

TI stands for an inverse trend rule

For example, the rule named TT-15-137, is a traditional trend rule applied to input series 15 (Cumulative Money Flow) using a look-back span of 137 says. A rule named TI-40-41 is an inverse trend rule applied to input series 40 (the quality spread BAA– AAA) using a look-back span of 41 days.

Extreme Values and Transitions

The second category of rules considered in the case study is "Extreme Values and Transitions" or E rules. This category is based on the notion that a time series conveys information when it assumes an extreme high or low value or as it makes the transition between extremes. High and low extremes can be defined in terms of fixed value thresholds if the time series has a relatively stable mean and fluctuation range (i.e., is stationary). All input series used for E rules were made stationary by applying the CN operator.

Thirty-nine of the 40 input series were used for the E-type rules. The open price of the S&P 500 was excluded on grounds of redundancy. The input series used for E rules were first smoothed with a four-day linearly weighted moving average (LMA) before applying the CN operator. The smoothing was done to reduce the number of signals that would have resulted from an unsmoothed version of the input series wiggling above and below the signal threshold. Though smoothing may have been inappropriate for series that were already smoothed, for example the 30-day moving average of negative volume, all series were treated with the LMA on grounds of consistency.

In ISL, the expression for the input time series used for E rules is given by the expression:

=CN (LMA (Input Series, 4), *N*-days)

Where:

CN is the channel normalization operator
LMA is a linearly weighted moving-average operator

This sequence of transformations is illustrated in Figure 8.10.

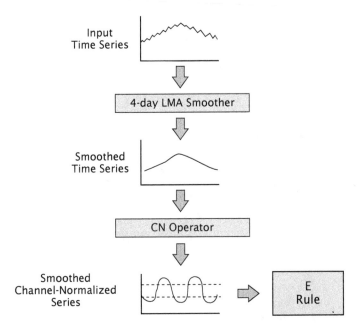

FIGURE 8.10 Smoothed channel normalized series.

E-rule signals were generated when the channel normalized smoothed series crossed a threshold. Given that there are two thresholds, an upper and lower, and given that there are two directions in which a crossing can occur (up or down) there are four possible threshold-crossing events:

1. Lower threshold is crossed in the downward direction.
2. Lower threshold is crossed in the upward direction.
3. Upper threshold is crossed in the upward direction.
4. Upper threshold is crossed in the downward direction.

These events are illustrated in Figure 8.11.

Each E rule was defined in terms of two threshold-crossing events: one specifying the long entry/short exit and the other specifying the short entry/long exit. This scheme yields 12 possible E-rule types. They are listed in Table 8.3. Because they cover all possibilities, there would be no point in including inverse versions. Note that type 7 is an inversion of Type 1, Type 8 is an inversion of Type 2, and so on.

The 12 E-rule types are illustrated in Figures 8.12 to 8.23.

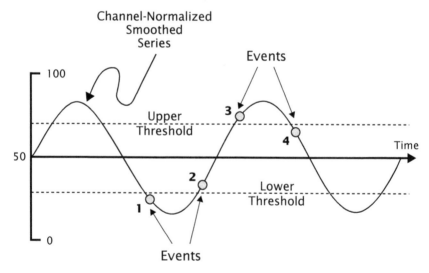

FIGURE 8.11 Threshold crossing events.

TABLE 8.3 The 12 E-Rule Types Defined in Terms of Threshold Crossing Events

E-Rule Types	Long Entry/Short Exit	Short Entry/Long Exit
1	Event 1	Event 2
2	Event 1	Event 3
3	Event 1	Event 4
4	Event 2	Event 3
5	Event 2	Event 4
6	Event 3	Event 4
7	Event 2	Event 1
8	Event 3	Event 1
9	Event 4	Event 1
10	Event 3	Event 2
11	Event 4	Event 2
12	Event 4	Event 3

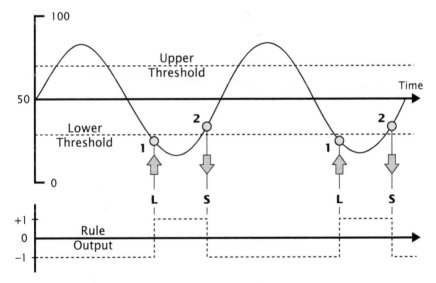

FIGURE 8.12 Extreme value and transition rule: Type 1.

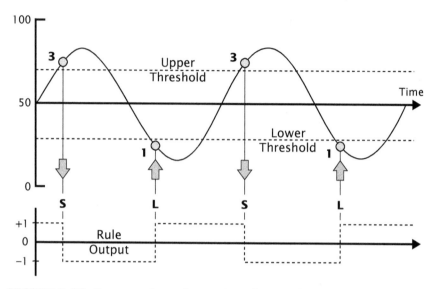

FIGURE 8.13   Extreme value and transition rule: Type 2.

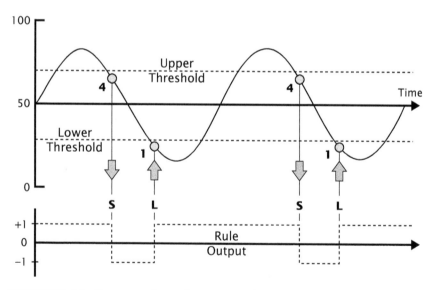

FIGURE 8.14   Extreme value and transition rule: Type 3.

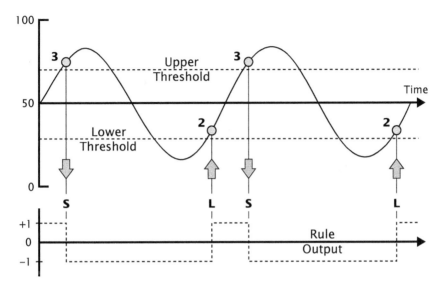

FIGURE 8.15 Extreme value and transition rule: Type 4.

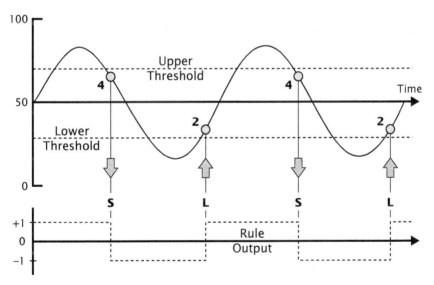

FIGURE 8.16 Extreme value and transition rule: Type 5.

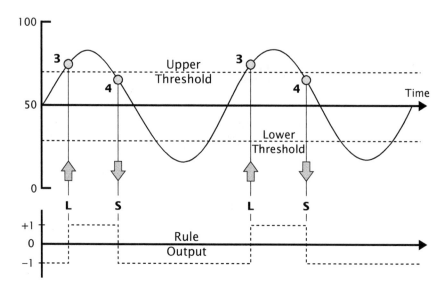

FIGURE 8.17   Extreme value and transition rule: Type 6.

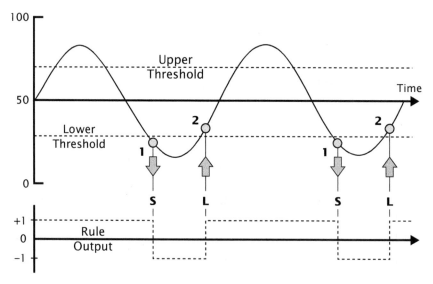

FIGURE 8.18   Extreme value and transition rule: Type 7.

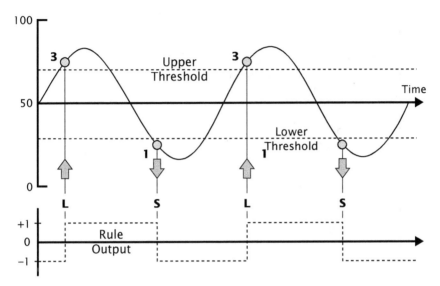

FIGURE 8.19 Extreme value and transition rule: Type 8.

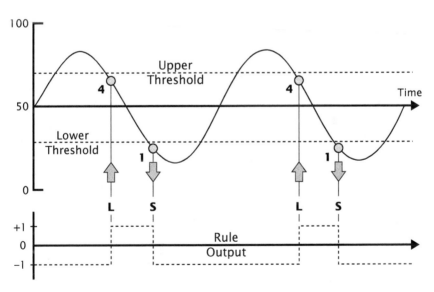

FIGURE 8.20 Extreme value and transition rule: Type 9.

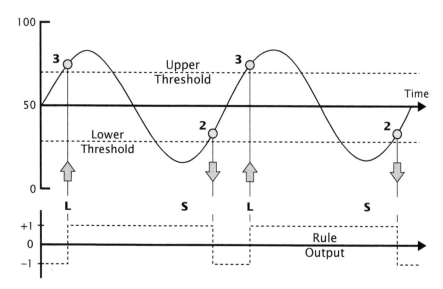

FIGURE 8.21   Extreme value and transition rule: Type 10.

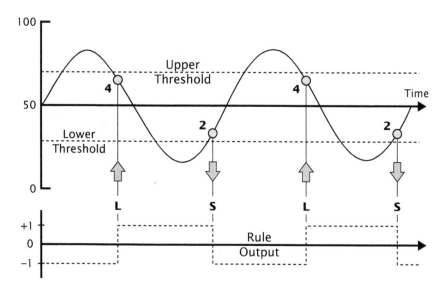

FIGURE 8.22   Extreme value and transition rule: Type 11.

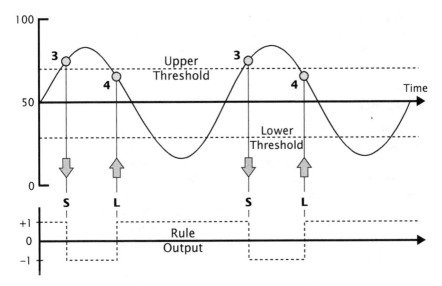

FIGURE 8.23 Extreme value and transition rule: Type 12.

Parameter Sets and Total Number of E Rules. An E rule is defined by four parameters: type (1 through 12), input series, displacement of the thresholds form 50, and look-back span for the channel normalization. Because both the upper and lower thresholds are displaced equally from the midvalue of 50, it is possible to specify them with a single number, their displacement from 50. For example, a threshold-displacement 10 places the upper threshold at 60 (50 + 10) and the lower threshold at 40 (50 – 10). Two different values for the threshold displacement parameter were tested: 10 and 20. The displacement value of 20 gave the upper threshold as 70 and the lower threshold as 30. Three different values were considered for the channel normalization look-back span: 15, 30, and 60. All parameter values were chosen without optimization on the basis of intuition.

Given 12 possible rule types, 39 possible candidate input series, 2 possible threshold displacements, and 3 possible channel normalization look-back spans, there were 2,808 E-type rules ($12 \times 39 \times 2 \times 3$).

Naming Convention for Extreme Value and Transition Rules. In Chapter 9, the following naming convention will be used to report results for E rules:

(E)-(type)-(Input Series)-(Threshold Displacement)-(Channel Normalization Look-Back Span)

For example, E-4-30-20-60 would be: E rule, type 4, input series 30 (cumulative new highs/new lows ratio), a threshold displacement of 20 (upper = 70, lower = 30), and a channel normalization look-back span of 60 days.

Divergence Rules

Divergence analysis is a foundational concept of TA that concerns the relationship between a pair of time series. It is premised on the notion that, under normal circumstances, certain pairs of market time series tend to move up and down together, and when they fail to do so it conveys information. A divergence is said to occur when one member of the pair departs from their shared trend. Typically, a divergence manifests itself as follows: both series have been trending in the same direction, but then one series reverses its prior trend while its companion continues its prior trend. This event, according to divergence analysis, is a potential signal that the prior shared trend has weakened and may be about to reverse. This is illustrated in Figure 8.24. Hussman contends that divergence signals are most informative when numerous time series are analyzed and a significant number begin to diverge.[42]

The Dow theory is based on divergence analysis. It asserts that when an index of industrial stocks and an index of transportation

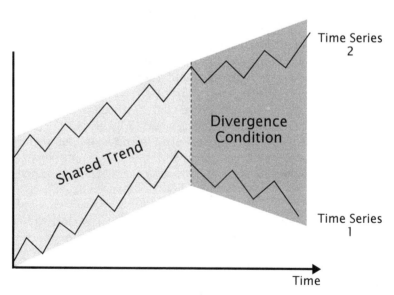

FIGURE 8.24 Divergence analysis.

stocks are trending in the same direction, the trend they share is healthy and likely to persist. However, if one series begins to diverge, it is taken as preliminary evidence that the trend is weakening and may reverse. Another application of divergence analysis considers the price of an instrument as one time series and its rate of change or momentum as the second series. Price/momentum divergence analysis is discussed by Pring.[43]

A divergence leads to one of two outcomes: either the series, for which the trend had remained undisturbed, will experience a reversal to join its diverging companion or the diverging series will end its errant ways and rejoin its companion. A completed signal of reversal is not presumed until both series have convincingly reversed and are again moving in the same direction. Thus, the fundamental idea behind divergence analysis is coherence, that is, the state of affairs when two waveforms are in phase with each other (see Figure 8.25). When two series are coherent, their common trend is considered strong and expected to continue. However, when their trends become incoherent, or out of phase, the future of the once shared trend is in question. Therefore, candidates for divergence analysis are pairs of time series that are generally coherent, but when they do diverge, one particular member of the pair tends to have leading information about the other. In other words, there is a rather stable lead–lag relationship.

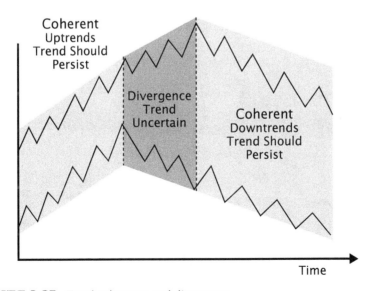

FIGURE 8.25   Trend coherence and divergence.

Subjective Divergence Analysis. Subjective divergence analysis typically involves comparing the peaks and troughs of the two time series under consideration. A negative or bearish divergence is said to occur if one series continues to register peaks at successively higher levels while the other series begins forming peaks at lower levels. The failure by the second series to form peaks at successively higher levels is also termed a bearish nonconfirmation. This is illustrated in Figure 8.26.

A *positive* or *bullish divergence* is said to occur when one series continues to register successively lower troughs in an established downtrend while the second series begins to form troughs at higher levels. This is also termed a *bullish nonconfirmation*. See Figure 8.27.

The problem with subjective divergence analysis, or any subjective method for that matter, is that it the procedure is neither repeatable nor testable. One issue requiring the analyst's subjective judgment is the timing of peaks and troughs. Because the two time series may not peak and trough at precisely the same time, it may be unclear which peaks and troughs should be compared. Another issue is related to duration: How long must the divergence be in existence before deciding that one has occurred? Still a third unresolved issue is how much upward (downward)

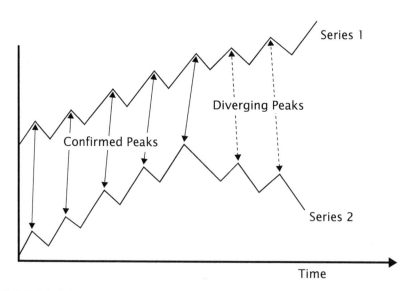

FIGURE 8.26   Negative divergence (peaks compared).

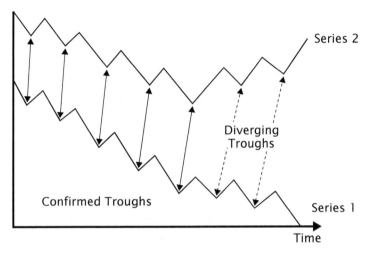

FIGURE 8.27 Positive (bullish) divergence: troughs compared.

movement in a series is required to establish that a new trough (peak) has formed.

An Objective Measure of Divergence. These problems can be addressed with objective divergence analysis. A method that objectifies peak and trough comparisons is discussed by Kaufman[44] and he provides computer code. Kaufman also discusses a second method that uses linear regression to estimate the slopes in the two time series being compared. A divergence is defined as the differences in their slopes. Both methods look interesting but no performance statistics are offered.

The divergence rules considered in this case study were inspired by the objective divergence method discussed by Heiby[45] in his book, *Stock Market Profits through Dynamic Synthesis*. The two series being examined by Heiby were first detrended with channel normalization. He defined a divergence to be in effect if one series had a channel-normalized value of 75 or greater while the other series had a value of 25 or less. Thus, divergence was quantified in terms of the difference in channel-normalized values.

This suggested an initial formulation for a divergence indicator that is defined in the equation that follows. Note that one series is always the S&P 500, the target market of the case study. The companion series, for example the Dow Jones Transports, is the series with which the S&P 500 is compared. The case study compared the S&P 500 to all the time series in Table 8.2, except the S&P 500 open price, which was excluded on grounds of redundancy with the S&P 500 close.

Divergence Indicator
(Initial Formulation)

$$= CN \, (\text{Companion Series, } n) - CN \, (\text{S\&P 500, } n)$$

Where:
CN = Channel normalization operator
n = Look-back span of the channel normalization

Because the channel normalized value of each series can vary between 0 and 100, this divergence indicator has a potential range of -100 to $+100$. For example, if the companion series is at the bottom of its channel range ($CN = 0$) and the S&P 500 is at the top of its range ($CN = 100$), the divergence indicator would have a value of -100. It should be noted that this quantification of divergence is merely one approach among several possibilities that may prove superior.

Limitations of the Proposed Divergence Indicator. The proposed divergence indicator measures the degree to which two times series have similar positions within their respective channels. In general, this will give a reasonable quantification of the degree to which the series are in phase with one another. For example, when the indicator registers a value of zero, it indicates that there is no divergence; both series have the same channel normalized values and can be presumed to be trending together. However, there can be cases for which a value of zero does not indicate that the two series are in phase. For example, if two time series are negatively correlated, that is to say, they tend to move inversely with respect to each other within their channels, the divergence indicator will assume a value of zero as the series-normalized values cross paths. In this instance, a value of zero would be an erroneous indication that the two series are trending together. This is illustrated in Figure 8.28 and is clearly a limitation of the proposed divergence indicator.

This problem could have been avoided with a more complex formulation of divergence indicator based on cointegration,[46] a concept developed in the field of econometrics. Cointegration was proposed in 1987 by Engle and Granger.[47] This more sophisticated and potentially more

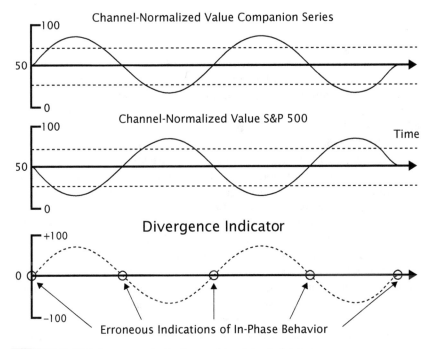

FIGURE 8.28 Erroneous indications of in-phase behavior.

accurate way of measuring divergences uses regression analysis to determine if a linear relationship exists between two time series. Because this method can easily accommodate the case in which the pair of series are strongly negatively correlated (180 degrees out of phase), it solves the problem discussed earlier that can occur with a divergence indicator based on channel normalization. An additional advantage of cointegration analysis is that it first applies a statistical test[48] to determine if the two series have related trends (i.e., that they are cointegrated). If the test shows that they are cointegrated, a stationary divergence indicator[49] naturally falls out of the analysis. In cointegration terminology, this indicator is referred to as the *error-correction model*. It measures the degree to which one series has diverged from the typical linear relationship between the two series.

In most applications of cointegration, the error-correction model is used to predict the behavior of the spread between the cointegrated time series. In these applications, the divergence is predicted to revert back to the normal state of a shared trend when the error-correction model becomes extremely positive or negative. In other words, when the error, which is a departure from the normal linear relationship between the two series, becomes extreme, it is predicted to correct back to its normal value of zero.

A typical application of this analysis is *pairs trading*. For example, if it has been determined that Ford and GM stocks are cointegrated time series and Ford has gotten high relative to GM, a short position would be taken in Ford against a long position in GM. Thus, no matter how the divergence is corrected (Ford falls, GM rises, or some combination) the pairs trade will generate a profit.

Fosback[50] made an innovative use of cointegration analysis to develop a stock market predictor. His innovation was to use the measurement derived from the error correction model as an indicator to predict the movement of a third variable, the S&P 500, rather than predict the behavior of the spread between the cointegrated variables. The indicator, called the *Fosback Index*, exploits the fact that interest rates and mutual fund cash levels are cointegrated time series. Fosback's work is particularly noteworthy because it preceded the Engle and Granger publication on cointegration by over a decade. The Fosback Index signals when the mutual fund cash level diverges significantly from a level predicted by its linear relationship with short-term interest rates. The premise is that when mutual fund managers are excessively pessimistic about stock market prospects, they hold cash reserves that are substantially higher than the that predicted by interest rates. Excessive optimism is the opposite situation. Fosback found that both excessive pessimism and excessive optimism, measured in this fashion, correlated with future returns on the stock market. In effect, the Fosback Index removes the influence of short-term interest rates from mutual fund cash levels, thus providing a purer measure of fund manager sentiment than that provided by the raw cash level, which is contaminated by interest rates.

In the interests of simplicity, the cointegration technique was not used for the divergence indicators in the case study. It was assumed that if a companion series was not related to the S&P 500, it would be revealed by the poor financial performance of the divergence rule. However, I[51] believe that the cointegration methodology warrants further investigation in development of indicators.

Need for Double Channel Normalization. A second problem with the initially proposed version of the divergence indicator was more serious and had to be remedied. The divergence rules in the case study involved pairing the S&P 500 with 38 other time series. Given that these series had varying degrees of co-movement with the S&P 500, the fluctuation range of the divergence indicator would vary considerably from one pair to the next. This would make it impractical to use the same threshold for all pairings. This problem is illustrated in Figure 8.29. Note that the high threshold displacement that would be suitable for a companion se-

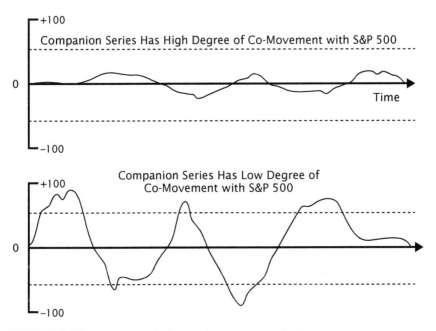

FIGURE 8.29 Divergence indicator: inconsistent volatility.

ries with a low degree of co-movement with the S&P 500 would never produce a signal for a companion series with a high degree of co-movement to the S&P 500. For this reason, the initial formulation of the divergence indicator was deemed impractical.

This problem was addressed with a modified formulation of the divergence indicator illustrated in the equation that follows. It employs the channel normalization operator twice. That is to say, the indicator is a channel-normalized version of the initial divergence indicator.

Divergence Indicator
(Double Channel Normalization)

$$= CN\{CN\,(\text{Series 1}, n) - CN\,(\text{S\&P 500}, n),\,10n\}$$

Where:
CN = Channel normalization operator
Series 1 = Companion series
n = Look-back span of the first channel normalization

The second layer of channel normalization takes into account the fluctuation range of the initial formulation of the divergence indicator. This solves the problem of inconsistent fluctuation ranges across the 38 pairs of time series. As a result, the modified version of the divergence indicator will have roughly the same fluctuation range irrespective of the particular pair of time series being used, making it practical to use uniform thresholds.

The look-back span for the second level of channel normalization was set at 10 times the look-back interval used for first level. Thus, if the channel normalization used a look-back span of 60 days, the second layer of channel normalization used a look-back span of 600 days. It was assumed that a 10-fold look-back span would be sufficient to establish the fluctuation range of the basic divergence indicator. Note that a modified divergence indicator has a potential fluctuation range of 0 to 100, similar to any channel-normalized variable. See Figure 8.30.

Divergence Rule Types.   Upper and lower threshold were applied to the modified divergence indicator to generate signals. A positive or bullish divergence was in effect when the divergence indicator was above its upper threshold. This occurred when the companion series was moving up more or moving down less than the S&P 500. This was evidenced by the companion series having a higher relative position within its channel than the S&P 500. Conversely, a negative or bearish divergence existed when the divergence indicator was below the lower threshold. This occurred when the companion series was moving down more or moving up less than the S&P 500, resulting in its having a lower relative position within its channel than the S&P 500. This is illustrated in Figure 8.30.

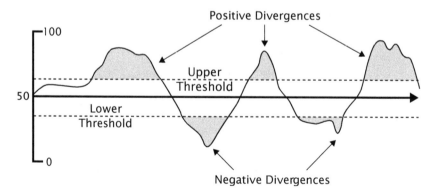

FIGURE 8.30 Modified divergence indicator.

The question was how to create signaling rules from the modified divergence indicator. Two rules seemed obvious: a bullish divergence rule, which would call for long positions in the S&P 500 when the divergence indicator was above the upper threshold, and a bearish divergence rule, which would call for short positions in the S&P 500 when the divergence indicator was below its lower threshold.

Both rules assumed that the companion series had leading information about the S&P 500. If the companion series was stronger than the S&P 500 (positive divergence), then a long position would be justified, whereas if the companion series was weak (negative divergence) a short position would be justified. However, this assumption may be incorrect. It may be the case that negative divergences are predictive of higher prices for the S&P 500, whereas positive divergences are predictive of lower prices. In other words, perhaps it is the S&P 500 that has the leading information. This suggests that inverse versions of each rule should be tried. In the end, it was determined that there are 12 possible divergence rule types, and all were tested.

These 12 rule types are exactly the same set used for the extreme value and transition rules. This makes sense because the modified divergence indicator is similar to the indicator used for the E rules because it has a fluctuation range of 0 to 100 and has two thresholds.

The 12 divergence rule types, presented in Table 8.4, include the basic bullish divergence (type 6), the bearish divergence (type 7) and their inversions (types 12 and 1). The 12 types are not illustrated because the illustrations would be redundant of those presented in the section on Extreme and Transition Rules.

Parameter Combinations and Naming Convention for Divergence Rules. Each divergence rule is defined by four parameters: type, companion series, threshold displacement, and channel normalization look-back span. There are 12 types of the divergence rules (see Table 8.4), 38 companion data series, 2 threshold displacement values—10 and 20, and 3 look-back spans—15, 30, and 60 days. This gives a total of 2,736 divergence rules ($12 \times 38 \times 2 \times 3$)

The naming convention used for reporting results of divergence or D rules in Chapter 9 is as follows: (D)-type-companion series-threshold displacement-channel normalization look back span. Thus, a rule is named

D-3-23-10-30

Divergence rule, type 3, companion series 23 (positive volume index 30-day moving average), threshold displacement = 10 (upper

TABLE 8.4 Divergence Rules and Associated Threshold Events

Divergence Rule Types	Long Entry/Short Exit	Short Entry/Long Exit
1	Down Cross Lower Threshold Down Cross	Upper Cross Lower Threshold Upper Cross
2	Lower Threshold Down Cross	Upper Threshold Down Cross
3	Lower Threshold Up Cross	Upper Threshold Up Cross
4	Lower Threshold Up Cross	Upper Threshold Down Cross
5	Lower Threshold Up Cross	Upper Threshold Down Cross
6	Upper Threshold Up Cross	Upper Threshold Down Cross
7	Lower Threshold Up Cross	Lower Threshold Down Cross
8	Upper Threshold Down Cross	Lower Threshold Down Cross
9	Upper Threshold Up Cross	Lower Threshold Up Cross
10	Upper Threshold Down Cross	Lower Threshold Up Cross
11	Upper Threshold Down Cross	Lower Threshold Up Cross
12	Upper Threshold	Upper Threshold

threshold = 60, lower threshold = 40), 30-day channel normalization look-back span.

This completes the description of the rules tested in the case study. Results are presented in Chapter 9.

CHAPTER 9

Case Study Results and the Future of TA

PRESENTATION OF RESULTS

The primary objective of the case study was to demonstrate the application of two statistical inference methods suitable for the evaluation of rules discovered by data mining. As explained in Chapter 6, traditional significance tests are not suitable because they do not take into account the biasing effect of data mining. The two methods used were White's reality check (WRC) and the Monte Carlo permutation (MCP).

A secondary objective of the case study was the possible discovery of rules with statistically significant returns when applied to the S&P 500 Index. Toward this end, a set of 6,402 rules described in Chapter 8 were back tested and evaluated.

With respect to the primary objective, the case study resoundingly demonstrated the importance of using significance tests designed to cope with data-mining bias. With respect to the second objective, no rules with statistically significant returns were found. Specifically, none of the 6,402 rules had a back-tested mean return that was high enough to warrant a rejection of the null hypothesis, at a significance level of 0.05. In other words, the evidence was insufficient to reject a presumption that none of the rules had predictive power.

The rule with the best performance, E-12-28-10-30,[1] generated a mean annualized return of 10.25 percent, on detrended market data. In Figure 9.1, the rule's return is compared to the sampling distribution produced by WRC. The p-value of the return is 0.8164, far above the 0.05 level set as the significance threshold. Figure 9.1 makes it clear that the performance of

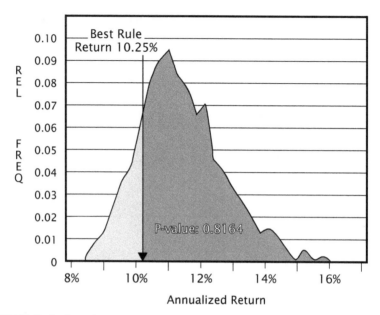

FIGURE 9.1 Sampling distribution for best of 6,402 worthless rules using White's reality check.

the best rule out of the 6,402 examined falls well within the range of ordinary sampling variability. In fact, it even falls below the sampling distribution's central value of 11 percent. Quite disappointing![2]

The sampling distribution was generated by 1,999 replications of the bootstrap procedure. Had a larger number of replications been used, the distribution's shape would have been smoother, but the conclusion would have been the same: the rule's performance was not high enough to reject the null hypothesis.

Figure 9.2 shows E-12-28-10-30 plotted on the sampling distribution produced by MCP. It produced a similar p-value of 0.8194.

Note that both sampling distributions are centered at approximately an 11 percent mean return. This particular value was a consequence of the specifics of the case study; the particular set of 6,402 rules, their return correlations, the number of observations used to compute their mean returns, and the particular set of S&P data. In other words, the expected return for the best rule of 6,402 competing rules with no predictive power under these specific conditions is approximately 11 percent. It is not 0 percent.

To recap a point made in Chapter 6, the sampling distribution for the mean return of the best-performing rule out of N rules (e.g., $N = 6,402$) is

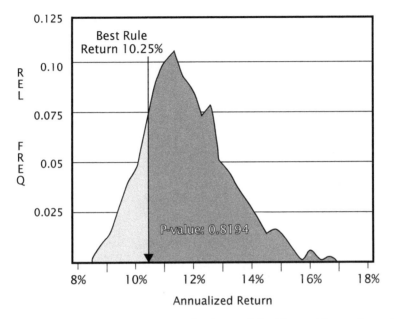

FIGURE 9.2 Sampling distribution for best of 6,402 worthless rules using Monte Carlo permutation.

not centered at zero. Rather, it is situated at a more positive value that reflects the sampling distribution for a statistic defined as the *maximum mean of N means.*

Figures 9.1 and 9.2 give an indication of what rate of return would have been required to be statistically significant. Returns in excess of 15 percent would have been significant at the .05. Returns in excess of 17 percent would have been highly significant (p-value < .001).

Ironically, the failure of any rule to generate statistically significant returns, after adjustment for data-mining bias, underscores the huge importance of using statistical inference methods that take the biasing effects of data mining into consideration. Had I used an ordinary significance test, which pays no attention to data-mining bias, the mean return of the best rule would have appeared to be highly significant (a p-value of 0.0005). This is dramatically illustrated in Figure 9.3. It shows the bootstrapped sampling distribution appropriate for a single rule back test (data-mining bias ignored). In contrast to the previous two Figures 9.1 and 9.2, the sampling distribution in Figure 9.3 is centered at zero. The arrow represents the mean return of the best rule E-12-28-10-30.

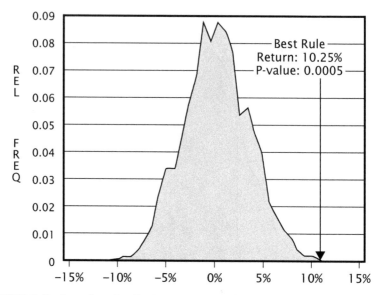

FIGURE 9.3 Sampling distribution appropriate for a single rule back test.

Had a conventional test of significance been used, about 320 of the 6,402 rules would have appeared to be significant at the 0.05 level. This is exactly what would be predicted to occur by chance. The naive data miner using a conventional test of significance would have concluded that many rules with predictive power had been discovered. In reality, mining operations conducted in this fashion would have produced nothing but fool's gold.

The full set of rule test results can be found on the web site www.evidencebasedta.com. The results for the 100 rules with the highest mean returns are presented in Table 9.1. The columns are: column 1—the rule's code according to the naming convention established in Chapter 8, column 2—the rule's mean return on detrended S&P data over the back-test period, columns 3 and 4—the single-rule p-values via bootstrap and Monte Carlo (note these p-values do not take account of the data-mining bias), columns 5, 6, and 7—significance at the 0.05 level, using three different inference methods in which data-mining bias is taken into account. Had any of the rules been significant, it would have been indicated by an asterisk. None were significant, hence there are no asterisks. Columns 8 and 9 are the lower and upper 80 percent confidence intervals.

TABLE 9.1 The Best Performing 100 Rules

Rule ID	Return	SR Boot p-value	SR MC p-value	B Sig	RC Sig	MC Sig	Lower 80% CI	Upper 80% CI
E-12-28-10-30	0.102501	0.0015	0.002				-0.02932	0.23527
D-8-4-10-60	0.102395	0.001	0.0015				-0.02943	0.23516
E-1-28-10-15	0.100562	0.0025	0.0005				-0.03126	0.23333
E-12-21-20-15	0.098838	0.0005	0.0015				-0.03299	0.23161
E-12-28-10-15	0.097502	0.001	0.0025				-0.03432	0.23027
E-12-24-20-15	0.095904	0.0005	0.001				-0.03592	0.22867
E-11-28-10-15	0.094635	0.003	0.002				-0.03719	0.2274
E-11-39-10-60	0.092282	0.001	0.0015				-0.03954	0.22505
D-7-37-10-30	0.092078	0.0025	0.003				-0.03975	0.22485
D-7-37-10-15	0.090196	0.0045	0.004				-0.04163	0.22296
TT-37-5	0.089024	0.0045	0.003				-0.0428	0.22179
TI-20-41	0.08862	0.0045	0.0045				-0.0432	0.22139
E-1-22-10-60	0.088591	0.0055	0.007				-0.04323	0.22136
TI-21-8	0.086963	0.0035	0.0075				-0.04486	0.21973
D-10-28-10-30	0.086939	0.004	0.0025				-0.04489	0.21971
D-11-28-10-15	0.085266	0.0055	0.0055				-0.04656	0.21804
D-7-38-10-30	0.085206	0.005	0.006				-0.04662	0.21798
TI-28-12	0.084912	0.0035	0.0035				-0.04691	0.21768
TI-24-8	0.084021	0.007	0.005				-0.0478	0.21679
E-2-28-10-15	0.083267	0.0075	0.0025				-0.04856	0.21604
E-5-36-10-30	0.083087	0.0055	0.0065				-0.04874	0.21586
D-9-34-10-30	0.081577	0.008	0.009				-0.05025	0.21435
E-11-15-20-60	0.08058	0.007	0.0075				-0.05124	0.21335
D-1-21-10-30	0.080499	0.008	0.008				-0.05132	0.21327
D-8-32-10-15	0.08048	0.006	0.0085				-0.05134	**0.21325**
D-7-36-10-30	0.079943	0.0065	0.0055				-0.05188	**0.21271**
D-8-27-10-30	0.079601	0.007	0.0085				-0.05222	**0.21237**
E-12-22-10-30	0.077796	0.009	0.008				-0.05403	**0.21057**
D-1-24-10-30	0.077582	0.01	0.0125				-0.05424	**0.21035**
D-7-36-20-30	0.077312	0.0095	0.0135				-0.05451	**0.21008**
D-8-33-20-15	0.077101	0.0095	0.0085				-0.05472	**0.20987**
E-1-19-10-60	0.077092	0.0075	0.0125				-0.05473	**0.20986**
D-8-32-20-15	0.076434	0.0105	0.009				-0.05539	**0.2092**
TI-8-18	0.076144	0.009	0.01				-0.05568	**0.20891**
TI-26-137	0.075767	0.009	0.0105				-0.05606	**0.20854**
TI-24-5	0.075732	0.008	0.009				-0.05609	**0.2085**
D-7-36-10-60	0.0755	0.0105	0.0105				-0.05632	**0.20827**
E-1-28-20-15	0.07541	0.013	0.0135				-0.05641	**0.20818**
E-6-38-20-30	0.074831	0.0085	0.0125				-0.05699	**0.2076**
E-12-24-10-15	0.074809	0.0115	0.0135				-0.05701	**0.20758**
TT-37-3	0.074756	0.0125	0.01				-0.05707	**0.20753**
TT-38-5	0.074579	0.0135	0.012				-0.05724	**0.20735**

(Continued)

445

TABLE 9.1 *(Continued)*

E-11-21-10-15	0.074168	0.0145	0.011			-0.05766	0.20694
D-9-4-10-60	0.07409	0.0125	0.0125			-0.05773	0.20686
E-1-25-10-60	0.073966	0.0155	0.01			-0.05786	0.20674
E-1-18-20-60	0.073439	0.015	0.0155			-0.05838	0.20621
E-11-25-10-15	0.073131	0.01	0.018			-0.05869	0.2059
D-10-32-20-15	0.072548	0.0205	0.0145			-0.05928	0.20532
E-5-38-10-30	0.07245	0.014	0.014			-0.05937	0.20522
D-11-28-10-30	0.07245	0.0185	0.013			-0.05937	0.20522
E-11-15-20-15	0.072363	0.012	0.018			-0.05946	0.20513
E-2-24-20-15	0.072286	0.018	0.011			-0.05954	0.20505
D-9-34-10-60	0.072065	0.012	0.016			-0.05976	0.20483
D-7-11-10-15	0.071859	0.0135	0.0115			-0.05996	0.20463
D-8-37-20-60	0.071562	0.0205	0.022			-0.06026	0.20433
E-2-21-10-15	0.071546	0.0175	0.015			-0.06028	0.20432
E-6-37-20-15	0.071509	0.016	0.0135			-0.06031	0.20428
TI-12-12	0.071403	0.0135	0.0095			-0.06042	0.20417
E-12-21-10-15	0.07114	0.016	0.0195			-0.06068	0.20391
TI-23-5	0.071013	0.0155	0.0115			-0.06081	0.20378
E-2-1-20-30	0.070897	0.016	0.013			-0.06093	0.20367
TT-36-5	0.070709	0.0235	0.017			-0.06112	0.20348
E-6-38-20-15	0.070681	0.017	0.021			-0.06114	0.20345
TI-21-12	0.070672	0.017	0.0105			-0.06115	0.20344
E-1-21-10-15	0.070672	0.02	0.016			-0.06115	0.20344
D-8-38-20-30	0.070308	0.02	0.0225			-0.06152	0.20308
D-10-4-10-60	0.070298	0.0145	0.016			-0.06153	0.20307
TI-32-61	0.070203	0.0215	0.0135			-0.06162	0.20297
E-2-19-10-60	0.070192	0.015	0.016			-0.06163	0.20296
TI-18-8	0.069985	0.019	0.0135			-0.06184	0.20275
TT-36-3	0.069962	0.0185	0.0195			-0.06186	0.20273
D-8-23-20-60	0.069884	0.0175	0.019			-0.06194	0.20265
D-7-16-10 -30	0.069749	0.013	0.0145			-0.06207	0.20252
D-7-34-10-60	0.069721	0.016	0.0235			-0.0621	0.20249
E-2-28-20-5	0.069572	0.017	0.02			-0.06225	0.20234
D-9-37-10-30	0.069551	0.0235	0.0195			-0.06227	0.20232
D-9-29-10-60	0.069538	0.013	0.0185			-0.06229	0.20231
D-9-36-20-30	0.069506	0.0225	0.018			-0.06232	0.20228
D-8-36-10-60	0.068993	0.018	0.022			-0.06283	0.20176
D-8-33-10-15	0.068802	0.025	0.023			-0.06302	0.20157
D-10-23-20-60	0.068752	0.0145	0.02			-0.06307	0.20152
D-7-37-20-30	0.068628	0.02	0.021			-0.0632	0.2014
E-2-1-10-30	0.068546	0.016	0.018			-0.06328	0.20132
D-8-31-10-30	0.06831	0.019	0.023			-0.06351	0.20108
D-9-32-10-15	0.068112	0.0175	0.022			-0.06371	0.20088
E-5-20-10-30	0.068035	0.0185	0.011			-0.06379	0.2008

TABLE 9.1 *(Continued)*

E-3-36-10-30	0.067922	0.0205	0.019			-0.0639	0.20069
TI-23-41	0.067856	0.0225	0.019			-0.06397	0.20063
E-2-9-10-15	0.067833	0.0185	0.0215			-0.06399	0.2006
E-7-36-20-60	0.067749	0.0255	0.0205			-0.06408	0.20052
TI-21-5	0.067723	0.022	0.0205			-0.0641	0.20049
E-6-38-10-30	0.067453	0.0225	0.024			-0.06437	0.20022
D-6-33-10-15	0.067088	0.023	0.022			-0.06474	0.19986
D-8-34-20-60	0.066988	0.025	0.023			-0.06484	0.19976
E-12-21-20-60	0.066859	0.0175	0.025			-0.06496	0.19963
E-1-18-10-60	0.066816	0.027	0.0235			-0.06501	0.19959
D-5-15-10-30	0.066604	0.024	0.017			-0.06522	0.19937

The three inference methods that take data-mining bias into account were used:

1. B (boot) is an improved version of WRC, which incorporates the enhancement suggested by Wolf and Romano[3] designed to improve the power of the test (reduce the chance of a type-II error) as discussed in Chapter 6.
2. RC (reality check) is the version of WRC that is currently available from Quantmetrics, which does not incorporate the Wolf and Romano enhancement.
3. MC is the Monte Carlo permutation method, developed by Masters, which incorporates the Wolf and Romano enhancement.

The upper and lower bounds of the 80 percent confidence intervals were derived on the basis of the mathematical theory first proposed by White,[4] using an algorithm that is described in Wolf and Romano. Dr. Tim Masters implemented the computer code for this. The confidence intervals presented take full account of the data-mining bias. That is to say, they are joint confidence intervals for which upper and lower bounds contain the true return of all rules, with a probability of 0.80. This means that if we were to redo the case study on 1,000 independent sets of data, an obvious impracticality given the existence of only one set of historical market data, in 800 of the tests the 6,402 confidence intervals would contain the expected returns for all rules.

It can also be said that, in 950 of these cases, we would not be fooled into an erroneous rejection of the null hypothesis, but in 50 we would. It so happens that in the particular experiment run for the case study, no rule showed up as significant. However, by setting the significance level to .05, the case study did in fact have a 1 in 20 chance of a type-1 error—that a rule with no actual predictive power would have displayed a p-value less than 0.05, thereby resulting in a false rejection of the null hypothesis.

CRITIQUE OF CASE STUDY

Positive Attributes

Use of Benchmarks in Rule Evaluation. One thing the case study did right was using a benchmark to evaluate rule performance. As pointed out in Chapter 1, the back-tested performance of a rule only makes sense in relation to a benchmark. Absolute levels of performance are uninformative.

The case study used the lowest reasonable benchmark, the performance of a rule with no predictive power. Under this standard, a rule is deemed effective if and only if it beats the performance of a nonpredictive rule by a statistically significant margin. Clearly, there are higher benchmarks that could make sense in specific cases. For example, suppose a claim is made that a superior version of the double moving average crossover rule has been developed. A sensible benchmark would be the performance of a conventional version of the rule.

Controlled for the Effect of Market Trends. As described in Chapter 1, the case study used detrended market data to compute rule returns to eliminate performance distortions. As explained, distortions result when a rule with a long- or short-position bias has its returns computed on market data that has a net upward or downward trend over the back-test period.

Controlled for Look-Ahead Bias. Rule studies that assume the availability of information that is not yet truly available at the time market positions are entered or exited are infected with look-ahead bias, also known as future information leakage. For example, if closing price information is needed to compute a rule's signals, it would not be legitimate to assume an entry or exit at the closing. The first legitimate price at which an entry or exit could legitimately be assumed is the next price. If the data is of a daily frequency, as was true for the case study, the first legitimate execution price does not occur until the market opens the day following the signal.

Look-ahead bias can also occur if a rule uses data series that are reported with a lag, such as mutual fund cash statistics, or that are subject to revisions, such as government economic statistics. When this is the case, lagged values must be used that take into account reporting delays or revisions.

The case study avoided look-ahead bias by assuming entries and exits on the open price of the day following a position-reversal signal. Moreover, none of data series used were subject to reporting lags or revisions.

Controlled for Data-Mining Bias. Few rule studies in popular TA apply significance tests of any sort. Thus, they do not address the possibility that rule profits may be due to ordinary sampling error. This is a serious omission, which is easily corrected by applying ordinary hypothesis tests.

However, ordinary tests of significance are only appropriate when only one rule has been back tested. When many rules have been tested and a best is selected, the ordinary hypothesis test will make the best rule appear more statistically significant than it really is (false rejection of the null hypothesis). Avoiding such type-I errors is the motivation for using advanced hypothesis tests such as WRC and Monte Carlo permutation method, as described in Chapter 6. The case study used such tests. As pointed out earlier, both WRC and MCPM revealed that the best-performing rule of the 6,402 tested was not statistically significant.

Controlled for Data-Snooping Bias. Data-snooping bias, which might be more properly named *prior-research-snooping bias*, occurs when data miners use the results of prior research to choose which rules to test. In other words, they use rules that have been previously found to be successful. This is an insidious problem because it is unknown how many rules were tested to find the successful rules. Because the number of rules tested is an important factor contributing to the magnitude of the data-mining bias it is impossible to evaluate the actual statistical significance of a rule that was included in a new data-mining venture because it had been successful in prior research efforts.

The case study mitigated the prior-research-snooping bias by not explicitly including any rules that were discovered by other researchers. Though many of the rules examined with the study's 6,402 rules were probably similar to those examined by other researchers, the similarity was coincidental. As explained in Chapter 8, the set of rules tested were arrived at by combinatorial enumeration of all rules possible within a set of specified parameter values. For example, trend rules were based on 11 possible values for the channel breakout look-back parameter and 39 possible time series. All 429 possible rules (11×39) were included in the case study. If one of these happened to be a rule discovered by some prior rule research, its inclusion was by happenstance and not a perusal of the prior research. Thus, the case study accounted for the full number of rules examined leading to the discovery of the best-performing rule.

Negative Attributes

Complex Rules Were Not Considered. Perhaps the biggest deficiency of the case study was the failure to consider complex rules. Complex rules result from combining and condensing, in some fashion, the information contained in a multiplicity of simple rules. This is a severe defect for several reasons. First, few TA practitioners, subjective or objective, restrict themselves to decisions based on one rule. In this sense, the case study did not replicate what subjective or objective analysts actually do. However, as commented on later in this chapter, subjective analysts are severely constrained in their ability to properly interpret the information pattern embodied in a multiple rule configuration.

Second, complex rules should produce superior performance on difficult prediction problems, such as financial markets. A nonlinear combination of simple rules allows the complex rule to be more informative than the summed information contained in its individual constituents. This allows the rule to comply with Ashby's Law of Requisite Variety,[5] which stipulates that a problem and its solution must have similar degrees of complexity. In the context of prediction, this implies that a model (rule) intended to predict the behavior of a complex system (e.g., a financial market) must also be complex. The general superiority of complex rules even of a linear form, was demonstrated in an analysis[6] of 39,832 rules, both simple and complex. This rule set was tested on four stock market indexes: Dow Jones, S&P 500, NASDAQ, and Russell 2000 over the period 1990 through 2002. Of the entire rule set, 3,180 or 8 percent were complex rules, but of the 229 rules that generated statistically significant profits, 188, or 82 percent, were complex rules. This study took account of the data-mining bias by using WRC to compute significance levels. Incidentally, the study showed that none of the rules produced statistically significant gains on either the Dow Jones Industrials or the S&P 500 Index.

The case study was restricted to simple rules to keep its scope manageable. However, I did so in the belief that at least a few of the 6,402 rules would prove significant. Clearly, I was overconfident.

Only Long/Short Reversal Rules Considered. Also in the interest of keeping the case study manageable, the rule set was restricted to one type of binary rule; long/short reversal. As discussed in Chapter 1, this restriction can distort the TA concept a rule is intended to express. This is an acknowledged limitation of binary rules in general and of long/short reversal rules in particular. The requirement that a rule always hold a market position, which is true of reversal rules, rests on the unlikely assumption that the market is in a perpetual state of inefficiency and continually presents profit opportunities. In contrast, rules that are more selective in identifying when market exposure is warranted are consistent with the more reasonable assumption that markets are occasionally inefficient. Therefore, tri-state rules, which would allow for long/short/neutral positions, or binary rules, which are long/neutral or short/neutral, may be superior. No such rules were examined by the case study.

Rules Limited to S&P 500 Trading. Also in the interest of limiting the scope of the case study, rules were applied to only one market, the S&P 500 Index. The large rule study[7] referred to earlier did not find any rules, either simple or complex, which were effective on the S&P 500. When I selected S&P 500 as the market to trade, I was unaware of the larger rule study, which did find useful rules for the NASDAQ and Russell 2000. Had I known of the study and decided to use either NASDAQ or Russell 2000 as the target market, I would have been guilty of snooping prior research, thereby compromising the validity of the p-values that were obtained in the case study. On the other hand, had I chosen the NASDAQ or Russell 2000 without knowledge of that study and found successful rules, they would have been discovered legitimately and the reported p-values would have been accurate.

POSSIBLE CASE STUDY EXTENSIONS

The aforementioned limitations suggest several possible extensions to the case study.

Application to Less Seasoned Stock Indexes

The Hsu and Kuan study referred to earlier that found statistically significant rules for the NASDAQ and Russell 2000 suggested that TA rules may be more successful on indexes of less seasoned stocks. Thus, one extension would be to apply the case study's rule set to stock market indexes of other countries with securities of less-seasoned companies. This would be practical if the raw data series needed to construct the indicators were available, such as advance/decline statistics, up and down volume, new highs and lows, and such. A literature search uncovered a number of studies[8] that lend credibility to the notion that newer stock markets may be more amenable to prediction than more developed and presumably more efficient markets. One practical limitation of

a newer stock market would be shorter market history and fewer historical observations.

Improved Indicator and Rule Specification

The profitability of a rule is determined by the information content of
the indicators on which the rule is based. The more effectively an indicator quantifies an informative feature of market behavior the higher
the rule's profit potential. The 6,402 rules used in the case study considered three TA themes: trends, extremes, and divergences. The indicators used were thought to be reasonable ways to quantify these themes.
No doubt there is room for improvement. As pointed out in a subsequent section, the most important future role of the TA practitioner will
be developing indicators that quantify market behavior in a more informative manner.

For example, as mentioned in Chapter 8, divergences might be better measured with indicators based on conintegration.[9] Indicators intended to measure extremes might prove more useful if they employed
the Fisher transform, discussed by Ehlers.[10] He points out that the frequency distribution of an indicator based on channel normalization has
an undesirable property, specifically, extreme values are considerably
more likely than values in the middle of the indicator's range. This is
hardly the behavior one would want in an indicator designed to detect
rare extremes. However, by applying the Fisher transform to channel-
normalized data, Ehlers claims that the resultant indicator is close to
normally distributed. An indicator with a normal distribution has the desirable characteristic that its extreme values are rare. This may, in turn,
make them more informative. Because Ehlers offers no data supporting
evidence of the Fisher transform's efficacy, at this time it is only an interesting conjecture worthy of further investigation.

Consideration of Complex Rules

Complex rules are derived by combining the information in two or more
simple rules in order to augment predictive power. There are two key issues in deriving complex rules: Which rules should be combined? and
How should they be combined? The *how* refers to the mathematical or
logical form used to combine the simple rules' outputs to produce the
complex rule's output.

The simplest method of combining is linear. A linear combination is
based on summing rule the outputs of simple rules. It treats the output of
each simple rule as if it makes an independent contribution to the output
of the complex rule. That is to say, the contribution of each simple rule is

unaffected by the output of any other rule. The simplest linear combination gives the same weight to each constituent. Thus, a simple linear combination of two binary reversal rules would assume a value of –2, when both are short; zero, when one is short and one is long; and +2 when both rules are long. A more sophisticated, though not necessarily superior, linear combination assigns varying weights to each rule, depending upon its predictive power. The relative weight of each rule is represented by a coefficient, designated by the letter a. The set of weights—which are best according to some figure of merit, such as minimum predictive error or maximum financial performance—can be found by optimization. The general form of a weighted linear combination is illustrated in the following equation:

Linear Combining Is Additive

$$Y = a_0 + a_1 r_1 + a_2 r_2 + \ldots + a_n r_n$$

Where:
Y is Output of complex linear rule
r_i is the output of ith rule
a_i is the weight for the ith rule
a_0 is a constant – y intercept

In contrast to a linear combination, a nonlinear combination considers interactions between the rules. In other words, the combined value, Y, is not simply a weighted sum of the individual rule values. In a nonlinear combination, the contribution of any individual rule to the combined output Y depends, in some way, on the output values of the other rules. In a linear combination, each rule's contribution to Y is unaffected by (independent of) the value of any other rule. The advantage of a nonlinear combination is that it can express more complex information patterns. This creates a disadvantage, however, in that a nonlinear combination may not be expressible as a neat easily understood equation. Because we are left in the dark about how the rule outputs are being combined (i.e., interacting), nonlinear models are sometimes referred to as black-box formulas. Nonlinear combinations produced by neural network software would be an example of a black-box formula.

The distinction between linear and nonlinear combining is more easily portrayed when one considers continuous variables rather than binary rule outputs. Continuous variables can assume any value within a range rather than being restricted to discrete values such as those of binary rule (–1 and +1). When a linear model is illustrated graphically, as in Figure 9.4, the response surface, which represents the complex rule's output (Y), assumes a flat shape. There are no hills and valleys. Another way to say this is that the slope of the response surface, with respect to each input (X_1 and X_2), remains constant throughout the entire range of the input. The slope of the surface with respect to input X_1 is designated by the coefficient a_1, and the slope with respect to input X_2 is given by coefficient a_2. The values a_1 and a_2 are typically discovered from a set of data by a statistical technique called regression analysis. The values a_1 and a_2 in combination with a third coefficient a_0, called the Y intercept, orient the plane so as to best slice through the set of data points used to estimate the model's coefficients. The fact that the slope of the response surface is constant (flat) tells us that there are no nonlinear interactions between the inputs. Said differently, the inputs X_1 and X_2 are interacting in an additive manner.

In a nonlinear model, nonadditive interactions between the inputs are allowed. This means that the value Y is not simply a weighted sum of the individual input values. In a nonlinear model, the contribution of any input (indicator) depends, in some arbitrary way, on the values of the other inputs. This manifests as a response surface with hills and valleys. In other words, the slope of the model's response surface with respect to any individual input, X_i, will not be constant throughout its range. This variation in the slope over the range of the inputs can produce a response surface like the one shown in Figure 9.5.

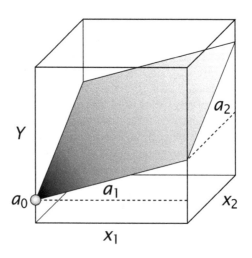

FIGURE 9.4 $Y = a_0 + a_1 x_1 + a_2 x_2$.

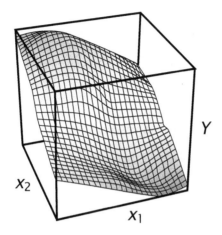

FIGURE 9.5 $Y = f(X_1, X_2)$.

Linear Combinations within a Theme. Despite the simplicity of combining rules via addition, complex rules with a linear form have proven useful. The study conducted by Hsu and Kuan[11] tried three methods for creating complex rules. Two of the methods were based on linear forms: voting rules and fractional position rules. The third type, which they referred to as a learning rule, did not combine rules, but rather was based on selecting the simple rule from a set of similar rules that had the best recent performance. The complex rules based on voting and fractional positions were essentially additive combinations of all simple rules within a given theme. Examples of themes would be all rules based on channel breakouts or all rules based on a moving average of on-balance volume. The output of a complex rule based on a voting scheme was derived by polling all rules within a theme (channel breakout) and taking a one-unit position that reflected the majority vote. For example, if the majority of rules were indicating a short position, a one-unit short position was taken. The output of a complex rule based on the fractional-position concept was also based on polling all the simple rules within a theme, however, the size of the position taken was proportional to the net percentage of rules that were long or short ([number long minus number short] divided by total number of rules). For example, Hsu and Kuan considered 2,040 on-balance volume rules. If 1,158 were signaling a short position and 882 were signaling a long position, a 0.135 unit short position would be taken ([882 − 1,158]/2,040 = −0.135).

Thus one logical extension of the case study would be to create linear complex rules based on voting or fractional-position schemes. This could be done for rules within a given theme, for example all divergence rules.

An indicator commonly used in TA, called a diffusion indicator, is based on a similar idea. An example of a well known diffusion indicator is the percentage of New York Stock Exchange stocks that are over their 200-day moving averages. In this instance the percentage is essentially an unweighted linear combination.

The diffusion indicator would simply be the net percentage of divergence rules that were long or short. Using a voting scheme, if more than 50 percent of the divergence indicators were in a +1 state, a long position would be held, else a short position. Using a fractional-position scheme, a partial long or short position would be held and adjusted as the net long/short percentage changed. It is important to note that the creation of diffusion indicators from the 6,402 rules used in the case study would require that inverse rules be eliminated. Their inclusion would cause a diffusion indicator to always assume a value of zero. Thus, a diffusion indicator based on the trend-rule category would be constructed only from TT rules and TI rules would be excluded. Likewise, a diffusion indicator based on rules in the extreme and transition category would be based only on types 1, 2, 3, 4, 5, and 6. Types 7 through 12 would have to be excluded inasmuch as they are the inverse of types 1 through 6.

Machine-Induced Nonlinear Combinations.   Complex rules that combine simple rules in a nonlinear or nonadditive fashion could also be derived from the case study's rules. However, this would require the use of autonomous machine learning (data-mining) systems such as neural networks,[12] decision trees and decision tree ensembles, multiple regression splines,[13] kernel regression,[14] polynomial networks,[15] genetic programming,[16] support-vector machines,[17] and so on. These systems employ inductive generalization to synthesize a complex nonlinear rule (model) by learning from a large set of historical examples. Each example is a a case, characterized by a set of indicator values as of a given date and the value of an outcome variable that the model is intended to predict.

Complex nonlinear rules could be derived in two ways. One would be to submit the rules in binary form, as the candidate inputs. A second approach would be to submit the indicators used by the rules.

To the best of my knowledge, there is no product currently available for generating complex nonlinear rules that incorporates a significance test that is robust to the data-mining-bias problem. In the absence of this protection, data miners searching for complex nonlinear rules must rely on the protection provided by a sophisticated form of out-of-sample testing that involves three data sets (training, testing, and evaluation). This is described later in this chapter.

Allowing the search to optimize a rule's complexity, rather than restricting it to finding the optimal parameter values for a rule whose complexity is fixed, has an upside and a downside. The upside is that allowing complexity optimization increases the chance of discovering a superior rule. The downside is that the added search dimension can greatly increase the number of rules considered before a best is selected. This increases the chance that the best-performing rule is overfitted. This refers to a rule that not only expresses the sample data's valid patterns but that also describes its random effects or noise. Overfitted rules do not generalize well. That is to say, their out-of-sample performance is typically poor relative to their in-sample performance. This is an example of data-mining bias.

To guard against the risk of overfitting when complexity optimization is allowed, three data segments are often used: *training, testing,* and *validation.* Recall from Chapter 6 that only two data segments are required when data mining is restricted to finding the optimal parameter values of a fixed-complexity[18] rule: training and testing.

In its search for the nonlinear rule of optimal complexity, machine learning algorithms cycle through the training and testing sets in two distinct loops. The inner loop searches for the optimal parameters at a given level of complexity. The outer loop searches for the optimal level of complexity. Once the best complex rule has been found, it is evaluated in the third data segment, called the *validation set.* This data has been held in reserve pending the discovery of the parameter values and complexity degree of the best-performing rule. Because the validation set was not utilized in this process of discovery, the performance of the best rule in this data set is an unbiased estimate of its future performance. This is shown in Figure 9.6.

This three-segment scheme can be conducted on a walk-forward basis. After the best rule has been found in the first data fold (train/ test/validation), the tripart data window slides forward and the entire process is repeated in the next fold. This is illustrated in Figure 9.7.

The motivation for the tripart data window warrants some additional explanation. Market behavior is presumed to be a combination of systematic behavior (recurring patterns) and random noise. It is always possible to improve the fit of a rule to a given segment of data by increasing its complexity. In other words, given enough complexity, it is always possible to fashion a rule that buys at every market low point and sells at every market high point. This is a bad idea.[19] Perfect timing on past data can only be the result of a rule that is contaminated with noise. In other words, perfect signals or anything approaching them almost certainly means the rule is, to a disturbing degree, a description of past random behavior (i.e., overfitted).

Overfitting manifests when the rule is applied to the test data segment. There, its performance will be worse than in the training data. This

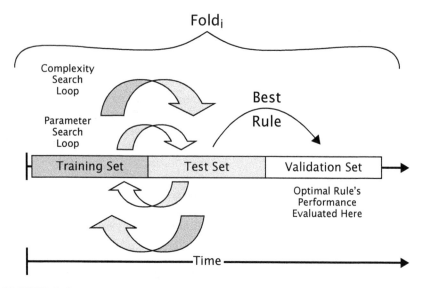

FIGURE 9.6   Searching for optimal parameters and complexity of best rule.

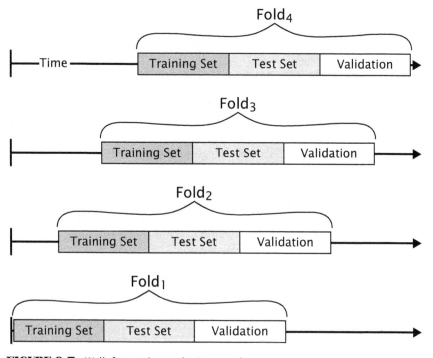

FIGURE 9.7   Walk-forward complexity search.

is because the legitimate patterns found in a training set recur in the test set, but the noise in the training set does not. It can be inferred that profitability in the training set that does not repeat in the testing set was most likely a consequence of overfitting.

During the process of complexity optimization, the first sign that the rule has become overfit is when its performance reaches a peak in the testing set and then starts to degrade. Complexity optimization proceeds as follows. It begins with a low complexity rule, which is run repeatedly over the training data set using different parameter values. Each run produces a performance figure (e.g., rate of return). The parameter(s) that yields the highest performance in the training data, let's call it *best-rule 1*, is then run on the test data set and its test set performance is noted. That completes the first complexity loop. The second complexity loop begins with a rule that is a notch higher in complexity than best-rule 1. That is to say, it has a greater number of parameters. Again, there is a search for the best parameter values of this more complex rule in the training set. The best rule at this complexity level, let's call it best-rule 2, will almost certainly perform better in the training set than best-rule 1 because of its additional complexity. Best-rule 2's performance is then measured in the test set. This process continues as a succession of rules of increasing complexity are mined from the training set and evaluated in the testing set. Typically, performance on the test improves as the rule's complexity is increased. The improvement is an indication that ever-more-intricate but valid patterns in the training set have been discovered. However, at a certain point in the rule's complexity growth, the performance in the testing set will start to decline. This indicates that the most recent increment in complexity has started to describe the random effects (nonrecurring noise) in the training set. In other words the rule has now become overfitted. Had the rule's complexity growth been stopped prior to this point, the rule would have failed to capture all the data's valid patterns. Such a rule is said to be underfitted. The phenomenon of underfitting and overfitting is illustrated in Figure 9.8. Note that increased complexity always produces improved performance in the training set, which is shown by the continual growth in training set performance. Also note that the boundary between underfitting and overfitting is defined by the point at which the test set performance peaks and begins to decline.

The concept of complexity search is abstract and may be new to some readers. In the interest of clarification, consider following the specific example of a human guided rather than a machine guided complexity optimization. We begin with a basic two moving-average crossover reversal rule.[20] The rule is defined by two parameters, the short-term moving-average look-back span and the long-term moving-average look-back span. Initially, all possible combinations of the parameters for the two averages

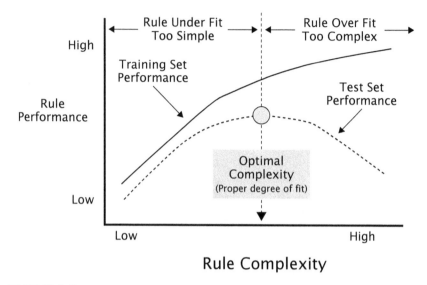

Rule Complexity

FIGURE 9.8   Optimizing rule complexity.

would be run on the training set. If each moving average were allowed 10 possible parameter values, a brute-force search would involve 100 tests.[21] The parameter combination with the highest performance in the training set (i.e., the best rule) would then be run on the test data set. Assume that the best rule earned a 30 percent annualized return in the training data and a 15 percent return in the test data. So far, this is nothing but ordinary parameter optimization, and because the test data has been used only one time, the 15 percent return is an unbiased estimate of the rule's future performance.

Now, suppose that we are not satisfied with a 15 percent annualized return, so we start to data mine a broader universe that includes complex rules that build on the simple two moving-average crossover rule.[22] We go back to the drawing board and propose a more complex rule by adding a rule based on an Wilder's Relative Strength Index (RSI), an indicator that measures the rate of price change. In this example, the addition of the RSI rule alters the original dual moving-average crossover rule from one that always reverses from long to short or short to long to a rule that can remain out of the market altogether. One way to do this would be to use the RSI indicator as a filter: If the RSI indicator is greater than a threshold, rsi_max, at the time of a sell signal by the basic dual-moving-average crossover rule, a neutral position would be taken instead of a short position. Conversely, and if the RSI were less than the threshold, rsi_min, at the time of a dual-moving-average buy signal, a neutral position instead of a long position would be taken. This more complex rule has four parameters that can be optimized: short moving-average span, long moving-average span, *rsi_max*, and *rsi_min*. A large number of parameter combinations are then run against the training data.

As expected, the increased complexity allows the four-parameter rule to earn a higher return in the training data. Suppose it makes 50 percent in the training data compared to 30 percent earned by its two-parameter predecessor. The increased performance in the training data was a predictable consequence of the increased complexity (additional parameters). We are, however, pleasantly surprised to learn that the four-parameter rule also does better in the testing set, earning 20 percent versus the 15 percent earned by the basic dual moving-average rule. When a more complex rule performs better in the test set, it is reasonable to assume that the additional complexity successfully exploited additional systematic aspects of market behavior.

Therefore, it's back to the drawing board again with another attempt to improve the rule performance with yet additional complexity. This involves new conditions with additional parameters. The new conditions might be other filters, or they could be alternative entry signals. At each increment in complexity, all the possible combinations of the parameter values are evaluated on the training set and the best performing combination is then run against the test set. The process of adding complexity is continued until performance in the test set begins to decline. This is the signal that the boundary between underfitting and overfitting has been crossed; the additional complexity has begun to fit the noise in the training data. The optimal rule is the rule of highest complexity that did the best performance in the test set.

What then is the purpose of the third data segment, the validation set? Thus far, it has not been touched. The astute reader will have realized that the performance attained by the optimal complexity rule in the test data set is positively biased. The repeated visits to the test set to find the rule of optimal complexity induced a positive bias—the data-mining bias. Hence, to obtain an unbiased estimate of the optimal complexity rule's expected performance in the future, we must go to the validation set. Because the validation set was not utilized in the search for optimal parameter values or optimal complexity, it remains untainted.

THE FUTURE OF TECHNICAL ANALYSIS

Technical analysis stands at a fork in the road. Its future depends on the path practitioners take. The traditional path continues the nonscientific subjectivist tradition of naive theories built on untestable propositions, anecdotal evidence, and intuitive analysis. The other path is the scientific approach, which I refer to as evidence-based technical analysis (EBTA). It is confined to testable methods and objective evidence, rigorously and skeptically examined with the appropriate tools of statistical inference. Thus, EBTA charts a course between foolish gullibility and relentless skepticism.

I now exercise literary license for literary effect and make the following unfalsifiable, forecast: *Technical analysis will be marginalized to the extent it does not modernize.* There are ample precedents in the history of science to substantiate this statement. Astrology, which gave birth to the science of astronomy, now languishes on the periphery while its offspring thrives as the mainstream discipline.

Will TA remain on its traditional unscientific path, thus fating it to be cast aside with other ancient practices, or will it adopt EBTA and remain vital and relevant? The historical precedents are not favorable. The history of science suggests that few practitioners who are committed to a given paradigm ever abandon it. This is consistent with evidence presented in Chapter 2, which established that beliefs are extremely resilient. Studies have shown that a belief can survive a complete discrediting of the evidence that originally gave rise to the belief. If TA were to remain on its traditional path, it would indeed be unfortunate. I believe that this will inevitably lead to TA relinquishing territory it originally staked to more rigorous disciplines, such as empirical and behavioral finance.

This is not to suggest that traditional TA will lose all its fans. There will always be consumers for the services of soothsayers and seers. Divining the future is, after all, the world's second oldest profession.[23] Some audience is assured because of a deep psychic need to reduce anxiety provoked by the uncertainty of the future. According to Scott Armstrong, an expert in forecasting theory, the brisk demand for the seers' services is most certainly not attributable to forecast accuracy. In his paper, "The Seer-Sucker Theory: The Value of Experts in Forecasting,"[24] Armstrong argues that people pay heavily for the experts' views, despite their lack of accuracy. What customers are really buying is an illusory reduction in uncertainty and an off-loading of responsibility onto the expert. Armstrong refers to these consumers as suckers because of the barrage of studies cited in his paper showing that experts' forecasts are minimally better than those of nonexperts. This lack of accuracy has been found to hold true across a range of disciplines, including financial predictions.

One seminal study cited by Armstrong is by Alfred Cowles,[25] who studied the track record of the market-guru of the early 1930s, Hamilton, the editor of the *Wall Street Journal*. Despite Hamilton's reputation among his readers, Cowles's study showed that, over the period 1902 to 1929, 50 percent of the guru's forecasts of directional change were wrong.

Cowles also reviewed the predictive performance of 20 insurance companies, 16 financial services, and 24 financial publications, all of which produced unimpressive records. The same conclusion can be found in the statistics provided by Hulbert's financial digest, which currently follows the performance of over 500 investment portfolios recommended by newsletters. In one Hulbert study, 57 newsletters were tracked for the 10-year period from August 1987 through August 1998. During that time, less than 10 percent of the newsletters beat the Wilshire 5000 Index's compound rate of return.

Armstrong also contends that expertise, beyond a minimal level, adds little in the way of predictive accuracy. Thus, consumers would be better off buying the least expensive predictions, which are likely to be as accurate as the most expensive, or investing the modest effort required to achieve a level of accuracy that would be comparable to the most expensive experts.

Recently, there have been signs that sophisticated consumers of Wall Street advice are unwilling to pay for traditional TA. During 2005, two of Wall Street's largest brokerage firms shut down traditional TA research departments.[26] Whether this is a random blip or the start of a trend remains to be seen.

Evidence-Based Technical Analysis: The Scientific Path

Adopting a scientific approach will have immediate benefits for technical analysis. The elimination of subjective TA, either by its being reformulated into objective testable methods or by jettisoning it altogether, would transform TA into a legitimate scientific activity. Only ideas that are testable would be entertained, and only those that prove themselves with objective evidence would be admitted to its body of knowledge.

This is not to suggest that, if EBTA were to be adopted, all answers will be clear-cut and all debate will end—far from it. Debate is part and parcel of the scientific process. Even in the hard sciences, important questions seek resolution, but the questions are about meaningful hypotheses that spin off testable consequences.

EBTA has limits. The major one is the inability to conduct controlled experiments, the gold standard of scientific investigation. In a controlled experiment, the effect of one variable can be isolated and studied by holding all other variables constant. TA is inevitably an observational science that must look to history for new knowledge.

Technical analysis is not alone in this regard. Archeology, paleontology, and geology also rely on historical data. Nevertheless, they are scientific disciplines because they deal in testable questions and look to objective evidence to separate useful from useless ideas.

There are statistical procedures that can partly ameliorate the lack of experimental controls. For example, when Fosback[27] quantified the optimism/pessimism of mutual-fund managers, he removed the confounding effect of short-term interest rates on cash reserves with regression analysis. By nullifying the powerful influence of short-term interest rates on mutual fund cash reserves, he was able to derive an uncontaminated measure of fund manager psychology called the Fosback Index. In a like manner, Jacobs and Levy[28] used multiple regression analysis to minimize the confounding effects of multiple variables. This allowed them to derive purified indicators for the prediction of relative stock performance. For example, they were able to measure the pure return-reversal[29] effect, thus revealing it to be one of the most powerful and consistent predictors of relative stock performance. In other words, they found a TA effect that works, namely, stocks that have been weak over the past month tend to have positive relative performance over the following month.

Another disadvantage of not being able to conduct controlled experiments is the inability to produce new samples of data. Technical analysis researchers have one body of market history that gets used over and over again. This contributes to the data-mining-bias problem. The more rules one tests in a given body of data, the more likely a rule will fit the data by accident. The inability to produce new sets of observations, which can be done in the experimental sciences, underscores the importance of using statistical inference methods that take the data-mining bias into account.

The Expert's Role in a Human-Computer Partnership

I assert that the future of TA would be best served by a partnership between TA experts and computers. This is not a new prescription. I was first exposed to it in the writings of Felsen[30] over 30 years ago, and leading edge TA practitioners have been taking advantage of advanced data modeling and machine learning for almost as long.[31] Within the past decade, numerous articles in peer-reviewed journals have shown the value of applying advanced data-mining methods to technical and fundamental indicators. Valid objective patterns have been found.[32]

This partnership exploits a synergy between human experts and computers. The synergy exists because the information processing abilities of these two entities are complimentary—computers are strong where humans are weak and visa versa. I am referring specifically to computers armed with data mining software and humans possessing expertise in a particular domain: TA, cytology, oil field geology, etc.

Though it is an oversimplification, people are inventive but computers are not. People can pose questions and hypothesize explanations that organize disparate facts into a pattern. However, this uniquely human ability has a dark side; it makes us gullible. Our gullibility is a consequence of a mind that evolved to be more prone to a state of belief than an attitude of skepticism. Therefore, although we are good at proposing ideas, like new indicators or new rules to test, we are ineffectual at the equally important task of disposing of poor ideas. Moreover, our intellect never evolved to interpret highly complex or random phenomena. This shows up in our limited abilities to engage in configural thinking, the intellectual task required when combining a multitude of variables into a prediction or judgment.

Though computers cannot invent, data-mining software allows them to dispose of irrelevant indicators and to synthesize complex models that can combine numerous variables into predictions. In other words, computers can engage in configural analysis. A computer's ability to synthesize complex high-dimensional models is only limited by the amount of data available. This constraint on predictive modeling, known as the *curse of dimensionality*, was named by mathematician Richard Bellman. In essence it says that as the number of indicators comprising a multidimensional space is increased, where each indicator is represented by a dimension, the observations populating the space become less dense at an exponential rate. A certain level of data density is required to allow data-mining software to distinguish valid patterns from background randomness. Maintaining a given level of data density as dimensions are increased thus requires an exponentially increasing number of observations. If 100 observations meet data density requirements at the two-dimensional level, 1,000 would be required at three dimensions and 10,000 at four dimensions. Despite this very real limitation on data mining, modern data-mining software is infinitely better at configural reasoning and complex pattern detection than the smartest humans.

The bottom line is this: Computers can do what people can't and people can do what computers can't. It is the perfect marriage.

The Futility of the Subjective Forecaster

Despite the potential of a human-computer synergy many traditional practitioners insist on using subjective methods to derive a forecast or signal from a multitude of indicators. They do so in the face of an overwhelming body of evidence, that has been accumulating over the last 50 years that demonstrates the futility of such an approach. These studies show that, for recurrent prediction problems, across a variety of fields, subjective predictions are rarely superior to predictions based on even simple statistical rules (models). A recurrent prediction problem is one in which the same type of prediction must be made repeatedly on the basis of a similar set of information. Examples of recurring prediction problems include technical analysis, predicting violence of prisoners being released, predicting if a borrower is likely to default on a loan, and so on. The information set that is available to the decision maker is a set of readings on a multitude of variables. In TA, this would be a set of technical indicator readings. In credit evaluation, it would be a set of financial ratios. The task is to determine if there exists a stable functional relationship between the indicators and the outcome that is to be predicted, to ascertain what the nature of that relationship is, and then to combine the variables according to that functional relationship. When the relationship is complex and involves more than just a few factors, the decision maker is faced with a configural thinking problem that exceeds human intellectual limits. The only choice for the subjective expert is to fall back on intuition.

The seminal study comparing the accuracy of subjective predictions (expert intuition) to predictions based on statistical rules (models) was done by Paul Meehl[33] in 1954. It was a review of prior studies, known as a meta-analysis, which examined 20 studies that had compared the subjective diagnoses of psychologists and psychiatrists with those produced by linear statistical models. The studies covered the prediction of academic success, the likelihood of criminal recidivism, and predicting the outcomes of electrical shock therapy. In each case, the experts rendered a judgment by evaluating a multitude of variables in a subjective manner. "In all studies, the statistical model provided more accurate predictions or the two methods tied."[34] A subsequent study by Sawyer[35] was a meta analysis of 45 studies. "Again, there was not a single study in which clinical global judgment was superior to the statistical prediction (termed 'mechanical combination' by Sawyer)."[36] Sawyer's investigation is noteworthy because he considered studies in which the human expert was allowed access to information that was not considered by the statistical model, and yet the model was still superior. For example, the academic performance of 37,500 sailors in naval training school was more accurately predicted by a model based on test scores than by judges who had access to test scores and who had conducted personal interviews. The judges apparently gave too much weight to the nuanced information they thought they had obtained in the personal interviews and gave too little to objective measurable facts.

An article by Camerer[37] compared the accuracy of experts' subjective predictions with two objective methods: the predictions of multivariate linear models derived with regression analysis and a second method based on a mathematical model of how the experts rendered their judgments. The least accurate predictions were the subjective judgments made by experts. The most accurate predictions were made by the linear regression model. Figure 9.9 was prepared from data presented by Russo and Schoemaker[38] summarizing Camerer's results. The figure of merit used to compare the forecasting methods was the correlation coefficient between predicted outcome and actual outcome. The correlation coefficient can range from 0, signifying the predictions were worthless, to 1.0 signifying perfect predictive accuracy. The prediction problems spanned nine different fields: (1) academic performance of graduate students, (2) life-expectancy of cancer patients, (3) changes in stock prices, (4) mental illness using personality tests, (5) grades and attitudes in a psychology course, (6) business failures using financial ratios, (7) students' ratings of teaching effectiveness, (8) performance of life insurance sales personnel, and (9) IQ scores using Rorschach Tests. Note that the average correlation of the statistical model was 0.64 versus the expert average of 0.33. In terms of information content, which is measured by the correlation coefficient squared or r-squared, the model's predictions were on average 3.76 times as informative as the experts'.

Numerous additional studies comparing expert judgment to statistical models (rules) have confirmed these findings, forcing the conclusion that people do poorly when attempting to combine a multitude of variables to make predictions or judgments. In 1968, Goldberg[39] showed that a linear prediction model utilizing personality test scores as inputs could discriminate neurotic from psychotic patients better than experienced clinical diagnosticians. The model was 70 percent accurate compared with expert accuracy that ranged from 52 percent to 67 percent. A 1983 study showed

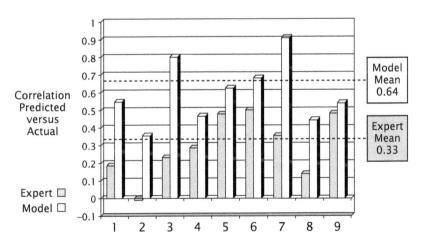

FIGURE 9.9 Predictive performance of subjective expert versus objective linear model in nine fields.

how poorly human experts do when the number of variables is increased. The task was to predict the propensity for violence among newly admitted male psychiatric patients based on 19 inputs. The average accuracy of the experts, as measured by the correlation coefficient between their prediction of violence and the actual manifestation of violence, was a poor 0.12. The single best expert had a score of 0.36. The predictions of a linear statistical model, using the same set of 19 inputs, achieved a correlation of 0.82. In this instance the model's predictions were nearly 50 times more informative than the experts'.

Meehl continued to expand his research of comparing experts and statistical models and in 1986 concluded that "There is no controversy in social science which shows such a large body of qualitatively diverse studies coming out so uniformly in the same direction as this one. When you are pushing 90 investigations [currently greater than 150[40]] predicting everything from the outcomes of football games to the diagnosis of liver disease and when you can hardly come up with a half dozen studies showing even a weak tendency in favor of the clinician, it is time to draw a practical conclusion."[41]

The evidence continues to accumulate, yet few experts pay heed. The most comprehensive study comparing the accuracy of experts' predictions with those produced by linear statistical prediction models was done by Grove and Meehl in 1996,[42] which covers 136 studies. In 96 percent of these studies, the rules either outperformed or equaled the experts. In a similar study in 2000, Swets, Monahan, and Dawes compared three methods of prediction in medicine and psychology: (1) expert subjective judgment, (2) statistical rules (models), and (3) a combination of the first two where the output of the statistical rule was modified by the expert's judgment. Their finding was consistent with prior studies, leading to the conclusion that experts who continue to operate on the basis of subjective judgment, are not only in error in a predictive sense but perhaps in an ethical one as well.[43]

From the foregoing, Hastie and Dawes[44] draw the following conclusions.

1. Experts and novices make subjective judgments by relying on a relatively small number of inputs (3 to 5). Assessments of livestock and weather forecasting are exceptions in that a larger number of inputs is typically used. The ability to use a larger set of information can be explained by the fact that immediate and precise feedback is available, which enables the experts in these two domains to learn. In other areas, like medical diagnosis, school admissions, and financial forecasting, feedback is often delayed or never available. Hastie and Dawes's conclusion suggests why subjective technicians do not learn from their mistakes—precise feedback is not

available because of the lack of objective pattern definitions and evaluation criteria.

2. For a wide range of judgment tasks, experts' judgments can be explained by an additive (linear) model of the inputs.

3. Few judges use nonlinear/configural thinking to combine inputs even though they are under the impression that they are doing so. However, when they do use configural reasoning, they tend to do it poorly.[45]

4. Experts do not understand how they arrive at their own judgments. This problem is most pronounced among highly experienced experts. As a result, their judgments are inconsistent when given the same set of inputs on different occasions.

5. In many domains, judges do not agree with each other when given the same set of information. The low level of interjudge agreement says that someone is wrong.

6. When irrelevant information is added to the set of inputs, judges become more confident although accuracy does not improve. Clearly, they are unable to distinguish relevant from irrelevant variables.

7. There are very few judges who are demonstrably superior.

Hastie and Dawes's conclusions have received additional support from Tetlock,[46] who evaluated predictions from experts in different fields and compares them to relatively simple statistical models that extrapolate recent trends. Tetlock's work, which appears to be the most rigorous long-term study ever conducted of expert judgment in the political and economic domains, does suggest that certain subjective cognitive styles of decision making are superior. He calls this style the fox. However, he shows that all human-based predictions, whatever their style, pale in comparison to formal model-based predictions. Using a two-dimensional framework for evaluating forecast accuracy, discrimination, and calibration, the accuracy of formal models, based on a method called generalized autoregressive distributed lags, far exceeds the performance of human experts.[47]

Why Are Experts' Subjective Predictions So Poor?

Although there is general agreement among those who study expert judgment, that it is rarely superior to objective forecasts, there is less agreement about why. A number of explanations have been proposed: the intrusion of emotional factors, the lack of consistency in how factors are weighted, excessive weight given to vivid concrete features that have little predictive power, inadequate weight given to abstract statistics that possess predictive power, the failure to use configural rules properly, falling prey to illusory correlations, failing to notice valid correlations, and being affected by the actions and statements of others. Many of these were covered in Chapter 2, with respect to the birth and maintenance of erroneous beliefs, and in Chapter 7, with respect to information cascades and herd behavior, and I will not repeat them here. Here, I will consider the intrusion of emotional factors on the subjective forecaster, which has not been discussed in prior chapters.

A number of investigators have considered the effect of emotions on subjective judgments made under conditions of uncertainty. One model, proposed by Loewenstein et al.,[48] suggests that a subjective forecast is impacted by the decision maker's anticipated emotional reaction to the prediction's outcome. Even though the expert's anxieties about the chance of being wrong have no valid role in a forecast, they appear to play a role. Nofsinger[49] presents Lowenstein's model in a diagram that I have reproduced in Figure 9.10. Note that when a person is making a prediction they are impacted by anticipating their emotions in response to the possible outcomes. This affects both the cognitive evaluation of information and the current emotional state of the decision maker.[50]

Slovic, Finucane, Peters, and MacGregor[51] explain the intrusion of emotions on the subjective decision maker in terms of *affect*. Affect refers to the good or bad feelings associated with a stimulus. These feelings often operate unconsciously and produce rapid reflex-like behaviors that

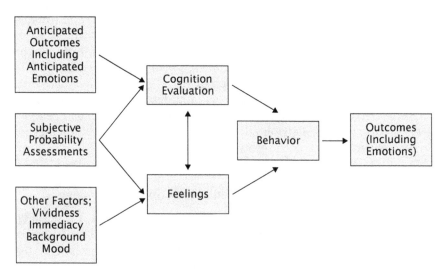

FIGURE 9.10 Lowenstein's model of judgment impacted by affect.

are not under the decision maker's conscious control. Slovic points out that feelings and images can weigh heavily in judgments that would be better handled by a purely analytical and rational consideration of evidence. For example, a market analyst who has negative feelings associated with a declining market is likely to remain more bullish than the evidence would warrant. However, not all judgments based on affect are bad. Some situations are accurately represented by the feelings they provoke and do demand the fast reflex-like decisions produced by this mode of thinking. Affective decision making was probably the dominant mode of judgment during the evolution of the human species. In other words, the speed of affective decision making had survival value. Fear of heights or of large predators demanded faster choices than those that a conscious weighing of pros and cons would have been able to produce. "However, like other heuristics that provide generally adaptive responses but occasionally lead us astray, reliance on affect can also deceive us."[52] This occurs when the relevant features of a situation are not well represented by the feelings they stimulate. Financial market prediction is such a situation, yet the subjective forecaster remains vulnerable to the automatic and subconscious judgments of a heuristic based on affect.

The model offered by Joseph Forgas further illuminates the futility of subjective forecasting.[53] It explains that "the greater the complexity and uncertainty in a situation, the more emotions will influence a decision."[54] This characterizes the task faced by the subjective TA analyst who operates against insurmountable obstacles when trying to evaluate a multitude of indicators in a rational manner. I contend that subjective forecasting is no longer the analyst's proper role.

The Expert's Proper and Crucial Role in Human-Machine Partnership

The proper role of the TA practitioner in the envisioned human-computer partnership is twofold: (1) proposing an information-rich set of candidate inputs suitable for presentation to the data-mining software, (2) specifying the problem to be solved by data-mining software (i.e., the target variable. In other words, the TA expert's proper role is to supply what the computer lacks, namely, expertise in the domain of TA and inventive talent.

It is somewhat ironic that in this high-tech era, the analyst's role has now taken center stage. This is a result of the changed economics of data mining. Within the last decade, the price of computing power and powerful data-mining software has declined sharply. Whereas these resources had been the exclusive domain of well-financed research organizations as recently as a decade or two ago, today they are commodities accessible to almost all market participants. These trends have democratized data mining. Most investors now have access to the same tools that once gave a huge competitive advantage to the largest institutional investors. That advantaged has been greatly diminished. Consequently, the competitive advantage—the source of added value—has now shifted back to the human analyst. The competitive advantage now lies with those TA experts possessing the best insights with regard to proposing indicators and specifying target variables. The TA practitioner who embraces the EBTA philosophy is well positioned to play this role.

Indicator design and target specification is a huge topic suitable for entire books. There are many books that cover indicators that are specific to TA.[55] There is no need to duplicate that here. There are other books that treat the more general problem of designing inputs (predictive variables) that are suitable for specific types of data-mining algorithms.[56] Different algorithms have different requirements. For example, although it is crucial that inputs to a neural net be properly scaled, inputs to decision-tree algorithms need not be. Masters,[57] Pyle,[58] and Weiss and Indurkhya[59] cover these issues nicely.

Indicator design refers to the specification of transformations applied to raw market data before it is presented to the data-mining tool. Data miners often refer to this as *preprocessing*. The task of proposing a list of information-rich and properly designed candidate indicators for a data-mining problem requires the domain expertise and inventive talents of the human analyst.

Anyone who has gotten their hands dirty in the data-mining trenches knows the following truth: a necessary condition for success in data mining is a good set of candidate indicators. *Good* does not mean that all inputs have to be informative. However, some of the proposed variables must contain useful information about the target variable. According to Dorian Pyle, a noted authority on data mining, "after finding the right problem to solve, data preparation is often the key to solving the problem. It can easily be the difference between success and failure, between useable insights and incomprehensible murk, between worthwhile predictions and useless guesses."[60] Dr. Timothy Masters, another data-mining authority, says, "Preprocessing is the is the key to success . . . even a primitive prediction model can perform well if the variables have been preprocessed in such as way as to clearly reveal the important information."[61] The message is amplified by Weiss and Indurkhya, in their book *Predictive Data Mining*. "The greatest gains in performance are often made by describing more predictive features (indicators). It is the human who specifies the set of features . . . and who investigates how to transform the original features into better features." "The computer is smart about deleting weak features, but relatively dumb in the more demanding task of composing new features or transforming raw data into more predictive forms ... the composition of features is a greater determining factor in the quality of results than the specific prediction methods used to produce those results. In most instances, feature composition is dependent on knowledge of the application."[62]

The TA practitioner who understands data-mining methods and the important issues in indicator design will be well positioned to play this crucial role in the human-machine partnership of twenty-first-century technical analysis. With the computer as an intelligence amplifier and a scientific orientation as the mindset, the EBTA practitioner is uniquely well positioned to push the frontiers of market knowledge forward at an accelerated pace. Given that human intelligence is essentially unchanging, but computer intelligence is increasing at an exponential rate,[63] no other approach to TA makes sense.

Proof That Detrending Is Equivalent to Benchmarking Based on Position Bias

In order to compensate for market bias interacting with long-short bias, one should compute the expected return of a random system with the same long-short bias, and subtract this bias-related return from the return of the candidate system.

The expected value of a single raw return drawn from the population of historical raw returns is, by definition, the mean of these returns.

$$E_{Raw} = \frac{1}{n} \sum_{i=1}^{n} R_i \qquad (A.1)$$

Let P_i signify the position of a trading system at opportunity i. This will be long, short, or neutral. The expected return of a trading system in which positions are random is:

$$E_{Random} = \sum_{P_i=Long} E_{Raw} - \sum_{P_i=Short} E_{Raw} \qquad (A.2)$$

The total return of the candidate system is the sum of the raw returns at those times when the candidate system is long, minus the sum of the raw returns when the system is short:

$$Total = \sum_{P_i=Long} R_i - \sum_{P_i=Short} R_i \qquad (A.3)$$

The total return of the candidate system (Equation (A.3)) is corrected for long/short prejudice by subtracting the expectation of a similarly prejudiced random system (Equation (A.2)). Subtraction distributes over the summation, giving:

$$Corrected = \sum_{P_i=Long} (R_i - E_{Raw}) - \sum_{P_i=Short} (R_i - E_{Raw}) \qquad (A.4)$$

Notice that the corrected return of Equation (A.4) is identical to the uncorrected return of Equation (A.3) except that the mean of the raw returns is subtracted from each individual raw return. In other words, to remove the effect of long/short imbalance in a biased market, all you need to do is center the raw returns.

Notes

INTRODUCTION

1. Data typically considered by TA includes prices of financial instruments; trading volume; open interest, in the case of options and futures; as well as other measures that reflect the attitudes and behavior of market participants.
2. J. Hall, *Practically Profound: Putting Philosophy to Work in Everyday Life* (Lanham, MD: Rowman & Littlefield Publishers, 2005).
3. Ibid., 4.
4. Ibid., 4.
5. Ibid., 5.
6. Ibid., 5.
7. Ibid., 5.
8. Ibid., 6.
9. Ibid., 5.
10. Ibid., 81.
11. R.D. Edwards and J. Magee, *Technical Analysis of Stock Trends*, 4th ed. (Springfield, MA: John Magee, 1958).
12. For a complete description of Elliott wave theory see R.R. Prechter and A.J. Frost, *Elliott Wave Principle* (New York: New Classics Library, 1998).
13. Any version of these methods that has been made objective to the point where it is back testable would negate this criticism.
14. The professional association of technical analysts, the Market Technicians Association (MTA), requires compliance with the National Association of Securities Dealers and the New York Stock Exchange. These self-regulating bodies require *"that research reports have a reasonable basis and no un-warranted claims."* Going even further, the MTA requires of its members that they *"shall not publish or make statements concerning the technical position of a security, a market or any of its components or aspects unless such statements are reasonable and consistent in light of the available evidence and the accumulated knowledge in the field of technical analysis."*
15. Some peer-reviewed academic journals include *Journal of Finance, Financial Management Journal, Journal of Financial Economics, Journal of Financial and Quantitative Analysis*, and *Review of Financial Studies*.

16. Outside of academia, there has been a move to greater emphasis on objective methods of TA, but often the results are not evaluated in a statistically rigorous manner.

17. F.D. Arditti, "Can Analysts Distinguish Between Real and Randomly Generated Stock Prices?," *Financial Analysts Journal* 34, no. 6 (November/December 1978), 70.

18. J.J. Siegel, *Stocks for the Long Run*, 2nd ed. (New York: McGraw-Hill, 1998), 243.

19. G.R. Jensen, R.R. Johnson, and J.M. Mercer, "Tactical Asset Allocation and Commodity Futures: Ways to Improve Performance," *Journal of Portfolio Management* 28, no. 4 (Summer 2002).

20. C.R. Lightner, "A Rationale for Managed Futures," *Technical Analysis of Stocks & Commodities* (2003). Note that this publication is not a peer-reviewed journal but the article appeared to be well supported and its findings were consistent with the peer-reviewed article cited in the prior note.

21. P.-H. Hsu and C.-M. Kuan, "Reexamining the Profitability of Technical Analysis with Data Snooping Checks," *Journal of Financial Economics* 3, no. 4 (2005), 606–628.

22. R. Gency, "The Predictability of Security Returns with Simple Technical Trading Rules," *Journal of Empirical Finance* 5 (1998), 347–349.

23. N. Jegadeesh, "Evidence of Predictable Behavior of Security Returns," *Journal of Finance* 45 (1990), 881–898.

24. N. Jegadeesh and S. Titman, "Returns to Buying Winners and Selling Losers: Implications for Stock Market Efficiency," *Journal of Finance* 48 (1993), 65–91.

25. T.J. George and C.-Y. Hwang, "The 52-Week High and Momentum Investing," *Journal of Finance* 59, no. 5 (October 2004), 2145–2184.

26. B.R. Marshall and R. Hodges, "Is the 52-Week High Momentum Strategy Profitable Outside the U.S.?" awaiting publication in *Applied Financial Economics*.

27. C.L. Osler, "Identifying Noise Traders: The Head and Shoulders Pattern in U.S. Equities," *Staff Reports, Federal Reserve Bank of New York* 42 (July 1998), 39 pages.

28. L. Blume and D. Easley, "Market Statistics and Technical Analysis: The Role of Volume," *Journal of Finance* 49, no. 1 (March 1994), 153–182.

29. V. Singal, *Beyond the Random Walk: A Guide of Stock Market Anomalies and Low-Risk Investing* (New York: Oxford University Press, 2004). These results are discussed in Chapter 4, "Short Term Price Drift." The chapter also contains an excellent list of references of other research relating to this topic.

30. A.M. Safer, "A Comparison of Two Data Mining Techniques to Predict Abnormal Stock Market Returns," *Intelligent Data Analysis* 7, no. 1 (2003), 3–14; G. Armano, A. Murru, and F. Roli, "Stock Market Prediction by a Mixture of Genetic-Neural Experts," *International Journal of Pattern Recognition & Artificial Intelligence* 16, no. 5 (August 2002), 501–528; G. Armano, M. Marchesi, and A. Murru, "A Hybrid Genetic-Neural Architecture for Stock In-

dexes Forecasting," *Information Sciences* 170, no. 1 (February 2005), 3–33; T. Chenoweth, Z.O. Sauchi, and S. Lee, "Embedding Technical Analysis into Neural Network Based Trading Systems," *Applied Artificial Intelligence* 10, no. 6 (December 1996), 523–542; S. Thawornwong, D. Enke, and C. Dagli, "Neural Networks as a Decision Maker for Stock Trading: A Technical Analysis Approach," *International Journal of Smart Engineering System Design* 5, no. 4 (October/December 2003), 313–325; A.M. Safer, "The Application of Neural-Networks to Predict Abnormal Stock Returns Using Insider Trading Data," *Applied Stochastic Models in Business & Industry* 18, no. 4 (October 2002), 380–390; J. Yao, C.L. Tan, and H.-L. Pho, "Neural Networks for Technical Analysis: A Study on KLCI," *International Journal of Theoretical & Applied Finance* 2, no. 2 (April 1999), 221–242; J. Korczak and P. Rogers, "Stock Timing Using Genetic Algorithms," *Applied Stochastic Models in Business & Industry* 18, no. 2 (April 2002), 121–135; Z. Xu-Shen and M. Dong, "Can Fuzzy Logic Make Technical Analysis 20/20?," *Financial Analysts Journal* 60, no. 4 (July/August 2004), 54–75; J.M. Gorriz, C.G. Puntonet, M. Salmeron, and J.J. De la Rosa, "A New Model for Time-Series Forecasting Using Radial Basis Functions and Exogenous Data," *Neural Computing & Applications* 13, no. 2 (2004), 100–111.

31. This firm was acquired by Goldman Sachs in September 2000.

CHAPTER 1 Objective Rules and Their Evaluation

1. A long position in a security means the investor owns the security and hopes to benefit by selling it in the future at a higher price.
2. A short position in a security means the investor has sold the security without owning it but is obligated to buy it back at a later point in time. The holder of a short position therefore benefits from a subsequent price decline, thereby permitting the repurchase at a lower level than the selling price, earning a profit.
3. *Neutral* refers to the case where the investor holds no position in the market.
4. It is assumed that all market information required by the method is known and publicly available at the time the method produces the recommendation.
5. The possibility of the time series being equal to the moving average is eliminated by computing the value of the moving average to a greater degree of precision than the price level.
6. J. Bollinger, *Bollinger on Bollinger Bands* (New York: McGraw-Hill, 2002).
7. T. Hayes, *The Research Driven Investor: How to Use Information, Data and Analysis for Investment Success* (New York: McGraw-Hill, 2001), 63.
8. A diffusion indicator is based on an analysis of numerous market time series within a defined universe (e.g., all NYSE stocks). The same rule, such as a moving average cross, is applied to all the series comprising the universe. Each series is rated as in an uptrend or downtrend, depending on its position

relative to its moving average. The value of the diffusion indicator is the percentage of time series that are in an upward trend. The indicator is confined to the range 0 to 100.

9. This analysis does not make clear how many rule variations were explored to attain this level of discrimination. As will be pointed out in Chapter 6, it is impossible to evaluate the significance of these findings without information on the amount of searching that led to the discovery of a rule.

10. Many of the rules tested in this book use data series other than the S&P 500 to generate signals on the S&P 500.

11. This law of statistics is discussed in detail in Chapter 4.

12. $(0.9) \times 0.035\% - (0.1) \times 0.035\% = 0.028\%$ per day or 7.31% annualized.

13. $(0.60) \times 0.035\% - (0.40) \times 0.035\% = 0.007\%$ per day or 1.78% annualized.

14. The look-ahead bias is discussed by Robert A. Haugen, *The Inefficient Stock Market: What Pays Off and Why* (Upper Saddle River, NJ: Prentice-Hall, 1999), 66.

15. The percentage of fund portfolios invested in interest-bearing cash instruments such as T-bills, commercial paper, and so forth.

CHAPTER 2   The Illusory Validity of Subjective Technical Analysis

1. J. Baron, *Thinking and Deciding*, 3rd ed., (Cambridge, UK: Cambridge University Press, 2000), 12.

2. This figure, redrawn by the author, is similar to and inspired by one found in G. Gigerenzer, *Calculated Risks: How to Know When Numbers Deceive You* (New York: Simon & Schuster, 2002). That book cites as the original source of the illustration R.N. Shepard, *Mind Sights: Original Visual Illusions* (New York: W.H. Freeman & Company, 1990).

3. T. Gilovich, *How We Know What Isn't So: The Fallibility of Human Reason in Everyday Life* (New York: Free Press, 1991).

4. See "Defying Psychiatric Wisdom, These Skeptics Say Prove It," *New York Times* (March 9, 2004), F1–F3.

5. Alpha refers to the capital asset pricing model term, which represents the Y-intercept obtained by regressing the returns of an investment strategy on the returns of a market index. It represents the portion of return that is not attributable to the volatility of the strategy (its beta). Meritorious investment strategies have alphas that are positive to a statistically significant degree.

6. J. Murphy, *Technical Analysis of the Financial Markets: A Comprehensive Guide to Trading Methods and Applications* (New York: New York Institute of Finance, 1999), 20, where market trends are said to be clearly visible.

7. H.V. Roberts, "Stock Market 'Patterns' and Financial Analysis: Methodological Suggestions," *Journal of Finance* 14, no. 1 (March 1959), 1–10.

8. F.D. Arditti, "Can Analysts Distinguish Between Real and Randomly Generated Stock Prices?," *Financial Analysts Journal* 34, no. 6 (November/December 1978), 70. An informal test of the same nature is discussed by

J.J. Siegel, *Stocks for the Long Run*, 3rd ed. (New York: McGraw-Hill, 2002), 286.

9. Gilovich, *How We Know.*
10. Shermer, M., *Why People Believe Weird Things: Pseudoscience, Superstition, and Other Confusions of Our Time* (New York: W.H. Freeman, 1997).
11. Gilovich, *How We Know.*
12. Ibid., 10.
13. H.A. Simon, "Invariants of Human Behavior," *Annual Review of Psychology* 41 (January 1990), 1–20.
14. Shermer, *Why People Believe*, 26.
15. Ibid., 26.
16. C. Sagan, *The Demon-Haunted World: Science as a Candle in the Dark* (New York: Random House, 1995), 6.
17. C. Sagan.
18. U. Neisser, *Cognitive Psychology* (Englewood Cliffs, NJ: Prentice-Hall, 1967).
19. D. Kahneman, P. Slovic, and A. Tversky, *Judgment under Uncertainty: Heuristics and Biases* (Cambridge, UK: Cambridge University Press, 1982).
20. H.A. Simon, *Models of Man: Social and Rational* (New York: John Wiley & Sons, 1957).
21. G.A. Miller, "The Magical Number Seven, Plus or Minus Two: Some Limits on Our Capacity for Processing Information," *Psychological Review* 63 (1956), 81–97.
22. J.R. Hayes, Human Data Processing Limits in Decision Making, Report No. ESD-TDR-62-48, Massachusetts: Air Force System Command, Electronics System Division, 1962.
23. The term *algebraic* in this context refers to the fact that numbers with both positive and negative values are being combined.
24. This is a simple linear combination. There are more sophisticated methods of linear combining where the variables are assigned weights (weighted algebraic sum).
25. R. Hastie and R.M. Sawes, *Rational Choice in an Uncertain World: The Psychology of Judgment and Decision Making* (Thousand Oaks, CA: Sage Publications, 2001), 52.
26. J.E. Russo and P.J.H. Schoemaker, *Decision Traps: The Ten Barriers to Brilliant Decision-Making and How to Overcome Them* (New York: Doubleday, 1989), 137. The authors cite 10 studies comparing the accuracy of intuitive expert prediction with predictions produced by objective linear models. The studies include prediction of academic performance, life-expectancy of cancer patients, changes in stock prices, psychological diagnosis, bankruptcy, student ratings of teacher effectiveness, sales performance, and IQ based on Rorschach test. The average correlation between prediction and outcome for expert judgment was 0.33 on a scale of 0 to 1.0. The average correlation for the objective model was 0.64. In a meta-analysis of over 100 peer-reviewed studies comparing expert judgment with statistical rules, statistical rules were more accurate in 96 percent of the cases. See J.A. Swets, R.M. Dawes, and J. Monahan, "Psychological Science Can Improve Diagnostic Decisions," *Psychological Science in the Public Interest* 1 (2000).

27. If each variable is assigned a value of 0 for low and 1 for high, the possible values of a sum are: 0 (all have values of zero), 1 (one variable has a value of 1 and two are zero), 2 (two variables have values of 1 and one has a value of zero), and 3 (all have values of 1).

28. If financial markets are complex nonlinear systems, a predictive model would have a nonlinear, functional form. Thus indicators would need to be combined in a configural (nonlinear) manner rather than a simple sequential-linear fashion.

29. B. Fischhoff, P. Slovic, and S. Lichtenstein, "Knowing with Certainty: The Appropriateness of Extreme Confidence," *Journal of Experimental Psychology: Human Perception and Performance* 3 (1977), 552–564; L.A. Brenner, D.J. Koehler, V. Liberman, and A. Tversky, "Overconfidence in Probability and Frequency Judgments: A Critical Examination," *Organizational Behavior and Human Decision Processes* 65 (1996), 212–219; R. Vallone, D.W. Griffin, S. Lin, and L. Ross, "Overconfident Prediction of Future Actions and Outcomes by Self and Others," *Journal of Personality and Social Psychology* 58 (1990),.582–592; A. Cooper, C. Woo, and W. Dunkeelberg, "Entrepreneurs' Perceived Chances for Success," *Journal of Business Venturing* 3, no. 97 (1988), 97–108

30. D.G. Myers, *Intuition, Its Power and Perils* (New Haven: Yale University Press, 2002).

31. J. Metcalfe, "Cognitive Optimism: Self-Deception of Memory Based Processing Heuristics," *Personality and Social Psychology Review* 2 (1998), 100–110, as referenced by D.G. Myers, in *Intuition, Its Powers and Perils* (New Haven: Yale University Press, 2002).

32. S. Lichtenstein, B. Fischhoff, and L. Phillips, "Calibration of Probabilities: The State of the Art to 1980," in *Judgment under Uncertainty: Heuristics and Biases*, D. Kahneman, P. Slovic, and A. Tversky (Eds.) (Cambridge, UK: Cambridge University Press, 1982), 306–334.

33. B. Fischoff and P. Slovic, "A Little Learning . . . Confidence in Multi-Cue Judgment Tasks," in R. Nickerson (Ed.), *Attention & Performance VIII* (Hillsdale, NJ: Earlbaum, 1980), the original source, as mentioned in *Judgment under Uncertainty: Heuristics and Biases*, D. Kahneman, P. Slovic, and A. Tversky (Eds.) (Cambridge, UK: Cambridge University Press, 1982).

34. L. Goldberg, "Simple Models or Simple Processes? Some Research on Clinical Judgments," *American Psychologist* 23 (1968), 338–349.

35. J.J.J. Christensen-Szalanski and J.B. Bushyhead, "Physicians' Use of Probabilistic Information in a Real Clinical Setting," *Journal of Experimental Psychology: Human Perception and Performance* 7 (1981), 928–935.

36. A.A. DeSmet, D.G. Fryback, and J.R. Thornbury, "A Second Look at the Utility of Radiographic Skull Examination for Trauma," *American Journal of Radiology* 132 (1979), 95–99.

37. Russo and Schoemaker, *Decision Traps*, 72.

38. Ibid.

39. D. Dreman and M. Berry, "Analysts Forecasting Errors and Their Implications for Security Analysis," *Financial Analysts Journal* 51 (May/June 1995), 30–41.

40. B. Barber and T. Odena, "Boys Will Be Boys: Gender, Overconfidence, and Common Stock Investment," Working Paper, University of California, Davis, 1998a.
41. Hersh Shefrin, *Beyond Greed and Fear: Understanding Behavioral Finance and the Psychology of Investing* (Boston: Harvard Business School Press, 2000), 51.
42. D. Kahneman and M. W. Riepe, "Aspects of Investor Psychology," *Journal of Portfolio Management* (Summer 1998).
43. T. Gilovich cites the following studies: N.D. Weinstein, "Unrealistic Optimism about Future Life Events," *Journal of Personality and Social Psychology* 39 (1980), 806–820; N.D. Weinstein, "Unrealistic Optimism about Susceptibility to Health Problems," *Journal of Behavioral Medicine* 5 (1982), 441–460; N.D. Weinstein and E. Lachendro, "Eco-centrism and Unrealistic Optimism about the Future," *Personality and Social Psychology Bulletin* 8 (1982), 195–200.
44. *Hulbert Digest*, www3.marketwatch.com/Store/products/hfd.aspx?siteid= mktw.
45. The self-attribution bias is discussed in the following studies: D.T. Miller and M. Ross, "Self-Serving Biases in the Attribution of Causality: Fact or Fiction?" *Psychological Bulletin* 82 (1975), 213–225; R. Nisbettand L. Ross, *Human Inference: Strategies and Shortcomings of Social Judgment* (Englewood Cliffs, NJ: Prentice-Hall, 1980); P.E. Tetlock and A. Levi, "Attribution Bias: On the Inconclusiveness of the Cognition-Motivation Debate," *Journal of Experimental Social Psychology* 18 (1982), 68–88; R.R. Lau and D. Russel, "Attributions in the Sports Pages," *Journal of Personality and Social Psychology* 39 (1980), 29–38; C. Peterson, "Attributions in the Sports Pages: An Archival Investigation of the Covariation Hypothesis," *Social Psychology Quarterly* 43 (1980), 136–141; R.M. Arkin and G. M. Maruyama, "Attribution, Affect and College Exam Performance," *Journal of Education Psychology* 71 (1979), 85–93; H.M. Dawes and W.G. Stephan, "Attributions for Exam Performance," *Journal of Applied Social Psychology* 10 (1980); T.M. Gilmour and D.W. Reid, "Locus of Control and Causal Attribution for Positive and Negative Outcomes on University Examinations," *Journal of Research in Personality* 13 (1979), 154–160; R.M. Arkin, H. Cooper, and T. Kolditz, "A Statistical Review of the Literature Concerning Self-Serving Attribution Bias in Interpersonal Situations," *Journal of Personality* 48 (1980), 435–448; D.T. Miller and M. Ross, "Self-Serving Biases in the Attribution of Causality: Fact or Fiction?" *Psychological Bulletin* 82 (1975), 213–225; R. Nisbett and L. Ross, *Human Inference: Strategies and Shortcomings of Social Judgment* (Englewood Cliffs, NJ: Prentice-Hall, 1980).
46. T. Gilovich, "Biased Evaluation and Persistence in Gambling," *Journal of Personality and Social Psychology* 44 (1983), 1110–1126; T. Gilovich and C. Douglas, "Biased Evaluations of Randomly Determined Gambling Outcomes," *Journal of Experimental Social Psychology* 22 (1986), 228–241.
47. R. Nisbett and L. Ross, *Human Inference: Strategies and Shortcomings of Social Judgment* (Englewood Cliffs, NJ: Prentice-Hall, 1980).

48. John R. Nofsinger, *Investment Madness* (Upper Saddle River, NJ: Prentice Hall, 2001).

49. D. Dreman, *Contrarian Investment Strategies: The Next Generation* (New York: Simon & Schuster, 1998) 80, regarding a study by Paul Slovic discussed in a speech before the IGRF, May 1973, entitled "Behavioral Problems Adhering to a Decision Policy."

50. J.E. Russo and P.J.H. Schoemaker refer to the following studies: E. Langer, "The Illusion of Control," *Journal of Personality and Social Psychology* 32 (1975), 311–328; L.C. Perlmuter and R.A. Monty, "The Importance of Perceived Control: Fact or Fantasy?," *American Scientist* 65 (November–December 1977), 759–765.

51. John R. Nofsinger references P. Presson and V. Benassi, "Illusion of Control: A Meta-Analytic Review," *Journal of Social Behavior and Personality* 11, no. 3 (1996), 493–510.

52. B. Fischoff, "Hindsight Is Not Equal to Foresight: The Effect of Outcome Knowledge on Judgment under Uncertainty," *Journal of Experimental Psychology: Human Perception and Performance* 1 (1975), 288–299; B. Fischoff and R. Beyth, "I Knew It Would Happen—Remembered Probabilities of Once-Future Things," *Organizational Behavior and Human Performance* 13 (1975); B. Fischoff, "For Those Condemned to Study the Past: Heuristics and Biases in Hindsight," in *Judgment under Uncertainty: Heuristics & Biases*, D. Kahneman, P. Slovic, and A. Tversky (Eds.) (Cambridge, UK: Cambridge University Press, 1982), 201–208.

53. Gary L. Wells and Elizabeth F. Loftus, *Eyewitness Testimony: Psychological Perspectives* (Cambridge, MA: Harvard University Press, 1984), and Eugene Winograd, "What You Should Know about Eyewitness Testimony," *Contemporary Psychology* 31, no. 5 (1986), 332–334.

54. Baruch Fischoff, "Debiasing in a Research Paper for the Office of Naval Research," in *Judgment under Uncertainty: Heuristics and Biases*, D. Kahneman, P. Slovic, and A. Tversky (Eds.) (Cambridge, UK: Cambridge University Press, 1982), Chapter 31.

55. R.F. Pohl. and B. Gawlik, "Hindsight Bias and the Misinformation Effect: Separating Blended Recollections from Other Recollection Types," *Memory* 3, no.1 (March 1995), 21–55; D. Stahlberg and A. Maass, "Hindsight Bias: Impaired Memory or Biased Reconstruction?," *European Review of Social Psychology* (1998).

56. R. Hastie and R.M. Dawes, *Rational Choice in an Uncertain World: The Psychology of Judgment and Decision Making*, Chapter 7, "Judging by Scenarios and Explanations" (Thousand Oaks, CA: Sage Publications, 2001); R.C. Shank and R. P. Abelson "Knowledge and Memory: The Real Story," in *Advances in Social Cognition*, vol. 8, R. Weyer (Ed.) (Hillsdale, NJ: Lawrence Earlbaum, 1995), 1–86.

57. R.E. Nisbett,E. Borgiada, R. Rich Crandall, and H. Reed, "Popular Induction: Information is Not Necessarily Informative," Chapter 7 in *Judgment under Uncertainty: Heuristics and Biases*, D. Kahneman, P. Slovic, and A. Tversky (Eds.) (Cambridge, UK: Cambridge University Press, 1982).

58. B. Russell, *Philosophy* (New York: Norton, 1927).

59. Gilovich, *How We Know*, 91.
60. Hastie and Dawes, *Rational Choice*, Chapter 7.
61. Ibid., 134.
62. Ibid., 135 .
63. Ibid., 136, referring to N. Pennington and R. Hastie, "A Cognitive Theory of Juror Decision Making: The Story Model," *Cardozo Law Review* 13 (1991), 519–557.
64. Gilovich, *How We Know*, 105.
65. For a definitive explanation of Elliott wave theory, see R. Prechter, *Elliott Wave Principle: Key to Stock Market Profits* (Gainesville, GA: New Classics Library, 1978).
66. M. Livo, *The Golden Ratio: The Story of Phi, the World's Most Astonishing Number* (New York: Broadway Books, 2002).
67. In a recent book, *Socionomics* (New York: New Classics Library, 2003), Prechter describes an objective computerized version of EWP that has been realized as an expert system. Prechter asserts that the system has produced profitable signals and should be able to distinguish real price histories from pseudo-price histories generated by a random process, though as of June 2006, these results have not been made public.
68. This criticism would be nullified if an objective method of wave counting can demonstrate the ability to distinguish random data series from authentic price data and predict better than an appropriate random benchmark. I recently learned that an objective EWP algorithm has been developed by Prechter's firm and is currently being tested. This program, called EWAVES, which is discussed in Precther's 1999 book *The Wave Principle of Human Social Behavior and the New Science of Socionomics*. Though EWAVES has not yet been tested as to its ability to discriminate real from random price data, if the program were able to do so, it would provide important confirmation that Elliott's original insights about market behavior have merit. This test, however, would not establish the predictive power of the objective signals. According to Prechter, a separate test of this assertion is also being carried out.
69. A falsifiable prediction is one that is sufficiently specific such that errors can be clearly identified. For example, the success or failure of a signal issued by an objective rule can be determined. It either made or lost money. Forecasts of a continuous target variable, such as in a regression model, are typically evaluated by a loss function, such as squared or absolute error, where error is equal to predicted minus actual.
70. *Hulbert's Financial Digest* is an independent newsletter that evaluates the performance of other financial advisory newsletters. According to the July 2005 long-term performance ratings, the annualized returns earned by the best known newsletter based on Elliott wave analysis, *The Elliott Wave Financial Forecast,* using both its long and short signals is given as: +1.1 percent for 5 years +1.1 percent, –28.2 percent for 10 years, –25.9 percent for 15 years, and –18.2 percent for the duration of the life of the service since 12/31/84. For the same time periods, Hulbert's gives the following annualized returns for the Dow Jones Wilshire 5000 index with

dividends reinvested: −1.3 percent for 5 years, +10 percent for 10 years, and +10.7 percent for 15 years. It should be pointed out that a buy and hold in a market index may not be a suitable benchmark for a timing service that assumes both long and short positions. Per recommendations in Chapter 1, a benchmark that represents the null hypothesis for testing the significance of a long/short signals returns is a random signal with the same proportion of long/short positions.

71. Regarding the author's self-interest in book sales, making the message more compelling serves this interest. Try as I might, I cannot completely eliminate bias from deciding what to say or not say. Ultimately, TA's best protection is objective evidence evaluated in an objective fashion. In Part Two of this book, evidence regarding the efficacy of 4,500 TA rules will be presented in as unvarnished and objective way I as know how.

72. David G. Myers, *Intuition, Its Powers and Perils* (New Haven: Yale University Press, 2004), 116.

73. Research articles on the confirmation bias can be found in P.C. Wason, "On the Failure to Eliminate Hypotheses in a Conceptual Task," *Quarterly Journal of Experimental Psychology* 12 (1960), 129–140; K. Klayman and P.C. Wason, "Reasoning about a Rule," *Quarterly Journal of Experimental Psychology* 20 (1968), 273–281; H.J. Einhorn and R.M. Hogarth, "Confidence in Judgment: Persistence in the Illusion of Validity," *Psychological Review* 85 (1978), 395–416; J. Klayman and Y.-W. Ha, "Confirmation, Disconfirmation, and Information in Hypothesis Testing," *Psychological Review* 94, no. 2 (1987), 211–228.

74. R. Park, *Voodoo Science: The Road from Foolishness to Fraud* (New York: Oxford University Press, 2000).

75. G.T. Wilson and D. Abrams, "Effects of Alcohol on Social Anxiety and Psychological Arousal: Cognitive versus Pharmacological Processes," *Cognitive Research and Therapy* 1 (1975), 195–210.

76. Gilovich, *How We Know*, 50.

77. M. Jones and R. Sugden, "Positive Confirmation Bias in the Acquisition of Information," *Theory and Decision* 50 (2001), 59–99.

78. L. Festinger, *A Theory of Cognitive Dissonance* (Palo Alto, CA: Stanford University Press, 1957).

79. S. Plous, *The Psychology of Judgment and Decision Making* (New York: McGraw-Hill, 1993), 23.

80. Practitioners who actually trade on their predictions do get clear feedback on results, but as pointed out in this chapter this feedback can be diluted by other cognitive distortions (e.g., self-attribution bias).

81. A bull trap, or breakout failure, occurs when shortly after the breakout penetration occurs, prices repenetrate the breakout level in the opposite direction. This has been referred to as a turtle soup signal because a contingent of commodity traders called the Turtles, who trade on the basis of breakouts, find themselves in hot water when breakout failures occur.

82. Gilovich, *How We Know*, 58.

83. Gilovich cites this from M. Gazzaniga, *The Social Brain* (New York: Harper & Row, 1985); R.E. Nisbett and T.D. Wilson, "Telling More Than We Can

Know: Verbal Reports on Mental Process," *Psychological Review* 84 (1977), 231–259.

84. T. Plummer, *Forecasting Financial Markets: The Psychological Dynamics of Successful Investing*, 3rd ed. (London: Kogan Page Limited, 1998). Plummer describes waves patterns similar to EWP but sometimes there are three waves and sometimes five.

85. Gilovich, *How We Know*, 53.

86. Ibid., 54.

87. C.G. Lord, L. Ross, and M.R. Lepper, "Biased Assimilation and Attitude Polarization: The Effects of Prior Theories on Subsequently Considered Evidence," *Journal of Personality and Social Psychology* 22 (1979), 228–241.

88. Gilovich, *How We Know*, 54.

89. Ibid., 54.

90. T. Gilovich, "Biased Evaluation and Persistence in Gambling," *Journal of Personality and Social Psychology* 44 (1983), 1110–1126; T. Gilovich and C. Douglas, "Biased Evaluation of Randomly Determined Gambling Outcomes," *Journal of Experimental Social Psychology* 22 (1986), 228–241.

91. This refers to the situation where a subjective method or some aspect of it has been objectified. For example, a study of the head-and-shoulders pattern is cited in Chapter 3 that provides an example of a subjective pattern that has been made testable, at least in one form. The evidence from that study contradicts the efficacy of the head-and-shoulders pattern.

92. L. Ross, M.R. Lepper, and M. Hubbard, "Perseverance in Self Perception and Social Perception: Biased Attributional Processes in the Debriefing Paradigm," *Journal of Personality and Social Psychology* 32 (1975), 880–892.

93. D.L. Jennings, M.R. Lepper, and L. Ross, "Persistence of Impressions of Personal Persuasiveness: Perseverance of Erroneous Self Assessments Outside the Debriefing Paradigm," unpublished manuscript, Stanford University, 1980; M.R. Lepper, L. Ross, and R. Lau, "Persistence of Inaccurate and Discredited Personal Impressions: A Field Demonstration of Attributional Perseverance," unpublished manuscript, Stanford University, 1979.

94. Failure would be if artificially created random charts cannot be discriminated from authentic price charts and if EWP signals do not generate profits superior to a random signals. Even if EWP signals prove to be useless on their own, they have proven to have value in a multivariate model due to synergies with other indicators.

95. Prechter, *Socionomics*, Chapter 4.

96. Gilovich, *How We Know*, 22.

97. L. Ross, M. Lepper, F. Strack, and J.L. Steinmetz, "Social Explanation and Social Expectation: The Effects of Real and Hypothetical Explanations upon Subjective Likelihood," *Journal of Personality and Social Psychology* 35 (1977), 817–829.

98. I should point out that in writing this book I have made myself vulnerable to this very problem. Explaining my position may make me resistant to evidence that invalidates said positions.

99. This study was quoted by Michael Shermer in *Why People Believe Weird Things*. Shermer also discusses the phenomenon of ideological immunity as defined by social scientist Jay Stuart Snelson.

100. J.S. Snelson, "The Ideological Immune System," *Skeptic Magazine* 1, no. 4 (1993), 44–55.

101. C.A. Anderson, M.R. Lepper, and L. Ross, "The Perseverance of Social Theories: The Role of Explanation in the Persistence of Discredited Information," *Journal of Personality and Social Psychology* 39, no. 6 (1980), 1037–1049.

102. Note, for purposes of this discussion the patterns, signals, and their expected outcomes are those employed by subjective analysts. Because we are dealing with the problem of faulty perceptions, what matters is the analyst's subjective perceptions of illusory correlations.

103. According to the subjective interpretation of the analyst.

104. As reported in T. Gilovich, L. Allen, and H.M. Jenkins, "The Judgment of Contingency and the Nature of Response Alternatives," *Canadian Journal of Psychology* 34 (1980), 1–11; R. Beyth-Marom, "Perception of Correlation Reexamined," *Memory & Cognition* 10 (1982), 511–519; J. Crocker, "Biased Questions in Judgment of Covariation Studies," *Personality and Social Psychology Bulletin* (1982), 214–220; H.M. Jenkins and W.C. Ward, "Judgments of Contingency between Responses and Outcomes," *Psychological Monographs: General and Applied* 79, no. 594 (1965), entire publication; W.D. Ward and H.M. Jenkins, "The Display of Information and the Judgment of Contingency," *Canadian Journal of Psychology* 19 (1965), 231–241.

105. A false positive signal occurs when the signal occurs but the expected outcome does not occur. A false negative signal (failure to signal) occurs when the pattern/signal does not occur but the outcome the signal/pattern is purported to predict occurs anyway.

106. In fact some studies show that people also consider the instances falling in the lower-right cell (correct identification of nonevents or nonopportunities), but by and large most attention is paid to those cases falling in the upper-left cell.

107. Gilovich,. *How We Know*, 30. Here, Gilovich makes reference to an earlier article: H.J. Einhorn and R.M. Hogarth, "Confidence in Judgment: Persistence of the Illusion of Validity," *Psychological Review* 85 (1977), 395–416.

108. The following studies discuss aspects of illusory correlation: R. Beyth-Marom, "Perception of Correlation Reexamined," *Memory & Cognition* 10 (1982), 511–519; J. Crocker, "Judgment of Covariation by Social Perceivers," *Psychological Bulletin* 90 (1981), 272–292; J. Crocker, "Biased Questions in Judgment of Covariation Studies," *Personality and Social Psychology Bulletin* 8 (1982), 214–220; H.M. Jenkins and W.C. Ward, "Judgements of Contingency between Responses and Outcomes," *Psychological Monographs: General and Applied* 79, no. 594 (1965), entire issue; J. Smedslund, "The Concept of Correlation in Adults," *Scandinavian Journal of Psychology* 4 (1963), 165–173; W.D. Ward and H. H. Jenkins, "The Display of Information and the Judgment of Contingency," *Canadian Journal of Psychology* 19 (1965), 231–241.

109. D.L. Jennings, T.M. Amabile, and L. Ross, "Informal Covariation Assessment: Data-Based versus Theory-Based Judgments," Chapter 15 in *Judgment under Uncertainty: Heuristics and Biases*, D. Kahneman, P. Slovic, and A. Tversky (Eds.) (Cambridge, UK: Cambridge University Press, 1982), 220–222.
110. The variables in these experiments were continuous, meaning that they can assume any value within a range, like temperature. Thus far, I have been referring to binary variables that assume only two possible values: pattern present or pattern not present.
111. Jennings, Amabile, and Ross, "Informal Covariation Assessment."
112. Smedslund, "Concept of Correlation in Adults."
113. J. Baron, *Thinking and Deciding*, 3rd ed. (Cambridge, UK: Cambridge University Press, 2000), 177. Baron cites the following studies as supportive: H. Shaklee and D. Tucker, "A rule analysis of judgments of covariation between events," *Memory and Cognition* 8 (1980), 459–467; M.W. Schustak and R.J. Sternberg, "Evaluation of Evidence in Causal Inference," *Journal of Experimental Psychology; General* 110 (1981); H. Shaklee and M. Mims, "Sources of Error in Judging Event Covariations," *Journal of Experimental Psychology: Learning, Memory and Cognition* 8 (1982), 208–224; H.R. Arkes and A.R. Harkness, "Estimates of Contingency between Two Dichotomous Variables," *Journal of Experimental Psychology: General* 112 (1983), 117–135.
114. For a discussion of the chi-square test, see R.S. Witte and J.S. Witte, *Statistics*, 7th ed. (Hoboken, NJ: John Wiley & Sons, 2004),. 469–492.
115. *Significant* in a statistical sense is a term that will be defined in Chapter 5.
116. Gilovich, *How We Know*, 32.
117. Gilovich cites a series of studies that discuss problem of illusory correlations in connection with asymmetric binary variables: R.H. Fazio, S.J. Sherman, and P.M. Herr, "The Feature-Positive Effect in the Self-Perception Process: Does Not Doing Matter as Much as Doing?," *Journal of Personality and Social Psychology* 42 (1982), 404–411; H.M. Jenkins and R.S. Sainsbury, "Discrimination Learning with the Distinctive Feature on Positive or Negative Trials," in *Attention: Contemporary Theory and Analysis*, D. Mostofsky (Ed.) (New York: Appleton-Century-Crofts, 1970); J. Newman, W.T. Wolff, and E. Hearst, "The Feature Positive-Effect in Adult Human Subjects," *Journal of Experimental Psychology: Human Learning*; and *Memory* 6 (1980), 630–650; R. Nisbet and L. Ross, *Human Inference: Strategies and Shortcomings of Social Judgment* (Englewood Cliffs, NJ:: Prentice-Hall, 1980); P.C. Wason and P.N. Johnson-Laird, *Psychology of Reasoning: Structure and Content* (London: Batsford, 1965).
118. In fact vague pattern/signal definitions and lack of objective evaluation criteria facilitate the discovery of seemingly confirmatory instances.
119. Gilovich, *How We Know*, 21.
120. A. Tversky and I. Gati, "Studies in Similarity," in *Cognition and Categorization*, E. Rosch and B. Loyd (Eds.) (Hillsdale, NJ: Lawrence Earlbaum, 1978).
121. D. Bernstein, E.J. Clarke-Stewart, A. Roy, and C.D. Wickens, *Psychology*, 4th ed. (Boston: Houghton Mifflin, 1997), 208.
122. Reference to this study can be found at www.azwestern.edu/psy/dgershaw/lol/ReinforceRandom.html.

123. Bernstein, Clarke-Steward, Roy, and Wickens, *Psychology*, 208.
124. Gilovich, *How We Know*, 10.
125. www.datamininglab.com/.
126. N. Jegadeesh and S. Titman, "Returns to Buying Winners and Selling Losers: Implications for Stock Market Efficiency," *Journal of Finance* 48 (1993), 65–91; N. Jegadeesh and S. Titman, "Profitability of Momentum Strategies: An Evaluation of Alternative Explanations," *Journal of Finance* 56 (2001), 699–720.
127. F.D. Arditti, "Can Analysts Distinguish between Real and Randomly Generated Stock Prices?" *Financial Analysts Journal* 34, no. 6 (November/December 1978), 70.
128. H.V. Roberts, "Stock Market 'Patterns' and Financial Analysis: Methodological Suggestions," *The Journal of Finance* 14, no. 1 (March 1959), 1–10.
129. Ibid.
130. Roberts' examples did not include volume data, which some claim is necessary for pattern identification.
131. Arditti, "Can Analysts Distinguish."
132. J. Siegel, *Stocks for the Long Run*, 3rd ed. (New York: McGraw-Hill, 2002).
133. Ibid., 286–288.
134. There are specific methods in statistics such as the runs test that detect departures from random behavior.
135. Gilovich, *How We Know*.
136. Ibid., 14–15.
137. Hastie and Dawes, *Rational Choice*, 4.
138. D.G. Myers, *Intuition: Its Powers and Perils* (New Haven: Yale University Press, 2004), 1.
139. Ibid., 4.
140. For example, if we always predict our grade on an exam to be higher than it turns out to be. An unbiased judgment can also be wrong, but its errors are not always on the same side of the true answer—for example, if you predicted a grade that was sometimes above and sometime below the grade you finally received.
141. Uncertain situations are those whose outcomes are difficult or impossible to predict.
142. B. Malkiel, *A Random Walk Down Wall Street* (New York: W.W. Norton, 1973).
143. There is a school of thought within probability theory that defines probability as the prior relative frequency, where relative frequency is the number of past events divided by the total number of instances in which the event could have taken place. We take up this topic in greater detail in Chapters 4 and 5.
144. This is true if events are independent. However, if events are dependent, then the occurrence of an event makes another more likely. For example, an earthquake is typically followed by a series of smaller quakes or aftershocks. Plane crashes are independent events—the occurrence of one has no bearing on the occurrence of another.
145. A. Tversky and D. Kahneman, "Judgement under Uncertainty: Heuristics and Biases," *Science* 185 (1974), 1124–1131.

146. A valid class trait is one that is truly indicative of class membership. Often the most obvious traits give valid signals of class membership, but not always.
147. Hastie and Dawes, *Rational Choice*, 116.
148. For a description of Bayes' law see S. Kachigan, *Statistical Analysis* (New York: Radius Press, 1986), 476–482, and Wikipedia, the online free encyclopedia, see reference to Bayes' theorem, 8 pages.
149. A conjunction refers to the logical operator AND; for example, the entity is an animal AND a horse.
150. A. Tversky and D. Kahneman," Judgments of and by Representativeness," in *Judgment Under Uncertainty: Heuristics and Biases*, D. Kahneman, P. Slovic, and A. Tversky (Eds.) (Cambridge, UK: Cambridge University Press, 1982).
151. The probability of a series of characteristics connected by the *AND* operator is equal to the product of the probability of each item in the list. Since the probability of any item is less than one, a product of terms all of which have a value less than 1.0 becomes smaller as the list grows larger. For example if X, Y, and Z are independent characteristics, and the probability of someone possessing characteristic $X = 0.5$, the probability of $Y = 0.5$ and the probability of $Z = 0.5$, then the probability someone possesses both X and $Y = 0.5 \times 0.5$ or 0.25, and the probability of X and Y and $Z = 0.5 \times 0.5 \times 0.5$ is 0.125.
152. This example comes from S. Plous, *The Psychology of Judgment and Decision Making* (New York: McGraw-Hill, 1993), 111.
153. Nassim Nicholas Taleb, *Fooled by Randomness: The Hidden Role of Chance in the Markets and in Life,* (New York: Texere, 2001).
154. This is the two-standard-deviation confidence interval for the proportion of heads in 100,000 coin tosses.
155. With regard to people's faulty expectations about how a tossed coin should behave, Gilovich refers to the following studies: R. Falk, "The Perception of Randomness," *Proceedings, 5th International Conference for the Psychology of Mathematics Education* (Grenoble, France: 1981); W.A. Wagenaar, "Generation of Random Sequences by Human Subjects: A Critical Survey of Literatures," *Psychological Bulletin* 77 (1972), 65–2; D. Kahneman and A. Tversky, "Subjective Probability: A Judgment of Representativeness," in *Judgment under Uncertainty: Heuristics and Biases*, D. Kahneman, P. Slovic, and A. Tversky (Eds.) (Cambridge, UK: Cambridge University Press, 1982), Chapter 3.
156. The probability of either sequence is $.05^6$, or 0.015626.
157. Gilovich, *How We Know*, 15.
158. Ibid., 20.

CHAPTER 3   The Scientific Method and Technical Analysis

1. M. Shermer, *Why People Believe Weird Things: Pseudoscience, Superstition, and Other Confusions of Our Time* (New York: W.H. Freeman, 1997).

2. C. Van Doren, *A History of Knowledge: Past, Present, and Future* (New York: Ballantine Books, 1991).
3. S. Richards, *Philosophy & Sociology of Science: An Introduction* (Oxford, UK: Basil Blackwell, 1983), 45.
4. Ibid.
5. Ibid., 189.
6. Ibid., 201.
7. As quoted by Shermer, *Why People Believe*.
8. Van Doren, *History of Knowledge*, 189.
9. Ibid..
10. Richards, *Philosophy & Sociology of Science*, 14.
11. D.J. Bennett, *Logic Made Easy: How to Know When Language Deceives You* (New York: W.W. Norton, 2004), 30.
12. Ibid., 31.
13. Ibid., 99 and 108; referring to P.C. Wason, "Self-Contradictions," in *Thinking: Readings in Cognitive Science* (Cambridge, UK: Cambridge University Press, 1977), 114–128; S.S. Epp, "A Cognitive Approach to Teaching Logic," *DIMACS Symposium, Teaching Logic and Reasoning in an Illogical World*, Rutgers, The State University of New Jersey, July 25–26, 1996, available at www.cs.cornell.edu/Info/People/gries/symposium/symp.htm.
14. The fact that a given set of observations can be consistent with (explained by) more than one theory or hypothesis and perhaps an infinite number of alternative theories is a problem known in philosophical and scientific circles as the *underdetermination of theories problem*. Because a multitude of hypotheses can be consistent with the same set of observations, the hypotheses are said to be empirically identical. The implication is that observational data, on its own, cannot tell us which of them is correct.
15. F. Schauer, *Profiles, Probabilities and Stereotypes* (Cambridge, MA: Belknap Press of Harvard, 2003), 59. References to studies on dog breed behavior are found in footnote 7.
16. In a subsequent chapter it will be shown that in this case the uncertainty would be 10 times greater with 10 observations than with 1,000 if price changes conform to the normal distribution, but may be far more uncertain if they do not.
17. http://en.wikipedia.org/wiki/Philosophy_of_science.
18. Shermer, *Why People Believe*, 24.
19. Richards, *Philosophy & Sociology of Science*, 45.
20. B.L. Silver, *The Ascent of Science* (New York: Oxford University Press, 1998), 15.
21. Ibid., 14.
22. R.S. Percival, *About Karl Popper*, adapted from his PhD thesis, available at www.eeng.dcu.ie/~tkpw/intro_popper/intro_popper.html.
23. This is the frequency definition of probability. There are others.
24. Richards, *Philosophy & Sociology of Science*, 52.
25. K.R. Popper, *The Logic of Scientific Discovery* (London: Hutchinson, 1977).
26. K.R. Popper, *Conjectures and Refutations* (London: Routledge & Kegan 1972).
27. This is known as the underdetermination of theories problem.

28. *If hypothesis is true, then X should be observed. X is observed* (affirms the consequent). Invalid conclusion: *The hypothesis is true* (fallacy of affirming the consequent).

29. A *necessary* condition is one that is required to produce an effect, but it alone is not enough to produce the effect. For example if X is a necessary condition of Y, it means that, if X is lacking, Y will not occur but the fact that X is present is not enough to insure Y. In shorthand: *If not X, then not Y.* A *sufficient* condition is more comprehensive in that its presence is enough (is sufficient) to produce the effect. Thus it means: *If W, then Y.*

30. Richards, *Philosophy & Sociology of Science*, 59.

31. My contention may be challenged in the near future by an objective version of EWT called EWAVES developed by Robert Prechter's firm, Elliott Wave International. Prechter claims it generates definitive signals for which financial performance can be measured.

32. Descriptions of EMH-weak vary. Some say only historical price data cannot be used to generated excess returns. Other versions say any stale market data, price, volume, or any other data series that TA practitioners study cannot be used to generated excess returns.

33. N. Jegadeesh and S. Titman, "Returns to Buying Winners and Selling Losers: Implications for Stock Market Efficiency," *Journal of Finance* 56 (1993), 699–720.

34. R.A. Haugen, *The Inefficient Stock Market: What Pays Off and Why* (Upper Saddle River, NJ: Prentice-Hall, 1999), 63.

35. F. Nicholson, "Price-Earnings Ratios in Relation to Investment Results," *Financial Analysts Journal* (January/February 1968), 105–109; J.D. McWilliams, "Prices and Price-Earnings Ratios," *Financial Analysts Journal* 22 (May/June, 1966), 136–142.

36. Because there are not infinite time and resources to test all ideas, receptivity is tempered with prior knowledge, experience, and intuition. Some new ideas merit more attention than others. However, being overly restrictive at this phase could have a big cost —missing a breakthrough. In this phase, if one is to err, it is better to err on the side of openness.

37. W.A. Wallis and H.V. Roberts, *Statistics: A New Approach* (New York: The Free Press of Glencoe, 1964), 5.

38. P.W. Bridgman, "The Prospect for Intelligence," *Yale Review* 34 (1945), 444–461, quoted in J.B. Conant,*On Understanding Science* (New Haven: Yale University Press, 1947), 115.

39. Wallis and Roberts,.*Statistics*, 6.

40. J.E. Russo and P.J.H. Schoemaker, *Decision Traps: The Ten Barriers to Brilliant Decision-Making and How to Overcome Them* (New York: Doubleday, 1989), 135.

41. L.R. Goldberg, "Man versus Model of Man: A Rationale, Plus Some Evidence for a Method of Improving Clinical Inference," *Psychological Bulletin* 73 (1970), 422–432.

42. P.H.K. Chang and C.L. Osler, "Methodical Madness: Technical Analysis and the Irrationality of Exchange-Rate Forecasts," *Economic Journal*,109, no. 458 (1999), 636–661; C.L. Osler, "Identifying Noise Traders: The Head-and-

Shoulders Pattern in U.S. Equities," Publication of Federal Reserve Bank of New York, 1998.

43. R.D. Edwards, J. Magee, and W.H.C. Bassetti (Eds.), *Technical Analysis of Stock Trends*, 8th ed., (Boca Raton, FL: CRC Press, 2001); M.J. Pring, *Technical Analysis Explained*, 4th ed. (New York: McGraw-Hill, 2002); J.J. Murphy, *Technical Analysis of the Financial Markets: A Comprehensive Guide to Trading Methods and Applications* (New York: New York Institute of Finance, 1999).

44. It may be possible to define chart patterns using fuzzy logic where class membership is given a class membership function (0 to 1.0) rather than a yes or no. However, evaluating pattern effectiveness will still require a threshold on the class membership function to decide which patterns belong in a given class and which do not.

45. S.S. Alexander, "Price Movements in Speculative Markets: Trends or Random Walks," *Industrial Management Review* 2 (1961), 7–26; S.S. Alexander, "Price Movements in Speculative Markets: Trends or Random Walks No. 2," *Industrial Management Review* 5 (1964), 25–46.

46. A.A. Merrill, *Filtered Waves: Basic Theory* (Chappaqua, NY: Analysis Press, 1977).

47. P.H.K.Chang, and C.L. Osler, "Methodical Madness: Technical Analysis and the Irrationality of Exchange-Rate Forecasts," *Economic Journal* 109, no. 458 (1999), 636–661.

48. C.L. Osler, "Identifying Noise Traders: The Head-and-Shoulders Pattern in U.S. Equities," Publication of Federal Reserve Bank of New York, 1998.

49. A.W. Lo, H. Mamaysky, and W. Jiang, "Foundations of Technical Analysis: Computational Algorithms, Statistical Inference, and Empirical Implementation," *Journal of Finance* 55, 4 (August 2000), 1705–1765.

50. Kernel regression estimates the value of a smoothed curve by averaging nearby or local observations, where the weight of each observation is inversely related to its distance from the location for which a smoothed value is desired. Thus, nearby observations are given the greatest weight. The term *kernel* refers to the shape of the weighting function used. One common weight function is based on the shape of the normal probability distribution (Gaussian kernel).

51. The authors of the paper do not come out directly and say the patterns are not useful for forecasting trends, but the data they present indicates this as does the commentary on the paper provided by Narasimahan Jegadeesh (pp. 1765–1770). In Table 1 he shows that the post pattern returns (trends) are not significantly different than when the patterns are not present.

52. T.N. Bulkowski, *Encyclopedia of Chart Patterns* (New York: John Wiley & Sons, 2000), 262–304.

CHAPTER 4   Statistical Analysis

1. David S. Moore, *The Basic Practice of Statistics* (New York: W.H. Freeman, 1999).

2. B. Russell, *A History of Western Philosophy* (New York: Simon & Schuster, 1945).

3. R.P. Abelson, *Statistics as Principled Argument* (Mahwah, NJ: Lawrence Erlbaum, 1995).

4. A.W. Wallis and H.V. Roberts, *Statistics: A New Approach* (New York: The Free Press of Glencoe, 1956), 101–110.

5. The method for detrending or zero normalizing the market data series to which the rules are applied is discussed in Chapter 1.

6. Probability density is formally defined as the first derivative of the cumulative probability of a random variable. For the purposes of this discussion, it can be thought of as chance or probability that something will happen.

7. Fractional area refers to the proportion of the area of the density function lying to the right of the observed performance relative to the total area covered by the density function.

8. Instances of dogs missing limbs are excluded from this discussion for purposes of simplification.

9. Wallis and Roberts, *Statistics*, 101–110.

10. D.S. Moore, *The Basic Practice of Statistics* (New York: W.H. Freeman, 1999).

11. S. Kachigan, *Statistical Analysis* (New York: Radius Press, 1986), 77.

12. In this example, it is assumed that the underlying phenomenon is stationary; that is, it remains unchanged over time. Financial markets are most likely nonstationary systems. In general, statistical inference is not intended to cope with nonstationary phenomena. Nonstationary is a risk inherent when investing on the basis of any sort of rule, statistically derived or not.

13. Daily returns refers to returns earned by a rule on zero-centered or detrended market data as defined in Chapter 1.

14. S.J. Grossman and J.E. Stiglitz, "On the Impossibility of Informationally Efficient Markets," *American Economic Review* 70, no. 3 (1980), 393–408.

15. Chapter 7, Theories of Nonrandom Price Motion, discusses the possibility that TA rules may be profitable because they signal opportunities to earn risk premiums. Under this notion, TA rule profits are compensation to the technical trader for providing valuable services to other market participants, such as liquidity, information in the form of price discovery, or risk transference. Because these are ongoing needs, profits earned by rules that result from fulfilling said needs are likely to persist.

16. This definition of stationary is not strictly correct but close enough for purposes of this discussion.

17. N.N. Taleb, *Fooled by Randomness—The Hidden Role of Chance in the Markets and in Life* (New York: Texere, 2001), 97.

18. The rigorous definition of a statistic is a function of the cases in the sample that does not depend on any unknown parameter. Thus, if computing the statistic requires a piece of information that is unknown, then it is not a statistic.

19. The trimmed mean is computed after removing the largest 5 percent wins and losses. This can provide a more accurate estimate of the population mean by removing outliers that can skew results.

20. In fact, the Law of Large Numbers refers to the convergence between a sample average and a population average. However, a relative frequency is

the same as an average if the occurrence of an event is given the value of 1 and the nonoccurrence a value of 0. *Relative frequency* refers to the proportion of event occurrences within an observed sample, whereas the theoretical idea of probability refers to the relative frequency of the event in the unlimited number of trials that constitutes the population of observations.

21. Kachigan, *Statistical Analysis*, 75.
22. The Law of Large Numbers requires that the number of observations in each interval be sufficiently large to reveal the true relative frequency of the values represented by that interval.
23. Probability density is the slope of the cumulative distribution function. For any point on the horizontal axis, the height of the probability density function at that point is the first derivative of the probability that an observation will be less than or equal to the point on the horizontal axis.
24. For example, the probability of obtaining the value 4.23 is zero. This is not so strange because a continuous random variable never assumes a value of exactly 4.23. The real value is either slightly higher or lower than 4.23, if it were given with additional accuracy (e.g., 4.229).
25. In fact each individual observation that winds up in the sample is a probability experiment.
26. A more technical definition of sample statistic: A function of one or more random variables that does not depend on any unknown parameters. This implies that a statistic is itself a random variable.
27. Kachigan, *Statistical Analysis*, 101.
28. R.S. Witte and J.S. Witte, *Statistics*, 7th ed. (New York: John Wiley & Sons, 2004), 230.
29. Other statistics include: Z, t, F-ratio, chi-square, and so forth. There are many.
30. The Sharpe ratio is defined as the annualized average return in excess of the risk-free rate (e.g., 90-day treasury bills) divided by the standard deviation of the returns stated on an annualized basis.
31. The profit factor is defined as a ratio of the sum of gains of profitable transactions to the sum of all losses on unprofitable transactions. The denominator is stated as an absolute value (no sign) so the value of the profit factor is always positive. A value of 1 would indicate the rule is break even. A superior way to calculate the profit factor to transform it to have a natural zero point is to take the log of the ratio.
32. The Ulcer Index is an alternative and possibly superior measure of risk that considers the magnitude of equity retracements, which are not directly considered by the Sharpe ratio. The standard deviation, the risk measure employed by the Sharpe ratio, does not take into account the sequence of winning and losing periods. For a definition of the Ulcer Index, see P.G. Martin and B.B. McCann, *The Investor's Guide to Fidelity Funds* (New York: John Wiley & Sons, 1989), 75–79. A similar concept, the return to retracement ratio, is described by J.D. Schwager, *Schwager on Futures—Technical Analysis* (New York: John Wiley & Sons, 1996).

33. This figure was inspired by a similar figure in Lawrence Lapin, *Statistics for Modern Business Decisions*, 2nd ed. (New York: Harcourt Brace Jovanovich, 1978), Figure 6-10, 186.
34. The qualifying condition for the mean of a sample to approach the mean of the parent population is that the mean in the parent population be finite.
35. This is true when the test statistic is the sample mean, but it is not true in general. A critical assumption is that the observations comprising the sample are independent. If the observations are serially correlated, as might be the case in a time series, the variance reduction is slower than the square root rule suggests.
36. The population has a finite mean and a finite standard deviation.
37. The general principle that bigger samples are better applies to stationary processes. In the context of financial market time series, which are most likely not stationary, old data may be irrelevant, or even misleading. For example, indicators based on short selling volume by NYSE specialists seem to have suffered a decline in predictive power. Larger samples may not be better.
38. The Central Limit Theorem applies to a sample for which observations are drawn from the same parent population, which are independent, and in which the mean and standard deviation of the parent population are finite.
39. This figure was inspired by a similar figure in Lawrence Lapin, *Statistics for Modern Business Decisions*, 2nd ed. (New York: Harcourt Brace Jovanovich, 1978), 216–217.

CHAPTER 5   Hypothesis Tests and Confidence Intervals

1. J.E. Burt and G.M. Barber, *Elementary Statistics for Geographers*, 2nd ed. (New York: The Guilford Press, 1996), 5.
2. We saw in Chapter 2 that because of the self-attribution bias, people can maintain a delusion by rationalizing a loss: headache, shoelaces were untied, argued with wife before game, the other player put an evil eye on me, and so on. Distasteful evidence can always be explained away if loose evidence standards are applied.
3. As discussed in Chapter 3, according to Popper and Hume, no amount of confirmatory evidence can provide certitude for a claim. However, evidence can be used to falsify a claim. For this reason, a science test claims by focusing on evidence that has the potential to show that the claim is false rather than on evidence that might confirm the claim.
4. R.S. Witte and J.S. Witte, *Statistics*, 7th ed. (Hoboken, NJ: John Wiley & Sons, 2004), 264.
5. Ibid.
6. Eric W. Noreen, *Computer Intensive Methods for Testing Hypotheses: An Introduction* (New York: John Wiley & Sons, 1989), 2.

7. David S. Moore, *The Basic Practice of Statistics*, 2nd ed. (New York: W. H. Freeman, 2000), 314.
8. As described in Chapter 1, detrending transforms the market data such that it has a mean daily change of zero. This eliminates the distortion in a rules performance due to the conjoint effects of position bias and the market's trend during the back-test period.
9. Randomly paired means that the historical daily price changes of the market are scrambled, and then each is randomly paired with a rule output value (+1 or –1).
10. Quantmetrics, 2214 El Amigo Road, Del Mar, CA 92014.
11. B. Efron, "Bootstrap Methods: Another Look at the Jackknife," *Annals of Statistics* 7(1979), 1–26.
12. E.W. Noreen in *Computer Intensive Methods for Testing Hypotheses* cites the following references to bootstrapping: B. Efron and G. Gong, "A Leisurly Look at the Bootstrap, the Jacknife and Cross-Validation," *American Staistican* 37 (February 1984), 36–48; B. Efron, "Better Bootstrap Confidence Intervals," *LCS Technical Report No. 14*, Department of Statistics and Stanford Linear Accelerator; B. Efron and R. Tibshirani, "Bootstrap Methods for Standard Errors, Confidence Intervals, and Other Methods of Statistical Accuracy," *Statistical Science* 1 (1984), 54–77.
13. Here, *ordered* means the values occur in their proper temporal order.
14. A channel breakout rule, under traditional TA interpretation, registers a buy (sell) signal when the rule's input series is at a maximum (minimum) value for the current day and all prior days in the rule's look-back window.
15. L.J. Kazmier, *Statistical Analysis for Business and Economics* (New York: McGraw-Hill, 1978), 217.
16. *Standard error* refers to the standard deviation of sample means around the population mean when many independent samples are taken from the same population.
17. Kazmier, *Statistical Analysis*, 216.
18. Ibid.

CHAPTER 6   Data-Mining Bias: The Fool's Gold of Objective TA

1. H. White, "A Reality Check for Data Snooping," *Econometrica* 68, no. 5 (September 2000), 1102, Proposition 2.1. The proof shows that as the sample size goes to infinity, the probability that the rule with the highest expected return will also have the highest observed performance approaches 1.0.
2. R.N. Kahn, "Data Mining Made Easy: Seven Quantitative Insights into Active Management: Part 5," www.barra.com/Newsletter/NL165/SevIns5NL165.asp.
3. Bible code scholars claim that a prediction that Israeli Prime Minster Yitzhak Rabin would be assassinated was made in advance of the event. They also claim that efforts were made to warn Rabin, but to no avail. I have been unable to authenticate the veracity of this claim.

4. The code scholars do not define in advance what constitutes a significant pattern. It can be any group of words that are deemed to be in close proximity in the text and to be related, in the opinion of the code researcher, to the purportedly predicted event. They are free to use any spacing interval they wish to define the pattern.
5. See "The Case Against the Codes," Professor Barry Simon, www.wopr.com/ biblecodes/.
6. Ibid.
7. Kahn, "Data Mining Made Easy."
8. Here, the term *prediction* does not necessarily mean foretelling the future, though forecasting is certainly the ultimate intent of TA. Rather, the term *prediction* refers to observations not yet made, regardless of whether they lie in the future. It is crucial that the observations have not yet been made because prior observations can always be explained after the fact by an infinite number of hypotheses or rules. The only way to determine which of these numerous hypotheses might be correct is for predictions to be made that are then compared with new observations. Thus the term *new observation* can refer to the back test of a newly proposed rule. (See Chapter 3 for a fuller exposition of this point.)
9. *Out-of-sample data* refers to data not used for back testing the rule.
10. R. Pardo, *Design, Testing and Optimization of Trading Systems* (New York: John Wiley & Sons, 1992).
11. A.W. Lo, "The Adaptive Markets Hypothesis: Market Efficiency from an Evolutionary Perspective," *Journal of Portfolio Management* 30 (2004), 15–29; A. Timmermann, "Structural Breaks: Incomplete Information, and Stock Prices," *Journal of Business & Economic Statistics* 19, no. 3 (2001), 299–314.
12. W.V. Kidd and W.B. Borsen, "Why Have Returns to Technical Analysis Decreased?" *Journal of Economics and Business* 56, no. 3 (May/June 2004), 159–176. The article examines the deterioration of technical system performance over the course of the out-of-sample data. Thus, it could not be due to data-mining bias.
13. D. Meyers, "Optimization: The World of Illusion," *Active Trader* (March 2004), 52; D. Meyers, "The Optimization Trap," *Active Trader* (November 2001), 68; D. Meyers, "The Siren Call of Optimized Trading Systems, 1996, available on the author's web site, www.MeyersAnalytics.com.
14. T. Hastie, R. Tibshirani, and J. Friedman, *The Elements of Statistical Learning: Data Mining, Inference and Prediction*, Springer Series in Statistics (New York: Springer, 2001).
15. S.H. Weiss and N. Indurkhya, *Predictive Data Mining: A Practical Guide* (San Francisco: Morgan Kaufmann, 1998).
16. I.H. Witten and E. Frank, *Data Mining: Practical Machine Learning Tools and Techniques*, 2nd ed. (San Francisco: Morgan Kaufmann, 2005).
17. D.D. Jensen and P.R. Cohen, "Multiple Comparisons in Induction Algorithms," *Machine Learning* 38, no. 3 (March 2000), 309–338.
18. The Ulcer Index was discussed by P.G. Martin and B.B. McCann, *The Investor's Guide to Fidelity Funds* (New York: John Wiley & Sons, 1989). A

similar measure of risk based on the average magnitude of equity retrace-ment was previously proposed by J.D. Schwager, *A Complete Guide to the Futures Markets* (New York: John Wiley & Sons, 1984), 471–472.

19. R. Pardo, *Design, Testing and Optimization of Trading Systems* (New York: John Wiley & Sons, 1992).

20. J.O. Katz and D.L. McCormick, *The Encyclopedia of Trading Strategies* (New York: McGraw-Hill, 2000).

21. P.J. Kaufman, *New Trading Systems and Methods*, 4th ed. (Hoboken, NJ: John Wiley & Sons, 2005).

22. Mean-reversion rules are based on the concept that when a data series moves to extreme high or low values relative to recent values, it should revert back to its mean value.

23. Divergence rules are based on the concept that if two data series typically move up and down together, it is important information when they diverge from each other. Thus, divergence rules give signals when data series depart from this normal pattern of activity.

24. Hastie, Tibshirani, and Friedman, *Elements of Statistical Learning*.

25. White, "Reality Check," proof of Proposition 2.1

26. This diagram is conceptual and is not intended to accurately convey the predictive power of scientific laws or of TA rules except in a general sense.

27. Jensen and Cohen, "Multiple Comparisons in Induction Algorithms."

28. White, "Reality Check."

29. Jensen and Cohen, "Multiple Comparisons in Induction Algorithms."

30. Although this is not an example of data mining, it is an example of using a multiple comparison procedure to find a best solution to a problem.

31. Actually, randomness has been put to good use in the design of some of the most powerful data-mining algorithms used for complex rule synthesis. An example of this is Random Forests, developed by the late Leo Brieman, professor of statistics, at the University of California, Berkeley.

32. E. Peters, *Fractal Market Analysis: Applying Chaos Theory to Investment & Economics* (New York: John Wiley & Son., 1994), 21–38.

33. A rule selected because of its superior performance in the mined data.

34. This figure was inspired by a similar figure in Lawrence Lapin, *Statistics for Modern Business Decisions*, 2nd ed. (New York: Harcourt Brace Jovanovich, 1978), Figure 6-10, 186.

35. Pardo, *Design, Testing and Optimization*, 108.

36. M. De La Maza, "Backtesting," Chapter 8 in *Computerized Trading: Maximizing Day Trading and Overnight Profit*, M. Jurik (Ed.) (Paramus, NJ: Prentice-Hall, 1999).

37. Katz and McCormick, *Encyclopedia of Trading Strategies*.

38. Kaufman, *New Trading Systems*.

39. P.-H. Hsu and C.-M. Kuan, "Rexamining the Profitability of Technical Analysis with Data Snooping Checks," *Journal of Financial Econometrics* 3, no. 4 (2005), 606–628.

40. H.M. Markowitz and G.L. Xu, "Data Mining Corrections: Simple and Plausible," *Journal of Portfolio Management* (Fall 1994), 60–69.

41. De La Maza, "Backtesting."

42. B. Efron, "Bootstrap Methods: Another Look at the Jackknife," *Annals of Statistics* 7 (1979), 1–26; B. Efron and G. Gong, "A Leisurely Look at the Bootstrap, the Jackknife, and Cross-Validation," *American Statistician* 37 (February 1983), 36–48.
43. Quantmetrics, 2214 El Amigo Road, Del Mar, CA 92014; contact Professor Halbert White, PhD.
44. Note that the subtraction of the average daily return from each daily return can also be done prior to bootstrapping. In this illustration it was done afterward.
45. P.R. Hansen, "The Reality Check for Data Snooping: A Comment on White," Brown University Department of Economics; P.R. Hansen, "A Test for Superior Predictive Ability," *Journal of Business and Economic Statistics* 23 (2005), 365–380.
46. J.P. Romano and M. Wolf, "Stepwise Multiple Testing as Formalized Data Snooping," *Econometrica* 73, no. 4 (July 2005), 1237–1282. Note, this paper and many others use the term data snooping for what I refer to as the data-mining bias.

CHAPTER 7   Theories of Nonrandom Price Motion

1. C.R. Lightner, "A Rationale for Managed Futures," *Technical Analysis of Stocks & Commodities* (March 1999).
2. Kepler actually proposed three distinct laws.
3. R.D. Edwards and J. Magee, *Technical Analysis of Stock Trends*, 4th ed. (Springfield, MA: John Magee, 1958).
4. J.J. Murphy, *Technical Analysis of the Futures Markets: A Comprehensive Guide to Trading Methods and Applications* (New York: New York Institute of Finance, 1999), 2.
5. E. Fama, "Efficient Capital Markets: A Review of Theory and Empirical Work" *Journal of Finance* 25 (1970), 383–417.
6. R.J. Shiller, *Irrational Exuberance* (Princeton, NJ: Princeton University Press, 2000), 135.
7. Ibid.
8. In this chapter in section "Nonrandom Price Motion in the Context of Efficient Markets," I state the case of those who say EMH allows for price predictability, namely, that random walks are not a necessary implication of EMH.
9. Updating a belief in a probabilistically correct way implies that new information impacts a prior belief in accord with Bayes' theorem, whereby the prior belief is altered in accord with the predictive value of the new information.
10. Correct prices induce the proper allocation of resources among different possible uses. For example, if the price of corn is too high, more of it than necessary will be produced, flooding the economy with more corn than is needed at the expense of something else such as wheat. Net result: too many

boxes of Corn Flakes and too few boxes of Wheaties to meet consumer demand.

11. P. Samuelson, "Proof That Properly Anticipated Prices Fluctuate Randomly," *Industrial Management Review* 6 (1965), 41–49.

12. B.G. Malkiel, *A Random Walk Down Wall Street* (New York: W.W. Norton & Company, 2003).

13. E. Fama, "Efficient Capital Markets: A Review of Theory and Empirical Work," *Journal of Finance* 25 (1970), 383–417, as cited by A. Shleifer in *Inefficient Markets: An Introduction to Behavioral Finance* (Oxford, UK: Oxford University Press, 2000), 1.

14. A. Shleifer, *Inefficient Markets: An Introduction to Behavioral Finance* (Oxford, UK: Oxford University Press, 2000), 1.

15. N.N. Taleb, *Fooled by Randomness: The Hidden Role of Chance in the Markets and in Life* (New York: Texere, 2001).

16. A money manager with no skill whatsoever has a 0.5 probability of beating the market in any given time period (e.g., 1 year). In this experiment, Taleb assumed a universe of money managers with a 0.50 probability of beating the market in a given year.

17. Actually there are three forms of EMH—strong, semistrong, and weak. The strong form contends that no information, including inside information, can be used to beat the market on a risk-adjusted basis. This form is impossible to test because it cannot be reliably ascertained who knew what and when they knew it. The testimony of those who trade on inside information is notoriously untrustworthy.

18. E. Fama, L. Fisher, M. Jensen, and R. Roll, "The Adjustment of Stock Prices to New Information," *International Economic Review* 10 (1969), 1–21.

19. These results conflict with later studies in behavioral finance that found markets did not properly discount surprising earnings announcements. My interpretation is that Fama's studies did not consider the degree to which earnings announcements differed from prior Street expectations. Later studies done by V. Bernard showed that stock prices do experience trends after earnings announcements, if the degree of surprise in the announcement is large. V. Bernard, "Stock Price Reactions to Earnings Announcements," *Advances in Behavioral Finance*, R. Thaler (Ed.) (New York: Russell Sage Foundation, 1992; V. Bernard and J.K. Thomas, "Post-Earnings Announcement Drift: Delayed Price Response or Risk Premium?," *Journal of Accounting Research*, Supplement 27 (1989), 1–36; V. Bernard and J.K. Thomas, "Evidence That Stock Prices Do Not Fully Reflect the Implications of Current Earnings for Future Earnings," *Journal of Accounting and Economics* 13 (1990), 305–341.

20. A noninformative event is one that carries no implications for the future cash flows of the asset or the future returns of the security.

21. The capital asset pricing model was proposed by William F. Sharpe in "Capital Asset Prices: A Theory of Market Equilibrium under Conditions of Risk," *Journal of Finance* 19 (1964), 425–442.

22. APT was first proposed by S. Ross, "The Arbitrage Theory of Capital Asset Pricing," *Journal of Economic Theory* (December 1976). APT says a linear

model relates a stock's returns to a number of factors, and this relationship is the result of arbitrageurs hunting for riskless, zero-investment opportunities. APT specifies factors, including the rate of inflation, the spread between low and high quality bonds, the slope of the yield curve, and so on.

23. In other words, the current price change is correlated with the prior change (i.e., a lag interval of 1), then with the change prior to that (lag interval = 2), and so forth. A correlation coefficient is computed for each of these lags. Typically, in a random data series, the correlations drop off very quickly as a function of the lag interval. However, if the time series of price changes is nonrandom in a linear fashion, some of the autocorrelation coefficients will differ significantly from the pattern of autocorrelations of a random sequence.

24. E. Fama, "The Behavior of Stock Market Prices," *Journal of Business* 38 (1965), 34–106.

25. E.E. Peters, *Chaos and Order in the Capital Markets: A New View of Cycles, Prices and Market Volatility* (New York: John Wiley & Sons, 1991); E.E. Peters, *Fractal Market Analysis: Applying Chaos Theory to Investment and Economics* (New York: John Wiley & Sons, 1994).

26. A.W. Lo and A.C. MacKinlay, *A Non-Random Walk Down Wall Street* (Princeton, NJ: Princeton University Press, 1999).

27. S.J. Grossman and J.E. Stiglitz, "On the Impossibility of Informationally Efficient Markets," *American Economic Review* 70, no 3 (1980), 393–408.

28. Shleifer, *Inefficient Markets*, 2.

29. V. Singal, *Beyond the Random Walk: A Guide to Stock Market Anomalies and Low Risk Investing* (New York: Oxford University Press, 2004), 5.

30. F. Black, "Noise," *Journal of Finance* 41 (1986), 529–543.

31. Shleifer, *Inefficient Markets*, 10.

32. D. Kahneman and A. Tversky, "Prospect Theory: An Analysis of Decision Making under Risk," *Econometrica* 47 (1979), 263–291.

33. R. Shiller, "Stock Prices and Social Dynamics," *Brookings Papers on Economic Activity* 2, (1984), 457–498.

34. Cited by Shleifer, *Inefficient Markets*; J.B. De Long, A. Shleifer, L. Summers, and R. Waldmann, "Noise Trader Risk in Financial Markets," *Journal of Political Economy* 98 (1990), 703–738.

35. R. Merton and P. Samuelson, "Fallacy of the Log-Normal Approximation to Optimal Portfolio Decision-Making over Many Periods," *Journal of Financial Economics* 1 (1974), 67–94.

36. The expectation of a game is (probability of a win × amount won) − (probability of a loss × amount lost). Thus, per dollar bet, the expectation is +50 cents. In investment-strategy terms, this would be called a profit factor of 2.0. Very few investment strategies have such a favorable edge.

37. R. Shiller, "Do Stock Prices Move Too Much to Be Justified by Subsequent Changes in Dividends?," *American Economic Review* 71 (1981), 421–436.

38. Cited by Shleifer, *Inefficient Markets*, 20; D. Cutler, J. Poterba, and L. Summers, "Speculative Dynamics," *Review of Economic Studies* 58 (1991), 529–546.

NOTES

39. Cited by Shleifer, *Inefficient Markets*; R. Roll, "Orange Juice and Weather," *American Economic Review* 74 (1984), 861–880; R. Roll, "R-squared," *Journal of Finance* 43, (1988), 541–566.
40. Singal, *Beyond the Random Walk*, ix.
41. *Relative performance* refers to the stock's performance relative to the performance of the average stock, or a benchmark. Relative performance is also known as excess return.
42. Stocks can also be ranked on the basis of a prediction model that employs a multitude of indicators, typically referred to as factors.
43. When multiperiod horizons are used, the number of independent observations are also reduced, so a one-month horizon, based on monthly data, is often used.
44. The strong form of EMH is broader yet in claiming that not even inside information is useful in generating superior returns, but this version is not testable.
45. R. Banz, "The Relation between Market Return and Market Value for Common Stocks," *Journal of Financial Economics* 9 (1981), 3–18.
46. E. Fama and K. French, "The Cross-Section of Expected Stock Returns," *Journal of Finance* 47 (1992), 427–465.
47. Cited by Shiller, *Irrational Exuberance*; S. Basu, "The Investment Performance of Common Stocks Relative to Their Price-Earnings Ratios: A Test of the Efficient Markets," *Journal of Finance* 32, no. 3 (1977), 663–682.
48. Cited by Shiller, *Irrational Exuberance*; E. Fama and K. French, "The Cross Section of Expected Stock Returns," *Journal of Finance* 47 (1992), 427–466.
49. Singal, *Beyond the Random Walk*.
50. Although the weak form of EMH typically only talks about past prices and past price changes, I believe advocates of this position would also claim that any other data relied upon by TA would be useless for predicting future returns.
51. N. Jegadeesh, and S. Titman, "Returns to Buying Winners and Selling Losers: Implications for Market Efficiency," *Journal of Finance* 48, (1993), 65–91.
52. E. Fama, "Efficient Capital Markets: II," *Journal of Finance* 46 (1991), 1575–1617.
53. W. De Bondt and R. H. Thaler, "Does the Stock Market Overreact?," Journal of Finance 40, no. 3 (1985), 793–805.
54. In this case, risk is as defined by CAPM, volatility relative to the market.
55. T.J. George and C.-Y. Hwang, "The 52-Week High and Momentum Investing," *Journal of Finance* 59, no. 5 (October 2004), 2145.
56. C.M.C. Lee and B. Swaminathan, "Price Momentum and Trading Volume," *Journal of Finance* 55, no. 5 (October 2000), 2017–2067; S. E. Stickel and R.E. Verecchia, "Evidence That Trading Volume Sustains Stock Price Changes," *Financial Analysts Journal* 50, no. 6 (November–December 1994), 57–67. It should be noted that when the forward-looking horizon is 3 to 12 months, high volume increases the price momentum's effect. However, when the return is looked at 3 years out, high-momentum stocks with low volume are more persistent on the upside, whereas negative-momentum stocks with high volume persist on the downside.

57. E. Fama and K. French, "1996 Common Risk Factors in the Returns on Bonds and Stocks," *Journal of Financial Economics* 33 (1993), 3–56; E. Fama and K. French, "Multifactor Explanations of Asset Pricing Anomalies," *Journal of Finance* 51 (1996), 55–84.
58. W. Sharpe, "Capital Asset Prices: A Theory of Market Equilibrium under Conditions of Risk," *Journal of Finance* 19 (1964), 435–442; also see J. Lintner, "The Valuation of Risk Assets and the Selection of Risky Investments in Stock Portfolios and Capital Budgets," *Review of Economics and Statistics* 47 (1965), 13–37.
59. Shleifer, *Inefficient Markets*, 19.
60. J. Lakonishok, A. Shleifer, and R. Vishny, "Contrarian Investment, Extrapolation, and Risk," *Journal of Finance* 49 (1994), 1541–1578.
61. Shleifer, *Inefficient Markets*, 24.
62. Ibid.
63. Ibid.
64. W. Edwards, "Conservatism in Human Information Processing," in *Formal Representation of Human Judgment*, B. Kleinmutz (Ed.) (New York: John Wiley & Sons, 1968) 17–52.
65. D.G. Myers, *Intuition, Its Powers and Perils* (New Haven: Yale University Press, 2004), 157.
66. A. Tversky and D. Kahneman, *Judgment under Uncertainty Heuristics and Biases*, in *Judgment under Uncertainty: Heuristics and Biases*, D. Kahneman, P. Slovic, and A. Tversky (Eds.) (New York: Cambridge University Press, 1982), 14.
67. George and Hwang, "52-Week High."
68. Shiller, *Irrational Exuberance*, 138.
69. Ibid., 139.
70. E. Shafir, I. Simonson, and A. Tversky, "Reason–Based Choice," *Cognition* 49 (1993), 11–36.
71. Systematic process can exhibit real trends, which are streaks that are longer in duration than those found in random walks, or they can exhibit true mean-reversion behavior, which means that streaks will be shorter in duration (i.e., more frequent flip-flops between positive and negative outcomes) than is true for random walks. In both truly trended processes and true mean-reverting process, prior observations contain useful predictive information. In true random-walk processes, prior observations contain no predictive information.
72. Shiller, *Irrational Exuberance*, 148–169.
73. A. Asch, *Social Psychology* (Englewood Cliffs, NJ: Prentice-Hall, 1952), 450–501.
74. M. Deutsch and H.B. Gerard, "A Study of Normative and Informational Social Influence upon Individual Judgment," *Journal of Abnormal and Social Psychology* 51 (1955), 629–636.
75. Shiller, *Irrational Exuberance*, 148–169.
76. R.J. Shiller cites D.D. Bikhchandani, D. Hirshleifer, and I. Welch, "A Theory of Fashion, Social Custom and Cultural Change," *Journal of Political Economy* 81 (1992), 637–654; A.V. Nanerjee, "A Simple Model of Herd Behavior," *Quarterly Journal of Economics* 107, no. 3 (1993), 797–817.

77. Shiller, *Irrational Exuberance*, 152.
78. Ibid., 164.
79. Ibid., 165.
80. Ibid., 166.
81. See Carl Anderson, "Notes on Feedback and Self-Organization," at www.duke.edu/~carl/pattern/characteristic_student_notes.htm.
82. Shiller, Irrational *Exuberance*, 67.
83. N. Barberis, A. Shleifer, and R. Vishny, "A Model of Investor Sentiment," *Journal of Financial Economics* 49 (1998), 307–343.
84. This assumption is consistent with studies showing that people have difficulty distinguishing random series from series that display systematic behavior such as mean-reversion or trending behavior. This failure accounts for sports fans' misperception of the hot hand and chartists' inability to distinguish real from random charts cited in chapter 2.
85. Shiller, *Irrational Exuberance*, 144.
86. R.J. Shiller cites Barberis, Shleifer, and Vishny, "Model of Investor Sentiment," and N. Barberis, M. Huang, and T. Santos, "Prospect Theory and Asset Prices," *Quarterly Journal of Economics* 116, no. 1 (February 2001), 1–53; K. Daniel, D. Hirshleifer, and A. Subrahmanyam, "Investor Psychology and Security Market Over and Underreaction," *Journal of Finance* 53, no. 6 (1998), 1839–1886; H. Hong and J. Stein, "A Unified Theory of Underreaction, Momentum Trading, and Overreaction in Asset Markets," *Journal of Finance* 54, no. 6 (December 1999), 2143–2184.
87. Daniel, Hirshleifer, and Subrahmanyam, "Investor Psychology"; and K. Daniel, D. Hirshleifer, and A. Subrahmanyam,"Overconfidence, Arbitrage and Equilibrium Asset Pricing," *Journal of Finance* 56 (2001), 921–965.
88. N. Barberis, "A Survey of Behavioral Finance," in *Handbook of the Economics of Finance*, Volume 1B, G.M. Constantinides, M. Harris, and R. Stulz (Eds.) (New York: Elsevier Science, B.V., 2003).
89. N. Chopra and R. Lakonishok, "Measuring Abnormal Performance: Do Stocks Overreact?," *Journal of Financial Economics* 31 (1992), 235–268; R. La Porta, R. Lakonishok, A. Shleifer, and R. Vishny, "Good News for Value Stocks: Further Evidence on Market Efficiency," *Journal of Finance* 49 (1997), 1541–1578.
90. J.B. De Long, A. Shleifer, L. Summers, and R. Waldmann, "Positive Feedback Investment Strategies and Destabilizing Rational Speculation," *Journal of Finance* 45, no. 2 (1990), 379–395; N. Barberis and A. Shleifer, "Style Investing," *Journal of Financial Economics* 68 (2003), 161–199.
91. Hong and Stein, "Unified Theory."
92. S.F. LeRoy, "Risk Aversion and the Martingale Property of Stock Returns," *International Economic Review* 14 (1973), 436–446; R.E. Lucas, "Asset Prices in an Exchange Economy," *Econometrica* 46 (1978), 1429–1446.
93. A.W. Lo and A.C. MacKinlay, *A Non-Random Walk Down Wall Street* (Princeton, NJ: Princeton University Press, 1999), 5.
94. Ibid.
95. S. Grossman, "On the Efficiency of Competitive Stock Markets Where Traders Have Diverse Information," *Journal of Finance* 31 (1976), 573–585.;

S. Grossman and J. Stiglitz, "On the Impossibility of Informationally Efficient Markets," *American Economic Review* 70 (1980), 393–408.

96. L. Jaeger, *Managing Risk in Alternative Investment Strategies: Successful Investing in Hedge Funds and Managed Futures* (London: Financial Times–Prentice Hall, 2002), 27.

97. Gains from a true inefficiency are not a free lunch, because it is costly to identify them, but they need not entail the risk of additional volatility in returns. Thus true inefficiencies can generate investment performance with a high relative Sharpe ratio.

98. H.D. Platt, *Counterintuitive Investing: Profiting from Bad News on Wall Street* (Mason, OH: Thomson Higher Education, 2005).

99. Equity and bond markets provide a quick way for owners of equities to sell their position to other investors. The liquidity of stocks and bonds thus makes them attractive to the initial investors, thereby making it easier for companies to raise debt and equity financing.

100. Grains (corn, soybeans, soybean meal, soybean oil, and wheat); financials (5-year T-notes, 10-year T-notes, long-term treasury bonds); currencies (Australian, British, Canadian, German, Swiss, and Japanese); energy (heating oil, natural gas, crude oil, and unleaded gas); cattle; metals (gold, copper, and silver); and soft/tropical (coffee, cotton, and sugar).

101. G.R. Jensen, R.R. Johnson, and J.M. Mercer, "Tactical Asset Allocation and Commodity Futures," *Journal of Portfolio Management* 28, no. 4 (Summer 2002).

102. An asset-class benchmark measures the returns earned and risks incurred by investing in a specific asset class, with no management skill.

103. Lars Kestner, *Quantitative Trading Strategies: Harnessing the Power of Quantitative Techniques to Create a Winning Trading Program* (New York: McGraw-Hill, 2003), 129–180.

104. The eight market sectors tested were foreign exchange, interest rates, stock index, metals, energy, grains, meats, and softs.

105. The nine industry sectors were energy, basic materials, consumer discretionary, consumer staples, health care, financials and information technology, telecom. The three stock indexes were S&P 500, NASDAQ 100, and Russell 2000.

106. The five trend-following systems were channel breakout, dual moving-average crossover, two version of momentum, and MACD versus its signal line. For more description see Kestner's *Quantitative Trading Strategies*.

107. M. Cooper, "Filter Rules Based on Price and Volume in Individual Security Overreaction," *Review of Financial Studies* 12, no. 4 (Special 1999), 901–935.

CHAPTER 8   Case Study of Rule Data Mining for the S&P 500

1. J.P. Romano and M. Wolf, "Stepwise Multiple Testing as Formalized Data Snooping," *Econometrica* 73, no. 4 (July 2005), 1237–1282.

2. J.J. Murphy, *Intermarket Technical Analysis: Trading Strategies for the Global Stock, Bond, Commodity and Currency Markets* (New York: John Wiley & Sons, 1991). I was first exposed to the idea of using relationships between markets for indicator development in 1979 by Michael Hammond and Norman Craig of Advance Market Technologies (AMTEC), Ogden, Utah. AMTEC was one of the first firms to apply artificial-intelligence methods to market prediction. AMTEC's modeling approach was based on the work of Roger Baron on adaptive learning networks, now known as polynomial networks, at Adaptronics Inc, in the 1970s. I routinely used intermarket indicators in work for clients of Raden Research Group, including Cyber-Tech Partners (1983), Tudor Investment Corporation (1987), and Manufacturer's Hanover Trust (1988).

3. P-H Hsu and C-M Kuan, "Reexamining the Profitability of Technical Analysis with Data Snooping Checks," *Journal of Financial Economics* 3, no. 4 (2005), 606–628.

4. Many of the automated methods are described in T. Hastie, R. Tibshirani, and J. Friedman, *The Elements of Statistical Learning: Data Mining, Inference and Prediction* (New York: Springer, 2001).

5. A segment of the future over which the rule's profitability persists that is long enough to compensate the effort required to discover the rule but not of unlimited duration.

6. H. White, "A Reality Check for Data Snooping," *Econometrica* 68, no. 5 (September 2000). Note that White uses the term data *snooping* to mean "data-mining bias," as used in this book.

7. Mathematical operators include add, subtract, multiply, divide, powers, roots, and so forth.

8. Logical operators include *and*; *or*; *greater-than*; *less-than*; *if, then*; *else*, and so forth.

9. Time-series operators include moving average, moving channel normalization (stochastics), breakout channels, moving slopes, and such (described later).

10. P.K. Kaufman, 249.

11. Ibid., 200.

12. Ibid., 202. Kaufman notes that a study done in 1970 by Dunn & Hargitt Financial Services showed that a channel breakout using a four-week span, known as Donchian's four-week rule, was the best of several popular systems when tested on 16 years of data on seven commodities markets. Kaufman also compares the performance of channel breakout rules to four other trend-following methods (exponential smoothing, linear regression slope, swing-breakout, and point-and-figure) to Eurodollars for the 10-year period 1985 through 1994. The channel breakout method had the highest risk-adjusted performance over the 10-year period.

13. A simple moving average is centered by plotting the moving-average value in the center of the moving-data window. If N is the number of periods used to compute the moving average, the average is plotted to correspond with a value that is lagged by $(n - 1)/2$ data points.

14. J.F. Ehlers, *Rocket Science for Traders: Digital Signal Processing Applications* (New York: John Wiley & Sons, 2001); J.F. Ehlers, *Cybernetic Analysis for Stocks and Futures: Cutting-Edge DSP Technology to Improve Your Trading* (New York: John Wiley & Sons, 2004).
15. Kaufman, 256.
16. Ehlers, *Rocket Science for Traders*, 27.
17. W.A. Heiby, *Stock Market Profits through Dynamic Synthesis* (Chicago: Institute of Dynamic Synthesis, 1965).
18. Although almost all sources attribute the development of this time series operator to Dr. George Lane in 1972, no source mentions the use of the same idea by Heiby at an earlier time. On this basis, I have attributed the development to Heiby. It is possible that Heiby based his work on yet an earlier author.
19. For information about various back-testing software platforms see: for TradeStation www.TradeStationWorld.com; for MetaStock www.equis.com; for AIQ Expert Design Studio www.aiqsystems.com; for Wealth-Lab www.wealth-lab.com; for eSignal www.esignal.com; for Neuroshell Trader www.neuroshell.com; for AmiBroker www.amibroker.com; for Neoticker, www.tickquest.com; for Trading$olutions www.tradingsolutions.com; for Financial Data Calculator www.mathinvestdecisions.com.
20. Ultra Financial Systems, PO Box 3938, Breckenridge, CO 90424; phone 970-453-4956; web site www.ultrafs.com.
21. Market Timing Reports, PO Box 225, Tucson, AZ 85072; phone 520-795-9552; web site www.mktimingrpt.com.
22. Studies showing that trading volume contains useful information include the following: L. Blume and M. Easley O'Hara, "Market Statistics and Technical Analysis: The Role of Volume," *Journal of Finance* 49, issue 1 (March 1994), 153–181; M. Cooper, "Filter Rules Based on Price and Volume in Individual Security Overreaction," *Review of Financial Studies* 12 (1999), 901–935; C.M.C. Lee and B. Swaminathan, "Price Momentum and Trading Volume," *Journal of Finance* 55, no. 5 (October 2000), 2017–2069; S.E. Stickel and R.E. Verecchia, "Evidence That Trading Volume Sustains Stock Price Changes," *Financial Analysts Journal* 50 (November–December 1994), 57–67.
23. J.E. Granville, *Granville's New Strategy of Daily Stock Market Timing for Maximum Profit* (Englewood Cliffs, NJ: Prentice-Hall, 1976). The attribution to Woods and Vignolia can be found in the body of knowledge section on the web site of the Market Technicians Association.
24. This formulation of OBV is as presented in *Technical Indicators Reference Manual* for AIQ Trading Export Pro, a software product of AIQ Systems, PO Box 7530, Incline Village, NV 89452.
25. The MTA Body of Knowledge on Technical Indicators attributes the accumulation distribution indicator to Marc Chaiken, as does R.W. Colby, *The Encyclopedia of Technical Market Indicators*, 2nd ed. (New York: McGraw-Hill, 2003). No specific publication is referenced. The accumulation distribution indicator proposed by Chaiken is similar to an indicator developed by Larry Williams, *The Secrets of Selecting Stocks for Immediate and Substantial*

Gains (Carmel Valley, CA: Conceptual Management, 1971), later republished by Windsor Books in 1986. Williams's indicator compares the open price to the close as the numerator of the range factor. Chaiken compares the close price to the midprice of the daily range.

26. As presented in *Technical Indicators Reference Manual for AIQ Trading Export Pro*, a software product of AIQ Systems, PO Box 7530, Incline Village, NV 89452.

27. Ibid.

28. Attribution of NVI to Norman Fosback can be found in the MTA web site Body of Knowledge and in S.B. Achelis, *Technical Analysis from A to Z* (New York: McGraw-Hill, 2001), 214.

29. Paul Dysart is credited with the creation of both positive- and negative-volume indexes by C.V. Harlow, *An Analysis of the Predictive Value of Stock Market "Breadth" Measurements* (Larchmont, NY: Investors Intelligence, 1968).

30. According to Fosback's study, the NVI identified the bullish phase of the primary trend with a probability of 0.96 over the time period 1941 to 1975. This compares to a base rate bull-trend probability of 0.70 over that time period.

31. N.G. Fosback, *Stock Market Logic: A Sophisticated Approach to Profits on Wall Street* (Dearborn, MI: Dearborn Financial Publishing, 1993), 120.

32. Ibid.

33. Harlow, *Analysis of the Predictive Value.*

34. R.W. Colby, *The Encyclopedia of Technical Market Indicators*, 2nd ed. (New York: McGraw-Hill, 2003).

35. Fosback, *Stock Market Logic*, 76–80.

36. This formulation of CNHL is as presented in *Technical Indicators Reference Manual* for AIQ Trading Export Pro, a software product of AIQ Systems.

37. C.R. Nelson, *The Investor's Guide to Economic Indicators* (New York: John Wiley & Sons, 1987), 129. The author points out that a positive spread (i.e., long-term rates higher than short-term rates) is often a bullish indicator for future changes in stock prices, especially for stock indexes that are not inflation adjusted.

38. Moody's Investors Service is a widely utilized source for credit ratings, research, and risk analysis for corporate debt instruments. Information can be found at www.moodys.com.

39. Aaa is the designated definition for the highest quality of corporate bond. Securities carrying this rating are judged to have the smallest degree of investment risk. The principal is secure and interest payments are protected by a robust margin. Although there is always a chance that various protective elements can change, these changes are easy to visualize. The Aaa rating means that it is highly unlikely for any drastic changes to occur that would erode the fundamentally strong positions on these securities. Definition provided: www.econoday.com/clientdemos/demoweekly/2004/Resource_Center/about bondmkt/morefixed.html.

40. Baa bonds are considered medium-grade obligations. They are neither highly protected nor poorly secured. Interest payments and security on the principal appear adequate for the present, but there may be certain protective ele-

ments lacking. These securities have the possibility of being unreliable over any great length of time. These bonds lack outstanding investment characteristics, making them attractive to speculators at the same time. www.econoday.com/clientdemos/demoweekly/2004/Resource_Center/aboutbondmkt/moreﬁxed.html.

41. For a full discussion of alternative trend analysis methods and rules derived from them see Kaufman, Chapters 5 through 8.
42. J. Hussman, "Time-Variation in Market Efficiency: A Mixture-of-Distributions Approach," available at www.hussman.net/pdf/mixdist.pdf.
43. M.J. Pring, *Technical Analysis Explained*, 4th ed. (New York: McGraw-Hill, 2002).
44. Kaufman, 394–401.
45. Heiby, *Stock Market Proﬁts*.
46. C. Alexander, *Market Models: A Guide to Financial Data Analysis* (New York: John Wiley & Sons, 2001), Chapter 12.
47. R.F. Engle and C.W.J. Granger, "Co-integration and Error-Correction: Representation, Estimation and Testing," *Econometrica* 55 (1987), 251–276.
48. Alexander, *Market Models*, 324–328, 353–361. One type of test used to establish the fact that a time series is stationary, called the unit-root test, is described.
49. The indicator is a time series of the errors (residuals) of the linear relationship between the two series.
50. Fosback, *Stock Market Logic*.
51. In 1983 the author, in association with Raden Research Group, developed a time series operator called *YY* that was similar in concept to cointegration analysis with the exception that *YY* values were normalized by the standard error of the regression and no explicit test was made for residual stationarity. *YY*'s development was inspired by an article by Arthur Merrill, "DFE: Deviation from Expected (Relative Strength Corrected for Beta)," *Market Technician Journal* (August 1982), 21–28. The *YY*-based indicators were used as candidate inputs for a variety of predictive modeling projects. One example was a sentiment indicator based on advisory sentiment on T-bonds. The predictive power of the raw consensus information was improved by a *YY* transformation that used past market changes as the regressor variable.

CHAPTER 9   Case Study Results and the Future of TA

1. This is an extreme rule, Type 12, based on input series 28 (10-day moving average of the up/down volume ratio), using threshold offset of 10 (upper = 60, lower = 40) and a channel normalization look-back of 30 days. Type 12 is short although the indicator is above the upper threshold, long at all other times.
2. The bias-compensated p-values were this bad (worse than p = 0.5) in part because half of the 6,402 rules were inverse rules. This guaranteed that *half* of

the competing rules would have a negative return, and, hence, have no chance of being a true competitor. In effect the test had twice as many rules being tested as were truly in competition. This makes your test overly conservative. That is to say, the chance of a Type-1 error (false reject of the null) was lower than 0.10. It also means that the power of the test (ability to correctly reject the null) was less than it would have been had the inverse rules been left out of the competition. However, as explained in Chapter 1, the inverse rules were included because it was not known if the traditional TA interpretation was correct.

3. J.P. Romano and M. Wolf, "Stepwise Multiple Testing as Formalized Data Snooping," *Econometrica* 73, no. 4 (July 2005), 1237–1282.

4. H. White, "A Reality Check for Data Snooping," *Econometrica* 68, no 5 (September 2000).

5. W.R. Ashby, *Introduction to Cybernetics* (New York: John Wiley & Sons, 1963). In fact, Ashby was referring to the problem of system control rather than system prediction, though there are obvious similarities between the two problems.

6. P-H Hsu and C-M Kuan, "Reexamining the Profitability of Technical Analysis with Data Snooping Checks," *Journal of Financial Econometrics* 3, no. 4 (2005), 606–628. Note the authors are using the term data snooping as I use the term data mining. They are checking and making adjustment for data-mining bias using a version of White's reality check, without the enhancements suggested by Wolf and Romano (see Chapter 6).

7. Ibid.

8. Eui Jung Chang, Eduardo José Araújo Lima, and Benjamin Miranda Tabak, "Testing for Predictability in Emerging Equity Markets," *Emerging Markets Review* 5, issue 3 (September 2004), 295–316; Malay K. Dey, "Turnover and Return in Global Stock Markets," *Emerging Markets Review* 6, issue 1 (April 2005), 45–67; Wing-Keung Wong, Meher Manzur, and Boon-Kiat Chew, "How Rewarding Is Technical Analysis? Evidence from Singapore Stock Market," *Applied Financial Economics* 13, issue 7 (July 2003), 543; Kalok Chan and Allaudeen Hameed, "Profitability of Momentum Strategies in the International Equity Markets," *Journal of Financial & Quantitative Analysis* 35, issue 2 (June 2000), 153.

9. C. Alexander, *Market Models: A Guide to Financial Data Analysis* (New York: John Wiley & Sons, 2001), 347–387.

10. J.F. Ehlers, *Cybernetic Analysis for Stocks and Futures: Cutting-Edge Technology to Improve Your Trading* (Hoboken, NJ: John Wiley & Sons, 2004), 1–10.

11. Hsu and Kuan, "Reexamining the Profitability."

12. T. Hastie, R. Tibshirani, and J. Friedman, *The Elements of Statistical Learning: Data Mining, Inference and Prediction* (New York: Springer, 2001), 347–370.

13. Ibid., 283–290.

14. J.R. Wolberg, *Expert Trading Systems: Modeling Financial Markets with Kernel Regression* (New York: John Wiley & Sons, 2000).

15. J.F. Elder IV and D.E. Brown, "Induction and Polynomial Networks," in *Network Models for Control and Processing*, M. D. Fraser (Ed.) (Bristol, UK: Intellect Ltd, 2000).
16. W. Banzhaf, P. Nordin, R.E. Keller, and F.W. Francone, *Genetic Programming: An Introduction; On the Automatic Evolution of Computer Programs and Its Applications* (San Francisco: Morgan Kaufmann, 1998).
17. N. Cristianini and J. Taylor-Shawe, *An Introduction to Support Vector Machines* (New York: Cambridge University Press, 2000).
18. Complexity can mean different things in data mining. In the case of data mining for TA rules, it refers to the number of separate parameters and conditional statements required to define the rule. Higher complexity rules have more parameters and conditions. A dual moving-average crossover rule has one condition and two parameter values. The condition is: If short-term moving average > than long-term moving average, then hold long position, else hold short position. The two parameters are look-back spans for the short-term and long-term moving averages.
19. N. Gershenfeld, *The Nature of Mathematical Modeling* (New York: Cambridge University Press, 1999), 147.
20. If shorter-term moving average > longer-term moving average, then hold long position, else hold short position.
21. There are more intelligent and efficient search methods than testing every possible combination. These include genetic algorithm searching, simulated annealing, guided searching based on gradient descent, and so forth. Two excellent treatments of these topics can be found in Katz and McCormick, and Pardo. See earlier footnote references.
22. In this example, the simple two moving-average crossover rule is a subset of a more complex set of rules of greater complexity.
23. W.A. Sherden, *The Fortune Sellers: The Big Business of Buying and Selling Predictions* (New York: John Wiley & Sons, 1998), 1.
24. J.S. Armstrong, "The Seer-Sucker Theory: The Value of Experts in Forecasting," *Technology Review* (June/July 1980), 16–24.
25. A. Cowles, "Can Stock Market Forecasters Forecast?" *Econometrica* 1 (1933), 309–324.
26. In February 2005, Citigroup terminated its technical research department. Prudential Securities disbanded its technical research department later in the year.
27. N.G. Fosback, *Stock Market Logic: A Sophisticated Approach to Profits on Wall Street* (Dearborn, MI: Dearborn Financial Publishing, 1993), 80.
28. B.I. Jacobs and K.N. Levy, *Equity Management: Quantitative Analysis for Stock Selection* (New York: McGraw-Hill, 2000), 27–37.
29. The return reversal effect is similar to the residual reversal effect, which is based on cointegration analysis.
30. J. Felsen, *Cybernetic Approach to Stock Market Analysis versus Efficient Market Theory* (New York: Exposition Press, 1975); J. Felsen, *Decision Making under Uncertainty: An Artificial Intelligence Approach* (New York: CDS Publishing Company, 1976).

31. Two firms with which I had contact in the late 1970s that were using statistical pattern recognition and adaptive learning networks were Braxton Corporation in Boston, Massachusetts, and AMTEC Inc. in Ogden, Utah. I started Raden Research Group, Inc. in 1982.

32. A.M. Safer, "A Comparison of Two Data Mining Techniques to Predict Abnormal Stock Market Returns, *Intelligent Data Analysis* 7, no. 1 (2003), 3–14; G. Armano, A. Murru, and F. Roli, "Stock Market Prediction by a Mixture of Genetic-Neural Experts," *International Journal of Pattern Recognition & Artificial Intelligence* 16, no. 5 (August 2002), 501–528; G. Armano, M. Marchesi, and A. Murru, "A Hybrid Genetic-Neural Architecture for Stock Indexes Forecasting," *Information Sciences* 170, no. 1 (February 2005), 3–33; T. Chenoweth, Z.O. Sauchi, and S. Lee, "Embedding Technical Analysis into Neural Network Based Trading Systems," *Applied Artificial Intelligence* 10, no. 6 (December 1996), 523–542; S. Thawornwong, D. Enke, and C. Dagli, "Neural Networks as a Decision Maker for Stock Trading: A Technical Analysis Approach," *International Journal of Smart Engineering System Design* 5, no. 4 (October/December 2003), 313–325; A.M. Safer, "The Application of Neural-Networks to Predict Abnormal Stock Returns Using Insider Trading Data," *Applied Stochastic Models in Business & Industry* 18, no. 4 (October 2002), 380–390; J. Yao, C.L. Tan, and H-L Pho, "Neural Networks for Technical Analysis: A Study on KLCI," *International Journal of Theoretical & Applied Finance* 2, no. 2 (April 1999), 221–242; J. Korczak and P. Rogers, "Stock Timing Using Genetic Algorithms," *Applied Stochastic Models in Business & Industry* 18, no. 2 (April 2002), 121–135; Z. Xu-Shen and M. Dong, "Can Fuzzy Logic Make Technical Analysis 20/20?" *Financial Analysts Journal* 60, no. 4 (July/August 2004), 54–75; J.M. Gorriz, C.G. Puntonet, M. Salmeron, and J.J. De la Rosa, "A New Model for Time-Series Forecasting Using Radial Basis Functions and Exogenous Data," *Neural Computing & Applications* 13, no. 2 (2004), 100–111.

33. P.E. Meehl, *Clinical versus Statical Prediction: A Theoretical Analysis and a Review of the Evidence* (Minneapolis: University of Minnesota Press, 1954).

34. R. Hastie and R.M. Dawes, *Rational Choice in an Uncertain World: The Psychology of Judgment and Decision Making* (Thousand Oaks, CA: Sage Publications, 2001), 55.

35. J. Sawyer, "Measurement and Prediction, Clinical and Statistical," *Psychological Bulletin* 66 (1966), 178–200.

36. Hastie and Dawes, *Rational Choice*, 55.

37. C. Camerer, "General Conditions for the Success of Bootstrapping Models," *Organizational Behavior and Human Performance* 27 (1981), 411–422.

38. J.E. Russo and P.J.H. Schoemaker, *Decision Traps: The Ten Barriers to Brilliant Decision-Making and How to Avoid Them* (New York: Doubleday/Currency, 1989).

39. L.R. Goldberg, "Simple Models or Simple Processes? Some Research on Clinical Judgments," *American Psychologist* 23 (1968), 483–496.

40. R.M. Dawes, "The Ethics of Using or Not Using Statistical Prediction Rules," an unpublished paper written at Carnegie Mellon University.

41. P.E. Meehl, "Causes and Effects of My Disturbing Little Book," *Journal of Personality Assessment* 50 (1986), 370–375.

42. W.M. Grove and P.E. Meehl, "Comparitive Efficiency of Informal (Subjective, Impressionistic) and Formal (Mechanical, Algorithmic) Prediction Procedures: The Clinical-Statistical Controversy," *Psychology, Public Policy, and Law* 2 (1996), 293–323.

43. Dawes, "Ethics of Statistical Prediction Rules."

44. Hastie and Dawes, *Rational Choice*, 54.

45. C.F. Camerer and E.J. Johnson, "The Process-Performance Paradox in Expert Judgment: How Can Experts Know So Much and Predict So Badly?" Chapter 10 in *Research on Judgment and Decision Making: Currents, Connections and Controversies*, W.M. Goldstein and R.M. Hogarth (Eds.), Cambridge Series on Judgment and Decision Making (Cambridge, UK: Cambridge University Press, 1997).

46. P.E. Tetlock, *Expert Political Judgment: How Good Is It? How Can We Know?* (Princeton, NJ: Princeton University Press, 2005).

47. Ibid., 77.

48. G.F. Loewenstein, E.U. Weber, C.K. Hsee, and N. Welch, "Risk as Feelings," *Psychological Bulletin* 127, no. 2 (2001), 267–287.

49. J.R. Nofsinger, "Social Mood and Financial Economics," *Journal of Behavioral Finance* 6, no. 3 (2005), 144–160.

50. Ibid., 151.

51. P. Slovic, M. Finucane, E. Peters, and D. MacGregor, "The Affect Heuristic," Chapter 23 in *Heuristics and Biases: The Psychology of Intuitive Judgment*, T. Gilovich, D. Griffin, and D. Kahneman (Eds.) (Cambridge, UK: Cambridge University Press, 2002), 397–420.

52. Ibid., 416.

53. J.P. Forgas, "Mood and Judgment: The Affect Infusion Model (AIM)," *Psychological Bulletin* 117, no. 1 (1995), 39–66.

54. Nofsinger, "Social Mood," 152.

55. Some books on the general topic of TA Indictors: S.B. Achelis, *Technical Analysis from A to Z*, 2nd ed. (New York: McGraw-Hill, 2001); E.M. Azoff, *Neural Network Time Series Forecasting of Financial Markets* (New York: John Wiley & Sons, 1994); R.W. Colby, *The Encyclopedia of Technical Market Indicators*, 2nd ed. (New York: McGraw-Hill, 2003); P.J. Kaufman, *New Trading Systems and Methods*, 4th ed. (Hoboken, NJ: John Wiley & Sons, 2005); J.F. Ehlers, *Cybernetic Analysis for Stocks and Futures: Cutting-Edge DSP Technology to Improve Your Trading* (Hoboken, NJ: John Wiley & Sons, 2004).

56. D. Pyle, *Data Preparation for Data Mining* (San Francisco: Morgan Kaufmann, 1999); T. Masters, *Neural, Novel & Hybrid Algorithms for Time Series Prediction* (New York: John Wiley & Sons, 1995); T. Masters, *Practical Neural Net Recipes in C++* (New York: Academic Press, 1993); I.H. Witten and E. Frank, *Data Mining: Practical Machine Learning Tools and Techniques*, 2nd ed. (San Francisco: Morgan Kaufmann, 2005); E.M. Azoff, *Neural Network Time Series Forecasting of Financial Markets* (New York: John Wiley & Sons, 1994).

57. Masters, *Neural, Novel & Hybrid Algorithms.*
58. Pyle, *Data Preparation.*
59. S.M. Weiss and N. Indurkhya, *Predictive Data Mining—a Practical Guide* (San Francisco: Morgan Kaufmann, 1998).
60. Pyle, *Data Preparation,* xviii.
61. Masters, *Neural, Novel & Hybriad Algorithms,* 2.
62. Weiss and Indurkhya, *Predictive Data Mining,* 21, 57.
63. R. Kurzweil, *The Singularity Is Near: When Humans Transcend Biology* (New York: Penguin Group, 2005).

Index

Printed in the USA
CPSIA information can be obtained
at www.ICGtesting.com
LVHW050805011123
761291LV00002B/7

9 780470 008744